THE OXFORD
COMPANION TO
AUSTRALIAN
CHILDREN'S
LITERATURE

From *The Hut in the Bush* (1883) by Robert Richardson. Illustrator unknown

THE OXFORD COMPANION TO AUSTRALIAN CHILDREN'S LITERATURE

STELLA LEES

AND

PAM MACINTYRE

Oxford University Press
in association with ALIA Press

Melbourne
OXFORD UNIVERSITY PRESS
Oxford   Auckland   New York

OXFORD UNIVERSITY PRESS AUSTRALIA

Oxford New York Toronto
Delhi Bombay Calcutta Madras Karachi
Kuala Lumpur Singapore Hong Kong Tokyo
Nairobi Dar es Salaam Cape Town
Melbourne Auckland Madrid
and associated companies in
Berlin Ibadan

OXFORD is a trade mark of Oxford University Press

Alia Press is the publishing division of the
Australian Library and Information Assocaition
PO Box E441, Queen Victoria Terrace, ACT, 2600

National Library of Australia
Cataloguing-in-Publication data:

Lees, Stella.
Companion to Australian children's literature.

Bibliography.
ISBN 0 19 553284 8.

1. Children's literature, Australian—Dictionaries.
2. Children's literature, Australian—Bio-bibliography.
3. Children's literature, Australian—History and criticism.
I. Macintyre, Pam. II. Title.

A820.9

Edited by Venetia Nelson
Printed by Impact Printing Pty Ltd, Victoria
Published by Oxford University Press,
253 Normanby Road, South Melbourne, Australia

PREFACE

As children, Patrick White wept over *Dot and the Kangaroo* by Ethel Pedley; Christina Stead absorbed *Seven Little Australians* by Ethel Turner; Hal Porter devoured the 'Billabong' books by Mary Grant Bruce; Max Harris and Randolph Stow adored the surrealism of *Cole's Funny Picture Book*; Thomas Shapcott had his ear to the wireless, listening to 'The Argonauts', with one eye on Ginger Meggs by James Bancks; Dorothy Hewett, surprisingly, loved *Elves and Fairies* by Ida Rentoul Outhwaite; Thea Astley laughed over *The Flyaway Highway* by Norman Lindsay. Perhaps the Whites, Steads and Astleys of the twenty-first century will recall similar reactions to *Lockie Leonard, Human Torpedo* by Tim Winton, *Brother Night* by Victor Kelleher, Daisy Utemorah's *Do Not Go Around the Edges*, or Nadia Wheatley's *The Blooding*.

In the 1600 entries that appear in this *Companion*, we have selected many of the authors and illustrators who have contributed most to Australian children's literature and culture during the past 150 years. Radio and television programs that have been a part of children's cultural life in the twentieth century are also included.

Australian authors and illustrators predominate, although the *Companion* also includes some from other countries, such as M. Ella Chaffey, Latharo Hoover or Elizabeth Beresford. We have not represented every work of an author or illustrator. A full bibliography of works published before 1989 can be found in Marcie Muir's and Kerry White's *Australian Children's Books: A Bibliography* (1992). Generally we have aimed to comment on an individual's contribution. Some authors, such as Olaf Ruhen or Ruth Park, have also written for adults, and the reader is advised to consult the *Oxford Companion to Australian Literature* (1985) for a discussion of that material.

Subjects are listed in the body of the *Companion*, and include topics such as Bushfires, Death, and Sport; historical events, such as the Eureka Stockade; places, such as Melbourne; genre, such as Science Fiction or Historical Fiction; and people of historical significance, such as Captain Cook.

The majority of individual volumes discussed in the *Companion* won or were cited as Honour Books in the Book of the Year Awards or were winners of the children's choice awards. Other books appear that were written before the establishment of those awards, such as *The Magic Pudding*. Where an author or illustrator's work has a title entry, 'q.v.' appears before the date of the work, for example, *Playing Beatie Bow* (q.v., 1980).

Where a group of books is identified with a character, the name of that character has been used for the entry, for example, 'Simon Black' or 'Ann Rankin' — arranged as 'Black, Simon' and 'Rankin, Ann' respectively.

The important role played by publishers — both corporate and individual — in developing Australian children's literature is also represented in various entries.

Institutions that promote children's literature are included, such as the Children's Book Council of Australia and the Western Australian Museum of Childhood.

The use of the term 'Aborigine' to refer to the traditional inhabitants of Australia has been questioned. Some have indicated that they are more correctly referred to as

Kooris (people of Victoria, NSW and Tasmania), Murris (Queenslanders), Nyunga (southern Western Australians) and Nungga (South Australians). We have used the general term 'Aboriginal People' in this *Companion*.

In general, non-fiction is not included, although individual titles may appear. For instance, *The Australia Book* won the Book of the Year Awards, and the 'Trend' series had an impact on later publishing.

Cross-references are given to the name by which the author is best known, for example for Jennifer Rowe see 'Emily Rodda'. Not all items that receive an entry are cross-referenced, and the reader is encouraged to see if an item not covered by a 'q.v.' is nevertheless the subject of an entry. For example, although authors are not cross-referenced, their names should be sought alphabetically for biographical material.

In cases where the date of a book or date of birth or death of an author or illustrator is uncertain, a question mark precedes the approximate date. Where a death date is unknown, a birth date only is given. Every effort has been made to identify biographical details and the authors would be grateful for any further information.

Where books are cited within entries only short titles and authors' surnames are given. Full references are found in the Bibliography.

Entries beginning with MAC or MC are listed as if they were all MAC.

There are some people without whom we would have been unable to proceed. Belle Aldermann and Laurie Copping from the Lu Rees Archives, Jim Andreghetti and the staff of the Mitchell Library, State Library of New South Wales, and the helpful staff at the State Library of Victoria, the National Library of Australia, John Arnold from the National Centre for Australian Studies at Monash University, Juliana Bayfield from the State Library of South Australia, Pat Brady from the Australian Institute for Aboriginal and Torres Strait Islander Studies, Chris Cuneen from the Australian Dictionary of Biography, Claire Forte and the staff at the Research Collection of Children's Literature at the State Library of Western Australia, David Hedges at the Museum of Childhood, Edith Cowan University, Robert Holden, Shirley King from the University of Tasmania, Mercedes Mordecai at the ABC Archives, Margaret Murphy and the staff of the McLaren Collection at the Baillieu Library, University of Melbourne, Terry O'Neill at the University of Melbourne, Peter Metherall, Bruce Smith, Kim Burrell, Joanna Durst, Berenice Dwyer, Kathryn Jowitt, Joan Orr, Helen Reid, Joan Rowe and Suzanne Thwaites from the Library and Information Studies Division at Melbourne University, Albert Ullin from the Little Bookroom, Catherine Johnson, Colin Lawn, Sean McMullen, Gordon Pickard and Maurice Saxby. Many people have generously supplied material on friends and relatives who are authors and illustrators included in the *Companion*.

Special thanks are due to Judy Bensemann, from the Department of Library and Information Studies, Institute of Education, University of Melbourne, who has allowed us access to her extensive personal collection of Australian children's books, and who has read the manuscript with a meticulous eye.

Any errors are our own responsibility, and in no way reflect on the help that these people have given us.

ABBREVIATIONS

ABC	Australian Broadcasting Corporation (formerly Commission)
ACT	Australian Capital Territory
A&R	Angus & Robertson
ALIA	Australian Library and Information Association
AMP	Australian Mutual Provident
BBC	British Broadcasting Commission
BILBY	Books I Love Best Yearly
CBC	Children's Book Council of Australia
COOL	Canberra's Own Outstanding List
CROW	Children Rate Outstanding Writers and Illustrators
CSIRO	Commonwealth Scientific and Industrial Research Organization
fl.	flourished
IBBY	International Board on Books for Young People
KOALA	Kids Own Australian Literature Award
KROC	Kids Reading Oz Choice
NSW	New South Wales
NTYRBA	Northern Territory Young Readers Book Award
NZ	New Zealand
OUP	Oxford University Press
RAAF	Royal Australian Air Force
RMIT	Royal Melbourne Institute of Technology
SA	South Australia
SBS	Special Broadcasting Service
WA	Western Australia
WAYRBA	West Australian Young Readers Book Award
YABBA	Young Australians Best Book Award

A

'A. A. B. AND HELUMAC'. For *Australian Wonderland: a Fairy Chain*, see **Fairies.**

ABBOTT, JOHN HENRY MAC-ARTNEY (1874–1953), born Hunter Valley, NSW, was a jackaroo, journalist, a trooper in South Africa, and a prolific writer. His work includes popular stories and historical novels in the NSW Bookstall Company's (q.v.) 'Bookstall Series'; and articles about bushrangers, explorers, the Boer War, irrigation and Australian life in general, many of these for the *Bulletin*. In *Bohemians of the Bulletin* (1965) Norman Lindsay says that Abbott 'helped to create the legend of courage and endurance in battle' of the Australian soldier at war. *The South Seas (Melanesia)* (1908) is in the 'Peeps at Many Lands' series, and *The Story of William Dampier* (1911) in the 'Australian Story' series for young readers. *The King's School* (1931) was written to celebrate the centenary of the school for the *Sydney Mail* and the *Bulletin*, and is a mixture of the real and fanciful experiences of boys and masters. *Dogsnose* (1928) is the name given to a schoolboy detective, Bill Carfax, whose miraculous sense of smell enables him to find anyone in hiding. Bill's hound-like gifts have him 'sniffing all the time at the walls of the corridor', and when he is enlisted by the local police, lead him to the perpetrators of a robbery at the school. The story is told by Abbott in a poker-faced narrative.

ABBOTT, JOYCE (?1912–90) wrote and illustrated *Playabout: a Picture-Story Reader* (1955) and *Ullagulbra: a Picture-Story Reader* (1959). In the first, Arua plays in a canoe with his friend Tidja, catches turtles, hunts, makes fire and dances in a corroboree. *Ullagulbra* has a similar focus. Abbott illustrated *Dawn Mother* (1942), *Grandpuff and Leafy* (1942), *Little Round Stairway* (1946), *Leafy and Prince Brumby* (1944), and *Leafy's Seventh Wave* (1948), by Gladys Lister, and *Goolara* (1943) by Pixie O'Harris.

ABBOTT-SMITH, NOURMA, see **HANDFORD, NOURMA**

A.B.C. Children's Hour Annual, The, see **Annuals**

ABC of Monsters (1976) by Deborah Niland was Highly Commended in the 1977 Picture Book of the Year Awards. Robust monsters and endearing characters romp through a monster party, which opens with 'annoying apes' and concludes with the monsters 'zig-zagging all the way home'. This was Deborah Niland's first picture-book illustrating her own text.

ABDULLAH, MENA (1930–), born Bundarra, NSW, edited *The Time of the Peacock* (1965) with Ray Mathew, a collection of stories drawn from the *Bulletin*, *Quadrant* and *Hemisphere*, about Nimmi, 'a dark girl in a white man's country, a Punjabi Muslim in a Christian land'. A little-known cultural group is brought to life through Nimmi's clear perceptions of childhood.

ABICAIR, SHIRLEY (1930–), born Melbourne, actor and musician, settled in London in 1952, where she established her own television program. She told stories about Aboriginal children, and *Tales of*

Tumbarumba (1962), illustrated by Margaret Cilento, arose from the program. It has four stories: 'Tumbarumba and Ali the Afghan', 'Tumbarumba and Whurlie the Wildcat', 'Tumbarumba and Dilbay-Dilbay', and 'Tumbarumba and King Billy the Eel'. See also **Aboriginal People in Children's Fiction**.

Aboriginal Children's History of Australia, The (1977), 'written and illustrated by Australia's Aboriginal children', was Commended in the 1978 Picture Book of the Year Awards. This unique book relates Aboriginal history from the Dreaming to today in six sections: Dreaming, Old Time, The Macassans, The Whitefellas, Today, and My Country. Rural and urban experiences are interspersed with traditional stories and with biographies of famous Aboriginal People such as Yagan, Nemarluk, Albert Namatjira, Sir Douglas Nicholls, Evonne Goolagong and Lionel Rose. Colourful illustrations show the exuberance and perceptions of self of Aboriginal children. The book was adapted by the Aboriginal Arts Board of the Australia Council in 1978 for the videotape, 'Dreamtime, This Time — Dreamtime'.

Aboriginal Dreaming Stories. The oral tradition of the Aboriginal People is integral to their rich spiritual life, and has fascinated collectors since the nineteenth century. One of the first collections was Mary Anne Fitzgerald's *King Bungaree's Pyalla and Stories Illustrative of Manners and Customs that Prevailed Among Australian Aborigines* (1891), which contains stories of the 'Koree' people told to the author in her childhood by Bungaree. It also has Fitzgerald's own stories describing customs and incidents of first contact. It has a glossary of words and an introductory poem which asks Bungaree to tell the children tales which he ... 'learnt in times long flown,/When none but tribes of Koree,/Called this golden land their own'. Better known are Katherine Langloh

Parker's collections *Australian Legendary Tales: Folk-lore of the Noongahburrahs as Told to the Piccaninnies* (1896) and *More Australian Legendary Tales* (1898), some stories of which have appeared in Henrietta Drake-Brockman's *Australian Legendary Tales* (q.v., 1953), and Enid Moodie Heddle's *The Boomerang Book of Legendary Tales* (q.v., 1957). *Tales told to Kabbarli* (1972), illustrated by the Aboriginal artist Harold Thomas, are Dreaming stories told to Daisy Bates — 'Kabbarli' or White Grandmother — while she was living at Ooldea on the Nullarbor Plain. The stories have been retold for children by Barbara Ker Wilson. Drawn from the Dreamtime — called the Yamminga, Dhoogoorr, or Nyitting — the stories include 'The Jandu who hunted Walle' (The women who hunted meat), from the people of Yardagurra; 'Walja and Weeloo' (Eaglehawk and Curlew), and 'Njannamurra sings' (The Mallee hen sings). Although the stories are an important resource for later collections, they have been criticised for their eclectic sources, which are not clearly attributed, despite the considerable use of Aboriginal languages. Other collections are the seventy-three stories in *Aboriginal Fables and Legendary Tales* (1965) by A.W. Reed, John K. Ewers's *Tales from the Dead Heart* (1944), Phyllis Power's *Legends from the Outback* (1958), illustrated by Ida Outhwaite, and Deborah Buller-Murphy's *An Attempt to Eat the Moon and Other Stories Recounted from the Aborigines* (1958), illustrated by Elizabeth Durack. Enid Bell's *Legends of the Coochin Valley* (1946) is a collection from the Ugarapul people, featuring heroes such as Butcha of the Ugarapuls. Bell refers to white settlement as 'the white invasion', an advanced concept in the 1940s.

The increasing influence of anthropological studies is evident in Erle Wilson's *Churinga Tales: Stories of Alchuringa — the Dream-Time of the Australian Aborigines* (q.v., 1950), an attempt to present the culture authentically. Ann E. Wells compiled

Tales from Arnhem Land (1959), *Rain in Arnhem Land: Further Adventures of Three Aboriginal Children on the Far North Coast of Australia and Some of the Stories of Their People* (1961) and *Skies of Arnhem Land* (1964), all illustrated by Margaret Paice, which draw on the culture of the Yulnu, of north-east Arnhem Land. Another series, 'Legends of Arnhem Land', began with *The Dew-Wet Earth* (1973) and included *Daybreak* (1973) and *Stars in the Sky* (1973), with stories gathered from the same region. The author acknowledges her debt to the elders at Milingimbi and Yirrkala, although the stories are presented like European tales. Madeleine Brunato's *Worra and the Jilbruke Legend* (1972) and *Worra and the Legends of the Booandiks* (1975) use a fictional character as a device for a retelling of the material, giving due acknowledgement to her sources.

Many collections, however, often labelled 'myths and legends', have been made without any acknowledgement of source or reference to the people who had related their beliefs to whites, such as *Wandjina: Children of the Dreamtime; Aboriginal Myths and Legends* (q.v., 1968), selected by Roland Robinson, Dorothy Carnegie's *Kaka the Cockatoo* (1967), *The Platypus: an Aboriginal Legend Retold and Illustrated for Young Children* (1974) by Katherine Morris, and *Wunnamurra & Noorengong: How the Animals Came to Australia* (1978) by Peter Davidson, illustrated by Tony Oliver.

Foreshadowing an upsurge in Aboriginal writing, *The Legends of Moonie Jarl* (1964), retold by 'Moonie Jarl' (Wilf Reeves), illustrated by 'Wandi' (Olga Miller) has stories from Fraser Island and the Butchulla people which bring to life the role of stories in Aboriginal culture, and their variation from people to people. The tales are accompanied by story patterns in which each symbol has a special meaning. Sylvia Cairns, in *Uncle Willie Mackenzie's Legends of the Goundirs* (1967), has tales of the Darwarbada people which

were told to the author by her uncle (also known as Doungunja), illustrated by Fred Cobbo. *Tales from Torres Strait* (1972) by Margaret Lawrie was selected from her *Myths and Legends of Torres Strait* (1970), a collection drawn from stories told to Lawrie by Moses Dau and Namai Pabai at Boigu Island. The sources and careful documentation are omitted from the children's version of this important work. The material in *Land of the Rainbow Snake: Aboriginal Children's Stories and Song from Western Arnhem Land* (1979) by Catherine Berndt, illustrated by Djoki Yunupingu, comes from the Oenpelli region, and is recorded from the Gunwinggu women. It includes songs in the original language. Catherine Berndt has also retold *Pheasant and Kingfisher* (1987), illustrated by (Arone) Raymond Meeks, from the telling by Nganalgindja in the Gunwinggu language. Oodgeroo Noonuccal (Kath Walker) wrote *Stradbroke Dreamtime* (1972), recollections of her childhood on Stradbroke together with traditional stories. She wrote and illustrated *Father Sky and Mother Earth* (1981), containing creation stories from the Dreamtime, and *Rainbow Serpent* (1988) with Kabul Noonuccal, her son, a plea for harmony between the varied people who live in Australia and the land itself. *Rainbow Serpent* uses Aboriginal English. *Australian Legends of Our Land* (1990) has her stories and illustrations, with photographs of Stradbroke, called Minjerribah, by Reg Morrison. *Joe Nangan's Dreaming: Aboriginal Legends of the North-West* (1976) by Joe Nangan and Hugh Edwards is a collection of twenty stories from the Nygina people. *Kamilaroi* (1978) by John Ferry, illustrated by Graham Wade, describes the life and customs of the Kamilaroi people around 1818, with traditional narratives interwoven. The setting is the junction of the Barwon and Namoi rivers. This is a fine example of the use of song and narrative in a cultural context.

The Goori Goori Bird: from a Legend of the Bidjara People of the Upper Warrego (1984) by Grahame L. Walsh gives the traditional origins of the Milky Way, and *Didane the Koala: from a Legend of the Bidjara People of the Upper Warrego* (1985) is an explanation of the fertility of the Carnarvon area. Dick Roughsey has retold stories from the Lardil of Mornington Island and the Yalanji people of Cape York Peninsula, including *The Giant Devil Dingo* (q.v., 1973), *The Rainbow Serpent* (q.v., 1975) and with Percy Trezise, *The Quinkins* (q.v., 1978). *Djet: Dhuwalny Dhawu Djetpuy* (1977), a story about a boy who became a sea-eagle, is told by Wakuthi Marawili of the Madarrpa clan of Eastern Arnhem Land, and translated and illustrated by Durdiwuy Wunungmurra. The text is in the first language and English, and is a moral tale about the punishment of a greedy boy who would not share his catch of fish. *The Birirrk: Our Ancestors of the Dreaming* (1984), with photographs by Neil McLeod, is a single narrative about the creation. *Gulpilil's Stories of the Dreamtime* (1979), compiled by Hugh Rule and Stuart Goodman and illustrated by Allan Hondow, is drawn from the stories told to David Gulpilil, the well-known dancer and actor, when he was a boy in Arnhem Land, and each story is prefaced by a personal comment by Gulpilil. Goodman's fine photographs were taken for a television series. The introduction to the book is an excellent account of Aboriginal history, cultural and social life.

Aboriginal Legends from the Bibulmun Tribe (1981) by Eddie Bennell, illustrated with fine ink drawings by Anne Thomas, are stories told by Bennell's grandparents and tribal elders from the south-west of WA. A glossary is included. Some are creation stories, others describe the spiritual values of the Bibulmun, which are based on co-operation, friendship and loyalty. Although the language used would suggest that the book is not written for children, the stories would be enjoyed by older children. *The Nearest the White Man Gets: Aboriginal Narratives and Poems of New South Wales* (1989), collected by Roland Robinson, is a collection of stories and story poems, retold as they were collected with a minimum of interference by the editor. The collection acknowledges the power and diversity of the oral tradition.

The Aboriginal publishing house Magabala Books (q.v.) produced Pat Torres's and Magdalene Williams's *The Story of Crow* (1987), which is a bilingual book, in Nyul Nyul and English, with a pronunciation guide. It relates how the crow's feathers became black and his throat red, and originates from the Ngarlin people of Beagle Bay. *Jalygurr: Aussie Animal Rhymes* (1987), written and illustrated by Pat Torres, has ten poems which deal with an assortment of creatures and spirit beings, also in a bilingual format, English and Yawurru, from the Broome area.

The Story of the Falling Star (1989) by Elsie Jones, illustrated by Doug Jones, with collages by Karin Donaldson, was sponsored by the Western Region Aboriginal Land Council. Photographs and speech balloons, with sand maps and collages of location, show how the storytellers and the listeners interact to transfer ancient knowledge. Books produced by the Western Reader Committee, based at Dubbo, NSW, recount traditional stories from the Darling–Barwon River region, such as *King Clyde of Brewarrina* (1980) by Doreen Wright. *The Legend of the Seven Sisters* (1990) by May L. O'Brien is a story of the Wongutha people of the eastern goldfields area of WA, and *Wunambi the Water Snake* (1991), illustrated by Sue Wyatt, is from the same source. Both use Aboriginal forms of English and the mother tongue of the People, with pronunciation guides. *Djugurba: Tales from the Spirit Time* (q.v., 1974) and *Kwork, Kwork: the Green Frog and Other Tales from the Spirit Time* (1977) are collections by Aboriginal People from the Darwin area; *Milbi: Aboriginal Tales from Queensland's Endeavour River* (1980), told and illustrated by Tulo Gordon and translated by John B.

Haviland, comes from northern Queensland. An explanation of how the stories teach cultural knowledge is contained in this excellent collection. *The Lost Boomerang* (1983), by Thomas Stevens Tjapangati, an artist working at Papunya, is the traditional story of how the caves of Uluru were formed, in picture-book format. It was told to the author by Pitjantjatjara and Yankuntjatjara elders. Pamela Lofts has compiled a group of traditional stories such as *How the Kangaroos got their Tails* (1987), told by George Mung Mung Lirrmiyarri, which is a translation from the Kija language of the Warmun people, illustrated by the children of the community; *Warnayarra — the Rainbow Snake* (1987) is told and illustrated by the Senior Boys Class at Lajamanu School. The story belongs to the Warlpiri people — Lajamanu is on the edge of the Tanami Desert. *The Echidna and the Shade Tree* (1984) by Mona Green, from the Djaru people of Hall's Creek, WA, tells of the origins of the echidna's spines and Lake Nongra. Daisy Utemorrah's *Dunbi the Owl* (1983) explains why it is forbidden to harm owls. Brilliant illustrations enhance these productions. From north Queensland to the Kimberleys, Aboriginal People are now telling their own stories. Retellings by Aboriginal People themselves centre these strong and compelling stories in their rightful place within the appropriate cultural and spiritual traditions.

Aboriginal People in Children's Fiction. From *A Mother's Offering to her Children* (1841), descriptions of Aboriginal People in children's books have been racist and denigratory, as has been well documented in the work of Lorna Lippman, Twila Herr, Marji Hill and Alex Barlow, and others. See the Bibliography. Nineteenth-century adventure stories are full of descriptions of the war against Aboriginal People, conducted by gun, poison and disease. The anonymous collection of stories, *The Black Troopers and Other Stories* (1887), for instance, contains an account of the hunting and killing of Bobby Peel, a rebellious Aborigine. The story concludes with an indemnity: 'There are still occasional outrages, but the reckless treatment of the blacks is now held in check by a healthier public opinion.' This contention is not borne out by *The Secret of the Australian Desert* (1896) by Ernest Favenc, which is contemptuous of every aspect of Aboriginal life, and in which the white protagonists deal violently with Aboriginal People. E. Harcourt Burrage's *The Wurra Wurra Boys* (1903) traces the toughening up of the soft and inexperienced Dick Chandler, through encounters with bushrangers, cattle and much shooting. An Aboriginal character, Bucko Boy, is subjected to various racist descriptions, although his skills as a tracker enable him to find 'Massa' Arkwright when he is entombed, warn the others of the bushrangers' attack, and save the day when the bushrangers try to burn the Wurra Wurra boys out. For all this he is rewarded with a second-hand scarlet coat. *Frank Hardinge: From Torrid Zones to Regions of Perpetual Snow* (1908) by Gordon Stables describes many murderous attacks on the Aboriginal People, after which one of the characters, Mamma Molly, reverently exclaims, 'De Lawd done go fight on our side'. The author then provides his own answer to the Aboriginal question: 'I may be blamed if I say that slavery would be a blessing in disguise for these poor benighted wretches. As this cannot be thought of the next best plan would be to place them on reservations, or form some great scheme of emigration for them ... '

Early twentieth-century depictions are less explicit, but in order to rationalise the dispossession and exploitation of traditional communities, Aboriginal People were depicted as inferior beings doomed to extinction. Such novels as Mrs Aeneas Gunn's *The Little Black Princess: a True Tale of Life in the Never-Never Land* (1905) or the early Billabong (q.v.) books by Mary

Grant Bruce described Aboriginal People as quaint and childlike, even silly. In *From Billabong to London* (1915) Jim refers to Aboriginal People as 'a most unpleasant crowd ... Useless, shifty, lazy, thieving ... ', despite the family's reliance on Billy as stockman, stableman, messenger, water-carrier and general rouseabout. In *Norah of Billabong* (1913) the Lintons and Wally are able to identify a white child living with Aboriginal People by the cut of her instep! Later well-meant attempts to improve the characterisation of Aboriginal People such as Frank Dalby Davison's *Children of the Dark People: an Australian Folk Tale* (q.v., 1936) or Kylie Tennant's *All the Proud Tribesmen* (q.v., 1959) purport to present traditional Aboriginal life, but the results are often ethnocentric. The first is a European fantasy with only pseudo-Aboriginal content and the second is a picture of childlike Islanders who always defer to their white schoolteacher.

Tarlton Rayment's *The Prince of the Totem: a Simple Black Tale for Clever White Children* (1933), despite its subtitle, is a portrayal of dignified Aboriginal People with a complex cultural life. Rayment makes the connection between the people, the land and their Dreamtime, and applauds a lifestyle attuned to the environment. The book is dedicated to 'Unaipon, Trusted and Wise Man of the Narrinyerri'. Rayment uses many Aboriginal words, but in his only acknowledgement of sources says that they are 'from many tribes'. His novel is more sensitive than many others, at a time when depictions of Aboriginal People were generally racist. Although a decade had elapsed, Jane Ada Fletcher's *Little Brown Piccaninnies of Tasmania* (q.v., 1950) describes the culture through what it does not have, rather than on its own terms. Fred Lane's *Patrol to the Kimberleys* (1958) paints a picture of treacherous and primitive Aboriginal People who are treated like naughty children by their benefactors, the whites, who always know better than the blacks. Only the black trackers earn honorary status. In

Phyllis Power's *Under Australian Skies* (1955) Nat Clarke, the station manager, contemplates drugging the flour which is handed out to the restive station Aboriginal People, as the 'Boer settlers in Natal doped the rations they gave their Kaffirs'. Less obviously repugnant, and better known, is *Walkabout* (1959) by James Vance Marshall, first published as *The Children*. Mary and Peter survive an air crash and meet an unnamed boy who teaches them how to survive. The novel has been widely acclaimed as a book which depicts the moral superiority of a culture which is not concerned with material advancement, but by placing cultures on a ladder from primitive to advanced, it perpetuates the myth of the Noble Savage. Aboriginal culture is as misrepresented as the locale of the novel.

Advances were made with Rex Ingamells's *Aranda Boy: an Aboriginal Story* (1952). It recounts Gurra's growth to manhood, and the Aranda's first contact with white pastoralists. The massacre of the people and their exclusion from their traditional hunting grounds is seen through Aboriginal eyes. However, the happy ending, when Gurra saves his group by drawing them under the benevolent care of Don Byrne, a local station-owner, suggests that this is the way forward for the Aranda. Such a view typified race relations of the period, which aimed to draw the Aboriginal People into the work of the pastoral industry. Nevertheless, Ingamells's knowledge of the culture and traditions of the Aranda, learnt from the anthropologists A.P. Elkin and T.G.H. Strehlow, and Bill Harney, a student of the Aranda people, give authenticity to Gurra's development. A more blatant attempt to portray white culture as the way forward for Aboriginal People is Stella Sammon's *The Lucky Stone* (1969), in which Quei and Bundjell are taken away from their people to learn white ways. M.E. Patchett's contribution to the portrayal of Aboriginal People was at first equally unenlightened. In her *Ajax* books,

Mitta, an Aboriginal girl, is frequently likened to some sort of animal and displays far less intelligence than either Ajax the dog, or Tam the horse. Patchett's approach changes in *Quarter Horse Boy* (1970), where Tod's horsemanship and courage are shown to be the backbone of the horse stud.

Mavis Thorpe Clark's *The Brown Land was Green* (q.v., 1956) raised the issue of the slaughter of the people through the character of Mundowie, although Clark weakens her sympathetic picture by providing Mundowie with a menial place as nursemaid at the conclusion of the novel. Similarly, in Clark's *Spark of Opal* (1968) acceptance for Steve and Kathy depends on disowning their own culture in favour of white ways. Fred Baxter's *Snake for Supper* (1968) recognises the diversity of Aboriginal culture through its juxtaposition of the Kurnai and the Bidwelli people of Gippsland, its use of Kurnai language and its strong setting. At the conclusion, however, Gurawin, Jirri and Babbilla desert their people to stay with Kathy. An international connection is made in Leslie Rees's *Boy Lost on Tropic Coast* (1968) when a group of racists with links with South Africa attempt to stop Brace Edwards, a Torres Strait Islander and the cleverest boy in the school, sitting a scholarship examination.

Australian authors and illustrators have also used Aboriginal characters to add exotic interest to their creations. During the 1960s, Brownie Downing created a series of picture-books using romantic pictures of neat Aboriginal children which had great popular appeal: *Tinka and his Friends* (1960), *A Tale of Mischief* (1963), *Children of the Dreaming* (1966) and *Tinka and the Bunyip* (1966). Downing commercialised the depiction of Aboriginal children even further by using them for prints and products, such as china plates and tea-towels. Shirley Abicair's stories in *Tales of Tumbarumba* (1962) present Aboriginal life without authenticity. At one point Tumbarumba charges his friends three

witchetty grubs to see a wildcat he has caught, a concept quite alien to traditional Aboriginal life. An example of the misuse of Aboriginal culture can be found in Ivan Southall's *To the Wild Sky* (q.v., 1967), where Carol, who 'has Aboriginal blood', miraculously discovers that by listening to the earth she can identify bush food.

During the 1950s, Aboriginal People became more insistent that their history be given its rightful place in society, and many authors took up the changes in attitudes which were occurring. The impact of white invasion is portrayed in Nan Chauncy's *Tangara: 'Let Us set off Again'* (q.v., 1960). The destruction of Merrina's people, the Tasmanians, is vividly drawn, even though it is seen at all times through the eyes of the white girl, Lexie. Chauncy later wrote *Mathinna's People* (q.v., 1967), again about the Tasmanian Aboriginal People, and attempted to create the situations in which first contact was made, this time through the eyes of the Aboriginal People themselves. Even in 1975, however, Fae Hewston Stevens in *The Mallee Riders* (1975) perpetuates the idea that Aboriginal People must put aside their concept of family and communal support in favour of progress, in a world where attending school, a neat house, and above all, the promotion of the individual, leads to success. Fifteen years earlier, Patricia Wrightson's *The Rocks of Honey* (1960) had been more in the vanguard of change. Barney, Winnie, and an Aboriginal boy, Eustace Murray, find a stone axe. The dilemma which Eustace faces is resolved when, persuaded by his Uncle Tom, he embraces his Aboriginal heritage, and returns the axe to its proper place. Wrightson went on to write the Wirrun (q.v.) trilogy. Amy Bunker's *Millingi* (1973) depicts life before the coming of the white people, with an adolescent girl at the centre. Millingi has some slight contact with whites, but the novel is mainly about her reluctance to marry the man chosen for her, and her love for a younger man. Mary Durack's *The Courteous Savage: Yagan of*

Swan River (q.v., 1964), in recognition of the racist overtones of 'savage', was retitled *Yagan of the Bibbulmun* in 1976. Despite her claim that the Bibbulmun have all vanished, which is challenged by their descendants' existence, Durack's treatment of Bibbulmun customs is knowledgeable. Her choice of an Aboriginal hero as a subject was unusual for the period. The first edition was illustrated by her sister Elizabeth, the second by Revel Cooper, a Bibbulmun descendant. *Hughie* (q.v., 1971) by David Martin examined a more contemporary political issue, based on an actual attempt to confront racism in a country town by a group of Sydney Aboriginal People.

The theme of *Hughie* points to the developments which were occurring in writing about Aboriginal People. Thiele's *The Fire in the Stone* (q.v., 1973) begins as a novel about Ernie, but the Aboriginal character, Willie Winnowie, becomes the centre of the action, and the treatment of Willie and his people is the main concern of the novel. The warmth and sense of community which characterises Willie's family contrasts with Ernie's isolation from his uncaring father. Willie's tenacity, courage and resourcefulness save Nick's life. After the rescue, while Ernie is congratulated, Willie is ignored, and Ernie recognises this injustice is a pointer to prevailing attitudes. Willie's death concludes the novel, and serves as a bitter comment on the treatment of Aboriginal People. Sensitivity continued to grow, so that Ralph Smart and Mary Cathcart Borer's *Bush Christmas* (q.v., 1947) was reissued in 1980 with racist references to Aboriginal People removed. Aboriginal People were being accorded a dignity and power which they had previously been denied, and authors were finding them a rich source of inspiration. Max Fatchen introduced Aboriginal characters in *The Spirit Wind* (q.v., 1973) and *Chase Through the Night* (1976). In these adventure stories the character who is able to save the main protagonists uses knowledge unique to

Aboriginal People. Similarly, Thomas Roy in his two novels about the Cape York people, *The Curse of the Turtle* (q.v., 1977) and *The Vengeance of the Dolphin* (1980), shows an understanding of Aboriginal life, although the books draw on details of culture found in different parts of the continent. Faith Bandler's two books about her ancestors, *Wacvie* (1977) and *Marani in Australia* (1980) (with Len Fox), describe the conditions suffered by Islanders kidnapped to work on the sugar-cane fields. Two authors who have based their novels on Aboriginal characters, creating fantasies which admit the sophistication of the complex cultural life of Aboriginal People, are Bill Scott and Patricia Wrightson. Scott's *Boori* (q.v., 1978) and *Darkness Under the Hills* (1980) deal with the adventures of Boori, a hero figure. His *Shadow Among the Leaves* (1984) gives the responsibility for saving the rainforest to Aboriginal spirits. Patricia Wrightson's trilogy about Wirrun, which begins with *The Ice is Coming* (q.v., 1977), is a fantasy about a man who fights the dark forces which threaten Australia. It is one of the few works written for children which acknowledges the source of the author's information, and her debt to the lore. Also, unlike Scott, Wrightson creates a successful representation of Aboriginal speech.

There has been a significant development in the use of Aboriginal characters since the 1960s. A comparison made between Colin Thiele's *Coorong Captive* (1985) and his earlier novel, *Storm Boy* (1963), shows this change in understanding. In *Coorong Captive*, the white boy, Fitzie, has a similar relationship to Goondalee as Storm Boy has to Fingerbone Bill in the earlier Thiele novel, but in *Coorong Captive* Goondalee is given greater prominence. He is the one who alerts Fitzie to the destruction of the environment which white people have perpetrated and he is also able to save Fitzie from the bird-smugglers. Goondalee's speech patterns, rather than the pidgin English which Fingerbone Bill uses, also show how Thiele attempted to represent Aboriginal People more accurately, despite the clairvoyance attributed to Goondalee, apparently drawn from his Aboriginality. However, in some modern novels, such as Pat Peatfield Price's *The Hills of the Black Cockatoo* (1981), there continues to be abuse of cultural knowledge. There is no acknowledgement of sources; terms such as 'part-Aboriginal', or 'tribe'; stereotyping of appearance, such as 'flashing white teeth', and racist illustrations occur. Typically, it is the intervention of a white scientist in Mary Small's *Night of the Muttonbirds* (1981) which convinces Matthew to return to school: his own people do not consider formal education as particularly important.

Strong portrayals of Aboriginal life should be mentioned. *The Day we Lost Forever* (1988) by Andrew Taylor, illustrated by Judy Leech, recounts the life of the Wurundjeri people, who lived on the site of Melbourne, and their reactions during the fateful time of John Batman's arrival. Jeanie Adams's picture-books *Pigs and Honey* (q.v., 1989) and *Going for Oysters* (1991) are set on Cape York Peninsula. The family hunts for wild pigs, bush honey, and oysters, guided by Grandma. Sophie Masson's *Sooner or Later* (1991) depicts the racism of a country town, and draws attention to its bloody history. The book deals with the need to take Aboriginal People for what they are, without constant comparisons, and the long battle which is required to overcome deeply ingrained prejudices. *The Fat and Juicy Place* (1992) by Diana Kidd shows a development in the depiction of Aboriginal People. The speech, cultural perspectives, and family relationships of an urban group are presented in a story of death, acceptance and love. 'I heard that wind crying. Crying like Birdman's mob when them gubbahs came and took their land … We don't want to leave that land … We love all them sacred rocks and caves and hills and trees.' The growth in pub-lishing by the People themselves during the late twentieth century promises major changes in stories about Aboriginal People in Australian children's books. Further reading: Hill and Barlow, *Black Australia*.

Aboriginal Studies Press, the publications unit of the Australian Institute of Aboriginal and Torres Strait Islander Studies, has published the work of Aboriginal and Torres Strait Islanders since the 1980s. The first children's book published by the press was *The Story of the Falling Star* (1989) by Elsie Jones. Other publications include *The Legend of the Seven Sisters* (1990) and *Wunambi the Water Snake* (1991) by May O'Brien, both illustrated by Sue Wyatt.

Aborigines, see **Aboriginal People**

Absolutely Rapt: a Collection of Love Stories for Young People, see **Collections**

ADAMS, ARTHUR H. For *Australian Nursery Rimes* (1917), *Fifty Nursery Rhymes with Music* (1924) and *A Second Set of Forty Nursery Rhymes* (?1924) see **Nursery Rhymes**.

ADAMS, BERTHA SOUTHEY (Mrs T.C. BRAMMALL) (1876–1957) wrote material for children's radio programs, and novels and short stories for adults. *Dusky Dell* (1898) was published by the *Launceston Examiner*, and is set in Tasmania. The orphaned Dell is taken in by a large family, where she is harshly treated before being rescued by her long-lost parent. See also **Germans**; Adams also wrote *The Little Sister* (1916).

ADAMS, JEANIE (1945–), born Hamilton, Victoria, lived at Aurukun for eight years as a community arts worker, and has written two picture-books out of that experience. *Pigs and Honey* (q.v., 1989) and *Going for Oysters* (1991) show through text and impressionistic pictures the pleasure of hunting and camping with the Aurukun on the Archer River and the beaches of the Gulf of Carpentaria. See also **Aboriginal People in Children's Fiction**. Adams has written a book about crafts at Aurukun, co-illustrated a dictionary of Wik-Mungkan, and, with Rachel Tonkin, illustrated *Biaga and Lagi* (1977) by Jack Goodluck.

ADAMSON, BARTLETT (1884–1951), born Ringarooma, Tasmania, was a journalist and poet. His novel, *Mystery Gold* (1926), illustrated by Edgar A. Holloway, is an adventure story set on a tropical island, Malusa, where Billy Gordon and Dan Rockley find treasure, defeating all other comers, just because they are white Anglo-Saxons. Adamson contributed stories to *Fatty Finn's Weekly* in 1934.

Adelaide on the Torrens River, at the foothills of the Mt Lofty Ranges, was settled by whites in 1836 on a plan designed by Colonel Light. As it lies on the edge of the great inland deserts of the continent, Adelaide is the starting point for many of the outback adventures of the nineteenth century. Mr Oliphant, the settler who welcomes Frank to SA, in Rev. T.P. Wilson's novel *Frank Oldfield; or, Lost and Found: a Tale* (1869), emphasises the possibilities for the new chum there, although there are the same wickednesses as can be found in London. The novel contains a description of the city in the mid-nineteenth century, including Hindley Street, Rundle Street and the Parklands. 'We have no gas as yet ... Well, then, look along each side of the street and you'll see ordinary lamps projecting from houses at tolerably regular intervals. These houses are all public-houses ... I fear it tells of abundant crime and misery.' James Skipp Borlase in *Daring Deeds; and Tales of Peril and Adventure* (1868) points to the German influence, so central to children's books about SA. The city was 'the chief German resort in Australia [where] the language of the "Fatherland" was as fre-

quently heard in its streets as the dialect of the Celt or Saxon'.

More recent immigrants are described in Christobel Mattingley's *New Patches for Old* (1977), where the family find the climate unforgiving and the housing less than they have expected. Geoffrey Dutton in his poem 'The Beatles in Adelaide' calls Adelaide 'the square city, named for a dull, dead queen', but his picture-book, *Tisi and the Pageant* (1968), shows the city celebrating in a colourful display, and some of its strong cultural life. Colin Thiele in *The Undercover Secret* (1982) describes Adelaide in the 1930s. When Jenny and her friend visit Aunt Olga, they pass Hackney Road tram depot, go through the Botanic Park, and catch a ride up Hindley Street, watching 'the buildings slide past — the Exhibition Building, the University, the Museum with its whale skeletons, the Public Library, the War Memorial', then return via King William Road, where 'the marble columns on the new Parliament House shone brightly in the sun but the Government Printing Office was dingy and drab ... '. Erica Hale's *Catch the Sun* (1984) shows a darker side, as Lennie and her unemployed friends share an old house in Brompton, or window-shop in the city, and fill in their days eating their lunch at the Memorial Garden beneath the Cross of Sacrifice.

Adolescence. In the nineteenth-century novels, heroes went from school to station or marriage in a swift and apparently painless transition from child to adult. As soon as a young person was able to leave the fireside of his or her parents, he or she was expected to find a way in the world. Arthur and James Gilpin are in their mid-teens in *The Gilpins and Their Fortunes, an Australian Tale* (1865) by W.H.G. Kingston, but are mature enough to run 'Warragong' Station. Dominic in *First in the Field: a Story of New South Wales* (1894) by G.A. Henty is 15 and an experienced bushman. Esther in *Seven Little Australians* (1894) by Ethel Turner is 20, with a baby and six stepchildren, the eldest 16. Mona in *The Noughts and Crosses* (1917) by Lilian Turner, is just 17 when she marries Stephen. Mary Grant Bruce's Norah Linton may blush a little at times, but she is not troubled by self-doubt. In *Possum* (1917), however, the young heroine yearns for something better for herself than what she is. Earlier, Louise Mack had recognised some of the uncertainty of adolescents in her trilogy, the first of which was *Teens: a Story of Australian Schoolgirls* (1897). Lenny and Mabel are tentative, passionate about each other, and interested in the opposite sex.

The lengthening period between childhood and adulthood has been a preoccupation of many novelists of the post-World War II years. Hesba Brinsmead, Ivan Southall, Colin Thiele, Mavis Thorpe Clark and others explored the widening horizons of youth as childhood was set aside. Bruno in *Sun on the Stubble* (q.v., 1961) has a physical and emotional separation from his childhood when he leaves the security of the landscape which has defined his earliest years for the unknown future awaiting him in Adelaide. Ivan Southall is absorbed with the pain of adolescence in *Josh* (1971) and *The Mysterious World of Marcus Leadbeater* (1990), as is Gary Crew in his first two novels, *The Inner Circle* (1986) and *The House of Tomorrow* (1988). The recognition of the burgeoning of sexuality during puberty received greater emphasis during the 1970s. *Puberty Blues* (q.v., 1979) by Gabrielle Carey and Kathy Lette embraces a new realism, as Debbie and Sue smoke, swear, deceive their parents, and discuss their sexual encounters. Margaret D. Clark's *Pugwall* (1987) and *Pugwall's Summer* (1989) and Jocelyn Harewood's *Voices in the Wash-House* (1990) speak with the same light-hearted voice as Carey and Lette. A humorous novel which shows the complexity of adolescent emotions and the need for recognising the responsibilities of the adult world is James Grieve's *A Season of Grannies* (1987).

Loosening the ties with the family is part of adolescence, and conflicts between young people, parents, and society, have also engaged writers. In *The Min-Min* (q.v., 1967) by Mavis Thorpe Clark Sylvie returns to the womb of the family, ultimately on her own terms, but for Brenton, in *Beyond the Labyrinth* (q.v., 1988) by Gillian Rubinstein, there is no such solution, and the future, like the times, is unclear. Other writers, such as Simon French, Allan Baillie, Libby Gleeson, Libby Hathorn and Robin Klein (in her books for older readers) also centre on the difficulty of growing up in a society of uncertainty and change. Mavis Thorpe Clark, Colin Thiele and Ivan Southall draw on an adolescence more innocent than that represented in the novels of younger writers. Gillian Rubinstein, John Marsden, Frank Willmott, Jocelyn Harewood, Maureen McCarthy and James Grieve present issues such as sexuality, family breakdown, and violence, in the distinctive idiom of the young and from the viewpoint of today. These young people often appear to be tough and streetwise, and life's ups and downs assault their vulnerability and youthful inexperience, but they are usually able to rely on someone who cares.

The adolescence of the less privileged has been examined by Erica Hale in *Catch the Sun* (1984); Frank Willmott in *Suffer Dogs* (1985) and *Here Comes the Night* (1986); Gary Crew in *The House of Tomorrow* (1988); Pina Grieco-Tiso in *Blitz: a Bomber's Nightmare* (1991); and Maureen McCarthy in her 'In Between' series (1985) and *Ganglands* (1992). These writers deal with adolescents who are on the fringes of insanity, criminality and violence. They reject the values of society and society has rejected them. On their own in a hostile world, they have no safety net to catch them but their own inner resources. Often those resources are insufficient and tragedy results.

Over a quarter of a century after *Sun on the Stubble* (q.v., 1961), Argus's growth, in

John Marsden's *The Journey* (1988), involves sexual encounters and the responsibility of a family. Young people are again being initiated into the world of adults at an early age, but the modern world is drawn as less accepting of them and the hurdles more difficult to overcome.

"*Advance Australia*" ABC, see **Alphabet Books**

'Adventure Island' was a television program produced by Godfrey Phillip which ran from 1967 to 1972 on the ABC. It was written by John Michael Howson and presented by Howson, Nancy Cato, Liz Harris and others, and set in the village of Diddley-Dum-Diddley. Children were invited to become a part of the eccentric world of Clown, Fester Fumble, Mister Meaney and Panda. It built on the format of the 'Magic Circle Club' (q.v.), and maintained the same high quality of content and production. Its axing (on its fifth birthday) provoked questions in Parliament. Books arising from the program were *The Birthday Party*, *Clown and the Pirates*, *Flower Potts and the Giant* and *Frosty the Snowman* (all 1969), all by John Michael Howson.

Adventure Stories. The adventure story dominated writing for young people during the late nineteenth and early twentieth centuries, presenting adventure through exploration and settlement, and as a part of the cultural function of Empire. The land was the arena where boys and men could test their endurance, either to restore lost fortunes or as a way of being won over to the new country, with its freer and more egalitarian life. There is also evidence of an emerging national identity, always within the confines of the British tradition. Control of the landscape involved the attempted subjection of the original inhabitants, and many of the nineteenth-century novelists have an incident involving Aboriginal People where the traditional owners are hunted off their land, such as E.T. Hooley's *Tarragal: or, Bush Life in Australia* (1897), or Ernest Favenc's *The Secret of the Australian Desert* (1896).

Typical of the early adventure story is William Howitt's *A Boy's Adventures in the Wilds of Australia: or, Herbert's Note-Book* (1854). It is loosely constructed and anecdotal, as many of these nineteenth-century books were, but it includes vivid and humorous descriptions of Australian life, including experiences on the goldfields, where the author had spent two years after 1852. Unencumbered by any pretence at plot, such novels depended on the rough life experienced by settlers for their action, and the daily hazards of life in the alien bush provided sufficient interest. Howitt had travelled in Australia, but many English writers who had never set foot on Australian soil still used Australia as they used Africa or Asia, as an exotic setting to provide adventures for their heroes. The prolific English writer W.H.G. Kingston wrote many novels about Australia, such as *Twice Lost: a Story of Shipwreck, and of Adventure in the Wilds of Australia* (1876), a title which says it all, and *Peter Biddulph: the Rise and Progress of an Australian Settler* (1881), an account of the hero's voyage to NSW and his experiences there when it was still a convict colony. Kingston's *The Young Berringtons: or, the Boy Explorers* (1880) is a similar account of adventures with bushrangers, floods and Aboriginal People.

The gold rushes and the ensuing heyday of bushranging provided colourful experiences which placed the hero in mortal danger, from which he could extricate himself without harm, possibly saving a woman or child in the process. *The Treasure Cave of the Blue Mountains* (1898) by William Henry Oliphant Smeaton provides such a picture, as does James Skipp Borlase's *The Night Fossickers and other Australian Tales of Peril and Adventure* (1867). The novels of Joseph Bowes also fit the pattern, such as *The New-Chums: a Jungle Story* (1915) and *The Jackaroos: Life on a Cattle Run* (1923): the villain is brought down by the youthful hero or heroes who find their fortune after considerable inconvenience. Similarly, A.A. Methley's *Bushrangers' Gold* (1930) contains all the clichés of Australian adventure. English brothers Jeff and Tom are brought to his Australian station, 'Anzac', by their uncle; they soon get themselves into difficulties, but eventually find enough gold to restore everyone's fortunes. Alexander and Robert Macdonald's heroes find gold and opals, at the expense of other fortune-seekers, in a larger-than-life landscape. Alexander Macdonald's adventures, such as *The Pearl Seekers: a Tale of the Southern Seas* (1908), were often set in the Pacific Ocean, as its myriads of islands with their rich cultural mix offered romantic possibilities for adventures. Louis Becke's real-life experiences roving and exploring around the Pacific and its lands provided the same copy, in *Tom Wallis: a Tale of the South Seas* (1900) and *The Settlers of Karossa Creek and other Stories of Australian Bush Life* (1906). Charles Barrett's *The Isle of Palms: a Story of Adventure* (1915) is another Pacific adventure, about a boy who prefers nature to sport. The novel begins in a private school for wealthy landowners' sons, and moves to Queensland and the South Sea islands, providing much incidental information about the flora and fauna of those places.

As the remoter parts of Australia became more accessible, writers at times pushed beyond the boundaries of credibility to retain an arena for their adventure. Written by Barrett under the pseudonym 'Donald Barr', *Warrigal Joe: a Tale of the Never Never* (1946) is a long-winded story which includes the discovery of long-lost cities and valuable idols, which Jim, Bob, Ted and the swagman, Warrigal Joe, loot with impunity. In a similar vein, Bernard Cronin's *The Treasure of the Tropics* (1928) has a lost city in central Australia, this time ruled by a Moon-God, whose eyes shine with the light apparently emanating from radium. The evil characters with whom

Jerry, Reg and Scissors tangle are exposed as spies from the 'Red Russian Soviet'. The young heroes come through the adventure with the lost city destroyed and a bag of green diamonds. More realistic and readable, the novels of 'William Hatfield' (q.v.) also range across the landscape, bringing fortune to those lads who dare to venture into its remoter parts. Some of these adventure stories suspend disbelief beyond reasonable limits. 'Boyd Cable's' *The Wrist-Watch Castaways* (1929) is an unintentionally funny account of two children washed up on a desert island, with only a watch and a biscuit tin to keep starvation at bay. Bosun, who is a Girl Guide, uses her watch to fashion fish hooks and make fire, and the biscuit tin is able to be converted into a distillery for fresh water. In Dorothy Mellor's *Enchanting Isles* (1934), illustrated by Ida Rentoul Outhwaite, David and Jeanette fly their gliders (from a standing start) around the Pacific, stopping off at Lord Howe, Norfolk, Fiji, New Caledonia and other islands to valiantly save white men from the traditional inhabitants, who are invariably savage and untrustworthy.

The adventure story was still identifiable as a genre in the 1940s. Mary Grant Bruce contributed many titles during the first half of the twentieth century, from her Billabong (q.v.) books to *Karalta* (1941). Ion Llewellyn Idriess's *Headhunters of the Coral Sea* (1940), *Nemarluk: King of the Wilds* (1941), *The Opium Smugglers: a True Story of our Northern Seas* (1948) and *The Drums of Mer* (1933) are adventure stories, which Morris Miller says are a 'combination of fiction, description, history, ethnology and anthropology'. Louise Kinch's *Stories of Adventure* (1945) is in the format of a picture-book, illustrated by Edith Grieve. The first story, 'The Bush Adventure', is a return to the romantic adventure story of colonial times, except for its sympathetic treatment of Aboriginal People. In a small and idyllic mining community, Joan and her brother find gold, rescue an Aborigine, and are themselves saved from bushrangers by friendly Aboriginal People. In Dorothy Ingle's *Three Girls and an Island: a Story for Girls* (1947) Pam, Betty and Sam camp on an island in the Hawkesbury River, and uncover the hide-out of a gang of counterfeiters. Violet M. Methley wrote many adventure stories for girls, such as *Dragon Island: an Adventure Story for Girls* (1938), illustrated by Stella Schmolle, and *Derry Down-Under: a Story of Adventure in Australia* (1943), illustrated by L.F. Lupton. *Scum o' the Seas* (1944) by Eric Bedford is set during the gold rushes. George Humbolt, the pure-hearted hero, keeps himself honest amid a gang of crooks and pirates, and finds his long-lost father at the end.

After World War II, new horizons opened up. The Cold War stimulated stories about spies, uranium and advanced technologies. In Bernard O'Reilly's *Wild River* (q.v., 1949), a search for pitchblende on a Queensland property involves outwitting rival prospectors. Allan Aldous's *Danger on the Map* (1947) has Bluey Dowd and his co-adventurers foiling the plans of international crooks over the same mineral. ' ... the whole plot to steal uranium from Australia was part of the machinations of a gang of munitions racketeers who had enlisted the aid of power-lusting scientists in an effort to achieve world gangster-domination.' During the 1950s, George Finkel, Ivan Southall in his Simon Black (q.v.) books, and John Gunn in his Peter Kent (q.v.) series used the experience of war and the political antagonisms of the post-war period to provide adventure. In Finkel's *Cloudmaker* (1965) Russian Communists kidnap a young scientist. David is saved by three men who are either friends from the war years or on the Allied side. *The Mystery of Secret Beach* (1962), also by Finkel, has local Communists doing some dirty work on the currency for their Chinese masters. In Richard Graves's novels about six boys, *Spear and Stockwhip* (1950) and its sequel *Tidinbilla Adventure* (1951), the Russians

spy on Australia, with the support of local Communists who hide behind the front of peace workers. Peter Keene, a British Naval Intelligence secret investigator in Michael Barrett's *Traitor at Twenty Fathoms* (1963), goes diving off the north-west coast, near Port Barrow, looking for a device on a sunken submarine. The traitors are working for a foreign power, and their Australian colleagues are involved in the deception because they believe in peace and disarmament, apparently a quaintly naive but dangerous goal. Jim Blair's *The Secret of the Reef* (1963) is set on a small island off the coast of Papua New Guinea, and describes the efforts of Rags Bunting, Podge Wiltshire and Tiny Lambert to identify the source of a cargo cult which has confused the local workers. After much use of judo and small arms, the culprits are finally identified as a group of Japanese who are searching for a sunken submarine which has a fortune in gold aboard. M.E. Patchett used the new skill of underwater diving in *Undersea Treasure Hunters* (1955), *Caribbean Adventure* (1957) and *The Quest for Ati Manu* (1960).

By the late 1960s, the Cold War story was losing favour to other themes, although Paul Buddee also uses the currency and some missing gold for the adventure in *The Unwilling Adventurers* (1967). The escapades of Bernie and Brian, who are kidnapped twice, is told by the entertaining Brian, a worthy descendant of Ray Harris's Turkey. Less entertaining, but also about gold-smuggling, is Mervyn A. Cooke's *A Date with Destiny* (1965), illustrated by Richard Ressom. A complicated plot, which ranges from Melbourne to the Yanchep Caves in WA, involves an orphaned Dutch boy, Pieter Doorn, and three cousins, who discover a hidden submarine being used by Asian and local smugglers. The children's search begins with a treasure-hunt for relics of *De Vergulde Draeck* (the *Gilt Dragon*), a Dutch ship lost off the WA coast in 1656. Lawrie Ryan's *Toog's Island* (1979) is set in 1883, on the Queensland coast. David Jones,

Amy and Jody take the enigmatic Hester for a picnic on Toog's Island, where they run into the brutal bosun of the *Nancy Belle*. An exciting series of events enlarge a story which has a mysterious edge and the flavour of *Treasure Island*.

From the 1970s the adventure as the central purpose for action in the children's novel was overtaken by characterisation, in the work of Joan Phipson, Ivan Southall and Colin Thiele. These writers, in books such as *Keep Calm* (1978), *What About Tomorrow?* (1977) and *Shatterbelt* (1987), have produced adventure stories, but the adventure serves to reveal a source of character previously untapped. Again the recent adventure story is more likely to end in disaster than the restoration of fortune. Thiele's *February Dragon* (q.v., 1965) concludes with everything lost, N.L. Ray's *Nightmare to Nowhere* (1980) with the death of a central character. A less optimistic view of life, and pressure to present fiction within the bounds of young people's experience, has led to the demise of the adventure story, although adventure still inspires other genres, such as the war story, the mystery story and science fiction.

Adventures of "Chunder Loo", The, see O'FERRALL, ERNEST

Agapanthus appears in three books by Barbara Macfarlane. See *Naughty Agapanthus*.

'AGATHA, MIRIAM', see LE BRETON, AGATHA

Air Patrol series, by Paul Buddee, includes *Air Patrol and the Hijackers* (1973), *Air Patrol and the Saboteurs* (1973), *Air Patrol and the Underwater Spies* (1973) and *Air Patrol and the Secret Intruders* (1973). Four helicopter crews carry out secret missions to protect Australian security. The commanding officer is Kim Kirwan; however, much of the adventure lies in the exploits of the four intrepid boys who are cadet officers: Sandy Muirhead, John Ashby, Peter Wilson and Tim Walker. The hijackers are after gold; the saboteurs are involved in the prevention of a satellite launch; the underwater spies transmit secret weather information to foreign atomic submarines; the secret intruders are drug-smugglers. The Air Patrol is at the cutting edge of the defence of the Australian Way of Life, and its cadet officers are models of courage, initiative and airmanship.

Aircraft of Today and Tomorrow (1953) by J.H. and W.D. Martin was joint winner of the 1953 Book of the Year Awards. Illustrated with many black-and-white photographs and sketches, it is a comprehensive general and historical account of flight. The emphasis is on the Australian experience, but new developments in Europe and the USA are also discussed. Although the style is straightforward, the facts are linked to the flamboyant personalities of aviators, so the text makes exciting reading. The authors also wrote *The Australian Book of Trains* (q.v., 1947).

Ajax is the dog who features in books by Mary Elwyn Patchett.

Alan Marshall Prize for Children's Literature is a division of the Victorian Premier's Literary Awards. **1988** *So Much to Tell You* ... (q.v., 1987) by John Marsden; **1989** *The Lake at the End of the World* (q.v., 1988) by Caroline Macdonald; **1990** *Onion Tears* (1989) by Diana Kidd; **1991** *Strange Objects* (q.v., 1990) by Gary Crew; **1992** *The House Guest* (q.v., 1991) by Eleanor Nilsson.

ALANSON, ALFRED GODWIN (1863–1943), born Hargraves, NSW, was a teacher in Sydney, establishing the reputation for excellence of Randwick Public School, where he taught from 1907 to 1929. He was active in teachers' associations, was president of the Australian Teachers' Federation in 1923, and edited the journal of the NSW Teachers' Federation from 1919 to 1939. He wrote three adventure stories. In *The Diggers of Black Rock Hill* (1908), after a disastrous bushfire, where the settlers only manage to save their houses, Tom Simpson and Jim Charlesworth leave their properties to seek shearing work and gold-fossicking, in the hope of finding a fortune. *Ben Halyard; a Story of Bass and Flinders* (1907) describes the first contact between Aboriginal People and the sailors, accompanied by their cabin boy, Ben. Dilba and Doonga set out to attack Bass and Flinders, but fail. See also **Bass, George**. As 'Russell Allanson', Alanson wrote *Terraweena: a Story of a Mid-Winter Vacation in Australia* (1905), which was first published in the English magazine *Chatterbox*. The novel opens at Sydney Grammar School, where Harry Austin invites Bob Walters, Arthur Clay and Tom Burrowes to his outback home. The boys hunt kangaroos, muster brumbies, visit an Aboriginal camp, and witness a bush wedding. In one incident Bob is kidnapped by Aboriginal People, but saved by his redoubtable chums.

ALDOUS, ALLAN (1911–), born Perth, has written drama, novels and material for radio. *Quitters Can't Win* (1946) is a conventional 'boy saves family honour' story. Ron Grant sets out to prove that his father has been falsely accused of embezzlement, a feat which he accomplishes through a straight defensive right and the spilling of much Irish blood. Aldous then built stories around the preoccupations of his times. *Danger on the Map* (1947), illustrated by Alan McCulloch, concerns a treasure-hunt on the Arnhem Land coast, where Bluey Dowd, Dr Taggart, and Johnny Jingo (the Aboriginal stockman who provides the comic relief), fight off mysterious gunmen and armed aeroplanes. *Kiewa Adventure* (q.v., 1950) features the Snowy Mountains Scheme. *The New Australians* (1956), illustrated by Selby Donnison, is the story of

the Gail family, brought out from England to work on the AMP's reclamation of the Ninety-Mile Desert. In an evocation of 1950s culture, Jo and Stan honeymoon at Ayers Rock, Gerry is beaten up by Bodgies after his radio class at the Royal Melbourne Technical College, and Mother improves herself by joining Council of Adult Education classes. See also **Perth**. *The Tendrills in Australia* (1959) is set on a NT cattle station. Donald wants to be a scientist, but his father expects him to take over Diana Downs. In a series of adventures in which Donald visits the Mary Kathleen mines, exposes cattle thieves and is lost in the desert, he develops a greater confidence and sees a way of pursuing his scientific interests and working on Diana Downs, where there is the promise of uranium. *Doctor with Wings* (q.v., 1960) is a Flying Doctor story. *Bushfire* (1967) set in Victoria, has another immigrant family, this time Greeks, who earn their acceptance through heroism. In *Olympic Kayak* (1968), illustrated by Barry Sutton, Bart lives beside the Yarra River, Melbourne, and eventually makes the Olympic team, coached by a defector from Rumania. See also **Sport**. Aldous has also written a children's play, *The Man with Three Hands* (1959), five McGowan books (q.v.), and two about Colin McKee, *Colin McKee Voyager* (1948) and *Colin McKee Adventurer* (1948). Colin's father is an airline pilot with a distinguished war record, and Colin battles to contain his fear of deep water and earn the respect of his father in an exploration of what constitutes courage. Aldous's novels can also be read as social documents dealing with the issues which stirred the decades in which he wrote, such as the Cold War, post-war immigration, new technology and national development.

ALDRIDGE, JAMES (HAROLD EDWARD JAMES) (1918–), born White Hills, Victoria, worked for many years as a journalist in Australia, the UK and USA, and has written many novels for adults. His first children's book was a fantasy for young readers about a London bus, *The Flying 19* (1966) illustrated by Raymond Briggs.

Aldridge has written a group of novels centred on the Quayle family, who live at 'St Helen', a vividly recreated town on the border of Victoria and NSW, based on Swan Hill, where Aldridge spent his youth. Two of these novels describe a conflict over a horse. *A Sporting Proposition* (1973), later called *Ride a Wild Pony* (1975), describes the conflict between a poverty-stricken boy, Scotty, and the disabled daughter of the wealthiest man in St Helen, Josie Eyre. Both believe that a Welsh pony, Taff or Bo, is theirs, and to finally determine who is the owner, the pony is given the right to decide. It was filmed in 1975 by Buena Vista, a subsidiary of the Walt Disney studios, as a US–Australian co-production, directed by Don Chaffey, with a script by Rosemary Anne Sisson. Robert Bettels and Eva Griffith played Scotty and Josie. *The True Story of Lola MacKellar* (1992) explores the mystery surrounding the identity of Lola's parents, and her close friendship with the same Josie Eyre. In *The Broken Saddle* (1982) Eric's father, whom he rarely sees, gives him a pony. Eric's determination to ride the wild horse impresses Mr Hunt, who has the pony shod and gives Eric a saddle. The novel traces the relationship between Eric and the horse, and the subtle changes which occur when Eric breaks him into the saddle. There is no happy ending, but a growth in Eric's understanding of his long-suffering mother and of life's possibilities. Other novels deal with religious conflict. *My Brother Tom* (1966) points to the prejudices which divide Catholic and Protestant. It was a successful four-part television series in 1986, directed by Pino Amenta and written by Tony Morphett. In *The Untouchable Juli* (1975) the brilliant and eccentric Juli is involved in an obscure evangelist sect. When his mother is murdered he is accused. Quayle

appears for his defence, and in his summing up shows how Juli is the victim of the philistinism of a small country town. Religion is again seen as a way of alienating people from each other in *The True Story of Spit MacPhee* (1986), which describes the antagonisms triggered off over the adoption of a local boy. It was a four-part television series in 1987, directed by Marcus Cole, written by Moya Wood, with Phillip Hancock as Spit and Sir John Mills as Fyfe, his grandfather. *The True Story of Lilli Stubeck* (q.v., 1984), although set in St Helen, has a different focus.

In a change of setting, Aldridge wrote *The Marvellous Mongolian* (1974). Tachi is a rare and fierce Mongolian wild horse which is sent by Baryut to Kitty, to mate with her gentle Welsh pony, Peep. The two horses escape, to travel across Europe back to Tachi's mountain home, where Peep dies giving birth to a foal. The story is told through the letters which Baryut and Kitty write to each other.

Aldridge's serious approach to his readers is leavened with humour and a pleasure in eccentricity. He takes the events of daily life and places them against a larger canvas, bridging the gap between children's and adult preoccupations, and while his style is conversational, it has a more sardonic edge than that of most children's writers.

ALEXANDER, GOLDIE (1936–), born Melbourne, was a secondary teacher. In *Mavis Road Medley* (1991), a time-slip fantasy, Didi and Jamie are transported to Depression times through an old film, *On Our Selection*, and a ring, and are taken in by a household of Jewish immigrants. The experience of the rebellious Didi, a girl of the 1990s, is measured against her life as it would have been in the 1930s. As 'Gerri Lapin', Alexander writes 'Dolly' fiction. Titles include *Everything Changes* (1989), *Understanding Jack* (1990), *Working it Out* (1990) and *Slim Pickings* (1992).

Alfred Dudley: or, the Australian Settlers
(1830), written anonymously by an
English writer, Sarah Porter (Mrs George
Richardson Porter, née Ricardo) (1791–
1862), is an early account of pioneering.
Porter acknowledges as her source for the
novel *The Present State of Australia: A
Description of the Country, its Advantages and
Prospects and a Particular Account of the
Aboriginal Inhabitants* (1830), an account by
Robert Dawson (1782–1826), who had
come to Australia in 1821 as chief agent to
the Australian Agricultural Company. Mr
Dudley's sudden loss of wealth leads him
to emigrate with his son, Alfred. They
decide against Sydney in favour of the
bush, where they capture the affections of
adoring Aboriginal People who delight in
working their land. They then renounce a
fortune left by an uncle and remain in the
colony to set up a feudal village.

ALGER, HORATIO (1834–99), born
Mass., USA, began his literary career with
Ragged Dick (1867) and went on to
become one of the most popular
American authors for the young in the
late nineteenth century. *The Nugget
Finders: a Tale of the Gold Fields of Australia*
(?1893) variously titled *In a New World: or,
Among the Goldfields of Australia* (1893) or
Harry Vane: or, In a New World (1910)
relates how Harry Vane and Jack
Pendleton, characters first encountered in
an earlier novel, *Facing the World* (1893),
reach Australia and strike gold at Bendigo.
See also **Bushrangers**.

*Alitjinya ngura Tjukurtjarangka/Alitji in
the Dreamtime* (1975) is a retelling by
Nancy Sheppard of *Alice's Adventures in
Wonderland* in Pitjantjatjara, illustrated by
Byron S. Sewell. The White Rabbit
becomes the Kangaroo, not because there
is no word for rabbit in Pitjantjatjara, but
because 'an Aboriginal Alice would natu-
rally have seen a kangaroo in her dream'.
Similar transformations occur to other
characters and events. The Caterpillar
becomes the Witchetty Grub, the

Dormouse becomes the Koala, and the
Queen's croquet party becomes the
Corroboree of the Witch Spirit. The bark
paintings of the Arnhem Land people,
although not a part of the culture of the
Ernabella people, are the basis of the illustrations. Nancy Sheppard had been a
teacher of Pitjantjatjara at Ernabella, and
the project, under the editorial guidance
of Barbara Ker Wilson, was supported by
the University of Adelaide and the
Department of Aboriginal Affairs. The
book was republished in 1992 as *Alitjinya
ngura Tjukurmankuntjala/Alitji in Dream-
land*, with illustrations by Donna Leslie, an
artist of the Gamileroi people.

*All About Anna and Harriet and
Christopher and Me* (1986) by Libby
Hathorn, illustrated by 'Steve Axelson'
(Stephen Axelsen), was an Honour Book
in the 1987 Junior Book of the Year
Awards. The Saturday visits of Anna to
her cousins Harriet, Christopher and
Lizzie bring escapades which get out of
hand. Hosing the passing cars is fun until a
passenger is soaked. Jumping from the
garage roof with an umbrella does not
work like parachuting. When Anna leaves,
the others are devastated, but the new
neighbours, Isabelle and Nellie, could well
replace her.

All the Proud Tribesmen (1959) by Kylie
Tennant, illustrated by Clem Seale, won
the Book of the Year Awards in 1960. Set
on an island in Torres Strait, the story is
told through a 12-year-old boy, Kerri,
whose upbringing has been given to the
schoolteacher Miss Buchanan, as a gift of
gratitude for her work with the local people. When Firecrest Island sinks beneath
the sea after its volcano erupts, Miss
Buchanan insists that the islanders go to
Malu Island, although they believe it is
cursed. Kerri and Miss Buchanan are able
to overcome the suspicions of the local
people and convince the Firecrest people
to stay on Malu. Kerri goes off to school
in Queensland, and returns for the long

holidays, when 'all the proud tribesmen [come] down to the shore' with songs for his homecoming. The novel depicts a caring and dignified society, although it is dated by the childlike faith of the local people in Miss Buchanan and white officialdom.

All We Know (1986) by Simon French won the 1987 Book of the Year Awards: Older Readers. It is Arkie's last year at primary school. Her teacher leaves, she grows away from her best friend, and a boy in her class is very unhappy. Life is changing, and so is Arkie. Her stepfather gives her his father's camera, and as she records the small events of her life she becomes increasingly aware of the emotions and experiences of other people. She wonders about the life which stretches before her, and the events of the past, and although this restrained novel does not present any major dramatic incidents, we watch Arkie show a new maturity.

ALLAN, HENRY. For *The Happy Forest: a Story Book for Boys and Girls* see **Fantasy**.

'ALLANSON, RUSSELL', see **ALANSON, ALFRED GODWIN**

ALLEN, LESLIE HOLDSWORTH (1879–1964), born Maryborough, Victoria, lectured at Sydney Teachers' College, was later Professor of English at the Royal Military College, Duntroon, and lecturer in English at Canberra University College. He published four books of verse, works on literary expression and criticism, and provided an introduction to the 1952 edition of Marcus Clarke's *For the Term of His Natural Life*. *Billy-Bubbles: Child Songs* (1920) is a book of verse for children which presents the small pleasures of innocence: 'It's good to be in bed at night/And hear the sweeping rain/Go patter patter on the roof/And knock against the pane.'

ALLEN, PAMELA (1934–), born Auckland, NZ, settled in Sydney in 1977. She illustrated N.L. Ray's *The Pow Toe* (1979) and Sally Fitzpatrick's *A Tall Story* (1981), about Clara's raid on Great Great Aunt Eliza's jellybeans. Allen's remarkable talents are best displayed in her own books. They are concerned with universal ideas: simple science in *Mr Archimedes' Bath* (q.v., 1980), or the human frailty of greed, in *Herbert & Harry* (1986). Displacement theory is explored in *Who Sank the Boat?* (q.v., 1982). *Bertie and the Bear* (q.v., 1983) is a cumulative story about a boy who is chased by a bear, and in its dream-like sequel, *A Lion in the Night* (1985), the same characters pursue a lion with a baby on its back. She has written a series of small books for pre-school children, *Simon Said* (1985) and *Simon Did* (1988), where Simon's boasts are taken to their illogical conclusions; *Watch Me* (1985) and *Watch Me Now* (1988), wordless picture-books of a small boy showing off; and *Mr McGee* (1987), a simple verse story. Mr McGee eats a magic apple which makes him grow to the size of a balloon. He floats over the town until he is pecked by a passing bird. In *Mr McGee Goes to Sea* (1990) he is swallowed by a fish. In *Fancy That!* (1988) Little Red Hen hatches out her chicks to the delight of the White Leghorns and the rooster. In *I Wish I Had a Pirate Suit* (1989) a small boy is always outsmarted by his older brother, Peter, because Peter has the pirate suit. As the younger brother grows older, he finds that it is not clothes which have the power, and Peter meets his match. Andrew adopts a stray cat in *My Cat, Maisie* (1990), but his rough play is too much for Maisie, as Andrew rides her, chases her, and swings her around. When Andrew experiences the same treatment from Lobo, the dog next door, he learns the need to be more gentle with his pet. *Black Dog* (1991) is more metaphorical. Christina's obsession with a blue bird causes her to ignore her loving dog, whose desperation is expressed in an

My Cat Maisie (1990) by Pamela Allen

attempt to fly. Pamela Allen's exuberant, spare illustrations, spontaneous humour and pared-down texts combine in deceptively simple picture-books.

Alphabet, An: Being a Book of Designs and Rhymes, see Alphabet Books

Alphabet Books. The earliest alphabet book in Australia is thought to be *The Australian Alphabet of Natural History* (1857) published anonymously, but there are no surviving copies. The extant material displays a variety of treatments, from the very simple to the highly complex. The former are often aimed at teaching letters to young children, such as Nan Fullerton's *The Alphabet from A to Z* (1945), a publication which sold over 50 000 copies. 'A is the aeroplane just overhead/B is the bear Jenny cuddles in bed./C is the clock Mummy winds every night/D is the dog with a big bone to bite.' *Apple to Zoo* (1975) by Christopher McKimmie is a simple, colourful alphabet, reminiscent of the work of Dick Bruna. Elaborate creations aimed at adult and child audiences are exemplified in the complex *Animalia* (q.v., 1986) by Graeme Base.

Subject alphabet books take a particular theme to illustrate the letters, such as Joyce Nicholson's *An ABC of Ships and the Sea* (1950), illustrated by Max B. Miller. *The ABC of Monsters* (q.v., 1976) by Deborah Niland has monsters capering through the alphabet, and *Alphabeasts* (1985) by Elizabeth Fuller has alliterative verse about nonsense animals, such as the Crackatt and Noseynast, accompanied by colourful pictures of the monsters. Other successful alphabet books include Nu

Lynch's *Australian Animals A to Z* (1976), illustrated by Kim Lynch, which places animals from Anteaters to Zebra fish in their environment. Marinella Bonini's *I Can be the Alphabet* (1986) uses pictures of people to form the shape of letters, and can be used as a frieze. Ann James's *One Day: a Very First Dictionary* (1989) combines the daily events in a child's life with a simple alphabet. *A Crazy Alphabet* (1990) by Lyn Cox, illustrated by Rodney McRae, is a cumulative story from A for Apple to Z for Zero, in the style of 'I know an old lady who swallowed a fly'. 'B is for bird which ate the apple/C is for cat which caught the bird which ate the apple … '

Local alphabet books, however, typically use names of Australian flora, fauna and places to illustrate the alphabet. *The Young Australian's Alphabet* (1871) by William Calvert is an early example of the use of Australian plants, animals and features, such as the Opossum, Quartz and the Parrot, and *The Australian A, B, C, Book, Large Letters* (?1875) by William and John Calvert has an Australian miner digging for gold. Amy Mack's *Bushland Stories* (1910) contains 'The birds' alphabet': 'A is for Avocet … B is for Bower Bird … C for Cockatoo … ' *Sunlight Australian ABC* (?1920) was produced for Lever Brothers, a soap company, 'with the help of the authorities of the Sydney Museum', and is a beautifully illustrated alphabet of Australian birds and animals 'to whet the appetite of young Australians for a deeper and more practical Nature Study'. *The Young Australia A.B.C.* (1922) has verses for each letter illustrated by lovely pastel and pen-and-ink drawings. A striking alphabet book, *An Alphabet: Being a Book of Designs and Rhymes* (1932), was produced by the students of the Applied Art School at the Melbourne Working Men's College. Black-and-white pictures of animals and birds are carefully designed and integrated with the clever verse and decorated lettering. 'J is for the jackass gay/Now laughing in the tree/I wonder if

he's listening in/To station 3DB.' The noted artist Napier Waller was a senior teacher at the school, and his influence can be detected in the strong illustrative material. In Hal Missingham's *Australian Alphabet* (1942) each letter represents an Australian plant or animal, such as Q for Quokka and X for Xanthorrhoea. *Australian Alphabet Book* (1964), illustrated by Emilie Beuth, uses Australian flora and fauna, with brief information about each accompanied by fine illustrations. *Eirene Mort's Australian Alphabet from the Collection of the Australian National Gallery* (1986), drawn in 1902, shows the strong design for which the artist was to become famous, in pictures of birds, animals and reptiles. In David Ridyard's *Koalas, Kites and Kangaroos* (1985), illustrated by Doreen Gristwood, goannas, koalas, quokkas and other animals skate across the page, catching kites or taking tea. *Animal Capers* (1986) by Kerry Argent has a wagtail guiding an animal on each page, until the last page finds them at the zoo. Will Douglas's *A Bush Alphabet* (1986) has Australian animals with facts about them as the text. Its clever illustrations present the animals in positions which follow the shape of the letter and the book includes a Snakes and Ladders variant: Spiders and Vines. In *Animal Antics ABC* (1988) by Moira Cochrane, illustrated by Armin Greder, verse accompanies illustrations of animals in unusual poses.

Nationalism was, and is still, a motivation for alphabet books. An early attempt to interpret the movement towards Federation was *"Advance Australia" ABC* (1893), an anonymous work, which begins: 'A is for Australia — Advance aye, advance!/"Forward" thy watchword, and upward thy glance./Land of the boundless plain, gem of the sea,/Health and prosperity ever to thee.' C is for Captain Cook, and the national religion also appears as F for Football. 'F for our football match, where we won fame/Playing our best at the old English game./Norwood, Ports, South Clubs are all playing strong./So are

Essendon, Carlton, Fitzroy and Geelong.' The brightly coloured and plentiful illustrations in another anonymous work, *The Australian A.B.C. Book* (1918), accompany the same sort of nationalistic verse: 'Z is the centre of a glorious word/That tells of bravery ever was heard/It begins with an A, and then an N/Wonderful deeds, and wonderful men./It ends with an A and then a C,/Boys of Egypt, France and Gallipoli.' In the 1920s Hugh McCrae wrote *The Australian Alphabet*, illustrated by the Sydney artist Norman Carter. Confident black-and-white illustrations are complemented by verse which takes up contemporary issues and uses Australian parlance, such as 'sundowner', 'tracker', 'Yarra-man', and Aboriginal words like 'Nulla' and 'Gunyah'. 'U stands for Union/The shearer's support … '

Later in the century, although nationalism remains a preoccupation, Australian icons are treated more humorously. In *Nonsense Places: an Absurd Australian Alphabet* (1976) by Michael Dugan,

An Alphabet: Being a Book of Designs and Rhymes (1932) by students of the Applied Art School, Melbourne Working Men's College

enhanced by Walter Stackpool's amusing illustrations, Australian towns are conjured up. 'With backs that ache/and straining necks/We've looked for towns/that start with X/But though we've trudged/all round Australia/We must report/our utter failure.' *Alphacats* (1989) by Nicholas Brash, illustrated by Wendy de Paauw, is more satirical, with alliterative verses about places in Australia. *The Australian ABC Book* (1984) by Louis Silvestro presents animals, including Australian, in a comical way. The brilliant *A is for Australia* (1984) by John Brennan, illustrated with photographs, includes 'O is for the Opera House', and 'V is for Vegemite'.

Looking back on alphabet books from the nineteenth century to the present reveals how much they have been influenced by the social preoccupations of the times. Again, advances in printing technology, with a greater emphasis on design and innovation, have overtaken the simple, often naive alphabet book, so that it has become a vehicle for artistic virtuosity.

ALSOP, EDITH ANNIE MARY (1871–1958), born Melbourne, painter and printmaker, studied at the National Gallery School, Melbourne, where she won second prize for anatomical drawing in the student exhibition of 1904. Alsop travelled widely, studying in London and Italy before returning to Melbourne in 1930. She was active in the Melbourne Arts and Crafts Society. Alsop illustrated *Some Children's Songs* (1910) by Marion Alsop and Dorothy Frances McCrae, and Joice Nankivell's *The Cobweb Ladder* (1916). The latter, in black and white, was eclipsed by Ida Rentoul Outhwaite's first book with coloured drawings *Elves and Fairies* (1916). Alsop's work is dramatic and full of movement, and displays her mastery over the representation of the human form.

AMADIO, NADINE, born Sydney, is a journalist, music critic, poet and biographer, a member of a well-known musical family. She has written three books illustrated with her photographs: *The Magic Shell* (1958), a record of Mark's visit to Sydney and Palm Beach; *Amanda and the Dachshund* (1965), which shows Amanda playing with her new puppy Seal, at the beach and at home. One day Seal brings home a friend, Orpheus, and Amanda acquires another dachshund; and *Jamie's Adventures in the Land of Music* (1965), in which Jamie's ambition to be a conductor leads him through the orchestra, a brass band, a jazz group and an early music concert. Amadio edited *Alice's Adventures in Wonderland* (1982) and *The New Adventures of Alice in Rainforestland* (1988) (for which she has written a libretto), both illustrated by Charles Blackman, the latter a plea for the conservation of the rainforests of northern Australia built around the Alice in Wonderland idea. Amadio has also written a collection of short stories for adults.

Ambrose Kangaroo is the animal character created by Elisabeth MacIntyre, which first appeared in *Ambrose Kangaroo: a Story that Never Ends* (1941). Ambrose runs away for a day in this story, and in *Ambrose Kangaroo Has a Busy Day* (1944) he is continually diverted from his task — to buy a bar of soap for his mother. In *Ambrose Kangaroo Goes to Town* (1964) Ambrose has to move when his home is destroyed by a bulldozer; he becomes a delivery boy in *Ambrose Kangaroo Delivers the Goods* (1978). This is a series of well-constructed and energetic stories for younger readers. Ambrose featured in a cartoon strip in the Sydney *Telegraph* in the 1940s.

AMOR, RICK (1948–), born Frankston, Victoria, trained at the National Gallery School. He illustrated *Jamie* (1976) by Maureen Stewart, *Weekend* (1976) by Michael Dugan and Joan Lindsay's *Syd Sixpence* (1982). Amor produced 'Falcon Comics' (q.v.) in 1978.

ANDERSON, FLORENCE S. For *Dramatised Fairy Tales and Nursery Rhymes Set to Music* (1928) see **Nursery Rhymes**.

ANDERSON, HUGH (1927–), born Elenore, Victoria, is a historian and biographer. *The Singing Roads: a Guide to Australian Children's Authors and Illustrators* (1965–70) was a pioneering account of the Australian contribution to children's books, with brief biographies and bibliographies of over 130 children's authors and illustrators.

Angus & Robertson was established in Sydney in 1888 by George Robertson (2) and David McKenzie Angus. Angus had opened a bookshop in Market Street, Sydney, in 1884, and was joined by Robertson, a fellow Scot, in 1886. George Robertson was the enthusiastic publisher of the partnership. The firm published books for use in Australian schools, covering such subjects as mathematics, geography, spelling, history and writing. Early in the twentieth century it set up the Junior Book Club, described as an 'up-to-date circulating library for young readers'. For 3s. 6d. subscribers could borrow books by Louisa Alcott, Hans Andersen, R.M. Ballantyne, Andrew Lang, Charlotte Yonge and many others. Australian writers were also represented, among them Ethel and Lilian Turner. For a short period in the 1920s, A&R changed its imprint to 'Cornstalk Publishing' (q.v.). A&R's juvenile list includes many landmarks in the field, such as *Teens* (q.v., 1897) by Louise Mack, which was the first novel published by Angus & Robertson, *Dot and the Kangaroo* (q.v., 1906) by Ethel Pedley, *The Magic Pudding* (q.v., 1918) by Norman Lindsay, the books of May Gibbs, Dorothy Wall, C.J. Dennis's *A Book for Kids* (q.v., 1921) and, more recently, the novels of Joan Phipson, Patricia Wrightson, Ivan Southall, and Simon French. In 1963 A&R appointed Joyce Saxby as children's book editor, the first Australian company to make such an appointment. Barbara

Ker Wilson, David Harris, Jenny Rowe, Margaret Wild and Cathie Tasker followed as children's editors. In 1970 Angus & Robertson became a subsidiary of IPEC, and in 1981, a part of News Limited.

Animal Stories. A fascination with the unique fauna of Australia has shaped the animal story in Australian children's books. Stories have ranged from realistic accounts of the drama inherent in the animal kingdom to romantic and sanitised versions of natural life. A great number of kangaroos, koalas, wombats and possums, together with much fewer numbats, quokkas, and echidnas, hop, climb, dig and create havoc in children's books. Many nineteenth-century and early twentieth-century writers were still overwhelmed by the range and curiosity of indigenous animals. Mrs

The Gilpins and their Fortunes (1889) by W.H.G. Kingston. Illustrator unknown

R. Lee's novel *Adventures in Australia* (1851) is more a vehicle for her descriptions of the local flora and fauna than an adventure story. Later, Henry Lamond and Charles K. Thompson used their own observations for stories about kangaroos, dingoes and birds which attempt an authentic representation of bush life. The development of the animal story can be traced through the treatment of the kangaroo. The national emblem was initially regarded as fair game, and instances abound in early adventure stories of kangaroo-hunts. Davenport Cleland's *The White Kangaroo: a Tale of Colonial Life — Founded on Fact* (1890) and 'Arthur Ferres's' *His First Kangaroo: an Australian Story for Boys* (1896) use a kangaroo-hunt as the turning-point of the action, and describe the slaughter of kangaroos with relish. Gordon Stables, in *Frank Hardinge: From Torrid Zones to Regions of Perpetual Snow* (1908), reveals some guilt: 'Dogs and men are now in full tilt, coming down on all sides of the frightened kangaroos. Their tender, deer-like eyes plead in vain for mercy. They are shot, clubbed by blacks, who join the cruel sport, and torn in pieces by dogs.' Walter Bone's *Hoppity: Being the Adventures of an Albino Kangaroo* (1933) also describes a kangaroo-hunt, but by the 1930s the tone is more sympathetic. Dorothy Cottrell's *Wilderness Orphan: the Life and Adventures of Chut, the Kangaroo* (1936) is a moving story of a kangaroo whose mother is shot when he is very young. He is taken home by the kangaroo-hunter, Tom Henton, and under the care of Tom and his wife, Chut grows up to be a powerful and gentle adult. When he and a doe, Blue Baby, are sold to be performing animals, the cruel treatment drives Chut to kill a keeper. He escapes and returns to the wild, to establish his own family. Cottrell avoids anthropomorphism in presenting the kangaroo's responses to kindness and brutality. Forty-six years after Stables, Dennis Clark's *Boomer: the Life of a Kangaroo* (1954) also opens with a kangaroo-hunt, but this time

Boomer falls into human hands, has a time with the kindly Tyler family, then kills his enemy, the cattle-worker Scanlan, and is left to his wild destiny. Authors such as Charles K. Thompson, in *King of the Ranges, the Saga of a Grey Kangaroo* (1945) and *Red Emperor* (1950), and Henry Lamond in *Big Red* (1953) present kangaroos as heroic figures, struggling to survive against their enemies, including Man. Infant kangaroos inspired *Andy's Kangaroo* (1964), by Joyce Nicholson, Margaret Paice's *A Joey for Christmas* (1960) and Patricia Bernard's *Kangaroo Kids* (1989). *Chai the Kangaroo* (1985) by Pam Blashki is based on the experiences of the author and the artist, Clifton Pugh, who reared a joey, and displays the delight and respect accorded the kangaroo in modern animal stories.

Dot and the Kangaroo (q.v., 1899) by Ethel Pedley picked up another strand in the treatment of animals, the animal fantasy. In Florence E. Lord's *Kangaroo Kingdom* (1914), 'dedicated to the boys and girls of Queensland', the kingdom is ruled by King Kangaroo. The kangaroos are dressed in the woven bark cloth of the kurrajong tree, and wear cabbage-tree hats. Dingoes draw their carts, bandicoots are used to gather the nut grass, and the kangaroos ride emu horses. Victor Barnes's domesticated, almost human, kangaroo Skippy (q.v.) endeared the kangaroo to a generation of television-viewers, and Dumper the kangaroo created by Evelyn Bartlett, and Elisabeth MacIntyre's Ambrose Kangaroo (q.v.) appealed to the very young. Pamela Lofts's traditional story *How the Kangaroos got their Tails* (1987), told by George Mung Mung Lirrmiyarri, recalls the Aboriginal People's regard for the animal. The transition from an animal to be hunted to much-loved symbol has been made, with the Aboriginal stories returning the kangaroo to its original place as respected inhabitant of the ancient land.

Early animal stories which combined natural history with an imaginative story include Edward S. Sorenson's *Spotty, the Bower Bird and Other Nature Stories: Life Histories of Australian Birds and Animals* (1921) and Alec and Catherine King's *Australian Holiday* (1945), illustrated by Marjorie Rankin, in which Walter, Francis and Elizabeth are provided with natural history stories as they walk and play in the bush. Leslie Rees has specialised in the animal story, taking a native bird or animal and developing a story around a typical life, such as *The Story of Shy the Platypus* (1944) or *The Story of Kurri Kurri the Kookaburra* (q.v., 1950).

The wild dog has also received a share of the action. Henry Lamond's *Dingo: the Story of an Outlaw* (1945) is an account of the dingo in the wild, and, like *Wild Brother* (q.v., 1954) by Mary Patchett, is based on an informed understanding of animals. Patchett's *The Terror of Manooka* (1966) includes much information on the animals of north Queensland, as Nicky overcomes his fear of crawling, flapping creatures in a search for animals for a wild life reserve. Elyne Mitchell's *Jinki, Dingo of the Snows* (1970) describes the harsh life of a dingo in the high country of south-eastern Australia. In Ivan Smith's *Dingo King* (1977) the dingo hero gives his life to save his mate and pups during a drought. Other writers have used the dingo as a metaphor for the confinement of people. Mark, in Ivy Baker's *The Dingo Summer* (1980), finds solace in his identification with an alpine dingo. In Michael Dugan's *Dingo Boy* (1980) Carl also allies himself with the wild dingoes. In Frank Dalby Davison's *Dusty: a Dog of the Sheep Country* (1946) the dog, half dingo, symbolises the tension between domesticity and the freedom of a life more closely linked to nature.

The possibly extinct thylacine, or Tasmanian tiger or wolf, has engaged the imagination of writers since Erle Wilson's *Coorinna: a Novel of the Tasmanian Uplands* (1953), a dramatic account of a Tasmanian wolf, depicting the natural life of the creatures who live far away from Man. Wilson

Tiger in the Bush (1957) by Nan Chauncy. Illustrator: Margaret Horder

has closely observed their environment and displays a sensitivity to animal behaviour. Nan Chauncy in *Tiger in the Bush* (q.v., 1957) took the secret nature of the tiger's existence to illustrate how dangerous civilisation's inroads are into the wild. Harry Frauca's *Striped Wolf: a Bush Adventure* (1969), illustrated by Genevieve Melrose, set in central Queensland, is less dramatic, but also provides much information on the life and habits of animals, as Mike, Carol and their zoologist uncle Ted track and capture a thylacine. Also set in Queensland, M.E. Patchett's *Tiger in the Dark* (1964) is by no means as convincing, although the story is similar. The habits of the tiger and the illustrations provided by Roger Payne suggest an Indian tiger rather than a thylacine. Mary Small's *Grandfather's Tiger* (1985) takes up Nan Chauncy's theme, and concludes with Alan and Kate sighting a tiger family, confirming Alan's trust in his grandfather, and his complicity in keeping the tiger secret. Barbara Bolton's fantasy *Ring, Rock and River* (1987) also explores the right of the thylacine to remain free. Beth Roberts's *The Magic Waterfall: A Tasmanian Tale of an Invisible Thylacine* (1990) is a fantasy in which Nenner is able to return to his home with the help of a waterfall which allows invisibility. The novel refers to Coorinna (see above) as Nenner's inseparable companion.

Possums appear frequently, around the house and in the wild. Veronica Basser's *Bright-Eyes the Glider Possum*, illustrated by Richard Richardson (1957), Joyce Nicholson's *Ringtail the Possum* (1965), Eve Pownall's *Squik the Squirrel Possum* (1955), Julie Morris's *Possums on the Roof* (1989), Noela Young's *Flip the Flying Possum* (q.v., 1963) and *Mundarda* (1988) by Belinda Brooker, which traces the life cycle of the pigmy possum through a simple story and fine illustrations, variously relate how possums live in natural and unnatural environments.

The determined wombat features in *Sebastian Lives in a Hat* (1985) by Thelma Catterwell, illustrated by Kerry Argent, and *Wombalong* (1985) by Judith Pugh. Both books show the nurturing of orphaned wombats. Other wombats appear in Jean Chapman's *Wombat* (1969), *A House for Wombats* (1985) by Michael Dugan, illustrated by Jane Burrell, *Wombats Don't Have Christmas* (1987) by Michael Dugan, and Joyce Nicholson's *Woop the Wombat* (1968). Jill Morris has written many animal stories, among them *Harry, the Hairy Nosed Wombat* (1970). Ivan Smith's *Death of a Wombat* (1972), illustrated by Clifton Pugh, describes how a wombat dies in a bushfire.

Perhaps the most popular animal to feature in children's books, often in fantasies, is the koala (sometimes misrepresented as a bear), the most well known being Blinky Bill (q.v.), created by Dorothy Wall in the 1930s. Blinky was preceded by Edward Dyson's koala Billy, in *Billy Bluegum or Back to the Bush* (1947), illustrated by Norman Lindsay, which was first published in 1912 in *Lone Hand*. Dyson's book was an adult satire, but Lindsay's Bunyip Bluegum, looking very much the same as Billy, appeared in *The Magic Pudding* (q.v., 1918). In the same era as Wall, Lydia Eliott wrote *Little Teddy Bear* (1939), *The Koala Family at Home* (1949) and *Tufty the Teddy* (1950). Charles Barrett and Isobel Shead wrote *Kooborr the Koala* (1941), and although the text accurately relates the life cycle of the koala, Kooborr, who survives a bushfire with his family, the illustrations by the English illustrator Joan Kiddell-Monroe portray Kooborr as a bear-headed frog, rather than as a recognisable koala. *Mr Koala Bear* (q.v., 1954) by Elisabeth MacIntyre is more realistically drawn. Esta de Fossard's *Koala and the Bunyip* (1982), *Koala and the Tasmanian Devil and the Possum Hunt* (1984) and *Koala and Emu and the Unexpected Box* (1984) are adventures illustrated with engaging photographs. *Koala Lou* (1987) by Mem Fox, *Little Koala* (1989) by Margaret Roc, Wish in *Wish and the Magic Nut* (q.v., 1956) by Peggy Barnard, and the koala in Eleanor Nilsson's *A Bush Birthday* (1985) are all in the tradition of Wall. *Didane the Koala: from a Legend of the Bidjara People of the Upper Warrego* (1985) by Grahame Walsh places the koala in a traditional context.

Not all animal stories represent animal life so well. Inaccuracies abound in *Australian Animal Wonderland* (1967) by Mary Brooks, as Jill and John examine an unlikely collection of animals, ranging from a tawny frogmouth to a black swan in a setting which includes a river, beach, palm plantation, and bushland. Nocturnal animals such as the platypus and the cuscus appear in broad daylight. This poor example of the depiction of Australian animals perpetuates such inaccuracies as

'koala bears'. In Anita Hewett's *Honey Mouse and Other Stories* (1957), which contains ten stories about Australian birds and animals, the animals are humanised, dressed, and the settings inaccurate. Koalas are again referred to as bears, and in the same natural environment the reader finds koalas, cassowaries, turtles, bats, dingoes and pythons.

Animal stories often express the stereotypes which humans have attached to the animal world. Koalas and possums are cuddlesome or cute, dingoes are wild, thylacines are mysterious. However, the empathy which children have with animals, possibly based on mutual powerlessness, is caught in the best animal stories.

Animalia (1986) by Graeme Base was an Honour Book in the 1987 Picture Book of the Year Awards, winner of the YABBA Picture Book in 1987 and Secondary Winner of KOALA in 1988. From armadillos to zebras, characters, animals, plants and objects beginning with the appropriate letter appear on each ornate page. There is a multitude of images of real and mythical animals, accompanied by an alliterative text. *Animalia* has been very popular, both in Australia and internationally. A wall frieze, eight metres long, was produced in 1987.

Annie's Rainbow (1975), written and illustrated by Ron Brooks, was Highly Commended in the 1976 Picture Book of the Year Awards. Annie searches for her own rainbow. She follows it into a dark garden, where she finds a fountain from which the rainbow gushes. An old man whom she meets there shows her his painting, which is of Annie and her rainbow. In its delicacy and suggestion of dark and secret places, *Annie's Rainbow* foreshadows Brooks's later work.

Annuals. Annuals provided reading pleasure for a generation of children, who looked forward to a book full of fascinating facts, exciting stories, pictures and

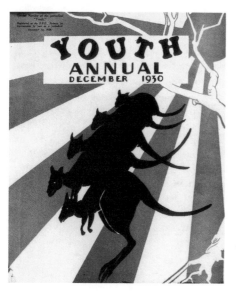

Youth Annual published by W.H. Honey, 1930

fifth annual volume' (1906–7) contains some stories by Australian writers, such as Amy Mack, but these annuals were aimed at an international market. They were advertised as companion collections to *Young England*. The *Empire Annual for Australian Boys*, published by the Religious Tract Society, appeared from 1900 to the 1920s, with more Australian references. One issue, edited by A.R. Buckland, contained three stories with an Australian setting: 'A kangaroo hunt and the sequel' by 'One who was there', 'The Killer' by Louis Becke, and 'A town paved with gold' by Phil Phillips. The *Empire Annual for Australian Girls* was a companion production. The 1910 volume had a story by Lilian Turner, and the pattern of one, two or three stories with Australian content or by Australian authors was followed over the next decade. For example, the 1919 volume contained 'The bush-fire brigade, a story of Australian adventure', by B.H. Righton.

The *Australian Girl's Annual* (1912–?), the feminine version of *The Boy's Annual* produced by the English publisher Amalgamated Press, and edited during the 1930s by Herbert Darkin Williams, occasionally had stories by writers such as Mary Grant Bruce which were set in Australia, but the same annual also appeared as *The British Girl's Annual*. Another *Australian Girl's Annual* was published in the 1920s by Cassell & Company, with its companion *Australasian Boy's Annual*, edited by Eric Wood, with more local content.

things to make, to be savoured and read again and again. *Australian Boys and Girls: an Illustrated Annual of Stories by Australian Writers, No. 1* (1895), edited by 'Armand Jerome' (Ernest Favenc) appears to be the first annual for young people published in Australia. It has stories by, and brief biographies of, Ernest Favenc, Louis Becke, Alex Montgomery, Louise Mack and Ethel Turner. There is a school story, three adventure stories and a family story. It also includes a history of Melbourne Grammar School; Scots College, Sydney; University High School, Melbourne; and Presentation Convent, Windsor. There were many annuals which included stories about Australia, such as *Boys of Our Empire* (1901), which had stories by Ernest Favenc, Edward Dyson, Alexander Macdonald and other Australian writers.

Young Australia was published in London from the 1870s by the Pilgrim Press. The 'Thirty second annual volume' with the subtitle *'An Illustrated Annual for Boys Throughout the English-Speaking World'* has very little Australian content except for a small paragraph on 'An Australian Robinson Crusoe'. Another, 'The Thirty

The Australian journal *Pals* (q.v., 1920–26) was annually combined into *Pals Annual: for the Boys of Australasia*, edited by Charles Barrett. William Honey edited *Youth*, a journal for children, which ran from 1930 to 1932. Two Christmas annuals arose from *Youth*: *Youth Annual* (1930) and *Father Time's Christmas Annual* (also 1930). The first was a lavish production, with full colour plates and contributions from Zora Cross, J.H.M. Abbott, A.H. Chisholm, Ion Idriess, Elizabeth Powell and others. Its aim was to encourage the youth of Australia 'to know more of their country, of its colour, its essence, its indefinable spirit'. The other, less lavish, but still a good production, has stories and verse by Ruth Bedford, Elsie Cole, Elizabeth Powell, Madeleine Honey and others, and on the cover, Father Christmas rides a kangaroo under a gum tree. 'I am proud to live in a country which gives so many beautiful flowers to its children at Christmas time', says Tom in one story. Popular comics were developed as annuals, such as the *Ginger Meggs' Annuals* which appeared from 1924, and the *Fatty Finn Annuals* in 1929 and 1930.

One of the best annuals of the 1940s was *The Boy Annual* published by International Distributors, an outcome of the journal *Boy*. The 1946–47 edition has a story by the cyclist Hubert Opperman about the Tour de France; Don Bradman on cricket; the naturalist David Fleay on wedge-tailed eagles; Douglas Nicholls on the earliest Australians; and 'Music — the Symphony' by Joseph Post and Colin Robin. Most of the entries are factual accounts of adventures, such as 'Australian Army Operations' from the Department of Information or 'Australian bravery in Burma' by Keith Welsh. *The Girl*, published by OPC Distributors, was its feminine counterpart. The 1948 issue has stories by H. Drake-Brockman, Mary Durack, and Marjorie (Eve) Pownall. The 1949 edition contains a story by Phyllis M. Power, 'Destination Oodoola'. Aimed at younger readers, *The Connie Christie Annual* (1947), written and illustrated by Connie Christie, includes fairy stories, verse, nursery rhymes and incidents in the life of small children. 'John Mystery's' *'Cobbers': Australian Children's Annual* appeared irregularly.

The A.B.C. Children's Hour Annual appeared from 1956 to 1960, with no issue in 1959. It was published for the ABC by the Educational Press under the managing editorship of Dr T.S. Hepworth, with stories by Ruth Park,

Leslie Rees, Denys Burrows, Claire Meillon, K. Langloh Parker and members of the Argonauts Club. After 1960, it became *The Australian Children's Annual*, also edited by Hepworth, and published by Angus & Robertson. There was no issue in 1962, and the last issue was in 1965. In 1963, another book of the same name, *Australian Children's Annual*, edited by Nance Donkin, and published by Lothian, had puzzles and activities, and stories by Nan Chauncy, Alan Marshall, Ivan Southall, Elyne Mitchell, Joyce Nicholson, Mavis Thorpe Clark and others. *Barrier Reef Annual 1972* is a collection based on a television series, with stories dealing with aspects of Australian life, such as the Flying Doctor, stone fish and bushranging.

By the 1970s, with publishing for children burgeoning, the annual ceased to be the favoured Christmas reading, and other publications, such as the collection, took over.

'Cobbers': Australian Children's Annual by 'John Mystery', 1938

Answers to Brut (1988) by Gillian Rubinstein was an Honour Book in the 1989 Book of the Year Awards: Older Readers. Kel takes home a bull terrier, knowing that Brut belongs to Caspian, Spirit and Skye. Kel's father sells the animal as a fighting dog, and in a tense conclusion, the children attempt to rescue Brut from an illegal dogfight. Rubinstein combines a study of insensitive parents, alienated from their children, with a strong adventure story.

Anzac Adventure: the Story of Gallipoli Told for Young Readers (1959) by Dale Collins, illustrated by Frank Norton, was Commended in the 1960 Book of the Year Awards. Collins drew on C.E.W. Bean's official history of Anzac, and the writings of the English war correspondent Ellis Ashmead-Bartlett. Written as a first-person narrative, it traces the historical background to the war, the role of the Australian Navy, the Egyptian campaign, the landing at Anzac Cove, and concludes with the evacuation. The stories of major figures such as General Sir William Birdwood, Major General Sir William Throsby Bridges, Private John Simpson Kirkpatrick and his donkey Duffy, and Private Jacka are related with humour and respect. There is no examination of the negative aspects of the landing, but the book is carefully researched, patriotic in tone and vividly written.

Aranea: a Story About a Spider (1975) by Jenny Wagner, illustrated by Ron Brooks, was Commended in the 1976 Picture Book of the Year Awards. Aranea spins her web each night, first in the garden, then on the clothes line. A storm drives her into the house, where she hides until she can return to the safety of the garden. Pen-and-ink illustrations reflect the drama of a spider's search for a place to spin.

ARCHER, ROBYN (1948–), born Adelaide, has written plays and stage pieces, and is noted for her interpretation of Brecht songs and the works of well-known women musicians. In *Mrs Bottle Burps* (1983), Mrs Bottle is temporarily unable to belch. The illustrations, by the cartoonist Victoria Roberts, add a sophisticated humour to the verbal joke. Mrs Bottle's problem is enlarged in *Mrs Bottle's Absolutely Blurtingly Beautiful World-Beating Burp!* (1990), illustrated by Ros Asquith.

ARGENT, KERRY (1960–), born Angaston, SA, illustrated *One Woolly Wombat* (1982), with Rod Trinca, six months before she graduated from the SA School of Design. The same wombat later appeared in *Friends, Hiding, At the Beach* (all 1988) and the novelty book *Surprise: A Woolly Wombat Flap Book* (1989). *A Bush Birthday* (1985) by Eleanor Nilsson features a koala; *Sebastian Lives in a Hat* (1985) by Thelma Catterwell is about a baby wombat; *Animal Capers* (1986), illustrated with her sister, Leanne Argent, is an alphabet book. Argent's animals are full of personality. *Thank You, Santa* (1991) by Margaret Wild, *Derek the Dinosaur* (1987) by Mary Blackwood, about a dinosaur who would rather knit than fight, *A Paddock of Poems* (q.v., 1987) by Max Fatchen, Jenny Boult's poetry collection *About Auntie Rose* (1988) and *Off the Planet* (1989), a poetry anthology by Jane Covernton, are other books illustrated by Argent. *Someone is Flying Balloons: Australian Poems for Children* (1983), a poetry collection compiled by Jill Heylen and Celia Jellett, demonstrates Argent's characteristic style, as she builds colour and form to create a visual and irreverent commentary.

ARGENT, LEANNE (1964–), born Cummins, SA, has illustrated *The Rainbow Stealer* (1984) and *Tatty* (1985) by Eleanor Nilsson; *Animal Capers* (1986) with her sister, Kerry Argent; and *Not Lost, Just Somewhere Else* (1990) by Hazel Edwards.

'Argonauts, The', had its beginnings in the ABC Children's Hour which operated during the late 1930s in Sydney and

Melbourne. The idea of a club for listeners built around Jason's search for the golden fleece had been suggested in the 1920s by Nina Murdoch at 3LO in Melbourne, in discussions with Frank Clelow and W.T. Bearup. At first Murdoch's idea was quashed as 'too hifalutin' for children', but in 1941 the Argonauts' Club was developed as a part of a national children's session, under the guidance of Nina Murdoch and Ida Elizabeth Osbourne (later Jenkins). The Argo, with Jason (Atholl Fleming) at the helm, enrolled rowers from all over Australia, although WA had its own Argonauts' Club. Ida Elizabeth Osbourne wrote the words, and Cecil Fraser wrote the melody which introduced the program to its avid listeners: 'Come, Old Mother Hubbard and Jack and Jill/And Tom the Piper's son,/Leave your troubles, forget your spill,/We're going to have some fun!/The wireless says to hurry and run/To leave your games and toys;/The wireless says the time has come/For all the girls and boys./So come with a hop, a skip and a run,/It's time for the Session, it's time for the fun.' The names of the Greek heroes were used as the names of the ships, and as these were filled, Greek rivers, cities, mountains and people were used. Each member was numbered as a rower on one of the ships, e.g. Agamemnon 43. Art, with 'Joe' (Albert Collins); music, with the 'Melody Man' (Lindley Evans); nature, with 'Jock' (A.J. Marshall); and writing, encouraged by 'Antony Inkwell' (the poet A.D. Hope), were some of the activities in which the Argonauts were urged to participate, and by 1945 there were nearly 40 000 members. Actors who were involved in the program included Leonard Teale, Patricia Lovell, Peter Finch, John Ewart, and John Meillon. By 1956 over 10 000 children were joining the club yearly, and writers such as Ruth Park, Claire Meillon, 'Musette Morell' and Rolf Harris were contributing material. In the 1960s, the membership wrote three books, edited by

John Gunn: *Dangerous Secret* (1960), *The Gold Smugglers* (1962) and *The Gravity Stealers* (1965), and contributed to *The Australian Children's Annual* and *The A.B.C. Children's Hour Annual*. See **Annuals**. The changeover to television seriously eroded radio audiences and, in 1967, in the face of declining membership, the club was confined to Sundays only, but could not survive beyond 1972, when it ceased, still with Atholl Fleming, now aged 77, as Jason.

Arkwright (1985) by Mary Steele won the Junior Book of the Year Awards in 1986. Captain Chilblain brings a giant South American anteater home to Candlebark, via Tumbalunda. Arkwright enlists the aid of Ethel the echidna to clean up the ants in the Bowling Club, but their success brings the undesirable Mr Wanderlust to the town. The resourceful Arkwright invents the disease of Blotch to frighten the odious Mr Wanderlust away and save Candlebark from becoming a safari park. Steele continued Arkwright's adventures with *Citizen Arkwright* (1990). When Arkwright's quick thinking saves a boy from drowning, he is made Citizen of the Year. Illustrated with whimsical line drawings by the author, *Arkwright* and its sequel are fast-moving and funny.

ARMITAGE, RONDA (1943–), born Kaikoura, NZ, is a writer and **DAVID** (1943–), born New Norfolk, Tasmania, is an illustrator. David studied at RMIT. The Armitages do not work in Australia, and many of their books are set overseas, but they have won two Australian awards, for *The Lighthouse Keeper's Lunch* (q.v., 1977) and *The Trouble with Mr Harris* (q.v., 1978).

ARNOLD, JOSIE (1941–), born Melbourne, has written *Getting There* (1988), a humorous look at the difficulties of the 15-year-old Jamie, whose real life becomes more exciting than his fantasies. His family connections with the music world complicate his life, as does his love affair at school with the lovely Anna. Arnold has also written educational and adult material, and a guide to books for young people, *A Practical Guide to Young Australian Fiction* (1985), with Tesha Piccinin.

ARONSTEN, JOAN (1914–), born Sydney, radio copywriter, poet and short story writer, contributed to 'Kindergarten of the Air' (q.v.) and scripts for the television program 'Kindergarten Playtime'. *Mrs Kind Rabbit and Five Other Playlets for Children 7 to 8 Years Old* (1952) was in Mullens's 'Plays for Children' series. *Charley the Concrete-Mixer* first appeared in the NSW *School Magazine* in 1951, with illustrations by Edwina Bell, and was published as a book, *Charley the Concrete-Mixer* in 1956, illustrated by Adye Adams and with music by Dulcie Holland. It and *Jolly the Polar Bear* (1957), illustrated by Florence Warburton, were used as supplementary readers for NSW schools. *Charley the Concrete-Mixer* has been translated into German by Frances Hill and published by Jos. Scholz, Mainz. It was also recorded with narration by Ruth Fenner. Aronsten contributed stories to *Listening Time* (1961), an anthology of the best of the 'Kindergarten of the Air' stories, including 'Shopping with Mother' and 'A Little Black Christmas Present'.

Art Folios Volume One: 12 Australian Paintings in the Art Gallery of New South Wales (1972) by Paul Milton, received a Special Mention in the 1973 Picture Book of the Year Awards. The folio sets out to teach basic art tenets to school students in six units: shape, composition, tone, colour, texture and media, using high-quality reproductions of the works of Australian artists. William Dobell, John Coburn, John Percival, Albert Tucker and Russell Drysdale are among those represented. Biographical details of the artists are supplied, with a critical discussion of each work, and accompanying exercises for students.

Arthur is a floppy-eared brown puppy created by Amanda Graham and Donna Gynell in *Arthur* (1984), *Educating Arthur* (1987) and *Always Arthur* (1989). Arthur first tries to imitate other animals in an effort to be selected for sale, is taught to be obedient by Melanie and Grandpa, and in *Always Arthur*, Melanie acquires Bonzer, who rivals Arthur so effectively that Arthur runs away. In 1985, *Arthur* won the Children's Book Award (UK), given for the favourite book selected by children throughout the UK.

Educating Arthur (1987) by Amanda Graham. Illustrator: Donna Gynell

Ash Road (1965) by Ivan Southall, illustrated by Clem Seale, won the 1966 Book of the Year Awards. Graham, Wallace and Harry inadvertently start a bushfire. As the fire threatens, a group of children, including the three responsible for the fire, are cut off from adult help. Disaster follows disaster: Lorna's father has a stroke; Pippa Buckingham desperately searches for her lost sister, Julie; Peter Fairhall has to save his ageing grandmother; Julie Buckingham and a baby are placed in a well by

Grandpa Tanner, and so on. The distraught behaviour of the children and the pent-up anger of the adults create a tension which catches the human agitation during an actual bushfire. See also **Bushfire**.

Ashton Scholastic was established in NZ in 1965, and Australia in 1968, a subsidiary of the US firm Scholastic. Initially organised by Alan and Olive Izod in Australia, the operation soon brought Terry Hughes, Myra Lee and Jim Reece from NZ, with the aim of making Ashton a major force in educational publishing in Australia. In 1980 Terry Hughes became an international vice-president of the company, and was replaced by Ken Jolly as managing director in Australia. In 1978 Ashtons acquired Oldmeadow Booksellers, including Dromkeen (q.v.). Ashton Scholastic's Book Clubs, 'Wombat', 'Lucky', 'Arrow', and 'Star', have been successful in both primary and post-primary schools, introducing inexpensive, quality material for the young reader. Ashton's are the largest distributor of children's paperbacks in Australia, selling most of these books through their book clubs and book fairs. The publisher has its own publishing program. Titles include *Tucking Mummy In* (1987) by Morag Loh and *Hattie and the Fox* (1986) by Mem Fox. In conjunction with Martin Educational, Ashton publishes the 'Bookshelf' series. Ashton Scholastic acquired Omnibus Books in 1991.

ATKINSON, REGINALD CYRIL EVERITT (d.1960), born NZ, and educated in medicine and public health at Edinburgh, Melbourne and Cambridge, was Commissioner of Public Health in WA from 1911 to 1944. As part of his major contribution to health in Australia, he wrote *Hygiene Jingles* (1924), a collection of verses for young people which suggest ways of maintaining personal health. There are poems on water, sewerage, baby care and even how to treat hairlice. 'With purpose keen / And kerosene/She soon will clean/Her pretty head./Thereafter she/Will ever be/Punctiliously/On watch for more.'

Augustus is the black-and-white kitten featured in a series by June Epstein, illustrated by Alison Lester. Augustus would prefer to be a person, and when he discovers that he has nine lives he decides to be a different person in each one. Titles include *Augustus*, *Augustus the Painter*, *Augustus the King*, *Augustus Teaches the Children*, *Augustus Plays Football*, *Augustus Flies a Plane*, *Augustus Conducts the Band* and *Augustus Works in a Factory* (all 1989). Augustus's pranks are extended by Lester's lively illustrations.

Australasian Boy's Annual, see **Annuals**

Australia Book, The (1952) by Eve Pownall, illustrated by Margaret Senior, won the Book of the Year Award in 1952. It is a history of Australia which begins

The Australia Book (1952) by Eve Pownall. Illustrator: Margaret Senior

before white settlement and concludes with post-World War II immigration. The clever balance between text and illustration unfolds events and periods of our past with distinction, and the large-format, eye-catching cover, careful design and succinct text combine in an original contribution to Australian books for children.

Australian A.B.C. Book, The, see **Alphabet Books**

Australian Alphabet of Natural History, The (?1858) by an anonymous author is thought to be the first Australian alphabet book, but there are no surviving copies.

Australian and New Zealand Ships of Today (1958) by Frank Norton, which was Commended in the 1959 Book of the Year Awards, describes the ships which pass in and out of harbours. Ships which are typical of their classes — steamers, passenger ships, cargo ships, ferries, tugs and merchant ships — are illustrated. Australasian shipping is detailed, from the paddle-steamer *Sophia Jane*, which arrived in Sydney in May 1831, to the Australian and NZ ships used in World War II. There are diagrams of the below decks areas, and facts on shipbuilding, ports, shipping routes and ships' flags in an authoritative account.

Australian Book of Trains, The (1947) by J.H. and W.D. Martin was Highly Commended in the 1948 Book of the Year Awards. It is a comprehensive account of Australian railways and rolling stock, describing 'an epic story of triumph over almost overwhelming difficulties.' The subject is initially treated State by State, then the role railways have played in the development of the country is described. Locomotives and their statistics, passenger services, transport of goods, and the building of trains in Australia is discussed, and particular trains, such as the Spirit of Progress, are examined in terms of safety and construction. The young

reader is also advised on how to become an engine-driver, and how to send a pet by train. The book is informative, written with clarity, and liberally illustrated with black-and-white and colour photographs.

Australian Boys and Girls: an Illustrated Annual of Stories by Australian Writers, No. 1, see **Annuals**

Australian Boys' Adventure Library, published by Alexander McCubbin, Melbourne, was a series of paperback adventure stories in magazine format distributed by Gordon & Gotch in Melbourne and Edwards, Dunlop in Sydney and Brisbane, in the 1930s. Titles included *The Veiled Riddle of the Plains*, *The Great Round Up*, set in the USA, *Adventures in the Gold Ridge, Outwitting the Spies*, set in England, *The Heroes of HMS Heroic* and *Life Among the Golden Grain*, set in Kansas, USA.

Australian Children's Annual, The, see **Annuals**

Australian Children's Folklore Collection, held at the University of Melbourne, contains over 10 000 playground rhymes, chants, games, insults, autograph album ditties, war-cries, divinations and other items, including cassettes and films of schoolyard play, and material from European, Asian and Aboriginal languages. The collection was begun by June Factor and Gwenda Beed Davey in 1979.

Australian Children's Television Foundation was established in 1982 with Dr Patricia Edgar as director. It is a national non-profit organisation, funded by the Commonwealth and the States, which has as its charter the development of high-quality children's television programs, and their promotion through tie-ins with books and other material. The foundation brings noted writers, directors and producers together. It has been responsible for the 'Winners' (q.v.) and

'More Winners' series, 'Touch the Sun' (q.v.) series, 'Round the Twist' (q.v.), 'Kaboodle'(q.v.) and 'Lift Off' (q.v.), as well as individual programs such as 'Five Times Dizzy' (q.v.), 'Fire in the Stone' (q.v.) and 'I Own the Racecourse!' (q.v.).

Australian Girl's Annual, The, see **Annuals**

Australian Junior's Journal appeared from 1952 to 1955, incorporating the *Australian Children's Pictorial*. It was published and edited by Oswald L. Ziegler, and contained book and film reviews, and articles on music, poetry, radio, and nature, as well as stories by Paul White, Ivan Southall and others. The photography section was run by Max Dupain, and cartoons by Emile Mercier were featured.

Australian Legendary Tales (1953), collected by K. Langloh Parker, selected and edited by Henrietta Drake-Brockman, illustrated by Elizabeth Durack, won the Book of the Year Awards in 1954. The stories were selected from the collections by Parker published in the 1890s, and are told with a sense of familiarity. They include children's stories and religious and initiation tales drawn from the Euahlayi people. A book with the same title was published in 1978, a compilation of Parker's two collections, with illustrations by Rex Backhaus-Smith. Vashti Farrer adapted six of the tales for *Tales of the Dreamtime* (1975), illustrated by Walter Cunningham.

Australian Museum of Childhood, see **Museum of Australian Childhood**

Australian Pet Book, The (1962) by 'John Wotherspoon', the pseudonym of Lady Ann Flora Flashman Rylah, a veterinary surgeon, with photographs by the author, was Commended in the 1963 Book of the Year Awards. How to choose a pet, then how to care, feed and train a dog, cat, fish, mouse, ferret, guinea pig, tortoise, rabbit or bird, is clearly described, with appropriate photographs. While some of the material has been outdated, such as the use of DDT as an insecticide, this handbook is still an excellent beginner's guide to pets.

Australian Wonder Book, The (1935) was published by the Home Entertainment Library, a Melbourne publisher. It contained four complete books: *The Little Black Princess* by Mrs Aeneas Gunn, which has a 'hitherto unpublished photograph' of Bett-Bett; *The Other Side of Nowhere* by Tarella Quin Daskein, illustrated by Ida Rentoul Outhwaite (although missing some of the original illustrations); *The Prince of the Totem* by Tarlton Rayment; and *Winks — The Mystery and Magic of the Bush* by J.J. Hall. The introductory note states proudly that it is a 'completely Australian production. The stories were written and illustrated by Australians, and every detail of printing, block-making and binding has been done by Australian craftsmen to provide a book of wonder and absorbing interest for young Australians.'

Australopedia: How Australia Works After 200 Years of Other People Living Here, The (1988), edited by Joan Grant, illustrated by Design students at Phillip Institute of Technology, Melbourne, was an Honour Book in the 1989 Book of the Year Awards: Younger Readers. This informative encyclopaedia of Australia is presented in a colourful format. Comic-strips, graphs, charts and straightforward language provide detail on people, objects, places, issues and events.

'Authors and Artists for Australian Children' was a series published by Cheshire, edited by Barbara Buick, which aimed to 'fill a cultural and aesthetic gap in the reading lives of younger Australians'. The series introduced to children 'the vitality of the best Australian art and design and true richness of artistic expression', and brought a leading writer and artist together in *Moggie and Her Circus Pony* (q.v., 1967) by Katharine Susannah Prichard, illustrated by Elaine Haxton; Geoffrey Dutton's *On My Island* (1967), illustrated by John Perceval; Ivan Southall's *Sly Old Wardrobe* (q.v., 1968), illustrated by Ted Greenwood; and *Yellow Jacket Jock* (1969) by Colin Thiele, illustrated by Clifton Pugh. Other books were planned, but Cheshire was amalgamated and the series abandoned.

AXELSEN, STEPHEN (1953–), born Sydney, re-illustrated some of Dorothy Wall's *Blinky Bill* titles in the 'Young Australia' series in 1976, and has illustrated many humorous picture-books. Titles include Cliff Green's *The Incredible Steam-Driven Adventures of Riverboat Bill* (1975), *The Further Adventures of Riverboat Bill* (1981) and *Riverboat Bill Steams Again* (1985); *Eli's Camel* (1978) by Vince Jones; *The Latchkey Dog* (1980) by Joan Dalgleish; Winsome Smith's *Elephant in the Kitchen* (1980); *The Racing Car Driver's Moustache* (1984) by Trevor Todd; *All about Anna and Harriet and Christopher and Me* (q.v., 1986) by Libby Hathorn; and *Little Sisters* (1988) by Jenny Axelsen. He illustrated some of Lorraine Wilson's *City Kids* series. His own texts and illustrations include *Eucalyptus Christmas* (1973), verse about Australian animals — 'The things that fill them up with bliss/The show they wouldn't want to miss' — and *The Oath of Bad Brown Bill* (q.v., 1978). He collected and illustrated *The Book of Australian Funny Poems* (1990), which has poems by Max Fatchen, Doug MacLeod, C.J. Dennis and others. Axelsen's humour is robust and earthy. For instance in *Eucalyptus Christmas* Father Christmas is a koala wearing thongs.

Ayu and the Perfect Moon (1984) by David Cox was Commended in the 1985 Picture Book of the Year Awards. Ayu tells three girls about the village ceremonial dances, recalling her youth when she performed for the whole village. Cox's illustrations evoke the lifestyle and landscape of Bali.

B

BACKHAUS-SMITH, REX (1935–), born Surat, Queensland, is an impressionist painter. He illustrated an edition of *Australian Legendary Tales* (1978) collected by K. Langloh Parker, and *The Curse of the Turtle* (q.v., 1977) and *The Vengeance of the Dolphin* (1980) by Thomas Roy.

BACKHOUSE, ELIZABETH (1917–), born Northam, WA, has written scripts for radio and television, scenarios, detective stories for adults, and a biography of her family, *Against Time and Place* (1990). *Enone and Quentin* (1946), illustrated by Irene Carter, is her only book for children. See **Fairies**.

Badge (Brian) Lorenny is the central character in *Tiger in the Bush* (q.v., 1957), *Devils' Hill* (q.v., 1958) and *The Roaring 40* (q.v., 1963) by Nan Chauncy. Badge is a child of the bush. In *Devils' Hill*, Chauncy introduces his more sophisticated cousin Sammy. Badge looks to Sammy to help him face the trauma of school, but at the beginning of *The Roaring 40*, Sammy has failed him, and Badge's homesickness is overwhelming. When he realises that Ned, a wild boy discovered on a fossicking trip, must also go to school, Badge is able to face leaving the valley to protect Ned at school.

BAILLIE, ALLAN (1943–), born Prestwick, Scotland, settled in Australia at the age of 7. Baillie has been a journalist with Melbourne and Sydney newspapers and the ABC. In his novels, Baillie examines the constituents of courage and the relationships within families. In *Adrift* (1983) Flynn and his sister Sally and a cat are accidentally set adrift in an old crate they have been playing on. Flynn finds he

has the inner resource to save his sister and himself, and comes to terms with his family situation. *Little Brother* (q.v., 1985) recounts the journey of 10-year-old Vithy from Cambodia to the border camp in Thailand, and then to Australia. *Riverman* (1986) is also a story of a boy's growth to adulthood, this time through his father's death, and a hazardous journey to save an ancient Huon Pine tree. The novel is set in the harsh mining settlements of western Tasmania and on the Franklin River. In *Eagle Island* (1987) a deaf boy, abandoned on an island, uncovers a smuggling operation. *Hero* (1990) takes place during the flooding of the Hawkesbury River, when Pam, Barney and Darcy each display heroism. *Bawshou Rescues the Sun* (1991), written with Chun-Chan Yeh, illustrated by Michelle Powell, is a Han folk-tale, in which Bawshou goes on a dangerous journey to retrieve the stolen Sun.

Megan's Star (1988) is a vivid portrayal of family life, with an irascible mother, a mischievous baby and a troubled, harassed girl. Megan meets Kel, who teaches her how to use the powers they both possess: to alter matter and travel into space. Kel, pursued on Earth by the menacing Hunters, goes off with the friendly aliens, but Megan is unwilling to give up her family. *Mates and Other Stories* (1989) is a collection of fourteen stories dealing with relationships. Topics include disabilities, immigrants, dangerous situations and science fiction. In *The China Coin* (1991) Leah's search for her cultural roots leads her to the Tiananmen Square massacre, through her involvement with Ke.

The picture-book *Drac and the Gremlin* (q.v., 1988) portrays the fantasy adventures of two children in a backyard garden. In another picture-book, *Little Monster*

(1991), illustrated by David Cox, Drew inherits an invisible creature, Queeg, who causes havoc in school and at home. *Creature* (1987), illustrated by Lorraine Hannay, is in Methuen's 'Dimensions' series, with excerpts from *Adrift* and *Little Brother*, two other stories, biographical information, and the sources of Baillie's inspiration.

Baillie's wide-ranging plots, from historical events to current political issues, from fantasy to realism, reveal his respect for the ability of young people to deal with complex questions of morality, identity and the fallible nature of the human condition.

BAKER, IVY (1922–), born Melbourne, has written novels which examine the close relationships between children and animals. *The Dingo Summer* (1980) is the summer after Mark is orphaned, when his observation of an alpine dingo helps

him adjust to his loss. In *If Wishes were Horses* (1984) Julie saves an old horse from the knacker's yard. *The Monday Sheepdog* (1987) is about a dog found by Ben in a box which has fallen off a truck. Charcoal becomes his companion when he is trying to manage the family farm alone. In *A Handful of Magic* (1988) Vicki calls up a genie when she rubs a piece of pottery she finds on the beach.

BAKER, JEANNIE (1950–), born Croydon, UK, studied art and design at Brighton Polytechnic before settling in Australia in 1976. In England she had illustrated *Polar* (1975) by Elaine Moss. *Grandfather* (1977) is also set in England, but *Grandmother* (1978) is set in Tasmania. *Millicent* (1980) is about an elderly woman who feeds the pigeons in Sydney's Hyde Park. The collages of the park, using real grass, clothing material, knitteds, clay

Millicent (1980) by Jeannie Baker

models and feathers are strikingly three-dimensional. *One Hungry Spider* (1982) is a counting book which describes the life of an Orbweb spider, and the various insects which are caught in or escape from her web. *Home in the Sky* (q.v., 1984) is set in New York, *Where the Forest Meets the Sea* (q.v., 1987) in the tropical rainforest at Daintree, and *Window* (q.v., 1991) in the expanding suburbs. Baker has said of her work that it is 'an illusion in perspective'. Her subtle exploration of sensory experience is presented through detailed, highly tactile relief collages which display her technical and artistic ability, and her control over the artistic miniature.

BAKER, ROBIN, see **BATEMAN, ROBERT**

BALDERSON, MARGARET (1935–), born Sydney, worked in Norway from 1963 to 1965, and her first novel, *When Jays Fly to Barbmo* (q.v., 1968), is set in that country. See also **War**. She has written *A Dog Called George* (q.v., 1975), for younger readers, and a picture-book, *Blue and Gold Day* (1979), illustrated by Roger Haldane, which represents the delight of two children playing on a remote beach.

BALDWIN, MAY was an English writer who wrote children's books in the first part of the twentieth century. Hilda de Trafford, the proud and lonely girl in *Hilda's Experiences* (1913), illustrated by W. Rainey, is so delicate when she comes to Australia that just scrubbing a floor makes her ill, but trial by fire and drought toughens her spirit, and she reluctantly returns to England, a changed girl. In *A Schoolgirl's Diary: the Story of Her Holiday Beyond the Seas* (1914) the orphaned Jean recounts incidents on the voyage to Australia with her uncle Ally. Jean's observations of the nuances of behaviour aboard ship and train are a perceptive account of social life in Australia before World War I.

BALL, DUNCAN (1941–), born Boston, USA, has lived in Sydney since 1974. He was trained as a mathematician and industrial chemist, and was editor of the NSW *School Magazine* in the 1970s. For his books about the ghost, *The Ghost and the Goggle Box* (1984), *The Ghost and the Gory Story* (1987) and *The Ghost and the Shutterbug* (1989), all illustrated by Noela Young, see **Taylor, Arnold**. For his three stories about a talking dog, *Selby's Secret* (1985), *Selby Speaks* (1988) and *Selby Screams* (1989), see **Selby's Secret**. In *My Dog's a Scaredy-Cat* (1987), with Craig Smith's funny illustrations, Stanley the dog is scared of many things — bees, birds, cars, cats — but dearly loved for all that. Jeremy tries to pin the tail on a donkey at the birthday party in *Jeremy's Tail* (1990), illustrated by Donna Rawlins, an effort completed after he travels, blindfolded, around the world, unaware of where he has been. *Comedies for Kids* (1988), also illustrated by Craig Smith, has 'preposterous plays, silly skits and daft dramas' — eight plays, ranging from stand-up comedy to a play with a cast of twenty. Ball has also written informational books.

BANCKS, JAMES CHARLES (1889–1952), born Sydney, was the creator of Ginger Meggs (q.v.). Leaving school as early as possible, Bancks worked as a lift-driver and in a woolstore until, to his amazement, the *Bulletin* accepted some of his illustrations and invited him to become a member of staff. After a period in Melbourne with the *Sun News Pictorial*, where he was influenced by Will Dyson, Bancks returned to Sydney to work for the *Sunday Sun*, to develop the newly created comic section. 'Us Fellers' was the result, soon taken over by a minor character, Ginger Meggs. Bancks also produced other cartoons, such as 'The Blimps', 'Napoleon Noodle' and 'Benno the Bear'. Like his creation, the cricket-loving, ginger-haired and iconoclastic Bancks was an amusing speaker and raconteur.

Band of Hope Review, The (1856–61), which later became the *Band of Hope Journal*, then the *Australian Home Companion and Band of Hope Journal* was the journal of the Band of Hope, a temperance organisation. The journal was aimed at educating the young, and included moral stories about the dangers of drink, models of good children for its readers to imitate, anecdotes and Christian poems.

BANDLER, FAITH (1918–), born Murwillumbah, NSW, has been active in the movement to obtain equal rights for Aboriginal People and Torres Strait Islanders. *Wacvie* (1977), illustrated by Robert Ingpen, is the story of her father who was kidnapped by white plantation owners from a Pacific island to work on the canefields of Queensland. In *Marani in Australia* (1980), written with Len Fox, Marani searches for his father while he works on the canefields. *Welou, My Brother* (1984) is about Wacvie's son, 12 when Wacvie dies, and Bandler traces the conflict between Ivy, his mother, who wants him to be educated in white schools, and Welou's need for his own people and their understanding of the world. Bandler's material has the tone of fiction, and although not specifically written for children, there are many child characters and childhood dilemmas. She describes the brutality meted out to the captured Islanders, their sorrow and loss of dignity, and their determination to keep their culture alive.

BARBALET, MARGARET (1949–), born Adelaide, has written adult novels, such as *Blood in the Rain* (1986), and a children's book, *The Wolf* (1991), illustrated by Jane Tanner. In a story rich in imagery and metaphor, Tal, Megan, Dai and their mother barricade themselves against a howling wolf, unseen until they recognise it for the poor bedraggled beast it is, and welcome it into their house.

Barjai (1943–47) was a magazine, begun when Laurence Collinson and Barrie (Barrett) Reid were in the senior class as Brisbane High School. It aimed to bring young people into contact with Australian literature, and encouraged writing on art, music and broad social issues. Material from authors aged 21 or under was accepted. Collinson was 18 and Reid 17 when the journal first appeared.

BARKER, Lady, see **BROOME**, Lady **MARY ANNE**

Barnaby and the Rocket (1972) by Lydia Pender, illustrated by Judith Cowell, was Commended in the 1973 Picture Book of the Year Awards. Barnaby first appeared in *Barnaby and the Horses* (1961), illustrated by Alie Evers, and re-illustrated by Inga Moore in 1980. In *Barnaby and the Rocket* it is bonfire night, and Barnaby waits anxiously for the moment when he can fire his rocket. Cowell expresses the magical excitement through evocative watercolours.

BARNARD, MARJORIE FAITH (1897–1987), born Sydney, was the librarian at Sydney Technical College for many years, and later at the National Standards Laboratories, CSIRO. She collaborated with Flora Eldershaw on novels for adults. Her children's book, *The Ivory Gate* (1920), illustrated by Leyshon White, contains fourteen stories, such as 'Shadows', about how fear is created; descriptions of magical places; and small adventures, such as 'The Runaways', about two boys who save an injured child. Barnard wrote an unpublished history of radar for the CSIRO.

BARNARD, PEGGY came to Australia from Malaysia during World War II and returned to England after 1945. She wrote the award-winning *Wish and the Magic Nut* (q.v., 1956), and *Michael the Mallee Chick in Search of a Mother* (1946), illustrated by

Mollie Quick. Michael is the last chick to hatch and has to fend for himself until he is cared for by Ma, a parrot.

BARNES, VICTOR DOMINIC SUTHERS (1913–89), born Sydney, was a teacher and the inventor of a range-finding device. He created the pet kangaroo Skippy (q.v.) and is the author of three books taken from the series. *Woobinda: Animal Doctor* (1969), illustrated by Walter Stackpool, is a picture-book in which John Stevens and his retinue care for the bush animals. *The Barrier Reef Adventures of Minus Five* (1971), illustrated by Walter Stackpool, and *Minus Five and the Mountain of Gold* (1974) are adventure stories. *The Legend of the Three Sisters* (1971), *Little Binjy* (1971), *The Bunyip and the Bul-Bird* (1971), *Three Aboriginal Legends* (1972) and *Aboriginal Tales* (1972) are all illustrated by Hal English. Little Binjy plays in the bush with Australian animals; Tyawan turns his three daughters to stone to save them from the bunyip; Dreaming stories, fire-making, sending signals, hunting and the use of weapons are described. Barnes edited the *Modern Encyclopaedia of Australia and New Zealand* (1964).

BARNETT, FREDERICK OSWALD (1887–1972), born Brunswick, Melbourne, was a poet, teacher and activist in the Methodist Church. Barnett established the Methodist Babies' Home in Melbourne in 1929, was a prominent member of the Slum Abolition Group, and became deputy chairman of the Victorian Housing Commission in the 1940s. He wrote *Happy Endings to Old Nursery Rhymes* (1945), illustrated by Dorothy Dibdin. See **Nursery Rhymes**.

BARNETT, GILLIAN (1948–), born Melbourne, has been a teacher and academic. *The Inside Hedge Story* (1981), illustrated by Geoff Todd, was serialised on the ABC. See **Conservation**. In *The Sack Man* (1987), illustrated by Lynda Taylor, Jess is afraid that an old man who carries a

sack around will kidnap her. When she exchanges gifts with him she finds that he is really a friend. In *Cat in Curlers* (1990), illustrated by Maya (Alexandrovna), Rachel wants to beautify her cat, with chaotic results. *Gumboots & Other Risks* (1989) is for older readers. Fourteen-year-old Katherine moves to the country with her family, and must adjust to difficulties, such as the death of her dog.

BARRETT, CHARLES LESLIE (1879–1959) (**'DONALD BARR'**), born Melbourne, joined the Melbourne *Herald* in 1906, and was on its staff for thirty-three years. He also edited the *Victorian Naturalist* from 1925 to 1939. He made no claims to being a scientific writer, but he was a bush rambler who popularised the riches of the bush, as well as developing public interest in the anthropology of Australia and New Guinea. His stories were written to introduce natural history to children. In *The Bush Ramblers: a Story for Australian Children* (1913), Robbie and Jean enjoy the untamed creatures of the bush, and travel around the Victorian countryside. Similar books are *Ralph in the Bush* (1921), *Rambles Round the Zoo* (1923), *The Penguin People* (1948), *Wild Life of Australia and New Guinea* (1954), and *Wild Life in Australia* (1950). In *Bushland Babies* (1924) Colin can talk to the animals; *Kooborr the Koala* (1941), with Isobel Ann Shead, illustrated by Joan Kiddell-Monroe, relates the life cycle of the koala. *The Fernland Story Book* (1922) edited by 'Donald Barr', illustrated by Betty Paterson, includes stories and poems by Donald Macdonald, Furnley Maurice, Mary Grant Bruce and Barrett himself. Barrett also wrote adventure stories, and for *The Isle of Palms: a Story of Adventure* (1915), *Warrigal Joe: a Tale of the Never Never* (1946), and *The Secret of Coconut Island: a Treasure Quest in Torres Strait* (1946) see **Adventure Stories**. *The Bunyip and Other Mythical Monsters and Legends* (1946) is an ethnological book which identifies places where the bunyip is said to appear, and legends about bun-yips. Barrett was the editor of the journal *Pals* from 1920 to 1928, and edited the *Australian Junior Encyclopaedia* (1951–61).

BARRETT, MICHAEL. For *Traitor at Twenty Fathoms* see **Adventure Stories**.

Barrier Reef Annual 1972, see **Annuals**

BARRY, JOHN ARTHUR (1850–1911), born Torquay, UK, joined the merchant navy at the age of 13. In 1870 he went to the Palmer diggings, and spent many years as a bushman, drover, gold-digger and boundary rider, as well as returning at times to his first love, the sea. In *A Son of the Sea* (1899), an adventure story for boys, the central character, Torre Leigh, starts as a midshipman, lands in Adelaide and wanders throughout south-ern Australia along the Murray and Darling rivers as far as Bourke, travels to Pacific islands, then settles in Sydney. Barry reveals the novel's autobiographical character at its conclusion, saying that none of the adventures is fictional. He also wrote *Sea Yarns* (1910), and novels for adults.

BARTLEET, MARGARET TRAILL (1916–72), born Cessnock, NSW, wrote *Wilderness House: a Story for Girls* (1952). Tess and Roddie are teenage orphans. They live at Wilderness House, and when Tess's dancing teaching is no longer viable, she takes in boarders. The family's for-tunes are secured when Roddie discovers limestone caves on the land Father had bought before he died, and the resourceful Tess keeps the family together. Bartleet also wrote novels and poetry for adults.

BARTLETT, EVELYN (1905–82), born WA, lived in Asia, England and Australia. For *Rosemary in Rhymeland* (1939) see **Nursery Rhymes**. Bartlett wrote two books about a small, energetic kangaroo, *Dumper the Kangaroo* (1955), illustrated by Audrey Addison, and

Dumper and the Circus (1958), illustrated by Irene Maher. Dumper leaves home to be an artist, with Scriggle, Scraggle and Scrum, three woolly caterpillars. He paints pictures of the bush animals to trick the bad dingo, and with his 'three hairy hin-drances' follows a circus to meet the beau-tiful Snowflake. They sail a boat, are attacked by pirate rats and are captured by the circus, but Snowflake sets them free. Bartlett also wrote books and short stories for adults.

BARTLETT, STEPHEN, see **'SLADE, GURNEY'**

BARTON, CHARLOTTE (1797–1862), born London, UK, was engaged to be governess to the children of Governor King's daughter, Mrs Hannibal Macarthur, but met and married James Atkinson before she took up the position. One of her children, Louisa Atkinson, was to become Australia's first woman novelist. After James Atkinson's death, Charlotte married George Bruce Barton. Charlotte Barton wrote the first Australian book for children, *A Mother's Offering to Her Children* (q.v., 1841). An account of her life appears in Marcie Muir's *Charlotte Barton: Australia's First Children's Author* (1980) and Patricia Clarke's *Pen Portraits* (1988).

BARTON, EMILY MARY (1817–1909), born England, settled in Australia in 1839. She was the grandmother of Andrew Barton Paterson. Her only chil-dren's book was a book of verse, *A Few of Grandmamma's Prizes for the Little Ones* (1885).

BASE, GRAEME (1958–), born Amersham, UK, artist and musician, came to Australia when he was 8. Base studied art at Swinburne Institute of Technology. He has illustrated *Adventures With My Worst Best Friend* (1982) by Max Dann, *The Rottnest Bike Business* (1982) by Susan

Animalia (1986) by Graeme Base

Burke, *The Day of the Dinosaurs* (1985) by Jan Anderson, and *The Creation Myths* (1987) by Maureen Stewart. He wrote and illustrated *My Grandma Lived in Gooligulch* (1983), a tall tale in verse in which Grandma and her pet wombat fly off to see the world. *Animalia* (q.v., 1986) is an original alphabet book about animals; *Jabberwocky: From Through the Looking Glass* (1987) is an interpretation of Carroll's poem; and *The Eleventh Hour: a Curious Mystery* (q.v., 1988) is a picture-story in verse, full of cryptic clues and hidden messages. Base's intricate, carefully designed picture-books, with their wealth of detail and verbal dexterity, offer a visual and aural feast.

Bass, George (1771–1803), born Aswarby, UK, mapped the southern coast of Australia with Matthew Flinders in 1795, and had the Strait between the mainland and Tasmania named after him. The journey and the natural world which surrounded the explorers is related through the eyes of a boy in *Bass & Billy Martin* (1972) by Joan Phipson. In *Ben Halyard: a Story of Bass and Flinders* (1907) by A.G. Alanson, illustrated by D.H. Souter, Ben is a cabin boy with Bass and Flinders, but Alanson's account of the reactions of the Aboriginal People is predictable and inaccurate: 'Never in the history of the world was a country occupied by an invading people so peaceably as was Australia by the British.' In contrast, in *Tom Fincham: the Boy who Sailed with Flinders and Bass* (?1922) by James Amess, a Whitcombe's Story Book, Tom also sails in the *Tom Thumb*, on the *Reliance* to Norfolk Island, and then to Shoals Haven, Point Hicks, and Bass Strait, including the Furneaux group and Western Port. This colourful novel, which examines the friendship of the two sailors, places Bass and Flinders against a background of colonial life.

BASSER, KATHLEEN VERONICA

(Mrs ABRAM), born Melbourne, has written for the NSW *School Magazine*. *Fria and the Sea Witch* (1944), illustrated by Silvia Tiarks, is a retelling of the old story of a fisher girl who is turned into a seal. Fria brings wealth to her lover in the form of a pearl, but when she becomes a human again she swears never to wear fur for the rest of her life. In *Glory Bird* (1947), illustrated by Elaine Haxton, a selfish and vain bird is stripped of his colourful feathers and banished from the forest. *The Martins of Montrose* (1948) is a domestic story of a very conventional family and their love affairs set around Sydney. *Ponny the Penguin* (q.v., 1948) traces the life cycle of a penguin, using humanised images such as an engagement between Ponny and Peter. *Bright-Eyes the Glider Possum* (1957), illustrated by Richard Richardson, is similar, except that Bright-Eyes is a children's pet for a time. *Round the Year Verses* (1956) is a collection of her poems, with activities, in three parts — First Term, Second Term and Third Term — which follow the seasons.

BASTIAN, GREG (1951–), born

Sydney, is a playwright and novelist. *The Great Secondhand Supper* (1989) is a complex picture of a boy growing up. Jason wants to win a competition to help his family out but is distracted by love. In *Lies and Alibis* (1992) the life of Hamish Kinsella, suspected of being a pyromaniac, is unravelled at home and at school.

Batavia was a Dutch ship which ran aground on Houtman's Abrolhos Rocks, off the WA coast, in 1629. Henrietta Drake-Brockman located the site of the wreck, and Hugh Edwards organised the diving party which discovered the wreck in 1963. The captain of the *Batavia*, Pelsaert, set off for Java in an open boat, but when he returned to the barren islands where he had left the survivors, he found that over 120 of them had been murdered by members of the crew. Captain Pelsaert then supervised the hanging of seven of the murderers and put some ashore to fend for themselves. Ernest Favenc's *Marooned on Australia: Being the Narration by Diedrich Buys of his Discoveries and Exploits in Terra Australis Incognita about the Year 1630* (1896) was an attempt to reconstruct their fate. After a description of the outrage, Favenc's two marooned sailors find a lost civilisation in the far north containing remnants of early contact with Europe. E.T. Hooley was also taken with the possibilities which the *Batavia* incident offered. Young Edwin Forrester in *Tarragal: or, Bush Life in Australia* (1897) recovers £40 000 worth of gold coins from a buried treasure, hidden by the ship's renegades. Melva Lear in *Dangerous Holiday, Five Young Treasure-seekers in the Abrolhos Islands* (1959), illustrated by Joan Abbott, touches on the romance of the incident, when her young adventurers find some of the *Batavia*'s treasure. Paul Buddee's *The Mystery of Moma Island* (1969) recalls Pelsaert's story, although the treasure found is not from the *Batavia*. In Deborah Lisson's *The Devil's Own* (1990), Julianna, a girl from the present day, finds herself as a survivor of the *Batavia*, after an argument with her parents. The horror of the massacres and the harshness of the times is softened by her love for Dirk. The story concludes with Julie restored to her own time, with a greater understanding of what love means. Gary Crew's *Strange Objects* (q.v., 1990) traces the plight of two survivors of the *Batavia*, who join a group of Aboriginal People and a white girl, Ela. The historical details of the tragedy are provided as background to the novel. Crew's novel is the most telling reconstruction of the mystery and brutality of the *Batavia* incident.

BATEMAN, ROBERT (1922–) wrote

A Map for Giants (1964), illustrated by Nancy Parker, based on the adventures of a real person, Robin Baker. Robin travels to the outback, contends with floods, dust, heat and every other possible difficulty, including crocodile-infested rivers and waterless deserts. *Quest for Nuggets* (1967) is based on the diary of the author's great-grandfather. Bill Wallace meets bushrangers on his way to the diggings, makes a very small fortune, and returns to England. The book describes roughing it on the Victorian and NSW goldfields.

BATES, DAISY (1863–1951), born Ireland, arrived in Australia in 1884, and worked at various locations with the Aboriginal People, to whom she was known as 'Kabbarli' (grandmother, wise woman, friend). Her collection of observations and tales is held in the National Library. Barbara Ker Wilson adapted some of these for children in *Tales Told to Kabbarli* (1972), illustrated by Harold Thomas. See **Aboriginal Dreaming Stories**.

BATES, DIANNE (1948–   ), born Peakhurst, NSW, teacher, journalist, and writer, was assistant editor of the NSW *School Magazine* and co-editor with Doug MacLeod of *Puffinalia*. She has contributed stories to anthologies. Her first novel looked at the results of divorce. *Terri* (1981) has a step-family in Sydney, but her favourite parent, Pa, lives in the country. Terri's life with her father is threatened when he tells Terri that he and Brenda will marry, and Terri's response is to reject Brenda and run away. In *Piggy Moss* (1982), illustrated by Bill Farr, the overworked and lonely Vivian is rejected by the children at school, who call her 'Pig Girl'. When her stepbrother Jack comes out from England, Vivian believes he will bring companionship and help. This is a study of a girl with demanding, cross parents, at a difficult stage in her life. Bates's concern for abused children motivates *Thirteen Going on Forty* (1986). Mitch Towers has an abusive and drunken father, and after a worse than usual bashing,

Mitch and her family find some peace in a refuge. Finally Father goes to prison and then Alcoholics Anonymous, Mother strengthens her resolve, and Mitch sees a better future.

Bates then moved to more humorous stories. Willie S. Macbeth, in *The Belligrumble Bigfoot* (1984), illustrated by Edwina Bates, has fantasies in which he catches the monster of Belligrumble, but the monster decides to live under his bed, and they are both happy. Grandma Cadbury in *Grandma Cadbury's Trucking Tales* (q.v., 1987) and *Grandma Cadbury's Safari Tours* (1989), both illustrated by Kevin Burgemeestre, is daring and larger than life, and attracts bizarre experiences from which she escapes with ingenuity. In *The Slacky Flat Gang* (1988), written with Bill Condon, Clarence Nickdorf, Spike Shilling, Sidney Custard and Dick Fink escape from prison and return to their childhood reform school, Buckingham Towers. Their intention to continue their lives of crime reckons without Miss Gloria Wangler, the retired headmistress, and Nettie Nickdorf, Clarence's formidable mother, in a tall story. In *Candy in the Kitchen* (1989) Candy and Sheree are twins. Candy wants to be a chef and Sheree wants to be a doctor. Some adventures in each vocation occur, with much funny dialogue and insult-trading. *The Boy Who Loved Chocolate* (1990) contains eight stories, realistic and fantastic, for younger readers. *The Worst Cook in the World* (1987), illustrated by Mary Davey, is a collection of six stories, extracts from *Terri*, *Piggy Moss*, and *The Belligrumble Bigfoot*, and three new offerings. *Madcap Cafe and Other Humorous Plays* (1986) with Bill Condon, *Operation Lily-Liver: a Shadow Play* (1987) with Bill Condon, illustrated by Jeff Hook, *The Little Red Hen* (1987), illustrated by Anne Sulzer, and *The Musicians of Bremen* (1987), illustrated by Bruce Rankin, are simple plays for early readers in Macmillan's 'Southern Cross' series. She has also contributed to other reading schemes.

Bates Family, The (1969) by Reginald Ottley was Commended in the 1970 Book of the Year Awards. This sombre novel is dedicated 'to all those who have moulded their lives to the harsh conditions of outback Australia'. Seventeen-year-old twins Albie and Linda are the eldest of eight. The Bates family, both girls and boys, are competent itinerant drovers. Through drought, flood and injury, the family cheerfully struggles on to a future without any promise of an easier life.

BATHIE, JUDITH (1938–90), born Melbourne, wrote *The Witch of Grange Grove* (1974), illustrated by Isabel Wicca, the first production of the Women's Movement Children's Literature Co-operative (q.v.), which also published *Alison and the Bear* (1975), illustrated by Carol Pavey, and *The Princess and the Painter* (1975), illustrated by Judith Crabtree. In these early non-sexist books, the witch encourages boys and girls to follow their own desires; Alison wants to catch a bear, but only her grandmother supports her; Amanda is an unhappy princess until she persuades one of the castle painters to let her do his job.

BAXTER, FRED, born Cheshire, UK, came to Australia in 1953. *All That Money* (1967), illustrated by Sandra Hargrave, is set in an isolated area of Gippsland, Victoria. Independent bush children find a suitcase full of money, which they suspect has been stolen. They take it for safe keeping, only to find that it is Sid's lottery winnings. *Snake for Supper* (1968), illustrated by Genevieve Melrose, is also set in Gippsland, this time a hundred years earlier. Jirri is a Kurnai who saves Kathy from drowning, and stays with her until she is reunited with her family. See **Aboriginal People in Children's Fiction**.

BAYLIS-WHITE, MARY, see **WHITE, MARY**

Beach, The in Australian children's books is generally represented as a place for holidays. Jeanie Adams's *Going for Oysters* (1991) shows the role of the beach in the life of the Aurukun people as a source of food as well as pleasure, but most Australians see a day at the beach as an opportunity for small children to discover the delights of swimming and beach-combing. Roger Haldane and Margaret Balderson's *Blue and Gold Day* (1979) and Geoffrey Dutton's *Seal Bay* (1966) and *On My Island* (1967) present the bliss of paddling and collecting shells as children wander along the shoreline. Jack Bedson's *Don't Get Burnt! or The Great Australian Day at the Beach* (1985), illustrated by Peter Gouldthorpe, takes the same approach, despite modern concerns about sunburn and its hazards. *Greetings from Sandy Beach* (q.v., 1990) by Bob Graham depicts a more chaotic holiday, this time camping beside the beach, and *Beryl and Bertha at the Beach* (1990) by Pippa MacPherson has two robust hens launching into surfing. Alison Lester's *Magic Beach* (1990) goes beyond reality to suggest the possibilities of imagination at the beach. A beach holiday has also provided a setting for a rite of passage for some characters. The delicate rarity of a starfish mirrors the changes which Patricia Wrightson's Lindy Martin undergoes on her beach holiday in *The Feather Star* (q.v., 1962). Jack Steadman, in Joan Phipson's *Six and Silver* (1964), discovers his own inadequacy when he is in danger in the water.

Claire Meillon's *The New Surf Club* (1959) introduces the drama of surfing, but her boys are involved in the club rather than the sport. J.M. Couper's *Looking for a Wave* (1973) uses the device of a surfing holiday, but Couper sees the experience as a way to maturity, and his characters do very little surfing. *Lockie Leonard, Human Torpedo* (q.v., 1990) by Tim Winton, on the other hand, has Lockie revelling in the surf itself, and Lockie's first loyalty, after his family, is to his surfboard. It was Roger Vaughan Carr's

Surfie (1966), a novel for adults about a young surfer, which caught the rebellious tone of youth, taken up by Kathy Lette and Gabrielle Carey in their seminal *Puberty Blues: a Surfie Saga* (q.v., 1979). The surf beaches here provide a setting for sexual adventures rather than sand castles, and it is the culture which surrounds surfing, not the sport, which is examined. Considering the popularity of surfing with young people, and its characteristic link with freedom from adults and youthful adventures, apart from Winton's novel, the surf and surfing culture is noticeably absent from contemporary settings, and reflects the cautious approach of writers for adolescents.

BEAR, CAROLYN, born UK, spent a year in Australia. For *Under Different Stars* (1988) see **Perth.**

Beat of the City (1966) by Hesba Brinsmead, illustrated by William Papas, was awarded a Special Mention in the 1967 Book of the Year Awards. It is set in Abbotsford, Melbourne, and follows the fortunes of Sabie, Syd, Mary and Raylene. When Raylene leaves home for the bright lights of the city, she falls in with a group of motorbike riders who lead her astray. Mary saves her from a life of crime. The novel provides a colourful picture of the youth scene in the Melbourne of the period. It was made into a television serial of eight thirty-minute episodes in 1976 by the ABC, featuring Liz Ryan, Joanne Simmons, Robert Hewett and Robert Ratti.

BECKE, 'LOUIS' (GEORGE LEWIS) (1855–1913), born Port Macquarie, NSW, wrote novels and short stories based on his own adventures. From the age of 14 he led a roving life throughout the Pacific, Queensland and on the east coast of the USA. He worked with the notorious 'Bully' Hayes, kidnapping Islanders to work on the canefields, and was once accused of piracy, experiences recalled in *Tom Wallis: a Tale of the South Seas* (1900). Becke's more legitimate occupation was that of an island trader. The legend goes that at the age of 38 he met Ernest Favenc and J.F. Archibald of the *Bulletin*, the latter in a hotel at Coogee, where Becke was holding the parlour audience enthralled with his accounts of adventures in the South Seas. Both Archibald and Favenc encouraged him to write. His reputation, according to H.M. Green, relies on his contribution to the short story, but his success with young readers rests on his powerful evocation of the Pacific islands, and his adventure stories. In *The Settlers of Karossa Creek: and Other Stories of Australian Bush Life* (1906), illustrated by J. Finnemore, William Kendall and his family take up land by free selection, earning the enmity of the local squatter, Major Vale Tarrant. Kendall and his son are accused of cattle-stealing, but are acquitted, and there is a reconciliation between the two families. See also **Bushfire.** Becke also contributed short stories to the annual *Australian Boys and Girls* (1895) and the magazine *Pals.* Further reading: Day, *Louis Becke.*

BEDFORD, ERIC, the son of Randolph Bedford, a member of the Queensland Legislative Council, and friend of Jack Lindsay, wrote *Scum o' the Seas* (1944). See **Adventure Stories**.

BEDFORD, H. LOUISA was an English author who set some of her books in Australia. In *A Home in the Bush* (1913) Prue and Bruce are English new chums on a farm in Tasmania. At first they find 'colonial life' frightfully exciting and interesting, despite having to go to the 'common State School where all the other children go'. Their colonial schoolmates confirm their misgivings and pronounce them to be 'too toffy, that is too soft to be any good!'. Bruce has to learn that he is not superior. He fights a boy who speaks disparagingly of the King, and the teacher remarks 'a new chum buys his experience'. See also **Death**; **Lost in the Bush**. Other novels include *Under One Standard: or, The Touch that Makes us Kin* (1923), illustrated by H. Piffard, about a family seeking their fortune in NZ at the time of the Maori Wars; *Jack, the Englishman* (1923), illustrated by W. Paget; and *Netta's Call* (1931), in which a girl's death inspires her brother to become a missionary. Bedford's novels were published by the Society for the Preservation of Christian Knowledge.

BEDFORD, RUTH MARJORY (1882–1963), born Sydney, poet and novelist, wrote *Rosycheeks and Goldenhead: Verses* (1913), illustrated by Mabel L. Webb; *Fairies and Fancies* (1929), illustrated by Mela Koehler Broman; and *Hundreds and Thousands* (1934), illustrated by Pixie O'Harris, all collections of poems. *Fairies and Fancies* touches on childhood experiences, such as trying on summer dresses, and imaginative encounters with fairies. *Hundreds and Thousands* used similar themes. 'The end of our garden is a good place to be,/There's a red wall with creepers and a mulberry tree,/And an old broken wheelbarrow lying in the shade,/Where I play the nicest games of all I've ever played./ ... For "I Spy" and "French and English", "Rounders" and the rest/You have to have a lot of children; I like it best/When there's no one to bother in a place of my own,/And the best games of all are the games I play alone.' *Who's Who in Rhyme and Without Reason* (1948) is a collection of satiric verses about familiar stereotypes. Katie Kaleidescope, for instance, believed everyone should always be happy. 'Now what a very surprising attitude,/What perversity, what ingratitude/Katie Kaleidescope's friends displayed!/They weren't impressed by her gay parade/Of helpful mottoes and quips and wiles,/They even jibbed at her ceaseless smiles./They said if they felt like being tearful/They jolly well wouldn't go looking cheerful.' *The Little Blue Devil* (1912)

and *Two's Company* (1914) were novels for adults written in collaboration with Dorothea Mackellar.

BEDSON, JACK (1950–), poet and librarian, wrote *Don't Get Burnt! or The Great Australian Day at the Beach* (1985), illustrated by Peter Gouldthorpe, which shows how easily Jack is sunburnt on an exuberant day at the beach. Mac and Kelly in *Sheep Dogs* (1990), also illustrated by Gouldthorpe, are family pets. They hear the farmer say that he needs a couple of sheepdogs, so they roll in tar and wool to look like sheep — hence, sheepdogs. With A.J. Bennett, Bedson co-edited a collection of poems for adults, *The Contents of Their Wallets* (1987).

Beetles Ahoy!: Being a Series of Nature Studies Specially Written for Children (1948) by Ada Jackson, illustrated by Nina Poynton, was Highly Commended in the 1948 Book of the Year Awards. Originally broadcast on the ABC, it is a novel about two children, John and Molly, who collect flora and fauna, particularly insects, under the guidance of their next-door neighbour, 'the Professor', to set up their own museum. There is much interesting scientific information included in the unlikely conversations between the three characters.

Behind the Wind (1981) by Patricia Wrightson was Highly Commended in the 1982 Book of the Year Awards. See *The Ice is Coming*.

BELL, EDWINA (Mrs EDWINA WILLIAMS) (1915–), born Sydney, is a painter and illustrator who studied at East Sydney Technical College. In the 1940s she illustrated Ella May McFadyen's 'Pegmen' books and *Little Dragons of the Never Never* (1948). McFadyen introduced Bell to Doris Chadwick, then editor of the NSW *School Magazine*, and many of Bell's illustrations can be found in that paper. She illustrated *Ponny the Penguin* (q.v., 1948) by Veronica Basser, *Bush*

Cobbers (q.v., 1948) by 'Musette Morell' and *The Adventures of Jan and Jennifer* (1948) by Don Edwards. Bell was also engaged for illustrations to some of the 'Australians in History' series published by Collins, such as *Margaret Catchpole* (1974) by Nance Donkin and *Merchant Campbell* (1976) by Ruth Park. *Rough Road South* (1975) and *Colour of Courage* (1978) by Valerie Thompson, and *The Best of the Bunch* (1978) by Nance Donkin show Bell's strong command of line and her capacity to reveal character using pencil, pen and ink. With *A Dream of Seas* (1978) by Lilith Norman she put aside her attention to outline and expanded into soft wash drawings to suggest the freedom of swimming in the open sea, and the vague longings of a boy whose life only becomes real in the water. Bell's later paintings have continued to express her fascination with the sea and coastal landscapes.

BELL, ENID (1889–1965), born 'Coochin Coochin' Station, Boonah, Queensland, gathered *Legends of the Coochin Valley* (1946), illustrated by Marjorie de Winter, from Bunjoey, one of the survivors of the Ugarapul people, who had lived in the valley before the arrival of whites. See **Aboriginal Dreaming Stories**. *David and his Australian Friends* (1952), illustrated by Noela Young, with a foreword by Sir Laurence Olivier, describes David's years in country Australia, where he learns to ride, finds a calf and fights off snakes and goannas. David's dreams are realised after returning to Scotland when his father buys a farm in Australia.

BELL, ESME ELLIOTT. For *The Rainbow Painter* see **Fairies**. Bell also illustrated *Peter Porter* (1952) by Olive Mason.

BELL, LEIGH (ALISON CLARE HARVEY BELL) (?–1943), born Tasmania, was a clerk at the University of Tasmania. *Colin's Story-Book* (1924), illustrated by Hugh McCrae, is a collection of stories about children and their adventures with Santa Claus, mermaids and fairies. *Breakers on the Beach* (1926), illustrated by Edgar Holloway, is set in Tasmania. Iris dallies with Tom's affections until he shows how brave and true he really is. See also **Romance**.

BENNELL, EDDIE, playwright, collected *Aboriginal Legends from the Bibulmun Tribe* (1981). See **Aboriginal Dreaming Stories**. Bennell headed the National Aboriginal Consultative Committee from 1972 to 1975.

BENNETT, DEBORAH ELIZA-BETH (1932–) wrote *Jean's Black Diamond: a Story of Australia* (1951), illustrated by L.F. Lupton, the first of two sanctimonious horse books about Jean Brownley, who lives with her family on a cattle station south of the Queensland border. The family falls on hard times, captures brumbies to help with horse-breeding, and Jean falls in love with a fine mare. When Jean wins first place in a gymkhana, complicated because she cannot ride on Sunday, she gives her money to Bob to pay for his university course. *Son of Diamond: a Story of Australia* (1952) takes the reader three years on, and introduces Hugh Durant, an English orphan who is to take over a nearby station. Jean gives Diamond's colt, Gem, to Hugh, and the story concludes with Hugh and Jean becoming engaged. *Susan's Conquest: a Story of Australia* (1956), also illustrated by Lupton, is set near Murwillimbah on a dairy farm. Susan wins over her cousins after some unhappy times at home and at school. In one scene she saves the day by smashing her head against an attacker. The blow breaks her spectacles, which are the bane of her life and the cause of much of her sorrow, and a piece of glass becomes imbedded in the ruffian's neck! Her conquest, brought about through her faith in God and much prayer, is over her feelings of rejection.

BENNETT, JACK (JOHN BAILLIE BENNETT) (1934–), born Cape Province, South Africa, wrote *Jamie* (1963), about a South African boy, set in the African bush. Four other novels followed. After settling in Australia, Bennett wrote *The Lieutenant: an Epic Tale of Courage and Endurance on the High Seas* (q.v., 1977), which follows William Bligh's extraordinary story of survival. *The Voyage of the Lucky Dragon* (1979) traces another journey, this time of a family who leave Vietnam. Quan and his father are threatened with re-education when the North Vietnamese take over Saigon, so the whole family set off for Malaysia in the *Lucky Dragon*. They are forced to sail on, attacked by pirates, and suffer terrible deprivations before reaching Australia. Only Quan, his sister Ly, Uncle Tan and Aunt Binh survive the journey. Bennett has written *Matilda Goodbucket* (1984) for younger readers, a picture-book with brilliant illustrations by Trish Hart, about a cat who lives near Sydney Harbour.

BENTLEY, JOHN CLIVE (1944–), born UK, has written three novels in the Longman Cheshire 'Triple Header' series. In *The Mark of the Swastika* (1985) finding a gun with a swastika on its handle leads Gary and Sarah to uncover gun-running on the French coast. In *The Rampage of Rampo* (1985) Frankie and Pat travel to prehistoric times. *Heads They Win, Tails We Lose* (1985) is set in contemporary Tasmania. Mike and Sandy, Scottish twins, meet Wendy, an Aboriginal girl, who reveals the beauty of the countryside to them. These well-written adventure stories are aimed at the school market, with questions appended for classroom use. Bentley has also written *The Bang on the Head: a Children's Novel* (1983).

BERESFORD, ELISABETH, born Paris, came to Australia for some years after World War II. Her research material on immigration interested her in outback areas. For *The Flying Doctor Mystery* (1958) and *The Flying Doctor to the Rescue* (1964) see **Royal Flying Doctor Service**. After her return to Britain, she wrote *The Wombles* (1968), about creatures who lived beneath Wimbledon Common, starting a popular series for British television.

BERNARD, PATRICIA (1942–) wrote *We are Tam* (1983), a science fiction story in which Tamarisk from the twentieth century connects with Tameron in the twenty-fifth to find a poet lost in the twentieth century. *Aida's Ghost* (1988) is a time-slip fantasy in which two teenagers involved as extras at the Sydney Opera House are drawn into the time of Rameses and Princess Aida by her ghost, and become caught up in the real events which inspired the opera. In *Kangaroo Kids* (1989) Tony overcomes his loneliness when he, Lillie and Mrs Thomas share a secret pet — a baby kangaroo. As **JUDY BERNARD-WAITE**, with Judy Nunn and Fiona Waite, Bernard has written *The Riddle of the Trumpalar* (1981) and *Challenge of the Trumpalar* (1986). Carl and Cass enter an enormous Moreton Bay fig tree in Trumper Park, Sydney, which leads them to Trumperland. By taking them into past times in Sydney, the Trumpalar shows them how to save the tree. In the other Trumpalar novel, the children travel forward into the future. Bernard also writes detective stories as P. Scot-Bernard.

BERNDT, CATHERINE HELEN (1918–), born NZ, married Professor Ronald Berndt and collaborated with him on anthropological studies. Both have worked on Aboriginal issues. *Pheasant and Kingfisher: Originally told by Nganalgindja in the Gunwinggu Language* (1987), illustrated by Arone Raymond Meeks is a story from the Western Desert. It was first published in Berndt's *Land of the Rainbow Snake: Aboriginal Children's Stories from Western Arnhem Land* (1979), illustrated by Djoki Yunupingu. *When the World was New: In Rainbow Snake Land* (1988) and *This is Still*

Rainbow Snake Country (1988), also illustrated by Meeks, are stories from western Arnhem Land, the latter dedicated to the women of Oenpelli. These are authentic recountals, placed in their correct location with the storyteller identified.

Bernice Knows Best (1983) by Max Dann, illustrated by Ann James, won the Junior Book of the Year Awards in 1984. Hugh's clumsiness is quite out of control until the irrepressible Bernice suggests practical ways to overcome his difficulties. The contortions she suggests fail to cure him, until he accidentally enters a bicycle race where he defeats the caddish Rotten Frank, because he just cannot stop the bike. Bernice, of course, takes the credit for curing him.

Bertie and the Bear (1983) by Pamela Allen won the 1984 Picture Book of the Year Awards. When Bertie is chased by a large brown bear, the Queen, the King, the Admiral, the Captain, the General, the Sergeant and the little dog chase the bear. After a noisy pursuit, the pace changes, and the bear dances with Bertie to music made by the courtiers. The same characters appear in *A Lion in the Night* (1985). The exuberance of the stories is expressed in text and picture.

Bertie and the Bullfrogs: an Australian Story for Big and Little Children (1874), which appeared in the 1873 Christmas number of the Adelaide *Observer*, was published anonymously and privately, by John Howard Clark, editor of the *South Australian Register* from 1870 to 1878. It is not illustrated. The book is considered a landmark, an Australian *Alice's Adventures in Wonderland*. In his preliminary poem, Clark apologises to Carroll for 'pluck[ing] this poor twig from out thy crown of laurel/To plant it in the far Australian land,/And grow, inspired by thee, a Christmas Carroll'. In Bertie's world at the bottom of the creek are bullfrogs, owls, kangaroos, mice, lizards and 'opossums',

and the verses mimic the Carroll style. ''Tis the voice of the bullfrog, I heard him complain,/You have waked me too soon, I shall wait for next train;/As a swell on his travels, so he for a swag/Bears his rug, and his hatbox, and his carpetbag.' The conversation, too, is Carroll-like: '"What is the first letter?" "A," said Bertie, thinking that if all the questions were as easy as that the owl would make a very nice examiner. "Wrong!" said the owl; "next boy!" "O," cried the first opossum. "Right!" said the owl. "Take him down." "But, please Sir," said Bertie, "A *is* the first letter." "That shows what *you* know about it," said the owl. "Only vulgar people say 'a possum'; we say 'o-possum', and I would like to know how you'd spell 'owl' if O isn't the first letter of that too!"' Clearly *Bertie and the Bullfrogs* is derivative, and the author was the first to claim that, but it is a thoroughly Australian derivation.

Best-Kept Secret, The (1988) by 'Emily Rodda' (Jennifer Rowe), illustrated by Noela Young, won the 1989 Book of the Year Awards: Younger Readers. Unhappy about her family's impending move, Jo is one of the few who is able to ride on the merry-go-round which has come into the town. The journey takes the riders seven years forward, where Jo is joined by Davy, who must be returned to his own time. In doing so, Jo recognises her parents, herself and the small boy as a family. The story is enriched with minor characters facing crises who are allowed to ride the merry-go-round. Themes invite exploration: the importance of imagination, the development of confidence and morality, the effects of change, and the nuances of family life.

Bett-Bett appears in *The Little Black Princess: a True Tale of Life in the Never-Never Land* (1905) by Mrs Aeneas Gunn. The real-life Bett-Bett became a nursemaid of the Ward family, and travelled with them to Melbourne. She married in

1913, and became Dolly Bonson. She had three sons and two daughters, and remained in contact with Jeannie Gunn's family, even after Jeannie's death in 1961.

BEUTH, EMILIE. For *Australian Alphabet Book* see **Alphabet Books**.

BEVAN, TOM (1868–?1930), born Monmouthshire, UK, was the education editor for the publishers Sampson Low & Marston. He wrote historical and adventure books for boys and contributed to the *Boy's Own Paper*. *Bob Blair — Plainsman* (1924) is a rags-to-riches adventure story. When Bob's father's property is burnt out by Malone and the cattle-thieves, Bob and his black retainer, Jimmy, rout Malone, find gold, and Bob sets up the Blair Mining Company. Bevan also contributed to *The Victorian Schoolboys' Story Book* (?1930), which despite its title, has no Australian content.

Beyond the Labyrinth (1988) by Gillian Rubinstein won the 1989 Book of the Year Awards: Older Readers. Brenton Trethewan is at odds with his family, and when Victoria Hare visits for a prolonged stay, the two are drawn together. They meet an alien, Cal, who is studying life on Earth. Cal contracts an illness (alienation?) from which she will certainly die unless she is helped to return to her own world. In alternative endings, Cal and Brenton return together, or Cal dies and Brenton sees some future for himself in a troubled world. The novel is a convincing examination of an anguished boy and a homesick girl, set within a family too concerned with materialism to recognise each other's needs.

'Bib and Bub' was a cartoon-strip created by May Gibbs (adapted from her book *Gumnut Babies* [1916]), which first appeared in the *Sunday News* in 1924. The comic appeared almost continuously until 1967, each picture accompanied by a witty verse caption. Bib and Bub's adventures include accompanying Mr Lizard to the theatre, where Mrs Chameleon gobbles up a group of baby flies; surviving Mrs Snake's stomach; and observing the tragic vanity of Mrs Bear. They were collected in *Bib and Bub, Their Adventures* (1925), *The Further Adventures of Bib and Bub* (1925), *More Funny Stories about Old Friends Bib and Bub* (1928), *Bib and Bub in Gumnut Town* (1929), *Bib and Bub Painting Book, New Stories* (1932) and *Gumnuts* (1940).

BIDWELL, DAFNE (1929–), born Hampshire, UK, settled in Australia in 1971. She has written *The Tiger Gang and the Hijackers* (1976), illustrated by Graham Bryce, and *The Tiger Gang and the Car Thieves* (1977). Simon and Claire Thompson, Mark, Nikki and Philip Trelawny, and Patrick Tierney operate from a school in Attadale, Perth. They foil a kidnap attempt and find a stolen car. *Seeker Seven* (1984), illustrated by Lorraine Lewitska, is an adventure story about six children holidaying in Singapore who unmask criminals working on an offshore oil rig.

BILBY Awards (Books I Love Best Yearly) are chosen by children under the auspices of the Children's Book Council of Australia's Queensland Branch, supported by the Department of Education and the State Library of Queensland. BILBY was instituted in 1990 in three categories, 'Read Aloud' (Primary to Year 12), 'Read Alone' (Primary) and 'Read Alone' (Secondary). **1990** *Matilda* by Roald Dahl; *Superfudge* by Judy Blume; and *The Secret Diary of Adrian Mole Aged 13 and 3/4* by Sue Townsend. **1991** *The BFG* by Roald Dahl in the first two categories; *The Outsiders* by S.E. Hinton.

'Billabong' is the sheep station located somewhere in northern Victoria created by Mary Grant Bruce. In her first novel about 'Billabong', *A Little Bush Maid*

(1910) Bruce introduced the core of characters who were to appear in the fourteen books which followed. Brownie is the housekeeper, cook and surrogate mother to the family; Murty O'Toole is the stockman and right-hand man; Lee Wing is the vegetable gardener and Hogg is the flower gardener; Black Billy is the rouseabout, and there are various other horse-breakers, stockmen and maids. In the comfortable, secure and snobbish world of the Linton family, wholesome rural concerns are directed by David Linton, the owner. Linton's son Jim is active and inarticulate, an image of Australian manhood, and his daughter is the renowned Norah, the original 'little bush maid'. Norah is essentially an outdoor girl, one of the 'mates of Billabong', but retains her femininity through knitting, cooking and charitable enterprises. As the series proceeds, Norah marries Jim's best mate, Wally Meadows, and has a son, Davie, and in *Son of Billabong* (1939) Jim marries 'Tommy' Rainham, an English immigrant. In *Bill of Billabong* (1931) Jim wins over a protégé from Melbourne, Bill Blake (a.k.a. Percival), who appears in subsequent novels. Through flood, drought and fire, war and domestic crises, 'Billabong' remains unchanged, rooted in the healthy nature of outdoor life, and founded on ideals of leadership, hard work, independence, and above all, mateship — for one's own class and race. The idealised world of 'Billabong' was much loved by its fans, both children and adults, and became a model of what it meant to be an Australian to a generation of readers. The Billabong books are: *A Little Bush Maid* (1910), *Mates at Billabong* (1911) (see also **Boys; Sport**), *Norah of Billabong* (1913) (see also **Aboriginal People in Children's Fiction**), *From Billabong to London* (1915) (see also **Aboriginal People in Children's Fiction**; **War**), *Jim and Wally* (1916) (see **War**), *Captain Jim* (1919) (see also **War**), *Back to Billabong* (1921), *Billabong's Daughter* (1924), *Billabong Adventurers* (1927), which deals

with the honeymoon adventures of Norah and Wally, *Bill of Billabong* (1931), *Billabong's Luck* (1933), *Wings Above Billabong* (1935), *Billabong Gold* (1937), *Son of Billabong* (1939), and *Billabong Riders* (1942) (see **Chinese**). Further reading: Niall, *Seven Little Billabongs*; Alexander, *Billabong's Author*.

BINGHAM, LORNA, see '**Search for the Golden Boomerang, The**'

BIRD, BETTINA LAWRIE SEA-WELL has written titles for Cheshire's 'Trend' series (q.v.), collaborated with Ian H. Falk and Tony Scanlon on other 'Trend' books, and in 1971 wrote a teachers' handbook to the series, with Ian Falk. Her pseudonyms include 'Dale Gordon', 'Kerry Martin', 'Scud Morgan', 'Jodie Rankin', 'Robby Reece' and 'Lawrie Seawell'. With Jeffrey Prentice, Bird wrote *Dromkeen: a Journey into Children's Literature* (1987).

Birds of Australia in Colour (1955) by Lyla Stevens, illustrated by Anne Lissenden, was Highly Commended in the 1956 Book of the Year Awards. Australian birds and their habits are described, and the folklore associated with them is related. Beautiful illustrations accompany accounts of the kookaburra, the magpie, the cockatoo, the wedge-tailed eagle and others.

BIRMINGHAM, KARNA (1900–87), born Sydney, was an artist and illustrator who studied with Julian Ashton at the Sydney Art School. Birmingham's sight failed in 1938. *Skippety Songs* (1934) is a collection of poems for children, illustrated by the author with graceful sketches. One of the poems is inspired by the children's game 'Mothers': 'When Gracie plays, she's not much fun;/She won't play any game but one./Because she's fat, and puffs a bit,/She likes a game where she can sit./I say, "Let's play at steps and stairs,/Or tipped-you-last, or hounds and

Brenda greeted all her Bads with a little irresistible giggle.

Teens (1897) by Louise Mack, 1927 edition. Illustrator: Karna Birmingham

hares,/Or I'll go hit and you can hide,/Or let's have chasings round the side,/Or play at pirates in the bath,/Or skippings up and down the path./Oh, what's the use of sitting still?/Let's roll each other down the hill!'/But no! She only wants to play Mothers!' Birmingham illustrated an edition of *Teens* (1897) by Louise Mack in 1923, Amy Mack's *Scribbling Sue* (1914) in 1923 and *Bushland Stories* (1910) in 1924. *The Fantail's House, The Little Black Duck and Other Stories of Bushland and Sea* and *The Flower Fairies and Other Stories of the Australian Bush* (all 1928) are all taken from *Bushland Stories*. Birmingham's children are beautiful, carefully dressed and aesthetically placed in full-page designs.

BIRTLES, DORA (1904–), born Wickham, NSW, joined the crew of a cutter in 1932 and made a journey from Newcastle to Singapore which lasted eight months, an experience which is described in *North-West by North* (1935). She was the research officer for the film *The Overlanders*, made by Ealing Studios, written and directed by Harry Watt, and in 1946 wrote a novel of the same name drawn from the story of the film. She has written two books for children about the restoration of fortune, *Bonza the Bull* (q.v., 1949) for younger readers, and *Pioneer Shack* (1947), set in the Newcastle district of NSW. The latter is a novel for older readers about Elsa Graham who, with resource and energy, builds her dream house on land left to her family.

BISSETT, PEGGY, poet, created Amber Mae, a small pig-tailed girl who features in two books, *Amber Mae Story Book* (1946) and *Amber Mae Goes to Kindergarten* (1947), both illustrated by Anne Drew. Amber Mae and her talking cat, Henry D., write stories and verse, dot-to-dots, mazes, and crosswords, and learn to count and read. Bissett also wrote a book of humorous verse for adults, *Sexes and Siphons* (1944).

Black, Simon was a character created by Ivan Southall, in *Meet Simon Black* (1950), *Simon Black in Peril* (1951), *Simon Black in Space* (1952) (later published as *Simon Black on Venus* [1974]), *Simon Black in Coastal Command* (1953), *Simon Black and the Spacemen* (1955), *Simon Black in the Antarctic* (1956), *Simon Black in China* (1959), *Simon Black Takes Over* (1959) and *Simon Black at Sea* (1961). Wing Commander Simon Black is a lean, dark, hard-muscled six-foot airman. His bosom pal is the younger Squadron Leader Alan Grant, a few inches shorter, but as ready with his fists as Simon. They usually fly successive models of the *Firefly*, a remarkably versatile aircraft, but anything else from a Sunderland to a Cessna will do. Under the orders of the irascible Mac, and often joined by the dog, Rex, and other loyal companions, they harry Australia's enemies, including fanatical Nazis and Chinese spies, even to the edges of the universe. See also **Science Fiction**. The Simon Black books were very popular and were translated into four languages. Southall wrote an unpublished spoof of the books in 1956, 'Simon Black in Arabia'. His parody of the clean-cut adventure story, entitled 'Real Adventure Belongs to Us', was given by Southall as the May Hill Arbuthnot Lecture, in 1974, and published in *A Journey of Discovery: on Writing for Children* (1975).

Black Troopers and Other Stories, The (1887) is an anonymous collection of four adventure stories, published by the Religious Tract Society. The prefatory note states that it is 'suited to readers of both sexes, and well adapted for circulation in Sunday school libraries, and as gift and prize books'. See also **Aboriginal People in Children's Fiction**.

BLACKMAN, CHARLES (1928–), born Sydney, is a figurative painter and printmaker. He has illustrated *A Cat-tale* (1987), a story by Mark Twain originally

Alice's Adventures in Wonderland by Lewis Carroll, edited by Nadine Amadio, 1982. Illustrator: Charles Blackman

published in 1880. He made a series of drawings and paintings in the early 1950s when he was working as a chef in Melbourne, and read Lewis Carroll's book for the first time. *Alice's Adventures in Wonderland* (1982) and *The New Adventures of Alice in Rainforest Land* (1988), edited by Nadine Amadio, reveal unusual insights into the strange world of Alice.

BLAIR, JIM (JAMES BEATTON BLAIR) (1903–), born Port Augusta, SA, was a short story editor and leader-writer for the *Bulletin* from 1946 to 1960. For *The Secret of the Reef* (1963) see **Adventure Stories**.

BLAKE, LES (1913–87) was a Victorian teacher who wrote many books on historical and literary topics. He edited a history of Victorian schools, *Vision and Realization*, and from 1974 to 1976 he was the Victorian State Historian. *Lost in the*

Bush (1964), the story of the Duff children, was made into a film in 1973, directed by Peter Dodds. See **Lost in the Bush**.

BLASHKI, PAM (1956–), born NZ, wrote *Chai the Kangaroo* (1985) and *A Sometimes River: the Story of a Kangaroo* (1986), both illustrated by Clifton Pugh. See **Animal Stories**.

Bligh, Sir **William** (1754–1817) commanded HMS *Bounty*. In 1789, after leaving Tahiti, the crew mutinied under the leadership of Fletcher Christian. Bligh and eighteen men were cast off in an open launch less than seven metres long, and through the exceptional navigational skill of Bligh, reached Timor, nearly 6000 kilometres away, in six weeks. Bligh became the Governor of NSW in 1806. Joyce Nicholson's *Man Against Mutiny: the Story of Vice-Admiral William Bligh* (1961) is an account for young people of Bligh's vicissitudes, from the mutiny to his governorship of NSW, written with the intention of clearing Bligh's name after what the author believes was a campaign of vilification, first by the relatives of well-connected mutineers, then by John Macarthur and the Rum Corps. Jack Bennett's *The Lieutenant: an Epic Tale of Courage and Endurance on the High Seas* (q.v., 1977) is based on Bligh's diary of the journey.

Blinky Bill is the adventurous koala character created by Dorothy Wall, who first appeared in *Blinky Bill, the Quaint Little Australian* (1933). Blinky had been glimpsed in Brooke Nicholls's *Jacko the Broadcasting Kookaburra* (1933), but Wall developed the character into what he is seen as today, a symbol of the characteristic Australian — confident, disrespectful, and always ready for a joke. Blinky Bill, his distracted mother, Mrs Magpie's sharp beak, the irascible neighbour Mrs Grunty, and the untrustworthy Mrs Snake appear in a series of episodes which conclude with Blinky threatened with Mrs Magpie's school. In *Blinky Bill Grows Up: Further Adventures of the Quaint Little Australian* (1934) Blinky runs away from home, and meets Percy Bull Ant, Bluey the Cattle Dog and Belinda Fox, until Blinky and his mother are rushed off to Taronga Park Zoo. *Blinky Bill and Nutsy: Two Little Australians* (1937) introduced a new friend for Blinky, after Mrs Bear and Blinky escape from the zoo with the kangaroo, Splodge. Nutsy is an orphan adopted by Mrs Bear, and after a tree warming, a visit to the pelicans and Walter Wombat, the three of them make their tree a guesthouse. In this book Wall simplified her drawings in an attempt to make them more adaptable for animation. *The Complete Adventures of Blinky Bill* (1939) contained the three previous books. In *Blinky Bill Joins the Army* (1940), Blinky Bill trains the soldier ants until he is chosen to become an army mascot. *A Tiny Story of Blinky Bill* (?1942) has Blinky, Splodge and Wally the Wombat embarking on a night-time escapade in Farmer Brown's boat. *Blinky Bill's Dress-up Book* appeared in 1942, and Blinky Bill acquired his own alphabet book in *Blinky Bill's ABC Book* (1947). There have been adaptations of Wall's work, such as *Fun with Blinky Bill* (1953), *Blinky Bill and the Pelicans* (1976) and *Blinky Bill and the Tree Warming* (1976) by Anne-Marie Willis, illustrated by Stephen Axelsen, in the 'Young Australia' series. 'Junior Bearbacks', a series developed by Angus & Robertson, includes extracts from *The Complete Adventures of Blinky Bill* in single volumes, such as *Blinky Bill Runs Away* (1977), adapted by Betty Boaden. Other titles were *Meet Blinky Bill*, *Blinky Bill at Frog Hollow*, *Blinky Bill and the Bull Ants*, *Blinky Bill Meets Nutsy* and *Blinky Bill Back Home*. Louis Silvestro illustrated *Blinky Bill Goes to School* (1982). Carol Odell wrote *Let's Call him Blinky Bill* (1970). Wall's illustrations have appeared in such oddities as *Blinky Bill Cookbook* (1977), a collection of recipes by Mary Coleman, including onion dip, french toast and kebabs. The strength of Blinky Bill's appeal to the national psyche is shown by an incident in 1977, when Mickey Mouse was chosen to be the King of Melbourne's Moomba festival. Public outrage led to an attempt to dethrone the 'middle-aged plastic rodent from California' and replace him with Blinky Bill.

Blue Above the Trees (1967) by Mavis Thorpe Clark, illustrated by Genevieve Melrose, was Commended in the 1968 Book of the Year Awards. The Whitburn family come to the Colonies from England to make their fortunes. They settle south of Drouin, Victoria, and remain longer than expected. The land they have fought so hard to subdue eventually claims their loyalty, so that they stay on. The experience is seen through the eyes of Simon Whitburn, who recognises the consequences of the destruction of the great rainforest, and persuades his family to retain twenty acres of untouched bush. The theme of conserving nature is seen in a context of the difficulties of pioneering, as the author regrets the irreversible passing of the forests, and their native fauna, while acknowledging the fine farming country created at that expense.

Blue Fin (1969) by Colin Thiele, illustrated by Roger Haldane, was Highly Commended in the 1970 Book of the Year Awards. The 14-year-old 'Snook', Stephen Pascoe, is disapproved of by his father, who thinks he is a clumsy good-for-nothing. Snook proves his worth by saving his unconscious father when their boat is hit by a storm during a tuna-fishing expedition. The novel is set around Port Lincoln, and was filmed in 1978 by the SA Film Corporation, directed by Carl Schultz, scripted by Sonia Borg, with Greg Rowe as Snook and Hardy Kruger as Mr Pascoe. Another edition of the novel was published to coincide with the film, with photographs by David Kynoch.

'**Blue Wren**' series, published by Angus & Robertson in 1951, was Highly Commended in the 1952 Book of the Year Awards. Titles covered nursery rhymes, alphabets, fairy-tales, poetry, fables, carols and Aboriginal Dreaming stories. Three illustrators contributed: Margaret Horder and Diana and Sally Medworth, and contemporary and classic authors are represented, e.g. Joan Phipson's *Christmas in the Sun* and William Makepeace Thackeray's *The Ballad of Little Billee*. Other titles were: *Lavender's Blue and Two other Rhymes* (see **Nursery Rhymes**), *What They Wore: a First Book of English Costume*, *Pretty Pollie Pillicote*, *Good King Wenceslas*, *Aesop's Fables Re-told: The Dove and the Ant* and *The Wind and the Sun*, *The 12 Days of Christmas*, and *Moograbah: an Australian Aboriginal Legend*.

Bluecap and Bimbi: the Blue Wrens (1948) by Leslie Rees, illustrated by Walter Cunningham, was Highly Commended in the 1950 Book of the Year Awards. Bluecap admires himself while Bimbi is busy nest-building, although he does keep other birds away from his territory. When a bronze cuckoo lays an egg in the nest, Bluecap and Bimbi lose their fledgelings, so they find another nesting place. The dramas which affect the life of birds are described, with the beautiful illustrations by Cunningham decorating every page. A 1975 edition, which included *Gecko and Mokee*, was illustrated by Tony Oliver.

BOARDMAN, ALAN wrote *Eureka Stockade* (q.v., 1981), *The First Fleet* (q.v., 1982), and *The Crossing of the Blue Mountains* (1984), all illustrated by Roland Harvey. Boardman follows the events as though he was a participant, providing historical detail in an easily assimilated form.

Bobbie in the Bush (?1940), a Peter Huston Playbook, is an early example of a moveable book. Jenny the Jackass's beak opens, Percy Peek the Platypus has eyes which roll, Kim the Kangaroo's tail moves and Billy the Koala Bear's arm swings as a tag is pulled.

BODSWORTH, NAN (1936–), born Swan Hill, Victoria, trained at Chisholm Institute, RMIT and Melbourne Teachers' College. She has been a teacher in schools and has taught fashion design. She wrote *Mike's Birthday Bulldozer* (1981), in which machinery bought for Mike's birthday clears the road and provides amusement for the whole family. In *Hello Kangaroo!* (1986) Dorothy and her bossy aunt visit the zoo, where Dorothy imagines a life among the animals while her aunt cautions her to stay away from them. A similar theme appears in *A Nice Walk in the Jungle* (1989). A schoolteacher and her class take an excursion where the children are eaten one by one by an oversized boa constrictor, while the teacher, unaware, points up details of animal life to the children. The beautifully designed, lush double-page illustrations are full of clever details, such as the tiger's kittens, caterpillars and athletic monkeys. In all her books, the fantasy life of children is nicely caught, and Bodsworth's text and illustrations display her ironic humour.

BOLTON, BARBARA MOLLY (1941–), born Hobart, examines the importance of family and relationships in her stories. *Jandy Malone and the Nine O'Clock Tiger* (q.v., 1980) describes how imagination is used to deal with family tensions. In *Edward Wilkins and his Friend Gwendoline* (1985), illustrated by Madeleine Winch, Edward is a large black cat who reminisces about his happy life with Gwendoline, whom he learnt to love so dearly that he taught her cat language — Siamese, Persian and Tabby. *Ring, Rock and River* (1987) is a fantasy in which Caron, Richard and Cilla enter the subterranean world of the Grokkots and learn to co-operate with each other. Bolton's unromanticised portrait of families and

growing old are underscored with warmth and humour. She edited the Salvation Army's journal for young people, *Young Soldier*, and has written *Booth's Drum: the Salvation Army in Australia, 1880–1980* (1980).

BONE, WALTER HENRY (?1863–1934), born Sydney, was the principal of one of the oldest family printing houses in Sydney, and both of his children's books were published by the firm. Bone lived in Zanzibar for part of his youth, and was a commandant of the Sultan's cavalry. He was also a big-game hunter, a skilled linguist, an expert shot and authority on ballistics, and a keen swordsman. *Hoppity: Being the Adventures of an Albino Kangaroo* (1933) is about a kangaroo who is chased by hunters because of his rarity. *What Became of Them? Australian Stories for Children* (1952) is a collection of Bone's contributions over thirty-five years to the *Sydney Mail*. The stories are fantasies explaining the origins of various animals. Bone illustrated all of his books himself.

BONINI, MARINELLA. For *I Can be the Alphabet* see **Alphabet Books**.

BONWICK, JAMES (1817–1906), born Lingfield, Surrey, UK, arrived in Hobart in 1841, where he opened the first free day school in Tasmania, established by Governor Franklin. He later moved to Adelaide where he was again a teacher, and secretary of the first Australian branch of the Young Men's Christian Association. After a time on the goldfields of Victoria, he became an Inspector of Schools. Bonwick had an enlightened approach to learning, stressing observation and experiment. Among the fifty or more books and pamphlets which he wrote were some of the first school textbooks produced in Australia. He returned to England in 1883, where he searched records for Australian material, later used as the basis for Watson's *Historical Records of Australia*.

He published the *Australian Gold-Diggers Monthly Magazine* (1852–53), one of the first Australian journals to have a children's section. Examples of his work include *Bible Stories for Young Australians* (1852), *The Reader for Australian Youth* (1852), *Early Days of England* (1857), *Early Days of Melbourne* (1857), *How Does a Tree Grow? or, Botany for Young Australians* (1857), *Astronomy for Young Australians* (1864), *Little Joe: a Tale of the Pacific Railway* (1862) and *Orion and Sirius* (1888).

Bonza the Bull (1949) by Dora Birtles was Highly Commended in the 1950 Book of the Year Awards. Baron Bonza of Bellanjuck is the last bull in the once famous Hereford stock of the Saunders. When Chris's father is killed, his mother decides to sell Bonza at the Royal Easter Show in Sydney. When the manager Sep has a domestic crisis, Chris and Sep's son, Nobby, take Bonza to Sydney on the train, a 1200-kilometre journey. Bonza wins first prize, Nobby and Chris are promised an Aboriginal initiation ceremony and Mrs Saunders is set to marry Uncle Charley, the boys' hero. Birtles's attitude to her Aboriginal characters, Sep and Nobby, is non-racist, and the novel moves along with pace and excitement.

Book of the Year Awards is the name given to the annual awards for the best books for young people published in Australia, selected by the Children's Book Council of Australia. The awards were instituted in 1946, when the responsibility for selection was rotated between the States. From 1959 the winners have been determined by a panel representing all States. Judges are elected for a two-year term. The awards were funded by the Australia Council, but since 1988 have been sponsored by Myer-Grace Brothers Stores. There are three awards: Book of the Year Awards: Older Readers; Book of the Year Awards: Younger Readers (until 1987 named the Junior Book of the Year

Award); and the Picture Book of the Year Awards. The book must have been published and submitted between 1 January and 31 December of the year before judging, although reprints are considered if the text or illustration is new. The author/illustrator must be of Australian nationality or normally resident in Australia. The awards are primarily for literary merit, including cohesiveness, plot, theme and style, but the quality and design of the book as a whole are also considered.

Criteria for the Book of the Year Awards: Older Readers are 1. appeal to children, 2. book design, production and quality of printing, 3. literary merit, 4. quality of illustration. The Book of the Year Awards: Older Readers is made to 'outstanding books which generally require mature reading ability to appreciate the topics, themes and scope of emotional involvement'.

When the Book of the Year Awards were begun there was no separate award for younger readers. An award for Junior Readers was begun in 1981, in an attempt to overcome the problem of books for older children dominating the Award. In 1982 this became the Junior Book of the Year, and in 1987 the Book of the Year Awards: Younger Readers. These awards are for 'books for readers who have developed independent reading skills but are still developing in literary awareness'.

The Picture Book of the Year Awards were instituted in 1952. In addition to the criteria applying to the other awards, the judges must consider the artistic and literary unity the author and illustrator have achieved, or the artistic unity in wordless books where the story, theme or concept is presented solely through the illustrations.

In 1982, judges of the Children's Book of the Year Awards proposed a short list of titles from which the three Australian awards were to be chosen. The short list is available for some months before the announcement of the award-winners.

Boomerang Book of Australian Poetry, The (1956) edited by Enid Moodie Heddle, illustrated by Margaret R. Dods, was Highly Commended in the 1957 Book of the Year Awards. It is an anthology of Australian poetry by poets such as Judith Wright, David Campbell, Douglas Stewart and others, arranged in five sections: People, the Land, Living Things, Adventures, Legend and Song.

Boomerang Book of Legendary Tales, The (1957) edited by Enid Moodie Heddle, illustrated by Nancy Parker, won the 1957 Book of the Year Awards. It is a collection of Aboriginal Dreaming stories and Maori song and narrative, tall tales, and stories from Micronesia and the South Pacific, including New Guinea. The material has been drawn from works by K. Langloh Parker, Roland Robinson, Lance Skuthorpe, Charles Barrett, A.W. Reed, Mervyn Skipper, Alan Marshall, Dal Stivens and others. A glossary is included.

'Boomerang Books' were produced by the Primary Schools Advisory Curriculum Board of the SA Education Department and edited by Enid Moodie Heddle. *Near and Far, Now and Then, Here and There*, and *New and Old* (all 1953) had graded material suitable for early readers to the more confident students. The last, *New and Old*, for example, is an attractive collection of extracts from John Masefield, Walter de la Mare, Edward Dyson, Lewis Carroll, Helen Jo Samuel and others, illustrated by Harold Freedman.

Boori (1978), by Bill Scott, illustrated by A.M. Hicks, was Highly Commended in the 1979 Book of the Year Awards. Scott used the traditions of the south Queensland coastal people. Boori is a Goundir, or magician, created by Budgerie under the orders of Ganba, the Rainbow Serpent, and raised with all the old man's wisdom. Boori undertakes his life tasks: freeing the mullet from a spell which keeps them in one place, defeating a bad magician, Bookal, enlisting the aid of Dingo, defeating the thieving Pukwudgies for the Lizard, Perentie, releasing the warrior, Bunya, from the Melong, the great water spirit, and returning fire to the tribes. His companion is a spirit, Jun Jaree, carried with him in a bag around his neck. Boori's story concludes in *Darkness Under the Hills* (1980), also illustrated by Hicks, which was Highly Commended in the 1981 Book of the Year Awards. He journeys north with Jaree and Dingo to bring together a force which will defeat Rakasha, who threatens the People and the Law. When his task is finished, Boori and his friends become stars, guarding the People forever. Boori's magical adventures are hero tales in the European tradition, using the idea of a quest, the difficult, magical task, and the final transformation. See also **Death**.

BOOTHBY, GUY NEWELL (1867–1905), born Adelaide, was a prolific author of mystery stories for 'grown-up boys'. Boothby left Australia for England in 1894, but many of his novels have Australian settings and characters. *A Bid for Fortune, or, Dr Nikola's Vendetta* (1895) introduces Dr Nikola, a perfect specimen of Victorian manhood with 'limbs perfectly shaped and plainly muscular, but very slim'. Other titles were *Dr Nikola* (1896), *The Lust of Hate* (1898), *Dr Nikola's Experiment* (1899) and *Farewell, Nikola* (1901). Nikola, accompanied by a black cat which perches on his shoulder, is a Sherlock Holmes-like character who manipulates other people's lives. Enigmatic, he will stop at nothing to get what he wants, but always remains a gentleman.

BOOTHROYD, ARTHUR S. (1910–), born Southport, UK, came to Australia in 1922. He is a figurative painter who has worked as an illustrator for magazines, including the *Australian Women's*

Weekly. Boothroyd illustrated Barbara Ker Wilson's *Daisy Bates* (1985) and *Broome Dog* (1989) by Mary Small.

BORDEN, CHARLES. For *He Sailed with Captain Cook* see **Cook**, Captain **James**.

BORER, MARY CATHCART, see *Bush Christmas*

BORG, SONIA (1931–), born Vienna, Austria, came to Australia in 1961. She was the scriptwriter for Colin Thiele's *Storm Boy* (q.v., 1963) and *Blue Fin* (q.v., 1969) which were filmed in 1976 and 1978. She adapted Alan Marshall's *I Can Jump Puddles* (1955) for television in 1980, and wrote the screenplay for the film of Frank Dalby Davison's *Dusty: A Dog of the Sheep Country* (1946) in 1983. Borg and Hyllus Maris wrote the television series 'Women of the Sun', screened in 1982 and published as a book in 1984.

Boris and Borsch (1990) by Robin Klein, illustrated by Cathy Wilcox, was an Honour Book in the 1991 Book of the Year Awards: Younger Readers. Eugene is the best-behaved child in the world; his cousin Patrick is the worst behaved. Their bears are Boris, daffy and lopsided, and Borsch, neat and polite. Bears and children are dreadfully mismatched. Boris is oppressed by Eugene's clean and healthy lifestyle: Borsch is dismayed by Patrick's sweaty and chaotic household. Both are happier when they swap owners, and so are the boys. Klein and Wilcox have made the most of the exaggerated contrasts to create a frolic.

BORLASE, JAMES SKIPP (b.1839), born England, came to Australia in 1862, and contributed stories and articles to journals such as *Hobart Town Fun* over a period of five years. He returned to England, where he wrote novels with Australian settings, and other thrilling romances, such as *The Police Minister: a Tale of St. Petersburgh*, and *For True Love's Sake: a Tale of Paris*. His short stories appeared in '105 lesser papers of Great Britain', as well as many boys' and girls' journals. Serials written for these journals included 'Both Princess and Police Spy: or, By Order of the Czar' and 'Nina the Nihilist: or, Death in the Palace'. Borlase also wrote under the name of 'J.J.G. Bradley' and 'Captain Leslie'. His Australian books include *The Night Fossickers and Other Australian Tales of Peril and Adventure* (1867), 'dedicated to His Excellency Sir Charles Darling K.C.B., Late Governor of the Colony of Victoria'. It is a collection of stories which examine the life of the Aboriginal People, outback and station life, a bushfire etc. The first story, 'The Shepherd's Hut', opens with a description of mid-nineteenth-century Melbourne. *Stirring Tales of Colonial Adventure: a Book for Boys* (1894), illustrated by Lancelot Speed, is an edition of *The Night Fossickers...*, and *Daring Deeds and Tales of Peril and Adventure* (1868) (see **Melbourne**) has many of the stories in *The Night Fossickers* .... It has a strong urban emphasis, with evocative descriptions of Sydney, Melbourne, Adelaide and Hobart, and their cosmopolitan life. *Blue Cap the Bushranger: or, The Australian Dick Turpin* (1885) appeared as a serial in the *Boy's Standard* 1876, and then became one of the Hogarth House Standard Library, 'price one shilling, with parts available at one penny a week'. It recounts with sardonic humour and skilful characterisation the adventures of three young heroes on the trail of the notorious Blue Cap. Despite the subtitle, *Ned Kelly: the Australian Ironclad Bushranger: By One of his Captors* (1881), there is no record of Borlase's presence at Ned Kelly's capture, and the account is much embellished by Borlase's imagination. Ned has an adopted 14-year-old daughter, Rose, entrusted to him by a dying woman he once loved. Ned is 35, and lusts after Lola Montez 'firstly, because she is beautiful and famous, and secondly, because a king has grasped her in vain'. Lola soon cools Ned's passion by shooting off his ear. Borlase himself put his success down to being 'very quick to gauge the taste of the reading public', and never wrote a story which he was unable to sell. To quote from an assessment of his work which was probably written by himself, 'He dashes at once into the full interest and excitement of his subject, and doesn't allow that excitement and interest to flag for a single instant (even in a full three volume length novel) until he has reached the last line of the last chapter. Of true genius he has none, but instead, that constructive ability which, heaping thrilling incident atop of thrilling incident, keeps the reader's attention on a perpetual strain, and his excitement at perfect fever heat, until the startling climax is at last reached.' (Quotations are from NLA Terry O'Neill Papers MS 7661.)

BOSWORTH, ELLEN, see **Peters, Shelley**

Bottersnikes and Gumbles are the fantasy creatures created by S.A. Wakefield. Bottersnikes are ugly and lazy, with noses like cheese-graters and ears that turn fiery red when they are angry. Their main occupation is snaring Gumbles and enslaving them by pushing them into old jam tins. Gumbles are cheerful, easily squashed and always giggling, cleverer than Bottersnikes and much more friendly. Both Bottersnikes and Gumbles live in the bush (the Bottersnikes on a rubbish dump) and mix with kookaburras, wallabies, koalas and other bush animals. *Bottersnikes and Gumbles* (1967) introduced the creatures and their rivalries, and some of the individual members, such as Tinkin-gumble, who is full of ideas; the Bottersnike, Smiggles, whose dreams come true; and the particularly odious Chank. In *Gumbles on Guard* (1975) the Gumbles defend a lyrebird chick from a hungry fox while they avoid the encroaching Bottersnikes. In *Gumbles in Summer* (1979) there is a contest over who

will be king of the Bottersnikes which the Gumbles use to advantage, including the invention of dry water. The fourth book in the series is *Gumbles in Trouble* (1990), where the Gumbles find a typewriter after a flood. All four books are illustrated by Desmond Digby, the first in black and white and the last three with some colour plates. Digby's nasty Bottersnikes and cuddlesome Gumbles match the robust and inventive humour of the series.

BOWES, Rev. JOSEPH (1852–1928), born NSW, was a Methodist minister in NSW and Queensland for forty-nine years. In *Pals: Young Australians in Sport and Adventure* (1910), illustrated by J. Macfarlane, Joe Blair, Sandy McIntyre, Tom Hawkins and their friends play games, win at cricket, battle floods, fight off sharks and strike gold. See also **Sport**. In *Comrades: a Story of the Australian Bush* (1912), illustrated by Cyrus Cuneo, Tony contracts pneumonia and is sent north to convalesce at the home of a Scottish relative who has lived in the NT most of his adult life. Tony's catalogue of adventures includes stowing away, shooting expeditions in pursuit of buffalo, birds and bandicoots, encounters with cattle-thieves, flash floods and being kidnapped by cannibal Aboriginal People. Tony and his friends come through it all with honour. *The New-Chums: a Jungle Story* (1915), also illustrated by Cuneo, follows the fortunes of Lionel and Alan, who are washed up on an uninhabited part of Australia after a mutiny and subsequent shipwreck. They fall in with local Aboriginal People, find their way to civilisation, and strike gold. *The Jackaroos: Life on a Cattle Run* (1923) relates the adventures of Aleck Winstanes and Jim Porter, who defeat the machinations of a gang of cattle-thieves. In *The Fur Hunters in Australian Wilds* (1925) the hunters' wallaroo skins are stolen, but Dick and Bill retrieve them after many snakes, terrible floods and much hard riding. *The Young Settler: the Story of a New-Chum in Queensland* (1927) is 'dedicated to all English, Irish and Scotch lads who are looking towards Australia'. After a short tour of the main cities, Julian Grey is initiated into life on the land. See also **Adventure Stories**; **Brisbane**.

His war stories include *The Young Anzacs: a Tale of the Great War* (1917). Jack Smith, Jock McThirst, and Tim, go off to the war and experience Gallipoli. *The Anzac War-Trail: With the Light Horse in Sinai* (1919), illustrated by Arch Webb, is another war story. In *The Aussie Crusaders with Allenby in Palestine* (1920) Major Jack Smith and Sergeant Jock McThirst are captured by Bedouins and Turks, escape, and are present at the fall of Gaza and Jerusalem. See also **War**. Bowes writes exciting stories for adults and young people, in an eloquent and flowing style, with much fervent sentiment of Empire and Australian nationalism. There is a memorial tablet to Bowes in the Albert Street Church, Brisbane.

BOWMAN, ANNE (*fl.* 1855–75), was an English novelist who wrote boys' adventure stories such as *The Castaways* (1857) and *Among the Tartar Tents* (1861). In *The Kangaroo Hunters: or, Adventures in the Bush* (1858), illustrated with plates engraved by Dalziel, a shipwrecked family cross the country to find their way to Melbourne. Mrs Bowman never visited Australia and her book reads as though she had a description of Australian flora and fauna beside her as she wrote. The Mayburns dine on pigeon pie made in an oyster shell, and 'opossum' stew flavoured with saltbush, decking themselves out in 'opossum' skins. They dodge snakes, mangrove swamps, deserts, bushrangers and 'the natives'.

BOYD, MARTIN (1893–1972), born Lucerne, Switzerland, was a member of the artistic Boyd family. He is the author of many novels for adults, but his only children's book is *The Painted Princess: a Fairy Story* (1936), illustrated with water-colours by Jocelyn Crowe, and dedicated 'for the grandchildren at Lee Priory'. Princess Erna falls over the parapet of a Tyrolean castle, and rolls over and over, down the hill, until she becomes the shape of a sausage. The fairies find her, and their Chamberlain, Florizel, conjures up Leonardo da Vinci to paint a face on the sausage. When Erna returns to reality, it is 400 years later, and the Leonardo face on her stomach is worth enough to save the fortunes of the family. Erna is kidnapped and the painting is removed, but her cousin's descendant, August, saves her from the evil Herr von Brenner, and marries her. The story is richly imaginative and full of clever asides, and the sensible Erna behaves like a real and sprightly child.

BOYLAN, Fr **EUSTACE** S.J. (1869–1953), born Dublin, Ireland, taught at St Aloysius College and Riverview in Sydney, and Xavier College and St Patrick's College, Melbourne. *The Heart of the School* (1919) opens with Peter Jackson being taught at home by a governess, Miss Moonlight. He leaves home for boarding school in 1907, and his experiences in the classroom and on the playing field are related with vigour. After initial adjustment problems, Peter embraces the school spirit wholeheartedly, particularly the many sporting events which are described in full. It delighted ex-students of Xavier College when it appeared, one saying, 'I will never part with the book as long as I live … get the book, read it, and read it again, and then keep it among your permanent treasures.' See also **Melbourne**. *Mrs Thunder and Other Stories* (1923) has six humorous stories for adults.

Boy Annual, The, see **Annuals**

Boys. The early stereotype of the rough colonial boy, more familiar with the saddle than book-learning, is found in many nineteenth-century novels, such as those of 'Arthur Ferres' and Richard Rowe. In

The Boy in the Bush (1869) Rowe describes his hero: 'Sydney was very proud of having the key of the store, counting the sheep, peppering mangled calves with strychnine to poison the native dogs that had mangled them, and riding about all day cracking his stockwhip, heading back bullocks that seemed inclined to make a rush at him, looking after the men, and when meat was wanted, driving the beast into the stockyard himself, and shooting it with his own gun. Sydney thought himself a man now.' In the same book 12-year-old Harry is described: 'Like most Australian boys, he was a very quick little fellow, but he was inclined to be rather lazy over his lessons.' 'Ferres' in *His First Kangaroo* (1869) comments on these young Australian lads, who 'can ride when they are not much bigger than monkeys', and presents them as skilled at horse-riding, bushcraft, shooting and survival, though not as skilled at education, learning and culture. The response of these boys to the pampered new chums is to deride their ineptitude, an attitude which continues into the twentieth century. Rowe goes on to say: 'the old hands are twice the men the new chums are that come nowadays. A set of stuck-up milksops. They don't know anything and they can't do anything.' Mary Grant Bruce's effete city boy, Cecil, in *Mates at Billabong* (1911) is in marked contrast to the responsible bush-bred lads, Jim Linton and Wally Meadows. Cecil does not ride well, deserts Norah when he is most needed, and causes the death of Norah's horse, Bobs. Lillian Pyke puts a sloppy character down to bad parenting, and sees some hope in a proper education and the character-building environment of the bush. *Bruce at Boonderong Camp* (1920) presents a boy spoilt by too much indulgence being shaped into a real man by hardship, responsibility, and the approach of a schoolteacher who believes that learning depends on motivation rather than drill, values which would be heartily derided by E.J. Brady's Tom Pagdin. *Tom Pagdin, Pirate* (1911) is about

rural boys who have the spirit of Huck Finn. Their escapades on the Broadstream, including a little theft, spying and other adventures, cheerfully defy the moral stereotype.

A direct descendent of Tom Pagdin is the hero of *Duck Williams and His Cobbers* (1939) by Fred Davison. The boys in Duck's gang, Baldy, Tut and Blue, play Ned Kelly, kill snakes, keep goats, rabbits and pigeons, go camping on the Whipstick (the book is set around Bendigo, Victoria) and fight with other gangs. In Ethel Turner's *The Little Larrikin* (1896) Lol, this time a city boy, races around the streets of Sydney confidently overcoming police, toughs and do-gooders, the 'head of a small-boy "push" he had organised and recruited lately with several lads of nine and ten'. The larrikin tradition was continued into the 1940s with Smiley (q.v.), in three novels by Moore Raymond: *Smiley* (1945), *Smiley Gets a Gun* (1947) and *Smiley Roams the Road* (1959). Smiley's milieu is the un-sophisticated pre-industrial world of rural Australia before World War II. His adventures have much of the rollicking humour of the later Ray Harris's *The Adventures of Turkey, Boy of the Australian Plains* (1952). These boys are made of honest fabric, straightforward, truthful, brave and humorous, but they have a great capacity to get into mischief. Tas, in Richard Parker's two books about the Pipers, *A Valley Full of Pipers* (1962) and *Perversity of Pipers* (1964), is resourceful and tough, with a dry sense of humour. Rafferty, in Joan Woodberry's *Rafferty Rides a Winner* (q.v., 1961) and its sequels, although an immigrant from Yorkshire, is in the same mould.

During the 1970s, with the rise of the women's movement, boys became more nurturing and more sensitive to their emotions. The boys in *The Racketty Street Gang* (1961) by L.H. Evers are like Lol in their adventures, but Anton's sensitivity prefigures later boys. One of the strongest representatives of these sensitive boys is

Ivan Southall's *Josh* (1971) whose emotional life can be traced through to Marcus, in *The Mysterious World of Marcus Leadbeater* (1990). Boys such as Ernie in *The Fire in the Stone* (1973) and Benno, in *The Valley Between* (1981), by Colin Thiele, although active rural boys, present a similar introspection.

Terry, in *Nicking Off* (1975) by Judith Crabtree, cares for an abandoned baby. Ant and Tim, in Christobel Mattingley's *Tiger's Milk* (1974) and *The Windmill at Magpie Creek* (q.v., 1971) overcome their fearfulness. These are pre-adolescent children. In *Cannily, Cannily* (1981) Trevor is on the verge of adolescence, and his problem is that he is different from the 'ocker' inhabitants of the country town, who sneer at his long hair, recycled clothes and itinerant lifestyle. In an unusual and challenging book, *The Blooding* (1987), Nadia Wheatley presents a young man, Colum, whose nature is divided between the tough male image of the timber-worker and the sensitive conservationist. The book examines the entrapment of many males in an aggressive gender role which denies any inner sensibilities. *Came Back to Show You I Could Fly* (q.v., 1989) by Robin Klein introduces another complex boy in Seymour. He is timid and repressed, but his sensitivity and growth in understanding lead him out of a very difficult time. Pina Grieco-Tiso's Len the Pen in *Blitz, a Bomber's Nightmare* (1991) is a graffiti artist, a rebellious outsider at school, constantly hounded by the school bully, and at odds with his father. There is no easy solution for Len, who is in an institution at the end of a novel touching on teenage suicide, accidental death and madness.

Max Dann's Roger Thesaurus and Peter Dusting, who first appear in *The Adventures of My Worst Best Friend* (1982), like their forebears Lol and Tom Pagdin, make us laugh because of their contrast — Roger so sensitive, Dusting completely oblivious to any higher feelings. Judith Clarke's Al Capsella, Tim Winton's Lockie

Leonard and David McRobbie's Wayne Wilson are naive and optimistic, without any 'machismo', but have all the clumsy energy of an adolescent boy. Allan Baillie, David Martin, Gillian Rubinstein, Frank Willmott, and Eleanor Nilsson, among others, have placed boys in a variety of contexts, characterising them as individuals within families or fighting for their lives, far removed in sensitivity and tenderness from the boys their fathers and grandfathers read about.

BOYD, SUZETTE. For *Between You and Me* see **Collections**.

Boy's Annual, The, see **Annuals**

Boy's Birth-Day Book, The: a Collection of Tales, Essays, and Narratives of Adventure, see **Collections**

Boys of Our Empire, see **Annuals**

BOZIC, MAGDA. For *Gather Your Dreams* see **Hodja Educational Resources Co-operative**.

BRACKEN, ANNE, born UK, came to Australia at the age of 10. In *The Adventures of Flopsie Flat-Foot, the Walking Toy* (1944) Flopsie floats down a drain to the sea, is carried to land by a seagull, picked up by a dog, dropped in a haystack, and taken home to the toymaker by a possum. Attractive illustrations appear on alternate pages. Patch in *The Tail (or Tale) of Patch the Puppy* (1944) is banished from the house, pecked by Mrs Hen, pricked by a hedgehog and laughed at by the other farm animals, until he returns home to be petted. Patch appears again in *Patch and his Friend Pom-Pom: a Tale of Two Tales* (1947). *Being the (Mis)adventures of Podgy the Penguin* (1946) is another adventure for young readers. *The Tuppity Twins* (1947) is about two tortoiseshell kittens, Timmy and Tilly. *Meg & Peg: Adventures of Two Peg Dolls* (1946), illustrated by 'Piers' (Margaret Senior), join Pamela's other dolls in a new doll's house. In *The Lost Toy Shop* (1946), also illustrated by 'Piers', Brenda discovers a fairy shop in which wonderful toys come to life. In *Penny and Dorabella at the Beach* (1947) a giant Penguin is revealed to Penny and her doll, Dorabella, who takes them under the sea to Lady Flora Mermaid and Sir Merry Merman. *Penny and Dorabella at the Circus* (1947) describes how Penny's toys perform for her and Dorabella.

For older readers Bracken wrote *The Twins Take Charge* (1946), which introduced Julie and Jon Howard. They rescue Lyle from her cruel kidnappers, find her a family, and save their father's fortune with the help of their mother's friend Candy and her friend Hal. *The Twins to the Rescue* (1947) also features Lyle, Candy and Hal, but this time there is a mysterious schoolmistress, who is finally revealed as a famous actress who has had a memory lapse. See **Jancy** for Bracken's four books about Jancine Mitford.

BRADY, EDWIN JAMES (1869– 1952), poet, novelist and short story writer, born Carcoar, NSW, edited the first Australian labour paper, the *Workman* at the age of 21. He was associated with many journals, and contributed to *Pals* (q.v.), the weekly boys' magazine. *Tom Pagdin, Pirate* (1911), illustrated by Lionel Lindsay, is a vivid portrayal of working-class life. Two runaway boys overhear two criminals plotting a crime, one instantly recognisable from his foreign accent, assumed to be German, although really French. He is Jean Petit, a murderer, born and bred in crime. He murders Hans Halterman, a German wine-grower, and is finally captured by the authorities with the help of the boys. Brady ridicules current xenophobia as the novel concludes, with Tom's observation about 'sour Kraut' (i.e. Petit), 'Oh, he's nothing — only a cold-blooded German. It's the Germans

that's ruinin' this country'. The irony is not lost on the reader. See also **Boys**.

BRAITHWAITE, ALICIA has written *Angry Albert* (1987), illustrated by Noela Hills. Albert's angry response to the world is converted into peace when he stops shouting and hears the silence. *The Horribubble* (1990) was illustrated by Shirley Peters. *Elephants Don't Like Tuna Casserole* (1990), illustrated by George Aldridge, describes the friendship between John and a baby elephant, which John's parents fail to see.

BRASH, NICHOLAS (1946–). For *Alphacats* see **Alphabet Books**.

Bread and Honey (1970) by Ivan Southall won the 1971 Book of the Year Awards. On Anzac Day unhappy Michael Cameron must choose between the scientific rationalism of his father and the imaginative faith of his grandmother. In a confrontation with a group of bullies, Michael finds a friend, Margaret, faces up to the choice and comes to terms with his own difficulties with his family. This novel is an examination of a confused boy, without the tense action which Southall developed in his earlier novels.

Breaking Up (1983) by Frank Willmott was Commended in the 1984 Book of the Year Awards. Fifteen-year-old Mark Wheeler writes a diary, struggling to make sense of a life which is becoming more perplexing. His relationships with his peers and his parents, Jackie and Alec, are changing as his parents part and his school friends face various crises. Willmott's account of Mark and Andy's distress when their father leaves is compelling. The inner-city setting, sharply observed, provides a rich background to a suffering family. Issues such as sexuality, violence, racism and child abuse are touched on, and no comforting solutions are provided. A film of the novel was made in 1985, directed by Kathy Mueller and written by the author. See also **Italians**; **Sexuality**.

BREEN, BARRY ANDREW (1938–), born St Arnaud, Victoria, wrote short stories set in the 1950s about the adventures of a group of boys. *Flop and Mick and John and Me* (1976), illustrated by Margot Kimber, and *Mick & His Mates* (1983), illustrated by Mary Davy, are about 'The Bad Deeds Gang'. Some of the stories were first broadcast on the ABC in the 'Listen and Read' and 'Storyteller' programs. A collection edited by L.M. Hannan and W.G. Tickell in 1971 used *The Bad Deeds Gang* as the title story. *Doing Nothing* (1989), illustrated by John Veeken, in Methuen's 'Dimensions' series, has excerpts, stories and biographical information.

BRENNAN, JOHN (1952–), born Melbourne, has driven taxis, and worked in advertising and television. For *A is for Australia* (1984) see **Alphabet Books**. *1,2,3 and What Do You See?* (1990) is a photographic counting book. See also **Counting Books**. *Zoo Day* (1990), with Leonie Keaney, describes a day in the life of the Royal Melbourne Zoo, illustrated with fine coloured photographs.

BRETT, BERNARD. For *Captain Cook* see **Cook**, Captain **James**.

BRIDGES, HILDA (1881–1971), born Hobart, wrote novels for adults and books for Whitcombe & Tombs, including *Jock Whitehead: an Australian Fairy Story* (1922), illustrated by Zoe Rothwell. In *Bobby's First Term: a Schoolboys' Story* (1924) Dick and Bob are boarders at Rockley school, where they are accused of theft. Their sworn enemy, Dalton, appears to be the real culprit, but things are not as they seem. *Connie of the Fourth Form* (1930) uses a formula later beloved of Enid Blyton. Connie goes to Lowbanks School as a boarder, discovers a secret room containing money and routs a mistress who

dislikes her. In *Carnaby's Boy: a Tale of the Founding of Melbourne* (1926) Bridges describes the journey of Dick Carnaby and Will Oakley on John Pascoe Fawkner's ship the *Enterprise*. The boys glimpse the site of Melbourne as the ship sails up the bay to the Saltwater River (now the Maribyrnong): ' ... the spreading plains, where scarce an axe would be needed before the plough. Here and there they saw swamps haunted by teal and ducks, geese and swans.' Bridges also wrote adult novels.

BRIDGES, ROY (1885–1952), born Hobart, journalist and novelist, brother of Hilda Bridges, wrote many novels for adults. *Dead Men's Gold* (1916) and *The Black House* (1920) are adventure stories, the latter about a pirate attack during a voyage to Australia. Bridges contributed to the magazine *Pals* (q.v.).

BRIDGES, THOMAS CHARLES (1868–1944), born France, was an English author of over sixty adventure stories. His first boys' story was *Paddy Leary's School Days* (1911), about an Australian boy in an English school. Further escapades of Paddy Leary appeared in 'The Boys' Friend Library' as *Paddy Leary, Millionaire* (1929). *On Land and Sea at the Dardanelles* (1915) is a novel about the Anzac landing. In *The Bush Boys: a Story of the Australian Desert* (1930) Tad, Bob and Jed are blown into the desert in a balloon, where they find that the evil Blayne is using slave labour to dig gold. The swindle is exposed after much fighting and dirty dealings. Bridges was also a contributor to *The Victorian Schoolboys' Story Book* (?1930).

BRINSMEAD, HESBA FAY (née HUNGERFORD) (1922–), born Berambing, NSW, has based some of her books on her childhood experiences in a remote part of the Blue Mountains, including *Longtime Passing* (q.v., 1971), *Once There was a Swagman* (q.v., 1979), *Longtime Dreaming* (1982) with Ken

Hungerford, *Christmas at Longtime* (1983), illustrated by John Caldwell, and *The Honey Forest* (1979), illustrated by Louise Hogan. This last novel was first published in the Victorian *School Paper*. See **Longtime Passing**. Her first novel was *Pastures of the Blue Crane* (q.v., 1964), which examines the family relationships of Ryl Merriwether, a snobbish girl who comes to her senses on a banana farm at Murwillumbah. The novel introduced Perry, a Torres Strait Islander. Brinsmead furthered her exploration of racial issues in *Listen to the Wind* (1970), illustrated by Robert Micklewright, in which Loveday Smith and another Torres Strait Islander, Tam Greenrush, join forces to build a prawn-trawler. Brinsmead's concern for environmental issues is at the forefront in *A Sapphire for September* (1967), illustrated by Victor Ambrus. Binny Flambeau and her friends attempt to save the Old Vale Settlement from the real estate developers. In *Isle of the Sea Horse* (1969), illustrated by Peter Farmer, Emma, George, Shem, Raquel and Mrs Mulvaney are reluctant to return to civilisation after they are shipwrecked off the Great Barrier Reef. They are apprehensive about the effect of tourism on the Reef. Brinsmead has written a book about the flooding of Tasmania's Lake Pedder and the attempts to save it, *I Will Not Say the Day is Done* (1983). For her series on Clippie the pilot, *Who Calls from Afar?* (1971), illustrated by Ian Ribbons, *Echo in the Wilderness* (1972), illustrated by Graham Humphreys, and *The Sand Forest* (1985), see **Nancarrow, Clippie**.

From *Season of the Briar* (1965), illustrated by William Papas, set in Tasmania, *Beat of the City* (q.v., 1966), *Under the Silkwood* (1976), illustrated by Michael Payne, *The Ballad of Benny Perhaps* (1977) to the *The Wind Harp* (1977), illustrated by Peter Dickie, Brinsmead has been concerned with young people at a turning-point in their lives. For younger readers, *Someplace Beautiful* (1986), illustrated by Betina Ogden, is about Miss Dove's Flying Trunk

Bookshop, where a group of children find the delights of reading, and save the bookshop from closure. *When You Come to the Ferry* (1988), illustrated by Dee Huxley, takes a summer in the life of Tracy and James and their parents, who visit their grandmother near Murwillumbah during a flood. Brinsmead has returned to the past for *Time for Tarquinia* (1981), illustrated by Bruce Riddell, in which Nusi lives in Etruria in pre-Christian times, and wants to be a sculptor. Using the 'Snow White and Rose Red' story, Brinsmead has explored a new direction, examining the delicate balance of opposites, in *Bianca & Roja* (1990), illustrated by Andrew McLean, set in Yugoslavia.

Hesba Brinsmead's evocation of her experience of childhood, her feeling for the landscape of the bush, and her acceptance of alternative lifestyles and children out of the mainstream of middle-class white Australia, prefigured the concerns of later writers.

Brisbane and its semi-tropical setting appears in Gordon Stables's *Frank Hardinge: From Torrid Zones to Regions of Perpetual Snow* (1908). Frank walks 'in the splendid botanical gardens, a favourite lounge of his. He was ... graciously permitted to lead his dog around the lovely tropical walks, adorned with trees and flowering bushes and wild heaths, that made the whole place, especially what is called the "bush-house", look like a terrestrial paradise or fairyland.' Joseph Bowes in *The Young Settler: the Story of a New-chum in Queensland* (1927) describes early Brisbane. Fred and Julian stay at the People's Palace, near Central Station, walk down Edward Street to the Botanical Gardens, catch a tram up Queen Street to the Museum, then to the Brisbane River and climb Mount Coot-Tha 'which the locals call One Tree Hill'. In Maureen Stewart's *Orange Wendy* (1974) Wendy goes to Centenary Pool, Myers, the Valley and the City Square. Modern Brisbane appears rarely in children's books, although it has been evoked in books for adults, such as David Malouf's *Johnno* (1975).

Broady Book of Stories, The, see **Collections**

BROGDEN, STANLEY MARCEL WILLIAM (1913–), born Malta, was an aviator and journalist, and edited the RAAF journal *Wings*. Brogden wrote short stories for children, and novels and short stories for adults. In *The Cattle Duffers: Adventures in the Kimberleys* (1948), illustrated by Bruce Crampton, John Hamilton discovers that he is part-owner of a cattle station in the Kimberleys. He tracks down cattle-thieves who are raiding stations in the far north-west. Information on the cattlemen and the stations in the area is woven into the action. See also **Perth**.

BROOKER, BELINDA (1967–). For *Mundarda* see **Animal Stories**.

BROOKS, EDWY SEARLES (1889–1965), born London, UK, was a writer of boys' adventure stories. His series about a group of schoolboys from 'St. Frank's', was first published as a serial in the popular boys' paper *The Nelson Lee School Story Library*, between 1917 and 1933. In 1933 this paper merged with the *Gem*. Nelson Lee was a detective who was invited to join the staff of St Frank's, and was responsible for uncovering shady machinations previously unsuspected. At one stage the boys travel to Australia and NZ to a Test cricket series. The titles were published by the Amalgamated Press between 1925 and 1929, and the Australian adventures included *The Boy from the "Bush"! or, the Brand of the Twin Stars* (1926), *The Isle of Coral! A Magnificent and Extra Long Story of the Wonderful Adventures of the Boys of St. Franks with Lord Dorrimore in the South Seas* (1925), *Beset by Cannibals!* (1925), *Trapped by Bushrangers! A Magnificent Long Complete Yarn of Schoolboy Adventure in Australia Featuring the Cheery Chums of St. Frank's* (1929), *Lost in the Bush! A Vivid, Long, Complete Schoolboy Adventure Yarn Featuring Archie Glenthorne and his Cheery Chums of St. Frank's in Australia* (1929), *"The Adelaide Test Match Sensation!"* (1929), *St. Frank's at the Test Match!*, *In Unknown Australia!*, *The Valley of Surprises!*, *"Hard Lines, Handy!"*, *The Melbourne Test Match Triumph!* and others, all with an exclamation mark. Brooks created the detective Sexton Blake.

BROOKS, MARY. For *Australian Animal Wonderland* see **Animal Stories**.

BROOKS, RON (1948–), born Pambula, NSW, was trained in illustration at RMIT and has been an artist and designer in theatre and journalism. He illustrated *Iron Mountain* (1970) by Mavis Thorpe Clark; *Hughie* by David Martin (q.v., 1971); *Bass & Billy Martin* (1972) by Joan Phipson; *Time Sweep* (1976) by Valerie Weldrick; *Go Ducks Go!* (1987) by Maurice Burns, which explores the journey down a river of two toy ducks; *The Macquarie Bedtime Story Book* (1987), edited by Rosalind Price and Walter McVitty; and *The Pochetto Coat* (q.v., 1978) by Ted Greenwood. Brooks was a contributor to Mitsumasa Anno's *All in a Day* (1986). He has also written and illustrated his own books, such as *Annie's Rainbow* (q.v., 1975). In *Timothy and Gramps* (1978) the timid Timothy finds friends when Gramps, reminiscent of the character in *Annie's Rainbow*, breaks the ice at school. Brooks joined with Jenny Wagner to produce three outstanding picture-books, *The Bunyip of Berkeley's Creek* (q.v., 1973), *Aranea: a Story About a Spider* (q.v., 1975) and *John Brown, Rose and the Midnight Cat* (q.v., 1977). He believes that a picture should be 'offered as an invitation to explore' so that children may 'find their own connections'.

Brooks, William & Co. were Sydney printers and publishers. Brooks published a series of books for use in schools, including spelling, reading, history, geography and arithmetic books. They also published Drill books, describing exercises with sticks, clubs and dumb-bells which could be performed in 'schools and private families'. William Brooks & Co. were also responsible for some fine early children's books, such as *Australian Nursery Rimes* (1917), *Bubbles: His Book* (1899) by R.F. Irvine, and *Gum Leaves* (1900) by Ethel Turner, the last two illustrated by D.H. Souter.

BROOKSBANK, ANNE (1943–), born Melbourne, has written material for television and film, including 'Archer', the story of the first winner of the Melbourne Cup. *On Loan* (1985) is her book from the script of the episode in the television series 'Winners' (q.v.). In a story of cultural discovery, Lindy finds that her real father exists, and wants to visit her. The conflict between her love for her adoptive Australian family and her gentle Vietnamese father is made even more difficult when Lindy, called Mai, is introduced to her large family of cousins. There is no easy resolution, although both families accept Lindy's decision.

BROOME, ERROL (1937–), born Perth, has worked as a journalist, and contributed to Macmillan's *Children's Encylopaedia* (1986). *A Year of Pink Pieces* (1987), illustrated by Lee Smith, explores a friendship between Yoshito of Japan and Ben of Australia; *Dear Mr Sprouts* (1991) is the correspondence between a city girl and a country boy which traces their developing friendship. Her picture-books include *Wrinkles* (1978), illustrated by Terry Dyer, in which Grandmother turns cartwheels to avoid wrinkles, *The Smallest Koala* (1988), illustrated by Gwen Mason, and a series of animal stories, *Bird Boy* (1986) and *Town and Country Ducks* (1986), both illustrated by Lindy Joubert. *Spooked!* (1990) explores the childish fear of a ghost in the wardrobe, and in *Garry Keeble's Kitchen* (1992) Garry becomes a

gourmand chef, with twenty-eight recipes provided. Her informational books treat sport, in *Have a Go!* (1988), and the racehorse Phar Lap in *Bobby Boy* (1990).

BROOME, Lady **MARY ANNE** (1831–1911), born Spanish Town, Jamaica, married Captain George Robert Barker, and later Frederick Napier Broome. While living in NZ, she wrote an account of early NZ settlement, *Station Life in New Zealand* (1870), as Lady Barker. Her second husband (after whom the town of Broome is named) was appointed as Governor of WA in 1882. Lady Broome's *Letters to Guy* (1885) recount her experiences travelling throughout WA with her husband. She contributed to children's magazines, including the *Boys' Own Paper*, and was a talented literary woman with considerable influence in WA society. She encouraged W.H. Timperley to write about his experiences, and edited his book, *Harry Treverton: His Tramps and Troubles* (1889). Lady Broome wrote other books for children, including *Ribbon Stories* (1872).

Brother Night (1990) by Victor Kelleher, was an Honour Book in the 1991 Book of the Year Awards: Older Readers. In a landscape which includes desert, jungle and a city built on water, Kelleher contrasts the giant Lal and the beautiful Ramon. Lal is animal-like, with a gentle disposition, while Ramon is beautiful and cold. With its many symbolic overtones, this novel draws on powerful myths in an exciting narrative. Kelleher's plea is for the acceptance of others and oneself, and of the balance in Nature and Life.

BROWN, BARRY, a UK author, wrote *The Flying Doctor: John Flynn and the Flying Doctor Service* (1960). See **Royal Flying Doctor Service**.

Brown Land was Green, The (1956) by Mavis Thorpe Clark, illustrated by Harry Hudson, was Highly Commended in the

1957 Book of the Year Awards. The Webster family arrive in Portland, Victoria, in 1844, from England. Mr Webster takes a position as a carpenter at 'Kammoora', near Wannon, under an unscrupulous manager. Fourteen-year-old Henrietta is appalled by the brutal attacks on Aboriginal People and saves Mundowie, who is wounded in one of the forays. The manager is exposed by the resourceful Henrietta, and the Websters are given a hundred acres to establish themselves. Despite its assimilationist approach, the novel is enlightened in its racial attitudes and its portrayal of a resourceful and assertive girl. It was republished as *Kammoora* in 1990. See also **Aboriginal People in Children's Fiction**.

BRUCE, MARY (MINNIE) **GRANT** (1878–1958), born Sale, Victoria, began her career as a journalist on the staff of the Melbourne *Age* and the *Leader*, where her early Billabong books first appeared. In 1912 she travelled to London where she met her second cousin, Major George Evans Bruce, whom she married in Melbourne in 1914. They returned to Ireland at the outbreak of World War I, and divided the rest of their lives between that country and Australia. Between 1910 and 1946 Bruce wrote thirty-seven novels, a collection of Aboriginal Dreaming stories, *The Stone Axe of Burkamukk* (1922), illustrated by J. Macfarlane, and a fantasy, *Timothy in Bushland* (1912). For her Billabong books see **'Billabong'**.

The bush was Bruce's favoured setting as a testing ground for character. An example is *Gray's Hollow* (1914), where the 'precocious' Horace, Thelma and Johnny Densham, who cannot ride, make a bed, or make themselves useful, are taught to 'go straight' through the example of their despised bush cousins, the Grays. Other novels which take up the same theme are *Glen Eyre* (1912), *The Twins of Emu Plains* (1923), illustrated by J. Macfarlane, *Robin* (1926), illustrated by Edgar A. Holloway,

and *Rossiter's Farm* (1920). The other side of the coin is examined in *The Cousin from Town* (1922), illustrated by Esther Paterson. Brenda Young's stay with her cousins, the Wyatts, transforms a 'bickering ... house that knows no mother' into a place where the happy children gather around the piano and sing every evening. Brenda's cheerfulness and ever-present goodwill shames the Wyatt children into better behaviour.

The bush, according to Bruce, can also cure those corrupted by the city. In *'Possum* (1917) Aileen, Tom Macleod and Garth, from Toorak, Melbourne, are transformed by 'Possum, the epitome of courage, strength, common sense and self-lessness. Aileen is able to bring some city refinements to the bush by teaching 'Possum how to speak properly and make herself dainty print frocks, but it is 'Possum who is the real educator. 'The fragile, willowy girl of Toorak had gone: in her place was a ... gracious woman, with perfect health on her brown cheek, and in her eyes perfect happiness.' *Anderson's Jo* (1927) and *Golden Fiddles* (1928), illustrated by Dewar Mills, take adult viewpoints. The first describes the reforming effect of a child on a dour and solitary adult, the latter the corrupting effect of the city. *Golden Fiddles* was made into a television mini-series in 1990, directed by Claude Fournier and scripted by Sheila Silby.

Lessons learnt in the bush have made Dick Lester the manly boy he is. In *Dick* (1918), illustrated by J. Macfarlane, he has rarely left 'Kurrajong' Station. After he and his mother explore caves near their property, and nearly lose their lives in the process, Dick reluctantly goes to school in Melbourne, where he soon learns to play a straight bat and take on the school bullies. See also **School Stories**. In *Dick Lester of Kurrajong* (1920), also illustrated by Macfarlane, Dick accompanies his mother to meet Mr Lester in Fremantle. On the way he saves Bobby Warner by leaping overboard when Bobby falls over the side of the ship. Later he makes it a double by saving Bobby's bad-tempered sister Merle during an attack by Aboriginal People, an escapade in which Dick's legs are injured. However Merle repays Dick by finding a surgeon who operates on him to give him back the use of his legs. Another surgeon cures Hugh Stanford's legs in *Hugh Stanford's Luck* (1925). Hugh comes to his uncle's property from Ceylon, bringing with him a jade image, his 'Luck', which has the reputation of bringing good fortune.

Sinister twins appear in *The Tower Rooms* (1926), illustrated by Dewar Mills, a novel for older readers. When Doris Earle obtains a position as governess to the McNab children, she becomes involved in an elaborate deception of the police by her employer and finds a benefactor who eagerly solves her family's financial problems. Also for older readers, *The Houses of the Eagle* (1925), illustrated by Harold Copping, describes how the Browne family convert an unhappy woman into a bride, through their cleanliness, politeness, general refinement, and fey younger son, John, who quotes poetry and is transfixed by music.

The Happy Traveller (1929), illustrated by Laurie Tayler, begins in an orphanage. Teddy Winter runs away and finds a friend in Bill Courtney, with whom he roams the bush. When Teddy is caught by the dreadful orphanage manager, Bill saves him. In *Road to Adventure* (1932), also illustrated by Tayler, Hugh Russell is left in the care of a circus company. He quickly learns the ropes, and is on the way to becoming one of its stars at the end of the novel. *Circus Ring* (1936), illustrated by J.F. Campbell, continues Hugh's adventures with Peterson's Circus as he wins over the stern owner, Dan Peterson, saves Peterson's daughter Nita from drowning, and develops his own circus acts. *"Seahawk"* (1934), also illustrated by Campbell, is the boat which takes twins Derek and Jill on the track of 'Chinese cocaine' smugglers. In *Told by Peter* (1938)

and *Peter & Co.* (1940), Peter and Binkie Forsyth, Peter's friend Clem, and Binkie's governess, Miss Tarrant, foil murderers and German and Japanese spies in exploits which range from the Forsyth's cattle station, 'Weeroona', to Kongai Island, on the Great Barrier Reef. Both stories are related by the schoolboy Peter. Peter's legs, like Dick's and Hugh's, are injured at the end of the first book, but are saved by some clever passes 'in long sweeping movements, an inch or so from the skin' by a footballers' masseur (who turns out to be also a secret service agent) and a lesson in positive thinking, which Bruce had expatiated on in four radio broadcasts 'The power within'. 'If we hold thoughts of courage, cheerfulness, unselfishness and hope, the power flows in, creating corresponding conditions.' It soon sets Peter right, at any rate. See also **Girls**. Other spies emerge in *Karalta* (1941), set during World War II. Jan, a fluent speaker of German, is evacuated to Australia and unmasks the local chemist by discovering a German note while snooping in the darkroom.

Bruce has been a major influence on the construction of the Australian ethos, particularly during the period before World War II, and has shaped the nature of how white Australians view their relationship with the land. She embraced and enlarged on the concept of neighbourliness in the bush, saw the rural life as the best upbringing for children, and wrote enthusiastically about the beauty of the landscape. The world which she wrote about was conservative and class-ridden, but her women and girls do not allow their refinement to interfere with their strength in emergencies or the capable management of their lives. Further reading: Niall, *Seven Little Billabongs*; Alexander, *Billabong's Author*.

BRUCE, Major **GEORGE EVANS** (1867–1949), born County Cork, Ireland, married his cousin, Mary Grant Bruce. After a military career, Bruce left England in 1918 with his wife to settle in Victoria. After another period in England and Ireland from 1926, they returned to Australia in 1939, where Major Bruce died. His children's books are not set in Australia. *The Lion's Son* (1928), illustrated by Edgar A. Holloway, is a story of the Indian frontier, and much of the action occurs in Afghanistan. *Tom in the Andamans* (1924) is a Whitcombe 'Southern Cross' Story Reader.

Brumby books, see *Silver Brumby, The;* **Patchett, Mary Elwyn**

BRUNATO, MADELEINE, born England, has written two collections of Aboriginal Dreaming stories, *Worra and the Jilbruke Legend* (1972) and *Worra and Legends of the Booandiks* (1975), both illustrated by C. Dudley Wood. The latter draws on the work of Mrs James Smith, a missionary who lived with the Booandiks around Mt Gambier. Brunato provides meanings of words and phrases, and locates her material clearly. She has also written a biography *Hanji Mahomet Allun: Afghan Camel Driver, Herbalist and Healer, and Australian* (1972).

BUDDEE, PAUL (1913–   ), born Mt Lawley, WA, poet and teacher, was a concert performer, and conducted the ABC's music broadcasts from 1946 to 1951. He began his novels for children with *The Comical Adventures of Osca and Olga: a Tale of Mice in Mouseland* (1943) and *The Remarkable Ramblings of Rupert and Rita* (1944), both illustrated by C.H. Percival. Both were broadcast by radio stations throughout Australia in 1944 and 1945, and *Osca and Olga* was serialised in the NSW *School Magazine*. *Six Comical Stories About Rattigan Rat* (1947), illustrated by Neves Cherry, was the third in the trilogy. The domestic adventures of Rattigan and his wife Patty, Wally Magpie, Osca and Olga are told with intriguing detail, reminiscent of Mary Norton's *Borrowers* (1952 ff.) series. Oscar and Olga's house is set up

with tiny furniture, with framed pawprints of their friends on the wall. Buddee then began to write adventure stories for older readers, with *The Unwilling Adventurers* (1967), illustrated by Gareth Floyd. See **Adventure Stories**. *The Escape of the Fenians* (1971), illustrated by Anne Culvenor, is a historical novel about the Irish political prisoners who were imprisoned in Fremantle from 1867 to 1875. They were freed by the Irish patriot John Breslin on the ship *Catalpa* in a daring rescue. Buddee dramatises the story which is seen through the eyes of Jamie O'Mara. *The Escape of John O'Reilly* (1973) is a biography of O'Reilly, a Fenian transported to WA, who had been sentenced to death in 1868, and later actively assisted Breslin's *Catalpa* expedition. *The Mystery of Moma Island* (1969), illustrated by Peter Kesteven, is an adventure story about three sea cadets who find that the contents of a historic Dutch ship off the WA coast are being pilfered by unscrupulous divers. He has also written pony club stories (see **Rankin, Ann**), outback adventures (see **Devlin, Peter**) and a series about a helicopter unit (see **Air Patrol** series). His informational books include a history of civil aviation, *Airways: the Call of the Sky* (1978), and *The Fate of the Artful Dodger* (1983), the story of the Parkhurst criminal boys sent to Australia and NZ between 1842 and 1852.

BULLER-MURPHY, DEBORAH (1887–1965) (née DRAKE-BROCKMAN) was the daughter of the heroine Grace Bussell, who participated in the rescue of eighty survivors of the wreck of the sailing ship *Georgette*. *An Attempt to Eat the Moon and Other Stories Recounted from the Aborigines* (1958), illustrated by Elizabeth Durack, contains fifteen stories from the Dordenup people, from the Margaret River region of WA. See **Aboriginal Dreaming Stories**.

Bumble's Dream (1981) by Bruce Treloar was Commended in the 1982 Picture

Book of the Year Awards. Mr Bumble and Timothy build a flying machine, the *Bumble Bee*, out of junk. In *Bumble's Island* (1984) Mr Bumble crashes on a desert island and his aircraft must become a boat; in *Bumble's Journey* (1986) Bumble and Timothy build a balloon. Treloar pictures the rich domestic chaos of Bumble's house shared with Emily the hen, and the exhilaration of flight.

BUNKER, AMY (1911–) taught creative writing with the Council of Adult Education. For *Millingi* (1973) see **Aboriginal People in Children's Fiction**. *Finders Keepers* (1977) and *Copper Cove* (1978) are short novels in the 'Flag' series. In the first Bob finds a wallet, spends the money, confesses and is given a job. In the second, Jim's predictive dreams uncover a mystery. Buggs and Tommo belie the title of *HMAS Unsinkable* (1976) in Macmillan's 'Orbit' series.

Bunyip Hole, The (1958) by Patricia Wrightson, illustrated by Margaret Horder, was Commended in the 1959 Book of the Year Awards. Intruders kidnap the Collins's dog, Homer. Binty Collins lacks confidence, but risks falling into the Bunyip Hole, a deep chasm, to recover him. In the process of being rescued by Ken and Valery, Binty finds that he has the resources to tackle a dangerous climb.

Bunyip of Berkeley's Creek, The (1973) by Jenny Wagner, illustrated by Ron Brooks, was Commended in the 1974 Book of the Year Awards and won the Picture Book of the Year Awards in the same year. Bunyip wakes in the depths of the swamps and asks the eternal question, 'Who am I?'. When Man tells him that bunyips do not exist, he returns mournfully to the swamp, only to find a female bunyip waiting for him. When she asks the same question, Bunyip assures her that she is a bunyip. Brooks's atmospheric illustrations echo the mystery of the bush and the question.

Bunyips, also called Yaahoos and Wowees, are mythical creatures who live in rivers, creeks and swamps. Descriptions can be found in Aboriginal Dreaming stories, and bunyips have featured in children's books, where they can be evil or benevolent presences. In William Howitt's *A Boy's Adventures in the Wilds of Australia: or, Herbert's Note-Book* (1854) Herbert comments on 'a strange reptile which lies at the bottom of waters and pulls people under when they are swimming. They [Aboriginal People] call this the Bunyup [*sic*], and are much afraid of it.' J.R. Lockeyear's *"Mr Bunyip"*: *or, Mary Somerville's Ramble, a Story for Children* (1871) is a cautionary tale in which Mary is instructed in moral precepts by a river monster. Mary's Mr Bunyip 'looks a little like an elephant' but has 'fins at his sides, which gave him more the appearance of a whale, and as he had difficulty in moving along the ground, and seemed so much more at home in the water, she came to the conclusion at last that he must belong

Children of the Dark People (1936) by Frank Dalby Davison. Illustrator: Pixie O'Harris

Whispering in the Wind (1969) by Alan Marshall. Illustrator: Jack Newnham

rather to the whale species'. Mr Bunyip is precisely 180 years old. *Mollie's Bunyip* (1904) by Annie Rentoul and Ida Rentoul (Outhwaite) is about 'a lost soul of the ancient forest', another kindly spirit. E. Dalrymple's *When the Stars Look Down* (1930) has the bunyip babes Nulla and Tilba as naughty and cheerful creatures with pointed heads, although their father is a little more fearsome. In Frank Dalby Davison's *Children of the Dark People* (q.v., 1936) the lost children are rescued by 'Old Mr Bunyip', who is like 'all the elders of the tribe in one figure'. Pixie O'Harris's illustration depicts a noble, bearded elder. Judith Whitlock's five stories for younger readers, *The Green Bunyip* (1962), *Bunyip at the Seaside* (1962), *Bunyip and the Brolga Bird* (1963), *Bunyip and the Bushfire* (1964) and *Bunyip and the Tiger Cats* (1965), all illustrated by Leslie Green,

have a small, fat, thinly whiskered, green and friendly bunyip (who is afraid of water), and information about the habits of bush animals and birds is woven into imaginative stories. The bunyip in Alan Marshall's *Whispering in the Wind* (1969) is more frightening, although soon friendly when Peter has given him the magic leaf. This bunyip has 'the body of a giant wombat, the thick, inflexible tail of a kangaroo, the long neck of a giraffe and the head of a dragon'.

The bunyip in *The Bunyip of Berkeley's Creek* (q.v., 1973) by Jenny Wagner is confused about his identity, and like that in Sally Farrell Odgers's *The Bunyip Wakes* (1984) eventually finds a mate in a creek. In *Gloop the Gloomy Bunyip* (1962) by Colin Thiele, illustrated by John Bailey, Gloop tries unsuccessfully to save his environment by frightening white people. *A*

Boggle of Bunyips (1981, revised 1989) is a collection of excerpts, newspaper articles and Aboriginal stories gathered together and edited by Edel Wignell, illustrated by Bob Graham, which all feature bunyips. It includes Wignell's outline for her later novel *Escape by Deluge* (1989), which has a bunyip struggling to escape from a building in modern Melbourne. Wignell presents the primeval longings of the bunyip, and although her picture is less defined than earlier writers, Wignell creates a satisfying creature, incompatible with the modern city, and representing the spirit of an ancient land.

BURGEMEESTRE, KEVIN (1957–), born Perth, has contributed illustrations to reading schemes, and illustrated Maureen Stewart's *Easy Plays for Junior Secondary Students* (1987); *Mr Lively's Lighthouse* (1988) by Antonia Feitz; Dianne Bates's *Grandma Cadbury's Trucking Tales* (q.v., 1987) and its sequel *Grandma Cadbury's Safari Tours* (1989); Diane Kupke's *The Secret of the Tower Room* (1991); and *Don't Forget Granny* (1991) by Michael Dugan.

BURKE, DAVID (1927–), born Melbourne, has worked as a journalist and has written books about steam trains. *Come Midnight Monday* (1976), illustrated by Janet Mare, is an adventure story about the efforts to restore a steam locomotive. It was serialised on ABC television in 1983, directed by Mark Callan, and scripted by Roger Dunn in seven half-hour episodes. In *Darknight* (1979) a young reporter, Steve Baird, discovers the secrets hidden in a strange and unfriendly town, Glenrock.

BURKE, SUSAN (1953–), born Perth, was program director of the ABC in Perth. Her first book was *Alexander in Trouble and other Stories* (1979), illustrated by Gavin Rowe, six lively stories about a boy in a wheelchair. Alexander has a birthday, lets others ride in his chair, makes a disastrous cake and gets bogged.

All Change at the Station (1980) is an informational book. *The Rottnest Bike Business* (1982), illustrated by Betty Greenhatch and Graeme Base, is an adventure story about a group of children who uncover drug-dealers disguised as a gang of bike-thieves. The novel weaves the history of the island and its unique animal life into the action.

BURNS, ROGER. For *Two Boys in Australia* see **Perth**.

BURRAGE, EDWIN HARCOURT (1839–1916), born Norfolk, UK, was a prolific writer of boys' stories. He created 'Handsome Harry of the Fighting Belvedere' for the *Boy's Standard*, introducing Ching Ching, who later had a magazine *Ching Ching's Own* entirely devoted to his exploits. For *The Wurra Wurra Boys* (1903) see **Aboriginal People in Children's Fiction**.

BURROW, AILEEN L. also wrote as **'NEELIA'**. Her books presented natural history to children. Titles include *The Think Man* (1911), *The Sunset Fairies* (1911), and *The Adventures of Melaleuca* (1928). In *The Magic Shell* (1939) natural history is explained through the story of Buddy, the black man-creature, who is taken by the bush animals and made into a fairy baby. He is given a pearly shell which will carry him anywhere, and discovers the origin of moonlight, the sources of the rainbow, and how the water cycle works. *Little Shepherd: the Life Story of a Little Dog Founded on Fact* (1920), *Goblin Greenleaf: Life Stories of Some Australian Insects* (1925) and *The Quest of the Crown Jewels* (1929) were Whitcombe's Story Books.

BURROWS, DENYS, born Lancashire, UK, came to Australia at the age of 4. He worked in radio for many years, and *Above the Snowline* (1959) was a radio serial on the ABC. The story is set on the Snowy Mountains Hydro-Electric Scheme.

Hungarian Nicky (or Miklosh) Kovash, Australian David, and Irish Doreen foil an attempt to rob the Authority. The novel presents a melting pot of cultures, with everyone eager to become Australians. Nicky refuses to speak Hungarian, and Nicky's mother cheerfully abandons her Hungarian heritage in favour of a new-found freedom. *Stagecoach West* (1964) describes the threat of bushrangers against a background of the rivalry between the stagecoaches and the railway between Bathurst and Sydney. See also **Bushrangers; Historical Novels**. *Clipper Ship* (1965) is set on a clipper ship transporting tea from China in the 1860s, and takes up characters such as the young hero, Ian Grey and his father, Captain Grey, and Barnacle, the old sea dog, who had appeared in 'Tall Ships', a radio serial written by Burrows for the ABC. *Fight for Gold* (1966) is set in the goldfields of Ballarat. See **Eureka Stockade**. Burrows's novels were illustrated by Graham Wade. *Living in Australia* (1967) is a book of description and travel.

BURSTALL, TIM (1929–), born Stockton-on-Tees, UK, film-maker, came to Australia in 1937. *The Prize* (1962), with photographs by Gerard Vandenberg, was based on a film directed by Burstall. When Snowy wins a goat at the Show, it is stolen by Dan and Marcus, so Snowy enlists the help of Lisa and a rabbiter. *Sebastian and the Sausages* (1965) was based on *The Adventures of Sebastian Fox*, a film with puppets made by Peter Scriven, in the Eltham Film Series, illustrated with photographs by Vandenberg. Both films had music written by Dorien Le Galliene.

Bush, The. The bush has always been an important motif in Australian writing, and this is also true of children's books. In the nineteenth-century novels of 'Arthur Ferres', Richard Rowe, W.H. Timperley, E.B. Kennedy, William Howitt and others, the bush plays the role both of a heal-ing agent for those who have fallen on hard times, or been corrupted by the exi-gencies of city life, and a wilderness which must be tamed to the white man's will. Enduring hardships rarely exist, although temporary sufferings of drought, flood and fire serve to temper the steel of the pio-neers. See also **Boys**. The beauty of the landscape has always been appreciated. Mary Grant Bruce drew bush scenes with delight. *Robin* (1926) is set in Gippsland, Victoria, and Bruce describes the lush temperate rainforest country: 'Below them a great veil of maidenhair fern trailed downward to the stream that washed its fronds: above towered the tall brown shafts of tree-ferns, their spreading crests min-gling with sarsaparilla and clematis. Just across the stream stood a clump of Christmas-bush, already a starry mass of white. There were birds everywhere among the bushes, happy and unafraid; bell-birds chimed ceaselessly in the tree-tops far above them.' In William Howitt's *A Boy's Adventures in the Wilds of Australia: or, Herbert's Note-Book* (1854) Herbert comments more wryly, 'For ever and for ever it is the gum-tree, it is the gum-tree, gum-tree, and still gum-tree'. Bruce con-trasted the corrupt city with the purity of country life. The theme is further devel-oped in the books of Nan Chauncy. Badge's knowledge of the bush is far more important than the cleverness of Lance, or the town lore of Sammy. In Libby Gleeson's *Eleanor, Elizabeth* (q.v., 1984) the rural life provides Eleanor with a rite of passage. Libby Hathorn's Lara, a city child, in *Thunderwith* (1989) is not corrupted by the city, but the bush provides her solace.

For almost thirty years the bush domi-nated children's books. In Patricia Wrightson's *The Crooked Snake* (q.v., 1955), Joan Phipson's *It Happened One Summer* (q.v., 1957), Eleanor Spence's *The Summer In Between* (q.v., 1959) and Hesba Brinsmead's *Pastures of the Blue Crane* (q.v., 1964) the story is thrown into focus by its bush setting. Hesba Brinsmead in her 'Longtime' series (see **Longtime Passing**), Eleanor Spence in *Lillipilly Hill* (q.v.,

1963), Patricia Wrightson in *The Book of Wirrun* (see **The Ice is Coming**), Joan Phipson in *The Way Home* (1973) and Allan Baillie in *Riverman* (1986) have treated the bush as a presence which shapes the Australian experience. See also **Lost in the Bush**.

As novelists turned to urban settings, the role of the bush in children's books has changed. It is now more distant, a place for holidays, or to be preserved in its pristine state. In a reversal of the idea of the pioneer as conqueror, Mavis Thorpe Clark showed regret for the inroads into the primordial wilderness by the early settlers, in such novels as *The Brown Land was Green* (q.v., 1956) and *The Blue Above the Trees* (q.v., 1967). *The Blooding* (1987) by Nadia Wheatley, Jeannie Baker's *Where the Forest Meets the Sea* (q.v., 1987) and *Window* (q.v., 1991), Rodney McRae's *Cry Me a River* (1991) and Lilith Norman's *The Paddock* (1992) suggest an urgent need to conserve the great forests or their remnants. See also **Conservation**. With its elemental mysteries and unexpected dangers, the bush continues to be a potent setting for the novel. In Eleanor Nilsson's *The House Guest* (q.v., 1991), although the house provides the *raison d'être* for Gunna's actions, the presence of the surrounding bush is the necessary background to a resolution. Even in the most urban of novels, such as Frank Willmott's *Breaking Up* (1983), the bush is not far away, and its silence and timelessness puts the rush of the city in perspective.

Bush Christmas: a Film Story Retold (1947) by Mary Cathcart Borer and Ralph Smart, illustrated with stills, was a retelling of the 1947 film made by the British company Gaumont. It was directed by Ralph Smart, starring Neza Saunders as Neza, Helen Grieve as Helen, Chips Rafferty as Long Bill, Morris Unicomb as John, Michael Yardley as Michael, and Nick Yardley as Snow. Neza was an Aboriginal child cast in the role of faithful attendant.

Set in the Blue Mountains around Christmas time, the adventure involves five children tracking a group of thieves who have stolen valuable horses. The novel was reissued in 1980, illustrated by Nan McNab, with racist references to Aboriginal People removed. Neza no longer speaks in pidgin English, his cultural background is explained and is not seen as a lack of civilisation. Another film was made by Barron Films in 1983, directed by Henri Safran, with Nicole Kidman as Helen, Mark Spain as John and John Ewart as Bill. Neza was played by Manalpuy, and some of the earlier characters were omitted.

Bush Cobbers (1948) by 'Musette Morell', the pseudonym of Moyra Martin, illustrated by Edwina Bell, was Highly Commended in the 1948 Book of the Year Awards. Spiny the Echidna, Platypus and Possum set out to seek their fortune. They meet an angry spider, a rude dingo, form a popular bush band, and have other adventures, to find that home is best after all. In the style of Kenneth Grahame's *Wind in the Willows* (1908), *Bush Cobbers* is enriched with poems and songs and Bell's fine illustrations.

Bush Holiday (1948) by 'Stephen Fennimore' (Dale Collins), illustrated by Sheila Hawkins, was Highly Commended in the 1950 Book of the Year Awards. Martin, who views the world as though it were new, travels to 'Tangari' to stay with the Macleods. His naive city ways and 'Pommyness' are made much of, but with the help of his friend Penny he proves himself by accepting the teasing in good spirits and becoming as good a bushman as the rest. *Bush Voyage* (1950) by 'Stephen Fennimore', illustrated by Margaret Horder, was also Highly Commended in the same year. It continues the adventures of Martin and Penny, this time aboard a Murray riverboat, the *Bunyip. Sunset Plains* (1953) by 'Stephen Fennimore' and Dale Collins, illustrated by Horder, takes the children to a 200 000 acre sheep station in the outback. There are the usual hazards of bush life — flood, fire, snakes, and being lost, and a large population of native birds and animals. Martin remains remarkably cheerful in the face of continual insults and dreadful catastrophes.

Bush Voyage (1950) by 'Stephen Fennimore' was Highly Commended in the 1950 Book of the Year Awards. See **Bush Holiday**.

Bush Walkabout, see **Piccaninny Walkabout**

Bushfire. The bushfire has endured in children's fiction since the nineteenth century, a capricious enemy to be overcome if the land is to be mastered. As colonial life is usually presented as a great romp, full of excitement, danger and challenge with little real hardship, the bushfire, along with droughts, floods, bushrangers and marauding Aboriginal People, appears as only a temporary difficulty. Often it must be fought by the new chums as a part of their initiation into bush life. William Howitt in *A Boy's Adventures in the Wilds of Australia: or, Herbert's Note-Book* (1854) shows some of the power of the bushfire, but it is never a threat to the lives of the Macdonald family, who sensibly move to the protection of the creek at the first crackle of the flames. Howitt's description of the aftermath is dramatic: 'Huge blackened boughs of trees on the ground, still unconsumed, writhed up into the air like monstrous serpents which had perished in torment ... In that burnt and blackened solitude, not a living sound [greeted] their ears.' George Sargent in *Frank Layton: an Australian Story* (1865) respects the uncontrollable nature of a bushfire, but is able to distance himself enough from its terror to appreciate its majestic beauty. 'Notwithstanding its alarming character, the scene was magnificent.' Sargent diverges from his story to examine the cause of fire (which he says is negligence) and its beneficial effects. He

sees great advantages in fire, as it clears the bush for the settlers, but he acknowledges that an 'occasional loss of life' is the price extracted. Sargent is one of the few early writers to describe the plight of bush creatures during a bushfire. In Louis Becke's *The Settlers of Karossa Creek and Other Stories of Australian Bush Life* (1906) the effects of a bushfire are far more devastating than in Howitt or Sargent, and eleven families are left 'ruined and homeless' by a blaze which burns 20 000 acres. Nevertheless, the setback is only temporary. Soon after the drought breaks, knee-deep luscious grass covers the blackened earth, and the settlers rebuild as if the fire had never happened. In Laura Bogue Luffmann's *Will Aylmer: a Tale of the Australian Bush* (1909) the bushfire which sweeps past the Aylmer family's hut causes momentary concern, but once the surrounds are cleared, all is well. 'The fire raged all night, but the household slept secure.' The bushfire is presented as an adventure in 'Arthur Russell's' *Dream Isle: an Australian Story* (1926), where it is never threatening but serves as a test of manhood. Harry says, '"I'd like to be in the thick of it over there with the men beating back the flames." "Me too," added Percy. "Still, we might get it hot enough up here [on the haystack] to satisfy even us."' The firefighters remain unhurt. The women gallantly produce buckets of tea, and are able to bake batches of scones and cakes while the bushfire rages around them. The local fire brigade arrives in the nick of time to rout the fire, which has actually caused very little damage. '"All's well that ends well."' A picture-book in similar vein is Joan Woodberry's *Ash Tuesday* (1968), in which the schoolteacher makes a game of the children's escape from the bushfire. '"Now we are going to play a little game. I am going to squirt you all with the hose and then you are to take hands and run down to the creek and jump in."' Predictably, no one is hurt, although there is some danger, and all ends happily. Two early fantasies which used the bushfire are J.M. Whitfeld's *The Spirit of the Bushfire and Other Australian Fairy Tales* (1898) and Donald Macdonald's *At the End of the Moonpath* (1922). In the former, fire is personified as a being with destructive powers; in the latter, the bushfire is the enemy defeated by ghosts of World War I soldiers. In *The Luciflins and the Duck that Laid Easter Eggs* (1945) by R.V. West, illustrated by Chas. H. Crampton, 'wanton destructive little demons' cause bushfires, with the aid of 'careless humans'.

Later novels have depicted the bushfire more realistically, such as the Lintons's battle with a bushfire early in Mary Grant Bruce's *A Little Bush Maid* (1910), where Norah resourcefully saves prize sheep from fire. Bushfires frequently threaten 'Billabong'. In *Norah of Billabong* (1913) one is deliberately lit by Harvey, a resentful employee, in retaliation for his dismissal. A particularly graphic account of a fire is found in Bruce's *Robin* (1926). 'High above the trees [the fire] towered in rushing tongues and solid roaring sheets, while the hills shook and echoed with the noise of crashing timber.'

A menacing bushfire is the dragon of the title in *February Dragon* (q.v., 1965) by Colin Thiele. *Ash Road* (q.v., 1965) by Ivan Southall uses the panic of a fire threatening a town as the background to his analysis of two boys' growth to maturity. In James Preston's *The Ring of the Axe* (1968) Noel proves his skill and courage when a fire threatens the lives of Yvonne and Mr Carpenter. Their behaviour during the fire in *Bushfire* (1967) by Allan Aldous is a test of a Greek immigrant family's acceptance into a prejudiced rural community. Mavis Thorpe Clark in *Wildfire* (1973) imparts much sensible information about preparation, dress and behaviour during and after a bushfire, and the invaluable role of the volunteer rural fire brigade. Clark also uses the 'trial by fire' theme as her teenage protagonists have their squabbles, inadequacies and jealousies set aside when they have to fight

the fire to save themselves and others. In Margaret Paice's *Blue Ridge Summer* (1979), for younger readers, a bushfire is the final factor in the Gillis family's decision to remain in the city rather than settling in the Blue Mountains. In *Eleanor, Elizabeth* (q.v., 1984) by Libby Gleeson, Eleanor, Mike and Ken, injured and terrified, are able to escape the fire which is about to engulf them only through Eleanor's knowledge of a cave described in her grandmother's diary. In *Nightmare to Nowhere* (1980) by N.L. Ray (Nan Hunt) the fearful experience of the threatening fire as Bryony has to keep her two younger brothers safe in a cave is vigorously conveyed, as is the horror of its tragic results. Two novels describing bushfires which are lit deliberately are Betty Roland's *The Bush Bandits* (1966), in which native animal smugglers start a fire to cover their tracks, and in Mavis Thorpe Clark's *The Brown Land was Green* (q.v., 1956) Aboriginal People start a fire as retribution for the settler's destruction of their camp. The fire then becomes a means of ambushing the settlers.

In a rare lighthearted account of a bushfire, *Riverboat Bill Steams Again* (1985) by Cliff Green, Bill enlists the aid of the Bunyip, whose fiery breath is used to burn a firebreak which saves the town. Michael Foreman vividly illustrates the ferocity of a bushfire in his picture book *Panda and the Bushfire* (1986). The heroes, Panda and Lion, help to fight the fire and save the koalas. The dreadful fires which swept through Victoria and SA in 1983 inspired both *Jodie's Journey* (1988) by Colin Thiele and *Firestorm!* (1985) by Roger Vaughan Carr. In *Firestorm!* Ben witnesses the destruction of his town, and incidentally, recognises the fallibility of his father. In the Thiele novel, Jodie, who is crippled by arthritis and trapped in the house alone, shows her resourcefulness and courage when she saves her beloved horse Monarch.

Contemporary writers reiterate the impact of the bushfire: its devastation, the deaths it causes, its lasting effect on a community, and the tests of maturity which such a crisis brings.

Bushland and Seashore: an Australian Nature Adventure (1962), written and illustrated by Robin Hill, was Highly Commended in the 1963 Book of the Year Awards. Each chapter describes the experiences of this naturalist and painter as he explores the Australian beach, bush, swamps, streams and arid inland. His sensitive observations of animal and plant life in the field are accompanied by accurate paintings of lizards, gulls, possums, wombats, platypuses, birds and many other creatures. The index identifies them with their common and scientific names.

'BUSHMAN, JIM', see **SAYCE, CONRAD H.**

Bushrangers. Ned Kelly, Mad Dog Morgan, Captains Moonlight, Starlight and Thunderbolt plunder and pillage through the pages of Australian children's books. No nineteenth-century adventure story was complete without the young heroes outwitting dastardly bushrangers, such as Bracebridge Hemyng's *Ballarat Bill: or, Fighting the Bushranger* (1894) and James Skipp Borlase's *Blue Cap the Bushranger: or, The Australian Dick Turpin* (1885) and *Ned Kelly: the Ironclad Australian Bushranger* (1881). The bushranger fascinated the foreign adventure story writer. W.H.G. Kingston's Australian novels always include one episode where the protagonists are threatened, including surely the most loquacious bushranger of them all, in *The Diary of Milicent Courtenay: or, the Experiences of a Young Lady at Home or Abroad* (1873). No 'Bail up!' for him. After a page of parleying about whether the girls will send him the watches and rings which they have at home, he says: 'Come, come ladies ... give up your valuables, and swear that you will do what we require, or we will put our threats into execution; we do not

want to hurt you, but if you delay you will drive us to do what we had rather not, and as we have our horses at hand, before tomorrow morning you will be far away from this, where your friends must look hard to find you.' Helen Courtenay responds in like manner: 'You use a powerful argument to induce us to do what you require, but at the same time I am not frightened by your threats ... '

The American author Horatio Alger in *The Nugget Finders: a Tale of the Gold Fields of Australia* (1893) has his young protagonists captured by bushrangers on their way to Bendigo. 'Harry didn't need to be told that bushrangers in Australia correspond to bandits in Italy and highwaymen in other countries. Stories of their outrages were common enough, and among the dangers apprehended in a journey to and from the mines, that of meeting with a party of this gentry was perhaps the most dreaded.' G.A. Henty's *Among the Bushrangers* (?1923) is an extract from his longer work *A Final Reckoning: a Tale of Bush Life in Australia* (1886) and recounts the experiences of Reuben Whitney, who is attacked by the bushrangers. *Strike-a-Light the Bushranger and Other Australian Tales* (1972), edited by Marcie Muir, has as its title story an extract from *Roughing it in Van Diemen's Land* (1880) by Richard Rowe. In the story 'Strike-a-Light', a convict, escapes and turns to bushranging. *Mad Dan Morgan, Bushranger* (1976) by John Anthony King portrays the bushranger as a terrifying, looming figure. Judith Wright's *Range the Mountains High* (1962), loosely based on a story about Thunderbolt, presents a more sympathetic, and romantic, view of the bushranger. Dick Faulkner, or the Hawk, escorts Hugh, Joanna and their mother on their journey through the mountains outside Port Macquarie to join their father. Dick is brave and gentlemanly, and the children take many risks themselves to help him escape the police. Less sympathetic to the bushranger is Denys Burrows's *Stagecoach West* (1964), which depicts Dandy Jack, dressed like a gentleman but at heart a criminal, who threatens Kit and Vicky on the road from Bathurst to Sydney. The bushranger, with his English Adams revolver, has the advantage over the troopers, who are armed only with Navy Colts. Dal Stivens's colourful *The Bushranger* (1978), illustrated by Bruce Treloar, is told by Jack Daly from the point of view of the bushrangers themselves.

Still rash and occasionally violent, but now more a figure of fun, the image of the bushranger has been softened over the years. Stephen Axelsen's picture-book *The Oath of Bad Brown Bill* (q.v., 1978) is a satirical look at the exploits of a bushranger, as is Randolph Stow's *Midnite: the Story of a Wild Colonial Boy* (q.v., 1967). In *Ned a Leg End* (1984) by Susan Ferrier, Ned is born fully armed and trains at Mad Dog Morgan's academy. The picture-book is in cartoon style, humorously misleading. Paul Williams's *The Adventures of Black Ned* (1990) has a Ned Kelly look-alike who attacks the Billabong Bend Bank, but he is thwarted when his ingenious metal monster, based on the wooden horse of Troy, is destroyed. *Bossyboots* (1985), written and illustrated by David Cox, is about Abigail, who is able to rout Flash Fred the bushranger. *Dirty Dave the Bushranger* (1987) by Nette Hilton, illustrated by Roland Harvey, is about a bushranger whose snappy clothes become the envy of his victims.

Rungawilla Ranger (1986) by Dan Vallely, illustrated by Trish Hart, is a ballad about two animal bushrangers, Butch Echidna and Koala Kid, who terrify a Queensland town but are captured by Queensland Red. The real threat of the nineteenth-century bushranger no longer exists, and modern children's writers present the bushranger as bumbling and rather stupid, often easily overcome by a clever child. See also **Kelly, Ned**.

By the Sandhills of Yamboorah (1965) by Reginald Ottley, illustrated by Clyde Pearson, was Highly Commended in the 1966 Book of the Year Awards. Against a desert landscape, a lonely unnamed boy forms a friendship with the dour trapper, Kanga, enriched through a dog, Rags. The boy cares for Rags although he knows that eventually Rags must fulfil a destiny as the leader of Kanga's hunting kangaroo dogs. In *The Roan Colt of Yamboorah* (1966), illustrated by David Parry, Commended in the 1967 Book of the Year Awards, the boy learns to ride, and is given a delicate colt. The trilogy was completed with *Rain Comes to Yamboorah* (1967) illustrated by Robert Halles. The relationship between the solitary boy and the tough bushman is powerfully drawn, and the setting, the remote world of an outback station, is seen through the eyes of a tough, hard-working but sensitive boy.

C

Cabbage Patch Fib, The (1988) by Paul Jennings, illustrated by Craig Smith, won YABBA for Younger Readers in 1989. Chris discovers a green baby under a cabbage, and the responsibility nearly ruins him. He is too young to be a father, he claims, but the baby will not go away. He is mortified when all the girls and boys at school bring their cabbage-patch dolls and follow him around, and when he has to change the baby in class. In desperation he tries to return it to its cabbage, and is jubilant when its real mother snatches it back. Chris's father is told to tell Chris the truth about babies, which results in a search for storks. An avoidance of sex education is made into a funny story, as a popular lie is taken to its logical conclusion.

'CABLE, BOYD', the pseudonym of **ERNEST ANDREW EWART** (1878–1943), born India, was a newspaper correspondent in World War I and a contributor to the *Lone Hand* and the *Bulletin*. He wrote *Between the Lines* (1915), a popular collection of short stories of experiences in the front line during World War I. *Mates* (1929) is set in NZ. Slim and Chummie cross flooded rivers to bring a doctor to Old Anzac, impressing a local business man who contributes £1000 to the struggling farm. In *The Wrist-watch Castaways* (1929), illustrated by A.S. Merritt, Bosun and Jim survive on a desert island by using the components of Bosun's wrist-watch. They use bird skins for head coverings, and are calm and inventive at all times. Only when they are about to be rescued is there any hint of emotional behaviour, but they quickly pull themselves together and help in the

discovery of a treasure ship. See also **Adventure Stories**. Ewart also wrote a history of the P & O line.

CAIRNS, SYLVIA. For *Uncle Willie Mackenzie's Legends of the Goundirs* see **Aboriginal Dreaming Stories**.

Callie's Castle (1974) by Ruth Park, illustrated by Kilmeny Niland, was Highly Commended in the 1975 Book of the Year Awards. Callie's grandfather Cameron restores a cupola above the family's Sydney house for Callie to use as her retreat, and her stepfather, Laurens, sacrifices his beloved vintage car to finance the restoration. Their efforts to provide Callie with her own private place reassure her that her needs are recognised by a loving family. In *Callie's Family* (1988), also illustrated by Kilmeny Niland, Callie is disappointed when the 5-year-old Rolf accompanies Laurens to Denmark instead of her. The novel examines the vulnerability of her sister and brother, Gret and Dan, and Callie grows up a little. The development of character and the arguments and disappointments which make up family life are realistically portrayed.

CALVERT, JOHN, WILLIAM and **SAMUEL** were printers and engravers, the sons of the English artist Edward Calvert. John and William had emigrated to Adelaide in 1843, and Samuel joined them in 1848. In 1852, Samuel (1828–1913), born London, UK, arrived in Melbourne, where he illustrated Bonwick's *Notes of a Gold Digger* (1852). In 1854 Samuel and William were working together as 'Calvert Brothers, Engravers, Lithographers and Draftsmen', producing illustrated periodicals such as *The Australian Home Companion* and *Victoria Illustrated*. Another brother, John, was a collector, and together they brought out two series of picture-books. 'Calvert's Australian series of six-penny picture books, printed in colours', published around 1871, consisted of *The Young Australian's Alphabet*, *This is the Hut that Jack Built in Australia*, *Little Chinky Chow-Chow: the Boy that Ran Away* and *The Australian ABC Book (Large Letters)*. 'Calvert's Australian series of three-penny picture books printed in tint' were reproductions of the alphabet books only. Another picture-book by the Calverts was *Pictures of Australian Birds*, delicately illustrated, with descriptions and anecdotes about birds. *This is the Hut that Jack Built* has an Australian Jack shooting a hawk: 'And this is Jack, who with a shout,/Caught up his gun and rushing out,/Did shoot the hawk with talons red,/That took it into his wicked head,/To seize the jackass laughing loud,/As he carried the snake up near a cloud,/With his poisonous fangs, and glittering beak,/And hissing tongue and sinuous track.' See also **Alphabet Books**. Samuel Calvert suffered financial difficulties, for which he was jailed for a period, but in 1886 he had his own business, and was joined by his son, William Samuel Calvert, also an engraver. In 1904, Samuel returned to England, where he lived until his death.

Came Back to Show You I Could Fly (1989) by Robin Klein won the 1990 Book of the Year Award: Older Readers. Timid Seymour is staying with Thelma while his mother organises her life. During a particularly boring day he escapes over the fence and meets Angie: beautiful, exciting, free and deeply troubled. Seymour wants to believe the best of her, but is forced to finally confront her drug addiction. Klein treats the subject with subtlety. See also **Boys**.

CAMERON, 'TOBY' (BARBARA, Mrs ALAN CAMERON) has written three clever fantasies. In *The Magical Hat* (1943) a witch called Elvira and her seven daughters all have very large noses. *Our Funny Mummy* (1943) is a tortoise, who cares for three children while their mother is away. In its sequel, *Dora Dromedary, Detective* (1944), Dora emerges from a magic crossword puzzle, and sets off in search of wings.

CAMPBELL, DAVID (1915–79), born near Adelong, NSW, was a poet. His collection of short stories about childhood, *Evening Under Lamplight* (1959) describe the delights and puzzlement with which Janet and Billy view adult behaviour, seen through clear and unsentimental eyes. *Flame and Shadow* (1976) contains *Evening under Lamplight*.

CAMPBELL, ELLEN wrote *An Australian Childhood* (1892), an autobiographical account of her youth in a small outback town, Carcoar, NSW. She relates how she could repeat pages of *The Old Curiosity Shop* by heart, and the desperation with which she saved her pennies to buy *Martin Chuzzlewit* from a travelling pedlar. She catches leeches by standing in the creek to earn sixpence a dozen from the local doctor. The family buys an Aboriginal child, Tommy, for one shilling and ninepence to turn him into a 'Christian baby', and the children call him 'our pet'. Tommy contracts measles from Ellen's brother Ted, and dies in a week. *Twin Pickles: a Story of Two Australian Children* (?1897) offers a similar view of childhood. The escapades of Ted and Grace, 8-year-old twins, include their 'Kind Deeds Society', a source of various disasters. At one point they let Toss, the dog, off the leash. Toss kills a kitten and a sheep, and after a severe admonishment to Toss, the children bury the kitten under a tombstone which says: 'Kity Templeton Merdered by Tos.' Two very naughty children are drawn with wit.

Canberra, the capital city of Australia and the site of national monuments, appears in Michael Salmon's *The Monster That Ate Canberra: a Book for the Younger Generations of Canberra* (1972) and *Son of the Monster: a Story of Canberra in the Year 2022* (1973). Margaret Balderson's *A Dog Called George* (1975) refers to the National University, the 'solid blue mirror of Lake Burley Griffin', suburbs such as Dickson and Watson, and the view from Mt Ainslie. In Marjorie O'Dea's *Six Days Between a Second* (q.v., 1969) the Collard children are involved in stopping the basilisks poisoning the city, as they fight them under Lake Burley Griffin. The city's lavish buildings such as Parliament House, the National Gallery and the High Court building have not yet inspired an equivalent to E.L. Konigsberg's novel *From the Mixed-Up Files of Mrs Basil E. Frankweiler* (1967), set in New York's Metropolitan Museum of Art.

Candle for Saint Antony, A (1977) by Eleanor Spence was Highly Commended in the 1978 Book of the Year Awards. Justin's affluent, philistine family is contrasted with Rudi's poor but cultured mother. When a school excursion takes the boys to Austria, the friendship which has developed between them becomes more intense, so that Rudi asks Justin to stay on in Vienna with him. Their loving relationship is observed by Greg, who publicly jeers at what he sees as 'queer'. Justin returns to Sydney and Rudi remains in Vienna. The developing friendship, with its tentative physical overtones, raises questions of culture, religion and sexuality.

Cannily, Cannily (1981) by Simon French was Commended in the 1982 Book of the Year Awards. Trevor Huon begins to dislike the itinerant and temporary existence he leads with his parents, and longs for a settled home near the sea. When he arrives in a conservative town, he finds himself isolated. He attempts to establish himself in his new school by boasting that he can play rugby league football. In a bleak picture of the narrowness of a country town, Trevor is persecuted by a nasty teacher, Mr Fuller, and learns painfully that he must be himself. His parents, Kath and Buckley, recognise that Trevor needs stability. The novel takes the view that home is best if it is in a fixed place, like Eleanor Spence's *The Green Laurel* (q.v., 1963). See also **School Stories**; **Sport**.

CANTY, JOHN. For *The Christmas Book* see **Collections**.

Captain Cook, see **COOK**, Captain **JAMES**

'Captain Leslie', see **BORLASE, JAMES SKIPP**

Carcoola: a Story for Girls (1950) by Nourma Handford was Commended in the 1951 Book of the Year Awards. It traces the developing romance between Hope Macairn and Andrew Garrick, whose properties adjoin. At first, Hope's father disapproves of Andrew, his mother and twin half-sisters, but the stalwart Andrew wins him over by neighbourly acts and having served as a prisoner of war in Burma with Macairn's head stockman. Andrew's mother Lucy also charms the Macairns, as well as transforming a run-down cottage into 'an old Dutch interior', like a 'Rembrandt painting'. Some of these characters first appeared in *Three Came from Britain* (1945). *Carcoola* was followed by *Carcoola Adventure* (1952), which was Commended in the 1952 Book of the Year Awards. Hope and Andrew's romance proceeds, this time in the presence of Fran Grant, who is visiting 'Carcoola' before her marriage to Charles, a naval officer. Discussions of weddings and romantic interludes occupy most of the novel. Other 'Carcoola' novels are *Carcoola Holiday* (1953), illustrated by Frank Hodgkinson, in which Hope has a temporary setback through an accident and Fran is married, and *Carcoola*

Backstage: a Career Novel for Girls (1956), illustrated by Kate O'Brien, which concentrates on Marion Grant and the other girls she meets at the Academy of Dramatic Art, Sydney. Handford's view of adolescence is coloured by notions of good and bad taste and the idea that marriage is the desirable goal for girls.

CAREY, GABRIELLE, see *Puberty Blues*.

CARMODY, ISOBELLE (1958–), born Wangaratta, Victoria, journalist and novelist, has written *Obernewtyn* (1987) and its sequel, *The Farseekers* (q.v., 1990). See also **Science Fiction**. *Scatterlings* (1991) is another futuristic fantasy, in which Merlin awakes after an accident with no memory, and sets off through the alien landscape to find who she is.

CARNEGIE, DOROTHY, born Ballarat, Victoria. For *Kaka the Cockatoo* (1967) see **Aboriginal Dreaming Stories**.

CAROZZI, BARRY (1943–), teacher and reading specialist, has written *Kid Rotten's Book of Stories for Rotten Kids* (1980) and *Aunty Joyce and the Water Rat* (1980). *The Greatest Juggler in the World* (1972) is a collection of fairy stories. *The Last Voyage and The Cruel Sister* (1974) is a heroic saga and a tragic romance. *New Axe Handle and Other Stories* (1983) and *Cranckworth Bequest and Other Stories* (1987), compiled with Jennifer Hayes for the Australian Association for the Teaching of English, are collections of short stories for secondary school students.

CARR, ROGER VAUGHAN (1937–), born Melbourne, began his career as a writer in 1957. He has written for school magazines, television, films and newspapers, and over twenty novels for children. He has contributed to many reading schemes, such as Cheshire's 'Trend', Macmillan's 'Flag' and 'Orbit',

Ashton's 'Bookshelf' and Dove's Primary Education Social Studies Scheme. Carr has also published longer novels. In *Firestorm!* (1985) Ben stays away from school and only narrowly escapes the bushfires which sweep Whaler's Wash in a dramatic reconstruction of the Ash Wednesday fires and their impact on a township. See also **Bushfire**. In *The Clinker* (1989) the American boy, Rust, visits his great-grandparents. They resist any changes to their lives and apply pressure to Rust to conform with their ideas of how Sealer's Inlet should remain. *Piano Bay* (1991) is a historical novel about Jonah Hatton and his son Tam. Jonah intends to wreck a ship and plunder its cargo, but his plans go awry as Tam's values are affected by the survivors. *The Split Creek Kids* (1988), illustrated by June Joubert, was one of Ashton's 'Bookshelf' series, and was for younger readers. It recreates a small country primary school in the 1950s through a group of memorable characters and incidents, such as Peter, Nipper and Mary, Nipper's nest of mice and the knitting of Mary's scarf. The story of the Split Creek kids is continued in *Nipper and the Gold-Turkey* (1991), also illustrated by Joubert. This time the story centres on the family, rather than the school. Nipper hopes that the Christmas turkey, Fossicker, will peck up alluvial gold, but when the turkey's time comes, it is too much of a pet to eat. Carr has written short adventure stories and mysteries about surfing, minibikes, football and other topical subjects which have caught the interest of developing readers. He has explored the realisation by young people that parents are not infallible, and has used his own childhood and the coastal locations he loves to create a sense of place and time.

CARROLL, JANE (1948–) writes about everyday problems in children's lives. In *Normie* (1989), illustrated by Lucinda Hunnam, Kate is bullied by a gang of Year Four students at her school, but through Normie, she learns to defend herself against the world. Merry in *First Born* (1990) is resentful of her younger siblings until an accident brings her closer to her mother. *Goose* (1989), illustrated by Lorraine Hannay, is Phillip, who feels abandoned until he is drawn into a rural community. These are unsentimental stories of likeable, realistic children and adults.

CARROLL, LEWIS (1832–98) has inspired Australian artists and illustrators, such as Graeme Base, Charles Blackman, Christian Yandell, Nan Fullarton, Kevin Burgemeestre, Marjorie Hann, John Anthony King, and Pixie O'Harris, who have variously illustrated *Alice's Adventures in Wonderland*, *Jabberwocky*, and *The Hunting of the Snark*, and extracts from them. Charles Folkard's illustrations to *Songs from Alice: Alice in Wonderland & Through the Looking-Glass* (1978) recall Arthur Rackham. The poems are set to music by the composer and violinist Don Harper.

Carson, Clare is the bush nurse featured in Mary Elliott's *Clare Carson and the Gold Rush*, *Clare Carson and the Sheep Duffers*, *Clare Carson at Wilga Junction*, and *Clare Carson and the Runaways* (all 1970), all with the subtitle *Bush Nurse in the Australian Outback* and all illustrated by Rachel Tonkin. Clare successfully attends to the inhabitants of Wilga Junction. Her romance with a local squatter, Gavin McIntyre, is traced throughout the books, and the exploits of her flighty sister Meredith. Clare has chosen to live at Wilga Junction to save Meredith from bad influences in Sydney, where she was joining peace rallies. While events are plentiful, characterisation is lean. The local farm workers are crude and ill-educated, and the resident squattocracy live gracefully, and show all the initiative.

CARTER, DOROTHY was an English writer who contributed to the *Girl's Own Paper* in the 1930s and 1940s. Her stories had many Australian characters, frequently resourceful and adventurous girls. In *Jan Flies Down Under* (1948) Janice Burton is a flying instructor with her own flying school. She teaches Chick Newton, an Australian station-owner to fly, then she and her entourage fly his plane to Australia. The girls in the book are strong and daring, but the plot is weak, and the recommendation that they eat 'a coney' or 'a squirrel' for supper shows the author's ignorance of the setting. *The Cruise of the Golden Dawn* (1949) has Admiral Craythorne and his daughter Sally embark on a weekend cruise out of Sydney Harbour, organised to toughen Sally up. The yacht is wrecked, and the Admiral, Sally, and the rest of the crew, including Helen Martin, a sensible Wren, fall in with a group of Aboriginal People, where Sally learns to cook and be resourceful. The descriptions of Aboriginal life include the construction of skirts of humming bird feathers.

CARTER, ROBERT (1945–), born Junee, NSW, has been a patrol officer in Papua New Guinea, a private detective and a teacher. His work is forceful, inventive, and often chilling. In *The Sugar Factory* (1986) the child whom Harris is babysitting dies. The novel examines how the boy deals with his devastating sense of guilt. *The Pleasure Within* (1987) is a collection of short stories in which traumatised children respond to an unforgiving society.

CASWELL, BRIAN (1954–), born Flintshire, Wales, came to Australia at the age of 12. *Merryll of the Stones* (q.v., 1989) was his first book for children. After this first book, a time-slip fantasy, Caswell has moved towards a more interactive mode, with multiple narrators, fragmented narrative, and shifts in character. *A Dream of Stars* (1991) is a short story collection, with thirteen stories ranging from the futuristic to modern realism, including 'And be one traveller', which has an intriguing psychological twist. *A Cage of Butterflies* (1992) is a science fiction novel in which Myriam and the Babies, a group of five telepathic children, are threatened with experimentation. Caswell's narrative style takes into account the sophisticated demands of a generation used to modern media techniques. Caswell says of his work: 'Plot development is cinematic; scenes, perspectives — and narrators — shift continuously … '.

CATO, NANCY (1917–   ), born Adelaide, poet and art critic, was a journalist for the *Adelaide News*, and later edited the children's page of the *Adelaide Mail*. She moved to Queensland in the 1960s and became active in the conservation movement, an interest taken up in *Nin and the Scribblies* (1976), illustrated with photographs by Stanley Breeden and set at Granite Bay, on the coast of Queensland. Nin finds tiny people under the bark of the scribbly gums threatened by the local council. Cato also has written books for adults.

Cats, The (1976) by Joan Phipson, which was Highly Commended in the 1977 Book of the Year Awards, is a novel of suspense, with a hint of the supernatural. After their parents win the lottery, Willy and Jim are kidnapped by Kevin and Socker. Willy has an empathy with cats and a foreknowledge of the future. At the bush hide-out to which they are taken, Socker brutally kills a kitten. The other feral cats turn on the kidnappers, who are forced to look to Willy for protection. There is a chilling build-up of tension which is maintained to the end, and the suggestion that Willy and the cats are actually in league.

CATTERWELL, THELMA (1945–   ), born Melbourne, has written two stories on the need to care for the world of nature. *Sebastian Lives in a Hat* (1985), illustrated by Kerry Argent, traces the life of a baby wombat orphaned by a road

accident, who finds the security of his mother's pouch in an old brown hat. *Aldita and the Forest* (1988), delicately illustrated by Derrick Stone, is the life story of a Gippsland butterfly, and calls for the conservation of what remains of the great forests.

CAWTHORNE, WILLIAM ANDERSON (1824–97) came to Australia in 1841, opened a school in Adelaide, became headmaster of Pulteney Grammar School, and later established a music warehouse and stationery business. His concern for the Aboriginal People inspired a commentary on their customs, *Manners and Customs of the Natives*, which was first published in 1927, thirty years after his death. He wrote and illustrated the black-and-white picture-book *Who Killed Cockatoo?* (?1860), based on the rhyme 'Who killed Cock Robin?'. A facsimile was issued in 1978. It was republished in 1988 with illustrations by Rodney McRae.

CAZALY, MERLEANNE (1912–   ), born Melbourne, has written the historical novels *Riding for Gold* (1973, revised 1981) and *The Squatter-Man* (1980), both illustrated by her daughter, Suzanne Massee. *Riding for Gold* is set in 1852, and describes how Mike and Oofa Sinclair undertake an adventurous journey to the Mt Alexander gold-diggings. *The Squatter-Man* is set fifteen years later, in 1867, when Susan, her parents and seven brothers and sisters select land near the Murray. The battle between squatters and selectors, and the hard work involved in pioneering, is brought to life.

CENTER, RUS (EDMUND GEORGE ALEXANDER CENTER) (1918–   ), born Melbourne, left school at an early age, travelled extensively and has taught in the Public Service. His firm friendships with Aboriginal People in Darwin and Ceduna inspired him to write *Nunga*

(1985), illustrated by Margaret Senior, which covers fifteen years in the life of the Bunurong people of the Mornington Peninsula, Victoria. Nunga and her friend Yamali confront tribal laws at the time of the arrival of Europeans. A present-day Aboriginal girl features in *Melissa's Bunyip* (1989). *If Wishes Were Tigers* (1987), illustrated by Terry Denton, strikes a lighter note, as Grandpa finds his place in the family by saving Mum and Katherine from being urinated on by an old tiger at the zoo.

Centre for Children's Literature was set up in 1991 by the University of SA to facilitate publishing, undertake research, promote children's literature and raise its academic profile. An early publication was *Young Adult Fiction: Yesterday, Today and Tomorrow* (1991) by Roxanne Kelly-Kobes.

CHADWICK, DORIS (1899–1979), born Grafton, NSW, was assistant editor of the NSW *School Magazine* from 1924 to 1950, and editor from 1950 to 1959. During her time at the *School Magazine*, Chadwick was a major influence on the high quality and innovative nature of the journal. For her three novels about early Sydney, *John of the Sirius* (1955), *John of Sydney Cove* (1957), and *John and Nanbaree* (1962), see *John of the Sirius*.

CHAFFEY, M. ELLA (b.1860), born Toronto, Canada, was the wife of Charles Chaffey, who came from California in 1888 to manage the property established by his brothers at Renmark. Renmark is the town in *The Youngsters of Murray Home* (1896), illustrated by A.J. Johnson, although the childhood which is described is within a domestic rather than a particularly rural setting. Olga, Hubert, Ralph, Katrina, Dorothy and Bertram Olsen lead a comfortable existence in a large home near the Murray. The novel is a documentary of their lives, including Christmas, snakes, cooking disasters when their parents are away, and fishing. Chaffey also wrote children's books on her return to Canada, including *The Adventures of Prince Melonseed* (1916).

Change the Locks (1991) by Simon French was an Honour Book in the 1992 Book of the Year Awards: Older Readers. Steven lives with his mother and half-brother on the edge of a country town. He has vague memories of a terrible experience in his earlier years, which are confirmed during a trip to Sydney. His trauma is transferred to a fear that his baby brother may suffer a similar fate. The sensitive 10-year-old Steven's relationships with his mother, brother and others, are drawn with empathy.

Changelings of Chaan, The (1985) by David J. Lake was Commended in the 1986 Book of the Year Awards. John Hastings is taken to the South East Asian kingdom of Chaan, where his mother is working as a doctor. Through Ajo, his astrological twin, John finds that he can move between different worlds, as Varuna, the time-traveller. He saves Andara from invaders and Chaan from foreign exploitation, but his most important lesson is to set aside individualism in favour of living in harmony with all people.

CHANT, BARRY (1938–), born Adelaide, is a teacher and cleric. *Spindles of the Dusty Range* (1975), *Spindles and the Eagles* (1976), *Spindles and the Wombat* (1978), *Spindles and the Orphan* (1980), *Spindles and the Children* (1983) and *Spindles and the Sleepy Lizard* (1989) are all illustrated by Lorraine Lewitzka. See **Religion**.

CHAPMAN, ERNEST, see '**HATFIELD, WILLIAM**'

CHAPMAN, FRANCES. For *The Witty Wizard of Warrandyte: a Magical Hour in Fairyland* see **Fairies**.

CHAPMAN, JEAN, born Sydney, has worked for twenty-five years as a scriptwriter for ABC schools' broadcasts and television programs, including 'Playschool' and 'Kindergarten of the Air'. She has contributed to the NSW *School Magazine*, and has provided material for many reading schemes. Her book about a loveable cat, *The Wish Cat* (q.v., 1966), brought her early recognition, although *Amelia Muddle* (1963), illustrated by Adye Adams, had shown her talent. Amelia is always getting into trouble because she is too impetuous and never listens. Chapman went on to write books for young readers, such as *Sandy the Cane Train* (1966), illustrated by Walter Cunningham; *The Someday Dog* (1968), with photographs by Dean Hay; *Cowboy* (1967), illustrated by John Watts; *Wombat* (1969), also illustrated by Watts; and *Do You Remember What Happened?* (1969), illustrated by Edward Ardizzone.

Chapman has written a series of books containing stories, poems, folk tales and creative activities for children in *Tell Me a Tale* (1975), *Tell Me Another Tale* (q.v., 1976), both illustrated by Deborah and Kilmeny Niland, with selections from these in *Tell Us Tales: Stories, Songs, Verses and Things to Do* (1978); *Mostly Me* (1989), illustrated by Shirley Peters; *The Sugar-Plum Christmas Book* (q.v., 1977), and *The Sugar-Plum Song Book* (1977), both illustrated by Deborah Niland. *Pancakes and Painted Eggs: a Book for Easter and all the Days of the Year* (1981), illustrated by Kilmeny Niland, and *Haunts & Taunts: a Book for Hallowe'en and All the Nights of the Year* (1983), illustrated by Deborah Niland, both with song settings by Margaret Moore, have stories, activities, verses and songs. *Cockatoo Soup* (1987), illustrated by Rodney McRae, published at the time of the Bicentenary, has stories and poems from a wide range of cultures, from Aboriginal to Japanese, representing the multicultural nature of Australian society. *Stories to Share* (1983), chosen by Chapman and illustrated by Sandra

Laroche, is a collection of thirty-one stories for reading aloud, such as Letitia Parr's 'A Mouse called Mouse', Michael Salmon's 'Don't do that, Mark!' and Ruth Park's 'The Cotton Cat'. Her interest in the variety and richness of cultures is seen in *The Tall Book of Tall Tales* (1985), illustrated by Deborah Niland, which contains thirty-one tall stories from various cultures. *Little Billy Bandicoot: Rhymes and Songs for Australian Children* (1991), illustrated by Sandra Laroche, is a rich collection of over two hundred rhymes and songs, from Christina Rossetti to Trad.

The Great Candle Scandal (1982), illustrated by Roland Harvey, is a verse story in which the candlemaker and his apprentice must make a candle as high as the ceiling. *My Mum's Afraid of Lions* (1989), illustrated by Astra Lacis, has six stories about Kate's life at home and school. *Supermarket Thursday: Six Stories* (1977), illustrated by Astra Lacis, contains stories about the daily adventures of Anne and Tom. Single stories which Chapman has retold or written are *Double Trouble: an Old Chinese Tale* (1984), illustrated by Maya Winters, in which Mr Huk-Tuk finds a magic pot which doubles anything or anybody which is put into it; *The Terrible Wild Grey Hairy Thing* (1986), illustrated by Vicky Kitanov, an adaptation of a traditional Danish story, in which a sausage grows into something horrible until a dog saves the village by eating it; and *Blue Gum Ark* (1988), illustrated by Sue O'Loughlin, a version of the Noah's Ark story using Australian animals in a counting rhyme. She has written stories about animals, such as the stray cat in *Moon-Eyes* (1978), illustrated by Astra Lacis, *Koala's Tail* (1982), illustrated by Carolyn Bull, and *Pine-Cone Possum* (1981), illustrated by Astra Lacis.

Chapman has also written informational books, such as *Beware, Take Care: a Safety Manual for Kids* (1977), illustrated by Aart van Ewijk, which covers every danger from hot water to bushfires. *Capturing the Golden Bird: the Young Hans Christian*

Andersen (1987), illustrated by Sandra Laroche, is a biography of Hans Christian Andersen and a selection of his stories. Chapman's lively and inviting collections of stories from around the world, combined with poetry, music, and games, have offered enjoyment and pleasure to nearly two generations of readers.

'CHARLES, HAROLD' was the pseudonym of **ROBERT CHARLES A. FAWCETT** (1885–1960), a Melbourne postmaster, president of the Henry Lawson Memorial and Literary Society from 1953 to his death, and the author of a poem to Lawson on the occasion of the unveiling of his monument in Footscray Park, Melbourne: 'Wistful his eyes seem to say "Henry knows,/Stick to your mates, you will reap as you sow."' He wrote *Australian Nursery Rhymes and the Playlet "Friends of the Bush"* (1945), illustrated by Betty and Esther Paterson. *New Nursery Rhymes* (1946), illustrated by 'Armstrong' in an attractive large format, contains some of the poems in the earlier book. His verse is simple, but appealing: 'A carrot, a pumpkin, an onion, a pea/All grow in my garden for somebody's tea./Now, who do you think that someone can be;/A lady, a gentleman? No; just me.' See also **Nursery Rhymes**. Fawcett also wrote *The Melody of the Garden* (1953), a collection of poems with an introduction by Dame Mary Gilmore. Fawcett was a friend of John Shaw Neilson, J.C. Davies of the 'Bread and Cheese Club' and Kate Baker.

CHARLWOOD, DONALD ERNEST (1915–), born Melbourne, was a navigator in the RAAF during World War II, an experience which he recounted in *No Moon Tonight* (1956). Like most of his books, *All the Green Year* (1965) was not written as a children's book, but it is a convincing novel about family and community in the 1930s, seen through the eyes of 14-year-old Charlie. It has been widely read and enjoyed by children and adults, and was made into a six-part television serial in 1980 by the ABC. The script was written by Cliff Green; it was directed by Douglas Sharp and featured Alan Hopgood, Alwyn Kurts and Monica Maugham. His book for children about air traffic control is *Take Off to Touchdown* (1967).

CHAUNCY, NAN (NANCEN BERYL) (1900–70), born Westerham, Kent, UK, emigrated to Tasmania in 1912 where her family set up an orchard forty kilometres north of Hobart, now called Chauncy Vale. She began her Tasmanian stories with *They Found a Cave* (1948), illustrated by Margaret Horder, an adventure story about children who live in a cave rather than stay with bad-tempered Ma Pinner. It was made into a successful film by the Tasmanian Department of Film Production, directed by Andrew Steane, the only feature film made in Australia in 1962. In *World's End was Home* (1952), illustrated by Shirley Hughes, Cobby and Dallie set off with Gran on a holiday to Tasmania, where the children find relatives. In *A Fortune for the Brave* (1954), illustrated by Margaret Horder, Huon Trivett leaves his houseboat to travel to Tasmania to find gold which he believes his father had left on an island off the east coast. There is no gold, but the prospect of bee-keeping at the novel's conclusion, and Huon has gained confidence and formed a strong relationship with his cousins. In *Half a World Away* (1962), illustrated by Annette Macarthur-Onslow, the Lettengar family set out for Tasmania in 1911, only to find that the house they were to occupy has been burnt down. Their mother, Momps, prefiguring Liddle-Ma, rallies the family and they quickly make a new life for themselves. In 1990 the novel was made into a television series of four fifty-minute episodes, directed by Marcus Cole and written by Shane Brennan and Ross Dimsey. *Tiger in the Bush* (q.v., 1957) introduced Badge Lorenny (q.v.) and his family, who appeared again in *Devils' Hill* (q.v., 1958) and *The Roaring 40* (q.v., 1963). *Tangara: 'Let Us set off Again'* (q.v., 1960) was the first of her two novels about the Tasmanian Aboriginal People, the other being *Mathinna's People* (q.v., 1967). *High and Haunted Island* (q.v., 1964) looks at an isolated religious group. *The Skewbald Pony* (1965), illustrated by David Parry, is one of the 'Salamander' series published by Thomas Nelson for early readers, aimed at an English audience. The setting is an outback station, complete with heat, dust, drought and School of the Air for Carrie. *Panic at the Garage* (1965), illustrated by Peter Lloyd, is in the 'Flamingo' series. *Lizzie Lights* (1968), illustrated by Judith White, is set on one of the remote lighthouses which dot the Tasmanian coast. Lizzie is afraid of the outside world until holidays with an aunt in country Victoria, and an accident, take her to Melbourne. In her last novel, *The Lighthouse Keeper's Son* (1969), illustrated by Victor G. Ambrus, Chessy and his family move from Maatsuyker Island to Queensland, then again to another lighthouse island. She has also written nonfiction, such as *Beekeeping* (1967), in Oxford's 'Life in Australia' series.

Nan Chauncy is credited with changing the direction of Australian children's books. She was the first Australian children's writer to express the movement towards a greater realism which can be identified in other English language children's books of the period. Her ability to create characters with strong internal lives, her attempt to represent Tasmanian Aboriginal People with sympathy and dignity, and her commitment to the natural beauty of the environment opened the way for succeeding authors, such as Patricia Wrightson, Eleanor Spence, Joan Phipson and Mavis Thorpe Clark.

CHEESMAN, LUCY (1881–1969) was a naturalist. Her books for children on the life of plants and insects include *Everyday Doings of Insects* (1924), *The Growth of Living Things: a First Book of Nature Study* (1932), *Camping Adventures in New Guinea* (1948), *Camping Adventures on Cannibal Islands* (1949) and *Look at Insects* (1960). *Landfall the Unknown: Lord Howe Island 1788* (1950) is a novel which describes the Robinson Crusoe-like existence of a man and three children. It was based on the records of the botanist John Price, who was inadvertently abandoned for fourteen months on Lord Howe Island in 1788, with his daughter Susannah and two boys, Dicky and Matt. *Marooned in Du-Bu Cove* (1950), illustrated by Jack Matthew, is a similar story of isolation, set on a coral reef in Papua New Guinea.

Cheshire, F. W. was a bookselling firm. In 1940 it appointed Andrew Fabinyi as a director, with the intention of expanding into publishing. Fabinyi served in the Australian Army from 1942, then returned to Cheshires in 1945. During the next twenty-four years Fabinyi was responsible for the development of a notable publishing list, including Alan Marshall, Robin Boyd, Joan Lindsay, Bruce Dawe and Judah Waten. It expanded into educational publishing, producing school texts. Cheshires was sold in 1969 to the Hamlyn group.

CHEYNE, IRENE (?–1951) wrote *A Magic Hour With the Leaf Fairies: Russet, Gold and Green* (1933) and *The Golden Cauliflower* (1937), illustrated by Jean Elder. Quincey's dull life is relieved when he discovers that by wearing a wonderful brooch he is able to understand the language of the insects, birds and animals. *The Golden Cauliflower* was placed first on Hutchinson's London Christmas list in 1937. *The Little Blue Mountain* (1944), *Dinnie, Binnie, and Jinks* (1945), *Packman's Pipe* (1946) and *David of the Stars* (1942) are also fantasies. In the first, Denny finds a talking pie which leads him into adventures with Constable Nabbemquickly, the Rabbit, Mary-Might-Have-Been and others in the land beyond the mountain. In the second the three children help Mr Doll to fight the goblins; in the third, Daffy meets Peter the Packman, who carries gifts for children; and in the last, David is left in charge of a curiosity shop where magical happenings occur. Cheyne wrote *Annette of River Bend* (1941) and *Annette & Co.* (1942) for older readers. In a confusing catalogue of relationships, Annette Linney discovers she is Annette Heriot, born Annette Dalvey, before she is adopted by a wealthy family. In *Annette & Co.* she arranges the same fortune for a young friend, Odd Wattier, by identifying his real father. Annette is always cheerful in adversity, is able to win over any heart, no matter how world-wearied, and is forever interfering in other people's lives, always for their own good.

Childhood in Bud and Blossom (1900) was a Souvenir Book of the Children's Hospital Bazaar, Melbourne, compiled and edited by Joshua Lake in a beautifully produced luxury edition published by the Atlas Press. It contained poems and stories, including a story by Ada Cambridge, and Donald MacDonald's *At the End of the Moonpath*, with illustrations by Arthur M. Boyd, E. Phillips Fox, Frederick McCubbin and other artists and writers.

Children of the Dark People: an Australian Folk Tale (1936) by Frank Dalby Davison, in 1946 subtitled 'An Australian Story for Young Folk', was illustrated by Pixie O'Harris. Nimmitybel and Jackadgery are separated from their people and pursued by the Evil witchdoctor, Adaminaby. They are befriended by the good spirits of the bush: the Spirit of the Billabong, Grandfather Gumtree, the Spirit of the Mist, Mickatharra, the Brumby Boy, and others. Finally they meet Old Mr Bunyip who leads them back home. See also **Aboriginal People in Children's Fiction**.

Children of the Desert (1968) by Phyl and Noel Wallace, illustrated with photographs, was Commended in the 1969 Book of the Year Awards. String games, storytelling, drawing, spear making, hunting and digging for food are described in this account of the children of the Pitjantjatjara people. The rich and busy life of the group is shown in a series of anecdotes about individual children, and the atmospheric photographs show the grandeur of the Musgrave Ranges. A new edition published in 1973 contained a record of what had happened to the children in the interim.

Children's Book Council of Australia began in NSW as a response to the Children's Book Council of America's attempt to start an International Children's Book Week in 1945. The Victorian Council began in 1954 at the initiative of the National Council of Women, and the CBC held its first national meeting in 1959. The main objective of the CBC is the encouragement of children's reading. Other activities include promoting the efforts of writers and illustrators through the annual Book of the Year Awards; exhibitions and activities during Children's Book Week; supporting children's library services; and the reviewing of children's books. *Reading Time*, a major source of reviews, is the official journal. The CBC has produced collections of short stories by Australian writers, such as *Dream Time* (1989), illustrated by Elizabeth Honey, and *Into the Future* (1991), illustrated by Lorraine Hannay, both edited by Toss Gascoigne, Jo Goodman and Margot Tyrrell. Archives and records are kept in Canberra at the Lu Rees Archives Collection. In 1973 the Literature Board of the Australia Council provided a grant to establish a national secretariat. In 1988, Myer-Grace Brothers guaranteed money for prizes and administration for five years.

Children's Choice Awards for the most popular books are given in seven States and Territories of Australia. See **BILBY** (Queensland), **COOL** (ACT), **CROW**

(SA), **KOALA** (NSW), **KROC** (NT), **WAYRBA** (WA), **YABBA** (Victoria).

Children's Hour, The. The first magazine for children in Australia, edited by A.J. Hartley, then Director-General of SA education, was produced by the SA Education Department in 1899. It included stories and poems from Adam Lindsay Gordon, Dorothea Mackellar and other Australian material, as well as the traditional English fare. *The Children's Hour* ceased publication in 1963.

Children's Library Guild of Australia, The was an attempt initiated by the publisher, Lloyd O'Neil (1928–92), during the 1960s, to encourage the production of high-quality material for young readers. An advisory committee of librarians and educators was established in association with Cheshire, Jacaranda and O'Neil's own Lansdowne Press, with Professor G.S. Browne, Barbara Buick, Catherine King, Joyce Fardell, Joyce Boniwell (Saxby) and Cynthia Paltridge on the panel. Books were made available on subscription, with reinforced binding for school and public libraries. Titles included Enid Moodie Heddle's *How Australian Literature Grew* (1962), Joyce Nicholson's *A Mortar Board for Priscilla* (1963), Robin Boyd's *The Walls Around Us* (1962), Robin Hill's *Bushland and Seashore* (q.v., 1962), Judith Wright's *Range the Mountains High* (1962) and Frank Kellaway's *The Quest for Golden Dan* (1962).

Children's Peace Literature Award is presented biennially by the Psychologists for the Prevention of War to recognise authors who through their work promote the peaceful resolution of conflict at the global, local or interpersonal level. **1987** Gillian Rubinstein *Space Demons* (q.v., 1986); **1989** Victor Kelleher *The Makers* (1987); **1991** Libby Gleeson *Dodger* (1990).

Children's Treasure House Book and Toy Museum. Founded in 1983, this private museum was developed by Hilarie Lindsay in Leichhardt, Sydney. It is housed in seven rooms attached to the toy factory founded by the Lindsay family in 1930. The collection includes dolls, toy bears, other toys and artefacts, such as moneyboxes and masks, and many items of Victoriana.

Chinese. The Chinese provided curiosity value only in the children's books of the nineteenth century, often as objects of fun or derision. Almost all reference to them was in the context of the bush or the goldfields, despite the fact that there were Chinese enclaves in the major cities. In an early allusion to the Chinese miners, Richard Rowe's *The Boy in the Bush* (1869) describes how they are taunted by a group of local boys, 'pelting the Chinamen and taking sly pulls at the dangling tails whenever they got the chance'. *Bluecap the Bushranger: or, the Australian Dick Turpin* (1885) and *Daring Deeds and Tales of Peril and Adventure* (1894) by James Skipp Borlase have Chinese characters on the goldfields, referred to as 'the butt of all practical jokers who no more consider his feelings than if he were a wooden puppet'. *Tarragal: or, Bush Life in Australia* (1897) by E.T. Hooley touches on the movement of Chinese immigrants from SA to the Victorian fields. 'Arthur Ferres', in *His First Kangaroo: an Australian Story for Boys* (1896) says that the Chinese are 'civil, cleanly and sober, and you can always place dependence on [them].' Nonetheless, one of his characters, Archie, curses the 'heathen Chinee'.

Twentieth-century books, on the whole, present a more tolerant picture of the Chinese. In *The Gold-Stealers: a Story of Waddy* (1901) by Edward Dyson, there is a small community of Chinese, who live an apartheid existence two miles from the town, making a precarious living by fossicking and growing vegetables. The thefts

Salt River Times (1980) by William Mayne.
Illustrator: Elizabeth Honey

in the town are blamed on them, providing the townspeople with an excuse for not taking any action. The laugh is more on the residents of Waddy than on the Chinese. In *Fortunatus: a Romance* (1903) by J.H. White a central role is given to the Chinese in an adventure story about the goldfields. Their victimisation is made very clear, and there is also an account of the violence which they suffered at the hands of other miners. *The Hidden Nugget: a Story of the Australian Goldfields* (1909) by Alexander Macdonald has incidental pictures of Chinese miners, but also, for the first time, Chinese as cooks, shop-owners, and traders. *Will Aylmer: a Tale of the Australian Bush* (1909) by Laura Bogue Luffmann has the first Chinese hero, Ah Ling. Ah Ling is presented with dignity and individuality, and saves the children and the homestead from a bushfire. *The Invisible Island: a Story of Far North Queensland* (1910), also by Alexander Macdonald, is set in northern Australia. The general picture of Chinese follows the racial stereotyping: the bad Chinese are sinister and threatening and the innocent are peculiar. However, one Chinese character, Quong Lee, although not a hero, is drawn with individuality, perhaps because he has been educated at Edinburgh University, and is a government agent. In Tarella Quin Daskein's *Freckles* (1910) Lee See, the gardener, is

clever enough to reappear under another name after banishment from the station, claiming that he is not Lee See — he only looks like him! His streak of wickedness makes him a likeable character. Ethel Turner has a Chinese character, Hop Ling, in *Fair Ines* (1910). Although his speech and his description follow the stereotype, he shows strength of character and refuses to be bullied by the unpleasant Mrs Wharton. The Chinese gardener in Mary Grant Bruce's Billabong books is Lee Wing, who is transformed from a comic stereotype in the early novels to become a 'trusty' in the station hierarchy, an equal of Murtee and Brownie. In *Billabong Riders* (1942) Norah admonishes a visitor for calling Lee Wing 'your old Chow', saying, 'I'd rather you said Chinese or just Lee Wing. We have a great respect for our Lee Wing, you see.'

More contemporary works have provided a new approach to Chinese characters, and have included Chinese children as well as adults. *The Chinese Boy* (1973) by David Martin is an account of the massacre of the Chinese on the goldfields, reminding us of real historical incidents. Ho, the young hero of the book, is portrayed as a participant in a rich cultural heritage, yet despised and victimised by the non-Chinese. Terry Ho, in *Nicking Off* (1975) by Judith Crabtree, is the victim of racist taunts because he happens to be Chinese, but the main theme of the novel is the possibility of a nurturing role for a boy. In *Salt River Times* (1980) by William Mayne, there is a Chinese boy, Joe, Mr Young and Mr Lee, and other Chinese market gardeners. Joe is abused by Ivan as a 'dirty Chinamen'. Although the jibe offends Joe and he and his friends decide to 'get' Ivan, the central issue of *Salt River Times* is that Australian society is multicultural, and while racist remarks are made, stereotyping has no place. Rusty in *The Rusty Kee Adventures* (1986) by Garry Hurle is the illegitimate son of a Chinese gold-prospector. His Chinese origins are of little consequence, except to provide the opportunity for villains to vent their spite. Allan Baillie's *The China Coin* (1991) is set in China. Leah is gradually drawn to an understanding of the Chinese side of her dual cultural identity.

The long-standing Chinese presence in Australia has ensured their inclusion in children's books from the nineteenth century to the present, and their treatment in these novels has ranged from abuse to an acknowledgement of their contribution to Australian life.

CHRISTIE, CONNIE (CONSTANCE MARY, Mrs PEMBERTON) (1908–89) was a designer working for a retail store, G.J. Coles, when she was encouraged to produce children's books during World War II. Drawing on European fairy-tales, Christie wrote around seven books a year for seven years, including an annual each year, such as *The Connie Christie Annual* (1947) or *Sunny Days Annual* (1948). Titles include *The Adventures of Pinkishell* (1939), her first book. Other books produced during the 1940s include *Hansel and Gretel* (n.d.), *Mother Goose* (1945), *Wee One: from Hans Andersen's 'Thumbelina': the Story of a Fairy Child who was no Bigger than Your Thumb* (n.d.), *The Fairy Mermaid* (1946), *The Queen of Hearts* (n.d.), *Little Red Riding Hood* (n.d.), *Puss in Boots* (n.d.), *Favourite Tales* (n.d.), *The Magic Shell* (n.d.), *The Magic Bucket* (n.d.), *Little Rhymes, Mary Lou in Candyland, Mops: a Fairy Story, Nursery Rhymes* (all 1945), *Animal Nurseryland* (1946), *The Fairy Knight* (1948), *Sally's Sea Party* (1948) and many other nursery rhymes and fairy stories. Her alphabet and counting books include *Let's Count* (1945), *Nursery Numbers* (1948) and *Number Fun* (n.d.). Other fairy books are *The Flower Babies, Happy Days, Jill's Bubble, The Fairy Balloon, Bunty's Pixies, Baby Bunting Comes to Town* and *Susan*. Her colourful illustrations are in the commercial tradition.

Churinga Tales: Stories of Alchuringa — the Dream-Time of the Australian

Aborigines (1950) by Erle Wilson, illustrated by Sally Medworth, was Commended in the 1951 Book of the Year Awards. Introduced as a series of stories told to a boy fascinated with Aboriginal life, it recounts the origins of people, language, animals, fire, and other phenomena, based on the traditions of various Aboriginal peoples, such as the Aranda. The sources are obscure, although the book represents Aboriginal life with integrity and suggests some of the complexity and diversity of the culture.

Cinderella Dressed in Yella, see **Folklore**

CLAIRE, STEPHANIE (1944–) has written *The Painted Statue* (1987), illustrated by Salvatore Zofrea from the statue of Saint Sebastian. The statue was a gift from the people of Cerami, Sicily, to the church at Earlwood, Sydney. The statue disappears, and Danny and Adam have twenty-four hours to find it before it must be placed in the church. *Three Golden Rainbows* (1989), also illustrated by Salvatore Zofrea, is a picture-book on how the child Dalai Lama is selected.

CLARK, DENIS (?–?1950), born England, travelled extensively, lived in Corsica and served in the Royal Air Force during World War II. He has written travel books, such as *The Sea Kingdom of Corsica* (1949). He wrote *Black Lightning*, a novel about a leopard, set in Ceylon, *Explorers and Discoverers* (1951), illustrated by L. Kenyan, and *Boomer: the Life of a Kangaroo* (1954), illustrated by C. Gifford Ambler. See **Animal Stories**.

CLARK, JOHN HOWARD (1830–78), born Birmingham, UK, was business manager of the *South Australian Register*, which he also edited from 1870 to 1878, and was influential in the establishment of the South Australian Institute, the predecessor of the State Library of SA. *Bertie and the Bullfrogs: an Australian Story for Big and Little Children* (q.v., 1874) was published anonymously.

CLARK, MARGARET DIANNE (1943–), born Geelong, Victoria, has written two books about an irrepressible teenager: *Pugwall* (1987), illustrated by Cathy van Ee, and *Pugwall's Summer* (1989). A serial of the books was made for the ABC in 1990. In *The Big Chocolate Bar* (1991) Spoonhead, Amy Yiu, Trash, Zits and others set up a blackmarket in junk food at a school camp. *Tina Tuff* (1991), illustrated by Lin Tobias, is about a tough and funny girl who is so out of control that she is sent to live with her grandmother, an equally tough customer. Tina learns about herself as she confronts her own anger and insecurity, brought on by her father's sudden death. Clark's understanding of the confusion of many young people is combined with tolerance and humour.

CLARK, MAVIS THORPE (1912–), born Melbourne, initially drew on the formula fiction of the boys' adventure. She wrote *Hatherly's First Fifteen* (1930), illustrated by F.E. Hiley, when she was 18. It opens and closes with a rugby match, the first match saved by Jim Manning, and the last by another 17-year-old, Bob Wentworth, who is a fine athlete, despite five years of blindness. 'The man who is fond of sport, and good at it, is not often a backslider,' thinks Bob. In *Jingaroo* (1951) Robin leads the local school cricket team to victory, although he has to accept the fact that the local lads are 'poor material', compared to those he had played with at school. The Melbourne Show features in *Pony from Tarella* (1959) illustrated by Jean M. Rowe. Sandy proves that his gentle riding technique is better than the harsh mastery favoured by Phil, when he wins a jumping contest on his horse Sunflower. Sport and school feature in *Missing Gold* (1949). Sunnymount and Findon are rival schools at football. Bob, star of Sunnymount's team, is injured and his Dad is too poor to pay for the operation that will fix his leg and restore him to the team. Bill, Dick, Debbie, the indomitable Judith Anne and her sidekick Mosquito set out to find gold to pay for the operation. *Dark Pool Island* (1949) is another school story in which the boys expose the bogus new headmaster and save the school by finding a fortune. *The Twins from Timber Creek* (1949) and *Home Again at Timber Creek* (1950) are family stories about Elizabeth May and Pete, staying with their grandmother for an adventurous Christmas holiday. The sequel continues the episodic adventures of the twins in a country town, this time shared by their baby sister, Wendy, and a faithful dog, Nigger.

Clark took a more complex direction with *The Brown Land was Green* (q.v., 1956), reissued as *Kammoora* in 1990. Other historical novels followed. *Gully of Gold* (1958), illustrated by Anne Graham, displays her attention to detail. She sketches Melbourne when gold was first discovered, and includes specific buildings, such as the Shakespeare Inn, in Collins Street. See also **Eureka Stockade**. *They Came South* (1963), illustrated by Joy Murray, follows the fortunes of Edward Foster and Angus McIvor, who open up grazing land in central Victoria. *Blue Above the Trees* (q.v., 1967) was set in early Gippsland. *Nowhere to Hide* (1969), illustrated by Genevieve Melrose, is also set in this area. The year is 1942, and the routine work required on their dairy farm distances the Brewsters from the war, until cousin Roger becomes involved with escaped prisoners of war. Clark evokes Gippsland not only directly but also through her references to the destruction of its forests and its wet climate. See also **War**.

Harsher settings are used in *Spark of Opal* (1968), illustrated by Genevieve Melrose, set in the opal-mining town of Coober Pedy. See also **Aboriginal People in Children's Fiction**. *The Min-Min* (q.v., 1966) is set in the SA desert. The mountain of *Iron Mountain* (1970), illustrated by Ron Brooks, is Mt Tom

Price in WA. In a pioneering environment, Joey, Leah and Mr Rose sort out their lives against a background of mining. *Wildfire* (1973) demonstrates the destructive power of nature. See **Bushfire**. Adding a fantastic element to her interest in mining in *A Stranger Came to the Mine* (1980), illustrated by Jane Walker, Clark has the alien Lu stranded on Earth, needing the fuel locked within the opal mine to return home. *New Golden Mountain* (1973), which was the name given to Australia by the Chinese immigrants, is set in Bendigo, where goldmining and Chinese history are brought together in a study of an adolescent girl. Louise plans to run away from poverty and her unambitious Aunt Eva, financing her escapade by stealing an old Chinese painting. But when she experiences a near tragedy, trapped in a mine, she recognises how much she means to her aunt, who has sacrificed her own plans to look after her. Another runaway appears in *The Sky is Free* (1974). Sam believes he is the failure of the family until he and Tony have to work hard in an opal town and begin to know themselves.

In *The Hundred Islands* (1976), illustrated by Astra Lacis, Greg is about to finish school, and his father wants him to help with the farm, but the boy wants to study environmental science so that he can preserve the wild birds and animals of Bass Strait. *Spanish Queen* (1977), illustrated by Joan Saint, is a short novel about Ben, who finds gold coins when he is running from his uncle's dog, and in *The Lilly-Pilly* (1979), illustrated by Prue Chammen, Maureen moves into a new neighbourhood and makes new friends through a duck which she finds in the yard. These are books for younger readers. Clark explores an unsympathetic domestic environment in *Solomon's Child* (1981). Thirteen-year-old Jude is confused when her father decides to return to his wife, and Jude's mother takes to drink. Jude becomes a shoplifter. She is asked to choose between her parents, a choice which is too painful for her until a benevolent teacher helps her through her trauma.

Clark's interest in the lives of Aboriginal People can be identified in her informational books, such as *The Boy from Cumeroogunga* (1979), a version for children of her earlier *Pastor Doug* (1965), a biography of Sir Douglas Nicholls, the prominent Aboriginal activist. It can also be traced in her novels, from *The Brown Land was Green* through *The Min-Min* to *A Stranger Came to the Mine*. Despite an occasional overdose of factual information, Clark writes with depth, demonstrated in her strong female characters, and her creation of setting. Girls such as Ettie in *They Came South* and Henrietta in *The Brown Land was Green* are resourceful and capable. These young women are often seen in an historical context, a far cry from the circumscribed and delicate portraits in many colonial novels. Clark re-creates historical and contemporary settings vividly, particularly the countryside, ranging from the lush Victorian rainforests to the arid central deserts. Her historical research is accurate and wide-ranging.

Clark contributed *A Pack-Tracker* (1968), illustrated by Shirley Turner, to the Oxford 'Early Australians' series, and *John Batman* (1962) to the 'Great Australians' series. She has also written other factual books, such as *Strolling Players* (1972), a biography of Joan and Betty Rayner, and *Young and Brave* (1984), stories of young Australians such as Tommy Woodcock, Donald Bradman, Grace Bussell, Undyarning, Alice Niemann and others. Her major contribution has been the historical novel, a fine example being *Blue Above the Trees*, although her stories about contemporary adolescents under stress, such as Sylvie, in *The Min-Min* and Jude in *Solomon's Child*, are written with poignancy.

CLARK, SAMUEL, see **'PARLEY, PETER'**; **'WILSON**, Rev. **T. P.'**

CLARKE, JOSEPH AUGUSTUS (1840–90), born Kent, UK, arrived in Brisbane in 1869. He was a painter and etcher, taught drawing in schools, and was the first teacher of drawing at Brisbane Technical College. Clarke was a leading artistic figure in colonial Brisbane. He illustrated J. Brunton Stephens's *Marsupial Bill: or, The Bad Boy, the Good Dog and the Old Man Kangaroo* (1879), matching the humour of the story with satirical sketches of a young larrikin, a smart dog and lordly kangaroos.

CLARKE, JUDITH (1943–), born Sydney, has written short stories for adults, and lectured in creative writing to adults. *The Boy on the Lake: Stories of the Supernatural* (1989) has eleven stories, each with a frightening sting in the tail. *Teddy Zoot* (1990) is a brave toy bear who helps Sarah with her mathematics homework. *Luna Park at Night* (1991) describes how the dreadful Sophia and Jezebel torment their parents, only to be foiled by a green frog. Her series about a bemused adolescent began with *The Heroic Life of Al Capsella* (1988), which chronicles 14-year-old Al's desperate struggle to be normal against such obstacles as a father who will not mow the lawn and a mother who writes romantic novels. Al's efforts founder on the example of his tedious but very normal maternal grandparents, the Blounts. His story is continued in *Al Capsella and the Watchdogs* (1990), the watchdogs being his parents. In *Al Capsella on Holidays* (1992) Al and his friend Lou set off for a beach holiday, which does not turn out as planned. Clarke's books examine Al's wry perceptions of life and his family, Mr and Mrs Capsella, his grandparents, Pearly and Neddy, and other characters, with wit and perspicacity.

CLARKE, MARJORIE (1907–63), born Newton Abbott, UK, worked as a governess in India, where she wrote children's stories for the *Times of India*, and beauty and household hints as 'Ellen Harriet'. She moved to Perth in 1949, worked for the WA Department of Education, and returned to England in 1959. *Sawdust and Spangles* (1959), illustrated by Irene Maher, was a serial on the ABC before its publication. Jim, Sue and Trevor stay with their aunt, who has a troupe of performing dogs. The children become friends with circus performers — Bettina the high-wire artist, Gekko the clown, and Benito the animal-trainer — and foil the despicable Simon. *Kangaroo Paws* (1959), illustrated by Leslie Green, is set in Yanchep National Park, WA. Robin and Marna (English), Don (Australian), Lolita (Italian), and Leonid (Czech), combine forces and expose an illegal immigration racket.

CLEARY, SHEILA wrote two books about Australian fauna. *Aussie Animals: Stories of Some Quaint and Wonderful Australian Animals* (1946), with verses by Bartlett Adamson and drawings by Harry MacDonald and Jack Childs, and *Aussie Birds* (1948), a companion volume with drawings by Tina Grace, present the study of animals and birds in stories and verse. 'The Platypus looks like a mixture of things,/A fish without fins and a bird without wings/He lives in a hole like a wombat or mole/And maybe he croons but I don't think he sings.' Both books were designed by the artist, Roderick Shaw.

CLELAND, ELPHINSTONE DAVENPORT (1854–1928), born Adelaide, was a journalist and mine-manager. His adventurous life took him to Broken Hill, Kalgoorlie, Coolgardie, Leonora and the Pilbara in search of minerals. His geological collection is held at the University of Adelaide. Cleland's *Mining Practice in Western Australia* (1911) was used as a textbook until the 1940s. *The White Kangaroo: a Tale of Colonial Life — Founded on Fact* (1890), which was serialised in *Sunday Reading for the Young* in twenty-nine instalments, is a novel about two boys kangaroo-hunting in northern SA. Fourteen-year-old Ralph Everdale and his cousin Ernest become lost when hunting a white kangaroo. They fall in with Aboriginal People, and finally shoot the white kangaroo. See also **Lost in the Bush**.

CLEMENT, ROD (1961–), born Sydney, spent over four years of his childhood in Papua New Guinea, and has worked as an illustrator for the *Sydney Morning Herald*, the *Australian Geographic*, and the *Australian Financial Review*. He illustrated *Snail Mail* (1986) and *The Imaginary Menagerie* (1984) by Hazel Edwards. *When Hippo was Hairy and Other Tales from Africa* (1988), told by Nick Greaves, is a collection of folk tales. The striking *Edward the Emu* (1988) by Sheena Knowles is a verse story with Clement's humorous illustrations of Edward and the other animals in unexpected poses and from unusual perspectives. *Counting on Frank* (q.v., 1990), which Clement wrote and illustrated, is another funny and richly illustrated picture-book. *Eyes in Disguise* (1992) shows two fish swimming in a polluted reef meeting two children in goggles.

Counting on Frank (1990) by Rod Clement

Climb a Lonely Hill (1970) by Lilith Norman was Commended in the 1971 Book of the Year Awards. Sue and Jack are taken on a holiday by the slapdash Uncle Bert. After a car accident they wander through the desert for two weeks, surviving on what little they are able to forage. The experience binds the two children into a closer relationship and reassures them that together they can overcome their difficult circumstances at home.

Clive Eats Alligators (1985) by Alison Lester was Commended in the 1986 Picture Book of the Year Awards. The seven children all eat, dress, and buy different things, from breakfast to bedtime expressing their own individuality. Lester's fluid shapes and clear colours combine in pictures of a childlike innocence. The adventures of others in the group are taken up in *Rosie Sips Spiders* (1988) and *Tessa Snaps Snakes* (1990).

CLUNE, FRANK (1893–1971), born Sydney. For *Ned Kelly* (1970) see **Kelly, Ned**.

COCHRANE, MOIRA. For *Animal Antics ABC* (1988) see **Alphabet Books**.

Cocky's Castle (1966) by Celia Syred, illustrated by Astra Lacis Dick, was Highly Commended in the 1967 Book of the Year Awards. When Aunt Pen decides to sell her old house, her great-nieces and nephews enter it into a historic homes competition. Fran discovers some old photographs and valuable paintings. Although the house is lost, Fran's own sketches, and the paintings, will remain, proof of the permanence of artistic endeavour.

Cocky's Circle Little Books are a series of paperbacks, published by Murdoch Books, for *Family Circle Magazine*, available at supermarkets. There are fourteen titles in the series, including *Sly, Old Lockjaw Croc* (1990) by Marcia Vaughan,

illustrated by Rodney McRae, *The Most Scary Ghost* and *The Yuckadoos* by Joy Cowley, illustrated by Jo Davies, and *Lavender the Library Cat* (1985), also by Joy Cowley, also illustrated by McRae.

COHN, OLA (1892–1964), born Bendigo, Victoria, was a sculptor, and her sculpture of the Fairies' Tree is at the Fitzroy Gardens, Melbourne. She studied at the Bendigo School of Mines, Swinburne Technical College and the Royal College of Art in London. Cohn's fascination with small creatures is shown in *The Fairies' Tree* (1932), *More About the Fairies' Tree* (1933) and *Castles in the Air* (1936). *Mostly Cats* (1964) contains reminiscences of her life in Bendigo, England and Melbourne.

COLE, EDWARD WILLIAM (1832–1918), born Woodchurch, Kent, UK, joined the gold rush to Victoria in 1852, settling in Melbourne. He began his bookselling in a barrow in Bourke Street, graduating to a shop close to the Eastern Market site, on the corner of Russell and Bourke Streets, in 1874. He was so successful that he was able to lease the whole of the Eastern Market (which he sublet) and construct a huge shop in Bourke Street which he had extended through to Collins Street by 1906. Howey Place still has the reinforced glass roof which Cole built. Under the sign of the rainbow, the symbol he adopted, Cole's Book Arcade flourished, and it was estimated that 5000 people used the Arcade daily. For many years the Cole family lived upstairs, and observers report that 'on washing day the Cole laundry could be seen fluttering from the gallery'. The family later moved to Essendon to a house which is now Lowther Hall Anglican Grammar.

Cole's particular gift was in advertising his books, and one of his ploys was to have thousands of medals struck, and then either dropped on the streets of Melbourne to advertise his wares or sold as tokens; these are now in much demand by numismatists. Ferneries, aviaries, cages of monkeys, trick mirrors and a large toy department attracted the customers. At its peak the shop was one of the largest in the world, with a stock of over a million books, and an annual turnover of over £100 000 pounds. Branches were opened in Sydney, at 333 George Street, and Adelaide, at 67 Rundle Street. The shop closed in 1929 and the site was purchased by G.J. Coles Pty Ltd. As well as *Cole's Funny Picture Book* (q.v., 1879) E.W. Cole was responsible for the Australian editions of many English titles. He was a great lover of books, a supporter of Federation and an opponent of alcohol, smoking and the White Australia policy. Many Australians, including Alfred Deakin, have paid tribute to his contribution to the intellectual climate of the times. Further reading: Turnley, *Cole of the Book Arcade*, and Dean, *A Handbook on E.W. Cole*.

COLERIDGE, ANN, born UK, has lived in Melbourne since 1981. *The Friends of Emily Culpepper* (q.v., 1983) is a fantasy about Emily's magical ability to shrink her friends. *Stranded* (1987), illustrated by Eric David, describes the efforts of a community to rescue the beached whales. In *Gertie the Fearless* (1987), illustrated by Mark Payne, the fertile imagination of a lollipop lady causes her to miss the real bank robber. *Jim's Last Ride* (1987), *Kitchen Physics* (1987) and *Longneck's Billabong* (1987) are in the Macmillan's 'Southern Cross' series. Coleridge has also written informational material on animals, such as *Biological Control* (1987) and *Protecting Themselves: Defence Mechanisms in Animals* (1987).

Cole's Funny Picture Book: the Funniest Picture Book in the World was first published in 1879, compiled by E.W. Cole with scissors and paste from books, newspapers, and magazines. Forty thousand copies were sold for one shilling each. Book No. 2 was issued in 1882. Forty five

editions were published, and by 1983 one million copies had been sold. Similar productions were *Cole's Rosebud Story Books* (n.d.), a collection of stories, songs, verses, and riddles, profusely illustrated with black-and-white pictures by various artists; and *Cole's Fun Doctor: The Funniest Book in the World* (n.d.), a compilation of excerpts, stories and poems under the headings 'Fun about Babies', 'Fun about Kissing' and so on. There is also a second series of *The Fun Doctor* (n.d.) which is not illustrated and not for children. Randolph Stow says of the *Funny Picture Book* that Cole managed 'to provide quite the best and funniest ragbag of Victorian sentimentality and domestic humour that this writer has seen, bound volumes of Punch not excepted' (*Australian Letters* 1 (3) April 1958). Cole's grandson, Cole Turnley, produced *Cole's Funny Picture Book No 3* (1951) and with Merron Cullum, Cole's great-granddaughter, *Cole's Funny Picture Book No. 4* (1991).

Collections. Collections of stories and extracts from longer works were a feature of nineteenth-century books for boys and girls. A typical example is *The Boy's Birth-Day Book: a Collection of Tales, Essays, and Narratives of Adventure* (1864), containing stories by Mrs S.C. Hall, Augustus Mayhew, Thomas Miller, George Augustus Sala and William Howitt. Over eighty years later, a fine and lavishly illustrated collection was compiled by Barbara Ker Wilson, *The Illustrated Treasury of Australian Stories and Verse for Children* (1987), with material drawn this time from Australian sources, including, again, William Howitt, joined by C.J. Dennis, Ellen Campbell, Ruth Park, Jean Chapman, and Nadia Wheatley, with illustrations by Ida Rentoul Outhwaite, Frank Mahony, Jan Ormerod and many more. Rosemary Wighton had edited an earlier collection, *Kangaroo Tales: Australian Stories for Children* (1963), illustrated by Donald Friend, which also contains extracts bridging a century and a half of

Australian writing, from Charlotte Barton to Elyne Mitchell. *The Land of Ideas: an Anthology of Stories for Children by South Australian Writers* (1986), edited by Pauline Wardleworth and Adam Dutkiewicz and illustrated by Michael Dutkiewicz, follows the history of SA writing through Tarella Quinn Daskein, 'Elizabeth Powell' and Rex Ingamells to contemporary writers such as Colin Thiele, Christobel Mattingley and Barbara Hanrahan.

Patricia Wrightson edited two collections, *Beneath the Sun: an Australian Collection for Children* (1972), which has stories, poems, comic-strips, party ideas, sport, hobbies and travel hints, and *Emu Stew: an Illustrated Collection of Stories and Poems for Children* (1976), drawn from material which appeared in the NSW School Magazine. *The Macquarie Bedtime Story Book* (1987), edited by Walter McVitty and Rosalind Price and illustrated by Ron Brooks, has stories, poems and extracts, and Jean Chapman's *Stories to Share* (1983) is a collection for the very young by well-known authors. *Rotten Apples: Top Stories to Read and Tell* (1989) by Virginia Ferguson and Peter Durkin, illustrated by Rolf Heimann, is another

outstanding collection for teachers and storytellers, but at a language level which children could read with ease, reminiscent of Virginia Tashjian's *Juba This and Juba That*. *All the Best: a Selection Celebrating Twenty-Five Years of Puffins in Australia* (1989), compiled by Kay Ronai, contains thirty extracts from the 'best bits from best Australian books', from *The Nargun and the Stars* to *Space Demons*.

Many editors have drawn on Australian writers to present short stories, either previously published or commissioned for the collection. Leon Garfield's *A Swag of Stories* (1977), illustrated by Caroline Harrison, contains ten new stories by Hesba Brinsmead, Max Fatchen, Christobel Mattingley, Joan Phipson, Ivan Southall, and Patricia Wrightson, among others. *The Cool Man and Other Contemporary Stories by Australian Authors* (1973) includes short stories by Ivan Southall, Nance Donkin, Kylie Tennant, and Geoffrey Dutton, with biographical information. Frank Willmott and Robyn Jackson edited an outstanding collection, *Crazy Hearts* (1985), which has eight tough, realistic stories by writers such as Michael Hyde, Isobelle Carmody, and

Kangaroo Tales (1963), edited by Rosemary Wighton. Illustrator: Donald Friend

Willmott himself, confronting many controversial issues, such as racism, sexism and power games. Other similar collections, for varying age groups, are Jo Goodman's *Win Some, Lose Some* (1985) and Suzette Boyd's *Between You and Me* (1989). Michael Kavanagh's *Telling Tales* (1986), illustrated by Anna Mertzlin, includes stories by Dianne Bates, Gary Hurle, Mary Roberts, and Robin Klein.

Some editors have centred on a subject or theme as the focus of a collection. *Dream Time* (1989), illustrated by Elizabeth Honey and *Into the Future* (1991), illustrated by Lorraine Hannay, both edited by Toss Gascoigne, Jo Goodman and Margot Tyrrell for the CBC, contain stories by authors who have won awards, such as Victor Kelleher, John Marsden, Gillian Rubinstein and Patricia Wrightson. The CBC asked each author to build a story from the title. *State of the Heart: Stories about Love, Life and Growing Up* (1988), *Bizarre: Ten Wonderfully Weird Stories* (1989), *Amazing* (1989) and *Weird: Twelve Incredible Tales* (1990), all compiled by Penny Matthews, have stories by writers such as Gillian Rubinstein, Allan Baillie, Libby Gleeson, Max Dann and Doug MacLeod. Edel Wignell's *Crutches are Nothing* (1982) deals with disabilities. Writers such as Colin Thiele, Barbara Hanrahan and Tim Winton have contributed to the love stories in the powerful *First Loves* (1989), edited by John Malone, as well as newer writers such as Richard Goodwin and Alan Close. *Absolutely Rapt: a Collection of Love Stories for Young People* (1990) is another collection about the pains of teenage love from eight writers, including Nadia Wheatley, Tony Lintermans, Mary Pershall, Debra Oswald, and Gillian Barnett. *A Teddy Bear's Picnic: Original Stories about Teddy Bears* (1986), enhanced by the whimsical illustrations of Terry Denton, is a collection of stories by such authors as Robin Klein, Kate Walker and Libby Hathorn. *The Christmas Book* (1989), illustrated by John Canty, has Christmas pieces, with ideas for activities.

Barbara Ker Wilson's *A Handful of Ghosts: Thirteen Eerie Tales by Australian Authors* (1976) includes stories by Ivan Southall, Hesba Brinsmead, Colin Thiele, Celia Syred and David Martin, and *Frightfully Fearful Tales* (1987), illustrated by Jiri Tibor Novak, has scary stories by Judith Worthy, Michael Dugan, Kath Walker, Patricia Wrightson and Bill Scott. *After Dark: Seven Tales to Read at Night* (1988) and *Before Dawn: More Tales to Read at Night* (1988), compiled by Gillian Rubinstein, are also mystery and adventure stories.

On a lighter note, *Money!* (1989), edited by Ruth Moline, is a humorous collection by Nadia Wheatley, Victor Kelleher and Libby Hathorn and others, and Michael Dugan's *The Hijacked Bathtub and Other Funny Stories* (1988) contains twelve funny stories, some original and others extracted from longer works by authors such as Hesba Brinsmead, Robin Klein, Doug MacLeod and Colin Thiele. Libby Hathorn asked writers to respond to a painting, resulting in the excellent collection *The Blue Dress* (1991). Nadia Wheatley's *Landmarks* (1991) has nine stories by Australian authors, each focusing on a facet of a contemporary adolescent experience. The immigrant experience is examined in *Goodbye and Hello: Sixteen Compelling Stories about Leaving and Arriving — From Irish and Australian Authors* (1991), edited by Clodagh Corcoran and Margot Tyrrell.

There are many collections published by individual schools and organisations. *A Picture Forms in My Mind: a Collection of Poetry, Prose and Illustrations by the Children of East Carnarvon Primary School* (1983) was published to celebrate the centenary of the school. Others include *The Meat in the Sandwich* (1988), written by students at Brunswick Technical School, Melbourne, edited by Michael Hyde and Marian Lees; *The Broady Book of Stories* (1987), an anthology of work written by students from Broadmeadows, Melbourne; and *Why Must We Go? Descriptions of Journeys* to *Australia from South-East Asia by South-East Asian Students of Richmond Girl's High School* (1981), compiled and edited by Valerie R. Falk, which was used by Diana Kidd for *Onion Tears* (1989). Some collections present the first commercially published work of young writers, an outstanding example being the *Youth Writes* collections edited by Marcia Kirsten. *Midnight Dip: Award Winning Stories from Young Australian Writers* (1990) is a selection by Catherine Hammond of the winning entries in the Sydney Morning Herald's Young Writer's Award. *If You Lose, You're Dead* (1988), edited by Diana Giese, contains twenty-two stories written by 14 to 18-year-olds for the same competition. *Turns of Phrase, Young Queensland Writers* (1988), edited by Lawrie Ryan and Ross Clark, has prose, verse and drama submitted by thirty-eight young people between 10 and 18 to a writing project organised by the State Library of Queensland. In *Kissing the Toad* (1987), edited by Doug MacLeod, young people write about their perceptions of beauty.

The flexibility and usefulness of a collection ensures its popularity, and a good collection, high-minded or frankly entertaining, can provide an introduction to the longer work of an author. (For collections of short stories by individual authors, see entry under author's name.)

COLLINS, ALAN (1928–), born Sydney, has worked as a journalist and in advertising, and has written short stories and novels. When Jacob and Solly Kaiser are orphaned, in *The Boys from Bondi* (1987), they are taken into a Jewish children's home where the other children are refugees from Nazism. Jacob begins an apprenticeship as a printer, boarding with Mrs Pearlman, although a butt of the casual racism of his workmates. Solly's decline into petty crime, and Jacob's politicisation and growing awareness of his own cultural heritage, are drawn against a background of pre-war Sydney and a rich gallery of characters and experiences.

COLLINS, DALE (1897–1956), born Balmain, Sydney, also used the pseudonyms 'Stephen Fennimore' and 'Michael Copeland'. Collins began in journalism when he was 14. He worked for the Melbourne *Herald* and the *Bulletin*, and wrote stories for the NSW Bookstall Company before travelling extensively. He returned to live in Australia in 1948. From these experiences he wrote *Robinson Carew — Castaway* (1948), in which a spoilt rich boy is shipwrecked on a Pacific island, and thrown on his own resources. *Storm over Samoa* (1954), illustrated by Vera Jarman, follows the fortunes of Nick Enderby in Samoa; and in *The Vanishing Boy* (1949), illustrated by Margaret Horder, set in London, Jonathan Johns develops the capacity to vanish, and is befriended by an African king and his son until his parents return to care for him. For his books about Martin, *Bush Holiday* (1948), *Bush Voyage* (1950) and *Sunset Plains* (1953), see **Bush Holiday**. Other adventure stories include *The Voyage of the Landship* (1947) and *Coral Sea Adventure* (1951). *Anzac Adventure: the Story of Gallipoli Told for Young Readers* (q.v., 1959) is an account of the landing at Anzac Cove. His adult novels include *Lost* (1933), *The Happy Emigrants* (1948), about shipboard romances seen through the eyes of a 12-year-old boy, and *By the Waters of Galilee* (1954), short stories using biblical sources.

COLQUHOUN, BRETT (1958–), born Albury, NSW, has illustrated Michael Dugan's *Billy the Most Horrible Boy in the World* (1981), *Aunts, Uncles, Cousins and All* (1987), *The Great Overland Riverboat Race* (1982) and Jason Timlock's *Basil, the Loneliest Boy in the Block* (1990). He contributed illustrations to Barbara Giles's *Spooky Poems and Jokes* (1983) and *A Second Australian Poetry Book* (1983), and illustrated the paperback publication of Morris Lurie's *Arlo the Dandy Lion* (1971) in 1983.

COLWELL, MAX (1926–), born Brompton, SA, has written educational radio and television scripts for the ABC, the NZ Broadcasting Service, the BBC and SA Youth Education broadcasts. His informational books include *Careers with Animals* (1968) and *The Journey of Burke and Wills* (1971). For *Peter the Whaler in Southern Seas* (1964), illustrated by Geoffrey C. Ingleton, see **'Great Stories of Australia'**. His semi-autobiographical trilogy is a series of loosely connected and humorous incidents about Mike. *Half Days and Patched Pants* (1975) begins in Mike's childhood. In *Full Days and Pressed Pants* (1978), illustrated by Aubrey Collette, he is 17 and takes his first job working for a wholesale grocery during the Depression. *Glorious Days and Khaki Pants* (1987) recounts Mike's experiences in the Army during World War II. Colwell has written a history of Adelaide, *Light's Vision: the City of Adelaide* (1983), with his son David Colwell.

Come Danger, Come Darkness (1978) by Ruth Park, illustrated by Tony Oliver, was Commended in the 1979 Book of the Year Awards. Otter (Octavius) and Paddy Cannon arrive in Norfolk Island to live with their uncle, the commandant of the penal colony. When Otter recognises his friend Corny Stack among the prisoners he is determined to help him, and as his own ambition to be a surgeon is being constantly thwarted, he throws everything he can behind an escape attempt. Park's historical accuracy and strongly realised characters give pace and colour to an exciting adventure story.

Conservation. An awareness of the fragile nature of Australian flora and fauna has been highlighted by many authors since Ethel Pedley's *Dot and the Kangaroo* (1899). Nan Chauncy, Mavis Thorpe Clark, Colin Thiele and Patricia Wrightson have all written novels which express concern about the damage to the environment caused by development, such as *Tiger in the Bush* (q.v., 1957), *Blue Above the Trees* (q.v., 1967), *Storm Boy* (q.v., 1963), *Yellow-Jacket Jock* (1969) and *The Crooked Snake* (q.v., 1955). Thiele's *The Sknuks* (1977) appeals for a recognition of the fragility of the planet.

The rise of environmental awareness during the 1970s has led to novels centred on conservation. Many describe the irretrievable loss of animals and birds and the destruction of the landscape or historic sites through pollution or 'progress'. Jeannie Baker's *Where the Forest Meets the Sea* (q.v., 1987) calls for the preservation of the Daintree, and *Window* (q.v., 1991) documents the effects of urban spread, also taken up in *Goanna* (1988) by Jenny Wagner. In Deirdre Hill's *Over the Bridge* (1969) Bob Burrow desperately wants to save a tram; in Ted Greenwood's *Joseph and Lulu and the Prindiville House Pigeons* (1972) the issue is the threat to an old building. Sam saves a stranded whale in Katherine Scholes's *The Boy and the Whale* (1985), and in *Riverman* (1986) by Allan Baillie Tim's concern is for an old Huon pine tree. In Christobel Mattingley's *The Battle of the Galah Trees* (1974) Matt saves the gum trees in the local park, home to the galahs. The illegal trapping for sale of animals and birds is explored in Mattingley's *Lizard Log* (1975), in which lizards are saved from capture, and in Joan Phipson's *The Bird Smugglers* (1979), in which Margaret discovers parrots in her neighbour's coat on a flight to London. Wilfred also saves the birds in Phipson's *No Escape* (1979). In Patricia Wrightson's *Moondark* (1987) logging is defeated through an alliance of animals and ancient spirits. In *Kenju's Forest* (1989) by Junko Morimoto, a boy's determination to plant a forest ensures that a factory town has its own breathing space. *Cry Me a River* (1991) by Rodney McRae expresses the concerns of the later part of the twentieth century, as the river is polluted almost beyond recovery.

Community action to conserve threatened species, land or property is a recurring theme, such as the attempt to save the gums in *Nin and the Scribblies* (1976) by Nancy Cato or Gillian Barnett's *The Inside Hedge Story* (1981), where the preservation of an old estate in a Melbourne suburb is at stake. Abby and Bereznicki develop support to keep its rambling garden. In Nadia Wheatley's *The Blooding* (1988) conservation is no a longer a simple exercise in protecting endangered species or the bush. The novel describes the conflict within Colum, whose father is a logger, and the boy's own desire to conserve the great forests. Both sides of the conservation debate are explored through the eyes and emotions of Colum, so that the complexities and ramifications of people's lives are pursued, beyond a theoretical debate.

COOK, HUME. For *Australian Fairy Tales* see **Fairies**.

Cook, Captain **James** (1728–79), born Marton-in-Cleveland, Yorkshire, UK, has inspired few Australian children's writers, despite his impact on the Pacific. *Under Cook's Flag* (1924), one of the Whitcombe's Historical Story Books, (No. 533, attributed by McLaren to Helen Turner) recounts the three voyages of Cook to the South Seas through the eyes of Dick Dalton, a midshipman. It concentrates more on the voyages and the response of the indigenous inhabitants than on the Captain, and displays hostile attitudes to Maoris and Aboriginal People. The English writer Aubrey de Selincourt's *Mr Oram's Story: the Adventures of Capt. James Cook, R.N.* (1949), a more ambitious work, is about David, to whom the story of Cook is told by an old sailor, Mr Oram. In the twentieth-century David lives out Cook's adventures as they are recounted, participating in the voyages as one of the crew. There is little mention of Australia apart from it being the setting for the *Endeavour*'s repair at Cooktown. More familiarity with Cook's arena is displayed in Charles Borden's *He Sailed with Captain Cook* (1952), illustrated by Ralph Ray. Tobias Whitechapel comments on the voyages as the midshipman who assists both Cook and Green, the astronomer. This is a well-researched account of the voyages. The excellent bibliography appended shows that the author has used Cook's Journal, as well as other written accounts. Borden has also used the tales about Cook and his voyages which were related to him by his Polynesian friends during the author's fifteen years as a sailor in the South Pacific. His enlightened attitude to South Pacific people distinguishes this novel from de Selincourt's. Josephine Kamm, another English author, wrote *He Went with Captain Cook* (1952), illustrated by G.S. Ronald, which features Nicholas Young, a real member of Cook's crew, although some of his adventures are imaginary. Nick is rescued from a cruel chimney-sweep to join the *Endeavour* as Banks's cabin boy. He remains with Cook for the Pacific voyages and witnesses his death. Bernard Brett's *Captain Cook* (1969) is a factual account in picture-book format. Frank Knight's *Captain Cook and the Voyage of the 'Endeavour' 1768–1771* (1968) is based on Cook's diaries. *James Cook, Royal Navy* (q.v., 1970) by George Finkel, writing in Australia, is another realistic account of Cook's life. In all of these informational books and novels, Cook is portrayed as a courageous, fair and generous man, fascinated with mathematics and map-making, and an outstanding seaman. Borden, Finkel and Kamm make a point of showing how Britain was using the first voyage not only for scientific purposes but also to pre-empt any other nation's occupation of Terra Australis, thus placing Cook's voyages in historical perspective.

COOK, PATRICK (1949–), born UK, is a cartoonist who has written comedy for television and the theatre, including a script for a puppet play *Captain Lazar and his Earthbound Circus* in 1979. Although Cook's trademark is a whimsical koala, his four novels for children introduce a more universal animal. In *Elmer the Rat* (1980)

Elmer stows away on a ship looking for food and is at the mercy of tough ship's rats. In *Elmer Makes a Break* (1982) Elmer discovers that the urban jungle of life outside his home at Mother Murphy's Fishburgers leaves much to be desired. He takes to the road in *Elmer Runs Wild* (1986), faces the vicissitudes of country life, and meets the lovely Alma. In *Elmer Rides the Rails* (1991), which first appeared as a serial in the *Australian Women's Weekly*, Elmer and Alma survive various train journeys before they are reunited over a smoked salmon and raspberry sauce sandwich. Cook's *Waltzing Matilda* (1988) is a pop-up version of A.B. Paterson's poem, with the troopers leaping out from behind a tree.

COOKE, MERVYN A. *Tell Me a Tale* (1940) has verse and stories, including 'Sonny Jim's Adventures with the Bushland Folk'. *More Adventures of Sonny Jim* (1944) followed. The settings are wartime — Sonny thinks the air-raid shelter makes a 'bonzer cubby house'. For *A Date with Destiny* (1965) see **Adventure Stories**.

COOL Awards (Canberra's Own Outstanding List) are the children's choice awards in the ACT. They were established in 1991 by the ACT Library Service, with the assistance of the School Libraries Branch, Children's Week Committee and the CBC's ACT Branch. The aims are to promote enjoyment of reading and develop a critical appreciation of Australian children's literature and authors. Titles which have previously won are no longer eligible. The awards are given in two categories. **1991** Secondary winner: *People Might Hear You* (q.v., 1983) by Robin Klein; Primary winner: *Round the Twist* (q.v., 1990) by Paul Jennings.

Cool Man, The, and Other Contemporary Stories by Australian Authors see **Collections**

COOPER, NELLE GRANT was a member of staff of Angus & Robertson during the 1930s. *Australians All: Bush Folk in Rhyme* (1934), illustrated by Dorothy Wall, is a collection of verses about animals and birds, such as 'The Opossum' and 'The Jabiru', enlivened with the characteristic Wall pictures. *More Australians: Land and Sea Folk in Rhyme* (1935) was illustrated by Phyllis Shillito. *Australians All: Land and Sea Folk in Rhyme* (1939) combined both books. Cooper's text has a modest wit: 'When swimming should a shark you see,/Make straight for shore — go home to tea,/Leave at once, don't waste a minute/Better far, outside than in it.' *Play Songs for Children* (1941), with music by Dorothy Mathlin and decorations by Pat O'Harris, has twelve songs with Australian themes, such as the magpie, kangaroo and bunyip. As 'Kay Grant' Cooper wrote a series of humorous verses, such as *It's 'Ard to go Wrong in the Suburbs* (1940) and *It's 'Ard to go Wrong in New Guinea* (1945).

CORCORAN, CLODAGH. For *Goodbye and Hello: Sixteen Compelling Stories about Leaving and Arriving — From Irish and Australian Authors* (1991) see **Collections**.

Cornstalk Publishing Company took its name from the term used to denote a colonial-born white Australian. It was the name adopted by Angus & Robertson (q.v.) from 1924 to 1930, so that books could more readily be sold by other booksellers without advertising the Angus & Robertson name. Australian and overseas children's books were also published in the 'Bellbird' and 'Platypus' series, with the Cornstalk imprint. Cornstalk authors included Mary Grant Bruce, May Gibbs, Ethel Pedley, Norman Lindsay, Louise and Amy Mack and Constance Mackness.

COSGROVE, MARILYN (1954–). For *The Surfing Kid* (1987) and *The Cricket Kid* (1989) see **Sport**.

COTTRELL, DOROTHY (1902–57), born Picton, NSW, had little formal education, as she contracted poliomyelitis when she was 6, and was confined to a wheelchair. She was encouraged to write by Mary Gilmore, and after spending some time on Dunk Island, Queensland, with her husband, Walter Mackenzie Cottrell, she wrote her adult novel, *The Singing Gold* (1928). It was accepted by the American *Ladies Home Journal*, and serialised in 1927, which enabled Cottrell and her husband to travel to the USA, where she lived for most of the rest of her life. *'Winks, His Book* (1934), illustrated by J. Nicolson and Paul Bransom, is the story of an Australian terrier on 'Grey Farm', NSW. *Wilderness Orphan: the Life and Adventures of Chut, the Kangaroo* (1936) was first published in *Cosmopolitan* July 1935, and was made into a film in 1936 by the pioneering film director, Ken Hall, titled *Orphan of the Wilderness*. See **Animal Stories**.

COULTER, REG. WALTER illustrated for the *Bulletin* and the *Lone Hand*. His powerful illustrations appear in *The Meeting Pool: a Tale of Borneo* (1929) by Mervyn Skipper, and *The Bubble Galleon: a Holiday Pantomime* (1934) and *Master Davy's Locker* (1935) by Ernest Wells.

Counting Books. The later half of the twentieth century has seen the development of the counting book as a vehicle for the expression of the picture-book artist. Early examples are Kathleen Mellor's *Gee Up, Bonny* (1945), a flap book, Connie Christie's *Let's Count* (1945), and the charming *Mrs Hen Counts Her Chickens* (1949) by Leila Pirani, illustrated by Norman Davis. Mrs Hen's ten eggs hatch out, and as each chick appears, it is named and counted by its mother. Traditional stories have inspired Elaine Haxton's *A Parrot in a Flame Tree* (1968), an Australian version of the old carol 'A Partridge in a Pear Tree.' The strong, colourful and

One Dragon's Dream (1978) by Peter Pavey

stylised illustrations of Australian animals and birds are mixed with less specifically local creatures such as locusts and owls. Jean Chapman's *Blue Gum Ark* (1988), illustrated by Sue O'Loughlin, is based on a traditional American counting rhyme, 'Old Noah He once had an Ark', using Australian animals, and Rodney McRae's *The Gaping Wide-Mouthed Waddling Frog: a Counting Book* (1989) on a nineteenth-century rhyme game.

Deborah and Kilmeny Niland's *Birds on a Bough* (1975) has a cumulative text, where the birds must be counted across each page. The humorous and exaggerated pictures of birds of all shapes and sizes conclude with a surprise at the end. Jeannie Baker's *One Hungry Spider* (1982) is another clever counting book, with insects hovering around a web. *1 is for One* (1985) by Nadia Wheatley, illustrated by Helen Leitch, is more than one book. Within a pocket inside the back cover is a smaller book, and so on, making three books in all, so that number and size can be examined. The same text is used, simple nonsense verses, but the illustrations are variations.

The Australian locale and indigenous animals are used in Michael Dugan's *Nonsense Numbers* (1980), illustrated by Jack Newnham, a companion to his alphabet book *Nonsense Places: an Absurd Australian Alphabet* (1976). The story in verse uses Australian animals who join in a run until there are ten of them, then fall by the wayside as they tire, until there are none. Michael Dugan's other counting book, *The Wombat's Party* (1990) is illustrated by Jane Burrell. Kerry Argent and Rod Trinca's *One Woolly Wombat* (1982), illustrated by Argent, uses Australian animals, birds and flora. The verses are complemented by Argent's whimsical drawings, such as koalas eating lamingtons. Wendy de Paauw illustrated *Ten Little Australians* (1984). At a party by the river, each child is disposed of one by one, until on the last page, they all peep from behind bushes. *The Hilton Hen House* (1987) by Jo

Hinchcliffe, illustrated by John Forrest, is in rhyme. What begins as a fowl house becomes a very large mansion as more and more animals are invited in. *1 2 3 and What Do You See?* (1985) by John Brennan is a book of striking photographs of characteristically Australian objects, such as Puffing Billy, thongs and sparklers, and the reader makes other associations arising from the text. *1 to 10 and Back Again* (1983) by Anne Ferns, illustrated by Susanne Ferrier, is aimed to teach children how to manipulate numbers, and includes concepts of addition and subtraction, but it goes beyond the didactic to entertainment as the elderly elephants, rascally robbers, whiskery walruses and floppy frogs romp across the pages. The most arresting counting book is Peter Pavey's *One Dragon's Dream* (1978). The lavish and intricate illustrations invite the reader to count the multitude of objects depicted on each double-page spread. The bizarre landscape and nightmarish animals suggest a dream, and unlike other counting books a narrative emerges from the pictures.

Young children enjoy counting and number games; adults want them to learn to count. While authors and artists of picture-books continue to offer inventive and artistic examples, the future of counting books seems assured.

Counting on Frank (1990), written and illustrated by Rod Clement, was an Honour Book in the 1991 Picture Book of the Year Awards, and won the YABBA Picture Book for 1991. The boy's father urges him to use his brain. So, while Dad snoozes and watches the television, the boy and his dog, Frank, both wearing studious spectacles, calculate how long a ballpoint pen can write, how many humpbacked whales would fit into the house, how high the toast would fly if the toaster was the size of a house, all depicted with wit. When there is a trip to Hawaii for the one who can guess how many jelly beans in a jar, the boy and Frank have no difficulty at all.

COUPER, JOHN MILL (1914–), born Dundee, Scotland, came to Australia in 1951. He has written books of verse for adults, including *The Book of Bligh* (1969), and two novels for young people. *The Thundering Good Today* (1970) examines the complacency of Australian society through the eyes of the 18-year-old Ian Guthrie, who must register for national service during the Vietnam War. Ian and his friend Limp have to decide whether to volunteer for service in a war they do not like, or be drawn into it by force. The title is based on the author's translation of Mallarmé's sonnet 'Le vierge, le vivace et le bel aujourd'hui'. In *Looking for a Wave* (1973) Mark sets off during a summer vacation to travel north on a surfing holiday. He gets a ride with an older woman, Biddy, and together they join up with Lin, whose feckless sister has had a baby. Couper charts the demands of the baby, Lin's care for it, and Mark's recognition that life is not always as one would like it to be. Through understatement and a poetic use of words, Couper explores the philosophical dilemmas of young people as they become adults.

COUPER, SUE (1934–) has written *The Lemon Thieves* (1972), illustrated by M.J. Couper and L.N. Mitchell, an adventure story in which Mark, Tom and Robbie save a valuable crop of lemons from thieves. *Pelican Point* (1977), illustrated by Patricia Mullins, is the diary of three days on an isolated beach. Each of the campers makes a written contribution, from 14-year-old William to small Susan. The Jamieson and Meredith cousins, with William Jamieson in charge, camp on Pelican Point, East Gippsland. Their discovery of rare birds saves the area from destruction by developers.

Courteous Savage, The: Yagan of Swan River (1964) by Mary Durack, illustrated by Elizabeth Durack, was Commended in the 1965 Book of the Year Awards, and retitled *Yagan of the Bibbulmun* in 1976.

The book is an account of the experience of Yagan and the Bibbulmun people who lived around Perth. Yagan, as is the custom with his people, takes retribution when a Bibbulmun is killed by the white settlers who arrived in Swan River in 1827. He becomes an outlaw, and is killed himself after seven years, for the £30 on his head. Yagan remains a heroic figure, a symbol of black resistance, in this confronting novel. See also **Aboriginal People in Children's Fiction**.

Cousins-Come-Lately: Adventures in Old Sydney Town (1952) by Eve Pownall, illustrated by Margaret Senior, was Highly Commended in the 1952 Book of the Year Awards. Emily and Ned and their parents arrive in Sydney during the governorship of Bourke. With their cousins Tom and Lucy they help Joe, who is being blackmailed by another convict, by pleading his innocence to Governor Bourke, and persuading Joe to return to his employment in a bird shop. Bourke's forgiving response to the children's pleas for Joe seems at odds with the strong discipline which characterised the management of the new colony. Pownall provides a picture of life in the convict settlement as jolly good fun.

'Cover to Cover' was a series of television programs produced by the Victorian Ministry of Education between 1983 and 1989. The programs were directed by Ann Grieve, John Marsh, Lily Steiner and Ivan Gaal, and contained interviews with authors and illustrators such as Gillian Barnett, Graeme Base, Bob Graham, Paul Jennings, Alison Lester and Jane Tanner.

COVERNTON, JANE (1951–), born Gawler, SA, established Omnibus Books with Sue Williams. In *Putrid Poems* (1985), *Petrifying Poems* (1986) and *Vile Verse* (1988), all illustrated by Craig Smith, the subjects are bodily functions and the less refined habits of insects and animals. *Four* *and Twenty Lamingtons* (1989), illustrated by Jenny Rendall, has traditional and modern rhymes, and *Off the Planet* (1989), illustrated by Kerry Argent, is a collection of funny poems about space and the universe.

COX, DAVID (1933–), born Goondiwindi, Queensland, trained at St Martin's School of Art, London, and was an artist for the Brisbane *Courier-Mail*. He has also written children's drama. *Miss Buncle's Umbrella* (1981) is a gentle satire on Miss Buncle's trip overseas; *Tin Lizzie and Little Nell* (q.v., 1982) describes a race between a mare and a motor car; in *Rightway Jack* (1987), Jack, who is an authority on the right way to do everything, is cured by an adventurous horse-ride. *Ayu and the Perfect Moon* (q.v., 1984) is a Balinese story. Cox illustrated *The Sugar-Gum Tree* (1991) by Patricia Wrightson. He has also written *Sometime Sam* (1973), *Gymkhana* (1974) and *Picnic* (1979). *Bossyboots* (1985) (see **Bushrangers**) was made into a children's operetta by his wife, Betty Beath. He also wrote *Spice and Magic* (1983), *Abigail and the Rainmaker* (1976), *In this Garden* (1976) and *Marco Polo* (1977) with Betty Beath, all musical pieces for children.

CRABTREE, JUDITH, born Melbourne, is a writer and illustrator who was a founding member of the Women's Movement Children's Literature Co-operative. She illustrated *The Princess and the Painter* by Judy Bathie (1975) and *A Family of Potters* (1975) and *Marina* (1977), both by Jan Harper. In *Carolyn Two* (1975), illustrated by Cresside, the brave Carolyn, hidden inside a timid child, takes over when she saves a kitten. *Emily Jean and the Grumphfs* (1975), illustrated by Susan O'Bryan, is a narrative poem about how Emily Jean faces her fears.

Her novels for older readers also question stereotypic roles. *The High Rise Gang* (1975) is a series of adventures set in a block of flats. Each chapter looks at the adventures of Tilly, Candy, Elly and others, in a multicultural environment. In *Nicking Off* (1975) Terry finds an abandoned baby and has to care for it. See also **Chinese**. In *Skins & Shells & Peelings* (1979), Liz is unhappy when her mother remarries. On a school camp, she and Ken, a sensitive boy, are lost and captured by thieves. In the process of rescue, Liz learns to care for others and recognise her own feelings more clearly. See also **Lost in the Bush**.

Crabtree has drawn on the style of the traditional story for *Legs* (1979), a moral tale of a pair of legs left incomplete by an artist, which symbolise beauty in different ways to different people. *The Sparrow's Story at the King's Command* (1983) is beautifully illustrated in medieval style with meticulously decorated borders and letters. An old storyteller tells his last story for the young prince, and a sparrow delivers it to the palace. *Stolen Magic* (1983) is part of OUP's 'Thematic Pack' on Witches, Ghosts and Hallowe'en. Peter, Sally and Emma discover real magic when they are preparing for a school party. *Song at the Gate* (1987) depicts a warrior king who preserves his solitude until he meets a mystery singer. In *The Night of the Wild Geese* (1990) Eliza can only be brought back to her human form when her father agrees to stop hunting. Crabtree's books have strong messages, often presented in symbolic settings.

CRANE, OLIVE (1902–35), born Sydney, studied at the Julian Ashton School. She designed bookplates and Christmas cards, and exhibited with the NSW Society of Artists after World War I. Crane provided the polished illustrations to *The City of Riddle-Me-Ree* (1918) by Zora Cross and *The Sleeping Sea-Nymph* (1924) by Agnes Littlejohn.

CREW, GARY (1947–), is a teacher, editor and writer. *The Inner Circle* (1986) describes the alienation of Tony, whose broken family do not understand his need for communication, and Joe, whose Aboriginality is used against him when he looks for work. They meet by chance, and find a mutual respect. Each chapter explores the search for solutions by one or other boy. In *The House of Tomorrow* (1988) Danny hears voices, and has premonitions of events to come, experiences described through his teacher, Mr Mac. At one level Danny tells Mac about his life, and at another the reader follows a stream of consciousness where Mac sees his past. Danny's family are Christian fundamentalists and speak in tongues. He is helped by Mac, and a music teacher, Liz, and her boyfriend Leigh. Balance, conflict and metamorphoses are touched on in this complex novel. Crew's next novel, *Strange Objects* (q.v., 1990) took the wreck of the *Batavia* (q.v.) as its background. *No Such Country: a Book of Antipodean Hours* (1991) again examines the first contact between black and white. Rachel and Sarah belong to a fundamentalist religious community which hides a dark secret, uncovered by the Aboriginal student, Sam. For a much younger audience, Crew has written the picture-book, *Tracks* (1992), illustrated by Gregory Rogers. Joel is intrigued by what animal makes the tracks, as he explores the garden at night. Crew's style challenges traditional storytelling techniques, and his thoughtful exploration of characters who are not immediately attractive is rarely attempted in books for young people.

Crichton Award is presented by the CBC, Victorian Branch, to an illustrator who has not previously had a major piece of work published. For over thirty years the Victorian Branch has given a book at Christmas to every child in an institution in the State, and Raymond Wallace Crichton was a generous supporter of the Children's Book Appeal. Mr Crichton made a legacy to the branch, and the award is made through that legacy. The first recipient of the Crichton Award in **1988** was Arone Raymond Meeks for

Pheasant and Kingfisher (1987) by Catherine Berndt. **1989** Marilyn Pride for *Australian Dinosaurs* (1988). **1990** Jeanie Adams for *Pigs and Honey* (q.v., 1989). **1991** Grace Fielding for *Bip the Snapping Bungaroo* (1990) by Narelle McRobbie. **1992** Kim Gamble for *The Magnificent Nose and Other Marvels* (q.v., 1991) by Anna Fienberg.

Cricket the Australian Way (1968) edited by Jack Pollard was Commended in the 1969 Book of the Year Awards. Twenty chapters by famous cricketers follow a Foreword by Sir Donald Bradman. Neil Harvey writes on 'Planning an innings', Keith Miller on 'The fundamentals'; Bill O'Reilly calls his chapter 'Defy the batsman', and Ray Lindwall describes 'The pace that kills'. Illustrated with outstanding black-and-white photographs of players, games and techniques, such as Keith Miller demonstrating an in-swinger, this conversational and useful book was part of a series designed by Lansdowne, which also included *How to Play Aussie Rules* (1960) and *Australian Golfing Success* (1961). Jack Pollard was the editor of the magazines *Sport* and *Outdoors*.

CRIST, ALICE GUERIN (1876–1941), born County Clare, Ireland, came to Australia when she was 2. She wrote poems for the Brisbane *Catholic Advocate*, two collections of poems, *When Rody Came to Ironbark* (1927) and *Eucharistic Lilies and Other Verses* (1929), and *"Go It! Brothers!!"* (1929), dedicated to the Christian Brothers of Australia, which first appeared as a serial in the *Catholic Advocate*. Cyril, alias 'Ginger', cannot join in the athletic pursuits so important to the school's life until a serious fall seems to overcome his frailty.

Criticism of Children's Literature. Despite the controversies which frequently surround children's books, critics have persisted in ignoring them as literature.

The many histories of Australian literature, such as Leonie Kramer's *Oxford History of Australian Literature* (1981) or the earlier John K. Ewers's *Creative Writing in Australia: a Selective Survey* (1966), and critical works such as John Docker's *In a Critical Condition* (1984), do not mention leading Australian children's writers such as Colin Thiele, Patricia Wrightson, Ivan Southall or Eleanor Spence, except where these writers make a contribution to the adult field. Where this has been the case, as it is with Judith Wright, her children's books are not dealt with. Docker allows Ethel Turner a small place in his *The Nervous Nineties: Australian Cultural Life in the 1890s* (1991), and Geoffrey Dutton's *Snow on the Saltbush: the Australian Literary Experience* (1984) recognises the significance of Ethel Turner, Mary Grant Bruce and Ethel Pedley, but the opus of recent writers is rarely discussed. Even in Carole Ferrier's *Gender, Politics and Fiction: Twentieth Century Australian Women's Novels* (1985) or Drusilla Modjeska's *Exiles at Home: Australian Women's Writers, 1925–1945* (1981), children's writers are not mentioned. Despite their contemporary popularity, neither Ethel Turner nor Mary Grant Bruce appear in *Exiles at Home*, although it might have been expected that they would be mentioned in Chapter 1, 'A prolific decade', about women writers of the 1930s, a period when both writers were producing novels. Margaret Smith's 'Australian women novelists of the 1970s: a survey' in Ferrier's book makes no mention of Patricia Wrightson or Eleanor Spence, who had produced novels widely translated and internationally acclaimed. Even where the purpose has been to explore the depiction of women in the Australian novel, as is the case in Shirley Walker's *Who is She? Images of Woman in Australian Fiction* (1983), Judy Woolcott and Nora Linton of Billabong do not appear. In one of the few texts devoted to an investigation of Australian popular culture, Peter Spearritt and David Walker's *Australian Popular Culture* (1979),

while there is a very inadequate bibliography of children's books, the only children's authors referred to in the text are Mary Grant Bruce and Ethel Turner, whose names appear twice. In the Susan Dermody et al. book about popular culture, *Nellie Melba, Ginger Meggs and Friends: Essays in Australian Cultural History* (1982), Ginger is discussed only in terms of his meaning for adult Australia. Ross Gibson's *The Diminishing Paradise: Changing Literary Perceptions of Australia* (1984) disregards children's writers.

Susan Drury's *Writers and Writing* (1979) is the exception to this general position. There are two chapters on children's books, one on the early years of writing for children in Australia, and a second chapter on writers such as Wrightson, Thiele, Spence and Southall. *The Oxford Literary Guide to Australia* (1987) is also more generous. Children's novelists such as H.F. Brinsmead, Mary Grant Bruce, Nan Chauncy, Ruth Park, Dick Roughsey and Patricia Wrightson are included. Similarly, *The Oxford Companion to Australian Literature* (1985) deals with many children's authors and titles. *The Penguin New Literary History of Australia* (1988), edited by Laurie Hergenhan, devotes thirteen of its 620 pages to children's books, in an excellent chapter on 'Children's Literature' by Brenda Niall.

There are three major critical works on Australian children's literature: Maurice Saxby's two-volume *A History of Australian Children's Literature* (1969; 1971) covering the period 1841 to 1970, which has been further updated with *The Proof of the Puddin': Australian Children's Literature 1970–1990* (1993); Walter McVitty's *Innocence and Experience: Essays on Contemporary Australian Children's Writers* (1981); and *Australia Through the Looking Glass: Children's Fiction 1830–1980* (1984) by Brenda Niall. These provide an overview of Australian children's books. Saxby's two-volume work was the first attempt to survey the field, and remains basic to the study of children's literature.

McVitty's aim is to show how eight well-known children's writers have improved their craft, in some cases over three decades, from 'uncomplicated songs of innocence ... towards sober songs of experience', and his essays examine themes, characters, settings and particularly style, *à la* E.M. Forster. Niall says that she will examine the 'perceptions of Australian life in books for children', and is increasingly drawn into an examination of children's books in terms of universal themes: survival stories, the outsiders, the uses of the past, and the communion with the land which Australian children's authors have achieved. Rosemary Wighton's historical and critical work, *Early Australian Children's Literature* (1979), first published in 1963, deals with nineteenth-century books, although there are some general comments on Ethel Turner's work. Maxine Walker's *Writers Alive! Current Australian Authors of Books for Children* (1977) has critical material on lesser known children's writers. Robert Holden's *Twinkle, Twinkle, Southern Cross: the Forgotten Folklore of Australian Nursery Rhymes* (1992) is an important history and analysis of early verse for children.

Invaluable for researchers is Marcie Muir's two-volume A *Bibliography of Australian Children's Books* (1970, 1976), which has been updated and enlarged to include material from 1973 to 1988 by Muir and Kerry White in 1992. Terence and Frances O'Neill's *Australian Children's Books to 1980: a Select Bibliography of the Collection held in the National Library of Australia* (1989) is equally important. John Simkin's *Subject Guide to Australian Children's Books in Print* (1991) contains 3430 titles, cross-referenced under 1800 subject headings. D.W. Thorpe and the National Centre for Australian Studies, Monash University, have produced *Who's Who of Australian Children's Writers* (1992) containing names, addresses, bibliographies, and awards of over 1000 writers for children.

Some books look at the life and work of individual writers and illustrators: Ira Nesdale's *The Little Missus: Mrs Aeneas Gunn* (1977); Philippa Poole's *The Diaries of Ethel Turner* (1979); Alison Alexander's *Billabong's Author: the Life of Mary Grant Bruce* (1979); Brenda Niall's *Seven Little Billabongs: the World of Ethel Turner and Mary Grant Bruce* (1979); Maureen Walsh's *May Gibbs, Mother of the Gumnuts: her Life and Work* (1985); Walter McVitty's *Dorothy Wall, Creator of Blinky Bill: her Life and Work* (1988); Marcie Muir and Robert Holden's *The Fairy World of Ida Rentoul Outhwaite* (1985); and Nancy Phelan's *The Romantic Lives of Louise Mack* (1990). Ivan Southall's *A Journey of Discovery: on Writing for Children* (1975) is a collection of his writings on children's literature and his own development as a writer. Artists and illustrators are considered by Marcie Muir in *A History of Australian Children's Book Illustration* (1982) and her earlier work, *Australian Children's Book Illustrators* (1977). Another introduction to illustration is Robert Holden's *Koalas, Kangaroos and Kookaburras: 200 Australian Children's Books and Illustrations 1857–1988* (1988).

Books which contain material on contemporary authors and illustrators, with statements by the subjects themselves, are Hugh Anderson's *The Singing Roads: a Guide to Australian Children's Authors and Illustrators Part I* (1965) and *Part II* (1969); Michael Dugan's compilation *The Early Dreaming: Australian Children's Authors on Childhood* (1980); Margaret Dunkle's *The Story Makers: a Collection of Interviews with Australian and New Zealand Authors and Illustrators for Young People* (1987) and *Story Makers II* (1989); Belle Alderman and Lauren Harman's *The Imagineers: Writing and Illustrating Children's Books* (1983); and Belle Alderman and Stephanie Owen Reeder's *The Inside Story: Creating Children's Books* (1987). Eleanor Stodart has edited *Writing and Illustrating for Children: Children's Book Council A.C.T. Seminars 1975–1980* (1985), a collection of papers. *The Authors and Illustrators Scrapbook: Featuring 24 Creators of Australian Children's*

Books (1991), published by Omnibus, is a collection of light-hearted autobiographies, with old photographs and mementos of each author, presented for children who want to find out more about their favourite author or illustrator. *Australian Children's Authors* (1986) by Walter McVitty deals with fifteen Australian authors, with brief biographies and photographs; a greater number of authors and illustrators are considered in his *Authors and Illustrators of Australian Children's Books* (1989). Agnes Nieuwenhuizen's *No Kidding: Top Writers for Young People Talk about Their Work* (1990) contains revealing interviews with twelve Australian writers for adolescents.

Other books containing general criticism are Moira Robinson's *Readings in Children's Literature: Proceedings of the National Seminar on Children's Literature at Frankston State College* (1977); Stella Lees's *A Track to Unknown Water: Proceedings of the Second Pacific Rim Conference on Children's Literature* (1980); Maurice Saxby's *Through Folklore to Literature* (1979) and Saxby and Gordon Winch's *Give Them Wings: the Experience of Children's Literature* (1987, 1991). *On Writing for Children* (1991), edited by Kerry Malan, is a collection of nine papers by Australian and overseas writers, including Max Fatchen, Mem Fox, Colin Thiele and Patricia Wrightson. Subjects of contemporary significance, such as the portrayal of girls and immigrants, are dealt with in Anne Hazell's *Reflections of Reality? Female Roles in Australian Adolescent Fiction since World War II* (1989) and *Children's Literature for Multicultural Australia* (1986) by Judith Crewe.

Children's books have not suffered the same neglect as children's authors in adult reviewing journals. Newspapers and general literary journals often include children's book reviews, even from the first issues. For instance *All About Books*, produced by D.W. Thorpe in the 1920s, had reviews of children's books by Nettie Palmer. From 1961 to 1970 *Australian Book Review* produced annual supplements devoted to children's books, edited by Barbara Buick, Anthony Ketley and Rosemary Wighton. Fiction was reviewed by Dennis Hall, then editor of the NSW *School Magazine*, who challenged the general approval accorded children's books. Hall's tough, penetrating criticism did much to raise the standard of writing for children. Hall's successors include Margaret Dunkle and Meg Sorensen. *Magpies: Talking about Books for Children* (1986–), a journal about children's books, is directed at teachers, students and parents. Articles, profiles of contemporary authors and illustrators, interviews and reviews are presented in an attractive format. Other journals which contain critical articles and reviews of children's books include *Reading Time: the Journal of the Children's Book Council of Australia* (1967–), *Orana: Journal of School and Children's Librarianship* (1965–), *Papers: Explorations into Children's Literature* (1990–), and publications by State ministries of education.

Apart from Saxby, McVitty and Niall's monographs, there is little material which examines children's books in depth, although biography, bibliography and description is increasing. The journal *Papers: Explorations into Children's Literature* (1990–) is an attempt to fill this gap, and a collection of articles, *Children's Literature and Contemporary Theory* (1991), edited by Michael Stone signals an increasing interest in examining Australian material in the light of literary theory.

CRONIN, BERNARD (1884–1968), born Ealing, UK, came to Australia in 1890. Cronin wrote thirty novels and many short stories and plays, sometimes using the pseudonym 'Eric North'. He was the first president of the Society of Australian Authors, from 1928 to 1934, and was at the centre of Melbourne literary circles during his lifetime. With Doris Boake Kerr, as 'Stephen Grey', Cronin wrote *Kangaroo Rhymes* (1922). For *The Treasure of the Tropics* (1928) see **Adventure Stories**.

Crooked Snake, The (1955) by Patricia Wrightson, illustrated by Margaret Horder, won the 1956 Book of the Year Awards. Jenny and Peter Conway, Roy and John Fenton and twins Spike and Squeak Kemp have a secret society, the Crooked Snake. They discover a flora reserve, and tangle with four boys who shoot protected animals in the reserve. After a fixed battle with the 'D.Ps' — Dangerous Persons — they confiscate their guns and enlist adult help to have the boys barred from the area. This modest adventure was Wrightson's first novel, and shows her gift for dialogue.

CROPP, BEN (1936–), born Buka Island in the Solomon Islands, is a naturalist and underwater photographer who has used his knowledge of sea animals for *Sammy the Seal* (1966) and *Cheeky the Dolphin* (1968), illustrated with photographs by the author. Both Sammy and Cheeky accept their fate as trained performers in an aquarium.

CROSER, JOSEPHINE CLAIRE (1943–), born Jamestown, SA, also writes as 'Susannah James'. *Roadmaker's Munch* (1986), illustrated by Beverly Allen, juxtaposes, on the left-hand page, a description of the crushing and rolling required to make truffles with, on the right-hand page, heavy vehicles seen in action. Croser has written animal stories, such as *Brella: the Story of a Young Fruit Bat* (1976), illustrated by Inga Moore, which traces the life story of a fruit bat found by Greg and Kerry, and is based on an event which occurred when the author was a biology teacher at a Brisbane school. *Crunch the Crocodile* (1986), illustrated by Carol McLean-Carr, is about a cowardly crocodile. *Clackymucky and the Bulldog* (1988), also illustrated by McLean-Carr, describes the warm relationship between

Ted, the old dog, who acts as temporary mother, and a small duckling who needs care until she is ready to join her family on the pond. In *Tiddycat* (1989), illustrated by Donni Carter, Ben's devotion to a cat that has been killed interferes with his response to a new kitten.

Other books consider human problems. *Matt's Marathon* (1987) is the story of a runaway boy living on the streets of Melbourne. *Let's Go* (1987), illustrated by Robert Roennfeldt, describes how Mr McGregor finds friendship with his neighbours, the Twiggs. He drives them around when they are small, and they take him out for excursions when he is past driving a car. In *The Talking Stone* (1989) Robin and her family move to a country town where Mr Saunders is the teacher. In this study of rural life in the 1950s, Robin meets a deaf girl, Kate, who is victimised by the locals. In *Hello There* (1989), illustrated by Vicky Kitanov, Toby foils an attempted kidnapping by going to a safety house, and in *Rotten Eggs* (1989), also illustrated by Kitanov, Jennifer finds a safety house where she is able to save Jamie from bullies.

Croser introduces fantasy in *Nanna's Magic* (1985), illustrated by Carol McLean-Carr. Nanna makes her walking frame a time machine to take her grandchildren to other worlds. In an attempt to make his parents take some notice of him, Max wins a school prize by deception in *Last Bus Home* (1991). A strange journey on a bus leads him to an apparently abandoned house where he and his companions are forced to confront their own difficulties. As 'Susannah James' she has written *Wingnut* (1989), in which Jay and Tim, alias Wingnut, unmask a gang illegally capturing native birds.

CROSS, ZORA BERNICE MAY (1890–1964), born Brisbane, was a teacher, actor, poet, journalist and critic, whose stormy relationships startled a generation. She wrote poems for many journals, among them the *Bulletin*. *The City of*

Riddle-Me-Ree (1918), delicately illustrated and decorated by Olive Crane, is a verse fairy-tale, in which Boy Blue and Bo Peep fall in love: 'And still they are running, Boy Blue and Bo Peep,/Along with the Queen by that dancing blue sea,/Where the lame and the weary forget how to weep/In the beautiful region of Riddle-Me-Ree.' See also **Nursery Rhymes**. Cross was commissioned by Angus & Robertson to produce a further book of nursery poems in 1924, but the two parties fell out, and it was not published.

CROW Awards (Children Rate Outstanding Writers and Illustrators) are the Children's Choice Awards given in SA, established by the Centre for Children's Literature in 1992. Voting is in two categories, Years 3, 4 and 5 and Years 6 and 7, and children are asked to vote on a list of books derived from their nominations.

Crusher is Coming (1987), written and illustrated by Bob Graham, won the 1988 Picture Book of the Year Awards. When Crusher comes to Peter's place, Peter is anxious to impress him by appearing tough and manly, because Crusher is his idol — a big red-haired football-player. As it turns out, the easygoing Crusher likes playing tea parties and reading to little sister Claire. During Crusher's visit, Peter learns to see his sister in a new light, and develops greater confidence in his own attitudes to his family, in this gentle tilt at stereotyped manly behaviour.

Cub, The is John Calthrop, in Ethel Turner's *The Cub* (1915), *Captain Cub* (1917), and *Brigid and the Cub* (1919). His career from unhappy schoolboy to army officer at Gallipoli concludes with his marriage to Brigid Lindsay. See also **War**.

CUNNINGHAM, WALTER (1910–88), born Surrey, England, the husband of Noela Young, arrived in Australia at the age of 14 and became a messenger boy for John Sands, Sydney printers and publishers. He studied at the National Art School, where he later taught illustration. Cunningham drew a comic-strip, 'Kaark the Crow' for the *Sydney Morning Herald* during the 1940s. He was a staff artist at Sands, and collaborated with Leslie Rees on the Digit Dick books and a successful series of animal stories, beginning with *The Story of Shy the Platypus* (1944) and including *The Story of Aroora the Red Kangaroo* (1952), *The Story of Sarli the Barrier Reef Turtle* (1947), *The Story of Karrawingi the Emu* (q.v., 1946), *The Story of Russ, the Australian Tree Kangaroo* (1964), *The Story of Shadow the Rock Wallaby* (1948), *The Story of Wy-lah the Cockatoo* (1959) and *A Treasury of Australian Nature Stories* (1974). Other animal illustrations appear in A.S. Le Souef's *The Brownie Twins: the Story of a Ringtail Family* (1955), *Eric Worrell's Australian Birds and Animals* (1970), *Quippy: a Story for Three Year Olds* (1946) by Olive Mason, *The Dove and the Eagle* (1956) by F. Moss and *Silvertail, the Story of a Lyrebird* (1946) by Ina Watson. Australian themes are pictured in *Sandy the Cane Train* (1966) by Jean Chapman, *Jackey Jackey* (1976) by Margaret Paice, *The Loaded Dog* (1970) by Henry Lawson, *The Old Man River of Australia: a Saga of the River Murray* (1945) by Leila Pirani, *River Rivals* (1975) by Ian Mudie, *They Live in Australia* (1960) by Eve Pownall and *Tales of the Dreamtime* (1975), a selection by Vashti Farrer from K. Langloh Parker's *Australian Legendary Tales* (1896). Cunningham's expert watercolours in effective double-page layouts were innovations during the 1940s, and marked a development in children's book design.

CURLEWIS, JEAN (1899–1930), born Sydney, was the daughter of Ethel Turner. In *The Ship that Never Set Sail* (1921), illustrated by J. Macfarlane, Brenda longs for adventure and a life at sea. She practices at sleeping out, making damper, and tying knots. As she grows older she meets Jimmy Stevenson, who shares her dreams, but he is forced to become a mundane shop assistant. Brenda at first rejects his practicality, but finally realises that his dreams are based more in reality than her own. In *Drowning Maze* (1922), also illustrated by Macfarlane, four schoolboys solve domestic crises, and find the crown jewels and the formula for an important dye process which belong to a Balkan country, Cadalia. In *Beach Beyond* (1923), illustrated by Macfarlane, Merrick leaves his desk job to act as lifesaver for a group of families at an isolated beach. When the obsessed millionaire, David Hartley, threatens to take the families to a Utopia he has been organising on a Pacific island, Merrick and the brilliant Egbert save the day. *The Dawn Man* (1924), illustrated by Harold Copping, is an adult romantic mystery story about Anthony Brant, aged 22, who is an anthropologist. Curlewis wrote a comic story with her mother, *The Sunshine Family: a Book of Nonsense for Girls and Boys* (1923) (See **Turner, Ethel**). *Verse Writing for Beginners* (1924) is a handbook on how to construct verse. Curlewis wrote with conviction, and her spirited characters, particularly Brenda in *The Ship that Never Set Sail*, suggest that she had a greater potential than was able to be realised before her untimely death.

Curse of the Turtle, The (1977) by Thomas Roy, illustrated by Rex Backhaus-Smith, was Commended in the 1978 Book of the Year Awards. The story is told by Jimmy Brent, the grandson of the white man who built 'Oonaderra' on a sacred Aboriginal site. Jimmy's friends are the traditional owners, the Oona people, whose totem is the great turtle. As he develops a respect for their culture and lifestyle, Jimmy finds himself increasingly alienated from his father's attitudes to the Oonas. He becomes an honorary member of the Oona people. When his father dies and the station is in the grip of a drought, Jimmy pleads with his mother to move the house away from the Bora Ring. The novel concludes with a well sunk near the house which has been moved, the end of the drought, and the curse lifted from 'Oonaderra'. In *The Vengeance of the Dolphin* (1980), also illustrated by Backhaus-Smith, Jimmy discovers a carved stick which he shows to his Aboriginal friends. They realise that it contains information on a murder, and with Jimmy's help they and the Burunjis, a neighbouring people, seek out the murderer and avenge the wrong done twenty-five years ago. See also **Aboriginal People in Children's Fiction.**

CUSACK, ELLEN DYMPHNA (1902–81), born Wyalong, NSW, wrote books and plays for adults. *Kanga-Bee and Kanga-Bo* (1945) illustrated by Matt-Slater-Wigg, is a mixture of fairy happenings and bush life in which the Rainbow Serpent sends two babies to Mother Murrimbidgee in gratitude for his reflection in the river. Mother Murrumbidgee discusses the future of Kanga-Bee and Kanga-Bo with Mr Yabbie, and they are taken in by Bidgee Bunyip, where they rescue Joey Kangaroo from Dingo's gang. Cusack collaborated with Florence James to write *Four Winds and a Family* (1947), illustrated by Virginia Sikorskis. Tess and Topsy look after their three nieces, Jay, Fan and Dee, for a summer. The novel describes the antics of the children and the animals they adopt, in a playful, indulgent tone. The same collaboration produced the adult novel *Come In, Spinner* (1951).

D

'**DALE, EDWIN**' was the pseudonym of **EDWARD R. HOME-GALL** (1899–), born London, UK. Home-Gall joined the Amalgamated Press as an office boy, and became the most prolific writer of boys' stories, next to Charles Hamilton ('Frank Richards'). He wrote for the *Champion* and *Triumph*, and produced the first story to feature speedway racing in Britain. In his series in the *Champion Library* were stories set in Australia. *From Bush to Speedway!* (No. 77, 1932) is a motorbike story about Jack Sterling, *Lone Hand Lawrence: the Aussie Speedster* (No. 145, 1935) also features motorbikes. At the conclusion, Lawrence's 'two enemies, Paola Martz and Jake Horde had been handed over to the police. He had recovered his father's lost fortune, making the Bush Speedsters the richest bunch of cinder pals in the world — and he had helped Australia to win the speedway Test.' *King Flame* (No. 194, 1937) is 'a thrill and laughter packed horse-racing story', in which Stocky Gordon rides a brumby to win the Australia Cup, with 'Swan Hill' sheep station thrown in with the prize. Villains are recognisable from their shifty eyes and mean streaks, and heroes are identified by their square jaws and riding finesse in these entertaining 'penny dreadfuls', which cost fourpence a copy.

DALE, RAE (1945–), born Melbourne, has illustrated *Fight for Life* (1972) by Alan Marshall, *The Greatest Juggler in the World* (1972) by Barry Carozzi, *The Three*

The Champion Library, 1932–1937

Dragons (1975) by Jenny Pausacker, *Fish, Chips and Jaws* (1987) by Hazel Edwards, *The Undoing of Jeremy Kite* (1988), by Maureen Stewart, *Heffalump?, Heffalump? and the Toy Hospital* (1989) and *Pomily's Wish* (1987) by Eleanor Nilsson.

DALGLEISH, JOAN (1938–), born Sydney, has written stage, radio and television plays. Her books featuring animals include *Dog on a Diet* (1989), illustrated by Stephen Axelsen. Strider's photogenic qualities turn him into a television star, solving the James family's straitened circumstances. In *Cats Don't Bark* (1978), illustrated by Walter Stackpool, Clarence the cat terrorises the gentle labrador dog Angel, and creates domestic chaos for Jeff's family. In *Clarence Settles Down* (1986), also illustrated by Stackpool, the temperamental Clarence violently resists the temporary invasion of his territory by the beautiful Clarissa, a persian. These are funny stories of an interesting and good-natured family and their assertive cat. *The Latchkey Dog* (1980), illustrated by Stephen Axelsen, is the disaster-prone labrador, Sebastian, who is dearly loved by his family, despite the damage he causes. *Kate and the Runaway Granny* (1980) in Rigby's 'Reading Rigby' series relates how Kate and the elderly Winifred are able to help each other when each of them becomes a problem to those who are caring for them. In *Kate and the Horse Camp* (1982) Kate's initial dislike of horses is overcome.

Holidays at Hillydale (1973) by Dame Mary Daly. Illustrator: Betty Paterson

In *Dim and Dusty* (1983), illustrated by Julie Vivas, two children meet on their first day at school. When hams are stolen from Dim Mavropoulou's family delicatessen, Dusty helps find the culprit.

DALY, Dame **MARY DORA** (?–1983), born Cootamundra, NSW, wrote *Cinty and the Laughing Jackasses and Other Children's Stories* (1961), fairy stories with fine illustrations by William Dargie, William Dobell, Betty and Esther Paterson, Hans Heysen and other artists. *Timmy's Christmas Surprise* (1967) was illustrated by George Arnold, Max Middleton, Dudley Drew, Betty and Esther Paterson and Ambrose Griffin. *Holidays at Hillydale: A Story for Children about a Family's Holiday Spent on an Australian Sheep Station* (1973) has seventeen illustrators, including Russell Drysdale, William Dargie and Kenneth Jack. The three books were published in aid of the Yooralla Hospital for Crippled Children, and were introduced by Sir Dallas Brooks, Dame Pattie Menzies and Sir Robert Menzies respectively.

DALZIEL, KEN (1916–), spent a year in Antarctica, an experience described in *Penguin Road* (q.v., 1955).

Dancing in the Anzac Deli (1984) by Nadia Wheatley, illustrated by Waldemar Buczynski, was Commended in the 1985 Book of the Year Awards. See ***Five Times Dizzy***.

DANN, MAX (1955–), born Yarraville, Victoria, who has worked as a carpenter's apprentice, handyman, factory worker and gardener, writes witty stories for 8 to 12-year-olds. *Adventures with My Worst Best Friend* (1982), illustrated by Graeme Base, introduced Roger Thesaurus, whose best friend is the redoubtable Dusting (q.v.). The vagaries of the friendship are continued in *The Mystery of the Haunted Theatre* (1983), in which Thesaurus and Dusting, in an attempt to make their fortune, run

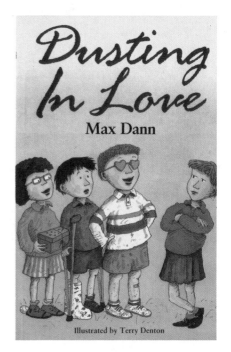

Dusting in Love (1990) by Max Dann. Illustrator: Terry Denton

up against the terrifying ghosts Marie Annabel Ashley and Douglas, and in *Going Bananas* (1983) and *Dusting in Love* (1990), all illustrated by Terry Denton, the last with Dusting in the throes of his first love affair. *Bernice Knows Best* (q.v., 1983) describes another friendship fraught with crises. In *Ernest Pickle's Remarkable Robot* (1984) Glen is a robot built by Ernest to solve problems with relationships, but Glen prefers to read *Home and Garden* magazine. In *One Night at Lottie's House* (1985) the timorous Arthur spends a night with the unconventional family of his friend Lottie. The hero of *Clark* (1987), illustrated by Carol Pelham-Thorman, is afraid of his new teacher, Mr Grimwraither. When the teacher comes to live at the end of Clark's street, and he is called on to save Grimwraither's life, Clark comes to understand a lonely man. *Horrible Humans* (1990), illustrated by Peter Viska, is a taxonomy of the more offensive aspects of humankind. *The*

Lonely Hearts Club (1987), written with Robin Klein, is for older readers, and describes how Donovan, Scuff and Rasputin engage in a frantic search for girls, only to be foiled by Tracee-Ann and Cheryl. *The Onion Man* (1988) is a novel for adults. Most of Dann's stories are set in Yarraville, an inner suburb of Melbourne, which is celebrated for its working-class traditions. The area was also the setting for the films *The Big Steal* and *Spotswood*. Dann collaborated on the script for both films. He has also written scripts for television, including 'The Fast Lane' and 'Fast Forward'. He has a sense of the absurd, an affection for the foibles of children and an understanding of their vulnerability.

Darkness Under the Hills (1980) by Bill Scott, illustrated by A.M. Hicks, was Highly Commended in the 1981 Book of the Year Awards. See **Boori**.

Darwin, capital city of the NT, appears to be off the map of children's books. It is the setting of *Top-Enders* (1988) by Jennifer Dabbs. Dabbs presents a multicultural town on the edge of the outback, with a modern casino, and the attractions of wilderness areas such as Kakadu for tourists. *When Tracy Came for Christmas* (1982) by June Epstein describes the terror of the cyclone which ravaged Darwin. Darwin still awaits a children's novelist to bring to life its cultural diversity.

DASKEIN, TARELLA QUIN (1877–1934), born 'Tarella' Station, near Wilcannia, NSW, was a major contributor to the Australian fairy story through her collections, all illustrated by her friend Ida Rentoul Outhwaite. The first of these, *Gum Tree Brownie and Other Faerie Folk of the Never Never* (1907), published by George Robertson with an introduction by Ethel Turner, was written and illustrated before either Daskein or Outhwaite were married, and working as Tarella

Quin and Ida S. Rentoul. There are eight stories: 'Gum tree brownie', about Martin, a woodcutter, who finds a brownie in a tree, 'Where stars abound', 'The other side of Nowhere', 'The Professor's dream', 'September gold', 'The Storm sprite', 'The City of dreams', and 'Exit to Faerieland'. It also contains music by Kenneth L. Duffield to a poem 'Over the water to Nowhere'. The stories are imaginative, and although calling on European fairy traditions, are set against the Australian landscape. Daskein followed this collection with *Before the Lamps are Lit* (1911), which has six stories: 'Before the lamps are lit', a sequel to 'Where stars abound' in *Gum Tree Brownie*, 'Ebenezer's anniversary', 'Constellation jam', 'Poppy and the pixies', 'The strange adventures of Aunt Martha', and 'The Binnajig and the Tattyoon'. *The Other Side of Nowhere* (1934) is a selection from the stories first found in *Gum Tree Brownie*. *The Other Side of Nowhere* is included in *The Australian Wonder Book* (q.v., 1935), and was republished by Angus & Robertson in 1983.

Chimney Town (1934) has four stories which show Daskein's inventive imagination. 'Chimney Town' is about a poor boy, Feathers, who spends time in a fairy town, described by the author in clever detail. 'Here come the bears' introduces a family of koalas who are the direct descendants of the famous Three Bears, and have Goldilocks's spoon and chair as family heirlooms. Mr Bear is terrified that Goldilocks will invade again, so the family emigrate to Australia, where they encounter Ravenlocks, the daughter of the Governor of NSW. Ravenlocks wants to stop the shooting of koalas, so she persuades her father to set aside a sanctuary for the Bear family. In 'The Stratosphere', three men, an inventor, a mathematician (Mr Add-em Smith), and a historian set out to discover the stratosphere only to find there are others there already. Janie in 'Janie of the magic shoes' has a fairy streak in her, which enables her to be taken by her magical fairy shoes to the outback, where she meets fairies and talks to animals. The Binnajig, in plaid suit and boxer hat, and the Tattyoon, in tattered clothes and walrus moustache, come from outer space to take the wisest man on Earth on a journey in a strongly realised story. Daskein's fairy creations display her originality, humour and sense of the Australian landscape. See also **Fairies**. Her realistic novel, *Freckles* (1910), illustrated by Jack Somers, relates the story of a small boy, Len Templeton, who goes to live with his uncle on 'Goonambery' Station. The novel is in the sentimental style of the period: an innocent and loveable boy wins over the crusty bachelors and brings joy to everyone. However, Freckles's charm is conveyed with flair, and Daskein's evocation of the countryside during a drought provides a strong picture of a uniquely Australian experience.

DAVEY, GWENDA BEED (1932–), born Melbourne, is a writer and folklorist. Davey worked with June Factor to develop the archive, the Australian Children's Folklore Collection (q.v.). *Snug as a Bug: Scenes from Family Life* (1990) and *Duck Under the Table* (1991), both humorously illustrated by Peter Viska, are collections of household sayings, family banter and rhymes. *The Great Australian Pumpkin* (1991), with Ron Edwards, is a tall story in the tradition of the Speewah, in which the pumpkin is so big that it hides a mob of sheep and a team of bullocks.

DAVEY, THRYZA (1931–), born Hahndorf, SA, is a writer and illustrator. *Waiting for May* (1984) is set in Queensland, on Bribie Island. Old Mr Thompson is saved from the threat of a nursing home when a cyclone destroys his houseboat, and he joins the family of his young friend, Chris. Lisa goes in search of her beloved cat, Poona, in *Yonderbeyonder* (1990), the land where dead pets go. Davey's atmospheric paintings of landscapes, interiors and people, provide

glimpses of life, often from a stairway or through a door.

DAVIDSON, PETER. For *Wunnamurra & Noorengong: How the Animals Came to Australia* (1978) see **Aboriginal Dreaming Stories**.

DAVISON, FRANK DALBY (1893–1970), born Melbourne, spent his childhood in Australia and his teenage years in the USA. Davison was a soldier settler in Queensland after World War I, then joined his father who was running a magazine in Sydney. After his marriage and during the Depression, Davison and his father printed *Man-Shy* themselves. 'We had a little old two-seater Rover car and loaded up the booby seat with copies of my book [*Forever Morning*] and the Smith and Ulm book [on their flight across the Pacific] — done up in pairs — and left them on doorsteps (street by street) in the more prosperous suburbs, and called round next morning, after the people had had time to examine them, to see if they wanted to buy. The wheeze worked, to the extent that my brother and I made a living — provided we didn't take the running costs of the car into account. It was in an effort to meet the latter — by including in the package a book that could be sold for the small sum of sixpence, as against the others at two and sixpence each — that *Man-Shy* came to be printed.' *Man-Shy: a Story of Men and Cattle* (1931) recounts the life of a red heifer and her struggle to remain free despite the efforts of men to contain her in the cattle herd. *Dusty: a Dog of the Sheep Country* (1946), like *Man-Shy*, is an animal story, this time about the offspring of a kelpie father and dingo mother. The dog's life is traced from birth to death, through his ownership by the bush worker, Tom, and Dusty's ever-present conflict between civilisation and the wild. In both *Man-Shy* and *Dusty* it is the spirit which remains untouched by the demands of the captor, Man. *Dusty* was filmed in 1982, directed by John Richardson, scripted by Sonia Borg, with Bill Kerr as Tom. In 1987 it was made into a television series of six one-hour episodes, directed by Colin Budds and scripted by John Misto and Graeme Farmer. *Man-Shy* and *Dusty* were not published as children's books but have been widely used as such since publication. Davison wrote *Children of the Dark People: an Australian Folk Tale* (q.v., 1936) for children.

DAVISON, FRED (1868–1942), born Mt Buninyong, Victoria, was the father of Frank Dalby Davison. For *Duck Williams and His Cobbers* (1939) see **Boys**.

DAWSON, ALEC JOHN (1872–1951), born London, UK, sailed to Australia as an apprentice, deserted his ship in Melbourne, and stayed for some years, working as a journalist. Some of the action of *Finn the Wolfhound* (1908) takes place in Australia, when Finn is stolen and taken to a circus. He escapes and learns to survive in the bush, mating with a dingo before returning to his owner, and then is taken back to Sussex. *Jan, Son of Finn* (1917) followed. Other books by this author are set in Canada and England.

DAWSON, DAGMA (1933–), born Sydney, wrote *Ladybird Garden* (q.v., 1949).

Day at the Zoo, A (1964) by Carol Odell was Commended in the 1965 Book of the Year Awards. Descriptions of animal families, feeding time and other daily events in the lives of the animals and birds at the Tooronga Zoo are brought to life in fine black-and-white photographs.

DE FOSSARD, ESTA (1934–) is a consultant in educational radio. *Puffing Billy: a Story for Children* (q.v., 1967) was illustrated by John Mason. In *Barrenjoey* (1971), also illustrated by Mason, the ferry which usually runs between Sydney and

Manly sails all the way to Melbourne for Moomba. *Let's Go Sailing* (1971) was also illustrated by Mason. For *The Alien* (1977) see **Immigrants**. De Fossard has published a series of animal books for young children, with photographs by Haworth Bartram, including *Monty Learns to Fly* (1982), *Friske, the Unfriendly Foal* and *Catkin the Curious Kitten* (both 1974). *Koala and the Bunyip* (1982), *Koala and the Tasmanian Devil and the Possum Hunt* (1984) and *Koala and Emu and the Unexpected Box* (1984), with photographs by Neil McLeod and illustrations by Lynn Twelftree, are animal adventures for young readers featuring Koala and his bush friends. De Fossard has also contributed many titles to reading programs. For her novels written as 'Estelle Grey' see **Gordon, Julie**.

DE GARIS, CLEMENT JOHN (1884–1926), born Mildura, Victoria, was a colourful businessman. He developed the Australian dried fruit industry through a very successful publicity campaign, made non-stop flights between State capitals in fragile aircraft, set up a commune in Pyap, SA, planned an agricultural future for Kendenup, WA, and proposed the greater development of Geelong, Victoria. His grand schemes eventually collapsed, and after a fake suicide, a court case and further economic difficulties, he died. An account of De Garis's life can be found in Keith Dunstan's *Ratbags* (1979). De Garis chose the name 'SUN-RAYSED' fruits from a competition he ran, and edited the *"Sun-Raysed" Children's Fairy Book* (1919). Fifteen prize-winning fairy stories, nursery rhymes, limericks, parodies and acrostics were selected. Reg Simpson, from Punt Road, South Yarra, Melbourne, wrote: 'Mary had a little lamb/And nearly every day,/From early morn till late at night,/You'd find them both at play./Mary's mother's SUN-RAYSED fruits/Disappeared too fast;/She set a trap each night for weeks,/And caught the thief at last./Mary had throughout these weeks/Suspected brother Sam;/But when her father forced the door,/He found inside — the lamb./Mary now has got a doll — /She wheels it in a pram,/For Sunday's dinner they will have/A leg of Mary's lamb.'

DE PAAUW, WENDY. For *Ten Little Australians* (1984) see **Alphabet Books**.

DE SELINCOURT, AUBREY (1894–1962). For *Mr Oram's Story: the Adventures of Capt. James Cook, R.N.* (1949) see **Cook**, Captain **James**.

DEANS, LESLIE. For *The Imp and the Fairy* (1945) see **Fairies**.

Death. Perhaps the most memorable example of the death of a character is that of Judy in *Seven Little Australians* (1894) by Ethel Turner. Judy's death occupies two chapters at the end of the novel. It is in the tradition of the Victorian novel for children that a child may die, and the passing of the child, often witnessed by the family, is described in detail. Turner's treatment is not as saccharine as many, and as Brenda Niall says, 'What makes the scene moving is the children's struggle to meet the demands of Judy's death, with an uncertain faith and no adult protection against their own fear.' '"Meg, I'm so frightened! I can't think of anything but 'For what we are about to receive', and that's grace, isn't it? And there's nothing in 'Our Father' that would do, either. Look at the dark, Meg. Oh, Meg, hold my hands! ... " The shadows were cold, and smote upon their hearts; they could feel the wind from the strange waters on their brows; but only she who was about to cross heard the low lapping of the waves ... Then the wind blew over them all, and with a little shudder she slipped away.' Judy's death concludes her story. Nearly a hundred years later, when Vasilios dies in Maureen McCarthy's *Ganglands* (1992), 'blood poured from the back of his broken skull and bone protruded from the end of a twisted leg. But the young man's face upturned in death was strangely peaceful.' McCarthy is concerned to show the effect of Vasilios's death on his grieving family, and his death provides the impetus for the story.

The death of a character, such as in Christobel Mattingley's *The Angel with a Mouth-organ* (1984), occurs as part of the action in many novels. In others it becomes the background to the plot, as in Eleanor Spence's *Miranda Going Home* (1985) or Lilith Norman's *Climb a Lonely Hill* (q.v., 1970). In some, death occurs but is not given any great significance. Valerie Thompson opens *Rough Road South* (1975) with the death of Rob's brother John. Rob's grief is short-lived. He is readily consoled by the doctor who attended his brother: '"Keep yourself warm and don't worry about a thing."' Some novelists, however, have explored the pain of grief and loss in greater detail. Little Ellie, in *Dusky Dell* (1898) by Bertha Southey Adams, dies in the arms of her 'dearest adopted sister, Dell'. For the 5-year-old it is a gentle release, but Dell has lost the only person who loved her. 'Side by side they lay when the parting came, and none could guess the agony the elder child suffered as the spark flickered and went out.' In H. Louisa Bedford's *A Home in the Bush* (1913) the lasting sorrow of Aunt Mary is that her only daughter, also called Mary, disappeared in the bush some years before. The mother is eventually able to reconcile herself to her loss when she discovers that her daughter died from exposure in the remote bush home of an elderly couple, and is buried there.

In later twentieth-century novels, writers have expanded on the emotional effects of death. Colin Thiele's *Storm Boy* (1963) describes the lingering death of Mr Percival, the pelican, who is capriciously killed by shooters. Thiele examines the grief of the boy during and after the bird's death, which marks the turning-point for Storm Boy, who then decides to leave the Coorong for school. Lilith Norman's *A Dream of Seas* (1978) deals with the grief of an unnamed boy who gradually retreats from life after his father drowns. His dreams involve images of seals. As the boy sets out on his final journey towards the ocean, he too becomes one of the seals. In Max Fatchen's *Closer to the Stars* (1981) the death of Nancy's lover is seen through the eyes of 13-year-old Paul as part of the cycle of life and death. Junko Morimoto's picture-book *Kojuro and the Bears* (q.v., 1986) again considers death as 'the turning of the wheel'. Morimoto tells the story of the annihilation of Hiroshima in *My Hiroshima* (1987). The horror of so many deaths is recollected in simple and powerful language against graphic images. In Barbara Bolton's *Edward Wilkins and his Friend Gwendoline* (1985) Edward the cat looks forward to joining in Heaven his beloved Gwendoline, who has cared for him until her death. Margaret Wild's *The Very Best of Friends* (1989), illustrated by Julie Vivas, has a cat which symbolises Jesse's grief for her husband, James. Jesse rejects James's cat, William, but after James's death she sees how William deteriorates from the loss of his love. Together, cat and woman are able to find comfort in each other. Letitia Parr's *Flowers for Samantha* (1975) concludes with the family burying the cat, a final ritual. In *John Brown, Rose and the Midnight Cat* (q.v., 1977) by Jenny Wagner, illustrated by Ron Brooks, the cat can be interpreted as Death, which wishes to gather up Rose; the dog, John Brown, is the life force.

Complex reactions to the death of a close friend or relative are explored in novels by N.L. Ray, Joan Phipson, James Preston, David Martin and others. Vicki in N.L. Ray's *Nightmare to Nowhere* (1980) dies by accident, and Ray describes Bryony's shock and loneliness powerfully. The reaction to his mother's enigmatic death in *A Tide Flowing* (1981) by Joan Phipson is resolved by Mark's relationship with the disabled Connie, who also dies. James Preston's *The Sky Between the Trees* (1986) deals with Peter's reactions to the death of his father, whom Peter is unable

to save from drowning. Peter is angry, confused and grief-stricken, and only his mother's understanding enables his distress to be resolved. The death of Bess's mother in David Martin's *The Cabby's Daughter* (1974) precipitates the disintegration of the family, just as their father's death in Alan Collins's *The Boys from Bondi* (1987) results in Solly and Jacob being sent to a home. Another death, the accidental death of Solly, occurs at the end of the same novel. In Bron Nicholls's *Mullaway* (1986) the impending death of her mother forces Mully, like Bess in the Martin novel, to reappraise her role in the family. Donna Sharp's *Blue Days* (1986) has a girl grieving for her father, which results in difficulties in her relationship with her mother. In Mary Pershall's *You Take the High Road* (1988) Sam blames her mother for the death of her baby brother Nicholas. In this poignant novel the death divides the family, and Sam's involvement with her own grief blinds her to other people's pain. The same occurrence, the death of a baby, is the catalyst in *Sophie's Island* (1990) by David Rish. In a sombre novel, *Black Sorrow* (1980), Reginald Ottley's central character, Jody, works through her reactions to her own disability and her mother's death as a result of a car accident. She rehabilitates a savagely treated brumby, Black Sorrow, who repays the debt with his own life. Joan Woodberry's *Come Back Peter* (1968) is set in outback Queensland, where Paul's older brother has recently been killed in a horse-riding accident. The plot revolves around the family's reaction to the death and particularly its effect on Paul, who feels guilty for remaining alive when Peter is dead. His sense of loss, the inability of adults around him to talk in other than euphemisms, the irrational overprotectiveness of his mother are all dealt with sensitively. At the conclusion of the book, Paul and his mother recognise that 'Death was a part of the law of the bush'. Colin's painful struggle to accept that his brother will die, in *Two Weeks with the Queen* (1989) by Morris Gleitzman, is told with humour. The lonely and violent death of Cal in Gillian Rubinstein's *Beyond the Labyrinth* (q.v., 1988) symbolises alienation, a condition which also affects Brenton, and to a lesser degree, Victoria. The final novel in Patricia Wrightson's Wirrun trilogy, *Behind the Wind* (1981, see **The Ice is Coming**) takes Wirrun 'behind the wind', 'grown out of now into forever' with the Murra as his bride. It is his symbolic victory over Death. Similarly, in Bill Scott's *Darkness Under the Hills* (1980, see **Boori**) Boori and Dingo's mortal battle with Rakasha concludes in their victory, but with their spirits taken to the sky.

The latter half of the twentieth century has seen a proliferation of books which include a death, a manifestation of the desire to inform children of the realities of life. Death is regarded as either a part of the life cycle, as in *Kojuro and the Bears*, or a capricious event which shatters those around it, as in *You Take the High Road*.

DEE, SHERYN. For *Tarin of the Ice* (1987) see **Science Fiction**.

Deezle Boy (1987) by Eleanor Spence was an Honour Book in the 1988 Book of the Year Awards: Older Readers. Grant's enthusiasm for trains and their engines is his main interest until he is abducted by a stranger, Laurie, who claims to be a relative. Laurie and her daughter Holly take Grant from place to place to avoid discovery, and their muddled life and Laurie's vagueness force Grant to learn how to assert himself. As his affection for Laurie grows, he begins to see some of the intricacies of family relationships.

Demon McGuire, The, see **GRUNDY, FRANCIS H.**

DENNIS, C. J. (CLARENCE MICHAEL JAMES) (1876–1936), born Auburn, SA, wrote *The Songs of a Sentimental Bloke* (1915) and *The Moods of Ginger Mick*

(1916). His children's book, *A Book for Kids* (1921), illustrated by the author, which was reissued as *Roundabout* in 1935, contains entertaining nonsense verse, poems and short stories, including 'The little red house', 'The ant explorer', 'The boy who rode into the sunset', 'Hist!' and 'Triantiwontigongalope', the latter reminiscent of Lewis Carroll's verse. *The Triantiwontigongelope and Other Funny Poems* was illustrated in 1989 by Patricia Mullins, and *The Ant Explorer* was illustrated by Rita Hall in 1988 and Vaughan Duck in 1990. *Hist!* (q.v., 1991) was illustrated by Peter Gouldthorpe with atmospheric linocuts and silhouettes. Further reading: Chisholm, *The Making of a Sentimental Bloke*.

DENTON, TERRY (1950–), born Melbourne, studied architecture before becoming an illustrator. He illustrated for *Comet*, a journal of the Victorian Ministry of Education, and contributed to *The All Australian Ha Ha Book* (1983). He has illustrated *Going Bananas* (1983) and *Mystery of the Haunted Theatre* (1983) by Max Dann; *The Story of Imelda, Who was Small* (1984) and *What's That Noise? What's That Sound?* (1991) by Morris Lurie; *A Teddy Bear's Picnic: a Collection of Original Stories about Teddy Bears* (1986) by various authors (see **Collections**); *Ten Monster Islands* (1987) by Doug MacLeod; *Meannie and the Min Min* (1987) by Pamela Shrapnel; *Night Noises* (1989) by Mem Fox; *Jimmy and his Fabulous Feathered Friends* (1988) by Peita Letchford; *Amy's Monster* (1990) by Jenny Wagner; and *Funky Man, Monkey Fan* (1991) by Paul Jennings and Ted Greenwood. He has written and illustrated *Felix and Alexander* (q.v., 1985) and *Flying Man* (1984), about Mungo Merryweather, who is obsessed with flight. Mungo's boarding house existence is relieved by his inventions, until the birds lend him a wing and he is really free. *At the Cafe Splendid* (1987) depicts ice palaces and huge waves in a fairy-tale city. In *Home is the Sailor* (1988) Claude and his penguin friend Sparky guide Captain Hagar, the seal, through bright seascapes to the Land of the Midnight Sea. In *The School for Laughter* (1989) Eddie loses his laugh and is sent to a very silly special school to learn to laugh again. Denton's comic figures and mastery of atmospheric colour convey strong emotions, laced with humour.

'DESDA' (Mrs DAVIES). For *The Rival Fairies: or, Little Maimie's Trouble, an Australian Story for Children* (1871) see **Fairies**.

DEVANEY, JAMES (1890–1976), born Bendigo, Victoria, was a nature writer, novelist and poet. His collection of short stories for adults, *The Vanished Tribes* (1929), drew on the life and culture of the Aboriginal People. The stories were adapted for children in four volumes, *The Girl Oona and other Tales of the Australian Blacks* (1929), *The Witch-Doctor and Other Tales of the Australian Blacks* (1930), *I-Rinka the Messenger and Other Tales of the Australian Blacks* (1930) and *The Fire Tribe and Other Tales of the Australian Blacks* (1930).

Devils' Hill (1958) by Nan Chauncy, illustrated by Geraldine Spence, was the joint winner of the 1959 Book of the Year Awards, and is the second book in the trilogy about the Lorenny family. Cousins Sammy, Bron and Sheppie (Soolvie) join Badge and his parents, in a search for a missing calf, camping out and travelling to a distant outcrop — Devils' Hill. Sophisticated, clever Sammy emerges as unreliable and self-centred, although his character improves towards the end of the book. Badge, more naive, is also more trustworthy, modest, caring and patient with the girls. Bron gains courage and self confidence. The missing cow is found, now with a calf of her own, and brought back to the farm. Although the plot of *Devils' Hill* is not as tightly developed as

the first of the Lorenny books, *Tiger in the Bush* (q.v., 1957), it is a well-paced adventure story with fine character studies. A version for television by David Phillips was included in the 1988 'Touch the Sun' (q.v.) series.

Devil's Stone, The (1983) by 'Helen Frances', illustrated by Kerry Argent, was Commended in the 1984 Book of the Year Awards. Present and past are entangled through a diary, geographical formations, and a pair of twins in each of two centuries. Emma Rose and Lauralei Tregarren are the children of the first whites to pioneer Bungaytown. They climb Crag Tor, a sacred place of the Aboriginal People, and find hidden caves, disturbing ancient spirits. The modern Emma and Leigh find a diary in the same caves, and the movement of the stones is re-enacted. Again tragedy looms, but is averted as the nineteenth-century twins appear to guide Emma and Leigh out of the caves. The novel draws on Aboriginal legend in a fast-moving fantasy.

Devlin, Peter is the central character in the series of that name by Paul Buddee. In *Peter Devlin Fights for Survival* (1973) Peter finds a job at 'Boolgana Downs' Station. On the way there he nearly dies of thirst, and is saved by Jet Mercedes Benz, who becomes Peter's friend. In *Peter Devlin — Range Rider* (1973), Peter and Jet are employed to help Harry Stewart of Yullamooloo muster his sheep. They find a sacred Aboriginal gorge which Jet unsuccessfully tries to conceal. At the conclusion of the book the gorge is threatened with iron ore mining. *Peter Devlin and the Road Bandits* (1973) opens with Devil's Gorge being mined by Harry Stewart's company. Peter and Jet discover the hide-out of a gang of road bandits who are looting vehicles. In *Peter Devlin — Buffalo Hunter* (1973) Peter and Jet hunt a gang who are smuggling wildlife out of Australia.

Gumbles in Summer (1985) by S.A. Wakefield. Illustrator: Desmond Digby

DICK, ASTRA LACIS, see **LACIS, ASTRA**

DICKINS, BARRY (1949–), born Melbourne, is a poet, playwright, cartoonist and novelist. A present-day visit to Nan and her recollections of her early life are juxtaposed on facing pages in *My Grandmother* (1989), a loving tribute.

DIGBY, DESMOND (1933–), born Auckland, NZ, studied at the Elam School of Art, Auckland, and at the Slade School, London. Digby is an illustrator, landscape artist and stage designer. He settled in Sydney in 1959 as a designer for the Elizabethan Trust, then for the Australian Opera Company in 1971. He has illustrated S.A. Wakefield's *Bottersnikes and Gumbles* (1967), *Gumbles on Guard* (1975), *Gumbles in Summer* (1979) and *Gumbles in Trouble* (1990), and A.B. Paterson's *Waltzing Matilda* (q.v., 1970).

Digit Dick was created by Leslie Rees. Dick is a tiny boy, only as big as his mother's big toe: hence his name. In *Digit Dick on the Barrier Reef* (1942), later published as *Digit Dick on the Great Barrier Reef* (1969), Dick goes to a sea party under the Reef with Miss Nautilus, where among other adventures, he is swallowed by a shark and is shot out of the spout of a whale. In *Digit Dick and the Tasmanian Devil* (1946) Dick and his budgerigar, Boska, travel on the back of an aeroplane to Tasmania where he meets Trucanini, who takes him to see a Tasmanian devil. WA is the setting for *Digit Dick in Black Swan Land* (1952). In *Digit Dick and the Lost Opals* (1957) Dick stows away in the Flying Doctor's bag to search for Mr Bradley's opals. He is joined by Wirra who is magically transformed into Dick's size, and together they survive the evil attentions of the bad witch-doctor, Jingara, and his lizard, Perentee. After a break of over thirty years Dick appeared again in *Digit Dick and the Zoo Plot* (1982), in which Dick foils a plot

Digit Dick and the Lost Opals (1957) by Leslie Rees. Illustrator: Walter Cunningham

to poison all the flightless birds. All of these stories were illustrated by Walter Cunningham. *Digit Dick and the Magic Jabiru* (1981) is illustrated by Sandra Laroche. Dick travels in a specially made tiny caravan pulled by G.B. Bandicoot, and collects six presents for the magic Jabiru, who lets Dick in to a secret: that his mother has a new child. *The Big Book of Digit Dick* (1973), illustrated by Latif Hutchings, contained the four books published in the 1940s and 1950s. In the tradition of Tom Thumb and the Gingerbread Boy, the figure of a very tiny boy allows a different examination of reality.

DILWORTH, MARY (1937–) has written poetry and short stories for adults, but has written one children's book. *Island* (1991) is the story of Judith Manning, whose mother has been killed. Judith and her brother and sister are sent to live with the reclusive Aunt Sarah on the vividly depicted Rottnest Island, where they become involved in the preservation of Parrot Bay. Judith finds romance with Gary, who understands her sense of loss.

'Dimensions' is a series produced by Methuen containing excerpts from novels, poetry and short stories for the middle and higher classes of primary schools. Twelve anthologies were compiled by Maurice Saxby and Glenys Smith, with illustrations by well-known artists. Teachers' books provided strategies and ideas for assistance in using the material. The Storytellers Strand features Allan Baillie, Diane Bates, Joy Cowley, Max Fatchen, Robin Klein, Barry Breen, Morris Lurie and others. Each has extracts and short stories, and also a biography and an account of how each writer works.

DISHER, GARRY (1949–), born SA, journalist and writer, has written novels (including crime thrillers), short stories and informational books such as *Bushrangers* (1984), illustrated by Rolf Heimann. He has written for students on creative writing, but his first novel for children is *The Bamboo Flute* (1992), adapted from one of his earlier short stories. Paul is a dreamer and longs for some beauty in his life. The harshness of his father's bitter struggle to make a living is ameliorated by a bamboo flute which Paul makes, at the instigation of a swagman. The story is a vignette of a boy learning to understand his father's complexity.

Displaced Person (1979) by Lee Harding won the 1980 Book of the Year Awards. The germ of the novel first appeared as a short story in *Science Fantasy*, 16, 46, April 1961. It is set in the seaside suburb of St Kilda, Melbourne. Graeme Drury, notable only for his ordinariness, finds that he is being increasingly ignored, even by his parents. His surroundings lose colour as he passes through into a cold grey world, 'Limbo', inhabited by an older man, Jamie, and a girl, Marion. As their lives darken, Graeme loses his two friends, and returns to reality with a tape recording to remind him of his experience. Harding challenges conceptions of reality, and considers the possibility of cosmic forces beyond our present understanding. He has said that the novel is 'a metaphor about the process of alienation — and perhaps ... the processes of schizophrenia and paranoia'. See also **Science Fiction**.

DIXON, JEAN (1915–), born Sydney, has written adult thrillers and mysteries. *Blue Fire Lady* (1977), based on a story by Robert Maumill, describes how Jenny overcomes her father's dislike of horses through her determination to make a success of riding. *Blue Fire Lady* was originally a film, made in the same year, directed by Ross Dimsey, with Cathryn Harrison as Jenny and Mark Holden as Barry. Dixon

also edited *Hello Mr Melody Man: Lindley Evans Remembers* (1983).

Djugurba: Tales from the Spirit Time (1974) by Aboriginal trainee students of Kormilda College, Darwin, was Commended in the 1975 Picture Book of the Year Awards. It is a collection of the 'myths and legends' of their own peoples, illustrated by themselves. This is an early example of high-quality publishing by Aboriginal storytellers and artists which acknowledges cultural origins, prefiguring later work in its respect for Aboriginal traditions. For instance, the point is made that all the stories here are neither secret nor sacred, one which has not concerned earlier (and some later) collectors. The illustrations reflect the deserts and forests of northern Australia, and the simple text imitates the oral tradition.

DOBSON, JILL (1969–), born Yorkshire, UK, came to Australia in 1974. *The Inheritors* (1988) was written when she was 16. See **Science Fiction**. *Time to Go* (1991) examines a watershed year in the lives of two girls, Laura, who wants to dance, and Danny, a flautist. Danny is haunted by the recent death of her sister, and Laura's ambitions are thwarted by an accident.

DOBSON, ROSEMARY (1920–), born Sydney, is a poet. In her novel for young people, *Summer Press* (1987), the Australian girl, Angela, meets the English Lily, and becomes absorbed in both the printing press Lily operates and a search for the story of the mysterious and long-dead Sarah. In the process, Angela finds acceptance in the English village. For *Songs for All Seasons: 100 Poems for Young People* (1967) see **Poetry**.

DOBSON, SONYA (1935–) came to Australia in 1969. *Hot on the Trail* (1989), illustrated by Bill Farr, is a clever and exciting mystery story. Theo's mother is ill, and he suspects that his worried green-grocer father is about to rob the next-door credit union. With the help of his friends in the Junior Detectives' Club, and particularly a small boy, Michael, who is fascinated by tyre rubbings, but has been excluded from the club, Theo catches the real thieves.

Doctor with Wings (1960) by Allan Aldous, illustrated by Roger Payne, was Commended in the 1961 Book of the Year Awards. David and the Locke family come to the outback from Scotland, where Dr Locke is to join the Royal Flying Doctor Service. With a minimum of disruption, the family adjusts to outback life. The Lockes soon come to terms with the 'Australian way', and the adoption of shorts, socks and sandals ensures acceptance. A sheep station for the Lockes is promised at the end of the novel. See also **Royal Flying Doctor Service**.

DOEDENS, CORRIE (?–1983), born Holland, came to Australia in the 1950s. Her three books were published posthumously. In *Cyclone Ruth* (1984) Ruth Conway goes to Hobart to live with the van Hoorn family, and finds her religious faith after much trauma. *Bonnie* (1986) is about the response of a girl to her new stepmother. *Tanzi's Search* (1986) examines the alienation of an adolescent. In each of Doedens's novels her young heroine develops a new piety after a struggle with her conscience. See also **Religion**.

Dog Called George, A (1975) by Margaret Balderson, illustrated by Nikki Jones, was Highly Commended in the 1976 Book of the Year Awards. Tony is overshadowed by older brothers and sisters, and finds that his life expands when he discovers the Old English sheepdog, George. The exuberant dog is the catalyst for new friendships and adventures. When George is claimed by Hob, a potter, Hob agrees to share the dog with Tony, so another friend is found for Tony. The picture of an introverted

boy who is released from his shyness by a dog is convincing, and Tony's thoughtful acceptance of Hob's claim to the dog provides a satisfying conclusion.

DOLESCH, SUSAN (1932–) came to Australia in 1970. She is a painter and designer, and also works in stained glass, tapestry and wrought iron. She has illustrated *The Dilly-Dally Man* (1975) by Jean Chapman; *Brumby Jack Saves the Wild Bush Horses* (1972) and *Pumpkin Paddy Meets the Bunyip* (1972) by Alex Hood; and *The Magic Fishbones* (1972) by Barbara Ker Wilson. Dolesch uses defined shapes, repetitive patterns and clear colours.

'Dolly' Fiction, see **Romance**

DONKIN, NANCE CLARE (1915–), born Maitland, NSW, contributed to the children's pages of the Sunday papers when she was a child, and joined the staff of the Maitland *Mercury* when she was 16. She began her career as a novelist with stories about ordinary families in small towns. In *Araluen Adventures* (1946), illustrated by Edith Bowden, Anne stays with her cousins and the children write a newspaper, swim, go to school together and join the Waverton centenary procession, where Anne distinguishes herself by making a speech. *No Medals for Meg* (1947), also illustrated by Bowden, describes the summer holidays of Meg, Bunny and Lois. They go to birthday parties, swim, consume much fruit and cake, and find the brother of Miss Bendison, who has lost her memory. *Julie Stands by* (1948) is the story of a developing friendship between Julie and Joan who meet on board the ship to Australia. *Blue Ribbon Beth* (1951) is a horse story. *Patchwork Grandmother* (q.v., 1975), also published as *Patchwork Mystery* (1978), illustrated by Mary Dinsdale, recalls these early novels.

Donkin's writing developed a historical perspective during the 1970s. *House by the Water* (1970), about the Reibey family, and *Johnny Neptune* (1971) are both set in

Sydney. *Johnny Neptune* begins in early Sydney, but the orphaned Johnny finds his fortune farming on the Hawkesbury, despite floods. *Two at Sullivan Bay* (1985), illustrated by Margaret Senior, is set at the first settlement in Victoria, near Sorrento, in 1803, from which William Buckley escaped. Will James and Ned Taylor observe the life of the convicts and free settlers, led by Colonel Collins. *The Best of the Bunch* (1978), illustrated by Edwina Bell, begins in Sydney in 1820, during the governorship of Macquarie. Girlie O'Leary searches for her father, and although her dreams of a red-coated soldier are dashed as he is found to be an old 'lag', Girlie swallows her disappointment and prepares for a better life with him. See also **Historical Novels**. *Green Christmas* (1976), illustrated by Gavin Rowe, highlights Donkin's view of Australian history as a continuum over 50 000 years, although it has a modern setting.

An issue which absorbed Donkin during this period was the experience of the immigrant. *A Friend for Petros* (1974), illustrated by Gavin Rowe, examines the loneliness of a newly arrived Greek child. *The Maidens of Pefka* (1979), illustrated by Bruce Treloar, relates how Shane has a mystical experience as she searches for the ancient figure of the twelfth maiden in an archeological dig on the island of Pefka. For *Nini* (1979), illustrated by Betty Greenhatch, see **Greeks**. In *A Family Affair* (1988), illustrated by Lynn Sikiotis, Stefi's father decides that he will sell his shop and return to Greece to set up a tourist hotel with his brothers. Her brother Mike and sister Alki soon make friends, but Stefi is often alone. When she discovers that her father is being duped by an aunt, Stefi saves him from a big mistake.

Yellowgum Gil (1976), illustrated by Margaret Loxton, is a novel about conservation. Gil's grandfather protects Yellowgum National Park from motor bikes and unthinking campers, and enlists Gil's help. In a return to her earlier novels,

Blackout (1987), illustrated by Sandra Laroche, is an adventure story about Mark, who witnesses a robbery in the local shopping complex. Donkin has retold *We of the Never Never* (1983), illustrated by Elizabeth Honey, and contributed *An Emancipist* (1967), illustrated by Jane Robinson, *A Currency Lass* (1968), illustrated by Jane Walker, and *An Orphan* (1969), illustrated by Jane Culvenor, to OUP's 'Early Australians' series. She has also edited *The Australian Children's Annual* (1963). Her other non-fiction includes *Stranger and Friend: the Greek-Australian Experience* (1983) and *Always a Lady: Courageous Gentlewomen of Colonial Australia* (1990). From her early adventures, Donkin went on to explore her interest in Australian history, and her appreciation of Greece, its people and its culture. Over a long career she has been concerned to represent for younger readers both the past of Australia and its contemporary changing face.

Donovan and the Lost Birthday (1968) by Marion Ord, illustrated by Penelope Janic, was Commended in the 1970 Picture Book of the Year Awards. Donovan is a donkey with a problem: his ears keep falling down. When Custer the cockatoo suggests that Donovan needs a birthday party, Donovan, Custer and Hegweg the emu set off to find Donovan's birthday. With helpful advice from Quincey the kangaroo, he finds his birthday; and Hegweg's present, two fine ear-rings, makes him happy about his ears. This is a gentle story, and Janic's pictures are full of character. Donovan's adventures were continued in *Donovan Saves the Skates* (1970) where the friends attempt a land speed record on Lake Eyre.

Dot and the Kangaroo (1899) by Ethel Pedley, illustrated by Frank Mahony, is the story of how Dot wanders into the bush and is befriended by its animals. Dot's fear of the 'cruel wild bush' is changed to a caring appreciation of the natural world. The transformation of Dot is effected by her communication with animals, particularly a 'big, grey Kangaroo', who teaches her about the destruction which people have brought. The innocence and selflessness of the Kangaroo is epitomised in the climax, where she faces the rifle of Dot's father, risking her life to take Dot home. The first Australian publication, by Angus & Robertson, with the sympathetic illustrations of Mahony, caught the spirit of pioneering life. The novel was influenced by *His Cousin the Wallaby* (1896) by 'Arthur Ferres' and by Lewis Carroll's *Alice's Adventures in Wonderland* (1865), but its direct approach, its lack of whimsy and

Dot and the Kangaroo (1899) Ethel Pedley. Illustrator: Frank Mahony

its expressed affinity with nature have made it a landmark in the development of Australian children's books. An excerpt, *In the Court of the Animals* (1976), was illustrated by Bob Smith. The novel was dramatised in 1924 by Stella Chapman and Douglas Ancelon, and Yoram Gross filmed an animated adaptation in 1977, with the voices of Lola Brooks, Ron Haddrick, Ross Higgins, June Salter, Barbara Frawley, Joan Bruce and Spike Milligan.

DOUGLAS, WILL. For *A Bush Alphabet* (1986) see **Alphabet Books**.

DOWNES, MARION GRACE (1864–1926), born Melbourne, poet and novelist, wrote romances with religious morals. *Flower o' the Bush* (1914) is set in Melbourne. Downes describes Wattle Day: Collins Street 'with its massive buildings, its throngs of well-dressed people, is at any time a goodly sight with its busy traffic, broad, clean pavements and mixture of "motors" and horse drawn vehicles'. In the novel, Dora rejects a faithful childhood sweetheart for a less worthy husband, only to be reconciled with her true love at the end. In *In the Track of the Sunset: an Australian Story for Girls* (1919) the heroine insists that she be permitted by her fiancé to see a male friend of whom he disapproves. ('Ah, the trail of the serpent, still in the garden of Eden!') *Swayed by the Storm* (1911) is another story of love and religion.

DOWNIE, JAMES M. Apart from *Warrigal: the Story of a Wild Horse* (1935), illustrated by his brother John C. Downie, which deals with the capture and training of a brumby, Downie wrote formula adventure stories. The enemies are foreigners or Aboriginal People, the adventures usually involve treasure, and the heroes are saved from certain death on the last pages. In *The Treasure of the Never-Never* (1936), also illustrated by John C. Downie, Pete Gilroy, Jerry Condor and

Orchard C. Maine, assisted by Sergeant Dale of the NT police, foil the attempts of unscrupulous foreigners and 'untrustworthy' Arnhem Land Aboriginal People to steal the plans of an aeroplane. In *Mutiny in the Air* (1937), illustrated by Reginald Cleaver, the adventure involves Al Maroni, 'America's Public Enemy Number 1', who demands £100 000 in ransom for a group of schoolboys from an English private school. Maroni is in league with the Baron, who is immediately identified as a German as soon as he clicks his heels, military fashion. Sergeant Dale also appears in this novel. *The Yellow Raiders* (1940) concerns a group of Japanese pearl-poachers, led by the Chinese merchant Ah Kwee, operating out of Broome, WA. They are defeated, of course, with the assistance of Major Cranston, who is made up as a sailor with a fake wooden leg. *The Pirates of Papua* (1949) introduced Air Commodore Christopher Gaunt of the Pearl Seas Patrol, who rescues Dick Hale, after he has been taken aboard by a gang of pirates under the command of Captain Kelly. *Alvacore's Island* (1951), illustrated by M. Mackinlay, is set in the New Hebrides, and describes the kidnapping activities of Captain Alvacore and an island rich in uranium. When Frank and his father fall foul of Alvacore, Air Commodore Gaunt steps in, and the island is taken over under the joint control of France and England. *The Mystery of the Santa Cruz* (1951) is set among the Pacific islands, where Keith Muir and Ray Allenby search for Spanish treasure, which they find despite the evil machinations of the Frenchman, Capitaine Barbier. *The Rocket Range Plot* (1952) is a plot designed by a cabal of Prussians, Russians, Poles, Jews and evil Aboriginal People in order to bomb secret rocket installations. Gaunt and his young assistants bring them all to heel. In *Gaunt of the Pearl Seas Patrol* (1950) another pearling lugger runs up against cannibals, wild South Sea islanders and Arnhem Land Aboriginal People, to be saved by the indomitable Gaunt. *The Flying Doctor*

Mystery (1954) is a complicated adventure in which the Flying Doctor, Stephen Rowe, sets off to help a phoney patient, a ruse to divert Rowe from a search for his son, Len. Len has been involved in an expedition led by Professor Wickham, to find the 'Hiding Tribe', who are ultimately revealed as escaped criminals. *The Secret of the Loch* (1954) is about an illegal transmitter operating in Scotland, which broadcasts scurrilous anti-British propaganda in the same breath as the latest cricket scores! Gaunt is called in to straighten things out, and reveals the spies, Kurt Wilkhelm, Pierre Laporte, Santo and Markoff. Other novels include *Killer-Dog* (1936) and *Skip of the Islands* (1948). The extent of Downie's xenophobia is equalled only by the contortions of his plots.

DOWNING, BROWNIE (VIOLA)

(1924–) studied at the Julian Ashton School. After World War II she developed prints and products out of Aboriginal motifs. *Tinka and His Friends* (1960), written with her husband John Mansfield, is about Tinka, Dinkydi the kangaroo, Widdy-Woo the koala bear (*sic*), and Nosey the bandicoot. In *A Tale of Mischief* (1963), Bosie the Koala teases the other bush animals, despite the efforts of Wiggy the Picaninny to discipline him. She also wrote *Children of the Dreaming* and *Tinka and the Bunyip* (both 1966). See also **Aboriginal People in Children's Fiction**. Downing left Australia in 1958.

Drac and the Gremlin (1988) by Allan Baillie, illustrated by Jane Tanner, was a joint winner of the 1989 Picture Book of the Year Awards. Drac, the Warrior Queen of Tirnol Two, and the Gremlin chase each other through a jungle until they must unite against General Min to save their world. The graphic illustrations show the reality of a girl and her small brother playing a game in a leafy suburban garden. General Min is a cat and the Hissing Horde her kittens; the Terrible Tongued Dragon is the family dog. The incinerator, garden sprinkler and fernery all play a part in the setting of the story.

Tinka and the Bunyip (1966) by Brownie Downing

This fine integration of story and illustration is an expression of imaginative play and the powerful creative skills of the child.

Dragon of Mith, The (1989) by Kate Walker, illustrated by Laurie Sharpe, was an Honour Book in the 1990 Book of the Year Awards: Younger Readers. A dragon appears in Mith, and only the practical Krissy has the good sense to find out what it wants. After a series of misunderstandings, Krissy uncovers the dragon's mission in a story which suggests the lesson of Andersen's 'The Emperor's New Clothes'.

DRAKE-BROCKMAN, HENRI-ETTA (1901–68), born Perth, was a novelist, playwright, and essayist, and editor and selector of K. Langloh Parker's *Australian Legendary Tales* (1953). She also wrote *The Lion-Tamer: a Comedy in One Act* (1948) in the 'Australian Youth Plays' series, and with Walter Murdoch, edited *Australian Short Stories* (1951). She was the first West Australian to edit *Coast to Coast*. Drake-Brockman was responsible for the identification of the correct position of the wreck of the *Batavia* (q.v.) through her examination of Pelsaert's original journal.

DREYER, ANNE HOPE (1905–), born WA, conducted the Melbourne sessions of the ABC's 'Kindergarten of the Air'. 'Good morning, children, this is Miss Anne Dreyer, with Kindergarten of the Air' resounded through Victorian households from the Mallee to Malvern, as children with ears glued to the radio hung on Anne Dreyer's words. The memory of Dreyer's warm and intimate presentation has remained with many who listened to her, including Roger Vaughan Carr and Phillip Adams. *The Little Coal Truck and Other Favourites Re-told for Very Little Children* (1944) contains well-known stories, such as 'The Three Bears', 'The Gingerbread Boy'and 'The Little Red Hen'. *Anne Dreyer's Little Songs for You and Me* (1950), with words by Dreyer and

music by George Santos, has ten songs, such as 'Clouds', 'The Bouncing Ball' and 'Mrs Henny Penny'. *Anne Dreyer's Aboriginal Songs for You and Me* (1954), illustrated by Marjorie Howden, also has ten songs, with music by Robin Wood. A similar collection is *Sing with Me, Children* (1951).

'Dromkeen' is a homestead at Riddells Creek, near Melbourne, which was built in 1889 by Judge Chomley, a prominent Melbourne jurist. The house and its twenty-five acres were bought in 1973 by Court and Joyce Oldmeadow, with the intention of making it a centre for children's literature and a repository for a national collection of original illustrations. The collection, opened in 1974, is formally named the Courtney Oldmeadow Children's Literature Foundation. Teachers and children are encouraged to use the resources of Dromkeen, which has a large and varied collection of artwork. It is now owned by the Ashton Scholastic Group. Associated with the Dromkeen collection is the 'Friends of Dromkeen'. The objective of this organisation is to promote children's literature through heightening interest in and arousing public awareness of the collection. Further reading: Bird and Prentice, *Dromkeen*.

Dromkeen Medal is awarded annually for a significant contribution to Australian children's literature by an Australian citizen. It was instituted in 1982 by the governors of the Courtney Oldmeadow Children's Literature Foundation. **1982** Lu Rees; **1983** Maurice Saxby; **1984** Patricia Wrightson; **1985** Anne Bower Ingram; **1986** Albert Ullin; **1987** Joan Phipson; **1988** Patricia Scott; **1989** Robert Ingpen; **1990** Mem Fox; **1991** Robin Klein. **1992** Julie Vivas.

DRUCE, KAY (1906–), born Montreal, Canada, was a fashion artist who came to Australia before World War II. Druce wrote and illustrated over thirty

Popsy and the Bunny Twins (1946) by Kay Druce

cheaply produced paper books during the war, published by the Children's Press, Sydney. Her many series include the 'Popsy' books, such as *Popsy's Picnic* (1945), *Popsy at the Sea-Side* (1946), *Popsy's Bumper Book* (1946), *Popsy's Adventures Down on the Farm,* also *Popsy's ABC, Popsy and Jimmy at the Zoo, Popsy's Holiday: More Adventures with the Bunny Twins, Popsy's Trip to Nurseryland* (all 1947), and *Popsy Goes Shopping* (1950); the 'Duffy' series, such as *Little Duffy: a Kay Druce Bumper Book* (1948), *Little Duffy at the Farm* (1948), *The Story of Little Duffy and his Dog* (1946) and *Little Duffy Goes Fishing* (1946); the 'Bunchy' books, *Bunchy and the Fairy,* and *Bunchy's Adventure* (both 1949); and *The Story of Small Sam* (1950) and *Small Sam at the Zoo* (1951). A typical plot has Sam leaving Whiffles the horse and Bounce the dog, and taking Nibs Bilikins the bear in his biscuit bag on the ferry to the zoo. Other books such as *Nursery Rhyme Book, Mother Goose Nursery Rhymes, Good Times: Stories and Pictures, My Big Book of Stories, The Toys Visit the Circus* (all 1947), *Little Thumbelina: a Fairy*

Tale (1948), *The Big Book for Little People* (1948), *Fun to Look at Pictures, Read the Stories, Play the Games* (?1950) and *Teeny Folk: Nursery Rhymes* (1950) were presented in large format. Druce's books suggest a local setting, as in *Small Sam at the Zoo,* and draw on traditional stories and the small adventures of childhood.

DUBOSARSKY, URSULA (1961–), born Sydney, has written *Maisie and the Pinny Gig* (1989) with Roberta Landers. Maisie dreams that her imaginary friend, which she calls a Pinny Gig, is eaten by a crocodile. When she is given a real guinea pig, she recovers from her despair. Phyllis receives a faded envelope addressed to her mother in *Zizzy Zing* (1991). When she arrives in Katoomba she slips into another time where she finds out about the tragic fate of her grandmother and aunt. Phyllis is staying in a nunnery while her mother is away, and Dubosarsky creates a picture of a happy community. *High Hopes* (1990), for older readers, has Julia contemplating murder when her father, George, falls in love with his English teacher, Anabel. Julia's plot is foiled when George cannot resist the cake Julia has made to poison Anabel. An incisive Argentinian grandmother is the mediator between Julia and her father. Dubosarsky has a buoyant style which confronts pomposity.

DUGAN, MICHAEL GRAY (1947–), born Melbourne, began publishing articles in the Melbourne *Age* while he was still at high school. He has edited *Crosscurrents* and *Puffinalia,* and *The Puffin Fun Book* (1980). His early work includes short pieces for series, such as *Weekend* (1976) for the 'Flag' series, about a group of teenagers testing their limits away from adults. Dugan has also contributed to the Macmillan series 'Australian Fact Finders', and 'People in Australia', and has written other informational material.

He has written poetry for Macmillan's 'Southern Cross' series, with *Spelling List* (1987), illustrated by Steve French; *Aunts,*

Uncles, Cousins and All (1987), illustrated by Brett Colquhoun; and *Aunt Fig Sells her Pig* (1987), illustrated by Anne Sulzer. Dugan's poetry compilations include *Stuff and Nonsense* (1974), illustrated by Deborah Niland; *More Stuff and Nonsense* (1980), illustrated by Roland Harvey; *The Moving Skull and Other Awesome Australian Verse* (1981) about the fearsome creatures of the night — wilderongs, witches, wizards and bunyips; and *Ten Times Funny: 100 Hilarious Poems* (1990), illustrated by Robert Roennfeldt. Original verse also appears in *Nonsense Places: an Absurd Australian Alphabet* (1976), illustrated by Walter Stackpool (see **Alphabet Books**), and *Nonsense Numbers* (1980), illustrated by Jack Newnham (see **Counting Books**); *My Old Dad* (1976); *Billy the Most Horrible Boy in the World* (1981), illustrated by Brett Colquhoun, a cautionary tale; and *The Worst Dream of All and Other Funny Poems* (1989), illustrated by Mark David.

Story collections include *The Ghost Trick and Other Stories* (1981) and *The Hijacked Bathtub and Other Funny Stories* (1988). See **Collections**. *Dragon's Breath* (1978), illustrated by Allan Hicks, is a picture-book about the defeat of a dragon feared by a fishing village. In *A House for Wombats* (1985) Kate builds a tree-house for wombats, where the animals themselves take part in its construction. The adventures are continued in *Wombats Don't Have Christmas?* (1987) and *The Wombat's Party* (1990), a counting book, all illustrated by Jane Burrell. In *The Great Overland Riverboat Race* (1982), illustrated by Brett Colquhoun, the unscrupulous Captain Coot and Captain Beejus, on boats pulled by bullocks or using steam engines, race on a dried-up river. *Bathing Buster* (1990), illustrated by Wendy Elks, is a picture-book about the tricks Buster the dog uses to avoid a bath. *Don't Forget Granny* (1991), illustrated by Kevin Burgemeestre, describes a disastrous party attended by nursery rhyme characters. *A Night for Frights* (1988), illustrated by Regina

Newey, is about a real ghost who is frightened by a boy dressed as Dracula. *Make it Fast* (1991) is a collection of exaggerated tales, such as 'My football career' and 'Bamboo bogey'.

Dingo Boy (1980) is a novel for older readers. Carl is sent to foster-parents, who use him as a source of unpaid labour. The boy identifies with the wild dingoes, and when he disobeys his foster-parents to save the dingoes, he has to return to the children's home where he had been happier. In *Melissa's Ghost* (1986), illustrated by Elizabeth Honey, Richard Starcrossed appears to Melissa and tells her where the family should dig for water in return for Melissa's help in discovering what happened to his parents. In *The Teacher's Secret* (1986), illustrated by Jacqui Young, Miss Lightfoot is building an aeroplane, and Evie becomes her co-conspirator. *Should We Tell?* (1990), illustrated by Allan Hicks, is a mystery story. Dugan also edited *The Early Dreaming* (1980), a series of interviews with noted Australian children's writers.

Dugan has written plays, radio scripts, picture-books, poetry, tall tales and novels. His promotion of children's books as editor, consultant and enthusiast and the diversity of his own creative work demonstrates his strong commitment to writing for children.

DUGDALE, JOAN (1943–), born Scotland, has written *City Bitten, Country Shy* (1989). Nellie, her father, and her brother and sister move from the inner suburbs, where the initially reluctant children adjust to rural life. Dugdale has also written *Radio Power: a History of 3ZZ Access Radio* (1979).

DUGON, NORA ISOBEL (1925–), born Northern Ireland, came to Australia as a child. She has written plays for radio and stage, and two novels for young people. *Lonely Summers* (1988) relates how 16-year-old Kelly Ryan comes to live with Mrs Kneebone, in Clare Street, when

Kelly's mother joins a group of travelling singers. Its sequel, *Clare Street* (1990), takes Kelly on another year in her life, suffering the pangs of love and unsure about where her future lies. Both novels have a wealth of characters: Kelly herself; the close family, headed by Kelly's Aboriginal grandmother, Gramma; Mr Ryan, Kelly's paternal grandfather; and the other inhabitants of an old Launceston street undergoing as much of a change as are its people. Dugon's work is reflective, paying more attention to emotions and relationships than events, and has a quiet strength.

DUNKLE, MARGARET (1922–), born Los Angeles, USA, came to Australia in 1959. She has worked as a librarian, storyteller, bookseller and editor. She co-edited with a panel of children *Our World, by the Kids of Australia* (1979). Her two collections of interviews with Australasian writers and illustrators are *The Story Makers: a Collection of Interviews with Australian and New Zealand Authors and Illustrators for Young People* (1987) and *The Story Makers II: a Second Collection of Interviews with Australian and New Zealand Authors and Illustrators for Young People* (1989). *Celebrating Australian Children's Literature* (1987) is a diary with information about children's literature and its contributors. *Growing Up with Books* (1991) is a list of recommended titles. Dunkle has been a reviewer and critic of children's books since the 1970s.

DUNN, ROGER (1939–), born Melbourne, contributed to reading series during the 1980s, such as *The Runaway Pig* (1980), illustrated by John Howell, for 'Australian Starters'. In *Matty Trakker and the Money Men* (1985) Matty is determined to find the hit-and-run driver who knocked her off her bike, and discovers counterfeiters during her investigations. Matty appears again in *Matty Tracker and the UFO* (1985), where she defeats the forgers and travels back in time to Atlantis

with her brother Tom and Uncle Arthur. See also **Science Fiction**. Dunn has also written one of the 'Touch the Sun' (q.v.) series, *The Gift* (1988) based on a screenplay by Jeff Peck and Paul Cox. *Percy* (1988), illustrated by Chantal Stewart, is an intriguing picture-book about a gardener who so loves his garden he takes on plant characteristics, such as eating humus and sprouting.

DURACK, Dame **MARY** (1913–), born Adelaide, and her sister **ELIZABETH** (1916–), born Perth, are descendants of a WA pioneering family from the Kimberleys. *Little Poems of Sunshine* (1923) was written when Mary was only 10 years old. The sisters collaborated on *All-About: the Story of a Black Community on Argyle Station, Kimberley* (1935) and *Chunuma: Little-Bit-King* (1936) which were first published by the *Bulletin*. The first is a series of vignettes of station life, which was followed by a sequel *Son of Djaro* (1940); *Chunuma* is an account of a boy's growth to adulthood, including his romance with Dingyerri.

During World War II, from 1942 to 1943, the Duracks wrote and illustrated a picture-strip for the *Sunday Telegraph* called 'Nungalla and Jungalla', which used Aboriginal stories and ran from February 1942 to February 1943. *Piccaninnies* (1940) is a verse collection. Elizabeth's artistry found richer expression in *The Way of the Whirlwind* (1941) and *The Magic Trumpet* (1946), both illustrated with her vivid and airy paintings. *The Way of the Whirlwind* tells how Jungaree and Nungaree search for their baby brother, Woogoo. In *The Magic Trumpet* an elfin child comes from a point beyond time to live with the Aboriginal People. His bamboo trumpet makes such beautiful music that adults want to tame his talent, but he escapes to enchant only children. The story is in verse. *Kookanoo and Kangaroo* (1963) describes Kookanoo's efforts to catch a kangaroo. For *To Ride a Fine Horse* (1963) see **Great Stories of Australia**.

Mary contributed *A Pastoral Emigrant* (1965), illustrated by David Parry, to Oxford's 'Early Australians' series, which recalls Tom Kilfoyle, who travelled with Patrick Durack, and later set up his own property. She wrote *The Courteous Savage: Yagan of Swan River* (q.v., 1964), also called *Yagan of the Bibbulmun* (1976). *Red Jack* (1987), illustrated by Michael Wilkin, is a poem about an enigmatic woman and her horse, Mephistopheles.

Elizabeth has held over fifty exhibitions of her work. Apart from her work with her sister, she illustrated *Australian Legendary Tales* (q.v., 1953), selected by Henrietta Drake-Brockman from K. Langloh Parker's collection; John K. Ewers's account of the journeys of Charles Sturt, *Who Rides on the River?* (1956); and *An Attempt to Eat the Moon and Other Stories Recounted from the Aborigines* (1958) by Deborah Buller-Murphy. Further reading: Hutchings, *The Art of Elizabeth Durack*.

DURKIN, PETER (1943–) is the co-author with Virginia Ferguson of *Let 'er Rip, Potato Chip: a Fresh Collection of Australian Children's Chants and Rhymes* (1988) and *That Awful Molly Vickers!: Poems and Rhymes Demanded by Children* (1989), both illustrated by Peter Viska. *Hedge Island* (1989), illustrated by Peter Viska and Con Aslanis, was one of the 'Kaboodle' series. Other collections include *Rotten Apples: Top Stories to Read and Tell* (1989) (see **Collections**) and *The Christmas Book* (1989), illustrated by John Canty.

Dusting appears in Max Dann's *Adventures with My Worst Best Friend* (1982), *Going Bananas* (1983) and *Dusting in Love* (1989). Dusting is a combination of larrikin and lair. He is untidy, rude, self-opinioned and very funny.

DUTTON, GEOFFREY (1922–), born Kapunda, SA, is a writer and critic. His books for children began with *Tisi and the Yabby* (1965), with photographs by Dean Hay of Dutton's family. Tisi's search for a lost yabby on a large SA sheep station leads her around the farm, until her brother brings the yabby home from school. Tisi's small adventures are continued in *Tisi and the Pageant* (1968), also with Dean Hay, as she goes to Adelaide for a Christmas parade. *Seal Bay* (1966), with Hay's fine atmospheric photographs, is an exploration of the beauty of a Bass Strait island. Two boys see a kangaroo, find a baby seal, discover a cave full of fairy penguins, and finally pick up a perfect nautilus shell on the beach. *On My Island* (1967), illustrated by John Perceval, is a collection of Dutton's poems for children, generally set on Kangaroo Island, where the children beachcomb and play in the sand. 'Sometimes my sister and I/Get scallop shells, and on their fluted backs/We paint a mouth or eye,/Or gaudy stripes of purples, greens and blacks./Then running to the beach/We lay them, front side up, down on the sand,/Just within the reach/Of some unsuspecting shell-collector's hand.' *The Prowler* (1982), illustrated by Craig Smith, is set in inner-suburban Sydney. Bottlebrush, a ginger cat who has been taught to knock by his owner, Miss Violet Nevertire, inadvertently terrorises the inhabitants of Samarkand Lane.

DWYER, VERA GLADYS (Mrs WARWICK COLDHAM-FUSSELL) (1889–1967), born Hobart, wrote books for adolescent girls. *With Beating Wings: an Australian Story* (1913), written with the encouragement of Ethel Turner, describes the domestic crises of the Pemelby family of Stome Lodge. Mr Pemelby is a snobbish martinet, whose pride leads the family into poverty. After driving his son away and alienating his daughters, he finally sees the error of his ways when he reads his daughter Gwen's novel. *Mona's Mystery Man* (1914), illustrated by J. Macfarlane, follows the fortunes of Mona and her cousins, Frieda, Dashie and Clive. Clive draws political cartoons, and the girls are artistic and skilful, assertive and competent. The superior Mona learns to appreciate others and develop more humility, without having her spirit quenched. *A War of Girls* (1915) describes the rivalries between two schools and the misunderstandings which dog the romance between Genevieve Stockley and David Chester. *The Kayles of Bushy Lodge* (1922) has some of the same characters as *A War of Girls*. It traces the efforts of the Kayle family to survive the neglect of their unobservant father, and their various romances. *Conquering Hal* (1916) is about Henry Trent, who 'had in him the spirit, the purely British spirit, of the pioneer and the adventurer'. Again, the intricacies of romances between various young people provide the action, this time as World War I begins. Dwyer also wrote *The Marches Disappear* (1929). Dwyer is in love with romance, and her outcomes are contrived, but in *With Beating Wings* she has depicted the misery of a family ruled by an oppressive despot, and in *Mona's Mystery Man* she has created interesting girls who are never too delicate to be practical. Dwyer also wrote romances for adults.

DYSON, EDWARD GEORGE (1865–1931), born Ballarat, Victoria, short story writer and novelist, left school at the age of 12, worked around the goldfields, and later became the sub-editor of the Melbourne journal *Life*. *The Gold-Stealers: a Story of Waddy* (1901), illustrated by G. Grenville Manton, set in a town based on Alfredton, near Ballarat, has Dicky Haddon as its central character. Haddon also appears in *Below and on Top* (1898), a novel for adults. *The Gold-Stealers* is an adventure story, full of humour, fun, and larger-than-life characters, about a group of schoolboys playing at being bushrangers who are able to expose the bogus superintendent of the local Sunday School. Waddy is peopled by 'lusty Wesleyan Cornishmen', Scots and Irish, which makes for a volatile mixture. *Billy Bluegum or Back to the Bush* (1947), illustrated by Norman Lindsay, was first published in 1912 in the *Lone Hand* as a serial. While it is presented as a children's story, it is really an adult satire of society. Billy brings civilisation to the koalas, introducing courtship and cottage pianos, pew rents, dentists, Parliament, cricket, washing day and gas stoves, among other hallmarks of civilisation. The various classes in Bruin are identifiable by the different ways they shave. There are frequent references to contemporary concerns, such as the Arbitration Act. The Bruin experiment fails because the bears must work, and 'no one can be content who is not thoroughly lazy'. Lindsay's illustrations are very similar to those in *The Magic Pudding* (q.v.).

E

EARLY, MARGARET (1951–), born New England, NSW, studied at the Shillito Design School and St Martin's School of Art, London. *Ali Baba and the Forty Thieves* (1988), richly illustrated in the style of Persian miniatures, retains the tension of the old story, and *William Tell* (q.v., 1991) suggests an illuminated manuscript.

EDWARDS, HAZEL (1945–), born Melbourne, has written plays and novels, material for radio, television and newspapers, and has contributed to reading series such as 'Flag' and 'Stoat'. Her first longer novel was *General Store* (1977), in which the Woods family must adjust to moving from the city to the country. Other adjustments occur: to her mother's pregnancy in *Kendall, Mim and Temporary Fred* (1980), to a disability in *Mum-on-Wheels* (1980), to a new stepmother in *The Pancake Olympics* (1981), illustrated by Tony Oliver, and to farm life in *Oinkabella!* (1990), illustrated by Dee Huxley.

One of Edwards's most popular books is the picture-book *There's a Hippopotamus on Our Roof Eating Cake* (1980), illustrated by Deborah Niland, in which a small girl projects her daily pleasures and disappointments on to an imaginary friend. *The Imaginary Menagerie* (1984), illustrated by Rod Clement, deals with fear of the dark, using the child from *There's a Hippopotamus on Our Roof Eating Cake*. A further adventure, this time at the beach, is *My Hippopotamus is on Our Caravan Roof Getting Sunburnt* (1989), also illustrated by Deborah Niland. Other picture-books are *Tolly Leaves Home* (1986), with dramatic illustrations by Rosemary Wilson, in which Tolly leaves his bossy family, heading for the Antarctic, on his BMX bike; *Snail Mail* (1986), with illustrations by Rod Clement, which views the world from a snail's eye; *Stickybeak* (1986), also illustrated by Rosemary Wilson; *Grandma Zed* (1986), illustrated by Carolyn Johnstone; and *Fish, Chips and Jaws* (1987), illustrated by Rae Dale. In *The Hundreds and Thousands Kid* (1987), illustrated by Rosemary Wilson, Quintana is fascinated by numbers. *Fey Mouse* (1988), illustrated by Kilmeny Niland, is about a kitten raised by mice. *Not Lost, Just Somewhere Else* (1990), illustrated by Leanne Argent, presents the imagination of a forgetful girl. Objects that are lost are found in unlikely places, such as a sneaker on a heron's leg, a note as a kite, a parka on a possum. The illustrations interpret the text with originality.

Leon invents an imaginary twin brother in the novel *Mystery Twin* (1983) and acts out his own fears. In *Skin Zip Me* (1986) Edwina loses her skin after sunburn. In *The 'O' Gang* (1985), illustrated by Chris Wilson, Jamie Chong, Tina and Emma Marinoff, Kate Savvas, and Mario Dominic investigate a bank robbery while orienteering. *Stowaway* (1987), illustrated by Megan Gressor, involves some detective work by Troy and the elderly Mrs Rose. Troy discovers that the 'Orange Hairy Man' he believes to be a stowaway is much more exciting than that. *So Who's the Misfit?* (1989) aims to make children aware of the need for religious tolerance. *Blue Light* (1989) is about Zandra, who is disenchanted with her life in the police force. *Axminster* (1991), also illustrated by Rosemary Wilson, is about a carpet snake.

Edwards has also developed educational material, such as *Understanding the Novel: a Study Manual* (1978), and *Life Writing: a Guide to Process Writing* (1987). In over forty books for children, Edwards has ranged from material for beginner readers to novels which address social issues.

EDWARDS, HUGH (1933–), born Perth, is a journalist and diver who contributed to the discovery of wrecks, particularly around the Abrolhos Islands. His adult work includes *Island of Angry Ghosts* (1966), an account of the discovery of the wreck of the *Batavia* (q.v.) in 1963, and *Captain William Bligh R.N.* (1972), illustrated by Arthur McNeil, a biography of the great sailor. His series for young readers about the *Sea Witch*, a ketch sailed by the Masterson family, began with *Tiger Shark* (1976), illustrated by John Richards, set off the WA coast. When Sam Masterson helps a wounded shark, he realises that all species, even a shark, have a place in the natural environment. *Sea Lion Island* (1977) describes how Sam, Michael and Amanda Masterson prevent the destruction of the habitat of the gentle sea lions by an oil company. *The Pearl Pirates* (1977), illustrated by John Richards, is an adventure story involving a fortune in pearls, and the Masterson's encounter with Malay and Chinese pirates. In *The Crocodile God* (1985) the Mastersons find a lost tribe who feed their victims to a giant crocodile. *Sim the Sea Lion* (1981), illustrated by Stephen Hederics, traces the life of a sea lion from his birth on Seal Rocks. Sophie and Christopher save Sim from Sru the shark when they are on holidays on Mutton Bird Island. With Joe Nangan, Edwards compiled a collection of Aboriginal Dreaming stories, *Joe Nangan's Dreaming: Aboriginal Legends of the North-West* (1976), illustrated with Edwards's photographs and Nangan's drawings.

EDWARDS, IAN (1948–), teacher and writer, has written *The Money Eaters* (1988) and *Papa and the Olden Days* (q.v. 1989), both illustrated by Rachel Tonkin. In *The Money Eaters* David and Briar are happy until they must move to Grimesville. Briar has to leave her beloved horse behind, David is terrorised by the Grimesville Greasers, Mother stops cooking and Dad is never home. Their problems are solved when they become friends with the Bui Thi Minh family, who help them stop the awful Stuffles eating money. Edwards has also written educational material.

EDWARDS, PAT (1925–), born Invercargill, NZ, has written *Granny Smith's Apples* (1978), illustrated by Chris Wilson, a picture-book describing the origins of the green apple, and *P.S! Write Soon* (1986). *Who Made the Sun?* (1980), illustrated by Walter Stackpool, is 'an Aboriginal legend retold'; *The Wild Colonial Boy* (1980), illustrated by Dee Huxley, a recounting of the life of Jack Doolan; *The Drover's Dream* (1980), also illustrated by Huxley, is a traditional poem; and *Crooked Mick of the Speewah* (1980), illustrated by Will Mahony, describes the competitions between Strong-arm Sam and the legendary Crooked Mick. Edwards was the general editor of the Reed Books series and the Bunyip Readers. See also **Lost in the Bush**.

ELDER, JEAN (Mrs TOWNS) (1915–), born St Arnaud, Victoria, trained at Swinburne Technical School, and has contributed artwork to the *Australian Women's Weekly*. She illustrated Irene Cheyne's *The Golden Cauliflower* (1937); Rosalind Miller's *The Adventures of Margery Pym* (?1939); Lyla Stevens's *Around the Corner* (1944), *The Land Where the Elephant Lives* (1960) and *A Dog Called Debbie* (1973); Phyllis Johnson's *Robbie's Trip to Fairyland* (1946) and *Robbie's Birthday Wish* (1950); and Dorothy Drewett's *Nurseryland Memories* (1947). In Sylvia Chew's *"Little Chiu": Kwong Chiu's New Year Clothes* (1947) Chui's clothes run

Robbie's Trip to Fairyland (1946) by Phyllis Johnson. Illustrator: Jean Elder

away from him because he is too lazy to dress himself, until he catches them with the help of his animal friends. She illustrated *Flip-Flop and Tiger Snake* (1970) by Colin Thiele, *Daughter of Two Worlds* (1970) by Audrey Oldfield, and wrote and illustrated *Soxy and the Bushland Queen* (1950). Elder's rosy and dimpled children, elves and fairies, and indigenous birds and animals merge the local and European traditions. Her work is seen at its best in her fine illustrations to H.C.F. Morant's *Whirlaway: a Story of the Ages* (1937), a geological history which presents evolution to children.

Eleanor, Elizabeth (1984), Libby Gleeson's first novel for children, was Highly Commended in the 1985 Children's Book of the Year Awards. Eleanor must adjust to a frugal existence in the country where she feels friendless and displaced, after living in comfort in the city. She discovers her Grandmother Elizabeth's diary, begun when she was 13, which documents her teenage years and a tragic love affair. Both Elizabeth and Eleanor undergo a transformation, Elizabeth with her love affair and Eleanor through a bushfire. The diary helps Eleanor come to terms with her new life and enriches her own relationship with her mother. See also **Bushfire**.

Eleventh Hour, The (1988) by Graeme Base was joint winner of the 1989 Picture Book of the Year Awards, winner of YABBA for Picture Books and Primary

Winner of KOALA in 1989. In an intriguing mystery story, food is stolen from Horace the elephant's birthday party. With Horace, the reader must track down the culprit through cryptic clues to be found in the verse and the pictures. Intricate illustrations complement a rhythmic text.

ELEY, ANNIE W. For *The Dawn Maiden: Dione's Visit to Australia* (?1922) see **Fairies**.

ELIOTT, LYDIA SUSANNA. *Little Teddy Bear* (1939), illustrated by Alan Wright, describes the koalas at Koala Park, north of Sydney, Edward the Koala, a pet koala who lives on Phillip Island, Victoria, and other pet koalas. *The Koala Family at Home* (1949) and *Tufty the Teddy* (1950) also celebrate the koala. *Kangaroo Coolaroo* (1950), illustrated by Joyce Horne, is about a small kangaroo, whose adventures include escaping from a storm, his first day at school, learning how to box, and escaping from captivity. Eliott also wrote for older readers. *Kangaroo Country* (1955) is a story of two orphans who come to Australia to live with their grandmother. The author draws moral and religious lessons for the reader, as Peter and Rosemary exhibit small selfishnesses, such as unpunctuality. Similarly, in *The Coconut Island Twins* (1956), set on a Pacific island, Rangi and Lulu learn forgiveness and love. *Australian Adventure* (1956), set on a Riverina sheep station, opens with Jenny suffering from jealousy because a younger brother has had the opportunity for further study. After many prayers and a broken back, she learns to control her jealousy, and wins a scholarship to university. *Glimpses of Family Life* (1959), with George Noyle, is a social studies textbook for schools. Eliott has also written novels with other settings. *The Chief's Secret* (1951), *Found in the Forest* (1958) and *The Young Explorers* (1958) are set in Canada, the last on Vancouver Island.

ELKS, WENDY (1957–   ), born Melbourne, teacher, has contributed to the magazines of the Victorian Ministry of Education. She has written and illustrated *Charles B. Wombat and the Very Strange Thing* (1987), about a travelling circus, and *The Platypus Who Saved the Sky* (1989), in which Polly Platypus catches the sky when it falls, saving the other bush animals. Buster is the dog, in *Bathing Buster* (1990) by Michael Dugan. Elks's illustrations of exaggerated animals are as energetic as the texts. Elks has also written a career guide, *The Salesperson: Retail* (1982).

ELLIOTT, MARY, see **Carson, Clare**

ELLIS, BOB (1942–   ), born Lismore, NSW, playwright and scriptwriter, wrote the script for the film, *Fatty Finn* (q.v.), produced in 1980. With John Hepworth he wrote *The Paper Boy* (1985) and *Top Kid* (1985) for the 'Winners' (q.v.) television series.

ELLIS, VIVIENNE RAE (1930–   ), born Wynyard, Tasmania, wrote *Menace at Oyster Bay* (1976), illustrated by Elisabeth Grant. Henry and his family are mena by Captain Matthew Brady, a bushranger, when his father is away. Pioneering life in Van Diemen's Land is seen through the eyes of an 8-year-old boy. Ellis has also written *Louisa Anne Meredith: a Tigress in Exile* (1979), a biography of the nineteenth-century author and artist.

EMBLING, JOHN (1952–   ), born Ballarat, Victoria, wrote a diary of his work with children, *Tom: a Child's Life Regained* (1978). Tom Goodwood was a disturbed boy from a brutal home who was taken in by Embling when he was teaching in a Melbourne school. Embling documents the process of his restoration, and the book is a critique of the social conditions which engender children like Tom. The book was made into the film *Fighting Back* in 1982, directed by Michael Caulfield, with Paul Smith as Tom, Lewis

Fitz-Gerald as John and Kris McQuade as Tom's mother.

EMERSON, ERNEST SANDOC (1870–1919), born Ballarat, Victoria, was a journalist and newspaper editor, who used the pseudonym 'Milky White'. He wrote *Santa Claus and a Sun-Dial: an Australian Christmas Fantasy* (1909), with illustrations and decorations by Percy Lindsay. Sim is crippled by a flagpole when he tries to raise a flag to his missing mother. Sim's nurse tells him about Santa Claus, and Sim is taken into the arms of Father Time and told the stories of the Christmas tree, the mistletoe, and how kangaroos and swans help Santa in Australia. The story ends with Sim's mother returning, and a reconciliation between Sim and his father.

Empire Annual for Australian Boys, The, see **Annuals**

Empire Annual for Australian Girls, The, see **Annuals**

EPSTEIN, JUNE SADIE (1918–   ), born Perth, has taught music in Melbourne at the Kindergarten Teachers' College, has been a broadcaster and scriptwriter for radio, and has made records of children's songs. *Big Dipper: Stories, Poems, Songs and Activities for Young Children* (1980) by Epstein, June Factor, Gwendda McKay and Dorothy Rickards, *Big Dipper Rides Again: Stories, Poems, Songs and Activities for Young Children* (1982) and *Big Dipper Returns: Stories, Poems, Songs and Activities for Young Children* (1985), all illustrated by Alison Lester, are collections for use with pre-school children. The music is collected in *Big Dipper Songs* (1985), also illustrated by Lester. Epstein created the **Augustus** (q.v.) books in 1989. *I Can't Find My Glasses* (1987), illustrated by June Joubert, is a simple text in Ashton's 'Bookshelf' series, as is *The Chocolate Frog* (1987), illustrated by Bruce Rankin. In *When Tracy*

Came for Christmas (1982), illustrated by Geoff Todd, Nicky and his family are caught in the Darwin cyclone. In *Scarecrow and Company* (1984) Peter Brown struggles to become a puppeteer, bedridden Liz is rehabilitated, and Penny is cleared from cheating at school. In *The Icecream Kids* (1984), illustrated by Sandra Laroche, Nico and Adam develop grand plans to sell ice-cream at school. *Password — Peggy Jones* (1986) is a detective story in which Nico, Adam and Caroline solve the mystery of the stolen pot plants. *The Blue Serpent* (1986) is another mystery, this time a spy thriller. Lien, from South East Asia, is haunted by dreams of her life before her adoption. Her essay, based on a computer image given to her by her brother, leads to the discovery of terrorists.

ERNST, OLGA DOROTHEA AGNES (Mrs WALLER) (1888–1972), born Melbourne, was a teacher. She has written *Fairy Tales from the Land of the Wattle* (1904), illustrated by Dorothy Ashley. In 'The origin of the wattle' Oberon turns a race of fairies with golden hair, living on Lake Eyre, into wattle trees. In 'The Mermaid' the mermaid swims in Hobson's Bay, near the mouth of the Yarra, and the giants of the Australian Alps become Eucalypts. See also **Fairies**. *Songs from the Dandenongs: Mountain Nursery Rhymes* (1939) has ten nursery rhymes set to music by Jean M. Fraser. Ernst also wrote a collection of philosophical essays for adults, *Magic Shadow Show* (1913).

Eureka Stockade was an uprising by the goldminers at Ballarat, Victoria, in 1854; an armed revolt which was quickly put down. The events of Eureka were given little prominence in nineteenth-century children's books, despite their historical significance. Eureka is described in Captain Thomas Mayne Reid's *Lost Lenore: or, the Adventures of a Rolling Stone* (1864), which is a picaresque tale of Rowland Stone, who is eluded by the love of his life, Lenore. There is a half-hearted account of the events leading to the Stockade, which Reid puts down solely to the licensing system. When the battle begins, the hero runs from it very quickly: "'I'm a Rolling Stone'", thought I, "and do not like staying too long in one spot. The Eureka Stockade is not the place for me.'"

With the rise of nationalism in the twentieth century greater attention was paid to the event. E.V. Timms's *Red Mask: a Story of the Early Victorian Goldfields* (1927) concludes with the Stockade, and although there is some criticism of the unbending attitude of the authorities, it is 'seditious foreigners' who are blamed for the bloodshed, and the dire threat of a revolution is raised. 'The moderate section of the diggers do not wish to overthrow the Crown ... but the extremist element, comprised mainly of designing aliens, are aiming straight at the Queen's power in this Colony. They desire a republic controlled by themselves.' William Thomas Hill's *The Golden Quest: a Story of the Eureka Stockade* (1935) is a Whitcombe's Story Book. Joe Bray and his parents, English immigrants, abandon Melbourne to find a fortune at Ballarat. The events of Eureka are described through the eyes of Joe, whose father disapproves of the rebellious miners. The troubles are laid at the feet of arrogant and corrupt officials, injustice, and foreign agitators. However, John Bray, Joe's father, does sympathise with the miners' complaints against the troopers, and hides one of those hurt in the battle. "'I'm an Englishman, Joe; and as such I can't raise my hand against my country,'" he says to his son. Peter Lalor, Carboni Raffaello, Frederick Vern, Captain Ross and other notables visit the Brays and discuss the situation with them. The outcome of the Stockade is not dealt with, as Joe and his family find their fortune soon after the event, and return to Melbourne.

A different light is cast by Jack Lindsay in *Rebels of the Goldfields* (1936), illustrated by George Scott, where the rebellion is seen as continuing the great Chartist tradition. Dick Preston, 15, becomes involved in the events of Eureka under the influence of his Irish friend Shane. After the event, Shane says: "'It's changed the face of the world ... The squatters have lost their grip on things, the old beastly landthieves ... because we didn't fight alone. There wasn't a man worth tuppence in the land that didn't speak up for us, and act too, after what we did ... They'll have to give the vote and ballot in England soon ... and after England the rest of the world will have to follow.'" Eighteen years later, written in the centenary year of Eureka, Helen Palmer's *Beneath the Southern Cross* (1954) also presented the rebellion as a blow for democracy and national pride. The 12-year-old hero, Davey, sets off for Ballarat to work with his Uncle Barney when his family falls on hard times. The disquiet on the fields is described in detail, and the decisions to take armed action are argued at length. The issue is one of the right of all citizens to vote, and thereby control a government run by landowners. Again, real historical characters are brought into the novel, although they remain public figures rather than intimates of the characters around whom the action of the novel takes place. One chapter describes the miners' wives sewing the Eureka flag. After the event, when Matt, Joe's friend is questioned as to his nationality by a trooper, he replies: "'Australian ... I want it written down — Australian.'" The novel concludes with Davey's proud thought that he had participated in a great moment in history. In *Gully of Gold* (1958) Mavis Thorpe Clark describes the clash between the gold commissioners, the troopers and the diggers at Golden Point, Ballarat, which was the first salvo in what was to become the Eureka uprising. The Bennett family and their friend, Peter Bracken, leave the fields of Ballarat before the Stockade occurs. *Fight for Gold* (1966) by Denys Burrows is the most searching account of the uprising, providing detail on the reasons why the events occurred, with Andrew and Jamie Murray, and Meg Colley, a girl who has been taken into the family, participating in the Stockade. Burrows's analysis puts the blame on the squatters, who encouraged the troopers to harass the miners in order to force them off the fields to become cheap labour on the land. The novel concludes with the assurance that the miners' demands will be satisfied, and the promise of a future for the family on the goldfields. Alan Boardman's *Eureka Stockade* (1981) treats the event as a result of the inequity meted out to the miners. Roland Harvey's illustrations add a humorous dimension, parodying the posturing of miners and politicians. The Eureka uprising still awaits a children's novel which will reveal its full political and human significance.

EVANS, GEORGE WILLIAM (1780–1852), born Warwick, UK, explorer, bookseller and publisher, arrived in Australia in 1802. After the crossing of the Blue Mountains by Gregory Blaxland, William Wentworth and William Lawson in 1813, he established the route, named the Bathurst Plains and was Surveyor-General of Van Diemen's Land until he retired in 1825. After a period in England he returned to Sydney, became the drawing master at the King's School, and opened a bookshop in George Street, where he also operated a circulating library. He published adult books and *A Mother's Offering to Her Children* (q.v., 1841) by Charlotte Barton, the first children's book published in Australia.

EVANS, MATILDA JANE, see 'FRANC, MAUD JEANNE'

Eve Pownall Award was awarded by the NSW Branch of the CBC in 1988 only, for the best informational book for children published in 1987, using the same rules of eligibility as for the Book of the Year Awards, with a primary requirement that the book 'contribute to children's understanding and knowledge of the natural or social environment'. It was awarded to *My Place* (1987) by Nadia Wheatley and Donna Rawlins.

EVERS, LEN H. (1926–85), born Brisbane, wrote *The Racketty Street Gang* (q.v., 1961) one of the first urban children's novels to give a central role to immigrants. It was televised for the BBC. In *Danny's Wonderful Uncle* (1963) Uncle William entertains Danny with tall stories. He fights dragons and pirates, saves Christmas, and feeds spacemen with saveloys. At the end of a humorous book, Danny and Uncle William watch a space satellite pass through the sky.

Everyday Inventions (1972) by Meredith Hooper, illustrated by Graham Wade, was Commended in the 1973 Book of the Year Awards. From nails to false teeth, from barbed wire to cornflakes, this is a fascinating book of facts about things which we take for granted, written in a conversational and lightly humorous style.

EWART, ERNEST ANDREW, see 'CABLE, BOYD'

EWERS, JOHN KEITH (1904–78), born Perth, was a novelist and critic. *Boy and Silver* (1929) is a verse story of a boy and a kangaroo. *Tales from the Dead Heart* (1944), illustrated by Leo Porter (published in the USA as *Written in Sand* (1947), illustrated by Avery Johnston), is a collection of traditional tales told by the carpet snake, Woma, to Ngangan, a small Aboriginal boy. It contains a glossary of Arunta words from the Wonkonguru people. *Who Rides on the River?* (1956), illustrated by Elizabeth Durack, is an account of Charles Sturt's epic journeys down the Murrumbidgee and Murray rivers to the sea and back. See also **Murray River**. His critical account of Australian literature is *Creative Writing in Australia* (1945).

Exploring Australia (1958) by Eve Pownall, illustrated by Noela Young, was Commended in the 1959 Book of the Year Awards. It begins with the Dutch sailors mapping the coast, and a picture of the map of Australia is developed through William Dampier, James Cook, the First Fleet and George Bass and Matthew Flinders. The interior of the continent with its network of rivers, mountains and deserts is also defined through the travels of Gregory Blaxland, William Lawson and William Wentworth, George Evans and John Oxley, Hamilton Hume, Charles Sturt, Major Thomas Mitchell and others.

EYRE, FRANK (1910–88), born Manchester, UK, was a publisher and author, who became managing editor of the children's book department at Oxford University Press, after World War II. In 1950 he came to Australia as editorial manager, then was general manager of OUP in Australia until his retirement in 1975. Eyre developed the Oxford children's list by encouraging authors such as Nan Chauncy, Hesba Brinsmead and Eleanor Spence, described in his book *Oxford in Australia: 1890–1978* (1978). He was an enthusiastic supporter of the Victorian Branch of the CBC, and its president from 1966 to 1968. His *British Children's Books in the Twentieth Century* (1952, reissued in 1973 as *Twentieth Century Children's Books*) was an evaluation of the genre, and included material on Australian children's books.

F

Faces in a Looking-Glass (1974) by Noreen Shelley, illustrated by Astra Lacis, was considered Worthy of Mention in the 1975 Book of the Year Awards. Set in Rose Bay, Sydney, it describes a misunderstanding of mother–child relationships which leads Kylie to believe that the young Mrs Garner is neglecting her baby daughter, Lurline. The baby is kidnapped and Kylie, through her involvement in the search, learns not to judge people too quickly.

FACTOR, JUNE (1936–), born Poland, academic, poet and writer, collaborated with Ian Turner and Wendy Lowenstein on the compilation of children's folklore *Cinderella Dressed in Yella* (1978). Her interest in the area led to her developing a large collection, some of which has appeared for children in her anthologies: *Far Out, Brussel Sprout!: Australian Children's Chants and Rhymes* (1983), illustrated by Peter Viska, *All Right, Vegemite!: a New Collection of Australian Children's Chants and Rhymes* (1985), *Unreal, Banana Peel!: a Third Collection of Australian Children's Chants and Rhymes* (1986), *Ladles and Jellyspoons: Favourite Riddles and Jokes of Australian Children* (1989), illustrated by Jeff Hook, and *Real Keen, Baked Bean: a Fourth Collection of Australian Children's Chants and Rhymes* (1989), illustrated by Annie Marshall. Factor has analysed the material in a definitive work, *Captain Cook Chased a Chook: Children's Folklore in Australia* (1988). See **Folklore**. She collaborated with June Epstein and others in the *Big Dipper* series. *Micky the Mighty Magpie* (1986), illustrated by Melissa Webb, is about a magpie remarkable for his immense size and his strange habits. *Summer* (1987), illustrated by Alison Lester, is a verse story describing the preparations for Christmas Day in the country. She has also compiled poetry collections: *A First Australian Poetry Book* (1983), *Jelly on the Plate: an Anthology of Poems* (1987) and *Mud in the Frying Pan: an Anthology of Poems* (1987), illustrated by Bob Graham, Rolf Heimann, Ann James, Ellen Jose, Alison Lester and others. With Gwyn Dow she edited *Australian Childhood* (1991), a collection of extracts dealing with childhood from 1788 to the present.

Fairies. Nineteenth-century writers drew on the work of the European collectors of traditional tales, such as the Grimms, Perrault and Lang, to create stories about creatures such as pixies, fairies, elves, brownies and goblins. James Lionel Michael wrote a fairy story for the journal *Month*, in 1858 — 'The Isle of vines, a fairy-tale for young and old', which is apparently the first fairy story to appear in Australia. Like other books for children of the period, moralism and didacticism motivated the fairy story. *Rosalie's Reward: or, The Fairy Treasure* (1870) by Mrs S.A. Roland ('Gumsucker'), set in Ballarat, Victoria, is a rags-to-riches story of a girl who is given grace and beauty by the flower fairies and a fortune by the garden's real owner. *The Rival Fairies: or, Little Maimie's Trouble, an Australian Story for Children* (1871) by 'Desda' (Mrs Davies) is a similar moral story. Charles L. Marson's *Faery: Stories* (1891) has nine imaginative horror stories which relate how bad fairies lead children astray, using trolls with names reminiscent of the Aboriginal —

Yewli, Wirra and Mukka. In 'The Blinding of Yewli', the boy Roland becomes a decrepit old man whose family no longer recognises him. In 'The Land of Cockain' George sees what becomes of children if they stay: 'The face was like that of a repulsive idiot, but very white. The eyes were tiny, and almost closed; the flat nose and mouth nearly joined; and four white teeth showed, like fishes' teeth, between the flexible lips... George saw with horror that two sets of little withered strings at the maggot's sides and end were shrivelled arms and legs.' Atha Westbury's *Australian Fairy Tales* (1897), illustrated by A.J. Johnson, is a collection of stories, less moralistic (and less fearful), of goblins, dwarves, fairies, princesses and toys which come to life in Ballarat, Fitzroy, Lake George and the River Torrens.

The Australian landscape began to have a greater impact on the fairy-story setting in collections such as J.M. Whitfeld's *The Spirit of the Bushfire* (1898), illustrated by George Lambert, which has the Spirit nurse a spark into life to threaten a typical Australian disaster, averted by the Raindrop Elves. Olga Ernst's *Fairy Tales from the Land of the Wattle* (1904), illustrated by Dorothy Ashley, uses the same idea, with roles reversed, in one of the stories, 'The Fire Elves'. 'A.A.B. and Helumac'

Australian Fairy Tales (1897) by Atha Westbury. Illustrator: A.J. Johnson

wrote *Australian Wonderland: a Fairy Chain* (1899), illustrated by Louise M. Glazier, in which Charlie Brendon meets gnomes on the road between Castlemaine and Muckleford, Victoria, who take on the appearance of their particular gift, e.g. an artist's palette, a book, a musical score.

Amy Mack's *Bushland Stories* (1910), later collected in *The Flower Fairies and Other Stories of the Australian Bush* (1928), illustrated by Karna Birmingham, uses some fairies, but the stories are mainly natural history. J.J. Hall's *"Winks": 'Winks' Tells Australian Children What He Saw in the Australian Bush* (1920), *The Crystal Bowl: Australian Nature Stories* (1921) and *The Kangaroo Paw: the Story of a Strange Australian Flower* (1922) also use fairies to introduce nature stories. In *Fairy Tales Told in the Bush* (1912) by 'Sister Agnes' the stories are not all set in Australia, nor are they all fairy stories. Some claim to draw on Aboriginal history, such as the life of King Barak, set in Healesville, or the origins of the Blue Lake at Mount Gambier. Others describe the adventures of Tom aided by an assortment of European fairies. One bizarre story has Tom steal an Aborigine's magic nail gun (*sic*) with which he has great fun killing kangaroos and nailing kookaburras to their trees. Even more gruesome was Henry Byron Moore's *How the Cruel Imp Became a Good Fairy* (1900), where an evil fairy roasts a live dog over a campfire and cuts the crest off a cockatoo. As punishment it is suggested that his leg be pulled off to beat him with the raw end! In Annie Eley's *The Dawn Maiden: Dione's Visit to Australia* (?1922) the childish form of the Queen of Love (Dione) comes to the Australian bush, where she is received by Prince Kalypto. A convoluted story is enlivened by inventive characters, such as the Kelpie Men, shaped from sea kelp, and some clever names, such as the Fici-Folia Sisters and Princess Melliodora.

Agnes Littlejohn wrote fairy stories, including *Star Dust and Sea Spray* (1918), illustrated by Sydney Ure Smith and Percy Leason, and *The Lost Emerald and Other Stories* (1924), illustrated by Pixie O'Harris. These collections use Australian birds and wildflowers mingled with traditional European fairies. Also illustrated by Pixie O'Harris was *Cinderella's Party: a Fairy Story* (1923) by Maud Renner Liston, another fairy story using traditional characters and a conventional moral tone: 'Always be happy, and then you'll be good. Think of others first, and get up bright and early in the morning.'

Ethel Jackson Morris wrote and illustrated two elegant collections of fairy stories, *All Among the Fairies* (1909) and *The White Butterfly and Other Fairy Tales* (1921), both with fairies, gnomes, elves, woods and even Merlin. In her first book she has a poem 'The Fairies', which contains an Australian reference: 'The willow trees by the lonely creek,/The tall grey gums on the mountain peak,/Welcome them all as they dance along,/Tripping it lightly to Bellbird's song.' Morris's fairy pictures exhibited between 1910 and 1920 rivalled Outhwaite's in their delicate style.

Australian Fairy Tales (1925) was written by Hume Cook, with illustrations by Christian Yandell (Waller). It arose out of a demand by the author's children for Australian fairies, and is introduced by a preface by the former Prime Minister, Billy Hughes. The fairies' names have become King Acacia, Queen Cootamundra, and Princess Wattleblossom. They live in central Australia, although their origins lie with Oberon, Titania and Puck. Yandell's striking illustrations are different from those which were favoured in fairy books of this period. She has created fairies with the strength and power of spirits, with adult bodies, sometimes halfnaked.

Spanning the first three decades of the twentieth century, the fairy stories of Tarella Quin Daskein stand out, filled with imaginative creatures described in close detail. *Gum Tree Brownie and Other Faerie Folk of the Never-Never* (1907), *Before the Lamps are Lit* (1911), *Chimney Town* (1934)

The Enchanted Forest (1921) by Ida Rentoul Outhwaite

and *The Other Side of Nowhere* (1934), were illustrated by Ida Rentoul Outhwaite. Daskein makes no concessions to language, and, like many writers of the period, she frequently has a child die. At times her settings appear to be very European — 'Ebenezer's anniversary' is located in a 'sleepy mountain village', but at other times she portrays the Australian scene with clarity. In 'The Strange Adventures of Aunt Martha', for instance, the adventures occur on the edge of the Australian desert. Her children are more innocent and much wiser than their elders.

The stories and verse by the talented Rentoul family were also fairy stories, such as *Mollie's Bunyip* (1904), *The Lady of the Blue Beads* (1908), *The Little Green Road to Fairyland* (1922) and *The Little Fairy Sister* (1923), all illustrated by Ida

Rentoul Outhwaite. Although the countryside is not typically Australian in either text or illustration, there are bunyips, koalas and kookaburras alongside brownies, elves, woodcutters and pixies. These beautifully produced books were stories to be read to children rather than by them, as they portray children as a quaint and amusing subspecies. The stories, which were written by the Outhwaites, Grenbry and Ida, lack the originality of Daskein's.

From the 1920s on, Pixie O'Harris wrote commercially successful fairy stories, often derivative of European fairy-tales, such as *The Pixie O'Harris Book* (1925), *Pearl Pinkie and Sea Greenie, the Story of Two Little Rock Sprites* (1935) and *Rondel the Fair* (1943). O'Harris also illustrated the fairy stories of Gladys Lister, such as *The Little Round Garden* (1938), which followed the same pattern.

Elizabeth Backhouse's *Enone and Quentin* (1956), illustrated by Irene Carter, relates how the mortal child, Enone, is taken to Cloud Land by the son of Mother and Father Sun. In a mixture of Australian and European themes, gumnuts and cockatoos appear in the 'dark woods'. An unusual fairy story is *Jean and the Shell Fairy* (?1920), illustrated by Sheila Hawkins and published as an advertisement for the Shell Company. 'Thanks to the fairy whose name is Shell/Who gives us Spirit and Oil as well/Motorists all his praises swell/All over the world each morning.' In an early conservation story, Annina E. Highfield's *The Wayward Fern Fairy* (1930), illustrated by Esme Duncan, the fairy remains when the railway goes through her fern gully, only to find her world destroyed. In Lyn Malin's *Stories of Faerieland* (1931), adventures of the spirits are enlivened by some droll twists. Princess Slumberlight has sky-blue eyes and a rosebud mouth, but is entirely bald, a situation which made 'the Queen weep half the night and the King drink more sherbet than was good for him'. A similar humorous note is struck in Frances Chapman's *The Witty Wizard of Warrandyte: a Magical Hour in Fairyland* (1944), illustrated in cartoon style by 'Armstrong'. Uncle Dogsbury tells Sally and her animal friends a series of stories about Bumblepump, the Threepenny Fairy and the Witty Wizard.

The tradition of European fairies has continued well into the twentieth century. In Ennis Honey's *Jennifer Jane* (1947), illustrated by L.G. Gordon, Fairyland is peopled by Cinderella, Santa Claus and other familiar characters. In Leslie Deans's *The Imp and the Fairy* (1945), illustrated by Esther and Betty Paterson, Mary is shown how to be naughty by Mischief, the Imp, only to be redeemed by Conscience, the Fairy. In *The Rainbow Painter* (1948) by Esme Elliott Bell, Sunshine, who lives in an old gum tree, blends colours from the bush flowers. The bush has native animals, elves and fairies, tortoises and squirrels. *Tales for Tinies* (1943) by Barbara Woods,

illustrated by Donald Gunn, is a collection of stories about elves, sea-horses and other fantastic creatures set in the Australian landscape. Peg Maltby's fairy folk and idealised Aboriginal children in bushland settings gained considerable popularity over two decades. *Peg's Fairy Book* (1944) went into five editions and sold over 180 000 copies.

The popularity of the fairy story declined after World War II. The self-conscious viewpoint and sentimentality which characterised the fairy story in the nineteenth and early twentieth centuries may seem cloying to the modern reader, but fairy stories expressed the powerful role of fanciful creatures in childhood imagination. The excellence of the work of Daskein and the Rentouls in the 1920s and 1930s recognised the serious adult acceptance of imagination as a vital force in the daily life of children. A changing world, where science presents its own imaginative challenges, and a taste for the epic rather than the domestic landscape has led to increased enthusiasm for a different imaginative dimension. Rather than in stories of imps, goblins, elves and fairies, the imagination of contemporary children is more likely to be animated by the space demons of science fiction (q.v.) or the Narguns of fantasy (q.v.).

'Falcon Comics' were twenty-one comic-books published from 1975 to 1978 by Macmillan for reluctant readers. Illustrators included Rick Amor, Peter Dickie, Geoff Cook, Chris Payne and Colin Stevens, and titles included *Rock Island Rescue* (1977) by Roger Vaughan Carr, *The Ghost of Gaffers Creek* (1975), *The Junk Shop* (1977) and *Star Bores* (1978) by Rick and Tina Amor, *Black Mountain Breakdown* (1976) by Colin Stevens, and *Tram Fury* (1976) by Geoff Cook.

'Falcon Island' was a television series which appeared in 1981. The thirteen half-hour episodes follow the exploits of three children as they attempt to save an old Dutch galleon from being destroyed by sand-miners. The series was directed by Paul Barron, and starred Francesca Shoesmith as Kate, Justin Hollyock as Jock and Greg Duffy as Paul. Joan Ambrose based the novel *Falcon Island* (1982) on the series.

FALK, VALERIE R. (1931–   ). For *Why Must We Go? Descriptions of Journeys to Australia from South-East Asia by South-East Asian Students of Richmond Girl's High School* (1981) see **Collections**.

Families. Death, separation, immigration and the industrialised economy have frequently disrupted the family. Nineteenth-century novels abound with accounts of families tearing up their roots and struggling to survive in the alien landscape of Australia, such as *The Young Berringtons* (1880) by W.H.G. Kingston or Mary Bradford Whiting's *Josee: an Australian Story* (1890). In some form or another, however, the family continues to be the setting against which children face the social complexities of their lives. *The Youngsters of Murray Home* (1896) by M. Ella Chaffey brings to life a stable nineteenth-century family, the Olsens, a group of realistic, sometimes naughty, children, and their cheerful existence on the Murray River. Dust storms, snakes and the new governess are managed with practicality and good humour. Ethel Turner's *Seven Little Australians* (q.v., 1894) remains the best-known example of a nineteenth-century family story. Both the Olsens and the Woolcotts are well-to-do, despite their references to 'making do'. In contrast, the family in Constance Mackness's *Gem of the Flat* (1914) is poor, and its members survive by pulling together to battle their way through hardships. Other writers, such as Lilian Turner, Lillian Pyke and Vera Dwyer all placed their protagonists within a family, not always ideally happy, and often held

together by an older girl. Mary Grant Bruce's Lintons are more a group of mates than a family — always co-operative, pleasant to each other, together in every adventure.

The families created by Joan Phipson in *The Family Conspiracy* (q.v., 1962), Eleanor Spence in *The Summer in Between* (q.v., 1959) and Patricia Wrightson in *The Feather Star* (q.v., 1962) are not affluent, but aspire to gentility and education, display good taste and solve any arguments harmoniously. Spence's *The Green Laurel* (q.v., 1963) is a more threatened family, where deeper issues are faced. Nan Chauncy's Lorenny family is less genteel and far less concerned with appearances.

During the 1980s the dislocation of family life was brought under closer scrutiny, and the changing family structures of the late twentieth century examined. *Solomon's Child* (1981) by Mavis Thorpe Clark introduced the dilemma of Jude, whose mother and father have separated. In Penny Hall's *Better for Everyone* (1992) goodwill between the adults is not enough to accommodate Meg, who is uncertain about her feelings towards her new stepmother and siblings. Hall touches on the insecurities which may arise after a divorce, and the difficult choices which children are frequently asked to make. *Thunderwith* (q.v., 1989) by Libby Hathorn is a frank account of a stepmother's refusal to accept her husband's daughter from a previous marriage. Bronwen Nicholls in *Mullaway* (1986) shows the shift in the family's relationships required when a parent dies. The boys in Frank Willmott's *Breaking Up* (q.v., 1983) must adjust to the collapse of what seemed to be an inviolable family, and the demise of a nuclear family contributes to Andrew's problems in *Space Demons* (q.v., 1986) by Gillian Rubinstein. The difficulties of blended families are treated in *Terri* (1981) by Diane Bates and the more positive results of remarriage in Simon French's *All we Know* (q.v., 1987) and Ruth Park's *Callie's Castle* (q.v., 1974). The links between generations are revealed in *The Family Book of Mary-Claire* (q.v., 1990) by Eleanor Spence, a history of a family which begins in convict times. Happy families are still found in children's books, such as Thurley Fowler's *The Green Wind* (q.v., 1985) and *The Wind is Silver* (1991) and Robin Klein's *All in the Blue Unclouded Weather* (1991), where a more innocent past is recalled, but the darker side of family life has emerged in *Letters from the Inside* (1991) by John Marsden, *Time to Go* (1991) by Jill Dobson, and Victor Kelleher's *Del-Del* (1991). The family as a bulwark against change is less likely, as optimism for the future is eroded.

Family at the Lookout (1972) by Noreen Shelley, illustrated by Robert Micklewright, won the 1973 Book of the Year Awards. When Uncle Joseph Wetherall bequeaths his large house in the Blue Mountains to his nephew, the family move from their flat in Melbourne to take up residence. Uncle Joseph's elderly housekeeper, Miss Caroline Hatch, seems to be hiding something, and Mark and his Dutch friend Joss do some detective work, discover some unfinished paintings of Uncle Joseph's bird studies, and help fight off a bushfire which threatens the house. In the excitement, prejudices against foreigners are tackled and largely overcome, and the Wetheralls are thoroughly accepted by the small community. This was Shelley's first novel for older readers.

Family Award for Children's Books has been presented by the NSW Family Therapy Association since 1988 as part of Children's Book Week. The award is made annually to acknowledge the strengths of Australian families in facing life's challenges. **1987** *Deezle Boy* (q.v., 1987) by Eleanor Spence; **1988** *You Take the High Road* (1988) by Mary K. Pershall; **1989** *The Blue Chameleon* (1989) by Katherine Scholes; **1990** *Two Weeks with the Queen* (1990) by Morris Gleitzman; **1991** *Change the Locks* (q.v., 1991) by Simon French.

Family Book of Mary-Claire, The (1990) by Eleanor Spence was an Honour Book in the 1991 Book of the Year Awards: Older Readers. The convicts Titus and Sarah Cleveland and their son Julius survive a shipwreck, and Marius is born. Four generations of Cleveland descendants — Marius, sent to live with free settlers, the Barrs; his daughter Miriam; her son Marion, the father of Mary-Claire — write about their perceptions of the family in a Bible rescued from the shipwreck. The complex inter-relationships, which include Aboriginal People, bushrangers, French aristocrats and Irish cedar-cutters, are seen through the eyes of carefully delineated individuals. See also **Historical Novels**.

Family Conspiracy, The (1962) by Joan Phipson, illustrated by Margaret Horder, won the 1963 Book of the Year Awards. Mrs Barker must have an operation, and Edward, Lorna, Belinda and Robbie decide they they will earn enough money to send her to a hospital in Sydney. Their efforts are a series of disasters, until each learns that rewards do not come quickly or easily. However, their mishaps bring out the best in each of them: Edward's determination saves some cattle he is droving, and Lorna's timidity is overcome when she has the responsibility of younger children. The Barker family are also the focus in *Threat to the Barkers* (1963). Jack, the eldest in the family, has bought some stud ewes, and when Edward uncovers a sheep-stealing racket he is torn between a responsibility to reveal the perpetrators and a need to protect the family from the threats made to keep him silent. Phipson has an assured grasp of rural life.

Fantasy. An endless pudding, a bumbling bushranger, a kangaroo with a bottomless pouch, wicked banksia men, creatures in jam tins, and incantations which bring up the past are the stuff of Australian fantasy. Apart from stories about fairies (q.v.), the

Coppertop (1919) by Harold Gaze

talking animal inspired early books, such as *Bertie and the Bullfrogs: an Australian Story for Little Children* (q.v., 1874) by John Howard Clark, *His Cousin the Wallaby: and Three Other Australian Stories* (1896) by 'Arthur Ferres', Mary Grant Bruce's *Timothy in Bushland* (1912), Donald MacDonald's *At the End of the Moonpath* (1922) and the most famous fantasy about Australian animals in a bush setting, Ethel Pedley's *Dot and the Kangaroo* (q.v., 1899). Animals continued to be a rich source of the fantastic, and in the first half of the twentieth century the bush fantasy reached its peak in the works of May Gibbs, Dorothy Wall and Norman Lindsay. Later writers, such as Pixie O'Harris, Leslie Rees, W. Lloyd Williams and Henry Allan have continued the tradition. In Henry Allan's *The Happy Forest: a Story Book for Boys and Girls* (1944), illustrated by M. Gilbert, the innocent Torty leaves Robert and Hilda Roo and Numbat to seek his fortune in the city, but is soon disillusioned by a sneering Pekinese and a bullying Great Dane who owns a pie stall, and returns, much wiser, to the bush. A sophisticated talking animal is found in Randolph Stow's *Midnite: the Story of a Wild Colonial Boy* (q.v., 1967) — the talking cat, Khat. This unique comic fantasy can be appreciated at a number of levels. The story of the inept bushranger is layered with satiric comments on Australian life and letters. Not a satire, but rich with Australian culture, Alan Marshall's *Whispering in the Wind* (1969) presents a traditional quest of a boy and Greyfur the kangaroo in search of a princess in the context of the bush — Crooked Mick, tall tales, magical creatures and bush lore.

Another lasting tradition has been the animal-like creature, first seen in the work of Harold Gaze, which appeared between the wars, in books such as *The Chewg-um-blewg-um* and *The Billabonga Bird* (both 1919). Their descendants are Michael Noonan's Jambies and Jeannies, in *In the*

Land of the Talking Trees, a Fantasy (1946), set in Papua New Guinea, and the characters invented by S.A. Wakefield for his *Bottersnikes and Gumbles* (q.v., 1967). Morris Lurie's *The 27th Annual African Hippopotamus Race* (1969) and *Arlo the Dandy Lion* (1971) present animals in a humorous way, mocking human foibles. The creatures of the Aboriginal Dreaming stories have been taken into children's literature, particularly the bunyip (q.v.), but also the Nimbin or Njimbin, used by Jenny Wagner and Patricia Wrightson. Wrightson, like Bill Scott, has increasingly turned to Aboriginal spirits for inspiration in the 'Wirrun' books and *Boori* (q.v., 1978) respectively. Aboriginal traditions also animate 'Helen Frances's' *The Devil's Stone* (q.v., 1983).

The more traditional magic of ghosts and the supernatural is represented in Duncan Ball's series on the ghost of Arnold Taylor (q.v.); in Nan Hunt's *The Pow Toe* (1979) and *Roma Mercedes and Fred* (1978); Michael Dugan's *Melissa's Ghost* (1986); and 'Emily Rodda's' *Something Special* (q.v., 1984). In Cassandra Golds's *Michael and the Secret War* (1985), Michael is enlisted as a Helper by ghostly people such as the Sparrow, and is called on to provide Sympathy, Empathy and Identity. This complex fantasy involves magic and religion. A sinister magic pervades Lilith Norman's *The Flame Takers* (1973), Victor Kelleher's *Baily's Bones* (1988) and Carolyn F. Logan's *The Power of the Rellard* (1986). Also returning to European traditions, David Martin uses the Faust motif in *The Devilish Mystery of the Flying Mum* (1977), and the defeat of the standard dragon is parodied in *The Dragon of Mith* (q.v., 1989) by Kate Walker. Ruth Park has drawn on the idea of a sea creature who is half-human in *My Sister Sif* (1986). The supernatural has also been introduced into the short story, such as in the short stories of Paul Jennings, Judith Clarke's *The Boy on the Lake* (1989), Ruth Park's *Things in Corners* (1989),

Robin Klein's *Against the Odds* (1989), *Before Dawn* and *After Dark* (both 1988), edited by Gillian Rubinstein, and *Bizarre: Ten Wonderfully Weird Stories* (1989), edited by Penny Matthews.

The idea that time is a dimension which can be explored outside present reality has fascinated twentieth-century writers. Examples include Ruth Hawker's *Yesterday: Being the Adventures of Us Three with the Early Colonists* (1936), illustrated by Nora Young; Nan Chauncy's *Tangara: 'Let Us set Off Again'* (q.v., 1960); Joan Phipson's *The Way Home* (1973); Valerie Weldrick's *Time Sweep* (1976); Ruth Park's *Playing Beatie Bow* (q.v., 1980); David Lake's *The Changelings of Chaan* (q.v., 1985) and *West of the Moon: a Fantasy Novel* (1988); Patricia Bernard's *Aida's Ghost* (1988) and John Marsden's *Out of Time* (1990). In Nadia Wheatley's *The House that was Eureka* (q.v., 1984) an old house provides the catalyst for a time-slip. In *The Best-Kept Secret* (q.v., 1988) by 'Emily Rodda', Jo finds reassurance in the future, rather than the past. An everyday saying is ingeniously actualised in the parallel world created by 'Emily Rodda' in *Pigs Might Fly* (q.v., 1986).

The epic fantasy has also found expression, though not always with an Australian setting. In the tradition of journey, task, and conflict between good and evil, Ruth Manley chose Japanese legend for the setting of her three books about Taro, beginning with *The Plum-Rain Scroll* (q.v., 1978). Welsh mythology inspires Brian Caswell's *Merryll of the Stones* (q.v., 1989). An earlier epic, in which the creatures of myth inhabit the Canberra landscape, is *Six Days Between a Second* (q.v., 1969) by Marjory O'Dea. Isobelle Carmody's *Obernewtyn* (1987) and *The Farseekers* (q.v., 1990) and Victor Kelleher's *Forbidden Paths of Thual* (1979), *The Hunting of Shadroth* (1981), *Master of the Grove* (q.v., 1982) and *The Red King* (1989) have links with J.R.R. Tolkien, Ursula Le Guin, and Robin McKinley. These books have a timeless setting, with prehistoric or medieval associations.

Politics, conservation, individualism, moral dilemmas, power and its use are all themes taken up in the fantasies of Ruth Park, Nadia Wheatley, Bill Scott, Patricia Wrightson and Victor Kelleher.

FARJEON, BENJAMIN LEOPOLD (1838–1903) lived in Australia from 1854 to 1861, mainly on the Victorian gold-fields either fossicking or editing goldfields newspapers. Out of these experiences, and his later life in NZ, where he became edi-tor of the *Otago Daily Times*, came a series of novels. In *The Golden Land: or, Links from Shore to Shore* (1886), a long-lost brother sends for a motherless family from England. Much of the book is taken up with the family's life in England and the voyage to the Colony. They arrive in Melbourne and set out through the bush via the gold-diggings for a property on the Murray River. *Grif* (1866) is about a Melbourne street urchin who befriends the lovely Alice, married to a drunken wastrel, Richard Handfield. Richard is accused of murder, is saved from the gal-lows by the dying testimony of Grif, and is reformed through Alice's love. Farjeon describes the poorer parts of Melbourne in the mid-nineteenth century, 'where poverty and vice struggle for breathing space', and his experiences of a Melbourne summer are recalled with clar-ity: 'The sky glared down whitely, and the blinding sun scorched up moisture and vegetation with its eye of fire.' *At the Sign of the Silver Flagon* (1876) and *The Sacred Nugget* (1885) are other goldfields stories. An account of Farjeon's life can be found in the autobiography of his daughter, Eleanor Farjeon, *A Nursery in the Nineties* (1935).

FARRELL, ANNE (1955–), born Latrobe, Tasmania, is the sister of Sally Farrell Odgers. Her books about the four Mitchell children are set on a dairy farm

in Tasmania, 'Guara'. They are *The Gift-Wrapped Pony* (1973), *The Calf on Shale Hill* (1974), *Eight Days at Guara* (1976) and *Shadow Summer* (1978), all illustrated by Astra Lacis. Horses and cows provide the drama in these family stories about Val, Lesley, David and Ian, and their toler-ant parents. Farrell has also contributed to reading schemes. *A Night to Forget* (1977), for instance, is in Hodder's 'Knight Riders' reading scheme.

FARRELL, SALLY, see **ODGERS, SALLY FARRELL**

The Farseekers (1990) by Isobelle Carmody was an Honour Book in the 1991 Book of the Year Awards: Older Readers. The novel is a sequel to *Obernewtyn* (1987), and continues the adventures of the Misfits, people who have been cast out from the prevailing society and hide at Obernewtyn, a place in the mountains. Elspeth and a group of her fol-lowers, including Jik, a novice, leave Obernewtyn with two tasks: to discover a Talent who has extraordinary powers of mind, and to find an enormous book stor-age from the Beforetime. Both are accom-plished with the assistance of the animal world, including the proud horse Gahltha and a group of dragon-like birds. Carmody creates a convincing alternative world in this quest fantasy.

FATCHEN, MAX (1920–), born Adelaide, was literary editor of the Adelaide *Advertiser* from 1971 to 1982. His poetry is collected in *Drivers and Trains* (1962), *Keepers and Lighthouses* (1963), *Songs for My Dog and Other People* (1980), illustrated by Michael Atchison, *Wry Rhymes for Troublesome Times* (1983), also illustrated by Atchison, *A Paddock of Poems* (q.v., 1987) and *A Pocket Full of Rhymes* (1989), both illustrated by Kerry Argent, and *A Country Christmas* (1990), illustrated by Timothy Ide, a collection of poems which affectionately recollects the festival through a boy's eyes. Fatchen knows what will amuse his young readers, from the delightful to the horrible. He has written novels for older readers. For *The River Kings* (q.v., 1966), and *Conquest of the River* (1970), which relate the adventures of Shawn, who runs away to work on a Murray River boat, see **The River Kings** and **Murray River**. For *The Spirit Wind* (q.v., 1973) and *Chase Through the Night* (1976), illustrated by Graham Humphreys, see **Aboriginal People in Children's Fiction**. *Chase Through the Night* was made into five half-hour television episodes in 1983, directed by Howard Rubie, with a script by Rob George and John Emery. In *The Time Wave* (1978), illustrated by Edward Mortelmans, Josef and Gina are thrown together through a kidnapping and a tidal wave. *Closer to the Stars* (1981), for older readers, is set during World War II. See **War**. *Had Yer Jabs?* (1987), illustrated by Sandra Laroche, first appeared as a short story in Leon Garfield's *A Swag of Stories* (1977). Tommy escapes his tetanus injection until he is cornered by the doctor just before a horse-race. The resulting tenderness in his rear end acts as a spur, and wins him the race. Fatchen has a keen perception of childhood and its difficulties.

Father Time's Christmas Annual, see **Annuals**

'Fatty Finn' was created as a Sydney *Sunday News* comic-strip by Syd Nicholls in 1923, first appearing as 'Fat and his friends'. Fatty Finn annuals appeared in 1929 and 1930, and *Fatty Finn's Weekly* (1934–35) was the first Australian comic-book, selling over four million copies. In 1953 Fatty Finn reappeared in the comic section of the Sydney *Sun Herald*, where it continued until 1977, the year of Nicholls's death. Hubert 'Fatty' Finn was at first a Billy Bunter type, but his persona changed over the years into more of a larrikin, to rival Ginger Meggs (q.v.) in

humorous appeal. Nicholls's style combined the cartoon-like figure of Fatty with more realistic figures of pirates, schoolmasters, and others. *The Kid Stakes*, a film made in 1927, was based on the Fatty Finn comic-strip. It was directed by Tal Ordell, who had appeared as Dave in the 1920 film of 'Steele Rudd's' *On Our Selection*. Another film version, *Fatty Finn*, was made in 1980, with a script by Bob Ellis, directed by Maurice Murphy, and starring Noni Hazelhurst and Bert Newton as Mr and Mrs Finn, and Ben Oxenbould as Fatty Finn. Ellis wrote a book for children based on the film, *The Adventures of Fatty Finn* (1980), with illustrations from the original cartoons by Syd Nicholls.

FAVENC, ERNEST (1845–1908), born Walworth, Surrey, UK, came to Australia in 1864. From 1865 to 1883 Favenc explored large areas of Australia throughout Queensland, the Gulf country and WA, experiences which are recalled in his novels, where he displays faultless bushcraft. In 1871 Favenc began contributing to the *Queenslander* under the pseudonym 'Dramingo'. He wrote a standard history of Australian exploration, *History of Australian Exploration from 1788 to 1888* (1888), novels and short stories. Favenc was influenced by the idea of the legendary 'Lemuria', a hypothesis developed by the zoologist C.L. Sclater in the 1850s to account for the distribution of the lemur. The proposition was that there was a lost continent which would be found to contain treasure, strange customs and a unique race of people. Favenc was not the only writer to suggest Lemuria within the continent. J.F. Hogan's *The Lost Explorer* (1890), J.D. Hennessey's *An Australian Bush Track* (1896) and G. Firth Scott's *The Last Lemurian* (1898) are based on the same concept. *The Secret of the Australian Desert* (1896), illustrated by Percy F.S. Spence, recalls the puzzling disappearance of the explorer Ludwig Leichhardt. Morton, Brown, Charlie and

The Secret of the Australian Desert (1896) by Ernest Favenc. Illustrator: Percy Spence

Billy Button set off to investigate the rumour of a burning mountain. Quickly overcoming all obstacles, such as desert, illness and strange cannibalistic inhabitants, the intrepid heroes discover a survivor of Leichhardt's party, a volcano-like mountain, inexplicable wall paintings and gold. See also **Aboriginal People in Children's Fiction**.

Marooned on Australia: Being the Narration by Diedrich Buys of His Discoveries and Exploits in Terra Australis Incognita About the Year 1630 (1896), also illustrated by Spence, uses Lemuria and the wreck of the *Batavia* as its inspiration. Diedrich and his companion Paul live for a time with the local Aboriginal People, then trek northwards, eventually finding 'cultivated fields, thickets of tall trees, low houses with white walls, and, above all, human beings, clothed and apparently wearing a kind of head-dress'. They fall in with the Quadrucos, both marry into the local aristocracy, and live happily for years with

these peaceful farmers until the lure of gold brings more Europeans to the coast and the Quadrucos are annihilated. Favenc's Quadruco Utopia is only vaguely realised, but the *Batavia* massacres are graphically recounted in the early part of the novel. See also **Batavia**. *The Moccasins of Silence* (1896), by Favenc under the pseudonym 'Armand Jerome', is a more adult romance in which Ruth Annett and her fiancé search for her father and his cache of priceless diamonds.

Tales for Young Australia (1900) with 'Mab' and James and Josephine Fotheringhame, (who according to Cheryl Frost's biography are probably pseudonyms for Favenc and his wife Bessie), illustrated by D.H. Souter, Percy F.S. Spence and others, is a collection of stories. *The Story of Our Continent, Told With Brush and Pen* (n.d.), illustrated by Spence, takes a historical approach, and was to appear as a serial, although it is doubtful whether more than the first issue was completed. As 'Armand

Jerome' Favenc edited *Australian Boys and Girls: an Illustrated Annual of Stories by Australian Writers* (1895), which contained stories by Louis Becke, Ethel Turner, Favenc himself and others. Further reading: Healy, 'The Lemurian Nineties'; Frost, *The Last Explorer*.

FAWCETT, ROBERT CHARLES A., see **'CHARLES, HAROLD'**

FAZAKAS, ALEX (1948–), born Sopron, Hungary, came to Australia in 1952. For *The Adonis Strategy* (1989) see **Science Fiction**.

Feather Star, The (1962) by Patricia Wrightson, illustrated by Noela Young, was Commended in the 1963 Book of the Year Awards. A beach holiday provides the setting for an examination of the embarrassments, mood changes, and growth in awareness of others which occur during a few weeks in Lindy Martin's fifteenth summer. Lindy becomes friends with Fleece (Felice), Bill and Ian, and while they have their disagreements, they begin to understand each other, with Bill and Lindy developing an even deeper affection. The only bitterness is the old man Abel, who is incapable of any tenderness, and maintains his anger towards the world. Wrightson's novel shows a sensitive girl moving towards adulthood within an understanding family.

February Dragon (1965) by Colin Thiele was Commended in the 1966 Book of the Year Awards. The novel was written with the encouragement of the Bushfire Research Council of SA. It is a series of anecdotes about the Pine children and their friends — fishing, going to school and life on the farm. In the second last chapter the dragon, a terrible bushfire, takes over to burn houses, stock and people, and to change the survivors' lives forever. The book closes on a threatening note, for the dragon 'was just waiting for another chance'.

Felix and Alexander (1985), written and illustrated by Terry Denton, won the 1986 Picture Book of the Year Awards. Alexander's best friend is Felix, a toy dog, as he is not allowed real pets in the high-rise building where he lives. When Alexander is lost, Felix leads him through a threatening city at night. The menacing buildings which loom down on the solitary Alexander and his dog are created through dark pages and the use of shadow. While the illustrations tower over the wistful boy, the reader is reassured by the sprightly confidence of Felix.

FENN, GEORGE MANVILLE (1831–1909), born London, UK, was the author of over 150 adventure stories. In *The Dingo Boys: or, The Squatters of Wallaby Range* (1892), illustrated by W.S. Stacey, a family of Bedfords, including uncles and cousins, fight off snakes and swim in crocodile-infested rivers on a journey across country to take up land and establish a property. At one point a kangaroo tries to drown one of the party by holding Shanter in his arms and plunging 'the poor helpless struggling fellow down beneath the surface [of the river], attentively watching the approach the while of a third enemy'. The colonisers' attitude to the land is expressed succinctly: 'There is plenty for all Englishmen, but those who are enterprising enough to do as we have done, of course get the first choice.' 'Dingo' Station is established in little more than a year, and the troublesome traditional owners dispensed with by the gun: 'If it were not for the thoughts of the black fellows, what a paradise this would be', says Ned Bedford. A similar experience is related in *First in the Field, a Story of New South Wales* (1894), which is an account of Nic Braydon's transformation from English schoolboy to bushman, playing his part in making 'Australia a big young England for John Bull's sons and daughters, who want room to move'. Interwoven with descriptions of the fauna of Australia, which the stalwart Nic takes

Felix and Alexander (1985) by Terry Denton

pleasure in shooting and stuffing, is the story of an assigned servant, Frank Mayne, who has been wrongfully sentenced to twenty-five years for embezzlement. Nic befriends Frank, helps him escape, and clears his name. *Bunyip Land: or, Among the Blackfellows in New Guinea* (1893), illustrated by Gordon Browne, begins in Australia, but quickly moves to New Guinea, as Joseph and his faithful Aboriginal servant, Jimmy, set off to find Joseph's naturalist father. Fenn never visited Australia, and uses the birds and animals to provide local colour, but his stories are exciting, if melodramatic.

FENNER, RUTH (1917–), born Toowoomba, Queensland, conducted the Sydney programs of the ABC's 'Kindergarten of the Air' from 1943 to 1961. *The Story House* (1960), illustrated by Elisabeth MacIntyre, has stories and verse for young children.

'FENNIMORE, STEPHEN', see **COLLINS, DALE**

FERGUSON, VIRGINIA (1940–) has co-authored books with Peter Durkin (q.v.).

FERNS, ANN (1942–) has written *Mungo the Mud Monster* (1984), illustrated by Susanne Ferrier. Mungo and the Drongo Bird sleep through the Ice Age and are awoken by Professor Platt, who returns them to the swamp when they fail his maths tests. Ferns has written three books about the mythical Yowie, a large, bumbling, Bunyip-like creature who overcomes his clumsy mistakes with the help of the other bush animals. *The Yowie That Nobody Wanted*, *The Yowie Finds a Home* and *The Yowie is Very Brave* (all 1981) are illustrated by Tristan Parry. *Once Upon an Australian Christmas* (1982), illustrated by

Murray Frederick, is a verse story. When Santa is late, the bush animals gather to take his place and provide gifts for the children. For *1 to 10 and Back Again* (1983), illustrated by Susanne Ferrier, see **Counting Books**. Ferns has also written *Starlight the Brumby* (1983), illustrated by Dee Huxley, and *Sacha the Fur Seal* (1983), illustrated by Ester Kasepuu, picture-books which examine the right of a wild animal to be free.

'FERRES, ARTHUR' was the pseudo-nym of **JOHN WILLIAM KEVIN** (?1843–1903), born Derry, Ireland. He was a school inspector, active in the school library movement, and edited *Poetic Selections for Schools* (?1882), an early collection for children to include Australian verse. *My Centennial Gift, or, Australian Stories for Children* (1887) first appeared in the *Sydney Mail*. *His Cousin the Wallaby and Three other Australian Stories* (1896), illustrated by Percy F.S. Spence, is a fantasy in which Dick begins to turn into a walla-by. *His First Kangaroo: an Australian Story for Boys* (1896) describes the adventures of schoolboys on a country holiday, and abounds with racist comments about Germans, Aboriginal People, Chinese and others, and episodes where emus, kanga-roos and snakes meet grisly ends. *The Ploughboy Premier: a Story for Boys* (1916), apparently published posthumously, has 'one, and only one, object — to show the influence for good that may be contained within the sphere of a bush school library'. A box of 115 books are sent to Cootawalla Public School, and Tom Skidmore's initial reluctance to read is overcome when he breaks his leg and is confined to bed. Although his studies are interrupted when his older brother dies, and Tom must leave school, he continues to read, attends the Mechanics Institute, joins a Debating Society, and finally becomes Prime Minister of NSW. 'His "luck" … is to be traced to the Cootawalla School Library (Heaven bless it, and all similar institu-tions!) and to nothing else.' The novel contains an account of recommended reading for young people in the nine-teenth century, including *A Basket of Flowers*, *The Life of Nelson* and *From Log Cabin to White House*.

FERRIER, SUSANNE (1934–), born Melbourne, studied at RMIT. She illus-trated Carol Mills's *The A to Z of Absolute Zaniness: an ABC Book* (1982), reissued as *A to Z and Back Again* (1984), which has a rhyme for each letter, with large, colourful and outrageous illustrations. Her grimy pictures of mud illustrate Ann Ferns's *Mungo the Mud Monster* (1984). For *1 to 10 and Back Again* (1983) see **Counting Books**. Taking figures from history, she has illustrated *Ned — a Leg End* (1984), see **Bushrangers**, and *Lola: a Doubtful Documentary of Her Doings at the Diggings* (1985), in which Lola Montez dances at Ballarat, is kidnapped by William Buckley, chased by Captain Moonlight and wins the Melbourne Cup on Archer. Ferrier uses cartoons and comic-strip styles for her humorous and exaggerated illustra-tions. She also illustrated *The Ashton Scholastic History of Australia* (1988) by Manning Clark and Meredith Hooper.

FERRY, JOHN. For *Kamilaroi* (1978) see **Aboriginal Dreaming Stories**.

FIELDING, GRACE (1948–), born Wandering, WA, is an artist and illustrator working in the Kimberleys. She has illus-trated *Bip the Snapping Bungaroo* (1990) by Narelle McRobbie. A film of the book, illustrated by Fielding, was made by the Australian Children's Television Foun-dation in 1992.

FIELDING, Rev. **SYDNEY GLAN-VILLE** (1856–1930), born Parramatta, NSW, was curate of All Saints' Cathedral, Bathurst, NSW, during the 1880s. *The Southern Light* (1895), a seafaring story set on the NSW coast, and *"Down to the Sea in Ships"* (1900), in which Dick Danvers runs away to sea and is shipwrecked off New Caledonia, take the high moral ground and draw lessons for the young reader.

FIENBERG, ANNA (1956–), born UK, came to Australia in 1959. She edited the NSW *School Magazine* during the 1980s. In *Wiggy and Boa* (1988), illustrated by Ann James, anti-heroic and thick-headed pirates are summoned up from the past by Boa, and restored to useful domesticity by Boa and her friend Wiggy. *Billy Bear and the Wild Winter* (1988), illustrated by Astra Lacis, was originally a serial in the NSW *School Magazine*. Billy objects to hibernating, so he arranges for the musical society to awaken the other bears for a feast and a dance. In *The 9 Lives of Balthazar* (1989), illustrated by Donna Gynell, scientific Harold sets out to test a theory. As Harold's ninth experiment on Balthazar is about to kill the cat, the boy realises that the old cat is more important to him than proving a theory. *The Magnificent Nose and Other Marvels* (q.v., 1991), illustrated by Kim Gamble, has six stories about children and magical happenings, linked by the wise Aristan the spider. She has also written *Ariel, Zed and the Secret of Life* (1992). Fienberg writes original and amusing stories for newly fluent readers.

Fighting Ships of Australia and New Zealand (1953) by Frank Norton was Highly Commended in the 1954 Book of the Year Awards. Aircraft-carriers, cruisers, destroyers, converted merchant ships, submarines and other ships are described, with diagrams. Information is included on ship construction, navigation, naval shore establishments, the hydrographic branch of the Navy, and the insignia of the officers, in a copiously illustrated and authoritative book.

FIGUEROLA, CARMEN, born Melbourne, was a violinist until she became a writer. She has written for the Victorian

School Paper and the NSW *School Magazine*. *The Family on Phillip Island* (1955), illustrated by Marguerite Mahood, is Da, the housekeeper, Aggie, and Teresa, Simon and Jennifer. The spirited children make their own entertainment (including producing a newspaper) enjoying the beaches, animals and birdlife of the Victorian island.

Finders Keepers (1990) by 'Emily Rodda', illustrated by Noela Young, won the 1991 Book of the Year Awards: Younger Readers, and YABBA for Younger Readers in the same year. When he tunes his television to a game show, Patrick is transported to a parallel world, where he becomes a Finder, who must locate the lost possessions of three people on the other side of the barrier. His first task does not present him with problems, but he is worried when he must steal a ring from Estelle's finger. An original explanation of the unaccountable loss of small objects is given in this fantasy. The novel was made into a five-part television series for the ABC in 1991, with Jeremy Schwerdt as Patrick and Paul Tresnan as the game show host.

FINKEL, GEORGE (1909–75), born South Shields, UK, served in the Royal Navy Volunteer Reserve as an aviation adviser. Finkel came to Australia in 1950, and his novels reflect his interest in history, the sea and flying. In *The Mystery of Secret Beach* (1962) Roger Ormston and his crew foil a plan devised by Chinese and local communists to corrupt the Australian currency in order to damage Australia's relations with her Asian neighbours. *Ship in Hiding* (1963) was the first of his novels to feature Group Captain Alan Metcalfe, 'Groupie' to his friends. Groupie and his mates unmask the 'Central Europeans who had worked together on the Snowy Mountains scheme' who are attempting to smuggle gold out of the country. In *Cloudmaker* (1965), set in the Blue Mountains, another Cold War adventure story, David has been kidnapped by Russian spies who want his knowledge of how to make a material with the strength of metal and the insulating properties of porcelain. See also **Adventure Stories**. In *The Singing Sands* (1966) Groupie Metcalfe assists a young Arab, Ali, to regain his kingdom through the possession of the Seal of Solomon, hidden by a group of Norsemen who travelled to the southern ocean and buried it on Squeaky Beach, at Wilson's Promontory, Victoria. Finkel displays his knowledge of early navigation and map-making.

Finkel's historical novels began with *Twilight Province* (1967), also known as *Watch Fires to the North* (1967), illustrated by George Tetlow, a reconstruction of the exploits of Artyr, after the Romans have left Britain. In *The Long Pilgrimage* (1967), also illustrated by Tetlow, a young outlawed Saxon carries out a mission for Charlemagne. *The 'Loyall Virginian'* (q.v., 1968) takes an episode in the English Civil War from the point of view of a young Virginian colonist. *Journey to Jorsala* (1969) is about the Crusades, in particular the exploits of Godric Anwulfsson. *The Peace Seekers* (1970) is set in 1170, and is an account of a rivalry between two Welsh princes. Madoc sails to North America as a child, becomes friendly with the Painted People, then returns to become Prince Llewellyn, the last prince of independent Wales.

In *The Stranded Duck* (1973), illustrated by Andrew Parnell, Finkel used his knowledge of boats to describe how three boys and their grandfather refloat a barge, or lighter, with much detail on how the operation is effected. *Operation Aladdin* (1976), illustrated by Walter Stackpool, continues the adventures of Ian, Jim and Stephen. Grandpa is setting up a Folk Museum around an old inn. He finds a headlamp which leads to the recovery of a vintage car, a Deutsche-Adler, which the boys call 'Aladdin'. Finkel has also written biographies, such as *James Cook, Royal Navy* (q.v., 1970), *William Light* (1972),

Matthew Flinders, Explorer and Scientist (1973), *The Dutchman Bold, the Story of Abel Tasman* (1975) and *Governor Lachlan Macquarie* (1975).

FINN, MARY AGNES wrote two religious romances, *Monica's Trial: a Story for Girls* (1929) and its sequel, *Monica's Victory: a Story for Girls* (1944). The novels set out to show the 'evils of a mixed marriage', as Monica battles to maintain her Catholicism in the Protestant household of her stepmother. 'That child is the stuff of which martyrs are made', comments Mrs Dale. Monica is sent home to Ireland, where she is visited by her stepsister, Stella. Monica's piety converts Stella, who is then a suitable proposition to marry Edward Farnleigh, who was not prepared to marry outside his faith. On Stella's return to Australia, there are numerous conversions, deathbed scenes and miraculous recoveries, before Monica marries Dick Kearney.

Finn's Folly (1969) by Ivan Southall was Commended in the 1970 Book of the Year Awards. In a dense fog by the side of a lake, there is a tragic accident. A truck careers off the road, and cyanide is strewn around the hillside. The intellectually disabled David is lost, and while his family frantically search for him, Max, David's brother, and Alison, the daughter of the truck-driver, fall in love beside the driver's body. Despite the crowded scenario, the tension is palpable.

Fire in the Stone, The (1973) by Colin Thiele was Commended in the 1974 Book of the Year Awards. The setting is Coober Pedy, where Ernie Ryan finds opal, only to have it stolen from him. He leaves town for the south after a mining tragedy, not knowing the fate of his friend Willie Winowie, but fearing the worst. Ernie sorrowfully concludes that in this uncaring world, there would be 'bigger headlines for a dead racehorse'. Despite some stereotyped descriptions of

Aboriginal People, the novel is complex and disturbing, and confronts the issue of racism. A film of the novel was made by the SA Film Corporation in 1983, directed by Gary Conway, with a screenplay by Graeme Koetsveld. See also **Aboriginal People in Children's Fiction**.

Fires and Firemen (1963) by Carol Odell was Commended in the 1964 Book of the Year Awards. Illustrated with photographs which have been gathered from newspapers, journals, and the NSW Fire Brigade, the vigorous text is given an impressive authenticity. Odell has shown the drama of a large fire, the courage of the firemen, and concludes with advice for young readers on fire prevention.

First Fleet, The is the name given to the first eleven convict ships which arrived at Sydney Cove in 1788, commanded by Arthur Phillip. An early fictional account for young people was Lillian Pyke's *Brothers of the Fleet* (1924), about a convict wrongfully accused, who is finally pardoned by the King himself. Doris Chadwick's three books *John of the Sirius* (q.v., 1955), *John of Sydney Cove* (1957) and *John and Nanbaree* (1962) are tightly written novels which keep to the known historical experiences. *Drummer Crispin* (1980) by Ronald Rose is more harrowing in its detail, describing floggings, courts martial, mutinies, and the starvation which attended the early colonists. A sombre note is also struck in *Bound for Botany Bay: Impressions of Transportation and Convict Life* (1976) by J.D. Shearer, where the grimness of convict life on the ships is presented, hard tack and all. John Anthony King's *An Uncommonly Fine Day: January 26, 1788* (1987), with its ironic title, also presents a pictorial view of the conditions under which the First Fleeters suffered. *Growing up in the First Fleet* (1983) by A.T. Yarwood builds an account of the times around a child and her convict mother.

With a humorous intent, *The First Fleet* (1982) by Alan Boardman, illustrated by Roland Harvey, has caricatures of the convicts, with faces which recall present-day politicians, and Meredith Hooper's *The Journal of Watkin Stench* (1988) takes a rat's eye view of the proceedings. As yet there is no novel about the First Fleet for young readers which approaches the strength of Eleanor Dark's *The Timeless Land* (1941) as an evocation of the first white settlement in Australia.

First Hundred Years, The (1954) by Helen Palmer and Jessie MacLeod, illustrated by Harold Freedman, was Commended in the 1955 Book of the Year Awards. The 'first' hundred years is from 1788, beginning with Captain Cook. First-hand accounts, newspaper reports, family documents and historical records and reports are used to advantage, so that the impressions of the people are given prominence. It was continued in *After the First Hundred Years 1900–1950* (1961), illustrated by Mary MacQueen, in a similar format.

First There was Frances (1985), written and illustrated by Bob Graham, was Commended in the 1986 Picture Book of the Year Awards. Frances meets Graham and a dog, Teak. Frances and Graham have Marisol and Fraser, then Grandma and Katy the goat arrive. The guinea-pigs Errol and Berryl, Triller the canary and a menagerie of other animals enlarge the family until Frances and Graham and all the others move to the country. A soberly told text heightens the humour of the illustrations, which show a happy and increasingly chaotic household.

First Walkabout, The (1954) by Norman B. Tindale and Harold Arthur Lindsay, illustrated by Madeleine Boyce, won the 1955 Book of the Year Awards. The migrations of the Negrito people from the jungles of South East Asia to Australia around one hundred thousand years ago to escape the depradations of the larger and more powerful Hunting Men are traced. The resourceful Gunju, and later his inquisitive son Pek, move southwards to the edge of the continent. Methods of hunting, family life and customs, and other inhabitants, such as the Diprotodon, who roamed Australia at the time, are presented through an adventure story. Since the novel was written the authenticity of some of the material has been questioned, but as an introduction to the concept of the migration of peoples, *The First Walkabout* still has power.

FISHER, MARJORIE, see **HANN, MARJORIE**

FITZGERALD, MARY ANNE wrote *Australian Furs and Feathers* (1889), illustrated by W.T. Anderson, and *King Bungaree's Pyalla and Stories Illustrative of Manners and Customs That Prevailed Among Australian Aborigines* (1891). See **Aboriginal Dreaming Stories**.

Five Times Dizzy (1982) by Nadia Wheatley, illustrated by Neil Phillips, was Commended in the 1983 Book of the Year Awards. The resourceful Mareka Nikakis tries to make her Cretan grandmother happy in Australia, but is continually thwarted by adults, who lack her sensitivity to the anguish brought about by Yaya's displacement from a small village to inner suburban Sydney. Mareka's plan is to buy Yaya a goat to replace the one left in Crete. A resolution of the well-drawn conflicts between family members and different cultures is found when the multicultural inhabitants of Smith Street, Newtown, join in a festival, presenting a vision of a new society where ethnicity is celebrated. Its sequel is *Dancing in the Anzac Deli* (1984), illustrated by Waldemar Buczynski, which was Commended in the 1985 Book of the Year Awards. The conflicts experienced by Yaya have been resolved, and she becomes the heroine of this novel. A mysterious character, whom Yaya calls the Munga, wants to have the Nikakises' delicatessen. The children discover that the Munga and his henchmen are dealing in shoddy refrigerators, and running a protection racket. Mareka and her friends enlist Yaya's aid, inspired by her account of her life in her homeland, and the heroism of Greek women during World War II. The atmosphere of an inner suburb of Sydney and its possibilities for adventure is captured realistically and stereotypes are challenged. *Five Times Dizzy* and *Dancing in the Anzac Deli* were dramatised in twelve half-hour episodes for SBS television in 1985, directed by John Eastway and scripted by the author with Terry Larsen.

FLANAGAN, JOAN (1931–), born Waverley, NSW, has written mysteries, science fiction, fantasy and picture-books, all laced with humour. Her first novel was *The Dingbat Spies* (1984), illustrated by Melissa Webb. *Danny Cassidy, P.I.* (1989) is a detective story in which Danny hides a boy from Hong Kong who is being chased by the KGB.

Mystery and magic combine in *The Ghost in the Gazebo* (1987), when a mysterious red-haired boy appears to a large and heterogeneous family. Only Eliza is able to discover his secret in this humorous mystery. In *Rose Terrace* (1986) Sophie's longing for her father transports her, through dreams arising from infant memories, across the city. *Sister* (1988), illustrated by Bill Wood, is about the destructive imaginary friend of Tom's sister, whose abilities seem far-fetched to Tom. On investigation, Tom discovers that a tiny sister really exists, and can only be routed by being trapped in a comic-strip. *The Witch's House* (1990), illustrated by Kay Stewart, is another fantasy about a woman who just may be a witch. *Miss Bossyboots* (1991) is about the selfish Chatty Bosenboom. When she discovers that people are being shrunk and kept in a doll's house by the evil Dawsons, Chatty's courage enables her to expose the Dawsons, restore their prisoners to normal, and develop a better image of herself.

Magic becomes science fiction in *The Squealies and other Extraordinary Stories* (1987), illustrated by Keith McKewan, a collection of stories about extra-terrestrials who visit an eccentric family. In *Musclenut and Brainbox: a Science Fiction Adventure* (1989) the Zalleons want to steal Laurence and Jessica to be their new king and queen.

Blinks (1986), illustrated by Robert Avitabile, is a picture-book. A bored Matthew visits the market, where a storyteller persuades him to see something new whenever he blinks his eyes. Another picture-book, *Mr Shanahan's Secret* (1988), illustrated by Bob Seal, explores the consequences of eavesdropping. Mr Shanahan's secret digging draws crowds, and the park is dug up. There is no treasure, but there are little green men. *The Murder Game* (1988) is a mystery for adults.

FLEMING, WILLIAM MONT-GOMERIE (1874–1961), born Avon Plains, Victoria, poet and novelist, was a State and Federal politician. *Bunyip Says So: a Tale of the Australian Bush* (1922), with illustrations by the painter R.W. Sturgess, is about a story competition between the bush animals. The concluding line to each story is 'Bunyip says so', an idea continued in *Bunyip Told Me* (1926), illustrated by H. Sands. *The Hunted Piccaninnies* (1927), illustrated by Kay Edmunds, is an imaginative account of Aboriginal life. *Jessie the Elephant: Her Life Story* (1939) describes the adventures of a real elephant which lived first at Moore Park, then at Taronga Park Zoo from 1883 to 1938; it is illustrated with photographs.

FLETCHER, JANE ADA (?1871–1956), born Penshurst, Victoria, wrote for the *School Paper* in Victoria, SA and Queensland. She was an active member of the Royal Ornithological Union, and *Stories from Nature* (1915) and *Nature and Adventure for Boys and Girls* (1916) are nature stories, such as 'Flyer and Grey

Fur', about two flying squirrels, and 'Fire, the destroyer'. *Brave Boys and other Stories of Australian Animals and Birds* (1922), *Wanna, A Small Tasmanian Aborigine Who Made Friends with Captain Cook at Adventure Bay* (1938) and *Tommy's Ride on the Emu* (1922) were all Whitcombe's Story Books, the last in the 'Australian Nature Story Reader' series. *Brave Boys* contains four stories: 'Brave boys: Arthur and Ned's visit to the cormorant rookeries'; 'One-ear the wild dog'; 'Will, Jock and the falcon's nest'; and 'Adventures of Old Grey and his mob'. The stories are set on Bruni Island in Tasmania, and evoke the dizzying experience of climbing the rocks. In *Wanna* the hero meets Captain Cook for a moment at the end of the book, which recounts Aboriginal life with questionable accuracy. In *Tommy's Ride on the Emu* Tommy is invited to watch Aboriginal People hunt, and see how 'birds … are teased to death by eagles, hunted by the blacks, shot down by careless men, and worried by dingoes'. Fletcher also wrote *Little Brown Piccaninnies of Tasmania* (q.v., 1950).

Flip the Flying Possum (1963), written and illustrated by Noela Young, was Commended in the 1964 Picture Book of the Year Awards. Flip is a feathertail possum who meets other bush animals before he finds another hole in a tree with his favourite gum blossoms. Accurate and delicate pencil illustrations picture a tiny, endearing animal.

FLINDERS, MATTHEW (1744–1814), born Lincolnshire, UK, circumnavigated Van Diemen's Land in 1798–99, mapped the east coast of Australia, and had sailed around the continent by 1803. Flinders suggested Australia as a name for the Great South Land. See also **Bass, George**. Flinders's account of his cat, written when he was a prisoner on Mauritius, was first published in 1973 in the literary magazine, *Overland*, and republished as *Trim* (1977), illustrated by

Annette Macarthur-Onslow. This faithful and intelligent cat, who faced the rigours of shipwreck and other adversities during four of Flinders's voyages, was lost during Flinders's imprisonment. Through his story of the cat shines the narrator, a courageous, generous and highly literate man. There is a small monument to Trim outside the State Library of NSW, in Macquarie Street, Sydney.

Fly West (1974) by Ivan Southall won the 1976 Book of the Year Awards. It is an account of Southall's experiences as a young man during World War II, his training and service in the RAAF and the other airmen with whom he served. He has drawn on his own history of his squadron for much of the material.

Flying Doctor Service, see **Royal Flying Doctor Service**

Folklore. Dorothy Howard, a US researcher, began a study of Australian children's folklore, traditional games and play in the 1950s. *Cinderella Dressed in Yella* (1969) by Ian Turner was the first published collection of playground rhymes, followed by a new edition in 1978 by Turner, June Factor and Wendy Lowenstein. The essay by Turner which concludes the book, 'The Play-rhymes of Australian children', is a study of the development of scholarly interest in the subject. The book provides an early record of a strong and dynamic oral tradition, based largely on playground games. Early in its publication life the Australian postal service refused to accept it as a mailed item on the grounds of obscenity, because many of the rhymes are associated with sex and excretion. A typical entry is: 'There was a little bunny/A-sitting on the dunny/Eating bread and honey/Waiting for his Mummy/To come and wipe his bummy.' With Gwenda Beed Davey, June Factor set up the Australian Children's Folklore Collection (q.v.) in 1979, and

Factor and Davey went on to publish popular collections for children, such as Factor's *Far Out, Brussel Sprout: Australian Children's Chants and Rhymes* (1983) and Davey's *Snug as a Bug! Scenes from Family Life* (1990), both illustrated by Peter Viska. Heather Russell's *Carmen Out to Play!: a Collection of Children's Playground Games* (1989), also illustrated by Viska, describes games played by children, with instructions for young players, drawn from her *Play and Friendships in a Multicultural Playground* (1986), a study of an inner-city school, and the influence, particularly of Indo-Chinese children, on play. Another collection has been made by Virginia Ferguson and Peter Durkin, *Let 'er Rip, Potato Chip* (1988), again illustrated by Viska. June Factor's definitive work, *Captain Cook Chased a Chook: Children's Folklore in Australia* (1988), discusses the nature of childhood, play, and cultural influences on the lore of children.

FOOTT, MARY HANNAY (1846–1918), born Glasgow, Scotland, poet and artist, came to Australia in 1853. She studied art under von Guerard, taught in schools and as a governess in Victoria, NSW and Queensland, and was literary editor of the women's pages of the *Queenslander*, as 'La Quenouille'. Her poem 'Where the pelican builds', contained in the collection *Where the Pelican Builds and Other Poems* (1885), is frequently found in anthologies, such as the Victorian Readers Sixth Book. *Sweep: a Comedy for Children in Three Acts* (1890) is a play.

FORBES, ALISON is an illustrator and book-designer. She was commissioned to illustrate school readers for Papua New Guinea, and later worked for the Melbourne *Herald* and *Sun*. She illustrated *Animal Talk and Other Stories for Boys and Girls* (1955) by Neville Smith; *I Can Jump Puddles* (1955) by Alan Marshall; *Boy on a Horse: the Story of Adam Lindsay Gordon* (1957) by Helen Jo Samuel and Enid

Moodie Heddle; *Patterson's Track* (1958) by Eleanor Spence; *New Land, New Language* (1957) by Judith Wright; and *World Unknown: an Anthology of Australian Prose* (1960), selected by Hume Dow and John Barnes. Forbes has also designed children's books, such as David Martin's *The Man in the Red Turban* (1978), illustrated by Genevieve Rees (Melrose).

Forbidden Bridge, The (1961) by Betty Roland, illustrated by Geraldine Spence, was Commended in the 1962 Book of the Year Awards, and introduced 7-year-old Jamie. Jamie and his widowed mother move to 'Cromarty', his uncle's property in the Goulburn Valley, Victoria. When Jamie crosses a dangerous railway bridge and is saved from death by his cousin Malcolm, he realises that others do care about him. His adventures are continued in *Jamie's Discovery*, also illustrated by Spence, and Commended in the 1964 Book of the Year Awards. When his dog is lost, Jamie discovers a cave with Aboriginal paintings. *Jamie's Summer Visitor* (1964), illustrated by Prudence Seward, Highly Commended in the 1965 Book of the Year Awards, introduces Nola, whom Jamie at first resents. Their differences are resolved when Jamie understands that she is a lonely girl who feels rejected. *Jamie's Other Grandmother* (1970), also illustrated by Seward, takes Jamie away from 'Cromarty' to visit his wealthy paternal grandmother at her sheep station, 'Arramagong', where he is given a horse to ride and a camera for Christmas. The visit results in a reconciliation between his mother and grandmother. The novels are aimed at younger readers, and each traces a development in Jamie's character.

Forbidden Paths of Thual, The (1979) by Victor Kelleher, illustrated by Antony Maitland, was winner of the Secondary section of WAYRBA in 1982. Quen undertakes a journey to rescue his people from the Mollag, and secures the Eye of Desire with the help of Nodak the

Woodsman and the animals of the forest of Thual. In this exciting fantasy, Kelleher creates a setting of dripping rainforest and wide grassland.

FOREMAN, MICHAEL (1938–), born Suffolk, UK, is an English writer who has written stories about Australia in the 'Panda' series, such as *Panda and the Bushfire* (1986). See **Bushfire**. In *Panda and the Bunyips* (1984) Panda and his friend Lion journey to Uluru, where they meet a bunyip and assorted Australian animals.

FOWLER, HELEN (1910–), born Sydney, has written *The Family at Willow Bend* (1955), illustrated by Irene Maher. Lance and Monica Carstairs are left in charge of their seven brothers and sisters. They deal with a serious car accident, a raging bushfire, an abandoned boy, snakes, amateur theatre and a feast for the whole district, and always keep their heads. Also books for adults, including *The Shades Will not Vanish* (1952) filmed as *Strange Intruder* in 1957.

FOWLER, THURLEY (1925–), born Griffith, NSW, has examined a range of family relationships. The odd one out appears as Robert in *Wait for Me! Wait for Me!* (1981), set on a rice farm. His clever and competent older brothers outshine him until he rescues them from a hut in which they are trapped by a murderer. In *Fall of a Clown* (1982) David Anderson treats life as a joke, until a crisis forces him to cope with catastrophe and find a place for himself. *Am I Going with You?* (1985) deals with Carlton, who is sent to stay with his Uncle Harry in a country town by his mother, and his difficulty in being accepted. In *A Hippo Doing Backstroke* (1988) the overweight Greg is put on a strict diet by his grandmother. He becomes a faster swimmer and decides on a future in farming. The effect of parents who have separated is explored in *The Youngest One* (1988) as the Martin family draw together when their father leaves. The story centres on Craig, who misses him the most. In *There's a Bushranger in My Bedroom* (1990) Rebecca follows clues which she believes will lead her to gold hidden by a nineteenth-century bushranger. In the process she learns to love and accept her new stepfather. In *A Horse Called Butterfly* (1984) a palomino is given to Susan for a birthday present after her parents have died, but she rejects him until she learns that her grief has made her hate people. *The Green Wind* (q.v., 1985) and its sequel *The Wind is Silver* (1991) are about Jennifer growing up. In *The Kid from Licorice Hill* (1988) Roger's enthusiasm for flying is the source of a new direction for his family. As his mother learns to fly, his father takes up cricket, and his brother and he discover a new companionship.

Fox Hole, The (1967) by Ivan Southall, illustrated by Ian Ribbons, was Commended in the 1968 Book of the Year Awards. During a visit to his uncle, Ken falls down a mine shaft. To his dismay, Uncle Bob is reluctant to rescue him until Bob is able to get a miner's right, because there may be gold in the tunnel. The panic and fear of the ordeal is exacerbated by the boy's overheated imagination, although Ken's good sense ultimately prevails. For Uncle Bob, too, there are turning-points, as he realises that a child's trust is being violated. Southall's ability to develop tension is sharply displayed, and the balance between self-interest and responsibility to others is explored.

FOX, MEM (MERRION) (1946–), born Melbourne, spent much of her childhood in Bulaweyo, Zimbabwe, where her parents were missionaries. Her skill as a storyteller has inspired her successful picture-books, including the popular *Possum Magic* (q.v., 1983), illustrated by Julie Vivas. Her interests are diverse. *Wilfrid Gordon McDonald Partridge* (1984), also illustrated by Vivas, has the elderly Miss Nancy helped by Wilfrid to replace her lost memories with new ones. Another older woman appears in *Night Noises* (1988), illustrated by Terry Denton. Lilly Laceby dreams of her childhood while her dog, Butch Aggie, hears strange noises, finally identified as the guests arriving for Lilly's eightieth birthday. *Sophie* (1989), illustrated by Craig Smith, shows the special relationship between Sophie and her Grandpa. When Grandpa dies, Sophie's grief is alleviated by the birth of her first child, and the cycle begins again.

In *Just Like That* (1986), illustrated by Kilmeny Niland, Harriet Harris's clumsiness is celebrated. *Goodnight, Sleep Tight* (1988), illustrated by Helen Semmler, is a series of play rhymes told by Skinny Doug when he is babysitting Vivienne Venn. In *Arabella, the Smallest Girl in the World* (1986), illustrated by Vicky Kitanov, a tiny child cavorts amid the everyday objects in a child's world; and in *Guess What?* (1988), illustrated by Vivienne Goodman, the reader must guess whether Daisy O'Grady is a witch. To assist hearing-impaired children, *Arabella* is supplemented with sign language. Fox uses animals to humorous effect in *A Cat called Kite* (1985), illustrated by K. Hawley, a rhyme in Dr Seuss style for early readers, and *Hattie and the Fox* (1986), illustrated by Patricia Mullins, where the fox is gradually revealed to the hen. Two dingo pups sail around Australia in *Sail away, the Ballad of Skip and Nell* (1986), illustrated by Pamela Lofts. *Koala Lou* (1987), also illustrated by Lofts, pits Koala Lou against her arch-rival, Koala Claws, in a tree-climbing contest, and although Lou tries very hard she does not win — but Mum loves her anyway. In *Feathers and Fools* (1989), illustrated by Lorraine Ellis, the peacocks fear the swans and the swans the peacocks. They sharpen their weapons and fight to the last. New hatchings stagger out of their eggs, saying, 'You're just like me!'.

A Bed-Time Story (1987), illustrated by Sisca Verwoert, *The Straight Line Wonder* (1987), illustrated by Meredith Thomas, and *Zoo-Looking* (1986), illustrated by Rodney McRae, are part of the Ashton Scholastic 'Bookshelf' series. In the verse story *Shoes from Grandpa* (1989), illustrated by Patricia Mullins, Jessie is provided with clothes from her relatives until she is thoroughly overdressed, when all she would like is a new pair of jeans. Fox's sense of the dramatic, her simple texts and comforting stories provide a secure world for younger readers. Her autobiography is *Mem's the Word* (1990). She was awarded the Dromkeen Medal in 1990.

'FRANC, MAUD JEANNE' was the pseudonym of **MATILDA JANE EVANS** (1827–86), born Surrey, UK. She came to SA in 1852, where her brothers and sisters were orphaned. Matilda supported the family first as a governess, then opened a school. She married Rev. Ephriam Evans, who died leaving her with two of her own children and various stepchildren to support. She opened another school, and continued to write more of her fourteen novels, poems and short stories.

Her novels were popular Sunday school prizes for older girls, and are fervently religious and teetotal. *Marian: or, The Light of Someone's Home* (1861) was her first book, a tale of bush life. Marian becomes the governess of the Burton children on a property fifty miles from Adelaide, where she eventually marries one of the sons. In *Emily's Choice* (1867) the young heroine must choose the right path when confronted by religious doubt, alcohol, true love, the Bible, good works, and selflessness, matters which are also taken up in Franc's other novels, including *Golden Gifts: an Australian Tale* (1869). In *Beatrice Melton's Discipline* (1880) the death of her beloved father leads Beatrice into a phase of religious doubt. See also **Religion**. In *Minnie's Mission* (1869) Minnie sets out to persuade her uncle and cousins to become total abstainers. Granting her dying wish, her friend, Dr Edwin Leigh, signs the pledge at her bedside. In *Hall's Vineyard*

(1875) the conflict is between two brothers, one who drinks and the other who is a teetotaller. *No Longer a Child* (1882) is set in the German community in SA. Lena Hartmann is forced to marry a man she does not love by her father. Lena dies soon after her marriage, when she hears of the death of her beloved, Lindsey. See also **Germans**.

Evans creates contemporary society with skill, peopled by well-meaning, naive heroines, conventionally pious. She collaborated with her son, William James Evans, on a collection of short stories, *Christmas Bells* (1882).

'FRANCES, HELEN' is the pseudonym of **HELEN GRANGER** (1939–), born Beechworth, Victoria, and **FRANCES PEARCE** (1942–), born Peak Hill, NSW. *The Devil's Stone* (q.v., 1983) is a time-slip fantasy. *Edge of Fear* (1986) recounts Lucy Talbot's perilous journey from nineteenth-century London to her grandmother in Tasmania. *The Deepwaterman* (1988) describes Tom's life aboard one of the last square-rigged ships, and his journey to adulthood.

FRANKLIN, MILES (1879–1954), born Talbingo, NSW, was a novelist, author of *My Brilliant Career* (1901). *Sydney Royal* (1947), with decorations by Nan Knowles, is a collection of stories for children about the people who live at the Royal Agricultural Show during Show Week in Sydney. Eccentric characters and the excitement of the Show are described in a souvenir of the event. Franklin recalls the first ten years of her childhood in *Childhood at Brindabella* (1963).

FRAUCA, HARRY (1928–). For *Striped Wolf: a Bush Adventure* (1969) see **Animal Stories**.

FREEDMAN, HAROLD (1915–), born Melbourne, is a painter, illustrator, cartoonist and teacher. He was an official war artist with the RAAF and later taught illustration at RMIT for twenty-two years. He painted the mural displaying the history of aviation at Canberra War Memorial and the historical murals at Melbourne's Spencer Street Station and at Melbourne Airport. He was State Artist for Victoria from 1972 to 1983. Freedman illustrated *Our Train Book* (1950) by Brenda Seeley; *Let's Go to the Circus* (1949), *Goldy* (1952), *Over the Hill* (1952) and *Pine Farm* (1952) by Kathleen Mellor; *Among Friends* (1954), a reader published by the Victorian Education Department; *Girdle Round the World* (1952), edited by Enid Moodie Heddle; some of the Boomerang Books produced for the SA Department of Education; and *The First Hundred Years* (q.v., 1954) by Helen Palmer and Jessie MacLeod.

FRENCH, JACKIE (1953–), born Sydney, is a radio commentator and has written books on organic gardening, and columns for magazines such as *Earthgarden* and *Organic Gardening*. *Smudge* (1988) is a picture-book which French wrote and illustrated. *Rainstones* (1991), a collection of five stories, expresses French's closeness to the natural world. One of the stories, 'Afternoon with Grandma', describes the childhood of an adventurous grandmother, whom the children know only as a victim of Alzheimer's Disease. *The Roo that Won the Melbourne Cup* (1991), illustrated by Carol McLean-Carr, is a story of a spirited woman who longs to train just one winner. The eccentric Aunty Mug has determination and style.

FRENCH, SIMON (1957–), born Sydney, wrote *Hey Phantom Singlet* (q.v., 1975), a study of an unhappy schoolboy, when he was only 16. French trained as a teacher, and worked in an inner-city child crisis centre. *Cannily, Cannily* (q.v., 1981) was written when he was completing his teacher training. Trevor, son of itinerant workers, is taunted by other children and his teacher for his atypical lifestyle in a narrow-minded country town. *All We*

Know (q.v., 1986) examines the emotions of an introspective girl. *Change the Locks* (q.v., 1991) is a more mysterious novel. French examines the world through the eyes of a boy or girl who does not go along with the crowd. Math, Trevor, Arkie and Steven have ideas and emotions which put them outside the conventional, and their struggles to retain their own individuality lead to a better understanding of themselves and those around them.

FRIEND, DONALD (1915–89), born Moree, NSW, was a painter who illustrated *Kangaroo Tales: a Collection of Australian Stories for Children* (1964), selected by Rosemary Wighton. *Coogan's Gully: a Young Person's Guide to Bushranging, Ecology and Witchcraft* (1979) is a satirical picturebook following the fortunes of Bold Dan Coogan's career as convict, bushranger, and devoted family man, until he is caught and hanged. His daughter Bridget takes over, using witchcraft to take her revenge on the law.

Friends of Emily Culpepper, The (1983) by Ann Coleridge, illustrated by Roland Harvey, was Commended in the 1984 Picture Book of the Year Awards. The elderly Emily is able to shrink her friends and keep them in bottles. When the policeman complains, she releases her friends, but keeps the policeman to play with. Harvey's illustrations are as whimsical as the text.

FULLARTON, NAN (1913–), born Melbourne, studied art at Sydney Technical College. Her first book was the very successful *The Alphabet from A to Z* (1945), with clear, warm pictures of a small girl and her daily activities. See also **Alphabet Books**. In *A Day in the Bush* (1946) Rabbit is frightened by a sound above him. He runs off to get help from Possum, Koala, Wombat, Bandicoot and others, so that they can kill the monster who becomes bigger with each recountal. They discover that the noise was Pigmy

Possum waking from his winter sleep. *Nest in the Bush* (1962) is similar, with Possum as a frightened animal and Hopping Mouse as the intruder. *Let's Read Thumbelina* (1948) is adapted from Hans Christian Andersen's story, and *Let's Say our Nursery Rhymes* (1948) has familiar rhymes. *Let's Visit the Zoo* and *Let's Walk in the Bush* (both 1948) are animal books.

Fullarton used a comic-strip format interspersed with conventional text for *Frisky, a Story of the Australian Bush* (1956) and *Further Adventures of Frisky* (1961), the adventures of a rabbit, who first appeared in a comic-strip in the *Sunday Herald*. Frisky and his friends, Scamp the kitten and Liebchen, a dachshund, have adventures in the bush, such as meeting a beaver (who says 'This'll be just swell,' and 'Sure will, honey'), visit Phillip Island and Lord Howe Island, and return to Healesville Sanctuary. At one point Frisky gets myxomatosis and has to be nursed back to health. Fullarton used the pseudonym 'Killibinbin' for the comic-strip, which ran for over twenty years. She also created the comic-strip 'Wippi', about a pygmy possum, and adapted *Alice's Adventures in Wonderland* as a comic-strip for the *Sydney Morning Herald* in 1949. Her comic-strips were taken up by other newspapers, such as the Melbourne *Age* and the Adelaide *Advertiser*.

Fullarton settled in London, where she continued to illustrate children's books, such as F.R. Ewell's *Mr Collins and Tony in London* (1960) and *Mr Collins and Tony by the Sea* (1960), and her own *Big Book of Animal Stories*, which includes koalas and wombats as well as elephants, hedgehogs, beavers and farm animals.

FULLER, ELIZABETH. For *Alphabeasts* (1985) see **Alphabet Books**.

FULLERTON, MARY ELIZABETH (1868–1946), born Glenmaggie, Victoria, was a novelist, poet, socialist and feminist, active in Melbourne literary society, who left Australia in 1921. *Bark House Days* (1921) is a re-creation of her childhood in Gippsland with a pioneering family, seen with a child's perception.

G

GALBRAITH, JEAN (1906–), born Tyers, Victoria, has written books and articles on Australian flora for journals and newspapers, including the Melbourne *Age. Grandma Honeypot* (1962), illustrated by Noela Young, was first published in the NSW *School Magazine*. John and Marigold observe the behaviour of animals, guided by their grandmother. Other nature books include *From Flower to Fruit* (1965) and *The Wonderful Butterfly* (1968).

GARFIELD, LEON (1921–), born Brighton, UK, is an English writer of historical novels. For *A Swag of Stories* (1977) see **Collections**.

GARNER, HELEN (1942–), born Geelong, Victoria, is a novelist. With Jennifer Giles she wrote *Moving Out* (1983), based on a film scripted by Jan Sardi, and starring Vince Colosimo as Gino. See **Immigrants**.

GAZE, HAROLD (1885–1962), born NZ, was a contemporary of Ida Rentoul Outhwaite, although his ideas of fairyland were in marked contrast to hers. *The Simple Jaggajay* (1919), *The Billabonga Bird* (1919) and *The Chewg-Um-Blewg-Um* (1919) were in his 'Merry Mite' series. The Billabonga Bird is no dainty bluebird but a gawky creature with the tail of a fish and carpet-bag shoes. He falls in love with the Fay, who rejects him because of his looks. In desperation, Billabonga takes the advice of a serpent: 'O never do a deed/Of kindness or of cheer,/And you will soon be rich and strong/Quite handsome too — not queer'. After being nasty to everyone, and falling on very hard times, Billabonga is saved by Merry Mite who destroys the fairy's tear Billabonga has in his possession. Gradually the bird becomes more beautiful, he rescues Fay from a bog and they sail away in Billabonga's shoes. The Chewg-Um-Blewg-Um is a one-legged creature with a camel's head on an emu's body. He has been accustomed to playing hopscotch with a lizard as his 'tipit' (taw), and when the lizard is parted from his tail and runs off, the Chewg-um-Blewg-um enlists the help of Merry Mite to find it. One lizard becomes two, and they are swallowed by the Bear. The Lobster saves them by shouting 'Flies!', and the two lizards emerge from the Bear's throat. The Chewg-um-Blewg-um and the Lobster are married. Gaze's clever verse carries the story, as in 'The Bear's song': ' ... Oh, just when I come/To a delicate trill/They butter their toast,/Till I really feel ill,/And when I sing bass — /With my throat open wide — /They jump up to see/What it looks like outside.' Gaze also wrote *The Wicked Winkapong* (1919), the only book in the 'Chap Happy' series.

Coppertop: the Queer Adventures of a Quaint Child (1919) tells how Celia Anagusta Sinclair visits the Clerk of the Weather. In an inventive and exciting fantasy, Coppertop and her imaginery brothers Tibbs and Kiddiwee are taken to the Castles of the Four Winds, the Himalayas and the Blarney Stone, meet Mr A. Tom, have adventures with whales, monkeys, crocodiles and spiders, and arrange a perfect day for Coppertop's parents' return from India. The adventures are continued in *Coppertop Cruises: the Wonderful Voyage of the Good Ship Queercraft* (1920). The funny verses and bizarre creatures are intended to make children laugh. In *War in Fairyland* (1921) the war is resolved when the Mosquitoes are defeated, pursued by the Horsefly Guards, and Tubberty Nose, the pride of the Garden (a lovely maid only 673 years old) marries King Cupid. In *Goblin's Glen: a Story of Childhood's Wonderland* (1924) Gaze's rich fantasy creatures include Inklewink the pixie, the Kingdom of the Trees, and the Blue Ming Cat, all met when Ruth and Norman take Uncle Hal to the Glen on a fairy adventure. Other books by Gaze include *China Cat* (1921), *The Enchanted Fish* (1921) and *The Merry Piper: or, the Magical Trip of the Sugar Bowl Ship* (1925). Gaze introduced the grotesque into illustration for children, and presented an alternative to the refinement of Outhwaite.

GENEROWICZ, WITOLD (1958–), born London, UK, artist and architect, came to Australia in 1969. He has written and illustrated *The Train: the Amazing Train Chase that Unfolds into one of the Longest Books in the World* (q.v., 1982), *The Escape of the Krollsnork: a Chase Through an Amazing Fantasy Land, That Unfolds Into One of the Longest Books in the World* (1987). Both are visual jokes — cops and robbers tales told without text, in books which unfold into friezes. In *The Mystery of the Missing Map* (1991) by Marcia Vaughan, Generowicz provides clues to where the map is to be found in intriguing pictures.

Germans. German settlers formed the largest non-Anglo-Celtic ethnic minority group in the latter half of the nineteenth century and have been subjected to racist treatment in children's books since that time. The settlements in SA are the setting for Matilda Jane Evans's *No Longer a Child* (1882), where the rude and domineering German men are contrasted with the sensitive Englishman, Lindsey. In *Dusky Dell* (1898) by Bertha Southey Adams, Annie, one of the children's school chums, is the daughter of a washerwoman, 'a poor German whose English was peculiar and her washing still more so'. Annie's fat brother has no name, but is referred to throughout the book as 'the German sausage'. When Annie's mother has twins, one of the children asks if they are 'both like the German sausage — fat and oily looking?'. In 'Arthur Ferres's' *His First Kangaroo: an Australian Story for Boys* (1896) the German teacher, Dr Wicker, is outsmarted by the clever wit of Tom Flood, who replies to Dr Wicker's admonishment: 'Here, none of that jaw, Mr Sauerkraut … we'll not stop here to be insulted by any walkin' larger-beer barrel that ever left Germany.' In Lillian Pyke's *A Prince at School* (1919) the year is 1914, with the villain of the adventure Mr Bernstein, who has designs on Lola and the island of Vilatonga. Bernstein is portrayed as nasty, scheming and brutal, and his sister, Katrina, as docile, clumsy and stupid. The German Greta Kowshorn in M. Ella Chaffey's *The Youngsters of Murray Home* (1896), however, is more sympathetically drawn, and her affectionate reactions are presented without her supposed racial identity or national characteristics determining her behaviour or the children's responses to her. Ethel Turner's Gertrud, in *John of Daunt* (1916), is another subtler picture. Gertrud is loyal to the Kaiser, but her dignity and affection for the family is in marked contrast to the unthinking prejudice of the Australian servant, Daisy.

Post-World War II immigration brought many German settlers to Australia in a period when Australia was eager to assimilate newcomers. In *The Racketty Street Gang* (q.v., 1961) by L.H. Evers, the boys are all full of goodwill towards the German Smertzers, and in Joan Phipson's *Helping Horse* (1974) the efforts of Simon, Bruce, Debbie and Hilary allay community suspicion of Horst, and ensure his acceptance. These novels reflect assimilationist attitudes. Paul Metzler's *A Foreign Father* (1979) considers attitudes to

Germans during World War II. Judith O'Neill's *Deepwater* (1987) also raises the issue of prejudice, when their neighbours turn against the Henschkes. The Henschkes have been Australians for generations, and their determination to keep their own culture alive against the ignorance of their neighbours is portrayed with sympathy and flair. The last two novels are concerned with German immigrants of past decades, and expose old prejudices. It has been the descendants of the first German settlers who have changed perceptions of Germans in Australia. The novels of Colin Thiele, beginning with *Sun on the Stubble* (q.v., 1961), about the German community in the Barossa Valley, present German traditions which sit comfortably in the Australian environment.

A Little Bush Poppy (1915) by Edith Graham. Illustrator: May Gibbs

Giant Devil Dingo, The (1973), written and illustrated by Dick Roughsey, was Commended in the 1974 Picture Book of the Year Awards. After a dangerous chase, the Chooku-chooku, or butcher bird brothers, kill Gaiya, the huge and savage devil dingo, who is controlled by Eelgin, the grasshopper woman. The medicine man, Woodbarl, makes friendly dingoes from Gaiya's kidneys, and the Chooku-chooku kill Eelgin, who becomes a grasshopper. Roughsey attributes the story to the Gugu-Yalanji people. This outstanding picture-book is a unity of vibrant illustrations and dramatically told story.

GIBBS, MAY (Mrs CECILIA MAY OSSOLI KELLY, née Gibbs) (1877–1969), born Surrey, UK, came to Australia with her family when she was 4, settling in WA. In 1905 she worked as an illustrator for the *Western Mail*. The early part of the twentieth century saw an increasing appreciation of native flora, and, influenced by the botanical illustrator Ellis Rowan, Gibbs produced watercolours of WA wildflowers. After studying art in London during three periods, she

returned to Sydney in 1913, and began her career as Australia's first full-time, professionally-trained children's book illustrator, with her first commission being the cover of Amy Mack's *Scribbling Sue* (1913).

She provided twenty-five covers for the *Sydney Mail* during this time, and illustrated books for many authors, such as Edith Graham's *A Little Bush Poppy* (1915), revealing a charm and liveliness in even her smallest sketches. In 1913 she created the characters which made her famous, two little creatures peeping around a gum leaf on a bookmark, inspired by her childhood pleasure in the life of the Australian bush. She says of their inspiration: 'When I stayed with my cousins in the Bush, I amused myself and them by telling stories about the little people I imagined to be there. They always took the form of sturdy, common-sense little persons living the same practical busy lives as ants and other intelligent bush creatures. Never did I find the elegant star-browed fairies that my old-world books showed me. The bush suggested always things grotesque, mirthful, cunning and quaint. Even the flowers held an eccentric charm for me, rather than an appeal by their beauty.' (*Woman's World* 1 Nov. 1924). In 1914 the Gumnut babies appeared on the cover of *Lone Hand*, and in 1916 she published *Gumnut Babies* and *Gum Blossom Babies*, followed by *Boronia Babies* (1917), *Flannel Flowers and Other Bush Babies* (1917) and *Wattle Babies* (1918).

In 1918 her most famous creations, Snugglepot and Cuddlepie (q.v.), came into being. Her early work displayed an imaginative style of illustration, and provided a world of fantasy based on the flora and fauna of the Australian bush, such as the bad 'Banksia Men'. The naked babies, wide-eyed and innocent, were popularised through a range of products, such as handkerchiefs, ornaments, tea-towels and fabrics. Further gumnut babies appeared in *Nuttybub and Nittersing* (1923), where Nittersing is kidnapped by Red Eye, the Banksia Man Chief, and rescued by Nuttybub, and *Chucklebud and Wunkydoo* (1924).

Gibbs also produced a weekly comic-strip, 'Bib and Bub' (q.v.), from 1924 to 1967, and other cartoons, such as 'Tiggy Touchwood'. From the latter she used Tiggy the pig in her later books about a Scotch terrier. In *Scotty in Gumnut Land* (1941) Scotty leaves home because he is unloved, and becomes involved with the Banksia Men, Boomer Roo the Kangaroo, Dr Stork, Mrs Kookaburra, Bib and Bub and others. *Mr and Mrs Bear and Friends* (1943) continues Scotty's adventures, and was Gibbs's last book about her gumnut characters. *Prince Dande Lion: a Garden Whim-Wham* (1953) was her last book.

Gibbs also created political cartoons, magazine covers, portraits and nature studies. A collection of 2000 watercolours and pen-and-ink works of the artist is held at the Mitchell Library, NSW, on permanent loan from the NSW Spastic Children's Society. The house which she and her husband built on the shores of Sydney Harbour is 'Nutcote' (q.v.). Further reading: Walsh, *May Gibbs, Mother of the Gumnuts*.

GIESE, DIANA. For *If You Lose, You're Dead* (1988) see **Collections**.

GILES, BARBARA (1912–   ), born Manchester, UK, came to Australia in 1923. She has written poetry for adults and edited anthologies for children, such as *Messages in a Bottle: Poetry by Young Australians* (1978), with Michael Dugan and J.S. Hamilton, and *A Second Australian Poetry Book* (1983). *Spooky Poems and Jokes* (1983), illustrated by Clare Balmford, Brett Colquhoun, F. Anne Ross and Michael Vale, is a collection of poems and stories about witches, Halloween and ghosts. Giles contributed poetry to Longman's 'Reading 360' series, for which she was the editor in 1982–83, including *People and Places* (1983). In *Bicycles Don't Fly* (1982), illustrated by Randy Glusac, and its sequel, *Flying Backwards* (1985), illustrated by Lin Tobias, magical bicycle oil makes Jack's bike fly. He thwarts a robbery, and with his friend Pug is transported to gold-rush times. *Jack in the Bush* (1983) is a striking picture-book illustrated by Betty Greenhatch in which a naked Jack runs with exhilaration through the bush at night. In *Alex is My Friend* (1984) the lonely Angelica finds Alex's diary in a secret room, unravelling the mysteries of an old house. *Bill* (1988), illustrated by Lisa Herriman, is set in Depression times, when Bill is sent to his bad-tempered grandfather's farm at Wombat Springs. The friendships which Bill develops at school and among the neighbours enable him to bear his stay, until he saves his grandfather's life, and the old man sees how much he needs the boy. *Gone Wild* (1990), 'tales at the edge of time', is a collection of science fiction and fantasy stories, each with a clever twist at

sailing under the command of Captain Roger Rove-Beetle, defeats the fierce pirate Ernest the Earwig. *Christopher Cricket's Favourite Tales* (1950) is a collection, and in 1979 Angus & Robertson published *The Adventures of Antony Ant and the Earwig Pirates* in the same volume as *Gregory Grasshopper* and *The Cruise of the 'Saucy Walnut'*. *The Little World of D.H. Gilmore* (1982) contains stories and verse about Bertie Beetle, Belinda Bumble, Selina Snail and others. In 1987 some of Gilmore's stories were collected in *The Delightful Adventures of Catkin and Codlin and Friends*. Gilmore wrote adult material as 'David Orr'. In his obituary, Gilmore is referred to as 'the Australian Walt Disney', and his illustrations are influenced by the Disney style.

Jack in the Bush (1983) by Barbara Giles. Illustrator: Betty Greenhatch

the end. Giles is concerned with the deeper human relationships, and her imagination and humour are underscored by her expression of the poignancy of childhood experiences.

GILMORE, DAVID HUNTER (1904–82), born NZ, worked as a teacher, a journalist and in advertising. He joined the staff of the NZ *Herald* in 1922, and later was with an advertising firm in Sydney. He lived in Sydney and Tasmania before returning to NZ. He wrote and illustrated a series of fantasies, beginning with *The Remarkable Adventures of Cuthbert the Caterpillar and Wilfred the Wasp* (1941), first written in 1928. *Antony Ant and the Earwig Pirates* (1942), *The Tale of Gregory Grasshopper* (1942), *The Adventures of Catkin and Codlin* (1946), *The Tale of Christopher Cricket* (1946) and *The Tale of Benjamin Bumble* (1947) followed. A typical story is *The Cruise of the 'Saucy Walnut'* (1948), in which Watkin Waterbeetle,

GILMORE, Dame **MARY** (1865–1962), born near Goulburn, NSW, poet, was the first woman member of the Australian Workers' Union. In 1896 she went to the New Australia settlement at Cosme, in Paraguay, led by William Lane, where she married William Gilmore. After working as a journalist in Argentina and Patagonia, she returned to Australia in 1902, and joined the Sydney *Worker* in 1908. During her long life Gilmore remained committed to social reform and the Aboriginal People, with whom she had spent her childhood. Her poems appear in *The Tale of Tiddley Winks* (1917), illustrated by Eirene Mort, and *Verse for Children* (1955), illustrated by Celeste Mass. *Poems to Read to Young Australians* (1968) is a collection of Gilmore's and Lydia Pender's poetry. Barbara Ker Wilson made a selection of her poetry for *The Singing Tree: A Selection of Mary Gilmore's Poetry for Young Readers* (1971), illustrated by Astra Lacis, and in her introduction quotes a verse from 'The Lesser Grail', written when Gilmore was 89: 'Age changes no one's heart; the field/Is wider, that is all./Childhood is never lost; concealed,/It answers every call.'

Ginger Meggs was created by James Charles Bancks for the Sydney *Sunday Sun*, where the character of Ginger Meggs first appeared in 1921 in the cartoon-strip 'Us Fellers', in the 'Sunbeams' section. Before long the comic was being published in all Australian States, and Bancks also produced books and annuals from the comics, such as *The Adventures of Ginger Meggs* (1924), *More Adventures of Ginger Meggs* (1937–42), *Ginger Meggs and Herbert the Billy Goat* (n.d.) and *Ginger Meggs' Lucky Break* (1957). The cartoon became international, appearing in the London *Referee*, the Boston *Post*, the *New York Mirror*, and in Montreal and Buenos Aires. Sarah Meggs, Ginger's mother, a powerful figure based on Bancks's own mother, is the second most important character in the strip. Ginger's main enemy is Tiger Kelly, and Eddie Coogan is his rival for Minnie Peters, his red-haired girlfriend. His companions are his younger brother Dudley; a monkey, Tony; a dog, Mike; and his best mate, Bennie Bolter. Ginger Meggs is the archetypal figure of the 'little Aussie battler' or larrikin, constantly being harassed by the police, ready with insults, opportunistic, self-confident, forever young, always ironically funny. 'Us Fellers' became 'Ginger Meggs' in 1939, and was continued by Ron Vivian, Lloyd Piper, and James Kemsley after Bancks's death. Kemsley has published *Ginger Meggs at Large* (1985), *The Comic Adventures of Ginger Meggs* (1986), *A Look Inside Ginger Meggs* (1987), *It's Sunday, Ginger Meggs* (1988) and *Wake Up, Ginger Meggs* (1989). Bill Peach wrote *Ginger Meggs Meets the Test* (1976), illustrated by Dan Russell. A pantomime was produced in the 1950s, written by Ray Lawler. *Ginger Meggs: the movie* began showing in 1982, produced by John Sexton and Michael Latimer, directed by Jonathan Dawson, with Paul Daniel as Ginger, and Garry Macdonald and Coral Kelly as Mr and Mrs Meggs. Further reading: Horgan, *The Golden Years of Ginger Meggs 1921–1952*; Dermody et al., *Nellie Melba, Ginger Meggs and Friends*.

Girl, The see **Annuals**

Girls. Domesticated and submissive or independent and assertive, girls have always been plentifully represented in Australian children's books. Nineteenth-century girls are generally characterised by their role as the carriers of civilisation and refinement, delighting in domesticity but prepared to take on the bush life with gusto. Helen Courtenay manages the home skilfully in W.H.G. Kingston's *Milicent Courtenay's Diary* (1873) but remains composed when she is faced by a bushranger; Maggie Stirling, in *The Early Start in Life* (1867) by Emilia Norris, can produce a crisp tablecloth when necessary, but she also rides and faces up to danger. Judy Woolcot, the heroine of *Seven Little Australians* (q.v., 1894) and *Judy and Punch* (1928) by Ethel Turner, is no civiliser, but a spirited and assertive girl. Turner had already created a tomboy, 'Miss Bobbie', who was not afraid to tear her dress or hole her stockings to perfect her skill at climbing, although she was yet to appear in the novel *Miss Bobbie* (1897), but Judy was of a different order again — a girl with initiative, imagination, contemptuous of the lily-livered, and fearless, qualities which were more associated with boys than girls. Lilian Turner's females are more conscious of being circumscribed by domesticity and attempt to break out of the home circle. Betty began as a tomboy, and in *Betty the Scribe* (1906) battles to assert her own individuality despite the family responsibilities thrust on her. Lennie Leighton and Mabel James in Louise Mack's *Teens* (q.v., 1897), *Girls Together* (1898) and *Teens Triumphant* (1933) are much more sedentary and urban, and more interested in relationships between friends and families.

Norah Linton, who first emerged in Mary Grant Bruce's *A Little Bush Maid* (1910), was Judy's rival in popularity. Norah can cook and sew, in fact 'she knew more of cooking and general housekeeping than many girls grown up', but

'Possum (1917) by Mary Grant Bruce. Illustrator: J. Macfarlane

her life is exciting, although always safe within 'Billabong', and while her character lacks the light and shade of Judy's, it is enriched by her confident outdoor life. Bruce's engaging heroine in *'Possum* (1917) is another strong girl, and this time she needs no father or brother to stiffen her backbone. She is the teacher, protector and rescuer of the Macleod family. Another of Bruce's heroines, Binkie Forsyth, in *Told by Peter* (1938) and *Peter & Co.* (1940) can also be relied on to hold her own with the best male protagonists. Binkie can run, swim and fish as well as her brother and his mate Clem, and is as resourceful and game as any boy. Even her appearance is the same, with hair 'a sort of dark bay and curly and generally untidy ... wearing riding-breeches or shorts practically all the time ... exactly the same kit' as her brother's. A natural successor to Judy Woolcot appears as Beatie in Ruth

Park's *Playing Beatie Bow* (q.v., 1980), who also refuses to accept society's prescription for her future, while Norah's successor could be Sylvie in Mavis Thorpe Clark's *The Min-Min* (q.v., 1966). Sylvie demands respect and has aspirations, but is domesticated by the desire for femininity and the situation of her family. Writers who developed female characters during the 1940s and 1950s were Irene Cheyne, Gladys Lister, and Pixie O'Harris. Annette, Jennifer Hogarth and Poppy Treloar show courage and initiative, but are not as memorable as their earlier counterparts. The post-war concentration on the domestication of women and the 'feminine mystique' is exemplified in Edna Roughley's *Ellice of Ainslie* (1947), where Ellice purposely loses a swimming race so that an over-confident Jeremy will not be humiliated before his friends.

The position as a surrogate mother is a frequent motif. Helen in *Milicent Courtenay's Diary* (1873) and Brenda in Ethel Turner's *A White-Roof Tree* (1905) nurture their brothers and sisters. David Martin's Bess in *The Cabby's Daughter* (1974) courageously battles to keep the family together after her mother's death. Mully in *Mullaway* (1986) by Bron Nicholls takes on a mothering role when her mother dies, but her strength of character (and new attitudes to women) ensures that her life is not subordinated to the family. A modern study of a strong girl which raises issues about independence and responsibility is James Aldridge's *The True Story of Lilli Stubeck* (q.v., 1984). Lilli is adopted by the wealthy and educated Miss Dalgleish, who tries to form Lilli into an image of herself, but the girl's passionate nature and her loyalty to her poverty-stricken family prevents her from being overwhelmed by the older woman. Scatty, irrepressible, imaginative and funny, Penny Pollard, who first appeared in *Penny Pollard's Diary* (q.v., 1983) by Robin Klein, is a rebellious girl who must find her own solutions to social expectations, which she does in a highly original manner. Erica Yurken in *Hating Alison Ashley* (q.v., 1984) and Isobel in *All in the Blue Unclouded Weather* (1991), both by Klein, are similar characters to Penny.

Many writers have taken a short period in a girl's life and traced the maturing process. Ryl in H.F. Brinsmead's *Pastures of the Blue Crane* (q.v., 1964) develops tenacity and sensitivity; Lindy grows up in Patricia Wrightson's *The Feather Star* (q.v., 1962); Susie accepts her true self in Libby Gleeson's *I am Susannah* (q.v., 1987); Lara finds a place in the family in *Thunderwith* (q.v., 1989) by Libby Hathorn. Ruth Park's books about Callie, *Callie's Castle* (q.v., 1974) and *Callie's Family* (1988), show turning-points in the life of a thoughtful girl, also explored in Gillian Rubinstein's *Melanie and the Night Animal* (q.v., 1988), in which Melanie learns courage from her friend Jasmine.

Changing attitudes to gender have affected the depiction of girls, so that girls are more likely to challenge the stereotypes. Perhaps Nette Hilton's picture-book *A Proper Little Lady* (1989) represents the contemporary view: Annabella loves pretty clothes, but they do not stop her playing adventurously.

GLASSOP, JACK LAWSON (1913–66), born Lawson, NSW, wrote a controversial adult novel, *We Were the Rats* (1944), which was banned on publication. *Susan and the Bogeywomp* (1947), illustrated by Ron Madden, is a fantasy about an 8-year-old who steps through her hoop. Characters such as the Oozle Bird, the Old Geezer, the Wild Garage and the Ziggle Zoggle, as well as the Bogeywomp, take her through a series of adventures until she is able to return to reality.

Glaxo Nursery Rhymes, see **Nursery Rhymes**

GLEESON, LIBBY (1950–), born Young, NSW, has written novels and picture-books. In *Big Dog* (1991), illustrated by Armin Greder, Jan is terrified of a big dog in her street until her brother helps her work out a plan to tame the dog and overcome her fear; the plan involves Anglo-Australians and Indo-Chinese working together. *One Sunday* (1988), illustrated by John Winch, describes Dad and Amy's visit to the dump with a truckload of rubbish. They return with the truck full of odds and ends which Amy has found, the detritus of a city. Annie, Jess, Baby Jack and Dad imagine the fairytale adventures which may have made Mum late in *Where's Mum* (1992), illustrated by Craig Smith. *Mum Goes to Work* (1992), illustrated by Penny Azar, describes what Mum does, paralleled by the activities of children at creche. *Uncle David* (1992), illustrated by Armin Greder, is about a giant who must be seen to be believed.

Her first two novels, *Eleanor, Elizabeth* (q.v., 1984) and *I am Susannah* (q.v., 1987), look at lonely girls working through their unhappiness. In *Dodger* (1990) Mick is shattered by the sudden death of his mother. He reluctantly accepts the part of the Artful Dodger in the musical *Oliver*, and finds that by working closely with the other students and a sympathetic teacher he is able to examine his feelings of guilt, his deep sense of loss, and his relationship with his father. Gleeson has used letters and snatches of memory to add layers to her narrative and complexity to her characters. Her analyses of young people experiencing painful periods in their lives are affecting and astute.

GLEITZMAN, MAURICE (1953–), born UK, came to Australia at the age of 16. He is a journalist and writer for television, and wrote for 'The Norman Gunston Show' for five years. For *The Other Facts of Life* (1985) and *Second Childhood* (1990) see **'Winners'**. He wrote the play *Skin Free* for Toe Truck Theatre in 1986; it was performed throughout NSW and Queensland.

In *Two Weeks with the Queen* (1989) Colin seeks a miracle cure for his younger brother Luke, who is dying of cancer. When Colin is in London he tries to find the Queen's doctor, but when he meets Ted, whose friend is dying of AIDS, Colin learns that although he cannot save his brother's life, he can be with him to help him die with dignity. Colin's relationship with his brother is examined against other relationships, and the seriousness of the subjects is explored without sentimentality, and with a light touch. For *Misery Guts* and *Worry Warts* (both 1991) see *Misery Guts*. Gleitzman's heroes are single-minded children with a self-deprecating humour.

Gold Rushes. The first gold rush was to Bathurst at the end of the 1840s, where Edmund Hargraves had found gold. A visit to the flourishing fields in WA, Victoria or NSW, was almost mandatory in the early adventure story. In William Howitt's *A Boy's Adventures in the Wilds of Australia: or, Herbert's Note-Book* (1854) Herbert travels to White Hills, near Bendigo, where he describes the cosmopolitan nature of the diggers, their costumes, how they wash the gold, inside a digger's hut, the sly-grog shops, and other details of diggers' lives. Howitt's view is by no means romantic: 'Dried bullocks' heads and feet, sheep's heads and feet, sheepskins and pieces of bullock-hides, all decaying and half trodden into the ground … Here and there amongst them rises an abode, half tent, half hut, with a wooden, or bullock-hide chimney, while projecting windlasses and here and there a blasted, leafless tree or bole deprived of its head … complete the scene.' The nugget in Alexander MacDonald's *The Hidden Nugget, a Story of the Australian Goldfields* (1910) is somewhere in WA. There are descriptions of the goldfields, as well as such colourful characters as Peter the Poet, the Chinese storekeepers and the Afghan drivers they employed. Other examples of adventure stories which include scenes of the diggings are Horatio Alger's *The Nugget Finders* (1893), Alfred Alanson's *The Diggers of Black Rock Hill* (1908), and Joseph Bowes's *Pals* (1910) and *The New-Chums* (1915). Robert Bateman's *Quest for Nuggets* (1967) is based on the diary of the author's great-grandfather. Bill Wallace meets bushrangers on his way to the diggings, makes a very small fortune, and returns to England. This book also describes rough life on Victorian and NSW goldfields.

In Frank Kellaway's *The Quest for Golden Dan* (q.v., 1962) Dan travels throughout the Victorian goldfields, including Bendigo and Beechworth. Pat Spencer's *Hustler's Gold* (1969) is set in Bendigo, Victoria, during the 1890s, where Albert and Jimmy discover the men who are smuggling gold from the mines on Hustler's Reef, and become involved in their capture. *Riding for Gold* (1974, revised 1981) by Merle Cazaly is another picture of the goldfields.

Writers about the gold rushes are inclined to see them as the matrix of an egalitarian Utopia, although also an unhygenic sewer. William Howitt in *A Boy's Adventures in the Wilds of Australia* (1854) said: 'And all people are equal at the goldfields; the Chinese fears here no cruel mandarin watching to squeeze him for his gold; the negro grins merrily and laughs and sings his chirpy, jolly song, freer even than if he were in Africa.' His view has been challenged only by David Martin in *The Chinese Boy* (1973). Martin sees the diggings more as a killing field: 'Black ropes of hair dangled from [the banner's] border. Severed pigtails, cut off and pinned to the flag-cloth for decoration. (There would be witnesses to say that often skin was torn away with the hair, that scalps were hanging there too.)' The gold rushes rarely led to fortune, and frequently to despair. Martin brings the romance into perspective.

Golden Lamb, The (1966) by Irene Gough, illustrated by Joy Murray, was

Commended in the 1967 Book of the Year Awards. Julie's father has a pure merino flock, and when a lamb is born with a straight golden fleece, Julie has trouble convincing the adults to allow it to survive. The lamb is saved by the CSIRO, who are collecting a flock of 'lustre mutant' sheep.

GOLDS, CASSANDRA (1962–), born Sydney, wrote *Michael and the Secret War* (1985). See **Fantasy.**

Good Luck to the Rider (1953) by Joan Phipson, illustrated by Margaret Horder, was a joint winner of the 1953 Book of the Year Awards. The timid Barbara, youngest in a family of four, finds an orphaned brumby foal which she names Rosinante. She cares for it, trains it and rides it to a first prize at the local Bungaree show. During the year it takes her to win with Rosinante, Barbara begins boarding school and develops a friendship with Will. Will's encouragement and her own growth in self-confidence are reflected in her increasing mastery of riding.

GOODE, ARTHUR RUSSELL (1889–1937), born Wedderburn, Victoria, used the pseudonym 'Arthur Russell'. He was the technical editor of the *Listener In*, a Melbourne radio journal. Out of that experience he wrote *Tony D'Alton's Wireless* (1931), *Twenty-Six Radio Stories* (1931), illustrated by V. Soper, and *Twenty-Six Australian Stories* (1934), illustrated by J.F. Campbell. Cattle-duffers, bushrangers, crocodiles, deserts, bunyips and bushfires are all here in these 'blood-stirring tales for the boy who loves the wide countryside, the crack of a whip, the loyalty of a good pal in a tight corner'. *Twenty-Six South Sea Stories* (1937) is in the same format. His books for boys were *Ginger for Pluck* (1926) and *Snowy for Luck* (1934), illustrated by Kurt Wiese. For *Dream Isle: an Australian Story* (1926), see **Bushfire.** *Bungoona: an Australian Story* (1928), illustrated by R.B. Ogle, *The Caves of Barakee*

(1936), *The Sky Pirates* (1946) and *Mason's Circus* (1947) are adventure stories with much gold bullion, deserted islands and submarines.

GOODE, EVELYN MARIA (1877–1927), born 'Canowie' Station, SA, was the wife of Crawford Vaughan, Premier of SA. *Days that Speak: a Story of Australian Child Life* (1908), illustrated by J. Macfarlane, is a collection of vignettes about three frolicsome children, seen from an adult's viewpoint. *The Childhood of Helen* (1913), also illustrated by Macfarlane, continues the story. Cousin Helen comes to stay with Polly-dear, Rod and Small, and is converted by their winning ways from an uncaring and selfish girl into a loveable future wife. Goode's gentle novels emphasize the need for selflessness in relationships.

GOODE, JOHN, born UK, wrote *Wood, Wire and Fabric: a Saga of Australian Flying* (q.v., 1968), *Smoke, Smell and Clatter: the Revolutionary Story of Motoring in Australia* (1969) and *Tortoises, Terrapins and Turtles* (1971), illustrated by Alec Bailey.

GOODMAN, JO (1940–), teacher, librarian and critic, edited the short story collection *Win Some, Lose Some* (1985). With Toss Gascoigne and Margot Tyrrell, she has compiled two collections for the CBC, *Dream Time* (1989) and *Into the Future* (1991). Goodman participated in the development of the reading program, 'RIB — IT' (Read in Bed — It's Terrific), for which she wrote the handbook in 1983.

GOODMAN, VIVIENNE (1961–), born Christchurch, NZ, studied art in SA. She has illustrated *Oodoolay* (1983) by Robin Klein and *Guess What?* (1988) by Mem Fox. Her surreal but photo-realist pictures challenge the observer to find references to places, objects, and other narratives.

GOODRICH, SAMUEL GRIS-WOLD, see **'PARLEY, PETER'**

GOODSIR, DONALD (1937–), born Sydney, wrote *The Gould League Book of Australian Birds* (q.v., 1979).

Gordon, Julie, a 14-year-old schoolgirl, appears in a series by 'Estelle Grey' (Esta de Fossard). In *Julie Gordon and the New Guinea Smugglers* (1972) she thwarts a bird-smuggling attempt; in *Julie Gordon and the School Fashion Contest* (1972) she wins second prize in a design competition run by the Wool Board; in *Julie Gordon and the Pony Club Camp* (1974) Julie and her friend Frankie uncover a plot to steal horses and help fight a bushfire; and in *Julie Gordon: Exchange Student* (1975) she exchanges to Cincinnati, Ohio, USA. Julie appears by courtesy of 'Trixie Belden'. See also **Peters, Shelley**.

GORDON, TULO. For *Milbi: Aboriginal Tales from Queensland's Endeavour River* (1980) see **Aboriginal Dreaming Stories**.

GOUGH, IRENE, born Tatura, Victoria, has written for the Victorian *School Paper* and the NSW *School Magazine*. *One Sunday Morning Early* (q.v., 1963) is a poetry collection. *The Golden Lamb* (q.v., 1966) is about a special sheep. Gough also wrote *The Cat who Belonged* (1969), illustrated by Sue Frankel, and poetry for adults.

Gould League Book of Australian Birds, The (1979) by Don Goodsir, illustrated by Tony Oliver, was Commended in the 1980 Book of the Year Awards. The author and artist have selected over forty of the better known Australian birds, such as the budgerigar, the rosella, magpie and kookaburra, as well as some introduced species such as the myna. The conversational text takes up some of the unusual aspects of each bird, and each description is accompanied by large and colourful illustrations.

GOULDTHORPE, PETER (1954–), born Melbourne, is a painter, illustrator, print-maker and teacher who studied at East Sydney Technical College. In *Jonah and the Manly Ferry* (1983), which is illustrated with coloured linocuts, Jonah is allowed to steer the ferry after he helps to rescue the passengers from a capsized boat. In *Walking to School* (1988), a poem by Ethel Turner, Gouldthorpe suggests the fear of a small boy as he walks to school alone for the first time, facing horses, dogs, 'fighting boys' and other terrors. His illustrations to C.J. Dennis's *Hist!* (q.v., 1991), dark linocuts, suggest the imaginary terrors of the night. He has illustrated two books by Jack Bedson, *Don't Get Burnt! or The Great Australian Day at the Beach* (1985) and *Sheep Dogs* (1990). The rapture of a day in the surf is caught in Gouldthorpe's luminous illustrations to *Don't Get Burnt!*. In *Sheep Dogs* each illustration is outlined in shapes which add a further dimension to the text. His surreal acrylic paintings in black and white for *Grandad's Gifts* (1991), a short story by Paul Jennings taken from *Unbearable! More Bizarre Stories* (1990), strike the appropriate chilling note. Gouldthorpe's work is unconventional, extending the narrative with flair.

GRAHAM, AMANDA JANE (1961–), born Adelaide, began writing picture-books with *Picasso the Green Tree Frog* (1985), illustrated by John Siow. Picasso can change colour to suit his environment, and when he jumps into a jar of jellybeans he becomes multicoloured. For her trilogy about the exuberant dog, *Arthur* (1984), *Educating Arthur* (1987), and *Always Arthur* (1989), illustrated by Donna Gynell, see **Arthur**. Graham contributed to Era Publishing's 'Magic Bean' series, with titles such as *Claude Money* (1987), about a train robber, illustrated by Gynell. In *So*

Hist! by C.J. Dennis. 1991 edition. Illustrator: Peter Gouldthorpe

What? (1987), illustrated by Debby Strauss, Max and Min boast about their mother's skills. *Sleepy on Sunday* (1988), illustrated by Donna Gynell, describes Grandma Speedy's week. Other titles in the same series are *In the Middle of the Night* (1988), *Wild Rose* (1988), *Help* (1988) and *Angus Thought He was Big* (1987). Graham has also written 'Dolly' fiction, including *Who Said Love was Easy?* (1989).

GRAHAM, BOB (1942–), born Sydney, studied painting and drawing at the Julian Ashton School. After a period in London he returned to Australia in 1969. He has written and illustrated his own books and also illustrated books for other writers, including *Jenny's Baby Brother* (1981) by Peter Smith. Graham writes a six-page monthly comic-strip, 'Charlotte et Henri', for a French children's magazine, *Les Belles Histoires*, and *The Adventures of Charlotte and Henry* (1987), five adventures of Henry, who is a worrier, and the wild and adventurous Charlotte, was first published in France.

Graham has written picture-books about the adventures of small children. Emily in *Libby, Oscar & Me* (1984) is a

Greetings from Sandy Beach by Bob Graham

master of disguise; in *Pete and Roland* (1981) Pete must come to terms with the escape of Roland, his budgerigar. In *Here Comes John* (1983) a snail has a hazardous journey across the garden, and just escapes being eaten by John. John's sister, Sarah, also appears in *Where is Sarah?* (1985). Theo the dog loves to jump on Sarah and John and give them 'the licking treatment' in *Here Comes Theo* (1984). William is learning to walk in *Has Anyone Here Seen William?* (1988) and his family is continually searching for him. Family life is further explored in *First There was Frances* (q.v., 1985). The restrictions in Arthur's life in a high-rise flat are overcome in *Pearl's Place* (1983), when Arthur meets the generous Pearl, with her rambling house. *The Wild* (1986) is a family story with a conservation theme. *Crusher is Coming* (q.v. 1987) is a gentle comment on sexism. In *The Red Woollen Blanket* (1987) Julia's favourite thing is her blanket, and Graham traces its fate from Julia's babyhood to when she starts school. In *Grandad's Magic* (q.v., 1989) Grandad may exasperate his daughter, but he enchants his granddaughter, Alison. Families are also at the centre of *Greetings from Sandy Beach* (q.v., 1990). In *Rose Meets Mr Wintergarten* (1992) Rose's friendliness and courtesy break through to the gloomy Mr Wintergarten, so that life becomes as happy for him as it is for Rose, her pet hen, and her family.

His non-fiction includes his own *The Junk Book: a Guide to Creative Uses of Recycled Materials for Children* (1984), *How*

Does Your Garden Grow? by Kevin Heinze (1985), *The Kids' Letter Writing Book* (1985) by Jenny Herbert and *Family Car Fun Book* (1986) by Anne Bower Ingram and Peggy O'Donnell. *It's Much Too Hot, Pig's Wild Cart Ride, Look Out for Rosie* and *Rupert's Big Splash* (all 1986) are titles in the 'Science Early Learner' series, and he has contributed titles to the 'I can' series, a reading scheme. *Waiting for the New Baby, Visiting the New Baby, Bringing Home the New Baby* and *Getting to Know the New Baby* (all 1989) aim to introduce the child to a new brother or sister. *Waking, Helping, Playing* and *Sleeping* (all 1988) are 'Busy Day' board books for pre-school children.

Graham's unstereotyped and humorous characterisation and his gift for seeing the world through the eyes of a very small child present the unusual in everyday experiences.

Grandad's Magic (1989) by Bob Graham was an Honour Book in the 1990 Picture Book of the Year Awards. Alison is fascinated by the magic which Grandad performs every Sunday at lunchtime. Her growing realisation that his magic is merely trickery does not alter her admiration for her wonderful grandfather. Graham presents Grandad, Rupert the dog and Alison and her brother in all the humorous nuances of family life.

Grandma Cadbury's Trucking Tales (1987) by Dianne Bates won the Primary category of WAYRBA in 1988. The novel and its sequel, *Grandma Cadbury's Safari Tours* (1989), both illustrated by Kevin Burgemeestre, relate the exploits of Grandma Cadbury, driving Tootsie, her 36-tonne truck or her 22-seater turbo-charged custom-built minibus.

GRANGER, HELEN, see 'FRAN-CES, HELEN'

GRASSE, WOLFGANG (1940–), born Dresden, Germany, is a painter and cartoonist. Grasse arrived in Australia in 1966, and worked as an illustrator for the *Bulletin*. Grasse's illustrations recall the settings of his stories: Japanese motifs in *Snowball* (1979). Yukio and Otomo have a beautiful cockerel who speaks to them. He flies to the Emperor's palace, where he is petted and spoiled, but Snowball longs for the love of Yukio and Otomo. *Kenji's Magic Kite* (1984) is another Japanese folktale. Kenji and his friend Saburo, a Sumo wrestler, build a kite on which they can fly. Japanese styles are also used in *Mai-Tzu and the Moon Princess* and *Mai-Tzu and the Kite Emperor* (1973). Mai-Tzu is a poor boy who is able to build his own kite from the offcuts given to him by Mr Fo, the kite-maker. It is destroyed by Kao the Kite Emperor, but the Emperor gives him the most beautiful kite of all. More sumptuous images inform *The Green Bamboo Flute* (1984), a Chinese folk-tale of courage and love. *Tataru* (1984), set in Brazil, is the story of an Indian boy in search of his sister Tanoa and the ancient treasures of his people. Tataru seeks help from the jungle creatures, and when he and his sister are united, discovers that love is more important than gold. The lush and verdant Amazonian rainforests are the background in this story.

GRATTAN-SMITH, THOMAS E. In *Three Real Bricks: the Adventures of Mel, Ned and Jim* (1920) Ned is given a hydroplane for his sixteenth birthday. Ned and his sister Mel (Meryl) and his chum Jim Stanley use it to advantage when tracking spies. See also **War**. Grattan-Smith wrote a sequel to *Three Real Bricks*, *The Cave of a Thousand Columns* (1938). *The Magic Billabong* (?1921), illustrated by Edgar A. Holloway, has three stories about Wattle Blossom and her friend Mr Plat. She travels with him to a kangaroo's wedding and to the seaside. In the middle story Wattle Blossom witnesses a trial of people who destroy the animals, birds and flowers of the bush. A woman guilty of having birds' feathers in her hat is punished with three weeks' hay fever.

GRAVES, RICHARD H. (1897–) wrote *Spear and Stockwhip: a Tale of the Territory* (q.v., 1950) and *Tidinbilla Adventure: a Sequel to Spear and Stockwhip* (1951). See **Adventure Stories**.

'Great Stories of Australia' was a series published by Macmillan, under the general editorship of Kylie Tennant, and was 'designed to introduce young people to the great stories of Australian history'. The material was presented in novelised form, written and illustrated to appeal to the young reader. *To Ride a Fine Horse* (1963), illustrated by Elizabeth Durack, is a children's version of Mary Durack's account of her pastoralist grandfather, Patrick Durack, in *Kings in Grass Castles* (1959). *Treasure from the Earth: Stories of the Adventurous men who Discovered Australia's Mineral Wealth* (1963) by Donald McLean, illustrated by Frank Beck, deals with the discovery of gold, opal, coal, iron, lead, zinc, uranium, bauxite and gemstones. *Riders to an Unknown Sea: the Story of Charles Sturt, Explorer* (1963) by George Farwell, also illustrated by Beck, is an account of Sturt's search for an inland sea. *By Gravel and Gum: the Story of a Pioneer Family* (1963) by Nancy Keesing, illustrated by Roderick Shaw, is an account of the pioneer Sarah White, whose husband first found gold at Lambing Flat (now Young), NSW, and who witnessed the massacre of the Chinese miners. In *Peter the Whaler in Southern Seas* (1964) by Max Colwell, illustrated by Geoffrey C. Ingleton, Peter Tregennis is 14 when the novel opens and his experiences over the next fifty years mirror the history of whaling in eastern Australia. *Trail Blazers of the Air* (1965) by Kylie Tennant, illustrated by Roderick Shaw, looks at the life of Ross Smith, Bert Hinkler, Raymond Parer and J.C. McIntosh, Kingsford Smith, Alan and Gordon Taylor, Lawrence Hargrave, John Duigan, and the origins of the Australian Flying Corps. *Strange Seeker: the Story of Ludwig Leichhardt* by Keith Willey, illustrated by William Mahony, describes Leichhardt's epic journey and his mysterious disappearance. *The Sliprails are Down* (1966) by Gordon Broughton, illustrated by Michael Brett, is the story of one of Broughton's ancestors who lived on the Durack's cattle station in the Kimberleys.

GREDER, ARMIN (1942–), born Biel, Switzerland, came to Australia in 1971, and has taught illustration in Queensland. He has illustrated an alphabet book, *Animal Antics ABC* (1988) by Moira Cochrane, *Danny in the Toybox: a Story* (1990) by Richard Tulloch, and *Big Dog* (1991) and *Uncle David* (1992) by Libby Gleeson.

Greeks. Greek characters rarely appear in novels before the immigration programs of the post-World War II period. One of the first Greek families is found in *Bushfire* (1967) by Allan Aldous. Here the immigrants confront a new culture, but, reflecting the community attitudes of the 1960s, they are either accepted or rejected, according to the class with which they are dealing. Working-class characters call them racist names, middle-class families patronise them. Mrs Koukoulas in Margaret Balderson's *A Dog called George* (q.v., 1973) is stereotyped, 'jabber[ing] away in an inexhaustible torrent of Greek'. She is drawn as a comic figure, and Tony concludes that 'with a mother like Mrs. Koukoulas, Helen didn't have much of a chance'.

Nance Donkin moved the acceptance of Greeks forward. In *A Friend for Petros* (1974) Donkin does not patronise, but her resolutions depend on small gestures which solve large problems. Petros's loneliness is overcome when he is given a dog by an Australian friend; in *Nini* (1979) the only family who do not support the establishment of an International Club in Bellfield conveniently move to Tasmania; and in *The Maidens of Pefka* (1979) Mrs Paniotis is made into a 'new, happy woman' through a kindness by her Greek-speaking Australian neighbour, Mrs

Stevens. There is more substantial treatment of the problems faced by Greek families in *The Alien* (1977) by Esta de Fossard. While cultural stereotypes appear, there is insight into Mrs Eliopolus, and her difficulties within her family and at her workplace in a new cultural environment.

The multicultural 1980s saw a major advance in the portrayal of Australian Greeks in *Five Times Dizzy* (q.v., 1982) and *Dancing in the Anzac Deli* (1885) by Nadia Wheatley. In inner-suburban Sydney, Yaya is homesick for her Cretan village, and the animosity of the Australian Wilsons towards the newly arrived Greek family is not immediately overcome. Mareka's parents are strong individuals, not types. Mareka's father feels that he must forsake his own cultural background and slavishly follow Australian customs to gain acceptance, while Mareka's mother wishes to retain her family's Greek heritage. The disagreement comes into the open over Mareka's idea of buying Yaya a goat. The text is sprinkled liberally with Greek words; the family's accent is conveyed by phrasing and expression, though they are competent in English. In the sequel, *Dancing in the Anzac Deli* (1985), the issues and conflicts of settling into a new culture are largely resolved. Sean, the 4-year-old dinkum Aussie who is slow to talk, utters his first words in Greek, a tribute to Yaya's skill and personality as a storyteller. Chapter 4 describes in moving detail Yaya's life in her homeland, and the heroism of Greek women during World War II. In Maureen Stewart's *Henry and Voula* (1989) the pair correspond because Henry is disguising his feelings for Voula under the pretext that he is studying Greek lifestyle for a project. Voula wants no one to know that she is writing to a boy, as her parents would not approve. Although Voula's parents are depicted as strict, not all Greek families in the novels are represented similarly. In fact, the families of Con, Liam, Ali, Sun, Hue, Tong, Phetdara and Julie are all different.

Eventually Voula and Henry's friendship is discovered and all contact must cease. Henry's acceptance of this is based on his respect for Voula's culture: 'Mum says I should respect other cultures and love you from afar.' Voula agrees, as she does not want to violate her cultural values. This light-hearted novel reflects the change occurring in the presentation of Greek Australians.

GREEN, CLIFF (1934–   ), born Melbourne, was a printer and teacher before writing for television. He wrote the script for the six fifteen-minute episodes of 'The Ballad of Riverboat Bill' in 1965, produced by the ABC, and directed by Peter Summerton. These were later extended into his novels, *The Incredible Steam-Driven Adventures of Riverboat Bill* (1975), *The Further Adventures of Riverboat Bill* (1981) and *Riverboat Bill Steams Again* (1985), illustrated by Stephen Axelsen. The crew of the good ship *Mystery*, with its steam created by Bunyip, the Patent Portable Firebox, suffer outrageous adventures, from which they manage to survive undaunted. A film was made in 1986, *The Steam-Driven Adventures of Riverboat Bill*, directed by Paul Williams, based on the three books. Green adapted Marshall's *I Can Jump Puddles* (q.v.) for television in 1981. He wrote *Boy Soldiers* (1990) for the 'Winners' series (q.v.).

GREEN, MONA. For *The Echidna and the Shade Tree* (1984) see **Aboriginal Dreaming Stories**.

Green Laurel, The (1963) by Eleanor Spence, illustrated by Geraldine Spence, won the 1964 Children's Book of the Year Awards. The Somervilles have to abandon the miniature train which they have operated at country shows, and move to Sydney to a settlement camp, providing a rare insight into a little-known aspect of post-war Australia. Lesley, an introverted 11-year-old, longs for a permanent home, to be ' ... like some green laurel, rooted in one dear perpetual place'. The camp at Blackbutt Hill is drab and monotonous, and at first Leslie dislikes it, but her maturing friendship with the immigrant children Carla and Stefan mirrors her own development. By the end of the novel, Lesley has won third prize in a design competition, grown to be 'pretty after all', and has come to realise that a family has roots regardless of where it resides. Assimilationist attitudes mark *The Green Laurel* as a novel of the 1960s, but it is a strong story of a realistic family developing strength during adversity.

Green Wind, The (1985) by Thurley Fowler, won the 1986 Book of the Year Awards. In 1948, on an irrigation area of the Murrumbidgee, Jennifer and her family adjust to their father's return from a prisoner-of-war camp and the hardships of rural life. Jennifer overcomes her problems through her lively imagination, and her father is rehabilitated. In *The Wind is Silver* (1991) Jennifer leaves school to manage the household when her mother is injured. Margaret, the eldest, goes off to Melbourne to study art; Jennifer takes up writing in earnest; the thoughtful Richard has a vocation, and tender-hearted Alexander decides to stay on the farm. The family rub along good-naturedly, with parents who are always ready to give support when it is needed. These are realistic pictures of the irritations, humour and affection found in a secure family.

GREENER, LESLIE (1900–75), born near Capetown, South Africa, was a journalist and teacher. Before World War II he was editor of *Pix*, and during the war was an intelligence officer with the Australian Army. He was a prisoner at Changi, and in 1942 he illustrated *The Happiness Box* (1947) by David Griffin, republished in 1991. Greener is remembered as one of the inspirational leaders of the Changi prisoners. After World War II he became

Director-General of Adult Education in Tasmania. For *Moon Ahead* (1951), illustrated by William Pene du Bois, see **Science Fiction**. *The Wizard Boatman of the Nile and Other Tales from Egypt* (1957) is a collection of Egyptian folk-tales.

GREENWOOD, TED (1930–), born Melbourne, was a primary teacher and lecturer in art before the publication of *Sly Old Wardrobe* (q.v., 1968) with Ivan Southall. Greenwood's picture-books and novels have two major themes: conservation and the pattern of existence. Early picture-books were *Obstreperous* (q.v., 1969), *Aelfred* (1970), about a drawbridge-keeper with a talent for engineering, and *Terry's Brrrmmmm GT* (q.v., 1974). *V.I.P.: Very Important Plant* (1971) depicts the growth of a tree until it is destroyed by Man, although with the promise of a new beginning; the life cycle of a mutton bird

Joseph and Lulu and the Prindiville House Pigeons (1972) by Ted Greenwood

is described in *Everlasting Circle* (1981); a rock is the focus of the passing of time in *Ship Rock* (1985). In *Joseph and Lulu and the Prindiville House Pigeons* (q.v., 1972) an old house is facing demolition. *A Day in the Life of Curious Eddie* (1979) has a lateral-thinking boy whose activities include giving himself a topiary haircut, oiling the clock with soap, and putting his thumb up the bath tap. *Uncle Theo is a Number Nine* (1990) relates a family's effort to survive the end of the world, predicted by Uncle Theo, a keen numerologist.

The Pochetto Coat (q.v., 1978) is a longer novel. *Ginnie* (1979) and *Marley and Friends* (1983) recount episodes in the lives of girls whose typically childish experiences are related in a series of adventures. *Flora's Treasures* (1982), illustrated by Elizabeth Honey, is set in the early twentieth century. Each event revolves around one of her collection of treasures, triggering a memory of an important incident in her life. In *The Boy Who Saw God* (1980) a religious but unhappy boy believes that God has demanded that he re-enact the sacrifice of Abraham. Leo kills a sheep, and the horror of the experience highlights his difficulties. Freya is recovering from glandular fever in *Windows* (1989) and by recording her impressions in her sketchbook she examines reality in different ways. *Warts and All* (1984) and *I Don't Want to Know* (1986), written with Shane Fennessey and illustrated by Elizabeth Honey, are factual books.

Greenwood has a diverse talent. His illustrations range from sketches to highly detailed drawings, and while they are sometimes not immediately appealing, they are always very demanding. His use of colour is restrained. In both his pictures and his stories, he stretches the imagination and intellect of his readers.

Greetings from Sandy Beach (1990) by Bob Graham won the 1991 Picture Book of the Year Awards. While they are on a camping holiday, the family meet and make friends with a gang of bikies (the Disciples of Death), battle to put the tent up, bury Mum in the sand and, although beset with other minor disasters, happily return home with their souvenirs. The witty illustrations explore a family holiday at the beach and its hazards.

'GREY, ESTELLE', see **DE FOSSARD, ESTA**

GRIEVE, JAMES (1934–), born Ireland of Scottish parents, came to Australia in 1960. In *A Season of Grannies* (1987) Jacqui Barclay is at a turning-point in her life. She is attracted to the handsome Garry, but she soon learns that he is not what he seems, and she is increasingly drawn to Looch (Luciano), the new boy in her class. She becomes involved in a bizarre attempt to help Looch's friend Beryl bury her lover. Meanwhile her troubles with her decidedly 'ocker' father and his plan for the family to adopt a grandmother are almost out of control. Grieve presents serious issues, such as racism and euthanasia, in the context of a credible family in which a girl is rapidly maturing away from her father's restrictions, all with a light touch and plenty of humour.

GRIFFIN, Sir **DAVID** (1915–), born Leura, NSW, was a prisoner of war in Changi during World War II, where he wrote *The Happiness Box* (1947), illustrated by Leslie Greener; it was republished in 1991. The book was intended as a Christmas present for the 300 children who were imprisoned at Changi. Winston the Chi-Chak (a lizard), Martin the monkey, and Wobbley the frog live in the jungle where they capture the winds to eat, grow food and keep house. One day the friends find a box which tells them that cleverness, generosity and kindness will teach the world the lesson of happiness. The text was typed by Bruce Blaikey, and bound into a small book, but the Japanese military tried to confiscate the only copy, because of its supposed allusion to Winston Churchill. After the liberation of Changi, the original *The Happiness Box* was deposited in the State Library of NSW. Griffin was prominent in national business companies, became Leader of the Opposition in NSW, and later Lord Mayor of Sydney.

GROCOTT, ANN (1938–), born Glenelg, SA, is an artist, illustrator and writer. In *Duck for Danger* (1985) Micky Massey is stranded in London, with a mother in hospital and a valuable jewelled duck smuggled into her luggage. Helped by the poor but kind Nizbo Natchett, her own resourcefulness and several coincidences, she is able to defeat the sinister Smalley-Hughes. Grocott combines adventure and humour in *Danni's Desperate Journey* (1987). See **Science Fiction**. She has also written the informational text *How to Write for Children* (1985).

GROSS, YORAM (1926–), born Poland, animator and film-maker, came to Australia in the sixties. *The Little Convict* (1979), illustrated by Greg Hyde, is a novel taken from the film, which featured Rolf Harris as the storyteller. Toby is assigned to a cruel master on his arrival in Botany Bay. *Sarah: the Seventh Match* (1985), retold by Ann Ferns, relates Sarah's survival after her family is taken by soldiers. Gross directed an adaptation of Pedley's *Dot and the Kangaroo* (1899) in 1977, with significant departures from the original novel. In continuations of Dot's adventures filmed by Gross, Dot meets a bunny, a bunyip, Santa Claus, a whale and smugglers, and sets off for Hollywood and space.

Grug is a small hairy creature with a large nose who appears in a series of over twenty books for early readers by Ted Prior.

From 1979, when Grug first appeared, he has had adventures with (and in) apples, gardens, playgrounds, rainbows, etc., and has learned to swim, fish, ride a bicycle, build a car, play cricket and soccer, and cook.

GRUNDY, FRANCIS H. (?1820–?), born UK, came to Australia in the 1850s. *The Demon McGuire* (1860), written anonymously by Grundy, is a verse story dedicated to D.J. Mitchell about an enormous demon who roams around Sydney causing havoc in his wake. 'He ne'er stirs abroad but on darkest of night,/The Aurora's bright streak is the flash of his sight;/And the earthquakes we fancied we felt t'other day,/Was merely the shake of his footstep, they say./A Norfolk Isle pine is his walking stick small;/As a snuff-box, he means to take George-street "Town Hall!"/The "New Post Office" building he lovingly eyes,/When complete, for cigar case, 't will just be the size.' The Demon is finally exiled to the Moon by Father Christmas and Father Time. The verse is accompanied by twelve fearsome black-and-white illustrations. Grundy

The Demon McGuire (1870) by F.H. Grundy

wrote an autobiographical account of his experiences in Australia, *Pictures of the Past: Memories of Men I Have Met and Places I Have Seen* (1879).

GULPILIL. For *The Birirrk: Our Ancestors of the Dreaming* (1984) and *Gulpilil's Stories of the Dreamtime* (1979) see **Aboriginal Dreaming Stories**.

Gumbles, see **Bottersnikes and Gumbles**

GUNN, Mrs **AENEAS** (JEANNIE TAYLOR) (1870–1961), born Melbourne, travelled to 'Elsey' Station with her husband in 1902. Aeneas Gunn died the following year, and Mrs Gunn left the property, but her stories are set on 'Elsey' Station, then situated at Warloch Ponds, south of Katherine, NT. *The Little Black Princess: a True Tale of Life in the Never-Never Land* (1905) also appears in *The Australian Wonder Book* (q.v.). See **Aboriginal People in Children's Fiction**; **Bett-Bett**. *We of the Never-Never* (1908) was written for adults, and was adapted for children by Nance Donkin in 1983. It was filmed in 1983, directed by Igor Avzins, with Angela Punch-McGregor as Jeannie Gunn. Further reading: Nesdale, *The Little Missus*.

GUNN, JOHN (1925–), born Northumberland UK, came to Australia at the age of 3. Gunn served in the Fleet Air Arm, an experience he drew on for many of his novels. He began his adventure stories with the Peter Kent series (see **Kent, Peter**), six novels published between 1955 and 1962. *Sea Menace* (q.v., 1958) and *Dangerous Enemies* (1961), both illustrated by Brian Keogh, are seafaring adventures set in the early days of settlement. *Dangerous Enemies* follows the land and sea adventures of Alan Johnson and his friend Midshipman Bruce Kemp, in their attempts to restore Alan's rightful ownership of a tract of land. In *The Humpy in the*

Hills (1960), illustrated by Noela Young, Col, Andrew, Ian and Barbara apprehend a bank robber and find the hidden money. *The Goodbye Island* (1963), illustrated by James Val, continues the adventures of the four children. They become 'the Black Hand Gang' with a German boy, Hans, challenge a rival gang, 'the Divers', and both gangs join forces during a flood. Two books drew on a television series: *Seaspray, The Man who Knew Too Much* (1967) and *Seaspray, the Spoils of War* (1967). Gunn edited three novels written and illustrated by members of the ABC Argonauts' Club: *Dangerous Secret* (1960), *The Gold Smugglers* (1962) and *The Gravity Stealers* (1965). He also wrote informational books for children, including *Flying for You, a Career in Aviation* (1955), *Sailing and Ships for You* (1957) and *Acting for You* (1957), with Barbara Bingham.

GUNN, THOMAS (1873–1950) was a NSW farmer. For *Nursery Rhymes* (1917) and *Bush Nursery Rhymes* (1920) see **Nursery Rhymes**.

GURR, ROBIN (1934–), born Sydney. While still at school, she wrote and illustrated *Red Pepper: the Story of an Australian Horse* (1954), about the changing fortunes of a thoroughbred racehorse. *Song is a Mirror* (1963), *Music in the Grass* (1971), *A House of Carols* (1975) and *Harvest of Birds* (1982) are collections of poems.

GURR, THOMAS STUART (1884–1967), born India, lived in NZ before he settled in Australia. He was general manager of the Melbourne *Herald and Weekly Times*, later working for the Sydney *Sunday Times*. Gurr wrote material for stage and radio, including *Collits' Inn*, a romantic opera with music by Varney Monk, about bushrangers in the Blue Mountains. It starred Gladys Moncrieff and the comedian George Wallace when it was first produced in 1933 at the Melbourne Princess Theatre. Gurr drew on his childhood in India for *Jungle Vagabonds* (1942), a collection of stories about Selim the Tiger, the Jackal and the Monkey. His books for older readers include *Mountain of the Sleeping Giant* (1948), set in Asia, and *The Valley of the Lost Trail* (1943), set in India, where Lakhsman struggles to gain a throne which is rightfully his. In *Jamaica Bay: a Fantasy for Children* (1945), illustrated by Stan H. Clements, a toy donkey comes to life to bring wealth to Teddy and his mother, and in *The Magic Hat: a Fairy Story* (1945), illustrated by Betty van der Pot, Hans plays his pipe beautifully when he wears the magic hat, but badly when he takes it off. *Roger the Rabbit* (1946) is an example of a picture-book which uses European landscapes 'Australianised' with an occasional gum tree, possum and wallaby. Roger, a vain rabbit, is born in the 'woods' on 'Farmer Cornford's' farm, and is chased down 'pretty country lanes' by a red fox. Gurr also wrote a history, *Blue Mountain Story* (1949), with Gwen Harrowsmith.

GYNELL, DONNA (1960–) illustrated *Arthur* (1984), *Educating Arthur* (1987) and *Always Arthur* (1989) by Amanda Graham (see **Arthur**), and her pictures of the clumsy, silly and endearing dog were as responsible for the series' popularity as its engaging text. Gynell also illustrated Graham's *Claude Money* and *Sleepy on Sunday* (both 1987) and *The 9 Lives of Balthazar* (1989) by Anna Fienberg.

H

Ha Ha Bird, The (1968), written and illustrated by Penelope Janic, was Commended in the 1970 Picture Book of the Year Awards. The Ha Ha bird is vain and arrogant, able to turn himself into any shape or colour he desires, until a seagull challenges him to catch fish, and the Ha Ha bird nearly drowns. Donkey saves his life and brings the bird to his senses. Janic's bold colours and cartoon-like shapes reflect the pomposity of the bird and the gentle perseverance of the donkey.

HAGINIKATIS, MARY (1950–) (MARY CONNELL), born NSW, is an illustrator, writer and bush guide. She illustrated *Platypus and Kookaburra* (1987) and *Black Duck and Water Rat* (1988), two poems by Rex Ingamells, *The Last of His Tribe* (1989) by Henry Kendall, and *Nungadin and Willijen* (1991) all with Percy Trezise.

HALDANE, ROGER (1945–), born Port Fairy, Victoria, was a member of the family which pioneered the tuna fishing industry at Port Lincoln, SA. He illustrated *Blue Fin* (q.v., 1965) and *Magpie Island* (q.v., 1974) by Colin Thiele, and *Blue and Gold Day* (1979) by Margaret Balderson. Haldane has also illustrated a sketchbook of Port Lincoln.

Blue and Gold Day (1979) by Margaret Balderson. Illustrator: Roger Haldane

HALE, ERICA (1936–) wrote *Catch the Sun* (1984), the story of 17-year-old Lennie, who leaves her mother and step-father in Queensland for Adelaide. At an unemployed youth centre she finds friends and a purpose to her life. When the novel opens, Lennie is reading *Puberty Blues*, and like that novel, *Catch the Sun* examines Australian society from a viewpoint differ-ent from most books for the young. Lennie and her friends swear, smoke mari-juana, brush up against the law, move from 'squats' to shared houses, and rage against the lack of concern with which they are treated. Young people facing unemploy-ment and a loss of their sense of worth are tellingly drawn in this convincing novel. See also **Adelaide**.

HALL, JAMES JOHN (1876–1936), born Victoria, worked as a tutor on coun-try properties, taught at Scotch College, Melbourne, and was a founding member of staff at Grimwade House, the junior school of Melbourne Church of England Boys' Grammar School. According to the introduction to *"Winks": 'Winks' Tells Australian Children What He Saw in the Australian Bush* (1920), his nature stories are the result of his success with young students at the school. Winks loves nature, and after he is saved from drowning by Jack, who is crippled in the accident, the two listen to stories told by the pixies about Australian native flowers, such as 'The Boronia' and 'The Quandong tree'. *'Winks'* was republished in *The Australian Wonder Book* (q.v., 1935). Hall's next book, *The Crystal Bowl: Australian Nature Stories* (1921), illustrated by Dorothy Wall, is in a similar vein. Writing in *Woman's World* (1 Nov. 1924), Hall complains that 'gloom and cruelty disfigured many of the old fairy stories, and sent children to bed to dream again their fear'. Yet, in 'The Clematis', Possie is made to suffer pain by Mother Nature in order to teach him to be kinder, because 'Pain cleanses the body and purifies the mind from evil thoughts'. *The Crystal Bowl* is notable for the strong

illustrations by Dorothy Wall, then under-taking her first book. It was republished by Angus & Robertson in 1981. *The Kangaroo Paw: the Story of a Strange Australian Flower* (1921) was a Whit-combe's Story Book, No. 209. Hall also wrote two unpublished manuscripts, 'The Beautiful Valley' (1928) and 'Between the Lines' (1933). The then headmaster of Melbourne Grammar asked Hall to defer publication of the latter because of con-cern that characters and events might be linked to the school.

HALL, PENNY (1941–), born Hobart, is a Sydney teacher and librarian. She has written two science fiction novels, *The Paperchaser* (1987) and *The Catalyst* (1989). See **Science Fiction**. Her concepts of the powerful forces of time are explored for younger readers in *Nim's Time* (1991), illustrated by Gwen Harrison. Nim 'rides the wind' to a parallel world. There he learns that chinks have developed in time. To prevent the resulting chaos and defeat the sinister cat people, Nim and his pet mouse repair the damage. See also **Sydney**. Sibling relationships are the crux of Meg's difficulties and their resolution in *Better for Everyone* (1992), a realistic study of personal disturbance. When her father and his wife invite her to stay with them in Sydney, Meg leaves her mother, brother and sisters behind to get to know her father better. But her life with the 'steps' is uneasy, and Meg feels that she has no real place with either family. Her grasp of reality falters until it can be no longer ignored by those around her.

HAMILTON, MARGARET (1941–), born Sydney, librarian, editor and pub-lisher, has been active in the CBC since the 1970s. She edited *Spooks and Spirits: Eight Eerie Tales by Australian Authors* (1978), illustrated by Deborah Niland. Hamilton established the publishing house Margaret Hamilton Books in 1988, open-ing the booklist with Rodney McRae's version of W.A. Cawthorne's *Who Killed*

Cockatoo? (1860). Other authors and illustrators published by Margaret Hamilton Books include Patricia Mullins, Dee Huxley, Margaret Wild, Libby Hathorn and Maurice Saxby.

HAMMOND, CATHERINE. For *Midnight Dip: Award Winning Stories from Young Australian Writers* (1990) see **Collections**.

HANDFORD, NOURMA (1923–), born Brisbane, is a writer of romantic novels. *Three Came From Britain* (1945) begins a saga about the Grant and Harvey families. In *Cottontrees* (1948), illustrated by David Christian, the summer holidays prove a turning-point in the lives of Fay Harvey and the Grant girls. Further romances are explored in *Carcoola: a Story for Girls* (1950), *Carcoola Adventure* (1952), *Carcoola Holiday* (1953), illustrated by Frank Hodgkinson, and *Carcoola Backstage: a Career Novel for Girls* (1956), illustrated by Kate O'Brien. See **Carcoola: a Story for Girls**. She has also written novels for adults.

HANN, MARJORIE (1916–), born Adelaide, illustrated *Alice's Adventures in Wonderland* in 1934, and produced an 82-episode newspaper cartoon of Thackeray's *The Rose and the Ring*. With Lloyd Wilson, Hann wrote *The Adventures of Charlie Cheesecake* (?1940), a flap book which shows the awful results of Charlie's reckless behaviour. As Marjorie Fisher, Hann illustrated Kathleen Mellor's *Stop Look Listen* (1945), *Now I'm Ready* (1947), *Splish-Splash Rainy Day* (1947), and *Let's Go to the Beach* (1947).

HANNAY, LORRAINE (1954–), born NZ, has illustrated for reading schemes, such as 'Beginnings', 'Dimensions' and the 'Patchwork' series. She illustrated the 1982 edition of *Stradbroke Dreamtime* (1972) by Kath Walker (Oodgeroo Noonuccal), *Simon's Secret* (1983) by Judith Worthy, *Kelly the*

Sleepy Koala (1983) by Barbara Ker Wilson, *The Cat* (1986) by A.B. Paterson, *Creature* (1987) by Allan Baillie, *Goose* (1989) by Jane Carroll, *Into the Future* (1991) by Toss Gascoigne et al., *Sam's Sunday Dad* (1992) by Margaret Wild, *Keep Me Company* (1992) by Gillian Rubinstein, and many book covers, including the covers of the 1992 editions of Mary Grant Bruce's Billabong books.

HARDING, LEE (1937–), born Colac, Victoria, is a science fiction writer, interested in possible futures, particularly the impact of social change on the individual. *The Fallen Spaceman* (1973), *Return to Tomorrow* (1976), *Children of Atlantis* (1976) and *The Frozen Sky* (1976) were books to encourage reluctant readers written for Cassell's 'Patchwork' and 'Encounter' series. *The Weeping Sky* (1977) suggests another outcome to a small change in historical events. *Displaced Person* (q.v., 1979) suggests another reality which exists parallel to our own. *The Web of Time* (1980) is another examination of time, as the Andersons journey in their time machine. *Waiting for the End of the World* (1983) describes a community on the edge of chaos, and Manfred's search for freedom. See also **Science Fiction**. Harding has written many adult novels, stories for science fiction journals and edited collections. Harding believes that for many young people 'the future begins to look dark and awesome', and while he predicts a difficult world, his books display confidence in the ability of the human spirit to survive.

HAREWOOD, JOCELYN (1942–), born NZ, writes humorously about the pleasure and heartbreak of being an adolescent. In *Voices in the Wash-House* (1990), when Peregrine breaks his leg he is relegated to the laundry. His mate, Mono, wires up the house so that he can listen to the family dramas which punctuate the day and night. *Movement on the Sofa* (1991) continues Peregrine's fortunes as he fails at school, tries work, observes the tempestuous love affairs of his mother and sisters, and participates in one of his own. In *Worms in the Night* (1991) Pen teaches her dyslexic friend Moose to spell, while trying to understand her father, grieve for her mother, and remain best friends with Lisa. Harewood has an ear for the cadences of young people's speech.

HARNEY, BILL (1895–1962), born Charters Towers, Queensland, was the first curator of Uluru (Ayers Rock) and a friend of the Aboriginal People. *Bush Stories* (n.d.), illustrated by Mary Gillham, has four simply told stories adapted from Aboriginal stories recorded by Harney, with exact locations defined.

HARPER, JAN (1934–) was a foundation member of the Women's Movement Children's Literature Co-operative (q.v.). In *A Family of Potters* (1975), illustrated by Judith Crabtree, Mr and Mrs Potter's creations would have been spoiled if Pamela had not had the wit to turn off the kiln. The story depicts a family where father takes the baby for a walk and mother takes the pots to the pottery shop.

HARRIS, RAY (1901–76), born Echuca, Victoria, wrote short stories for adults. His first novel, *The Secret of the Tide-Race* (1948), was an action-packed adventure for 'grown-up boys'. Tom, Ted and Barry run up against some nasty types when they sail up the Jamieson River to a lonely shore in north WA. They dig up treasure, nearly perish in the desert, find Ted's long-lost son, and are saved by Aboriginal People and wild camels. *The Opal Seekers* (n.d.) is equally outlandish. The trio here are Geoff Mason, Blue Campbell and the giant Aboriginal Dogfoot, who save someone's life each week, shoot with deadly accuracy, drive a powerful Minton sportscar through the roughest outback tracks, and ride as

though they were born in the saddle. They find the opals in an underground cavern and become very rich.

Harris's best work is his depiction of bush boys like Turkey Matthews and his mates, based on his own childhood at Barmah, Victoria, and Caroona, NSW. Turkey, or Ossie, as his parents know him, is tough, humorous and intelligent, completely lacking in self-pity or selfishness, and always resourceful. *The Adventures of Turkey: Boy of the Australian Plains* (1952), illustrated by Geoffrey Whittam (who illustrated all the Turkey books), traces his experiences at school with 'Old Go', the lugubrious schoolmaster, working on a farm in the summer, roving along the river with his mate Dick Harding, and appearing as the maiden Koong Shee in the end-of-year concert, all related with gusto. Further adventures are *Turkey and Partners* (1954), in which Turkey and Dick are joined by Possum, and *The Cruise of the Nifty Duck* (1955), in which Turkey, Possum and Dick revitalise the 'Nifty Duck' and journey down the Namoi to the Darling, pursued by Morgan and Horse Face, whose attempt at robbery is foiled by the boys. The series concludes with *Turkey and Co.* (1961), in which Turkey, Dick and Possum stop an attempted sabotage of an engineering firm. Photographic negatives are stolen, and Turkey's expertise as a photographer comes into play. See also **Boys**. The first of the Turkey books touches on the pleasure, drama and humour of bush life, before the introduction of the stereotyped Possum and the increasing exaggeration of the boys' adventures.

HART, GERTRUDE (1873–1965), born in Melbourne, poet and novelist, lived in Geelong, Victoria for a period, and ran a circulating library in Sandringham in 1930 and 1931. In 1927, with Bernard Cronin, she founded the Old Derelicts, which became the Society of Australian Authors. She wrote *Nora's Night of Terror: an Australian Story* (?1898), a 'Horner's Penny Story', and *Wanted —* *a Servant: an Australian Story* (n.d.). In *The Laughter Lady,* *a Story for Children of Different Ages* (1914), illustrated by O.A. Garland, Jill Mainwaring is taken on a journey by a fairy. *Chubby* (1937), also illustrated by Garland, chronicles the relationship between a tomboy, Chubby, and her shrewd but irascible Aunt Anne. In *Chubby and Pip* (1940), illustrated by Joan Kiddell-Monroe, she is joined by Phillip Penrose. They discover the source of the ghost stories which surround a haunted house and Chubby is the heroine of a devastating bushfire. Hart wrote novels for adults, song lyrics and poetry.

HARVEY, ROLAND (1945–), born Melbourne, is an illustrator, painter and writer, who established Five Mile Press and later Periscope Press. He illustrated *The Friends of Emily Culpepper* (q.v., 1983) by Ann Coleridge; *The Great Candle Scandal* (1982) by Jean Chapman; *Dirty Dave the Bushranger* (1987) by Nette Hilton; *Milly Fitzwilly's Mouse Catcher*

My Place in Space (1988) by Robin and Sally Hirst. Illustrator: Roland Harvey

(1991) by Marcia Vaughan; and *Crisis on Christmas Eve* (1991) by Harvey and Scott Riddle. *Roland Harvey's Book of Christmas* (1982), and *Roland Harvey's New Book of Christmas* (1986) look at Christmas traditions throughout the world. *Incredible Book of Almost Everything* (1984), *The Book of Australian Trivia* (1985) by Jim Converse, *Roland Harvey's First Ever Book of Things to Make and Do* (1980), and *Roland Harvey's Second Ever Book of Things to Make and Do* (1983) include stories, information, puzzles, body tricks, recipes and cartoons.

He takes a wry look at Australian history in his *Eureka Stockade* (1981), *The Voyage of the First Fleet* (1983) and *The Crossing of the Blue Mountains* (1984), all by Alan Boardman, and his own *Burke and Wills* (1985). He has provided a witty pictorial commentary to *My Place in Space* (q.v., 1988) by Robin and Sally Hirst, which he illustrated with Joe Levine. Harvey's outlined watercoloured illustrations, with their wide-angled views of incident, often skewed, contain details which make fun of pompous history or people who take themselves too seriously.

'HATFIELD, WILLIAM' (1892–1969), born Nottingham, UK, was the name used by **ERNEST CHAPMAN**, who came to Australia in 1911 and travelled and worked throughout the outback for many years. *Sheepmates* (1931) is a semi-autobiographical account of his early experiences. In *Buffalo Jim* (1938), illustrated by Norman Hepple, Jim Westcott completes his apprenticeship as an all-round bushman. The novel opens with the hero only 17, and suffering from Depression times — out of work and thoroughly dispirited. His adventures include stowing away aboard a ship bound for Fremantle, WA, becoming an expert cook in Adelaide, prospecting for gold, and buffalo-hunting. Jim's exploits follow the pattern of the manly romance: a naive, honest boy, very capable of defending himself in a hand-to-hand fight, is toughened by hardship, while retaining his

principles. Hatfield's attitudes are typical of the time: a decent white man is always preferable to one of another colour, and the land is always open for exploitation. In *Barrier Reef Days* (1948), illustrated by Pat Terry, set on Green Island, Queensland, Keith and Joan Heath live on board ship while they are making a film about the Reef. Hatfield also wrote *Wild Dog Frontier* (q.v., 1951), about outback life in the NT, and books for adults.

HATHORN, LIBBY (1943–), born Newcastle, NSW, has brought to her writing for children her interests and experiences as a parent, librarian, scriptwriter for television and stage, librettist and poet. Her early books deal with friendship and responsibilities. Her first-picture book was *Go Lightly* (1974) with John Hathorn, illustrated by Joan Saint. *The Tram to Bondi Beach* (q.v., 1981), *Stephen's Tree* (1979) (also published in a dual-text edition, in Italian and English) and *Lachlan's Walk* (1980), both illustrated by Sandra Laroche, in which a toddler escapes through an open garden gate, established her as a writer for younger readers. In *Paolo's Secret* (1985) Paolo finds a kitten and makes a friend. The theme is developed further in *All about Anna and Harriet and Christopher and Me* (q.v., 1986) and *Looking out for Sampson* (q.v., 1987). *So Who Needs Lotto?* (1990), illustrated by Simon Kneebone, has the over-confident Denise and the timid Cosmo finding a common interest in their dogs, and both decide that friendship is more satisfying than winning a lot of money. In *Jezza Sez* (1990), illustrated by Donna Rawlins, Jezza makes outrageous plans to raise money for a boat he desperately wants, but his capacity for compassion forces him to send the money raised for it to a child in Honduras.

Hathorn examines the possibilities of imagination in *Freya's Fantastic Surprise* (1988). Freya is so keen to have something wonderful to show and tell at school that her imagination runs wild, until her parents present her with a real surprise. In

The Extraordinary Magics of Emma McDade (1989), illustrated by Maya, Emma is able to stop the robbers with her magical powers. *Stuntumble Monday* (1989), illustrated by Melissa Wood, pictures an exuberant girl who wants to skip a week and rush to her birthday on Sunday, until her wiser older brother persuades her not to throw a week of her life away. Jack and Mrs Paddy in *The Garden of the World*, illustrated by Tricia Oktober, learn that beauty is where you least expect to find it. *Thunderwith* (q.v., 1989), for older readers, allows Hathorn to develop her preoccupation with the loner through more complex characters. *Love Me Tender* (1992), illustrated by Kate Linton, another book for older readers, is set in the 1960s. When their mother leaves them Alan and his family are farmed out. Alan persuades Aunt Jessie to acquire a jukebox for her Coogee milkbar, which releases her from her bitterness, although Alan still longs for his mother's return.

Talks with My Skateboard (1991), illustrated by Matt Mawson, is a collection of her poetry. Hathorn has also produced a literacy series, and edited short stories such as *The Blue Dress* (1991), inspired by a painting of her daughter, and written a collection of short stories, *Who?* (1992). The bulk of her work has been funny stories with impish characters for young readers.

Hating Alison Ashley (1984) won YABBA for Older Readers in 1986 and was the Secondary Winner of KOALA in 1987. Erk suffers from a huge superiority complex and uses her fertile imagination to create a perfect family for herself, but when Alison comes to tea, the truth is out. To Erk's surprise, Alison appreciates the warmth of the Yurkens, and when Erk visits Alison's tasteful but sterile home she can see why. The horse-mad Jedda, the boy-mad Valjoy, and Erk's de facto father, a loveable roughneck, have much more to offer than the detached Mrs Ashley. Erk

sees her family afresh and gains a new perspective on her own life, with the help of Alison. Klein has examined the formation of a friendship against a humorous portrayal of class.

HAWKER, RUTH MARJORIE (Mrs A.K. GAULT) (1897–1976), born UK, poet and novelist, came to Australia in 1906. She has written three books, all illustrated by Nora Young, about three children in the bush. *Us Three* (1929) is a collection of verses. *Us Three Outback* (1932) includes verses and stories, such as Pete the dog confronting a wildcat, and Neenie hiding in an Afghan's cart. *Yesterday: Being the Adventures of Us Three with the Early Colonists* (1936) relates how Yolande, Richard and Neenie meet their ancestors from the earliest settlement, then their neighbours, the Barkers, from the 1850s. *Two New Australians* (1949) is about Bob and Janice, sent to Australia during the war, where they run the gamut of Australiana, from the Flying Doctor to swagmen. In *Treasure at Prince's Point* (1949) three country children visit their uncle and aunt by the sea, and find a hidden house containing a lost treasure. In *Heather at Magpie Creek* (1950) Heather spends her summer holidays learning to ride, cook and enjoy her independence. In *The Warrens of Wombat Flat* (1950) the Warrens set off to manage a property out of Adelaide. Despite their sickly father, the children succeed in coping with rural life. Hawker's stories depend on supportive families who work hard for a living, and present girls who are active and assertive. *An Emu in the Fowl Pen* (1967), illustrated by George Tetlow, republished as *Growing Up in the Outback* (1977) is an account of her childhood between the wars at 'Anama', her father's property in SA.

HAWKINS, SHEILA (1905–), born on the goldfields of Kalgoorlie, WA, has done most of her work in England. *Black Tuppeny* (1932) is about a small child who goes to London to see the King. This picture-book, *Eena-Meena-Mina-Mo-and Benjamin* (1935) and *Appleby John the Miller's Lad* (1938) are for early readers. *Appleby John* was the first children's book to be wholly printed in offset lithography in England. *Pepito* (1938) displays Hawkins's strong line and sense of design. It is set in Spain and the pictures are in black and red. Each page is designed to reflect the text: a crowd walks across the page, Pepito chases his donkey across a page opening. She then wrote and illustrated *Little Gray Colo: the Adventures of a Koala Bear* (1939), *The Panda and the Piccaninny* (1939), and *Bruzzy Bear and the Cabin Boys* (1940). In *The Bear Brothers* (1942) Big Bear and Little Bear run a grocer's shop, and in *The Bear Brothers' Holiday* (1942) Little Bear rescues people and is given the freedom of the Fair. She has illustrated a series of legends, *A Book of Fables Adapted from Aesop* (1942), *Where the Leopard Passes: a Book of African Folk Tales* (1949), *The Long Grass Whispers: a Book of African Stories* (1949) and *The Singing Chameleon: a Book of African Stories Based on Local Custom, Proverbs and Folk-Lore* (1957), all by Geraldine Elliot. Hawkins's *Animals of Australia* (1947) represented indigenous animals with accuracy. *Bush Holiday* (1948) by Dale Collins captured life in the bush. Hawkins was illustrating the novel in a cold English winter, but Collins said of them: 'These pictures … are almost uncannily the scenes which remain bright in my memory … This effect is really quite weird — just as if I were revisiting the actual scenes in a dream.' She wrote and illustrated *Homes and Families: Africa* (1955) and *Australian Animals and Birds* (1962), informational books illustrated with handsome lithographs. She re-illustrated Mervyn Skipper's *The Meeting Pool* (1929) in 1954, and worked with Peggy Barnard to produce *Wish and the Magic Nut* (q.v., 1956).

Hawkins returned to Australia between 1948 and 1952, contributing a coloured strip to the *Sydney Morning Herald*, 'Bruzzy Bear and the Cabin Boy', based on her earlier book, and also illustrated for the NSW *School Magazine*. She drew six posters for schools on Australian birds, commissioned by Vincent Serventy. *Airlift for Grandee* (1964) by Ruth Park was her last Australian book, and the last book she has illustrated is *More Animals* (1966) by Maurice Burton.

Hawkins has worked as a commercial artist, including drawing a series of cats for the company which made the pet food 'Tibs'. She was one of the six illustrators commissioned by Penguin for their first Puffin Books. She painted portraits of Australian airmen during World War II, and her murals of the activities of Australian forestry units in Scotland are at the Australian War Memorial Gallery. She has continued to exhibit her work, the most recent solo exhibition being held in Hampstead in 1990. She was an innovative illustrator whose fine lithographs of animals, and attention to page design, are outstanding.

HAXTON, ELAINE ALYS (1909–), born Melbourne, painter, designer and illustrator, studied at East Sydney Technical School and in London. She has won major awards for her artistic work, the Sulman Prize in 1943, and the Crouch Prize in 1946. Haxton illustrated the John Sands publications *The Vain Red Fox* (1947) by Franklin Moss, with three-colour drawings of personable animals, Veronica Basser's *The Glory Bird* (1947) and a book of poems by Alex Scott, *Come Night, Come Ninepence* (1947). Her illustrations for *Moggie and Her Circus Pony* (1967) by Katharine Susannah Prichard are highly atmospheric, evoking the swirling life of a circus horse. In 1968 Haxton wrote and illustrated *A Parrot in a Flame Tree: Adapted from a Medieval Christmas Carol. The Story of China* (q.v., 1970) by Lo Hui-Min also shows the artist's grasp of her medium. She draws on the formality and colour of ancient Chinese art, and intersperses these pictures with her stylish designs. Haxton illustrated Meredith Hooper's *The Story of Australia* (1974).

HAY, DEAN (1911–), born SA, photographer, collaborated with Geoffrey Dutton for *Tisi and the Yabby* (1965), *Seal Bay* (1966) and *Tisi and the Pageant* (1968); with Jean Chapman for *The Wish Cat* (q.v., 1966) and *The Someday Dog* (1968); and with Barbara Drew for *Let's Dress More Dolls* (1974). *I See a Lot of Things* (1966), *Now I Can Count* (1977), *On the Farm* (1977), *Things We Do* (1971), *What Shape is It?* (1974), and *What Size is It?* (1974) have Hay's colour photographs of simple objects.

Hebe's Daughter (1976) by Celia Syred, Commended in the 1977 Book of the Year Awards, is a novel about the red-haired Elizabeth Pollard, set at the time of the French Revolution. When her father dies, she must leave Polstead Manor in Essex, where she has lived for most of her life, confident that she will return to claim her inheritance. After adventures in London and France, she finds out about her real origins, and settles in Hastings.

Hector and Maggie (1990), by Andrew and Janet McLean, was an Honour Book in the 1991 Picture Book of the Year Awards. Hector is a rooster, and the bane of the farmyard. He pecks and pesters all the other animals until he is challenged by Maggie, the new sheepdog. Although she is only young, Maggie knows how to keep a boastful rooster in check, and Hector has met his match. Hector's strut, with lost tail-feathers and dignity, is a parody of its former arrogance.

HEDDLE, ENID MOODIE, see **MOODIE HEDDLE, ENID**

HEDDLE, JOHN FOSTER, see **MOODIE HEDDLE, JOHN FOSTER.**

HEIMANN, ROLF (1940–) has illustrated *Festivals* (1984) by Dorothy Rickards; *Bushrangers* (1984) by Garry Disher; *The Peace Garden* (1989) by Lucy Sussex and *Rotten Apples: Top Stories to Read and Tell* (1989) by Virginia Ferguson and Peter Durkin. *A City by a River* (1987) is a history of Melbourne in pictures. *For Eagle Eyes Only* (1988), *More for Eagle Eyes* (1990) and *Amazing Mazes: Mind Bending Mazes for Ages 6 to 60* (1989) are puzzle books in which the reader is asked to solve a mystery.

HEMMINGS, ERNESTINE (ERNESTINE HILL) (1899–1972), born Rockhampton, Queensland, wrote books for adults. When she was only 16 years old, the Brisbane *Catholic Advocate* published a collection of her poetry, *Peter Pan Land and Other Poems* (1916). It contains her own work and poems by other contributors to the children's pages of the paper. Hemmings's poetry is at its best when it is dealing with natural subjects, such as her 'Ode to the Jelly-fish', written when she was 14, or 'The Song of the Curlew' written when she was 15: ' ... Then down the creek with a great, weird shriek,/And over the writhing river,/And up the hill with a cry so shrill/That even the ti-trees shiver;/Then back again, and across the plain,/And never I cease my crying,/Now loud and long like a witch's song,/And now in an echo dying.'

HEMYNG, SAMUEL BRACE-BRIDGE (1841–1901) was a London, UK, barrister whose adventure stories about the fearless Jack Harkaway thrilled a generation of readers in the last quarter of the nineteenth century. Jack Harkaway first appeared in 1871 as a serial in the magazine *Boys of England*, as a schoolboy at Pomona House School, where he defeats all bullies, including the execrable masters. The world was his oyster, however, and his triumphant adventures ranged all over the world, from China to

Cuba. He spawned a son, another Jack, and the two, with their faithful Aboriginal attendants Sunday and Monday, defeat a gang of bushrangers led by Captain Morgan and his more fearsome wife, Fighting Sue, in *Jack Harkaway and His Son's Adventures in Australia* (1893). Hemyng was untroubled by any attempt at accuracy in the representation of landscape or customs. Another young hero, Ballarat Bill, appears in *Ballarat Bill: or, Fighting the Bushranger, Ballarat Bill: or, Lumps of Gold* and *Ballarat Bill in Search of the Great African Diamond* (all n.d.). Hemyng created other redoubtables, such as Tom Tallyho and Hal Harkforward, but they have sunk into oblivion.

HENTY, GEORGE ALFRED (1832–1902), born near Cambridge, UK, was a war correspondent during the Austro-Italian war, the Franco–German war and the Turkish war with Serbia. He was the author of nearly eighty adventure stories, and a leading contributor to the *Boy's Own Paper*. *A Final Reckoning: a Tale of Bush Life in Australia* (1886) is used by Rosemary Wighton in her *Early Australian Children's Literature* (1979) as an example of the 'horrifying casualness' with which Aboriginal People were slaughtered in nineteenth-century books for the young. The novel begins in England, and there is much attention devoted to the trial of the innocent hero. Reuben is acquitted of theft, but comes to Australia because his reputation is ruined. *A Soldier's Daughter and Other Stories* (1906) contains a novella, *A Raid by the Blacks*, in which Effie Roberts and her father fend off an attack by Aboriginal People, armed with blazing arrows, for four days. No whites are lost, but at least fifteen Aboriginal People are killed in retribution for the attack.

HEPWORTH, JOHN (1921–), born Pinjarra, WA, collaborated with Bob Ellis on *The Paper Boy* (1985) and *Top Kid* (1985), and with Steve Spears on *The Big*

Wish (1990), all of which were produced as part of the 'Winners' (q.v.) television series.

HEPWORTH, Dr T. S. (1916–85), born Brisbane, edited the *Australian Children's Newspaper* and *The A.B.C. Children's Hour Annual*. See **Annuals**. Hepworth was a director of the Australian Reading Research Foundation, and an officer with the Commonwealth Office of Education. In *Castaways of the Monoboola: a Story for Boys* (1948) Michael O'Brien and Stephen Barker, 16-year-old convicts transported for political crimes and poaching, are shipwrecked while being taken to more severe punishment. They live with Aboriginal People, and are pardoned by Governor Bourke at the end of the book. Hepworth used the advice and writings of Daisy Bates and the accounts of Eliza Fraser for his novel.

'Here's Humphrey', see **Humphrey B. Bear**

HETHERINGTON, NORMAN and **MARGARET**, see **Mr Squiggle**

HEWETT, ANITA. For *Honey Mouse and Other Stories* (1957) see **Animal Stories**.

Hey Phantom Singlet (1975) by Simon French, illustrated by Alex Nicholas, was awarded a Special Mention in the 1976 Book of the Year Awards. French was 17 when the novel was published, although he wrote it when he was about 14. Math's father is absent, his mother overworked, and his only adult male friend has left the district. On a school camp in the Snowy Mountains he and his friend, Stu, run away. Their plans come to grief, and Math returns to Sydney to find his father has returned. Details such as Math's passion for a fur hat and orange singlet heighten the novel's youthful style, and this study of a troubled boy sensitive to the feelings of others shows a remarkable maturity. See also **School Stories**.

HEYLEN, JILL (1942–), born Adelaide, teacher and editor, wrote *The Empire Strikes Again* (1981), with Wendy Legge and Graham Jenkin, a history kit on convicts for primary students. *Someone is Flying Balloons: Australian Poems for Children* (1983), illustrated by Kerry Argent, and *Rattling in the Wind: Australian Poems for Children* (1987), illustrated by Maire Smith, are collections of poems selected with Celia Jellett and edited by Jane Covernton.

High and Haunted Island (1964) by Nan Chauncy, illustrated by Victor Ambrus, was Commended in the 1965 Book of the Year Awards. Tess and Vicky are marooned, then found and taken to a remote and isolated island off the Tasmanian coast run by a religious group, the Circlists. They adjust to their life there, marry and have children, and are discovered by Tess's brother John who is sailing in the vicinity.

HIGHFIELD, ANNINA E. For *The Wayward Fern Fairy* (1930) see **Fairies**.

HILL, DEIRDRE (1925–), born Sydney, also writes as Deirdre O'Donnell. Hill spent her childhood in Northbridge, the setting for *Over the Bridge* (q.v., 1969). *Bridge of Dreams* (1982) follows the construction of the Sydney Harbour Bridge. Lydia Martin dislikes the bridge because it has caused her friends to move away, but when she meets Florrie O'Riley she learns to be more assertive and ambitious. As the great edifice arises over the Harbour, and the Depression looms, Lydia and Florrie become involved in the social and political upheavals of the time. We follow the families' fortunes over nine years, until the bridge is opened and the girls are ready for higher education. A faithful picture of family life is also an accurate portrait of the ups and downs of a long friendship. See also **Sydney**.

Hill has also explored the immigrant experience. Mario is a boy from Rome who stays with his Australian grandparents in *Mario Visits Australia* (1978), illustrated by Helena Karnolz. See also **Italians**. In *Flight from Fear* (1988) Tommy's mother and sister have been killed in an air raid during World War II. At Tiboorie his clothes are too hot and his shorts too long, but some sympathetic pilots and a friend ensure his eventual acceptance. In *The Smiling Madonna* (1989) Maria travels to her father's people in Siena after her mother's death. When it seems that her father wants to marry and stay on, Maria is resentful until a romance also blossoms for her. *A Writer's Rights* (1984) is a history of the Australian Society of Authors, for which Hill was executive secretary from 1971 to 1981.

HILL, ERNESTINE, see **HEM-MINGS, ERNESTINE**

HILL, ROBIN (1932–), born Brisbane, wrote and illustrated *Bushland and Seashore: an Australian Nature Adventure* (q.v., 1962).

HILL, W. FITZMAURICE (1898–), born Melbourne, was a writer and broadcaster for the ABC. He adapted Hans Andersen's and the Grimms' fairy stories for radio, and worked with Isobel Ann Shead and Elizabeth Ann Jenkins on the children's sessions. *Southward Ho with the Hentys … (q.v., 1953) is a historical novel, and *By Their Endeavours: a Pageant and Two One-Act Plays of the Pioneer Men and Women of Australia, who, "by Their Endeavours" made Australia a Nation* (1956) are historical dramas.

HILL, WILLIAM THOMAS wrote books on explorers, and *The Golden Quest: a Story of the Eureka Stockade* (1935). See **Eureka Stockade**; **Melbourne**. In *The Magic Spear: or, Camped with the Blacks* (1929) Harry Pascoe lives with Aboriginal People when he is lost, observing and admiring their culture.

HILLS, NOELA (1954–87), born Brisbane, studied graphic design at Brisbane College of Art and Printmaking and in London. She illustrated *Wild and Woolly* (1983) and *Prisoner of the Mulligrubs* (1985) by Nan Hunt; Alicia Braithwaite's *Angry Albert* (1987); and *Goanna* (1988) by Jenny Wagner. Hills's arresting pictures have spontaneity and overtones of pop art.

HILTON, NETTE (1946–), born Bairnsdale, Victoria, teacher and writer, has written picture books which reject conventional gender roles. In *The Long Red Scarf* (q.v., 1987) Grandpa learns to knit. *Prince Lachlan* (1989), illustrated by Ann James, is about a clumsy prince, the depair of his parents, until his lack of co-ordination routs the enemy Great One. In *Dirty Dave the Bushranger* (1987) the hero is tough, his sister Sue is rough, his mother Maude is fierce, but his father Dan just likes to sew. It is Dan who makes their fortune. In *The Hiccups* (1992), illustrated by Craig Smith, anxious Tim does a good deed which he knows is in his own self-interest, but which his mother and his rival Coralie interpret as kindness. Notions of timorous girls are questioned in *Good Morning, Isobel* (1990), illustrated by Robert Roennfeldt. In *A Proper Little Lady* (1989), illustrated by Cathy Wilcox, Annabella Jones delights in dressing in her best clothes, but finds that a pretty dress and smart shoes are inappropriate for climbing trees and playing football. See also **Girls**. *A Monstrous Story* (1989), illustrated by Donni Carter, is a story in verse in which a savage sea monster is converted to vegetarianism by a small girl. The townsfolk are then able to protect themselves with carrots and celery. In *The Friday Card* (1989), illustrated by George Aldridge, Cecilia, who has no father, defies convention and makes a Father's Day card for her mother. *The Web* (1992), illustrated by Kerry Millard, describes a relationship between Jenny and her great grandmother, Violet-Anne.

Hilton has contributed to reading schemes, with titles such as *Oobley-Gum Chasing Game* (1990) and *Alison Wendlebury* (1990). Nette Hilton suggests possibilities for boys and girls outside the conventional stereotypes, without preaching and with humour.

HINCHCLIFFE, JO. For *The Hilton Hen House* (1987) see **Alphabet Books**.

HIRST, ROBIN (1944–), born Leeds, UK, who came to Australia in 1951, and **SALLY** (1951–), born Swansea, UK, who came to Australia in 1975, are museum administrators. They wrote *My Place in Space* (q.v., 1988). Robin has also written material on astronomy for young people.

Hist!, a poem by C.J. Dennis, published in 1921 in *A Book for Kids* and illustrated in 1991 by Peter Gouldthorpe, was an Honour Book in the 1992 Picture Book of the Year Awards. As three children come home through a park at night, the noises of an owl, a cat, and a frog seize their imaginations to create unseen terrors. These temporary fears are actualised in Gouldthorpe's black linocuts, within borders which tell a story of their own.

Historical Novels. Major contributions to the historical novel have been made by Mavis Thorpe Clark, Nance Donkin, Judith O'Neill, Ruth Park, Eleanor Spence, and David Martin. Writers of historical fiction have concentrated on the period since white invasion, although some have touched on the first collision between black and white. *Manganinnie* (1979) by Beth Roberts attempts a description of the feelings of a woman whose people have been killed, and Amy Bunker's *Millingi* (1973) has the girl observing early white landings. Novels such as *Tangara: 'Let Us set off Again'* (q.v., 1960) and *Mathinna's People* (q.v., 1967) by Nan Chauncy, *Hills of the Black Cockatoo*

(1981) by Pat Peatfield Price, and *Yagan of the Bibbulmun* (1974) by Mary Durack look at the conflict from a white view-point, but attempt to reconstruct the impact on Aboriginal People. See **Aboriginal People in Children's Fiction**.

One approach to white Australian histo-ry for children has been through the his-torical fantasy. Ruth Hawker's *Yesterday: Being the Adventures of Us Three with the Early Colonists* (1936) is an early time-slip fantasy set against colonial life in SA. The period in which Abigail finds herself in Ruth Park's *Playing Beatie Bow* (q.v., 1980) is central to the story. Park has researched Victorian life carefully and re-creates the streets of nineteenth-century Sydney. Attention to historical detail is also seen in Nadia Wheatley's *The House that was Eureka* (q.v., 1984), which contrasts the difficulties facing young people in Sydney in the Depression of the 1930s with the problems of the late twentieth century; two historical periods also used by Goldie Alexander in *Mavis Road Medley* (1991) set in Melbourne.

Historical events have provided a source for novelists. Paul Buddee's *The Escape of the Fenians* (1971) deals with the daring rescue of Irish political prisoners in the WA *Catalpa* incident; Allan Baillie's *Riverman* (1986) recreates the Tasmanian mine disaster of 1912 at Zeehan; and the massacre of the Chinese on the goldfields informs David Martin's *The Chinese Boy* (1973), which is loosely based on the events at Lambing Flat. There are novels on the Eureka Stockade and the gold rushes (qq.v.). Historical figures also appear. Arthur Phillip walks the deck in *John of the Sirius* (q.v., 1955) by Doris Chadwick; W.C. Wentworth appears as a shadowy figure in Eleanor Spence's *Jambaroo Road* (1969); Verity is presented to Governor Macquarie in Ruth Williams's *Verity of Sydney Town* (q.v., 1950), and the same eminence rides by in Nance Donkin's *The Best of the Bunch* (1978).

Joyce Nicholson's *The Convict's Daughter* (1976) shows life on the convict ships and the squalor of convict life. Early colonial times provided inspiration for *Verity of Sydney Town*, Eve Pownall's *Cousins-Come-Lately* (q.v., 1952) and Nance Donkin's *The Best of the Bunch* (1978), the last book providing a clearer picture of the times than either the Williams or the Pownall. Donkin looks at the seamier side of the first white settle-ment, presenting the necessary resource-fulness required for survival in Sydney in the 1820s, where Girlie makes a living as a 'finder', just short of thief. Donkin has written other historical novels, including *Two at Sullivan Bay* (1985), about the first white settlement in Victoria, near Sorrento, in 1803. Ruth Park's *Come Danger, Come Darkness* (q.v., 1978) explores the relationships between jailers and convicts on Norfolk Island, through the eyes of Octavius. Melva Lear's recre-ation of the landing at Albany, WA, *A Secret to Sell: a Story of the First Settlement in Western Australia* (1965), is based on the writings of Major Lockyer, who was in charge of the settlement. The novel recounts the activities of Snark, a convict, and two children of a soldier, Robert and Charlotte. Lear presents a sanitised picture of black–white relationships, although her characterisation is convincing and her research excellent. Kate Walker's *The Letters of Rosie O'Brien: a Convict in the Colony of New South Wales 1804* (1988), illustrated by Paul Borg, also provides an understanding of early settlement, and the injustices of transportation. Judith Wright's *The River and the Road* (1966) draws attention to the injustice meted out to many of the convicts when they were assigned to callous masters.

The vicissitudes of early white settle-ment are drawn in *West of Sunset* (1949) by the historian Margaret Kiddle, which details the experience in western NSW, and Diana Mercer's *Cows Can't Eat Cedar* (1957), which is set on the Clarence and Richmond Rivers. *Baker's Dozen* (1969) by Celia Syred is the story of an immigrant family during the 1860s; Ira Nesdale's *The Bay Whalers* (1985) deals with the harsh life on a whaling station in the nineteenth century, *Deepwaterman* (1988) by 'Helen Frances' with seafaring life in the same period. Catherine Shepherd's *Tasmanian Adventure* (1964) is set in Van Diemen's Land in 1825. The Crome family enjoy a charmed life as they camp out, build their house, fight off bushrangers, reap a bumper harvest, and finally call Australia home in this romantic picture of pioneering outside Hobart. Mavis Thorpe Clark's *The Brown Land was Green* (q.v., 1956) and *The Blue Above the Trees* (q.v., 1967) provide more realistic insights into early Portland and Gippsland. Eleanor Spence's *The Family Book of Mary-Claire* (q.v., 1990) is at its best describing the first Clevelands, escaped convicts, but the later descendants are also shown in the context of increasing settlement on the northern rivers of NSW. The expansion of settlement into the hinterland is recalled in Will Lawson's *When Cobb and Co. was King* (1937), a colourful picture of coaching times in Victoria and NSW, and Denys Burrows's *Stagecoach West* (1964), which describes the decline of the coaches when the railway was extended to Bathurst, and the construction of the Great Zig-Zag at Lithgow. Judith O'Neill's *Stringybark Summer* (1985) highlights the disruption of the change from horses to engines in the logging camps of the early twentieth century. O'Neill's *So Far from Skye* (1992) is a poignant account of the immigration of Scottish crofters to Victoria during the 1850s.

Margaret Paice's *Colour in the Creek* (1976) and *Shadow of Wings* (1978) recall Depression times, in 1932 and 1933. Paice draws a grim picture as the Fletcher family travel through the country looking for work, and her use of historical detail, such as the swagmen who work for a meal, the bitterness of the unemployed, and the stress on the children, forced to make do with less than ideal conditions, gives the

reader a rich understanding of hard times. Using the format of a picture-book, Ian Edwards's *Papa and the Olden Days* (1989), illustrated by Rachel Tonkin, evokes turn-of-the-century life in a rural town through closely observed illustrations of a general store.

Nadia Wheatley and Donna Rawlins's *My Place* (q.v., 1987) is an outstanding contribution to the genre. Wheatley and Rawlins have taken one place and traced it back to its origins to show the history of Australia, from the present, when the Moreton Bay fig gives way to a McDonalds fast-food store, to the past, when the traditional owners belonged to the place. See also **Eureka Stockade**; **First Fleet**; **Gold Rushes**; **War**.

Hobart is the capital city of Tasmania, or Van Diemen's Land, as it was known until 1854. In Richard Rowe's *Roughing it in Van Diemen's Land* (1880) the Norman family's first impressions must reflect those of many travellers who finally arrived in Tasmania: 'The magnificent estuary of the Derwent up which they sailed, looking, when the sunlight fell upon it, like polished steel inlaid with gold, seemed a sweet haven of peace after the wild waste of waters over which they had wandered. In the distance, Mount Wellington raised his hoary head — snow on his summit, and fern of almost tropical luxuriance on his sides.' 'Helen Frances's' *Edge of Fear* (1986) describes the city in 1821. 'Why it's little more than a village in a wilderness … All I can see is hovels', says Margaret MacDonald when her ship arrives. The town is further described: 'Hobart Town huddled at the foot of Table Mountain no bigger than a fishing village … Close to the waterfront stood a fine new church and the rambling pile of wooden buildings that was the Governor's residence.' For contemporary writers, the rugged interior of Tasmania is a more inspiring setting than this old and picturesque city on the Derwent River.

Hobyahs, according to Katharine Briggs in *The Personnel of Fairyland* (1953), are 'a nasty swarm of malignant fairies ... different from the generally harmless hobs. A dog is great protection against them.' Joseph Jacobs in *More English Fairy Tales* (1894) ascribes his source as *American Folk-Lore Journal*, iii, 173, for the version of the Hobyahs which appears in his collection, and remarks that the Hobyahs originated in Scotland. The creatures became well known in Victoria because of the version of the tale published in the Victorian Reader's Second Book. In the Australian version, it is 'the little old woman' who is taken by the Hobyahs, not a little girl, and Dog Turpie's name is changed to Dingo.

HOCKING, GEOFF (1947–), born Bendigo, Victoria, is an illustrator and graphic designer. He illustrated *The Boy Who Painted the Sun* (1983) by Jill Morris; *Adventures at Bangotcher Junction* (1985) by Morris and Mary Lancaster; and *I Shot an Arrow* (1987) by Robin Klein. He wrote and illustrated *It's One World* (1989), which describes a day at school when all the children wear their national costumes. Hocking also illustrated *'We'll All be Rooned' said Hanrahan* (1991), a classic poem about an eternal pessimist, written by 'John O'Brien' (P.J. Hartigan 1879–1952).

HODGES, MORWELL (b.1896). For *Bob Berrell in North Australia* (1947) see **War**.

HODGETTS, JAMES FREDERICK (1828–1906) wrote *Tom's Nugget: a Story of the Australian Goldfields* (1888). In 1851, when Tom is a child, Mr Hardy takes the family in search of gold, via Melbourne and Geelong. At his first sight of the city, he comments, 'A fouler sink of iniquity than Melbourne in 1852 cannot be imagined.' At 'Bendiggerat' the precocious Tom finds an enormous nugget which makes their fortunes. He twice saves the life of an older boy, rescues his father from a gambling den, nurses both parents back to health simultaneously, is rewarded by the Governor for taking prisoner Captain Galton, 'chief of the bushrangers', all when he is only 8 years old. After a time in England Tom returns to Port Phillip, visits the person who had bought the nugget from him, and then inherits it when the owner dies. The good fortune of the Hardy family arises from their superior gentility, which carries them through straitened circumstances and lifts them above the rough ways of other diggers.

Hodja Educational Resources Cooperative was a non-profit organisation founded by the Schools Commission in 1981 to produce teaching materials for multicultural education. Hodja produced a series, 'Hodja's Australian Stories for Kids', acknowledging the multicultural nature of Australian society, and focusing on various factors of culture, such as ethnicity, class, gender, age and religion. Titles include *Papou and the Magician* (1983), *Ali's Holiday* (1983) and *Vietnam, Australia and Me* (1985). *Kaiyu's Waiting* (1984), by the Aboriginal storyteller Maureen Watson, is set in Sydney. Kaiyu waits for a present to wear on National Aboriginal Day. Another series was aimed at teachers, the 'Hodja's Festival' series, which included *New Year for Children, Easter for Children* and *Christmas for Children* (all 1982) by Cavell Zangalis. Hodja also published Magda Bozic's *Gather Your Dreams* (1985), the story of an immigrant coming to terms with Australia.

HOLDEN, ROBERT (1948–), was the director of the Museum of Australian Childhood. *The Fairy World of Ida Rentoul Outhwaite* (1985), with Marcie Muir, is a biography and analysis of Outhwaite's work. *D.H. Souter's Cats* (1988) looks at the graphic style of Souter, and *Twinkle, Twinkle, Southern Cross: the Forgotten Folklore of Australian Nursery Rhymes* (1992) is a historical account of lesser known verse for children. Holden has written a history of photography in early Australia, *Photography in Colonial Australia: The Mechanical Eye and the Illustrated Book* (1988).

Hole in the Hill, The (1961), Ruth Park's first children's novel, illustrated by Jennifer Murray, was Commended in the 1962 Book of the Year Awards. Two Australian children, Dunk and Brownie, explore their NZ property with Tom te Taniwha, discovering sacred caves of the ancient Maoris. A shorter version first appeared in the NSW *School Magazine*.

HOLE, QUENTIN (1923–), born Charleville, Queensland, is a painter and designer. He has worked in theatre, television and opera, and was responsible for the design of the television production of *Seven Little Australians* (q.v., 1894). His illustrations for *The Man from Ironbark* (1974) and *A Bush Christening* by A.B. Paterson (1976) have the unsophisticated style of early twentieth-century Australia. *How to Demolish a Monster* (1981) is set in the lush subtropical scenery of a banana plantation. Paul talks his way through Danny's imaginary monsters, as the two boys take their father his lunch. When they meet a real frill-necked lizard, Paul is terrified and Danny not at all afraid. 'Meet anything interesting on the way?' asks father. 'Nothing much,' replies Danny. The static human figures of the boys emerge from a fantastic background of dramatic monsters. In *Dancing Phoebe and the Famous Mumblegum Piano* (1987) Phoebe loves to dance, but her mother thinks it unladylike and has her taught the piano. When a fire destroys the piano, Phoebe can return to dancing, to finally become the greatest dancer in the world, 'better even than Ludmilla Hopsteppanova'.

HOLKNER, JEAN (1926–), born Perth, has written *Taking the Chook and Other Traumas* (1987), also published as

Aunt Becky's Wedding and Other Traumas (1989), a droll autobiographical account of a Jewish childhood in Melbourne. See also **Melbourne**. *Children of the New Galaxy* (1989) is a humorous short story collection. *Aviva Gold* (1992) is set in Palestine in the 1930s, when Aviva and her family return to Haifa to what her father hopes will be an ideal life. But the times, like the family, are troubled, and Aviva's feelings mirror the dislocation. Holkner has also written literature texts for schools.

HOLLOWAY, EDGAR A. (c.1870– 1941), born Bradford, UK, had completed a series of watercolours on the uniforms of famous British regiments before he came to Australia in 1930. He contributed to the *Sydney Morning Herald* and the *Sydney Mail*, the annual *Pals*, illustrated George Bruce's *The Lion's Son* (1928), Bartlett Adamson's *Mystery Gold* (1926) and some of Constance Mackness's novels. He wrote and illustrated *Tiny Toddler's A.B.C.* (1931) for John Sands's 'Sunny South' series.

HOLMAN, ADA AUGUSTA (1869– 1949), born Ballarat, Victoria, novelist, was an active feminist, married to William Holman, Premier of NSW. *Little Miss Anzac, the True Story of an Australian Doll* (1917), reissued as *The Adventures of Woodeny* (1923), illustrated by Nellie Rodd, portrays the innocent misdemeanours of Molly and her doll through an amusing, anecdotal story of the gradual destruction through 'adventures' of the much-loved Woodeny. Woodeny survives a series of potential usurpers in her young owner's affections to the point where she is *sans* arms, legs, hair — even face. *Elka-Reva-Ree, a Story for Children* (1931) continues the domestic crises of Molly, still accompanied by Woodeny. They include going to the beach where the inquisitive Molly has her finger caught in a wooden seat, and playing her own interminable tunes on the piano to a frantic father.

Molly is a vigorous and independent child, and her exploits are astutely observed.

Home in the Sky (1984) by Jeannie Baker was Commended in the 1985 Picture Book of the Year Awards. Using her skilful collage technique, Baker creates a picture of New York. The pigeon, Light, flies over Central Park and travels in the subway until he is almost adopted by a boy before returning home to his owner, Mike. The bird's eye perspectives and three-dimensional effects are brilliantly realised.

HONEY, ELIZABETH (1947–), born Wonthaggi, Victoria, studied film and television at Swinburne College of Technology. Honey has illustrated a variety of publications, including reading schemes, such as Cheshire's 'Trend' and Macmillan's 'Southern Cross' series; informational books such as *Growing Things: Nature Study Ideas for the Primary School* (1979), and *History at Your Fingertips* (1979), both by Brian McKinlay; her own *Princess Beatrice and the Rotten Robber* (1988), and longer works. Her range is demonstrated in the exuberant sketches of endearing and lumbering beasts of *The 27th Annual African Hippopotamus Race* (q.v., 1977) by Morris Lurie and the reflective portraits in Christobel Mattingley's *Brave with Ben* (1982) and William Mayne's *Salt River Times* (1980).

HONEY, ENNIS JOSEPHINE (1919–), journalist and music teacher, wrote historical features for the Argonauts (q.v.). *Janey of Beechlands* (1947) is a school story about a scholarship girl who is received coldly by the other girls because of her dowdy clothes. She wins popularity by being friendly with Wendy, finding invisible ink on a plan and discovering a secret passage. Books for younger children include *Jennifer Jane* (1947), illustrated by L.G. Jordan (see **Fairies**), *Busy Mr Toot-Toot* (1948), illustrated by Gloria Bowiner,

Three Little Bunnies (1948), illustrated by Marjorie Pritchard, and *Mother Goose* (1946), illustrated by Rufus Morris (see **Nursery Rhymes**).

HONEY, LUCY MADELEINE (1890–1943), born Sydney, was the niece of Ethel Turner and the first wife of William Henry Honey. While living in NZ, Honey edited the children's pages of newspapers as 'Aunt Roberta'. *Dancing Lady* (1946) traces the domestic crises in a growing family. Little Boo, the dancer, gladly gives up a career for marriage to the man of her dreams. *The Secrets of River Valley* (1947), told with frequent capital letters and exclamation marks, is the story of the Meredith family, beset by alcoholism, poverty, and neighbours they do not like. *Diana* (1948) describes the pranks of Diana and her sisters and the romance between their widowed father and Miss Thompson, the governess. Lucy edited William Honey's journal *Youth*.

HONEY, WILLIAM HENRY (1879–1959), born Melbourne, was a Sydney publisher who also wrote his own material. He worked in advertising, and was responsible for Christmas pageants in the Sydney Town Hall during the 1920s and 1930s, such as 'A Dream of Fair Women'. Rufus Morris illustrated *The Story of Hanky, Panky* (1945) in Honey's 'Golliwog' series, *A Mother Goose Fantasy*, and *Smookie & Co.* (1947). *The Exciting Adventures of Smookie* (1945) was illustrated by L.G. Jordan. Smookie is a mouse who seeks advice from the other animals to outwit the cunning cat, Dusky. Honey also wrote *How They Coloured Australia* (1945), verse, and *A Mother Goose Fantasy and Other Stories* (?1944). *The Story of Towser* (1945) began a series of four Towser books, the last being *Another Story of Towser* (?1945), illustrated by L.G. Jordan. They are stories about a pup in rough blank verse: 'And Towser then lived the life of a lord until very restless he grew./One day he resolved, "I must go abroad, fresh parts of the big world to view."/The passion for goodness stayed with him such a very short while, I deplore,/and mischievous thoughts came to him so much and tempted him more and still more.' Honey published a children's paper, *Young Australia*, in 1923, which ran for a year, and *Youth*, which ran from 1930 to 1932. Two Christmas annuals arose from *Youth*: *Youth Annual* (1930) and *Father Time's Christmas Annual* (also 1930). See **Annuals**. There is a monument in Melbourne to William Honey's brother, Edward George Honey, who was responsible for the introduction of the two minutes' silence kept in November each year in memory of the Armistice after World War I.

HOOK, JEFF (GEOFF) (1928–), born Hobart, is a cartoonist and illustrator, whose work has appeared in the Melbourne *Sun*. *Kangapossum and Crocoroo* (1969) by David Rankine is in verse. Each page is split, so that fantastic creatures are made when the half-pages are turned. In the picture-book *Jamie the Jumbo Jet* (1971) Jamie tires of the constant racing from continent to continent, and deserts Captain Machbuster to join his African friends, the Elephants. His adventures with them make him happy to return to his old life. Jeff Hook illustrated Osmar White's *The Super-Roo of Mungalongaloo* (1973), *The Further Adventures of Dr. A.A.A. McGurk M.D.* (1981) and *McGurk and the Lost Atoll* (1983). *Animal Olympics* (1982) by Stan Marks is a variation on the race between the tortoise and the hare, this time won by Ron Reindeer. Hook's humorous, exaggerated illustrations for *Operation Lily-liver: a Shadow Play* (1987) by Dianne Bates and Bill Condon, *Tall Tales from the Speewah: Australian Stories that are Bigger and Better* (1988) by Maureen Stewart and *Ladles and Jellyspoons: Favourite Riddles and Jokes of Australian Children* (1989) by June Factor all contain his hidden insignia, a hook.

HOOLEY, EDWARD TIMOTHY (1842–1903), writer and explorer, was born at sea on the *Bolivar*. After exploration in WA, he worked in the pearling industry, then became a pastoralist. *Tarragal: or, Bush Life in Australia* (1897) was written while he was 'whiling away the lonely evening hours spent in a bush-hut in North-West Australia while engaged in forming a new sheep-station in that isolated portion of her Majesty's dominions'. 'Tarragal' itself is situated on the southern coast of Victoria, where the Forrester family, particularly Edwin, experience romance, excitement, adventure and danger. Edwin outwits the infamous bushranger, Gardiner, finds a fortune in gold from the *Batavia* and marries Ida, to live happily ever after. See **Adventure Stories**; **Chinese**.

HOOPER, MEREDITH (1939–) is a writer and historian. *Everyday Inventions* (q.v., 1972) and *More Everyday Inventions* (1976) describe the small items we use constantly. *The Story of Australia* (1974), beautifully illustrated by Elaine Haxton, presents Australian history from the first European landings until after World War II, in a conversational style. The text is interspersed with personal anecdotes from ordinary people. With Manning Clark, she wrote *The Ashton Scholastic History of Australia* (1988), illustrated by Susanne Ferrier. Hooper wrote the first twenty-three chapters using Manning Clark's multi-volume history and other sources; Clark wrote the last chapter. *Doctor Hunger and Captain Thirst: Stories of Australian Explorers* (1983) deals with the explorations of Eyre, Sturt, Burke and Wills and others, and *God 'elp All of Us* (1986) is an account of three important flights by Ross Smith, Bert Hinkler and Kingsford Smith. She has also written *A for Antarctica: Facts and Stories from the Frozen South* (1991), illustrated by Sally Townsend. *The Journal of Watkin Stench* (1988) is a novel about a rat who arrives on the First Fleet, the title a parody of the diary kept by Watkins Tench, an officer in the First Fleet. Watkin sees the Hefties and Skirts as clumsy incompetents. The more terrifying Locals are a different matter.

HOOVER, LATHARO was a US writer who wrote adventures about a group of boys set in many locations, such as the Brazilian wilderness, the African jungle, Borneo and the Philippines. *The Camp-Fire Boys in Australian Gold Fields* (1932) are Dick, Waddy, Hal and Dr Miller, forced down in Queensland when their biplane fails. Among their adventures in the 'canyons', 'corrals' and 'trails' of Australia is an attack by a bird six foot high and covered in coarse hair. Their courage and virtue is rewarded by the discovery of huge nuggets of gold.

HORDER, MARGARET L'ANSON (1903–78), born Sydney, studied at the Julian Ashton School and in London. She illustrated for the Melbourne *Sun* and the *Australian Woman's Mirror* during the 1920s, and worked in England for OUP in the 1930s. She illustrated children's books in England, including *A Laverlock Lilting* (1945) by Dorita Fairlie Bruce and *The Vanishing Boy* (1949) by Dale Collins, which is set in London. *They Found a Cave* (1948) by Nan Chauncy was her first children's book set in Australia, for which she was commissioned by Frank Eyre of OUP. 'Here was something from home, something I could get my teeth into!' she said. Horder returned to Australia in 1949.

The 'Blue Wren' series (q.v.) was largely her inspiration, and she wrote and illustrated *Moongrabah: an Australian Aboriginal Legend* (1951) for the series. She went on to illustrate *A Fortune for the Brave* (1954) and *Tiger in the Bush* (q.v., 1957) for Chauncy; *Good Luck to the Rider* (q.v., 1953), *Six and Silver* (1954), *It Happened One Summer* (1957), *The Boundary Riders* (1962), *The Family Conspiracy* (q.v., 1962), *Threat to the Barkers* (q.v., 1963) and *Birkin* (1965) for Joan Phipson; *The Crooked Snake* (q.v., 1955), *The Bunyip Hole* (q.v., 1958), *The Rocks of Honey* (1960), *Down to Earth* (1965), *'I own the Racecourse!'* (q.v., 1968) for Patricia Wrightson; and *Songs for All Seasons: 100 Poems for Young People* (1967) for Rosemary Dobson. She illustrated *Listening Time: "Kindergarten of the Air" Stories and Verses* (1961). Horder superintended the design of Phipson's *It Happened One Summer*, which is remarkable in the books of the period for its integration of illustration and text. Horder and her husband, Arthur Freeman, were active in the CBC, and Margaret designed the medal for the Book of the Year Awards.

Horder brought back to Australia her strong overseas experience in illustration and her serious commitment to design. She worked closely and enthusiastically with the authors whose work she was illustrating, so that her pictures not only interpret but expand the text. Horder set new standards in Australian book illustration.

HORNER, ARTHUR (1916–), born Melbourne, is a cartoonist who created the 'Colonel Pewter' comic-strip in 1952 while living in Britain. The strip appeared for almost twenty years in various papers, including the Melbourne *Age*. Horner returned to Melbourne in the late 1960s. He illustrated Morris Lurie's *Toby's Millions* (q.v., 1982).

Horse stories. Unlike their English counterparts who have preferred to write about pony clubs, Australian writers of horse stories have been attracted to the brumby horses which inhabit the wilder places of Australia. The best known of these is the series by Elyne Mitchell about Silver Brumby (q.v.) and his various offspring and Mary Elwyn Patchett's 'Brumby' series. Mitchell and Patchett both have an understanding of horses and riding and a wide knowledge of the ways of the brumby herds. Henry Lamond is another authoritative writer about horses, displayed in *Amathea, the Story of a Horse* (1937).

The affection which their owners have for horses is examined in Reginald Ottley's *Roan Colt of Yamboorah* (1966) and Nan Chauncy's *The Skewbald Pony* (1965). In the latter Carrie longs for a skewbald but is eventually won over to Chark, the horse she has to bring back to health. Eugene Lumbers's *A Taste for Blue Ribbons* (1969) describes the struggle to keep a foal with five legs which has been rescued from slaughter. James Aldridge's *A Sporting Proposition* (1973) is about a Welsh pony and the legal and moral battle over whether the horse really belongs to Scott or Josie. Aldridge's *The Broken Saddle* (1982) and *The Marvellous Mongolian* (1974) are novels about horses and horse-riding.

Competitive horse-riding has had its enthusiasts in Australian books for children, often providing for girls what cricket has done for boys — a test of character. In Joan Phipson's *Good Luck to the Rider* (q.v., 1953) Barbara learns to ride Rosinante, developing her confidence in the process. Dinah, in Meg Lewis's *It All Began with Calamity* (1962), trains a wild roan horse to the point where she and Calamity win a blue ribbon at the Granthorpe Show, although it is the character of the horse which is on trial not the character of the heroine. Less a test of character than a reward for hard work is the prize awarded to each of the McDonald girls in Nance Donkin's *Blue Ribbon Beth* (1951). Beth wins a blue ribbon for riding and her sister Mollie wins the prestigious riding prize, the Garryowen, at the Royal Melbourne Show. Mavis Thorpe Clark uses the same show in *Pony from Tarella* (1959). Jean Dixon's *Blue Fire Lady* (1977) is another success story of a young rider, and in Betty Roberts's *A Pony to Keep* (1985) Natalie, who rides her mother's horses before they are sold, is able to train her own horse when she wins one in an essay competition.

The affinity between child and horse, whether wild brumby or show pony, has been a fruitful source for children's writers since Anna Sewell's *Black Beauty* (1877) galloped across the page.

HOULDING, JOHN RICHARD (1822–1918), born Essex, UK, arrived in Sydney in 1839, spent a year in NZ and returned to Sydney where he kept a store. Houlding wrote short stories under seventeen pseudonyms. *Launching Away; or, Roger Larksway's Strange Mission* (1882) is about a new chum sheep farmer on an outback station. *In the Depths of the Sea* (1885) written by 'Old Boomerang' describes the life of Ben who finds employment in a factory in Flinders Street for fifty shillings a week, spends time at the Melbourne Free Library and joins a school of design in Carlton. Houlding's books were popular as Sunday school prizes.

House Guest, The (1991) by Eleanor Nilsson won the 1992 Book of the Year Awards: Older Readers. Gunno and a gang of children who call themselves the Home Burglary Service rob houses for money. During one expedition Gunno is intrigued by a bedroom which has been occupied by a missing boy Hugh. Gunno explores Hugh's past and finds an empathy with him which takes him to Hugh's last moments. The experience which Gunno undergoes leads to a resolution of his uncertainties about his mother and brings a sort of peace to Hugh's mother. The destinies of Gunno and Hugh are slowly revealed, and their subtle connections with the adults are thrown into focus.

House that was Eureka, The (1985) by Nadia Wheatley was Commended in the 1986 Book of the Year Awards. Two adjoining houses exist in the 1930s and

the 1980s. Both times converge as historical events increasingly impinge on Noel
and Evie, the contemporary young people, who are paralleled by Nobby and
Lizzie from the earlier time. The events
which trigger the convergence are the
evictions in the Depression and a campaign to assist the unemployed of the
1980s. Wheatley uses political writing,
including that of Karl Marx, songs, children's rhymes, letters and newspaper
reports to create the atmosphere of both
historical periods. See also **Historical
Novels**; **Sydney**.

HOWDEN, MARJORIE BEATRICE
(1911–88), born Melbourne, studied and
taught at RMIT. She painted murals for
public institutions in Melbourne, including the Royal Children's Hospital in 1962,
the Altona Public Library and the
Victorian School for the Deaf in 1974.
She illustrated many of the Victorian
School Papers and Readers, including *John
and Betty* (1951), *Playmates* (1952) and
Holidays (1953) and contributed illustrations to *High Spirits* (1963), *Roundabout*
(?1964) and *Gather Round* (1965). She
wrote and illustrated *Half-Way House*
(1951). Howden observed the details of
daily life and with simplicity of line displayed the pleasure of helping mother or
running on the beach. Apart from her

murals and illustrations, Howden exhibited her landscapes and flora and fauna studies at the Victorian Artists' Society and the
Lyceum Club.

HOWITT, WILLIAM (1792–1879),
born Heanor, Darbyshire, UK, and his
wife, Mary Botham Howitt, wrote many
books for children and were active in literary life, numbering Hans Christian
Andersen among their friends. William
spent two years on the Victorian gold-
diggings, arriving in 1852 aboard the *Kent*
with his two sons, Alfred and Charlton. *A
Boy's Adventures in the Wilds of Australia, or,
Herbert's Notebook* (1854) is based on these
experiences. It is a witty and enjoyable
story told by a fluent raconteur with a
'keen and detailed vision' (Green, *A
History of Australian Literature*). Herbert's
adventures are embellished with the experiences of those he meets. Life in the outback, including hunting for lost cattle,
bushfires and floods and the frantic pursuit
of gold on the diggings is interspersed
with acute observation of the natural environment. See also **Adventure Stories;
Bunyips; Bush; Bushfire; Gold
Rushes**. Howitt contributed a short story
to *The Boy's Birth-Day Book: a Collection of
Tales, Essays, and Narratives of Adventure*
(1864): 'Nipper and Toby, the Australian
Shepherd Boys'. Nipper is a stowaway and

Holidays (1953). Illustrator: Marjorie Howden

Toby a 'steward's fag'. They jump ship at Hobson's Bay to set off for the diggings and on the way are employed as shepherds by Mr Lassetter, fight off wild dogs, intercept bushrangers and remain at Lassetter's station at Upotipotpon. Howitt wrote a novel for adults set in Australia, *Tallangetta, the Squatter's Home* (1857). Alfred Howitt later settled in Victoria where he wrote a book about the Aboriginal People of south-east Australia and led the search party which found King, the only survivor of the Burke and Wills Expedition.

HOWSON, JOHN MICHAEL (1936–), born Melbourne. See **Adventure Island**.

Hughie (1971) by David Martin, illustrated by Ron Brooks, was Commended in the 1972 Book of the Year Awards. Hughie opposes the segregation of the new Merringee swimming pool and calls on his cousin who brings a busload of students from Sydney to help. Hughie and his school friend Clancy fall out, but their friendship is restored when Clancy refuses to compete in the swimming championships and returns to the river with Hughie. The novel has been criticised because it suggests that Hughie's artistic and athletic gifts are inherent to his Aboriginality, but this early attempt to present a modern boy taking a determined stand in defence of his rights and its support for Aboriginal militancy broke new ground in the representation of Aboriginal People.

Hugh's Zoo (1964) by Elisabeth MacIntyre won the 1965 Picture Book of the Year Awards. Hugh decides to make a zoo. He puts a kookaburra in a cage, a wombat in the dog's house, a koala in a wardrobe, a kangaroo in a clothes-peg bag and a platypus in a tub. The animals are not at all grateful and when Hugh goes walking he finds that they are much happier in the bush. Hugh and the animals are represented in bold stylised illustrations in three colours.

Humour. Tall stories, the ridicule of human foibles, verbal dexterity, slapstick, the scatalogical, and ludicrous incongruities abound in children's books. The irreverent humour of Norman Lindsay's *The Magic Pudding* (q.v., 1918) with its cheeky language, boisterous verse and eccentric characters sets the scene for subsequent comic novels with a distinctive Australian flavour. Lindsay's command of the insult is inventive. 'Of all the swivel-eyed, up-jumped, cross-grained, sons of a cross-eyed tinker ... If punching parrots on the beak wasn't too painful for pleasure, I'd land you a sockdolager on the muzzle that ud lay you out till Christmas.'

Lindsay uses satire, a tradition continued in *Midnite* (1967) by Randolph Stow, where the fearsomeness of the bushranger is mocked in the timid thick-headed Midnite, a bushranger doomed to failure were it not for his brilliant cat Khat. In a similar vein Osmar White's books about McGurk and his faithful Afghan Camel Cathie Khan, *The Super-Roo of Mungalongaloo* (1973), *The Further Adventures of Dr. A.A.A. McGurk M.D.* (1981) and *McGurk and the Lost Atoll* (1983) take the reader on outrageous adventures and laugh at the Australian idiom and landscape. Super-Roo is the head animal at the Willawallawalla waterhole at the foot of the Mungalongaloo mountains near the Deadibone Desert. Geoffrey McSkimming works within the traditions of Osmar White and Max Dann, but provides an exotic setting in *Cairo Jim & Doris: In Search of Martenarten* (1991). Doris is a Shakespeare-quoting macaw who reads hieroglyphs and with Cairo Jim, the archeologist and awful poet, and the redoubtable Brenda the wonder camel, they discover the tomb of the Pharoah Martenarten. Cairo Jim reappears in the Peruvian jungle in *Cairo Jim on the Trail to Chacha Muchos* (1992).

Patrick Cook's Elmer in *Elmer the Rat* (1980), *Elmer Makes a Break* (1982), *Elmer Runs Wild* (1986) and *Elmer Rides the Rails* (1991) is the eternal pessimist to whom the worst always happens. Peter Dusting, Roger Thesaurus and Grotty in Max Dann's *Adventures with My Worst Best Friend* (1982), *Going Bananas* (1983) and *Dusting in Love* (1990) are optimists but their optimism is based on such a lack of realism that, inevitably, their plans go awry in the most unlikely way. 'The Headmaster had said that the best place for Dusting was somewhere quiet and as far away as possible from contact with other human beings' after 'he set fire to the music room and burnt half of it down trying to electrify his drums'. Margaret Clark's *Pugwall* (1987) suffers from the same problems as Dusting and Maurice Gleitzman's Keith in *Misery Guts* (q.v., 1991) and *Worry Warts* (1991) is constantly putting his foot in it, although with the best of intentions. After he has painted the fish shop in tropical mango tint to cheer up his parents, he 'half-closed his eyes and banged himself on the head with his knuckles to see what it would look like with temporary (*sic*) bad eyesight due to a tension headache'.

Irreverence is the source of Doug MacLeod's humour in *Sister Madge's Book of Nuns* (q.v., 1986), a catalogue of the snuff-taking, motor-bike riding nuns in the Convent of Our Lady of Immense Proportions. Paul Jennings often uses children's delight in the scatalogical for his short stories, such as 'Birdscrap' in *Unbelievable!* (q.v., 1986) or 'Cowdung Custard' in *Unreal!* (q.v., 1985), combining it with a strong ear for dialogue. In *The Paw Thing* (q.v., 1989) the cat earns its name by swallowing and then defecating a transistor radio, hence — Singenpoo. In *All in the Blue Unclouded Weather* (1991) by Robin Klein, the girls carve a vulgar alphabet into the plaster surrounding the fireplace: 'A for Abscess, B for Buttock, C for Catsick ...', and play a rude game called 'Rin-Tin-Tin with a Rusty Sword'

where the potstick is twirled in the lavatory pan, or lie on the conveyor belt at the sawmill playing 'The Perils of Pauline'.

Penny Pollard (q.v.) in the Penny Pollard series and Erica Yurken in *Hating Alison Ashley* (1984) by Robin Klein display their original view of the world providing an unexpectedness which draws laughter. In the latter, Erica's sister Jedda imagines herself as a horse and Erica responds with 'I wasn't going to walk through Barringa East with a little kid who whinnied and got down on her hands and knees to eat the grass on people's nature strips.'

Judith Clarke's Al Capsella in *The Heroic Life of Al Capsella* (1988) suffers adolescent angst because he is embarrassed by his eccentric parents and very conventional grandparents. 'Mrs Capsella does the one thing a parent should never do: she stands out. She's like an alien who's dropped in from another planet and doesn't know the customs — and she doesn't even try to learn.' Wayne Wilson, in *Waxing with Wayne* (1991), is constantly outmanoeuvred by his parents, who are acutely aware of Wayne's transparent adolescent ploys.

We can be made to laugh at anything and the means by which our laughter is provoked are as various as the predicaments in which the characters in these novels find themselves.

Humphrey B. Bear is a television character. Humphrey originated in 1966 in Adelaide on a program designed for preschool children which began on the Nine Network, becoming national a few months later. The program has gone through various names, such as 'The Humphrey B. Bear Show', 'Humphrey' and 'Here's Humphrey'. Humphrey Bear Bear, aged about 4, is a child talking to children, suffering the same puzzles, pleasures and difficulties as the small people who watch him. The program has generated a series of books written by Gordon A. Rule, gathered together in *The Adventures of Humphrey Bear* (1974). *Here's*

Humphrey (1981), with contributions from various authors, has games, riddles, stories and activities.

HUNT, NAN (1918–), born Bathurst, NSW, also writes as N.L. Ray. Hunt wrote for the children's pages of newspapers when she was at school. After World War II, she was introduced to Cole Turnley by Bernard Cronin and wrote a story for one of E.W. Cole's annuals and verses for *Cole's Funny Picture Book No. 3* (1951).

As N.L. Ray she has written five novels. In *The Pow Toe* (1979), illustrated by Patricia Allen, Rory's life changes when his itching toe develops magical powers. A mysterious stranger involves a family in an extraterrestrial adventure in *There Was This Man Running …* (1979). *Nightmare to Nowhere* (1980) describes Bryony's prophetic dreams when she visits her new grandmother, and her friendship with the ill-fated Vicki. In *Roma Mercedes and Fred* (1981), illustrated by Walter Stackpool, Fred is a flying horse who takes Roma from her high-rise flat on a series of exciting adventures. *The Everywhere Dog* (1978) is a mystery story. While Breck is staying with his grandmother, his search for a dog leads him to a drug ring. *We Got Wheels, Man! and Other Stories* (1988), illustrated by Mark David, is a collection of seven humorous short stories. For *Never Tomorrow* (1989) see **Religion**.

For her series about Mrs Millie Mack, *Whistle Up the Chimney* (1981), *An Eye Full of Soot and an Ear Full of Steam* (1983) and *The Whistle Stop Party* (1990) see **Whistle Up the Chimney**. Her picture-book texts range from stories about the weather to feeling sick. *Rain, Hail or Shine* (1984) follows the effects of changing weather. Rain makes mud and rivers, hail chops up plants and damages windows and the sun and rain together make everything grow. In *Wild and Woolly* (1983), illustrated by Noela Hills, Mr Martin counts sheep to go to sleep, but buying them, getting them home and shearing them is

so exhausting that he falls asleep over a cup of tea. *When Ollie Spat on the Ball* (1985), illustrated by Mark David, is in the form of a comic-strip. An American boy, Ollie, joins the cricket game, and although he plays it like baseball, he annihilates the opposition at the critical moment. Jonathan has the measles in *Prisoner of the Mulligrubs* (1985), illustrated by Noela Hills, and his recovery is colourful and mischievous. In *A Rabbit Named Harris* (1987), illustrated by Betina Ogden, Granddad is losing his memory and Julio, misunderstanding his parent's irritation, decides to take him away to escape the threat of an old people's home. Mary waits for her uncle in *The Show* (1988). *Families are Funny* (1990), illustrated by Deborah Niland, shows how the family rallies when the young hero is sick. Hunt has contributed titles to reading schemes, such as *The Junk Eaters* (1987) illustrated by Peter Viska for Macmillan's 'Southern Cross' series.

In *The Dove Tree* (1991), a picture-book illustrated by Alison Kubbos, the narrator is seriously ill. Her friend Hannah gives her a dove tree when she is 5, hoping she will live long enough to see it flower. Hunt treats serious issues with a gentle touch, and is able to present the ludicrous as though it were matter of fact.

HURLE, GARRY (1942–), born Melbourne, teacher and farmer, wrote *Quickhoney* (1979) set near Buchan in east Gippsland. Anne and Jamie fear that developers will destroy the forests near their home, but they understand the secret messages of the wild bees and avert a disaster. *The Rusty Kee Adventures* (1984) describes the search which Rusty makes for his long-lost mother. Rusty is brought up in Gippsland near Walhalla, during the gold rushes of the last century. He is found abandoned on the doorstep by Ah Kee, Smiler Harris and Mrs Morgan. Smiler's specialty is making false teeth, a profession which Rusty supports enthusiastically. His adventures also include the discovery of a rich gold reef using the pattern of a key as a guide. *The Saddler's Grand-Daughter* (1986) is set on a farm in Gippsland. Francy and Pa restore an old saddle and Pa makes Fran a fine stockwhip and reins. The three stories are connected through the characters and the setting. The last story, 'Gum Nut Reins', won the Gippsland writer's section of the Mary Grant Bruce Award in 1985. *Angie's Ankles* (1990) is an adventure story about illegal crops told through Angie's letters. With *Trubb's Gift* (1992) Hurle has returned to the historical novel. Trubb and Catherine are washed ashore on a deserted beach near Port Jackson. Hurle's writing has offbeat detail, strong themes and memorable characters.

HURLEY, FRANK (1885–1961), born Sydney, was a pioneer photographer and adventurer. He shared a cockpit with Ross and Keith Smith, made films about pearl-divers and whalers and the seige of Tobruk, was rescued from the inside of a whale and accompanied Sir Douglas Mawson and Sir Ernest Shackleton on their Antarctic expeditions. He wrote *Shackleton's Argonauts: a Saga of the Antarctic Ice-Packs* (q.v., 1948), which is illustrated with his photographs.

HUTCHINS, ELIZABETH (1941–) was an administrator with the Australian Association of the Teachers of English. In *Lucky* (1987), Lucky is the kitten which Luke nurtures when he is staying with his grandparents. When the mother cat is missing, Lucky's life is threatened, but Luke finds Tortle just in time. *There's Something About Mondays* (1988) relates how Anna, who is partially deaf, adjusts to new surroundings.

HUXLEY, DEE (1947–), born Sydney, has worked as a teacher and graphic designer in television. She illustrated *The Raven and the Dove: the Story of Noah's Ark* (1980) by Heidi Lee, *Marzipan* (1984) by

I Wish … I Wonder (1989) by Dee Huxley

Virginia Arpadi, about a cat who loses his owner, *When You Come to the Ferry* (1988) by Hesba Brinsmead, *Mr Nick's Knitting* (1988) and *Remember Me* (1990) by Margaret Wild, *Sally and Rebecca* (1989) by Mary Baylis-White and *Oinkabella* (1990) by Hazel Edwards.

Huxley has written and illustrated *Tiffany's Own Story* (1979) about a lonely girl who makes friends by using her imagination rather than becoming a television addict, *I Wish … I Wonder* (1989) in which a boy daydreams in a stream of consciousness text, and *Rainbow Rabbits* (1991). She illustrated Pat Edwards's texts for *The Wild Colonial Boy* and *The Drover's Dream* (both 1980) and has collected and illustrated works of Australian writers, such as *Banjo Paterson, A Children's Treasury* (1984), *Henry Lawson, An Illustrated Treasury* (1985) and *Australian Poems are Fun* (1982), which has poems by C.J. Dennis, D.H. Souter, Irene Gough and others. Huxley's large watercolours, often exten-ding across a double page, are delicate and arresting.

HYDE, MICHAEL (1945–), teacher and writer, has written plays and short stories. *Working with Tommy* (1982) has three stories. 'The Day the Bridge Fell Down' recalls the tragedy of the collapse of Melbourne's Westgate Bridge, when Jim Guzman's father is killed. The other stories are the title story and 'The Marauding Pirate of Maribyrnong'. *Eagle* (1988) draws a group of children together in an inner suburb of Melbourne, as they battle to keep a wedge-tailed eagle alive. *Will You Shut Up about Spiritmen!* (1982) is set in the Lerderderg Gorge, outside Melbourne. Four young people become lost, and are shown the way to safety by a mysterious Aboriginal figure who disappears as strangely as he has appeared. With Marian Lees, Hyde edited *The Meat in the Sandwich* (1988). See **Collections**. Hyde's work reflects his sympathy for young people who are struggling to survive in a world which is not affluent or always caring.

Hyland House, a Melbourne publisher, established in 1977 by Anne Godden and Al Knight, published its first children's book in 1979, Lee Harding's *Displaced Person* (q.v., 1979). Authors published by Hyland House include James Aldridge, June Epstein, David Lake, Donna Rawlins, Gillian Rubinstein and Mary Steele. Other prize-winning books published by Hyland House are *The True Story of Lilli Stubeck* (q.v., 1984), *Arkwright* (q.v., 1985) and *Beyond the Labyrinth* (q.v., 1988).

I

I am Susannah (1987) by Libby Gleeson was an Honour Book in the 1988 Book of the Year Awards. Susie feels betrayed when her friend Kim leaves for Melbourne. Her other school friends are only interested in boys and clothes, and her problems are made more difficult because she is angry with her mother's reluctance to discuss her estranged father. Kim's house is occupied by a woman whom Susie secretly observes drawing and collecting leaves. On a traumatic night when all her troubles seem to close in on her, she is taken in by the Blue Lady, discovers a common interest in art, and is able to call herself by her full name for the first time.

'I Own the Racecourse!' (1968) by Patricia Wrightson, illustrated by Margaret Horder, was Highly Commended in the 1969 Book of the Year Awards. Andy Hoddel and Joe and his friends play a game in which they 'buy' local places, such as the police station, the parks, and the Town Hall. When Andy 'buys' the racecourse for $3 from a drunk, his friends realise that Andy cannot distinguish the game from reality. The racecourse authorities play along with Andy until he becomes a nuisance, and the dilemma is how to extricate Andy without breaking his heart. This sensitive novel portrays a likeable and disabled child as an accepted part of the neighbourhood. It was made into a 26-minute film in 1976 as a part of the 'Stories Around the World' series co-produced by Britain, Canada and the USA, featuring John Meillon Junior as Joe. In 1985 a feature-length film was made, directed by Stephen Ramsey, with Gully Coote as Andy and Norman Kaye as the drunk.

IBBY. The International Board on Books for Young People was established after World War II by Jella Lepman, working in Germany. She founded the International Youth Library in Munich with funds from the Rockefeller Foundation in 1949, and in 1951 organised a meeting of people involved with children's books, with the aim of promoting international understanding through books. IBBY was established in 1953. It has national sections throughout the world, and awards the Hans Christian Andersen Medal every two years to a living author and illustrator whose complete oeuvre has made an important contribution to children's literature. Patricia Wrightson and Robert Ingpen were awarded Hans Christian Andersen Medals in 1986. The Australian National Section was established in 1968, under the presidency of Ena Noel. IBBY in Australia publishes bibliographies and the proceedings of conferences and workshops. Titles include *Through Folklore to Literature* (1979), edited by Maurice Saxby; *Able to Enjoy: Books and the Young Disabled* (1982), edited by Ena Noel; *The Art of Storytelling* (1980), four videotapes; and *Books in Which Disabled Young People Play a Role* (1982), a bibliography by Ena Noel of books by Australian writers. Each year a celebration is held on 2 April, International Children's Book Day, the birthday of Hans Christian Andersen.

Ice is Coming, The (1977) by Patricia Wrightson won the 1978 Book of the Year Awards. It is the first part of a trilogy about Wirrun, completed with *The Dark Bright Water* (1978) and *Behind the Wind* (1981), which was Highly Commended in 1982. Wirrun fights off the Ninya, the ice people, in the first book; the Yunggamurra, a temptress, in the second; and meets the ultimate adversary, Walgaru, the death spirit, in the third. Wirrun's journey of discovery is in the tradition of the European hero tale, although Wrightson has used Aboriginal spirits and the Australian landscape to locate her novels. Wirrun is a combination of mythic hero and present-day Aboriginal man. In 1985 the series appeared in the Puffin edition as *The Book of Wirrun*.

'IDIE' (ANNIE FROST). For *Stories Told by 'Little Miss Kookaburra' of 3LO, Melbourne* (1925) see **Nursery Rhymes**.

IDRIESS, ION LLEWELLYN (1889–1979), born Sydney, spent twenty-five years as a boundary rider, drover, opal-digger, prospector, and buffalo-hunter, and travelled extensively throughout Australia and the Pacific, living with Aboriginal and Island People. During World War I he served with the Light Horse. Between 1927 and 1969, Idriess published fifty-six books. Much of his work recalls actual events, such as *Lasseter's Last Ride* (1931). *The Great Trek* (1940) is based on the expedition of Frank and Aleck Jardine, who walked the western coast of Cape York Peninsula to survey the mineral resources of Northern Queensland. Idriess used the family diaries and papers of the journey. A version for students aged 11 to 14 was published in 1954. *Headhunters of the Coral Sea* (1940) is drawn from the real story of Jack Ireland and Will D'Oyly, who survived the wreck of the *Charles Eaton* in 1834 and lived with the Islanders. *Nemarluk, King of the Wilds* (1941) is the life story of the chief of the Cahn-mah of NT. The battles which the people conducted against other jealous warriors, and against the whites, are described. Idriess calls him 'a living Tarzan

of the wilds', and had earlier touched on Nemarluk's struggles in *Man-Tracks* (1935). In *The Opium Smugglers, a True Story of our Northern Seas* (1948), Dick and Jack want to earn money to buy prospecting equipment, but become involved with Cross-eyed Joe, an opium-smuggler. *The Drums of Mer* (1933), about the survival and escape of two castaways, is an adventure story: a 'combination of fiction, description, history, ethnology and anthropology', says Morris Miller. *Gems from Ion Idriess* (1949) is a collection for schools of extracts from Idriess's work, such as *Headhunters of the Coral Sea*, *Lasseter's Last Ride* and *Forty Fathoms Deep*.

Illustration. Illustration has always been a strong feature of the children's book, from Comenius's *Orbis Sensualium Pictus* (1658) until recently. Marcie Muir suggests that the first coloured illustrations in a children's book relating to Australia are found in 'The Happy Grandmother, and her Grandchildren who went to Australia', a story in 'Peter Prattle's' *Amusing and Instructive Tales* (?1832), but *The Australian Picture Pleasure Book: Illustrating the Scenery, Architecture, Historical Events, Natural History, Public Characters &c. of Australia* (1857) by Walter G. Mason is regarded as the first illustrated Australian book for children, with its sedate and static wood engravings, depicting the current state of the colonies.

Nineteenth-century Australian children's books were often illustrated by English artists, at times inaccurate in their representations of the Australian landscape, most obviously seen in the depiction of Aboriginal People or the Australian bush. In W.H.G. Kingston's *Australian Adventures* (1884) an English forest or farmyard is supposed to illustrate an Australian scene. A.J. Johnson's interiors depict the typical middle-class house of Victorian times, which translated effectively to the Australian scene. John Macfarlane's nationality is unclear, but his outdoor girls provided a model of appearance which

Australian Adventures (1884) by W.H.G. Kingston. Illustrator unknown

their readers copied with enthusiasm. Australian artists such as Cyrus Mason and W.A. Cawthorne produced nursery rhymes and alphabet books, but novels such as *Seven Little Australians* (q.v., 1894) by Ethel Turner, and Mary Grant Bruce's *A Little Bush Maid* (1910) continued to be illustrated by English artists. An example is *Gray's Hollow* by M.G. Bruce, possibly illustrated by Stanley Davies. Australian flora and fauna found accurate representation in the work of the botanical artist Louisa Anne Meredith.

During the 1890s Angus & Robertson and William Brooks, Australian companies, commissioned Australian artists such as Frank Mahony, Percy Spence and George Lambert to illustrate books for young people. Frank Mahony's illustrations to Ethel Pedley's *Dot and the Kangaroo* (q.v., 1899) are recognisably Australian through landscape and the realistic portrayal of native animals. Percy Spence's illustrations to Ernest Favenc and 'Arthur Ferres's' books are also definitively local. Markedly different from these naturalist illustrators was the artist D.H. Souter,

Seven Little Australians (1894) by Ethel Turner. Illustrator: A.J. Johnson

ILLUSTRATION 228

who illustrated R.F. Irvine's *Bubbles: His Book* (1899) and Ethel Turner's *Gum Leaves* (1900). Souter's work draws on the English children's illustrator Walter Crane, although his striking images mark a change towards the modern in the illustration of Australian children's books. The talented Lindsay family all illustrated children's books before and after World War I, with *The Magic Pudding* (q.v., 1918) as the most outstanding example. *The Magic Pudding* exemplifies a successful marriage of text and picture, so that Bunyip Bluegum, Sam Sawnoff and the irritable Puddin' are defined for all time.

The realm of the fairy inspired the work of Ida Rentoul Outhwaite, who illustrated the fairy books of her own family and for Tarella Quin Daskein. Ethel Jackson Morris and Olive Crane illustrated fairy stories in a similar ethereal style. Christian Yandell's (Waller) illustrations show her

Gray's Hollow (1914) by Mary Grant Bruce. Illustrator: Stanley Davies?

profound sense of design, in a more formal unreality. Harold Gaze's work introduced the grotesque, in contrast to Outhwaite's romanticism. Pixie O'Harris began her large number of illustrated books during the 1920s. Also working in this period were two illustrators who were inspired by Australian animals and bush. May Gibbs, with her gumnut babies, and Dorothy Wall, with her Blinky Bill books, show a substantiality and innovation lacking in their contemporaries. The influence of Walt Disney is identifiable in Kay Druce, Rufus Morris and Walter Cunningham's pictures for Leslie Rees's Digit Dick books. Peg Maltby and Brownie Downing popularised images of quasi-Aboriginal characters. During the 1950s and 1960s, Edwina Bell, Walter Cunningham, Elizabeth Durack, Harold Freedman, Sheila Hawkins, Margaret Horder, Elaine Haxton and Elisabeth MacIntyre presented rural and urban Australia with authenticity and style.

The emergence of the picture-book during the 1970s provided opportunities for expression in a more direct way, however good illustration enhances narrative, and artists continue to illustrate novels. Robert Ingpen produced a gift edition of Colin Thiele's *Storm Boy* in 1974 and Sandra Laroche illustrated a new edition of Ethel Turner's *Seven Little Australians* in 1983. Dramatic covers which attract and entice the reader are now a feature of novels for adolescents, rather than illustration within the text. The latter is reserved for novels for younger readers, where it is used to break up the text, an excellent example being the work of Kim Gamble in *The Magnificent Nose and Other Marvels* (q.v., 1991) by Anna Fienberg. Astra Lacis's illustrations for Christobel Mattingley's *The Angel with the Mouth Organ* (1984), Ann James's illustrations for Robin Klein's Penny Pollard series and Jane Tanner's illustrations for Margaret Barbalet's *The Wolf* (1991) reaffirm the tradition. See also **Picture-Books**.

Immigrants. The history of white Australia is a history of immigration. The convicts and settlers of the First Fleet, those attracted to the colonies from all parts of the world by gold in the mid-nineteenth century, the political refugees from Europe between the wars, the massive post-World War II migration, and the Indo-Chinese and South American refugees of the 1970s and 1980s have all contributed to the multicultural nature of Australian society. The portrayal of immigrants has matched changes in society. Underlying the attitudes to racial minorities for all periods is the concept of class. The nationalities and the status and occupations of the characters frequently reflect the middle-class experience of the authors.

Generally, early books take up the idea of racial 'types', which was an accepted belief of nineteenth-century thought, with undisputed supremacy and superiority lying with the white Anglo-Saxon. For example, most female French or German characters act as governesses to squatter families, while the Irish are given roles as servant girls if they are female, or if they are male, bushrangers, cattle-duffers or other villains, invariably drunk. Mike Regan and Black Bob in *The Treasure Cave of the Blue Mountains* (1898) by William Smeaton are villainous and cowardly rogues who speak unintelligible brogue. The physical description of the two and their speech mark them as lower in status to the Scots, who are men of breeding, taste and discernment, a common stereotype.

After the turn of the century ethnic minorities were developed as central characters, acknowledging their visibility in Australian society of the time. These characters are drawn with some reality, though minor characters remain stereotypes, and racial generalisations are still popular. But there is a change in attitude towards racial prejudice. Prejudices are presented where they exist, but are more likely to be chal-

lenged; attempts to understand other cultures rather than denigrate them become evident. The school stories of Lillian Pyke show an ambivalence towards prejudice and racism; sometimes prejudice is acceptable, particularly against the Germans and Chinese, while in other cases it is not. The schoolboys who call Andi a 'nigger' in Pyke's *A Prince at School* (1919) are soon told he is a 'real white man underneath'. The conflict is again related to class. The books dealing with World War I show a similar dichotomy towards the Turks and Germans in the battlefield and at home in Australia.

A study of Mary Grant Bruce's novels which span a thirty-year period provides documentation of changing attitudes towards ethnic minorities. Her early novels are racist, particularly in their portrayal of the Chinese and Aboriginal People. In the later novels Chinese characters are given central roles and some eventually become heroes. But class continues to determine attitudes towards the immigrant, bound up with notions of caste, breeding, and occupation. Lower-class characters are more likely to express blatant racist attitudes than those from the genteel class, who are too well bred to be so crass. If characters from ethnic minorities remain stereotypes it is on the basis of their occupation and status, rather than on race. Bridget, the Irish servant girl in 'Tasman's' *A Little Aversion* (1910), is a stereotype because she is an uneducated, ignorant servant who could not possibly take part in the conversations and arguments of the young protagonists. Brian, also of Irish descent, is recognisable as an individual, not a mere racial type because he belongs to the right class.

During the 1950s, when there was large-scale European immigration to Australia, the policy of the Commonwealth Government was to assimilate everyone into a homogeneous Anglo-Celtic society. In the novels of the period, ethnic characters are urged to learn

English as quickly as possible, to abandon their cultural roots in favour of being 'Australian', and to recognise that the 'old' ways had nothing to offer Australian society. Typical of the children's books written during this period is *The Racketty Street Gang* (q.v., 1961) by L.H. Evers. The novel sets out to reassure the reader that Australian life will remain unaffected by the immigrants swelling the population, for they will soon become just like 'us'. At the conclusion the German Mrs Smertzer has taken the first steps towards learning English, Mr Smertzer's trucking business is assured, and Anton has become a fully accepted member of the gang.

Official policies to immigrants in Australia moved to a position of multiculturalism from the early 1970s. Early in this period children's novels portrayed some of the difficulties of the immigrant, but often provided easy solutions. A dog replaces the donkey left behind in Greece in *A Friend for Petros* (1974) by Nance Donkin, and a goat appeases Yaya's longing for Crete in Nadia Wheatley's *Five Times Dizzy* (1982). Later novels present a more searching appraisal of the immigrant experience. *Moving Out* (1983) by Helen Garner and Jennifer Giles, based on a film scripted by Jan Sardi, is a perceptive portrayal of the tension between Gino Condello and his parents, when his family prepares to go to the outer suburb of Doncaster from the less affluent Fitzroy. Gino is torn between a desire to be 'one of the boys' and his Italian family's demands for a better life. The conflicts bring him to an appreciation of his family and his culture.

The unique experiences of Indo-Chinese are considered in Diana Kidd's *Onion Tears* (1989) for younger readers. Nam-Huong's traumatic experiences aboard a small boat with her grandfather are related through letters which she writes to the people and animals she has left behind in Vietnam. Gradually the kindness of her 'Aunty' and another refugee, Chu Minh, who works in the restaurant where they live, and the understanding offered to her by her teacher, Miss Lily, enable Nam-Huong to weep for her lost relatives and speak again. There is no promise that Nam-Huong's unhappiness is over, but a recognition that Australia can offer her a new life. *Little Brother* (q.v., 1985) by Allan Baillie dramatically recounts the dislocation of Cambodian families during the dominance of the Khmer Rouge through the eyes of Vithy. Vithy finds his brother, but such a happy ending is not provided for the Cambodian Saret and Kanya in Maureen McCarthy's *Saret* (1987), one of the 'In Between' series (q.v.). These illegal immigrants have seen their father die, and the rest of their family is in a refugee camp in Thailand. Both young people are homesick and exploited in their Australian life. Kanya is raped and bashed and Saret faces deportation. While they find friendship with Jean-Louis, Kanya's employer, and Fatima, Angie and Alex, they are finally overpowered by a system which will not admit any special cases. While these novels provide some understanding of the displacement suffered by Indo-Chinese in Australia, there is no children's novel from a commercial publisher by a Cambodian or a Vietnamese writer, although in many schools stories by children who have settled in Australia provide inspiration such as *Why Must We Go?: Descriptions of Journeys to Australia from South-East Asia by South-East Asian Students of Richmond Girls' High School* (1981), compiled and edited by Valerie R. Falk.

Stereotypes, notions of Anglo-Saxon superiority, ethnocentrism, and the view of immigrants as untrustworthy aliens or inscrutable foreigners are now rarely found. Gone also are kind paternalism, the simplistic notions of solving cultural displacement by a gesture, and the happy endings, which deny the reality. What it means to live at the ethnic, social, and economic periphery of society is now being explored. Publications such as

Maureen McCarthy's 'In Between' series and Ursula Dubosarsky's *High Hopes* (1990) show us the common experiences shared by a variety of people from various ethnic backgrounds. The dilemmas that immigrants have are seen as the dilemmas of society as a whole. But there are few immigrant writers in Australia writing for children from their own experience, and some immigrant groups, such as Turks, Lebanese, Chileans or Salvadorans, have been virtually ignored by the writers. What has been achieved is a climate in which it is expected that books about the needs, interests, differences and similarities of the various ethnic groups in Australia will be written, and will be written free from bias, prejudice and stereotypes. See also **Chinese**; **Germans**; **Greeks**; **Italians**.

'In Between' series written by Maureen McCarthy and Shane Brennan, was produced for SBS television by Trout Films and Open Channel in 1987. Each of the four episodes is set in an inner-city suburb of Melbourne, and examines one of the characters. Four novels by McCarthy were published in 1987: *Fatima*, *Alex*, *Angie* and *Saret*, and have the same moving impact as the outstanding program. The lives of four school friends are examined: Fatima's battle to remain at school, Alex's forays outside the law, Angie's pregnancy and Saret and his sister's racial victimisation. See also **Immigrants**.

Inch Boy, The (1984), illustrated by Junko Morimoto, was Highly Commended in the 1985 Picture Book of the Year Awards. It is a Japanese folk-tale adapted by Helen Smith. Issunboshi is born so small that he can sail off in a walnut shell to seek his fortune. He rescues the princess by attacking the demon's stomach after he is swallowed, and is transformed into a beautiful Samurai. The dramatic illustrations follow the spare Japanese style.

Indonesian Journey (1965) by Ivan Southall, illustrated with photographs, was Commended in the 1966 Book of the Year Awards. It is a record of Southall's experiences in Indonesia living with Indonesian families as a volunteer graduate, and includes detail on the daily life and culture of Indonesian people, rich and poor. During the latter half of the book, Southall recounts his journey with Indonesians and other Australians across the country to Gunung Semeru, an erupting volcano.

INGAMELLS, REX (REGINALD CHARLES) (1913–55), born Orroroo, SA, was a founder of the Jindyworobaks, a group of poets devoted to the cause of Australianism in literature. His only book for children is *Aranda Boy: an Aboriginal Story* (1952). See **Aboriginal People in Children's Fiction**. Mary Haginikatis and Percy Trezise illustrated two of his poems, *Platypus and Kookaburra* (1987) and *Black Duck and Water Rat* (1988).

INGLE, DOROTHY. For *Three Girls and an Island: a Story for Girls* (1947) see **Adventure Stories**.

INGPEN, ROBERT (1936–), born Geelong, Victoria, is an author, illustrator and designer. He studied at RMIT and worked as a designer and illustrator for CSIRO. He was awarded the Hans Christian Andersen Medal for illustration in 1986. His early work includes *Storm Boy* (q.v., 1974) by Colin Thiele and *The Runaway Punt* (1976) by Michael Page. Ingpen wrote three books about gnomes. *Australian Gnomes* (1979) was not specifically for children, although of great interest to them. He used his gnomes again in *The Voyage of the Poppykettle* (1980). Seven Hairy Peruvian gnomes fit out the clay Poppykettle, and weight it with brass. They are towed out to sea by the Silver Fish, joined by El Nino, and cross the Pacific, to be saved by a dolphin and brought to land at Indented Head, near Geelong, Victoria. Ingpen's story is built around two ancient brass keys which were

River Murray Mary (1979) by Colin Thiele. Illustrator: Robert Ingpen

dug up on a cliffside in 1847. *The Unchosen Land* (1981) has the gnomes exploring the land, led by Don Avante. The series follows Australian history, using magic and real events to create a fantasy world.

Folk Tales and Fables of the World (1987), retold by Barbara Hayes, draws on a more international source, as does *Out of This World: the Complete Book of Fantasy, Folk Tales and Fables of the World* (1985) by Michael Page, which describes the creatures of imagination. *Idle Bear* (1986) has two discarded bears reminiscing about their past, involving philosophic dilemmas such as Who am I? In *The Age of Acorns* (1988) a bear who is left in a tree is frightened by a witch and an ugly doll until he is rescued. *The Child's Story* (1988) by Charles Dickens is the remembrance of the journey through life from childhood to old age, and *A Strange Expedition* (1988) is a story by Mark Twain, originally titled 'Some Learned Fables for Good Old Boys and Girls'. *Beginnings and Endings with Lifetimes in Between* (1983) by Bryan Mellonie and *Religious Worlds* (1985) by Max Charlesworth have also allowed Ingpen to explore the philosophic. Ingpen has also illustrated *I Rhyme My Time* (1980) by David Martin.

His dramatic landscapes and powerful portraits, often sombre, appear in *The Night of the Muttonbirds* (1981) by Mary Small; *Click Go the Shears* (1984) and *Clancy of the Overflow* (1982) by A. B. Paterson; *River Murray Mary* (q.v., 1979) by Colin Thiele; *The Great Bullocky Race* (1984) by Michael Page; his illustrations to a new edition of *The Nargun and the Stars* (q.v., 1973) by Patricia Wrightson in 1988; and *Conservation* (1987), with Margaret Dunkle. Ingpen designed the Dromkeen Medal, and was awarded the medal in 1989.

INGRAM, ANNE BOWER (1937–), born Manilla, NSW, has been active in editing and publishing since the 1960s. She edited *Reading Time* from 1970 to 1978, and made a selection of reviews and articles from the journal, *Reflections* (1974). She reviewed children's books for the *Sydney Morning Herald* from 1970 to 1972. Ingram was the children's book editor for William Collins, publishers, from 1971, where she was responsible for the publication of works illustrated by Desmond Digby, Patricia Mullins, Judy Cowell, Quentin Hole and the Nilands, among others. She became a consulting editor for publishers in 1980, and in 1988 established her own publishing house in association with William Collins, Ann Ingram Books. She has developed recommended reading lists, such as *Let's Read: a Guide to Children's Fiction* (1966), *Hurrah for Books: a Selection of Children's Non-Fiction* (1967) and *It's Reading Time: Books for the Under Fives* (1972). *Making a Picture Book* (1987), illustrated by Bob Graham, is a description of the process of creating picture-books.

She has edited collections, such as *Too True: Australian Tall Tales* (1974), twenty-four stories by Lilith Norman, Alan Marshall, Henry Lawson, Ruth Park and others, and *Shudders and Shakes: Ghostly Tales from Australia* (1972), a collection of extracts from newspapers and novels by well-known adult and children's writers. *The Pickled Boeing: an Illustrated Collection of Stories and Poems* (1982) was published for the silver jubilee of the Children's Medical Research Foundation, and has contributions from Joan Flanagan, Letitia Parr, Mary Durack, Patricia Wrightson, Lydia Pender, Bob Graham, Pamela Allen, Dee Huxley and others. She has also edited *Ford Family Car Fun Book* (1986), illustrated by Bob Graham, *Summer Fun Book* (1987), illustrated by Mary Davy, *Winter Fun Book* (1988), illustrated by Mark David, *Bedtime Fun Book* (1988), illustrated by Dee Huxley, and *Rainy Day Fun Book* (1988), illustrated by Shirley Peters, all with Peggy O'Donnell. Ingram's diverse talents have embraced the compilation of collections, the encouragement and promotion of authors and illustrators, and a valuable publishing program. She was awarded the Dromkeen Medal in 1985.

Irish National Readers were produced in Ireland and used in Victorian schools from 1848 to 1877, and in NSW schools until around the turn of the century. They contained religious material, moral tales, geography, and stories of classical and war heroes, with an overriding emphasis on Britain (then including Ireland) and British history. In 1872 Australian editions of the readers appeared, and stories of children lost in the bush, or the drama of bushfire, were included.

It Happened One Summer (1957) by Joan Phipson, illustrated by Margaret Horder, was Highly Commended in the 1958 Book of the Year Awards. Ten-year-old English Jennifer joins the affluent Walker family on a large property. Her pleasure in the companionship of Michael and

Tommy, the life of the station and its animals is complete, but her ultimate initiation occurs when single-handedly she saves the sheep, her dog and pony from a bushfire. Uncle Tom pronounces: 'You're the best stockman I've got on the place.'

Italians. From the time of the gold rushes, immigrants from Italy have contributed to Australian society, although their treatment has not always been just or welcoming. Even after there had been eighty years of the Italian presence in Australia, Mary Grant Bruce, in *Road to Adventure* (1932) refers to 'greasy little Italians'. The immigration program of the 1950s brought the largest group of Italians, who were expected to assimilate quickly and painlessly. Denys Burrows's *Above the Snowline* (1959) documents the Snowy Mountains Scheme and the ethnocentric views of the time. When Hungarian Nicky says to Italian Mario that he expects Mario has been yarning with his countrymen, Mario replies: '"Me? ... What you talk about, Nick? 'My own countrymen,' you say. You mean Italian? Me, I am two hundred per cent Australian!"' After the assimilationist thrust of the 1950s and 1960s, the policy towards immigrant groups altered to one of integration. David Martin's *Frank and Francesca* (1972) attempts to show the ethnic mix of Melbourne, but the Terranovas continue century-old vendettas, speak little English and make grappa in the bath. When Frank says, 'Blood, blood, and more blood. What's wrong with you Italians?', Francie expostulates 'What have you to be so proud of? Don't you know you got everything from us?' Sandra McCuaig's *Spaghetti Connections* (1990) also connects Italians with drugs and the Mafia.

Deirdre Hill prefigured the new policy of multiculturalism, and the importance of immigrants retaining the culture of their origins. Hill looks at immigration from the immigrant's viewpoint, in *Mario visits Australia* (1978). Mario finds suburban Sydney very different from Rome and his

family life there. At first he is homesick, and feels excluded because he cannot speak English, and he does not like the food. He is delighted when he finds 'patatine' — potato chips. There is some Italian text, a new development. David Martin's series of books for younger readers about Peppino introduced a family working on the tobacco farms of north-eastern Victoria. In *Peppino Turns His Luck* (1982) the Australians taunt Peppino, and the other Italian boys who have already survived the prejudice offer him no help at all, telling him that the correct response to not understanding what someone has said is 'Bugger off'. When Peppino finally solves his problems at school, it is at the expense of his relationship with his parents. Such an open-ended conclusion raises real issues of cultural conflict. In *Moving Out* (1983) by Helen Garner and Jennifer Giles, similar insights are given into an Italian family. Gino lives in two cultures, and the complexities, inconsistencies and realities of cultural conflict faced by a teenager in this situation are effectively portrayed. Prejudice is not glossed over, but presented where it exists. The resolution is not imposed on the novel but arises out of an acceptance by Gino of his parents and his situation. Contemporary novels see the Italian community as a part of the larger society, acknowledging its pluralistic nature, through the unselfconscious inclusion of Italian characters as part of life in the suburbs. In *Breaking Up* (q.v., 1983) by Frank Willmott Mark's friends include the Italian Charlie. Mark feels a part of this family: 'His parents are great ... His dad makes his own wine and we drink it with our meals while he tells stories about the war and living on a farm in Sicily. He always gives Charlie and me a big squeeze which nearly kills us because he's short and fat and has huge hands and hair all over his body ... Charlie also has two sisters; one who's married and lives in Adelaide and another one who is seventeen and looks beautiful and is a dental nurse.'

Maureen Pople's *The Other Side of the Family* (1986) takes racism head on. The intolerance which Kate shows towards her poor, deaf and 'dilapidated' grandmother is juxtaposed against her lack of sympathy for the outcast Bellini family who live next door. Gradually, Kate comes to love and admire her grandmother and she and the community begin to appreciate the courage of the Bellinis. In this novel, intolerance exists in the family as well as society, and at the conclusion the Bellinis have still to deal with prejudice. Diana Kidd's *The Day Grandma Came to Stay (and Spoilt my Life)* (1988), for younger readers, examines the changing relationship between Lucy and Nonna, who comes to visit from Italy. Lucy is self-conscious about her Italian relatives and particularly her grandmother, who wears black and speaks no English. The problems are all in Lucy's perception: others, such as Mango, Mrs Timmings, Miss Martin, her teacher, and Lucy's friend John, enjoy Nonna for her delightful individuality. In James Grieve's *A Season of Grannies* (1987) Jacqui's father's racism is challenged when he gets to know Luciano. Grieve does not shrink from portraying the day-to-day racism which Looch suffers in and out of school, but the Italian boy's resilience and good nature enable him to survive. In *The Smiling Madonna* (1989), by Deirdre Hill, Maria embraces the culture of her father's Sienna and stays on in Italy, although she still finds a place in her heart for the Australia of her childhood.

From derogatory dismissal to the recognition of the individual rather than the racial type, Italians are now included within the children's book as part of the multicultural society.

J

JACKSON, ADA ACRAMAN (née FAWCETT) (1902–) wrote *Beetles Ahoy! Being a Series of Nature Studies Specially Written for Children* (q.v., 1948).

Jam Roll Press was set up in 1988 in Queensland by Robyn Sheahan, Leonie Tyle and Robyn Collins. Early titles were *Message from Avalon* (1990) by Jenny Wagner and *The Bunyip in the Billycan* (1991) by Mavis Scott.

JAMES, ANN (1952–), born Melbourne, studied art at Melbourne Teachers' College, and worked as a graphic designer and illustrator for the Victorian Ministry of Education. She is the co-director of Books Illustrated, a Melbourne gallery specialising in children's book illustrations. *A Pet for Mrs Arbuckle* (1981) was the first book she illustrated, later illustrating another 'Mrs Arbuckle', *A Hobby for Mrs Arbuckle* (1987), both by Gwenda Smyth. She illustrated two multi-language texts, *Ston Kathrephte (In the Mirror)* (1982) and *Ti Eimai? (What am I?)* (1982) by Barbara Athanasioy-Ioannoy and others. She has illustrated *Jo-Jo and Mike* (1984) by Jenny Wagner; *Bernice Knows Best* (q.v., 1983) by Max Dann; *Penny Pollard's Diary* (q.v., 1983), *Penny Pollard's Letters* (1984), *Penny Pollard in Print* (1986), *Penny*

One Day: A Very First Dictionary (1990) by Ann James

Pollard's Passport (1988), *Penny Pollard's Guide to Modern Manners* (1989) and *Snakes and Ladders* (1985) by Robin Klein; *Where's My Shoe?* (1987) by Pat Edwards; *Looking Out for Sampson* (q.v., 1987) by Libby Hathorn; *Wiggy and Boa* (1988) by Anna Fienberg; *Prince Lachlan* (1989) by Nette Hilton; the rollicking *Beryl and Bertha at the Beach* (1990) by Pippa MacPherson; *First at Last and Other Stories* (1990) by Julia McClelland; *Dial-a-Croc* (1990) by Mike Dumbleton; *Amy the In-de-fat-ig-able Autograph Hunter* (1990) by Judith Worthy, and *Dog In, Cat Out* (1991) by Gillian Rubinstein. Two of her alphabet books are *ABC of What You Can Be* (1985) and *One Day: a Very First Dictionary* (1990). James uses loose line drawings and watercolour which she combines in a strong sense of page design. The delightful dog, Jo-Jo, the sturdy hens, Bertha and Beryl, and her illustrations to the Penny Pollard books have established the characters just as firmly as has the text. Her pictures 'see around the corners and under the skin'.

James Cook, Royal Navy (1970) by George Finkel, illustrated by Amnon Sadubin, was Commended in the 1971 Book of the Year Awards. The novel takes the life of Cook from his childhood to the conclusion of his first voyage to the southern oceans, and contains extracts from the sailor's journals as well as some fictional letters and diary entries. Cook's diligent apprenticeship on the coastal colliers, his distinguished service in the Royal Navy, and his selection as Captain of the Endeavour is detailed. Finkel reconstructs Cook's courtship and marriage to Elizabeth Batts, who survived both Cook and their six children.

JAMES, FLORENCE (1902–), born Gisborne, NZ, wrote *Four Winds and a Family* (1947) and the adult novel *Come In, Spinner* (1951) with Dymphna Cusack. See **CUSACK, DYMPHNA**.

JAMES, SUSANNAH, see **CROSER, JOSEPHINE**

Jamie's Discovery (1963) by Betty Roland, illustrated by Geraldine Spence, was Commended in the 1964 Book of the Year Awards. See **The Forbidden Bridge** (1961).

Jancy is the central character in four books by Anne Bracken: *Jancy Wins Through* (1945), *Jancy Scores Again* (1947), *Jancy in Pursuit* (1950) and *Jancy Stands Alone* (1955). The inquisitive and extraordinarily resourceful Jancy, with her girlfriend Rusty (Russel) Richmond, solves kidnappings, thefts and other minor and major misdemeanours. Jancy runs away from school when a necklace disappears; she and Rusty save the fortunes of Brigit and Giralda, who has a split personality (cured by a hard bump on the head); Jancy unmasks a kidnapper and confidence woman, finds new friends, Geoff and Marney, is caught in a bushfire, and is promised a future romance with Geoff. The police are called in as a last resort, often only in time to thank Jancy effusively for her brilliant detective work.

Jandy Malone and the Nine O'Clock Tiger (1980) by Barbara Bolton, illustrated by Alan White, was Commended in the 1981 Book of the Year Awards. Jandy's fertile imagination has invented a tiger which stalks the house between nine and nine thirty at night. Her younger siblings, Samantha and Peter, beg her to see if the tiger is in the house, and although Jandy's 'heart and feet turn to ice' she dares to look, and learns that when you look a tiger in the face, there is really nothing to be afraid of. In the process of telling the story, Jandy describes the loss of her father, and her admiration for her mother. A story of mastering fear and facing up to life is accompanied by pictures which show Jandy's apprehension, and give insights into her family.

JANIC, PENELOPE (1940–) (Penelope Welch), studied art at Sydney Technical School. She worked in film animation and design for commercial television and the ABC. She illustrated and wrote *Japhet, the Tiger* (1965), as Penelope Janjic. A tiger without stripes, Japhet, is taken to the zoo, where he leans against the newly painted cage and proves his tiger's heart by setting free all the other tigers. *The Ha Ha Bird* (q.v., 1968) shows how pride comes before a fall. *The No Such Thing* (1970) is a large ugly beast conjured up by Benjamin's wizard father for Benjamin's birthday. In *Peri and the Willow's Song: or, Tree Magic* (1971), Peri learns magic music from a willow tree. It brings happiness to everyone until Peri boasts that it is his own creation, when the lovely music disappears. *Too Many Guinea Pigs* (1974) are born too often after Hamish buys a pair at the market. Janic has illustrated *Wake Up! It's Night* (1966), by Carol Odell, which describes the work which is done while most of the city is asleep; *Donovan and the Lost Birthday* (q.v., 1968) and *Donovan Saves the Skates* (1970) by Marion Ord; and *Let's Have a Pet Show* (1978) by Mary Madgwick.

Jean and the Shell Fairy, see **Fairies**.

JELLETT, CELIA (1951–), born Henley Beach, Adelaide, is an editor who has worked with Omnibus publishing. She edited *Someone is Flying Balloons* (1983) and *Rattling in the Wind: Australian Poems for Children* (1987), with Jill Heylen, illustrated by Maire Smith.

JENKINS, WILLIAM STILL ('Stitt'). For *The Lost Children: in Perpetual Remembrance of Jane Duff* (1864) see **Lost in the Bush**.

JENNINGS, PAUL (1943–), born UK, came to Australia when he was 6. In his search for 'material which is easy to read and compelling in content', he has written books which engage readers of a wide age range and ability. His first collection was *Unreal! Eight Surprising Stories* (q.v., 1985). *Unbelievable! More Surprising Stories* (q.v., 1986), *Quirky Tales* (1987), *Uncanny! Even More Surprising Stories* (q.v., 1988), *Unbearable! More Bizarre Stories* (1990) and *Unmentionable!* (1991) followed, full of humorous and spooky stories on supernatural subjects, spiked with childish vulgarity. *Burp! Blue Jam: Two Short Stories* (1985) reveal a blacker side, as Jennings describes the events surrounding a magic feather which causes its discoverer to explode, and bewitched jam which brings evil to its maker. *The Paw Thing* (q.v., 1989) is a novel about the cat, Singenpoo, who swallows a transistor radio. In *The Cabbage Patch Fib* (q.v., 1988) Chris finds a baby when his father is too embarrassed to tell him the facts of life. *Round the Twist* (q.v., 1990) documents the making of the television series of the same title by the Australian Children's Television Foundation. The series was an adaptation of Jennings's stories from earlier collections. *Flutter* (1990) describes Phillip, who hates to lose anything, but when he finds that his budgerigar Melody prefers its freedom he lets it go. *Teacher-Eater* (1991), illustrated by Jeanette Rowe, is a picture-book featuring a stray dragon who saves a school from the ravages of a fearsome dragon who eats teachers. In *Grandad's Gifts* (1991), illustrated by Peter Gouldthorpe, and first published in *Unbelievable!*, the gifts are not what they seem. Jennings's direct language and his intriguing characters make his short stories funny and entertaining. They are strongly plotted, surprising, and free of pretension.

John and Betty: the Earliest Reader for the Little Ones (1951), illustrated by Marjorie Howden for the Education Department of Victoria, replaced the Victorian Readers First Book. We are introduced to the nuclear family, Father, Mother, John, Betty, Scottie the dog and Fluff the cat, who can run and jump and bang and rock and skip. In *Playmates* (1952), for first-grade pupils, the young protagonists continue to repeat themselves on every page: '"Let us wash our hands", says Betty. John will wash his hands. Peter will wash his hands.' *Holidays* (1953) followed. With Baby, the family go to the beach, the zoo, the circus and celebrate Christmas. *Among Friends* (1954), the Victorian Readers Third Book, illustrated by Harold Freedman, moved the young reader on to folk tales, poems and stories.

John Brown, Rose and the Midnight Cat (1977) by Jenny Wagner, illustrated by Ron Brooks, won the 1978 Picture Book of the Year Awards. The dog, John Brown, is jealous of the intruder, a black cat, despite Rose's affection for it. Only when Rose continues to stay in bed does John Brown allow the cat a place by the fire. Sombre illustrations create a mood of loneliness and regret in an outstanding work which can be interpreted on a number of levels. See also **Death**.

John the Mouse who Learned to Read (1969) by Beverly Randell, illustrated by Noela Young, was Commended in the 1970 Picture Book of the Year Awards. It had first appeared in the NZ *School Journal* in 1955. John lives in a cupboard in the classroom. He creeps out one morning and hears the children reciting their reader: 'Here is John … ' The mouse observes the teacher writing 'John' on the board, writes his name on the floor in front of all the children, and becomes the school pet. Young creates a small mouse, towered over by chairs and human legs, but full of character.

'JOHN MYSTERY', see **'MYSTERY, JOHN'**

John of the Sirius (1955) by Doris Chadwick, illustrated by Margaret Senior, was Highly Commended in the 1956 Book of the Year Awards. The story had appeared in the NSW *School Magazine* as a picture-serial in 1945, and was rewritten for publication in 1955. John, the son of a soldier, becomes Arthur Phillip's cabin boy, and Lieutenant Dawes, Tench, Hunter and other real First Fleet people appear. John's adventures were continued in *John of Sydney Cove* (1957), illustrated by Adye Adams, and *John and Nanbaree* (1962), illustrated by Senior, Nanbaree being the orphaned Aboriginal boy who is John's friend. Chadwick has shown some of the difficulties of life during the early days of the colony, particularly for the soldiers and their families, although the fun the children have far outweighs any deprivations.

JOHN SANDS, see **SANDS, JOHN**

JOHNS, Captain **WILLIAM EARLE** (1893–1968), born Hertford, UK, served in the Royal Flying Corps during World War I. From this experience, and at the instigation of the British government to assist its wartime recruiting drive, he created the very popular 'Biggles' and his female counterpart, 'Worrals', who figure in some Australian adventures. While investigating the possibility of establishing their own airline in Australia, Worrals and Frecks meet an old chum, Janet, who has been having trouble locating the opal cache left to her by her late Aunt Mary, in *Worrals Down Under* (1948). The three girls then proceed to tough it out at 'Wallabulla' against unidentified moaning at night, opal-thieves, murdering half-wits (black and white), poisoned water, and sugar in the aeroplane's fuel tank — at all times keeping their nerve and shooting straight.

There is a much more sinister force at work in *Biggles in Australia* (1955). Biggles and his fawning aides, Algy, Ginger and Bertie, expose a plot to turn the Aboriginal People of northern Australia into Mau-Mau, instigated by Biggles's old enemy Von Stalheim, who has 'sacrificed his sense of humour to have another crack' at Biggles, and joined forces with

Russians, communists and other 'Iron-Curtainmongers'. To outsmart this formidable alliance, Biggles et al. swim in waters stiff with sharks, and estuaries swarming with crocodiles, fight off giant decapods which attack aircraft with their tentacles, and always display the hearts of oak and deadly aim which have made them the heroes of a generation. Angus & Robertson brought out a new edition of *Biggles in Australia* in 1981, illustrated with cartoons by Patrick Cook.

Johnson, Frank C. was a Sydney publisher of paperback material during the 1940s, including comic-books such as *Amazing*, *Marvel*, and *Magic*, and a series, 'Johnson's Children's Books'. These, and the comics, featured the works of Unk White, Ralph and Noreen Shelley, Ruth and Rhys Williams, and Sydney Miller. Johnson published the children's books of 'Willo and Billo', Maria Wolkowsky, Evelyn Bartlett, Hilda Bridges and Arthur Goode, among others.

JONES, CAROL (1942–). For *Hickory Dickory Dock* (1991) see **Nursery Rhymes**.

JORGENSEN, GAIL (1951–) has written *Crocodile Beat* (1988), illustrated by Patricia Mullins. A crocodile waits in the river to eat the animals which come to play, but, in a cumulative tale, he is foiled by a clever lion. *Beware!* (1988), illustrated by Craig Smith, is another warning to watch out for unexpected terrors. Other titles include *On a Dark and Scary Night* and *Bubble Gum* (both 1988), both illustrated by Craig Smith.

Joseph and Lulu and the Prindiville House Pigeons (1972) by Ted Greenwood was Highly Commended in the 1973 Picture Book of the Year Awards. Prindiville House is threatened by a developer who wants to build a skyscraper to link the two adjoining buildings. Joseph, the caretaker who operates Lulu the lift, dreams of a way of saving Prindiville which satisfies tenants, developers and the pigeons who call it home. Greenwood uses unusual perspectives to incorporate the text into the illustrations.

JOUBERT, JUNE (1931–), born Perth, painter and illustrator, has illustrated books in reading programs for Nelson, Macmillan and Oxford. She illustrated Roger Vaughan Carr's *The Split Creek Kids* (q.v., 1988) and *Nipper and the Gold-Turkey* (1991), Robin Klein's *Get Lost* (1987) and June Epstein's *I Can't Find My Glasses* (1987).

Journey Home, The (1989), written and illustrated by Alison Lester, was an Honour Book in the 1990 Picture Book of the Year Awards. Two children, Wild and Woolly, dig a hole to the North Pole. On the way home they meet Father Christmas, the Good Fairy, Prince Charming, the Little Mermaid and other fairy tale characters.

'Joy' series is a series of twelve colourful paperbacks published by Barker & Co. in 1941. They are *David's Seaside Holiday* and *Jonathan and His Billy-Goat Cart*, written and illustrated by C.E. Stamp, *Philip the Frog*, *Peppo the Pony*, *Betty Ann's Birthday*, *Rupert the Rabbit*, *A Surprise for Shirley*, *The Misdoings of Mickey and Mack*, *Kenny the Koala*, *Judy's Joyous Day*, *Fun on a Farm* and *Trouble in Toyland*. Large format and print and plentiful illustrations are combined to show eventful happenings. Although they are dated by attitudes to gender and class, these gentle stories retain their appeal. *Trouble in Toyland*, for instance, describes how a small girl pleads with Father Christmas in future to bring only peaceful toys to Toyland.

Junior Book of the Year Awards, see **Book of the Year Awards: Younger Readers**.

K

'**Kaboodle**' was a television series produced by the Australian Children's Television Foundation in 1986 and 1990, with Patricia Edgar as Executive Producer. 'Kaboodle 1' had thirty-two segments over thirteen half-hours, mixing drama, live action and animation. Writers included Peter Viska, Paul Cox, Jeff Peck, Jill Morris, Morris Gleitzman, Hazel Edwards and others. Teachers' notes were produced from the series. 'Kaboodle 2' was fully animated. It had six half-hour episodes, each with four regular segments. Books produced from this series include *The Wheelie Wonder* (1987) by Hazel Edwards; *The Wizards of Solmar* (1988) and *Grandfather's Dream Machine* by Bronwen Scarffe; *Echidna Crossing* by Maggie Geddes and Neil Robinson; *Hedge Island* by Virginia Ferguson and Peter Durkin; and *The Great Detective and the Case of Captain Blunderbuss's Secret* by Susan Green (all 1989).

KAMM, JOSEPHINE (1905–) is an English author. For *He Went with Captain Cook* (1952) see **Cook**, Captain **James**.

Kapper Collection is housed at the J.B. Chifley Library, Australian National University. It contains material from 1880 to 1920, largely overseas fiction for young adults. Its special strengths are Religious Tract Society publications and the works of E. Evelyn-Green, R.M. Ballantyne, and W.H.G. Kingston.

Karrawingi the Emu, see *The Story of Karrawingi the Emu*

KAVANAGH, MICHAEL. For *Telling Tales* (1986) see **Collections**.

KAY, TIMOTHY wrote *Bobby Rubbernose: a Story about a Little Koala Bear who Lost Himself and Was Found Again* (1944). When he falls out of a tree Bobby is helped by rabbits, kangaroos and other koalas, then captured and taken home to Jimmy and Agnes who feed him the wrong food. He runs away and finds his own mother. In *The Adventures of Joker Jack* (1944) Jack is a kookaburra who learns to hunt and build a nest and is adopted by a human family. In *Koo-Loo the 'Roo* (1947) the kangaroo is rescued from the river and becomes Mary's pet. Koo-Loo's brother Kanga misses her and, with the help of all the other kangaroos, restores Koo-Loo to her family. *Flop the Platypus* (1946) is in the same series. All of Kay's books were illustrated by Rufus Morris.

KEESING, NANCY (1923–93), born Sydney, is a writer, critic and poet. For *By Gravel and Gum, the Story of a Pioneer Family* (1963), illustrated by Roderick Shaw, see '**Great Stories of Australia**'. *The Golden Dream* (1974), illustrated by Walter Stackpool, is a fictionalised account of George Preshaw's search for gold in Victoria and NSW. She has also written books for adults.

KELLAWAY, FRANK GERALD (1922–), born London, UK, wrote *The Quest for Golden Dan* (q.v., 1962), revised for schools as *Golden Dan* (1976), and one of the Oxford 'Early Australians' series, *A Whaler* (1967), illustrated by Patricia Thomas. Kellaway wrote two libretti for children, *The Takeover: a School Opera in One Act* (1968) and *Song of the Maypole: a Cantata for Children's Choruses* (1968), both with music by George Dreyfus. He also wrote poetry for adults.

KELLEHER, VICTOR (1939–), born London, UK, lived in Central Africa and NZ before settling in Australia in 1976. His African background can be identified in many of his settings, such as the deserts in *Brother Night* (q.v., 1990), or the jungles in *Papio* (1984). His first children's book was *Forbidden Paths of Thual* (q.v., 1979). In *The Hunting of Shadroth* (1981) the outcast, Tal, and Lea, his friend, defeat the monster Shadroth, who kills by freezing his victims to death. Tal and Lea use courage and some magic, and are helped by a beautiful animal, the Feln. It is set in an imaginary prehistoric time, among a clan of hunter-gatherers living in a lush setting. *Master of the Grove* (q.v., 1982) has a more medieval tone. *The Green Piper* (1984) is a modern retelling of the Pied Piper, though centred on the plant world. Tom, a sinister evil clone, is the representative of intruders from outer space. See also **Science Fiction**.

With *Papio*, Kelleher explored his fascination with the nexus between humans and the animal world. Jem and David release a pair of baboons which are being used for experimentation, and travel with them until they are absorbed into a wild group. The responsibility for the tragedy which the children bring about through their impulse to protect Papio and Upi is examined in this thoughtful and exciting novel. Kelleher's respect for animals can be traced from his earliest works: his depiction of the fox in *Forbidden Paths of Thual*, the lion-like Feln in *The Hunting of Shadroth*, the gleaming black bird, Craak, in *Master of the Grove*, the baboons in *Papio*, and the fearless tigers in *Taronga* (q.v., 1986). *The Red King* (1989) is a fantasy about Petie the enigmatic magician, Timkin the acrobat, Crystal the monkey and Bruno the bear, who set out to defeat a powerful ruler who subjugates through infecting dissidents with a fatal disease. Once again Kelleher has energetic animal and human characters. *Brother Night* (q.v., 1990) examines the need for balance in

action and emotion. For *The Makers* (1987) see **Science Fiction**.

Contemporary settings are found in the ghostly mystery *Baily's Bones* (1988), in which a family's peace is shattered when a convict's bones are unearthed and Baily takes over the mind of the disabled Kenny. *Del-Del* (1991) is a psychological thriller, in which Sam appears to be possessed by a malevolent being, perhaps from another world. In a family beset by deep differences of outlook and recent tragedy, the intruding spirit has its origins in the unresolved trauma of a child who has suffered a terrible loss. Kelleher writes strong, spare prose and has the ability to elicit a powerful emotional response. His well-sustained stories are concerned with the violence of modern society, the creative and destructive impulses of the human heart, and the issue of individual freedom in an increasingly restricted world. He has also written books for adults.

Kelly, Ned (1855–80) was a bushranger in northern Victoria. He was caught at Glenrowan in a spectacular confrontation with the police, where he and his gang donned a set of armour to protect themselves, and after a trial for murder, Kelly was hanged in Melbourne. The Kelly legend invokes a Robin Hood figure, and has inspired adult and children's novels, plays, songs and picture-books. James Skipp Borlase's *Ned Kelly: the Ironclad Australian Bushranger* (1881) is an early, though fanciful, retelling of the events. A century later, David Martin's *The Girl Who Didn't Know Kelly* (1985) is a more accurate account, woven into the life of Kit Grimshaw, the girl of the title. Kit is growing up in Beechworth at a time when Kelly is captured. Her father is a bank manager, and despises the heroism accorded Ned Kelly by the common populace, but Kit is not so sure that the bushranger is the villain her father thinks he is, and, influenced by one of her school friends, Dan Trevena, she begins to understand that justice is not always as simple as it seems. Frank Clune's *Ned Kelly* (1970), illustrated by Walter Stackpool, tells Ned's story from his father's transportation to his last words, 'Such is life'. *Ned Kelly* (1978) by Ken Little, illustrated by Dee Huxley, is a picture-book about the traditional Kelly story.

Ned — a Leg End (1984) by Susanne Ferrier parodies the legend and the times, and in Paul Williams's *The Adventures of Black Ned* (1990) Ned lives on in the scrap-heap, builds a solar-powered monster from a windmill and robs the bank.

KENIHAN, KERRY (1944–) (née WALSH), born Mildura, Victoria, set *Red and the Heron Street Gang* (1985) on the Murray River. See **Murray River**. *By Lexie Roberts* (1989) describes the crisis facing a rural family, which Lexie averts by writing a teenage romance. As Kerry Walsh she has written *How to be the Parents of a Handicapped Child — and Survive* (1981) and *Quentin* (1985), the story of her disabled son.

KENNEDY, EDWARD B. arrived in Australia in 1864. *Blacks and Bushrangers: Adventures in Queensland* (1889) is an adventure story about the exploits of Mat Stanley, who arrives in Australia with his brother Tim to avoid imprisonment in England. After a shipwreck, they survive in the bush, live with the Aboriginal People, and defeat a gang of bushrangers who have kidnapped Mat's true love, Annie Bell, to whom Mat finally proposes (on one knee). The arrival of a new chum, Lionel Fulrake, with his English pretensions and his total inability to 'rough it', is a source of amusement. Lionel writes home giving his impressions of colonial society, including 'the offensive independence of the so-called labouring classes'. He complains that there is ' … little comfort and no furniture in the place and the food is of the coarsest'. Lionel, despite his sophistication, is unable to carry buckets of water without spilling their contents and eventually sitting in one. However, he betters a Sydney ruffian in a fight and has therefore proved himself to be brave, tough, manly and above all, a good fighter. Despite this he cannot take to station life, and returns to England. 'The little chap has tremendous pluck and nerve but he is such a lazy fellow, and so full of fads about his grub and everything', comments the Australian Tim. Kennedy also wrote *The Black Police of Queensland* (1902), which describes his experiences in Queensland as an overlander, gold-fossicker, policeman and cane-grower. *Out of the Groove: a Romance of Australian Life* (1892) is an autobiographical novel for adults.

Kent, Peter appears in six novels by John Gunn. *Barrier Reef Espionage: a Thrilling Adventure Story for Boys with an Authentic Naval and Flying Background* (1955), illustrated by Edward Osmond, introduced the 17-year-old Kent in his fourth year at Flinders Naval College. On holidays with his uncle-guardian, Dr Robert Lassiter, he and his uncle are saved from drowning by HMAS *Kalda*. When they are set ashore on a Barrier Reef island, Black Island, they meet crocodiles and a python before being threatened with death in a pool containing Portuguese men-o'-war, sea snakes and ribbon fish. Joined by Lassiter's son, Allen, they assist in the exposure of a group of spies bent on discovering the secrets of atom bomb testings at Monte Bello. In *Battle in the Ice* (1956), illustrated by George Lane, Kent is aboard an aircraft carrier, HMAS *Legend*, when it is called to the Antarctic to help the *Kalda*. *Gibraltar Sabotage* (1957) finds Kent, now a midshipman, on a destroyer, *Fearless*, investigating an attack on a yacht in the Straits of Gibralter. In *Submarine Island* (1958), illustrated by George Lane, Kent is back on the *Legend*, and discovers an enemy submarine which he despatches from the air. Further adventures occur in *Peter Kent's*

Command (1960), and *City in Danger* (1962), illustrated by Noela Young. The villains, always dark and foreign, and clean-cut heroes (including Peter himself) are involved in adventures which are often repetitive, although Gunn's knowledge and experience of naval and air procedures gives an authentic ring to the stories.

KER WILSON, BARBARA (1929–), born Sunderland, UK, worked for OUP in England, and later worked as an editor with Bodley Head, William Collins, Angus & Robertson, Hodder & Stoughton and Reader's Digest. She edited C.S. Lewis's *The Last Battle* (1956) while she was with Bodley Head. *Path-Through-the-Woods* (1958), *The Wonderful Cornet* (1958), *The Lovely Summer* (1960), *Last Year's Broken Toys* (1962), *Ann and Peter in Paris* (1963), *Ann and Peter in London* (1965) and *Beloved of the Gods* (1965) were written before Ker Wilson came to Australia in 1964, where she has continued her commitment to publishing, including the development of Queensland University Press's teenage list. Over a long career in publishing Ker Wilson has written many books for children and adults. *A Family Likeness* (1967), illustrated by Astra Lacis, draws on Australian history, as Deborah Armstrong's life in the mid-twentieth century is compared to the lives of her nineteenth-century ancestors, Celandine, Tansy, Sorrel and Vervain Pratt, recalled through a family photograph.

Ker Wilson selected poems by Mary Gilmore for *The Singing Tree: A Selection of Mary Gilmore's Poetry for Young Readers* (1971), illustrated by Astra Lacis. She edited *Australian Kaleidoscope* (1968), illustrated by Margery Gill, a collection of poems, excerpts and short stories under the headings of 'City', 'Country', 'Outback' and 'Shoreline'. For *Tales told to Kabbarli: Aboriginal Legends* (1972) see **Aboriginal Dreaming Stories**. She has also collected folk-tales from other countries, such as

The Magic Fishbones (1972), illustrated by Suzanne Dolesch, and *Scottish Folk Tales and Legends*. *The Willow Pattern Story* (1978), illustrated by Lucienne Fontannaz, tells the old Chinese legend. *The Persian Carpet Story* (1981), with Jacques Cadry, illustrated by Nyorie Bungey, is set in Iran, and describes the life of a poor family, whose fortunes are improved when they sell their carpets to a kindly Australian. *A Story to Tell: Thirty Tales for Little Children* (1964) and *Hiccups and Other Stories: Thirty Tales for Little Children* (1971), illustrated by Richard Kennedy, are collections of Wilson's own stories for pre-school children. For *The Illustrated Treasury of Australian Stories and Verse for Children* (1987) and *A Handful of Ghosts: Thirteen Eerie Tales by Australian Authors* (1976) see **Collections**. She has also edited *Brief Encounters: Short Stories* (1992).

Kevin the Kookaburra (1983), illustrated by Sue Price, is a series of loosely connected episodes on a farm. To protect themselves from being dive-bombed by a nesting magpie, Martin and his friend wear safety helmets in *Max the Magpie* (1983), written with Brian Mackness, illustrated by Wendy de Paauw. *Molly* (1983), based on a film, with photographs by Carol Duff and Mark Manion, is a singing dog who is saved from being stolen by Maisie.

Ker Wilson wrote the text for picture-books published for the Golden Press, including *Katy the Grey Kangaroo* (1986), illustrated by Peter Townsend, about a zoo-keeper's search for the animal; *Tiddalick the Frog* (1986), illustrated by Jan Holloway, which places the legend in a modern context; *Yellow Dog Dingo* (1986), illustrated by Kathleen Phelps, an imaginary account of how the dingo came to Australia; *Danny the Dolphin* (1986), illustrated by Peter Townsend, about whaling in Twofold Bay; and *Tatsu the Frilled Necked Lizard* (1986), also illustrated by Townsend, set in outback Queensland. Japanese Noriko goes to school with Susan, contends with the positive and negative reactions of children and adults, and is excited to see a lizard one weekend.

Ker Wilson is an enthusiastic promoter of Australian children's books and while she was with Angus & Robertson instigated the Australian exhibitions at the Bologna Book Fair.

KEVIN, JOHN WILLIAM, see **'FERRES, ARTHUR'**

KIDD, DIANA (1933–) taught English to immigrant children, where she recognised the need for minority cultures to be nurtured rather than subsumed within the mainstream. In *The Day Grandma Came to Stay (and Spoiled My Life)* (1988) Nonna transforms Lucy's life for the better, despite the title. Nonna plays the mouthorgan, catches yabbies and makes delicious pasta for the school fête. In the process, she shows Lucy how to be proud of her Italian heritage. *Onion Tears* (1989), illustrated by Dee Huxley, describes in letters and story how Nam-Huong comes to terms with her past. See also **Immigrants**. *The Fat and Juicy Place* (1992), illustrated by Bronwyn Bancroft, is about the paradise up north which the Birdman evokes for urban Jack. Jack absorbs the rich Dreaming stories of the Birdman, and is able to confront his father's death. See also **Aboriginal People in Children's Fiction**. Kidd's novels for young readers present the richness found in a multicultural Australia without glossing over its problems.

KIDDELL, JOHN (1922–87), born Melbourne, wrote short stories, critical material, documentaries and radio plays. *The Day of the Dingo* (1955), illustrated by W. Neave Parker, is an animal fantasy. When Redda the red setter escapes from his cruel mistress, he is accepted by the animals of Gumbarumba Gully, despite the fears of some that he is a dingo in disguise. When a dingo does come, Redda saves the animals from the dingo pack. In *Giant of the Bush* (1962), illustrated by Richard Kennedy, Arnold, a bushman

eight feet tall, is befriended by David Morgan, who saves him from the hostility of the locals by taking on the mob who set out to lynch him. *Tod* (1968) is an account of the adventures of Tod Booth, which begins in King's Cross. In *Euloowirree Walkabout* (1969) David, Hamish and Bottle are determined to prove their mettle by walking from Sydney to Adelaide, each with only one dollar in his pocket. Their adventures involve organising a wedding, a near tragedy in the desert and pursuit by an angry husband. Each young man understands himself and his friends better after the experience, and each is ready to face the future with greater optimism, a future which they are aware may include being conscripted for the Vietnam War. Kiddell has also written factual material for children, such as *Choogoowarra: Australian Sheep Station* (1972).

KIDDLE, MARGARET LOCH (1914– 58), born Melbourne, wrote the fairy story *Moonbeam Stairs* (1945), illustrated by Anne Montgomery. The fairy Swiftwings takes David to Fairyland, a crystal sphere which circles the earth. David and Swiftwings ride in Ferloppity's pouch, then travel under the sea to Lob's Island, where they are joined by another boy, Jack. Together, Jack and David find the moonbeam stairs in an imaginative story. *West of Sunset* (1949), also illustrated by Montgomery, is a historical novel about two immigrant cousins, Jane and Harriet, who become protégés of Caroline Chisholm. Mrs Chisholm arranges for the girls to travel to 'Mirrabooka' Station to assist the widowed Mrs Browning, and their life there is detailed, as they assist with the household, learn the ways of the Aboriginal People, kill snakes, and capture bushrangers. See also **Lost in the Bush**.

Kiewa Adventure (1950) by Allan Aldous was Commended in the 1951 Book of the Year Awards. Mr Shapley is accused of theft, and the family move to the Kiewa Valley where he works for the State Electricity Commission ('it's the life for a real man') as a truck-driver, despite the associations he is forced to have with men who 'are only interested in race horses'. There are descriptions of the Kiewa scheme and the Bogong High Plains. Shapley's children, John and Erica, board at school during the week and ski during the weekend. In one of these expeditions John saves a crashed airman, which results in his father's name being cleared, and a bonus and promotion for Mr Shapley.

KINCH, LOUISE. For *Stories of Adventure* (1945) see **Adventure Stories**.

'Kindergarten of the Air' began in 1942 in Perth, on the suggestion of Miss Olga Dickson, Director of the Hazel Orme Free Kindergarten, Fremantle, which was the first kindergarten closed during World War II, as Fremantle was seen as an enemy target. With the help of Catherine King, the Kindergarten Union in WA developed the radio program, which was conducted by Margaret Graham, a kindergarten director, with a pianist and two children. Other States soon followed, and in 1943, a national program was begun, with Anne Dreyer in Melbourne, accompanied by Marjorie Boyes on the piano, and Ruth Fenner in Sydney, presenting on alternate days. Margaret Graham continued to run the WA sessions. *Listening Time: "Kindergarten of the Air" Stories and Verses* (1961), illustrated by Margaret Horder, arose out of the program.

KING, ALEC (ALEXANDER) (1904–70), born Dorset, UK, was an academic in WA and Victoria. With his wife **CATHERINE** (1904–), the daughter of Sir Walter Murdoch and an initiator of 'Kindergarten of the Air', he wrote *Australian Holiday* (1945). See **Animal Stories**. Catherine King conducted a radio session in Perth from 1944 to 1966.

KING, JOHN ANTHONY (1949–), born Sydney, studied at the National Art School, Sydney, and designed sets for the Nimrod Theatre. His picture-books on Australian life have the atmosphere of colonial times, such as *Mad Dan Morgan, Bushranger* (1976) or *The Wild Colonial Boy* (1985), an enigmatic interpretation of the story of Jack Doolan. *An Uncommonly Fine Day: January 26, 1788* (1987) illustrates the First Fleet landing. The diaries of the officers are used for the text, and the country and its inhabitants are interpreted with sympathy and dignity. In *Farewell to Old England Forever* (1984) the music-hall ballad is used to make an ironic background to the misery of convict times, while *The Book of Australian Songs* (1988), which has 'The Ballad of the Drover', 'Click Go the Shears', 'Waltzing Matilda' and other early poems, has a rural setting. *The Book of Australian Ballads* (1989) followed. These two books have also been issued in large format. *The Teams* (1986), *Andy's Gone with Cattle* (1984) and *Mary Called Him "Mister"* (1991) are poems by Henry Lawson. *The Circus* (1987) by C.J. Dennis is illustrated with exuberant pastels which show the excitement and daring of the circus. *Mother Monster!* (1986) by Jan McKeever is a scary verse story, accompanied by large and creepy illustrations, of a mother who dresses up to scare her children — who want the game again and again. *Teddy Bears Forever* (1988) by Barbara Hayes has thirteen stories about bears. He has also illustrated two poems by Lewis Carroll, *Father William* (1988) and *The Lobster Quadrille* (1989). King's bold and challenging pictures suggest contexts beyond the narratives.

KINGSLEY, HENRY (1830–76), born Northhamptonshire, UK, came to Australia in 1853. Soon after his return to England in 1858, he published the colonial romance *The Recollections of Geoffry Hamlyn* (1859). *The Boy in Grey* (1871) is a fairy story full of literary illusions, in which Prince Philarete of Liberia travels the world in search of the Boy in Grey. Philarete converses with hedgehogs, elephants, the Ancient Mariner and the Flying Dutchman, and eventually arrives in Australia where he finds the Boy, returning home after eleven years to take up his kingdom.

KINGSTON, WILLIAM HENRY GILES (1814–80) spent his youth in Portugal, and after settling in England, became a prolific writer of boys' books, including *Peter the Whaler* (1851). He translated a new edition of *The Swiss Family Robinson* in 1879, and edited many journals for boys. Adventure stories set in the Pacific and Southern ocean include *At the South Pole: or, The Adventures of Richard Pengelley* (1870), *The South Sea Whaler, a Story of the Loss of the "Champion" and the Adventures of Her Crew* (1875), and *The Three Admirals and the Adventures of Their Young Followers* (1878).

Although Kingston did not visit Australia, some of his books had Australian settings. When Arthur and James Gilpin arrive in Australia, in *The*

Gilpins and Their Fortunes, an Australian Tale (1865), they immediately master a bolting horse and are given £500. They take charge of 'Warragong' Station, the journey there providing them with the opportunity to observe unusual birds and animals, including one called a 'toombat'. At 'Warragong' they find the station in the hands of drunken rascals who become restive when the Gilpins insist on honesty, but the Gilpins win over the best of them and get rid of the others, and prosper to the point where they bring out the rest of their family. *Twice Lost: a Story of Shipwreck, and of Adventure in the Wilds of Australia* (1876) is another rambling adventure, including a hazardous journey by sea, after which Godfrey Raynor and his family suffer the obligatory misfortunes until they prosper in Australia. In *Australian Adventures* (1884) (later published as *Adventures in Australia*) Maurice and Guy Thurston also make their fortunes. Kingston built the story around illustrations he was given which had some reference to Australia. *The Young Berringtons: or, The Boy Explorers* (1880) first appeared in the English magazine

Adventures in Australia (1895) by W.H.G. Kingston. Illustrator unknown

Little Folks. It describes the adventures of Harry and Paul Berrington and their cousins, Reginald and the odious Hector. The English cousins are unable to milk a cow and are terrified of snakes, in contrast to the more resourceful Australians. They are attacked by Aboriginal People, suffer terrible storms, spend forty-eight hours up a tree after a flood, and hunt kangaroos and emus. Harry and Paul are already 'cornstalks', and when Hector, 'more bored than tired', says, 'I didn't imagine such a country as this was to be found in the Queen's dominions … It's a horrid country, to say the best of it …' Harry answers, 'It is my country, and I'll not have it abused.' See also **Families**. *Peter Biddulph: The Rise and Progress of an Australian Settler* (1881) is a similar series of adventures, told by Peter when he is a grandfather, to a sea captain. A lucky discovery enables the orphaned Peter to return a lost ring to Mr Wells, who becomes his benefactor. Peter becomes a sailor, and after marriage and the birth of his children, sets off on his own ship to Australia. Much of the novel is taken up with the perilous voyage, including raging storms, fear of the French, and being becalmed. There is the usual attack by bushrangers, observation of the flora and fauna, and an encounter with Aboriginal People. Despite early problems, Peter's 'trust in God, industry and perseverance' conquers all difficulties and leads on to success. In *The Diary of Milicent Courtenay: or, The Experiences of a Young Lady at Home and Abroad* (1873), Helen, Milicent, Mabel, Ranald, their guardian, Mrs Markham, and an entourage of servants set off for Australia after the loss of their father and brother. Half-way through the novel they arrive at 'Auburn' Station and later take up their own station, 'Rosella'. They observe an enormous variety of animal life, including kangaroos, native companions, platypuses, dingoes, 'opossums', koalas, parrots, and budgerigars, and cheerfully shoot lyre-birds and bell-birds

as specimens. Ranald is lost in the bush (and found by a stranger who finally identifies himself as his father), they experience a bushfire, are saved from incineration by a long-lost brother, and have a startling encounter with bushrangers. See **Bushrangers**. The novel concludes with all the Courtenays settled in Australia and happily married. Kingston's novels promoted Australia as a place welcoming the British settler, but one of a particular type. Peter Biddulph says, 'Australia still affords a fine field for settlers, but they must be industrious, persevering, and energetic; idlers, rogues and vagabonds will starve there as everywhere else', a sentiment echoed by his younger contemporary, Gordon Stables (q.v.).

KIRSTEN, MARCIA MEYMOTT (1902–83) was the editor from 1967 to 1981 of *Youth Writes: Original Writings by Young Australians of Secondary School Age* (1967) and further collections of the same name. The collections had contributions from young Australians from 11 to 14, and included poems and stories by authors who were later to become more familiar, such as Kerryn Goldsworthy and Anna Maria Dell'oso. The first volume was published by Kirsten on her own initiative, but a Fellowship was established in 1970 for the later collections. In 1984 *An Australian Youth Anthology* appeared, a selection from the previous volumes.

KITANOV, VICKY (1958–), has illustrated *Arabella, the Smallest Girl in the World* (1986) by Mem Fox; *The Terrible Wild Grey Hairy Thing* (1986) by Jean Chapman; *Hello There* and *Rotten Eggs* (both 1989) by Josephine Croser; *Santa Claws* (1989) by Mary Small; *Night at Benny's* (1990) by Dianne Bates; *Swap Shop* (1990) by Ian Bone and Judith Simpson; and May Gibbs's *Ten Little Gumnuts* (1990).

KLEIN, ROBIN (1936–), born Kempsey, NSW, became a full-time writer in 1981 after various jobs as teacher, nurse, library assistant, and craft worker. Klein's novels, short stories and poems appeal to a range of age groups. Her work for younger readers began with *The Giraffe in Pepperell Street* (1978), illustrated by Gill Tomblin, a verse story about a family's response to a giraffe who follows a girl home. *Thing* (q.v., 1982) and *Thingnapped* (1984), illustrated by Alison Lester, have a pet dinosaur at the centre of the action. In *Oodoolay* (1983), illustrated by Vivienne Goodman, the residents of a country town trick a lazy station master into cleaning up the station. *Junk Castle* (1983), illustrated by Rolf Heimann, deals with children in an inner-city environment. In their struggle to keep a playground, Mandy, Irene, Con and Splinter learn a lesson in how to co-operate and win over the cranky opposition. *Boris and Borsch* (q.v., 1990) is a romp, in which two fuzzy bears are given to inappropriate owners.

Honoured Guest (1979) was the first of her novels for older readers, and takes up themes Klein was to explore later, such as a friendship between a girl and an elderly woman, friends manipulating each other, and family life. For her books about Penny Pollard see ***Penny Pollard's Diary***; **Girls**. Klein's exploration of the outsider is found in her humorous novels for young readers: *Thalia the Failure* (1984), illustrated by Rhyll Plant, about a young witch with learning problems; *Birk the Berserker* (1987), illustrated by Alison Lester, about a timid Viking; and *The Princess who Hated It* (1986), about a princess who despises her role. *Boss of the Pool* (1986), illustrated by Helen Panagolopoulos, is an examination of disability. Shelley is handicapped in her inability to look beyond Ben's physical self into his heart, until her disgust is transformed into understanding and respect for Ben's courage as she teaches him to swim. A group of three novels, *Serve Him Right!*, *You're on Your Own* and

Good for Something (all 1985) were produced as a kit in Edward Arnold's 'Battlers' series. Each has a child with a particular problem — stammering, deafness and clumsiness. In *Get Lost* (1987), illustrated by June Joubert, after an accident the irascible Brad finds friendship and acceptance with an Aboriginal boy, Jamie. *Separate Places* (1985), illustrated by Astra Lacis, deals with the effects of divorce on Karen, aged 10. *Hating Alison Ashley* (q.v., 1984) (see **Girls**; **Humour**) and *The Enemies* (1985), illustrated by Noela Young, also deal with friendship, as does *Laurie Loved Me Best* (1988), where Klein is writing for an older audience. Julia and Andre, misfits at a snobbish school, fall out over the handsome Laurie, but their friendship survives through their sensitivity to each other's feelings. *The Lonely Hearts Club* (1987), with Max Dann, has Scuff and Donovan setting up a club in their desperate search for girlfriends. The tables are turned when Cheryl and Tracee-Ann take it over.

Klein's interest in fantasy is expressed in *Halfway Across the Galaxy and Turn Left* (1985) (see **Science Fiction**) and *The Ghost in Abigail Terrace* (1989), illustrated by Margaret Power, in which Mr Claude fails to haunt successfully, but finds a friend in the real-life Joanna. *People Might Hear You* (q.v., 1983) is an unusual novel about religious fanaticism. In *Games* (1986), illustrated by Melissa Webb, lonely Patricia and popular Kirsty and Genevieve plan to have an illicit party. They conduct a seance, where they fear they have called up Dorothea, who was murdered. Throughout the night they are terrified by inexplicable noises, smells and moving objects. Patricia sees through the superficiality of the two other girls, and finds a friend in a local boy, Darcy. There is a fine build-up of suspense, and the supernatural element is created with skill. There are three levels of games played: the malicious games of Kirsty and Genevieve, which are played on Patricia; the menacing game that Darcy plays on the girls; and the game the author plays on the reader. *Annabel's Ghost and Don't tell Lucy* (1983) were published together in OUP's 'Witches, Ghosts and Hallowe'en' thematic pack. *Don't Tell Lucy* was also republished in 1987, illustrated by Kristin Hilliard, in Methuen's 'Dimensions' (q.v.) series.

Ratbags and Rascals: Funny Stories (1984) and *Snakes and Ladders* (1985), both illustrated by Alison Lester, are collections of humorous and fantasy stories, and *Against the Odds: Extraordinary Stories about Ordinary People* (1989) has five fantasy and science fiction stories. *Tearaways: Stories to Make You Think Twice* (1990) are also stories to shock and disturb complacency. *Robin Klein's Crookbook* (1987), illustrated by Kristen Hilliard, contains activities for the bedridden child. Klein's narrative poem, *I Shot an Arrow* (1987), illustrated by Geoff Hocking, is a parody of Longfellow's poem. In a portrait of colonial Australia, she describes the chaos and mayhem which occurs when Tim O'Grady fires his arrow.

In *Came Back to Show You I Could Fly* (q.v., 1989), lonely Seymour meets the beautiful Angie. In the course of their friendship, Seymour learns to stand up for himself and Angie has to confront her addiction. *All in the Blue Unclouded Weather* (1991) is a series of vignettes, set during the late 1940s. Grace, Heather, Cathy and Vivienne and their cousin, Isobel, live in a country town where stickybeaks abound, money is scarce, and games are rough and inventive. There is freedom for the girls in a family where Mother is preoccupied with writing verse for the 'In Memoriam' section of the local newspaper, and Dad is either prospecting or weeding his tung-oil plantation. See also **Humour**.

Apart from her mastery over the craft of writing, Klein's talents include shrewd observation of people and situations, an ability to connect with children outside the mainstream, compassion, and an overriding sense of humour. She was awarded the Dromkeen Medal in 1991.

KNIGHT, FRANK (1905–), born London, UK, served in the merchant navy for many years, and with the RAF during World War II. He has written over twenty books for children, mainly about the sea and ships. The first novel in his 'Clipper' series was *The Golden Monkey* (1953), illustrated by J.S. Goodall, set in Australia at the time of the gold rushes. Johnny Spinner goes to sea on the *Merry Maiden*, bound for Australia. Knight's collections include *Stories of Famous Ships* (1963), *Stories of Famous Explorers by Sea* (1964) and *Stories of Famous Explorers by Land* (1965). For *Captain Cook and the Voyage of the 'Endeavour' 1768–1771* (1968) see **Cook**, Captain **James**.

KOALA (Kids Own Australian Literature Award), awarded in NSW and the ACT, was inaugurated in 1987. In 1991, the ACT instituted its own award, COOL (q.v.). The aim of KOALA is to involve young Australian readers in nominating and voting for their favourite books and to promote their enjoyment and critical appreciation of Australian literature. Representatives on the Council for the Award include the School and Children's Sections of ALIA; the CBC, NSW; the Australian Reading Association, NSW; Primary English Teachers' Association; School Libraries Association of NSW; Australian Booksellers and Publishers Association; and the English Teachers' Association. **1987** Primary winner: *Possum Magic* (q.v., 1983) by Mem Fox; Secondary winner: *Hating Alison Ashley* (q.v., 1984) by Robin Klein. **1988** Primary winner: *Sister Madge's Book of Nuns* (q.v., 1986) by Doug MacLeod; Secondary winner: *Animalia* (q.v., 1986) by Graeme Base. **1989** Primary winner: *The Eleventh Hour* (q.v., 1988) by Graeme Base; Secondary winner: *So Much to Tell You …* (q.v., 1988) by John Marsden. **1990** Primary winner: *Where the Forest Meets the Sea* (q.v., 1987) by Jeannie Baker; Secondary winner: *Unreal! Eight Surprising Stories* (q.v., 1985) by Paul Jennings. **1991**

Primary winner: *Unbelievable! More Surprising Stories* (q.v., 1986) by Paul Jennings; Secondary winner: *The Red King* (1989) by Victor Kelleher.

Kojuro and the Bears (1986), illustrated by Junko Morimoto, a text adapted by Helen Smith from a story by Kenji Miyazawa, won the 1987 Picture Book of the Year Awards. This Japanese folk-tale tells of a hunter who deeply respects the animals he must kill to support his family. When Kojuro's turn for death has come, he faces it with acceptance as a part of the cycle of life. Each opening is designed to convey the melancholy mood of the tale. Brilliant colour and perspective are used in a book about the dignity of human existence.

KRAUTH, CARON and **NIGEL** (1949–) were both born in Sydney. *Sin Can Can* (1987) is set in Bali and involves Balinese spirits and a budding romance between Ashlie Fallowfield, aged 14, and the Indonesian Rai. *Rack off, Rachmaninoff* (1989) introduces Zoe Asken and the war between the Sunny Corner pacifists and the Rathdowney ratpack for peace on the school bus. *I Thought You Kissed With Your Lips* (1990) describes Zoe's trip to Surfer's Paradise, where her passion for the cetaceans leads her to try to free them. Nigel Krauth has written novels for adults, including *JF was Here* (1991).

KROC Awards (Kids Reading Oz Choice) are the annual awards for the most popular children's author read in the NT. It was originally NTYRBA, Northern Territory Young Readers Book Award, which ran from 1983 to 1986. **1983** *Superfudge* by Judy Blume and *Watership Down* by Richard Adams. Through the national Reading 1990 Program, it was redesigned as KROC, and administered by the NT Library Promotion Council. **1990 and 1991** *Round the Twist* (q.v., 1990) by Paul Jennings.

L

LACIS, ASTRA (1937–), born Riga, Latvia, settled in Australia in 1949. Lacis studied at East Sydney Technical school, and has worked as a painter, illustrator and graphic artist. Since 1960, as Astra, Astra Dick or Astra Lacis, she has illustrated novels and informational books, magazines, educational materials, and reading schemes. Her large body of work includes novels and picture-books for Jean Chapman, Nance Donkin, Anne Farrell, David Martin, Christobel Mattingley, Carol Odell, Maurice Saxby, Noreen Shelley, Celia Syred, Edel Wignell and Patricia Wrightson. A characteristic example of her later work is *The Angel* *with a Mouth-Organ* (1984) by Christobel Mattingley, in which her delicate pictures evoke the European landscape, and display the pain and triumph of a family separated by war.

Lady Cutler Award for Distinguished Services to Children's Literature in NSW. Lady Helen Cutler (1923–90) was the patron of the CBC, NSW Branch, and the award has been given by that organisation since 1981. **1981** Eve Pownall; **1982** Joyce Fardell; **1983** Ena Noel; **1984** Anne Bower Ingram; **1985** Walter Cunningham; **1986** Patricia

The Angel With A Mouth Organ (1984) by Christobel Mattingley. Illustrator: Astra Lacis.

Wrightson; **1987** Val Watson; **1988** Lydia Pender; **1989** Maurice Saxby; **1990** Jean Chapman; **1991** Margaret Hamilton; **1992** June Smith.

Ladybird Garden (1949), written and illustrated by Dagma Dawson when she was eleven years old, gained a Special Mention in the 1950 Book of the Year Awards. Miss Dotty and Mr Spotty Ladybird are married, and move into Pumpkin House, with its lovely garden. Dotty hangs rose petal curtains, puts glow-worms in the lamps, and has five babies, the naughty Spik, Spak and Spek, and the well-behaved Flit and Glitter. Mature writing and well-executed illustrations combine in a surprisingly accomplished work.

LAKE, DAVID JOHN (1929–), born Bangalore, India, came to Australia in 1967 as Associate Professor of English at the University of Queensland. His science fiction novels for adults include *The Man who Loved Morlocks: a Sequel to The Time Machine Narrated by the Time Traveller* (1981). His two fantasies for children are *The Changelings of Chaan* (q.v., 1985), set in Asia, and *West of the Moon* (1988), in which Mark and Meg travel to Middleworld and Vornemarna, where they battle with the forces of evil.

Lake at the End of the World, The (1988) by Caroline Macdonald was an Honour Book in the 1989 Book of the Year Awards: Older Readers. After a world environmental disaster, Diana and her parents have found a refuge on the edge of Redfern Lake. When flying on her 'wingset', Diana meets Hector, a member of an underground community ruled by the tyrannical Counsellor. Diana and Hector save the lake and confront the Counsellor. The children tell their stories in alternate chapters, struggling towards understanding their dilemma, and determined to work with adults for an unpolluted earth. See also **Science Fiction**.

LAMBERT, ERIC (1918–66), born Stamford, England, arrived in Australia in 1919. Lambert wrote novels for adults about the experiences of the Australian soldier, such as *The Twenty Thousand Thieves* (1951). *The Tender Conspiracy* (1965), illustrated by Iris Schweitzer, is an autobiography of part of his childhood. Herman Hart, 'Toowoomba Jack', is an Austrian immigrant adopted by a group of children when he becomes blind. Jack reveals to the young Eric that a decision between courage and fear must often be made in a moment. The book demonstrates Lambert's preoccupation with courage, friendship and morality, issues which inform his adult work.

LAMBERT, GEORGE WASHING-TON (1873–1930), born St Petersburg, Russia, artist and illustrator, came to Australia in 1887. He studied at the Sydney Art School under Julian Ashton, and in Paris. He was an artist for the *Bulletin*, where his fine illustrations of bushmen and horses regularly appeared. He was also an official war artist in Palestine with the Australian Light Horse. Lambert's illustrations can be seen in *The Spirit of the Bushfire and Other Australian Fairy Tales* (1898) by Jesse Whitfeld and *Girls Together* (1898) by Louise Mack.

LAMOND, HENRY GEORGE (1885–1969), born Carl Creek, Queensland, worked on stations throughout northern Australia. Stories and extracts from Lamond's work are used in schools and in anthologies, although Lamond's intended audience was adult. The eleven stories in *Tooth and Talon: Tales of the Australian Wild* (1934) first appeared in the USA in the *Atlantic Monthly*, *Adventure* and *Short Stories*. His short stories and novels display his understanding of the lives of animals and birds in the wild or in domesticity, such as *An Aviary on the Plains* (1934) (which has a dustjacket by Dorothy Wall), *Amathea, the Story of a Horse* (1937), *Brindle Royalist: a Story of the*

Australian Plains (1946), *The Manx Star* (1954), *Towser, Sheep Dog* (1955), *The Red Ruin Mare* (1958), *Sheep Station* (1959) and *Etiquette of Battle* (1966).

Originally a serial in the *Australasian*, entitled 'White Ears the Outlaw', *Dingo, the Story of an Outlaw* (1945) is the life story of a big dingo which becomes such a skilful hunter that it defies capture. Another powerful account of life in the wild is *Big Red* (1953), the story of a red kangaroo, marked in its youth by a professional kangaroo hunter, Larry Grant, who puts a bullet hole in the joey's ear. Using this mark of identification, Larry observes the animal's development from joey to 'kangaroo-king of Boori'. Big Red's experiences include bushfire, dingo and eagle attacks, and the fight for dominance which concludes the book. With humour and without sentimentality, Lamond pays a tribute to the courage of animals.

The author's experiences as a bushman provide the background to all these novels. The animals' crises are discussed in bars and camps by the bushmen who share the land with sheep, cattle and the creatures of the wild, so that the novels show outback life in the early part of the twentieth century.

LAMONT, PRISCILLA. For *Ring O' Roses: Nursery Rhymes, Action Rhymes and Lullabies* (1990) see **Nursery Rhymes**.

LANAGAN, MARGO (1960–), born Newcastle, NSW, is a poet, writer and editor. In *Wildgame* (1991) Macka is pulled into a computer game where she becomes a small animal. When she returns to reality, the animal comes too, creating a dilemma which she must resolve. *The Tankermen* (1992) is set in Sydney's Kings Cross. Finn is a street kid who discovers a sinister gang pumping evil sludge into Sydney's waterways. Lanagan has used pseudonyms for her novels in Bantam's 'Wildfire' series: 'Melanie Carter' for *The Cappuccino Kid* (1991), 'Mandy McBride' for *Temper, Temper!* (1991) and 'Belinda Hayes' for *Star of the Show* (1991) and *Girl in the Mirror* (1991).

LANE, FRED. For *Patrol to the Kimberleys* (1958) see **Aboriginal People in Children's Fiction**.

'LAPIN, GERRI', see **ALEXANDER, GOLDIE**

LARDNER, KYM (1957–), born Adelaide, is a storyteller and illustrator. His ability to engage the interest of small children is seen in his picture-books. In *The Sad Little Monster and the Jelly Bean Queen* (1981) the life of a lonely monster is brightened by a friendly princess; *Grandpa's Horses* (1986) is about rocking-horses, and *Arnold the Prickly Teddy* (1989) is about a bad-tempered toy transformed by love.

LAROCHE, MICHEL (1948–), born France, is a museum consultant and writer. *The Snow Rose* (1983) is a fairy-tale set in the eighteenth century. Roland the troubadour must perform a series of tasks to win the hand of Princess Ermina, but eventually realises that it is Rose, the innkeeper's daughter, whom he really loves. *The Mushroom Feast* (1988) is eaten by a king who is so fond of food that he ignores everything else. Both are illustrated by Laroche's wife, Sandra Laroche.

LAROCHE, SANDRA (1944–), born Brisbane, has illustrated *Firebrand* (1968), *Wings on Wednesday* (1968), *Please Sit Still* (1969) and *Hullabaloo* (1969) by Natalie Scott; *The Wizard of the Umbrella People* (1971) by 'Louise Kent' (Natalie Scott); *It's Fun to Go to School* (1974) by Joan Mellings; *Grandpa Pearson* (1979) by Letitia Parr; *Stephen's Tree* (1979) and *Lachlan's Walk* (1980) by Libby Hathorn; *Digit Dick and the Magic Jabiru* (1981) by Leslie Rees; *A Gift from the Past* (1984) by Mavis Scott; *The Key and the Fountain* (1985) by John Pinkney; *Stories to Share*

(1983), *Capturing the Golden Bird: the Young Hans Christian Andersen* (1987) and *Little Billy Bandicoot: Rhymes and Songs for Australian Children* (1991) by Jean Chapman; *Had Yer Jabs?* (1987) by Max Fatchen; and *Angie the Brave* (1987) by Sally Farrell Odgers. Laroche illustrated Ethel Turner's *Seven Little Australians* (1894) in 1983. She has also illustrated two books by her husband, Michel Laroche (q.v.). Her careful research results in soft watercolours which recreate in detail the historical period in which the books are set.

LAW, WINIFRED. For *Through Space to the Planets* (1944) and *Rangers of the Universe* (1945) see **Science Fiction**.

LAWRIE, MARGARET (1936–) was a liaison officer with the Department of Aboriginal Affairs and matron of a home for Aboriginal women in Adelaide. She wrote *Myths and Legends of Torres Strait* (1970) and *Tales from Torres Strait* (1972). See **Aboriginal Dreaming Stories**.

LAWSON, WILL (1876–1957), born Durham, UK, novelist, journalist and poet, came to Australia as a child. He spent some years in NZ and wrote travel books about that country. *When Cobb and Co. was King* (1936) begins when its hero, Buster White, is around 14 years of age, and his fascination and rapport with horses get him a position with Cobb & Co. He rises from stable-boy to driver, fights off bushrangers and flood, goes to Melbourne and sees Archer win the first Melbourne Cup in 1861, buys shares in Cobb & Co., and wins Mary Lester from her handsome bushranger lover, Garston. Lawson credits the story's inspiration to William Williamson, a Cobb & Co. manager, and Frank Smiley, an old driver. The novel, historically accurate, was widely read for its romance and action. *Galloping Wheels* (1947), written with Tom Hickey, is the story of the rise of Jimmie McLernon from country boy to engine-driver.

Jimmie's work in the railway workshops, his experience as fireman and his journeys across the country are described, interspersed with the story of his romance with Nessie. Lawson edited *Australian Bush Songs and Ballads* (1944).

LE BRETON, AGATHA (1886–?), born Maryborough, Queensland, used the pseudonym 'Miriam Agatha' for the children's stories she wrote for the Australian Catholic Truth Society, in a series called 'Penny Publications'. Produced around the time of World War I, and 'designed to teach young Catholic children', they include *Benny and the Bishop*, "*Medically Unfit*", *Some Xmas Letters*, *A Soldier's Son*, *An Australian Mother*, *Soldier Stories*, *A Failure* and "*Little Therese*". *Grannie's Rosary Beads and Other Stories*, *Peggy's Present and Other Stories*, *For the Holy Souls and Other Stories* and *Roses and Rosaries and Other Stories* (all 1910) were written for the same society. *Eastwood Ho! Stories of Young Crusaders* (1925) are accounts of missionaries in China first published in the journal *Far East*. Her longer novels include *Nellie Doran: a Story of Australian Home and School Life* (1914), in which shy and homesick Nellie from outback Queensland is transformed as her talent emerges at St Mary's. This pious story conveys the peer-group pressures of school life, and its underground world of jealousies and friendships. *Dolour D'Arcy: or, The Church Between, an Australian Story* (1915) describes the romance between a Catholic girl and a non-Catholic man. When John Deraway is refused by Dolour, he marries Molly, but will not allow the children to be brought up as Catholics. Catastrophe results. Le Breton also wrote a history book, *The Story of Australia for Catholic Schools* (?1921).

LEAR, MELVA GWENDOLINE (1917–), born Pingelly, WA, has set three novels in WA. In *Dangerous Holiday: Five Young Treasure-seekers in the Abrolhos Islands* (1959), illustrated by Joan Abbott, Tony van Raaltes, Ken, Kate, Jean and Alan, foil the attempts of a foreign spy to steal secret equipment from the Woomera Rocket Range, and discover jewels from the wreck of the *Batavia*. *River Fugitive: the Story of a Boy with a Secret* (1963), illustrated by Walter Stackpool, is set on the Swan River. Kevin and his sister Jill become friends with the enigmatic Andy. They discover an illegal car-wrecking operation, and Andy finds a home with a French neighbour, Madam Roberts and her son. Although the novel has a leisurely pace, tension is created, and the characterisation of the young people who live on the river front is telling. They listen to pop music, try out smoking, and do not always do as they are told. For *A Secret to Sell, a Story of the First Settlement in Western Australia* (1965) see **Historical Novels**.

LEASON, PERCY (PERCIVAL ALEXANDER) (1889–1959), born Kaniva, Victoria, was a painter, illustrator and cartoonist. In 1906 he was apprenticed as a lithographer to John Sands, and in 1916 he became the chief designer for Sydney Ure Smith. Leason's laconic depiction of the landscape and population of a mythical bush town, 'Wiregrass', for the *Bulletin*, earned him the affection of its readers. Leason produced a series of portraits of Victorian Aboriginal People. In 1924 he became the chief cartoonist of the *Melbourne Punch*, but, disappointed with his success as a cartoonist and lack of recognition as a painter, he left Australia in 1938 for the USA, where he taught at the Staten Island Institute of Art. *Here is Faery* (1915) is a collection of his poems and stories for adults, which use fantasies of gypsies, princesses, and Father Time to reveal the power of love and art. He illustrated *Australian Nursery Rimes* (1917) selected from the *Bulletin*; Edward Cole's *Tales of Magic and Might* (1902); Agnes Littlejohn's *Star Dust and Sea Spray* (1918), illustrated with Sydney Ure Smith; Lillian Pyke's *Cole's Happy Time Picture and Nursery Rhyme Book* (1925); and *Red*

Poppy and Other Stories for Use in Schools (1911). He illustrated a version of L. Frank Baum's classic as *The Wizard of Oz Picture Book* (1939). His pictures of animals and humans are often wry caricatures, frequently observed from unusual perspectives, but always displaying precise execution, masterly craftsmanship and an understanding of the foibles of human nature.

LEE, LESLIE. In *The Road to Widgewong* (1928), illustrated by Edgar A. Holloway, Joe and Bob run away from Sydney to return to Joe's home at Widgewong. Their adventures along the way include encounters with swagmen and being lost in the bush. See also **Lost in the Bush**. *Furry Tales* (1928) and *More Furry Tales* (1953), illustrated by Angus McGregor, are legend-like stories about Australian animals.

LEE, Mrs **ROBERT** (1791–1856) was an English writer and artist of natural history. She first married the naturalist Thomas Edward Bowdich, with whom she travelled extensively before his death, although she never visited Australia. She wrote *Adventures in Australia: or, the Wanderings of Captain Spencer in the Bush and the Wilds. Containing Accurate Descriptions of the Habits of the Natives, and the Natural Productions and Features of the Country* (1851), illustrated by the colonial artist J.S. Prout. Mrs Lee used the journals of Stokes, Grey, Sturt, Eyre and others, and 'the works of Professor Owen and Mr Gould's works', as her sources. The novel is a Robinsonade, in which Spencer is shipwrecked and crosses the continent from north to south, then travels east with his horse Tiger, his dog Gipsy, his parrot Charlie and Kinchela, his Aboriginal mentor. The resourceful Captain Spencer undergoes every difficulty and privation imaginable, all the time observing the remarkable animals, birds and insects around him, the scientific names of which are provided for the reader. He makes hats for himself out of grass, shoes for himself and his horse from kangaroo skins, and is able to feed himself more than adequately off the land. When he meets another traveller, Spencer supplies the food: ' ... the supper was set out in pieces of bark, in a profusion which surprised [Mr St John]. There were stewed Kangaroo meat, baked Duck, boiled Trefoil, which resembled spinach; Sorrel salad, Crayfish, cakes of Grass-seed by way of bread and some powdered dust which resembled mustard, and salt was supplied by small pieces of salcolaceous plants.' Spencer survives snakebite and spearing before arriving full of health in Sydney. See also **Sydney**. Mrs Lee wrote other books for children, such as *The Juvenile Album: or, Tales from Far and Near* (?1846), which contains eight stories set in India, the West Indies and England.

LEES, MARGARET (1936–), born Melbourne, painter, illustrator and teacher, trained at the Art School at Melbourne Teachers' College. She has illustrated Barbara Macfarlane's *Zop, King of the Fireflitters* (1971), *Jenny and the Magic Ball* (1974), *The Birds and Hetty* (1974), *The Mouse Keeper* (1976), *Naughty Agapanthus* (q.v., 1966), *Queen Agapanthus* (1970) and *Agapanthus is Lost* (1970).

LEES, MARIAN (1957–), born Melbourne. For *The Meat in the Sandwich* (1988) see **Collections**.

Left Overs, The (1982) by Eleanor Spence was Highly Commended in the 1983 Book of the Year Awards. When Drew finds that Barnfield, the children's home where he lives, is to be sold, he decides that the best solution to avoid splitting up the only family he has known, is to find foster-parents for Jasmine, James, Straw and himself. He tries advertising in the paper, and even appeals through a television show. Spence's four child characters, Auntie Bill (their house mother) and Mick Mulvaney, the man who understands Drew's predicament, have individuality and humour.

LEOPOLD, KEITH (1920–) was Professor of German at the University of Queensland. *When We Ran* (1981) is the story of Christamarie and her mother, Ulrike, who was a member of the Baader-Meinhof group, trained by the PLO. Ulrike's past catches up with her, and she is threatened with blackmail. Mother and daughter escape to Queensland, pursued by the IRA, where they adopt new identities and are befriended by Nazis who are themselves wanted as war criminals. Baader-Meinhof, PLO, IRA and the Nazis have replaced the flood, fire and drought with which the nineteenth-century adventure writers spiced their stories.

'LESLIE, J.' was the pseudonym of **J.L. HADDON**, born on the NSW Tablelands. He was an engineer who worked in the lumber camps of Canada, the salmon canneries in Alaska and the railways in NZ, as well as in Australia. *Home is the Sailor* (1934) recounts the search for Jimmy Brent's long-lost sister after Jimmy is taken in by Captain John Hardy, aboard the *Mary Ellen*. *Youth Builds a Monument* (1933) is dedicated 'to Australian boys, whatever their ages, wherever they live'. The games and escapades of 'Podge' Lindsay, a train-driver's son, and his mates, during their school-days in a small town close to Sydney, are related in detail, in a poignant and amusing tribute to working-class life at the turn of the century.

LESTER, ALISON (1952–), born Foster, Victoria, studied at the Art School at Melbourne Teachers' College, and worked as a teacher. She has illustrated books by other writers, such as the *Big Dipper* series, edited by June Epstein and others, and Epstein's Augustus books. Her work includes Robin Klein's *Thing* (1982), *Ratbags and Rascals* (1984), *Thingnapped* (1984) and *Birk the Berserker* (1987); *A First Australian Poetry Book* (1983), compiled by June Factor, and *A Second Australian Poetry*

Book (1983), compiled by Barbara Giles; Summer (1987) by June Factor; and Night-Night! (1986) by Morris Lurie.

Lester has also written and illustrated her own material. In *Ruby* (1987) the heroine has a quilt, Besty, which, one magical night flies Ruby to an island where she rescues lion cubs. *Clive Eats Alligators* (q.v., 1985) is about individuality, and in the two books which follow, *Rosie Sips Spiders* (1988) and *Tessa Snaps Snakes* (1990) the same children imagine what they would like to be when they grow up, and do real-life things— earning pocket money, having secrets, running messages or having midnight snacks. *Imagine* (1989) requires the reader to find the animals, birds, dinosaurs and other creatures which are pictured on double-page spreads. Its sequel, *Magic Beach* (1990), explores the fantasy world of children playing on a beach. *The Journey Home* (q.v., 1989) uses characters from nursery rhymes. *Isabella's Bed* (1991) has a South American motif, where Anna and Luis dream of travelling in search of their grandmother's lost heart. Lester has produced a series of board books for very young children: *Bibs and Boots, Bumping and Bouncing, Crashing and Splashing* and *Happy and Sad: an Australian Baby Book* (all 1988). Lester takes the everyday world of the young child and invests it with romance and adventure, using childlike figures and a rich sense of design.

Let the Balloon Go (1968) by Ivan Southall, illustrated by Ian Ribbons, was Commended in the 1969 Book of the Year Awards. John Clement Sumner has cerebral palsy, and when his overprotective mother leaves him for the day, he climbs a tree. The consequences show his parents that he prefers the 'knocks and bruises' of life to their too careful protection. In a moving portrait of determination and courage, John persists despite his fears and a body which refuses to co-operate. *Let the*

The Journey Home (1989) by Alison Lester

Balloon Go was filmed by Film Australia in 1976, directed by Oliver Howes, with Bruce Spence, Ray Barrett, and Robert Bettles as John Sumner.

LETCHFORD, PEITA (1951–) is a television producer and writer. *Matthew and the New Baby* (1986), illustrated by Kilmeny Niland, describes how Matthew ultimately pacifies his crying baby sister; and *The Very Sniffy Dog* (1990), illustrated by Deborah Niland, relates how an irritating dog wins acceptance by rescuing the baby. In *Jimmy and his Fabulous Feathered Friends* (1988), illustrated by Terry Denton, the rooster seeks Jimmy's help when the neighbours threaten the fowls. Jimmy responds first by hiding them, then by encouraging them to disguise themselves, in a humorous romp.

LETTE, KATHY (1958–), born Sydney, was half of the 'Salami Sisters', a cabaret act, and has worked as a journalist and for television. She is also a novelist and playwright. With Gabrielle Carey, she wrote *Puberty Blues* (q.v., 1979).

LEWIS, MEG. For *It All Began with Calamity* (1962) see **Horse Stories**.

LEWITT, MARIA (1924–), born Poland, came to Australia in 1949, and has written about the immigrant experience for adults in *Come Spring* (1980) and *No Snow in December* (1985). The theme is also explored in *Just Call Me Bob* (1976), in Macmillan's 'Orbit' series, about the life of Giancarlo in inner-suburban high-rise flats, and in *Grandmother's Yarn* (1985) which recalls Babcia's childhood in Poland.

Liddle-ma Lorenny is the mother of Badge, Iggy and Lance, first introduced in Nan Chauncy's *Tiger in the Bush* (q.v., 1957). She is a large, sensitive, loving and active character who can turn her hand to fencing, which she does quite as well as

cooking kangaroo patties. Not surprisingly, Dad calls her 'mate'. Her disregard for her appearance, her contempt for material acquisitions, her empathy with Badge, and the equal respect she shares with Dad in the eyes of her children mark her as an unusual character in novels for children of the period. Few mothers in Australian children's books challenge Liddle-ma's unstereotypic appeal.

Lieutenant: an Epic Tale of Courage and Endurance on the High Seas, The (1977) by Jack Bennett was Commended in the 1978 Book of the Year Awards. It relates the journey of Captain William Bligh to Dutch Timor after the mutiny on the Bounty. Bligh's self-discipline, his efforts to control his rage, and the reactions of the eighteen men, which range from admiration to angry discontent, are explored in an accessible account of Bligh's journey. See also **Bligh, William**.

'Lift Off' was a television series developed by the Australian Children's Television Foundation for 3 to 8-year-olds in 1992. A blend of live action, puppetry and animation, it was designed to contribute to children's development in key areas such as linguistic skills, musical appreciation, logic and human relations. The action centres around a block of flats, where the officious Mr Fish and Beverley, an all-seeing pot plant, inhabit the lobby. At the Wakadoo Cafe the suave Wolf, and the pigs, Boris, Morris, Doris and Lonely, hold sway. The Burke, Garcia, Jordan and Stinson families are involved in various issues, with the androgenous rag doll puppet, EC (Every Child), who is shared and loved by all the children, responding to crises and supporting any character in trouble.

Lighthouse Keeper's Lunch, The (1977) by Ronda Armitage, illustrated by David Armitage, was Highly Commended in the 1978 Picture Book of the Year Awards.

Mrs Grinling foils the seagulls who continually steal her husband's lunch when it is sent over by cable. The adventures continue in *The Lighthouse Keeper's Catastrophe* (1986) and *The Lighthouse Keeper's Rescue* (1989). Mrs Grinling sends her husband across on the cable to rescue the cat and keep the light shining, and Mr Grinling is able to put off enforced retirement by rescuing a whale and taking on a young assistant. Mrs Grinling's solutions to the problems which confront her husband require lateral thinking and are always inventive.

Lillipilly Hill (1960) by Eleanor Spence, illustrated by Susan Einzig, was Commended in the 1961 Book of the Year Awards. Only Harriet Wilmot and her father are prepared to like Australia; the others want to return to London as soon as they are able. Aidan, her older brother, earns acceptance on the cricket field and changes his mind about Australia once he 'had seen the beauty of his new country and could begin to realize why Harriet loved it so much'. Harriet's mother is won over when she is reassured that Harriet 'would not turn into a little savage through living in the bush', despite Harriet's egalitarian behaviour. The bush works its magic on the family, and they decide to stay. Spence recognises the cost of immigration in a strong re-creation of period and place.

LINDSAY, HAROLD ARTHUR (1900–69), born Adelaide, wrote an adventure story set in WA, *The Arnhem Treasure* (1952), which was used in the ABC schools broadcasts, and a seafaring story, *The Cruise of the Kestrel* (1960). *The First Walkabout* (q.v., 1954), *Rangatira, the High Born: a Polynesian Saga* (q.v., 1959) and *Aboriginal Australians* (1963), an account of Aboriginal life, were written in collaboration with Norman Tindale.

LINDSAY, HILARIE (1922–), born Sydney, is the curator of the Children's Treasure House Book and Toy Museum (q.v.). Her work includes books on cookery, nutrition and toy-making for children and adults, handbooks on local history and writing, such as *One Hundred and One Toys to Make* (1972) and *The Gravy Train* (1981), a history of mankind through food and eating. *Midget Mouse Finds a House* (1978), illustrated by Marenelle, and *Midget Mouse Goes to Sea* (1989) describe the adventures of an albino mouse who finds a home in a paper bag. In *Mr Poppleberry and the Dog's Own Daily* (1983), illustrated by Gavin Ryan, Mr and Mrs Poppleberry show how to resolve conflict without resorting to violence, a theme which is also developed in *Mr Poppleberry and Fred the White Cockatoo* (1983) and *Mr Poppleberry and the Milk Thieves* (1983).

LINDSAY, JACK (1900–90), born Melbourne, the son of Norman Lindsay, left Australia in 1926 for London. He wrote many books for adults, and four children's books: *Runaway* (1935), a historical novel about ancient Rome, *To Arms! A Story of Ancient Gaul* (1938), *The Dons Sight Devon: a Story of the Defeat of the Invincible Armada* (1941), and a novel about the Eureka Stockade, *Rebels of the Goldfields* (1936). See **Eureka Stockade**.

LINDSAY, Lady **JOAN A'BECKETT** (1896–1984), born Melbourne, was a painter, the wife of Sir Daryl Lindsay. Her only children's book is *Syd Sixpence* (1982), illustrated by Rick Amor, a fantasy about a sixpenny coin which comes to Australia from London. After adventures with the Winkle family, Mr Gabb and Tramline the cat, Syd settles on South Melbourne beach. Lindsay's best known work is *Picnic at Hanging Rock* (1967), made into a film in 1975.

LINDSAY, Sir **LIONEL** (1874–1961), born Creswick, Victoria, with his brother, Norman Lindsay, drew the illustrations to

The Adventures of Chunder Loo (q.v., 1916) and the covers of many paperbacks produced between the wars.

LINDSAY, NORMAN ALFRED WILLIAM (1879–1969), born Creswick, Victoria, joined the staff of the *Bulletin* in 1903 as a writer and illustrator. Apart from his many novels for adults, he illustrated *The Animals Noah Forgot* (1933), a book of poems for children by A.B. Paterson. His best known book for children is *The Magic Pudding: Being the Adventures of Bunyip Bluegum and His Friends Bill Barnacle and Sam Sawnoff* (q.v., 1918). His other children's book, *The Flyaway Highway* (1936), recounts with characteristic humour and robust illustrations the adventures of Egbert Tomkins and Murial Jane, who accompany 'a bloke with cow's hooves', Sylvander Dan (Pan). Together they save a daughter and her lover from an enraged father, protect Dan from a furious abbot, and extricate him from various other predicaments caused by his tendency to drink too much.

LINDSAY, RUBY (1887–1919), born Creswick, Victoria, sister of Lionel and Norman Lindsay, left Australia in 1909 with her husband, the artist Will Dyson, and died in London during an influenza epidemic. Like her husband and brothers, Lindsay was a *Bulletin* artist. Her illustrations for children's books by English writers such as Winifred Letts and Eden Phillpotts, although less boisterous, display the same fine draughtsmanship as her brothers' work.

Lindsay Shaw Collection of Australian Children's Books is housed at Monash University Library, Victoria. It contains around 1350 titles in two parts. The main group consists of fiction and informational material from the nineteenth century to contemporary works, with an emphasis on fiction. A smaller group of around 200 titles gathers together the work of Mary Grant Bruce, Ethel Turner and their families.

LINTON, KATE (1969–), born Melbourne, trained at Swinburne Institute of Technology as an illustrator and graphic designer. Miranda's fantasy world emerges in the illustrations to *Miranda* (1991). The story tells us that she has left her toys in the garden during a storm, but the illustrations show her as a light-house keeper and her toys in danger from a stormy sea. Linton illustrated *Love Me Tender* (1992) by Libby Hathorn.

LISSON, DEBORAH (1943–), born UK, came to Australia in 1962. For *The Devil's Own* (1990) see **Batavia**.

LISTER, GLADYS (1887–1957), born Melbourne, wrote *The Little Round Garden* (1938), *The Little Round House* (1939), *The House That Beckons* (1940), all decorated by Pixie O'Harris, *Little Round Stairway* (1946), illustrated by Joyce Abbott, and *The Little Round World* (1954). *Grandpuff and Leafy* (1942), *Leafy and Prince Brumby* (1944), *Leafy's Seventh Wave* (1948), all illustrated by Joyce Abbott, and *Tubby the Little Round Bear* (1949) are romantic fairy stories about a gnome-like human, the Gardener; the wind, Grandpuff; and the young platypuses, 'platykittens'. Lister also wrote novels for older readers, *Jennifer Stands By* (1941), which appeared in an abridged version as a serial in the *Sydney Morning Herald*, and *Whither Jennifer?: a Story of Adventure* (1948). Jennifer Hogarth's stern English grandmother agrees to bring her to Australia when Jennifer finds that she has a father and twin brother. She discovers a bag of gold, secures the family's fortunes, and wins over her brother John after an aeroplane crash. In *Dawn Mother* (1942), illustrated by J. Abbott, Pixie O'Harris and others, Minetta and her four stepsisters come to Australia to avoid the air raids in England, and are looked after by the open-hearted but impoverished Dawn. Fortunately, a wealthy relative appears. In *The Song Goes On* (1941), illustrated by R.M. Thompson and the author, Betty and Bryan Lindsay are jolly evacuees from Britain who are taken in by Mrs Sue, a benevolent landlord who forgoes the rent from her ten tenement houses when the tenants are ill, or when a grandmother dies. *Starlight Belongs to Me* (1951), *A Star for Starlight* (1953) and *Quest for Starlight* (1956), all illustrated by Frank Varty, are three books in breathless prose about a charismatic white horse.

LISTON, MAUD RENNER. For *Cinderella's Party* (1923) see **Fairies**.

Little Brother (1985) by Allan Baillie, illustrated by Elizabeth Honey, was Highly Commended in the 1986 Book of the Year Awards. Vithy and his brother, Mang, flee the Khmer Rouge across the Cambodian border into Thailand. Vithy continues the journey when Mang is lost, a journey which further reveals the tragedy and courage of his people. The novel is a tribute to the tenacity of the Cambodian refugees. See also **Immigrants**.

Little Brown Piccaninnies of Tasmania (1950) by Jane Ada Fletcher, illustrated by Margaret Senior, was Highly Commended in the 1950 Book of the Year Awards. Fletcher concentrates on deficits: Tasmanian Aboriginal People did not know how to make fire, did not wear clothes, and had no 'proper' boats. The novel emphasises the 'strangeness' of the Tasmanians, and perpetuates the myth that no Tasmanian Aboriginal People remain.

Little Fear, A (1983) by Patricia Wrightson won the 1984 Book of the Year Awards. The independent Mrs Agnes Tucker leaves the retirement village against her family's wishes to live on a farm inhabited by an ancient Aboriginal spirit, a Njimbin. The Njimbin is 'a small spirit, but it had lived among these ridges while the forests grew and fell and the men came and went'. A struggle ensues over who will control the farm, until Mrs Tucker accepts that the ancient presence must prevail. Although she has lost this battle, the experience has ensured her own freedom. Wrightson continues her blend of Aboriginal tradition and modern predicament in an unusual juxtaposition of elderly woman and mischievous creature.

LITTLEJOHN, AGNES, poet and novelist, wrote stories and poems for children and adults. *The Silver Road and Other Stories* (1915) first appeared in the *Sydney Mail* and the *Presbyterian*. It is a collection of twenty-four stories and poems. In 'The Silver Road' a fairy is left behind on a lily pad, and in 'Zep's Betrayal', a dingo pup chooses his master's child rather than the wild pack. *Star Dust and Sea Spray* (1918), illustrated by Sydney Ure Smith and Percy Leason, is also a collection of fairy stories. In 'The Magic Thread' a princess knits a scarf until a prince awakens her to love. In 'The Magic Spectacles' Vera's lover Randolph loses his love for her when he dons the magic white spectacles, but sees her real worth when he breaks them. Star Dust and Sea Spray also appear in *Rainbow Dreams* (1919), illustrated by Alek Sass. A third collection appeared as *The Lost Emerald and Other Stories* (1924), illustrated by Pixie O'Harris.

These fairy stories of magic and transformation are in the Romantic tradition. 'Poets are in love with Love!/The joy! the joy of dreaming!/Colour, form and beauty rare— /An ecstasy of "seeming!"' *The Sleeping Sea-Nymph* (1921), illustrated by Albert Collins and Olive Crane, a tale of nymphs, princes and mermaids, is another story catering more for the adult taste for romance and rapture than for children. An example is the poem 'Song of the Sea Prince'. 'This is our light of love and joy a'quiver— /Love's everlasting Flower has bloomed for me!/As it enriches me— the happy giver— /So also dearest, it enricheth thee!/For we are lost in sweetest Love's illusion,/And rapturous enchantment makes the whole ...' Littlejohn's books were beautifully produced and delicately decorated by fine artists.

LO, HUI-MIN was Professor of Asian Studies at the Australian National University and wrote *The Story of China* (q.v., 1970). Professor Lo now lives in Cambridge, UK.

LOCKEYEAR, J.R. In *"Mr Bunyip": or Mary Somerville's Ramble. An Australian Story for Children* (1871), also issued as *Old Bunyip: the Australian River Monster* (1871), Mary, a very good girl just turned 8, always obedient, 'light-hearted and cheerful as people always are who do that which is right', walks through the bush gathering flowers for her mother, and is given a lecture by the Bunyip on the need for temperance, charity and good behaviour. See also **Bunyips**.

Lockie Leonard, Human Torpedo (1990) by Tim Winton, won the WAYRBA Hoffman Award in 1991. Lockie and his family have moved to a coastal town, Angelus. His mother has an uncanny understanding of him; his father, Sarge, is a pacifist policeman who reads books; and his brother Phillip has a problem with bed-wetting. It is Lockie's first year at the local secondary school where he falls in and out of love with the sophisticated Vicki Streeton. Lockie's thoughts about his sex life, family, surfing and the future are conveyed with veracity and self-deprecating humour. 'What do you reckon, Lock?' asks Phillip. 'Well, Phillip, I'd say life has its mysteries,' Lockie replies.

LOFTS, PAMELA (1949–), born Sydney, illustrator and animator, has created films based on Dreaming stories such as 'How the birds got their colours' and 'Dunbi the owl'. After visiting the Kimberleys, she retold and illustrated Aboriginal Dreaming stories: *How the Kangaroos Got Their Tails* (1987), told by George Mung Mung Lirrmiyarri; *Warnayarra— the Rainbow Snake* (1987) told and illustrated by the Senior Boys Class at Lajamanu School; *The Echidna and the Shade Tree* (1984) by Mona Green; Daisy Utemorrah's *Dunbi the Owl* (1983);

Wombat Stew (1984) by Marcia Vaughan. Illustrator: Pamela Lofts

The Bat and the Crocodile (1987), told by Jacko Dolumyu and Hector Sandaloo; *When the Snake Bites the Sun* (1984), told by David Mowaljarlai; *How the Birds Got Their Colours* (1987), with Mary Albert; and *The Kangaroo and the Porpoise* (1987), with Agnes Lippo. She has given Australian animals a humorous character in her illustrations to *Wombat Stew* (1984) by Marcia Vaughan, and *Koala Lou* (1988) and *Sail Away: the Ballad of Skip and Nell* (1986) by Mem Fox.

LOGAN, CAROLYN F. (1934–), born Iowa, USA, spent thirteen years in Peru as a teacher. She was the first editor of the reviewing journal *Fiction Focus*, and has edited *Orana*. In *The Power of the Rellard* (1986), a sinister force operates against Lucy, Shelley and Georgie. Only by using her gift, which Lucy obtains through an old game, can the evil teachers, Mrs Gibbs and Mr Boaz, be defeated in their plan to freeze the Earth. *The Huaco of the Golden God* (1988) is set in Peru, where Huascar finds an Inca pot linking him with the ancient people.

LOH, MORAG (1935–), born Melbourne, has examined the immigrant experience in *Immigrants* (1977), with Wendy Lowenstein, and *Stories and Storytellers from Indo-China* (1982). Her history of Australian childhood, written with Sue Fabian, is *Australian Children through 200 Years* (1985). Loh's picture-books *The Kinder Hat* (1985) and *Tucking Mummy In* (1987), both illustrated by Donna Rawlins, explore the everyday experiences of small children. Mother wears an ice-cream container as a hat when walking home, and a weary Mum is put to bed by her children.

LONG, CHARLES (1860–1944), born Wallan, Victoria, was an inspector of schools from 1890 to 1925. In 1896 Long established the *School Paper* in Victoria, and in 1900 founded the *Education Gazette*, the official journal of the Education Department of Victoria. In 1927 he returned from retirement to edit the Victorian School Readers, using much of the material already published in the *School Paper*. His informational books include *Stories of Australian Exploration* (1903), and *Stories of British Worthies* (1913). He also wrote a history of Victorian education.

Long Red Scarf, The (1987) by Nette Hilton, illustrated by Margaret Power, was an Honour Book in the 1988 Picture Book of the Year Awards. Grandpa teaches himself how to knit when Aunt Maude and Cousin Isobel are too busy to make him a scarf. He is so pleased with his new skill and the result that he knits a scarf for Baby Susan. By placing an accepted female skill in the hands of an elderly man, and providing a similar reversal of roles for Maude and Isobel, Hilton and Power show that we do not have to be restricted by convention.

Longtime Passing (1971) by Hesba Brinsmead won the 1972 Book of the Year Awards. Four brothers, including Edwin Truelance, take up Crown Land in the Candlebark Country, a remote area of the Blue Mountains. The family lived in a bark hut, then a rough-and-ready log house (both built by Father) before Teddy, the fifth and youngest child, is born. The small crises of childhood, against the background of the wild and unpredictable setting, are always softened by her loving family. As the book ends, a road is being surveyed and Teddy must go off to school. The story of the Truelances at 'Longtime' is continued in *Once There was a Swagman* (q.v., 1979); *Longtime Dreaming* (1982), in which Brinsmead uses the reminiscences of her father, Ken Hungerford, and takes the history of the family up to the end of World War II; and *Christmas at Longtime* (1983), illustrated by John Caldwell, which looks back to when Teddy was 10, during the Depression. Details and rituals of a family Christmas are recalled: making the pudding, selecting the presents, and an excursion to Mount Victoria, where Teddy has her first lemonade. In *The Honey Forest* (1979), illustrated by Louise Hogan, Dad and Mickey, from 'Longtime', camp out collecting honey. The resourcefulness of a close-knit family in the face of isolation is central to Brinsmead's 'Longtime' books.

Looking Out for Sampson (1987) by Libby Hathorn, illustrated by Ann James, was an Honour Book in the 1988 Book of the Year Awards: Younger Readers. When Cheryl comes to stay, Bronwyn is depressed by her rosy stories about previous experiences, but when Bronwyn's brother is lost at the beach, Cheryl's support becomes vital, and Bronwyn begins to understand why Cheryl has been so difficult. Sampson's rescue establishes a friendship.

LORD, FLORENCE E. For *Kangaroo Kingdom* (1914) see **Animal Stories**.

Lost in the Bush, a real danger in the large areas of wild country which are still found on the continent, has become a repeated motif in Australian children's books. In August 1864, thirty miles from Horsham, Victoria, the Duff children: Isaac, aged 9, Jane, aged 7, and Frank, aged 3, were lost in the bush. Black trackers led by Worroral found the children after nine days. During their ordeal the children had displayed great courage, and Jane had shown selfless concern for her small brother. The experience of the Duff children was not an isolated one, but their saga has continued to inspire writers.

Shortly after the event, William Stitt (i.e. Still) Jenkins wrote *The Lost Children: in Perpetual Remembrance of Jane Duff* (1864), a poem with sixteen verses to commemorate Jane's bravery. 'Come, let us sing of this fair child heroic,/And let her name in Austral history glow!' *Station Dangerous: or, The Settlers in Central Australia, a Tale Founded on Facts* (1866) by

O.F. Timins used the incident and its detail, when the three Ames children are lost in the bush gathering broom. Like the real Jane, Jane Ames takes off her dress to cover her little brother, Willie. Sophia Tandy's *The Children in the Scrub: a Story of Tasmania* (1878), published by the Religious Tract Society, has the statement 'The chief incident in the following story is strictly true'. Edward, Janey and Tommy Mullings are gathering sticks when they wander too far away. In anguish, Janey cries 'Cooey, Ned, cooey loud for father, for we are lost in the bush!' They are found after five days by an older brother, and the incident converts their parents to religion. William Strutt illustrated the event, and wrote about it in 1901 in an account first published in 1989, *Cooey: or, The Trackers of Glenferry,* changing only the names of the children to Roderick, Bella and David Duncan. Strutt expresses his admiration for the children, but 'Not less extraordinary was the sagacity and intelligence shown by the Australian Aborigines through whose persevering efforts the lost children were found at last. With unerring accuracy these Sons of the Desert advanced step by step, having only the faintest indications to guide them in their search …'. Robert Richardson also took up the story in *A Little Australian Girl: or, The Babes in the Bush, and Other Stories* (1881). In *Dot and the Kangaroo* (1899) by Ethel Pedley, Dot's adventures occur after she becomes lost while gathering wildflowers: the Duff children were gathering broom for their mother. Les Blake's *Lost in the Bush: the Story of Jane Duff* (1964), a detailed and factual account of the Duff children's experience, was the basis for a film in 1973. The incident was retold in various school papers and readers, most tellingly in the Victorian Readers Fourth Book (1930), and more recently in a reading scheme for schools, the 'Eureka Treasure Chest' by Pat Edwards, again called *Lost in the Bush* (1987).

The story appeared frequently in children's books from the nineteenth century to the present. Aunt Mary's daughter is lost and not found in Louisa Bedford's *A Home in the Bush* (1913). Donald MacDonald describes Ita's adventures in *At the End of the Moonpath* (1922) when she is lost in the bush. Violet Methley's *The Bunyip Patrol: the Story of an Australian Girls' School* (1926) has lost children found by the Girl Guides. Joe and Bob are lost in the bush for part of *The Road to Widgewong* (1928) by Leslie Lee. In Rosalind Miller's *The Pyms at Yarrambeat* (1940) Marjory, her brother David and Wilfred Gellibrand become lost in the Gippsland bush. In Allan Aldous's *The Tendrills in Australia* (1959) Donald becomes lost in the desert. Joan Phipson's *The Boundary Riders* (1962) uses the incident as a means of assessing the character of the three children. James Preston's *Jeedarra Country* (1971) describes the resourcefulness of a 12-year-old boy, Greg, who saves his small sister from death when they are lost on the Nullarbor, and the anguish of their parents. In Alan Marshall's *Fight for Life* (1972) the young hero is lost in the bush for five days, and, like Liz and Ken, in Judith Crabtree's *Skins & Shells & Peelings* (1979), the ordeal enables him to find inner strength. Miranda is lost in Judith Worthy's *Finch's Island* (1985), and in Ivan Southall's *Rachel* (1986) Eddie's worth is discovered when he is able to help Rachel find her way.

A variant is found in the stories of children whose survival depends on being taken in by Aboriginal People. Near Fremantle, WA, Bonny Dutton, aged 6, was lost in the bush in 1830 and returned home after a month of living with Aboriginal People. In E. Davenport Cleland's *The White Kangaroo: a Tale of Colonial Life — Founded on Fact* (1890) Ralph and Ernest Everdale become lost and are cared for by traditional inhabitants. Margaret Kiddle draws on the Dutton story directly in *West of Sunset* (1949). Little Joe Browning wanders off and is later brought back by the people with whom he has been living. Phyllis Power

uses the device twice, in *Lost in the Outback* (1954) and *Nursing in the Outback* (1959). In each book Hannah and Mary survive because of help from Aboriginal People. In James Vance Marshall's *Walkabout* (1961) the lost children symbolise the intrusion of 'civilization' into the purity of Aboriginal life, and the children survive, although the Aboriginal boy does not.

Perhaps the most convincing of all the 'lost in the bush' stories is Frances Margaret McGuire's dramatic account of a child lost in the outback, *Three and Ma Kelpie* (1964). Six-year-old Martin Blake wanders off from 'Akerriga' Station, over 200 kilometres north-west of Broken Hill, in search of a missing puppy and baby goat. McGuire forcefully portrays Martin's journey through the terrible heat, the desperate search by the outback people, the brilliant tracking of Tracker Jim, and the intelligence of Ma, the kelpie. Together they avert a tragedy. These novels capture the ever-present perils of exposure and thirst, and the vulnerability of the inexperienced, when lost in the Australian wilderness.

'Loyall Virginian', The (1968) by George Finkel, was Commended in the 1969 Book of the Year Awards. When Roger Bolynge's friends are killed by the American Indians, he seeks retribution by slaughtering the Opechancanough people. Bolynge then turns his attention to raising a vessel, the *Loyall Virginian*, in which he travels to England. He is involved in the English Civil War, returns to America, and takes up the cause of Independence. *The Loyall Virginian* is narrated in a semi-documentary style.

Lu Rees Award was established in 1988 to recognise an outstanding contribution to Australian children's literature. The award has been given twice, in 1988 to Laurie Copping and in 1989 to Belle Alderman.

Lu Rees Archives were established by the ACT branch of the CBC, and named after Mrs Lucy Frances Harvey Waugh Rees. The Archives' basis was the correspondence and collection which Mrs Rees began in the 1950s. It has been housed at the University of Canberra, formerly the Canberra College of Advanced Education, since 1980, and the library publishes an irregular journal: *The Lu Rees Archives: Notes, Books and Authors*. The collection's strength is in the post-1950 period. All foreign language editions of Australian children's authors are acquired. Manuscripts and photographs are also held.

LUFFMANN, LAURA BOGUE (LAURETTA MARIA LANE) (1846–1929), born Bedford, UK, had written children's books for the Society for the Preservation of Christian Knowledge as Laura M. Lane before she came to Australia with her husband, the Superintendent of the Burnley Horticultural Gardens, Melbourne. Luffman was a journalist with *Women's Voice* and the Sydney *Daily Telegraph*. *Will Aylmer: a Tale of the Australian Bush* (1909) was published by the Religious Tract Society. The novel describes farming life in Gippsland, Victoria, at the turn of the century. When the children are orphaned, they keep the farm and the family together, as they fight off bushfires and floods and generally support each other. Through Will's growing appreciation of the work of his sister Annie, this novel recognises the essential contribution of the women of the bush.

LUMBERS, EUGENE (1916–), born Adelaide, wrote *A Taste for Blue Ribbons* (1969), illustrated by George Tetlow, the story of a foal with a fifth leg which is found in a sideshow by the Byrne family. After treatment by a friendly vet, Blue Ribbons promises to be a Melbourne Cup winner. The novel has unusual twists, and became a popular ABC television serial in 1973, with ten thirty-minute episodes,

directed by Keith Wilkes, starring Gary Gray, Sally Conabere, Syd Conabere, Sheila Bradley, John Williams and Ron Graham. *I, Smocker* (1971), and *Smocker Takes Off* (1972), both illustrated by Robin Goodall, are based on an ABC children's program. In *I, Smocker* Smocker the cat and his friend the Irish terrier Patrick pursue their enemy, Norton, the cat next door. In *Smocker Takes Off* Smocker sets off on a round-Australia safari. Smocker is clever and cowardly, Patrick is loyal and not so smart. Lumbers has also written *The Art of Pro Hart* (1977) and *Pro Hart's Silver City* (1985).

LURIE, MORRIS (1938–), born Melbourne, writes books for children and adults. His first children's book was *The 27th Annual African Hippopotamus Race* (q.v., 1969), a comic account of an unlikely competition. *Arlo the Dandy Lion* (1971), illustrated by Richard Sawers, struts about in the elegant clothes he has found in a trunk in the jungle. But when he is captured and taken to the London Zoo, his clothes are discarded, and his true self revealed. Arlo learns that pride can lead even a lion into problems, and returns to Africa, an ordinary lion— deflated, but at peace with what he is. In *Toby's Millions* (q.v., 1982) Toby finds a pirate's treasure which he distributes more wisely than any advice he is given. The problems of tiny Imelda, in *The Story of Imelda, Who was Small* (1984), illustrated by Terry Denton, are solved by an elderly aunt, who suggests that a bed be provided for Imelda to grow into, rather than a tiny shoebox. *Night— night!* (1986), illustrated by Alison Lester, is a collection of bedtime stories. In *Alison Gets Told* (1990) the information is 'facts' about Father Christmas. Lurie's clever dialogue and inventive solution ensures that the magic of Christmas remains. In *What's that Noise? What's that Sound?* (1991), illustrated by Terry Denton, the small hero resolves his own fears by exciting imaginary solutions to the noises of the night. *Heroes* (1987) in Methuen's 'Dimensions' series, has excerpts, stories and biographical information. Lurie's autobiography is *Whole Life* (1987). He has a wry sense of the absurd and a fellow feeling for the small, clumsy, timid or powerless animals and children who populate his books for the young.

LYNCH, NU. For *Australian Animals A to Z* (1976) see **Alphabet Books**.

LYNE, NAIRDA (1929–84), born Melbourne, artist and writer, studied at Swinburne Technical School and the National Gallery School, Melbourne. She wrote and illustrated stories for the NSW *School Magazine* and the Victorian *School Paper*, and was a contributor to the Adelaide *Chronicle*, *Woman's Day*, *Woman's World* and the *Australian Women's Weekly*.

Tasmanian Tales (1965) and *Adventures at Powranna: More Tasmanian Tales* (1969) are collections of stories about farming life in Tasmania. The elephant, in *One-Tooth and Whirly-Bird* (1975), illustrated by Valerie Urquhart, has to work in a sawmill until he is returned to his village by helicopter. In *Granny Stayput* (1983) an elderly woman defies the building of a car park on the site of her home. *Vaulting Horse* (1984), illustrated by Astra Lacis, is based on the author's own experience of disability. Tim's spina bifida embarrasses him at school, until he learns that one cannot be good at everything, and the other children learn to respect his courage. Lyne produced commercial greeting cards for over twenty years. The Nairda Lyne Award for Writing for Children is awarded by the Tasmanian Fellowship of Australian Writers.

M

MACARTHUR-ONSLOW, ANNETTE (1933–), born Sydney, studied at the National Art School, Sydney and in London. Her early work for overseas authors included *Dog about Town* (1959) by Ashley Davey; *Children of the Red King* (1959) by Madeline Pollard; *Circus Boy* (1960) and *Animal Stories* (1961) by Ruth Manning-Sanders; *Otter's Path* (1961) by J. Ivester Lloyd; *Victoria* (1962) by Elizabeth Kyle; *Tim Fireshoe* (1963) by Ursula Wolfel; and *Nordy Bank* (1964) by Sheena Porter. *Birds: Poems* (1962) by Judith Wright; *Half a World Away* (1962) and *The Roaring 40* (1963) by Nan Chauncy; and *Pastures of the Blue Crane* (1964) by Hesba Brinsmead, gave her the opportunity to interpret her homeland. She depicted the Australian Alps in *Winged Skis* (1964), *Silver Brumbies of the South* (1965) and *Silver Brumby Kingdom* (1967) by Elyne Mitchell and A.B. Paterson's *The Man from Snowy River* (1977). Animals are her focus in *Uhu* (q.v., 1969), *Minnie* (q.v., 1971), and *Trim* (1975) by Matthew Flinders (q.v.). The

Minnie (1971) by Annette Macarthur-Onslow

Giant Bamboo Happening (1982) illustrates the carol 'The Twelve Days of Christmas' through the magical happenings in a garden among the bamboos where the birds feed. *Round House* (1975) is a description of a house in Gloucestershire, UK. Macarthur-Onslow believes that her work is interpretation rather than illustration, and carefully researches detail. Her impressionistic line drawings and understated watercolours have strength and fluidity.

McCARTHY, MAUREEN (1953–), born Melbourne, is a novelist and writer for television. She wrote the script and novels for the 'In Between Series' (q.v.): *Alex, Fatima, Angie,* and *Saret* (1987). Multicultural inner Melbourne is also the setting for *Ganglands* (1992). A tragedy occurs at Kelly's birthday party, involving Kelly's friend Phil, son of a lawyer, and Con, a Greek boy. Kelly saves Con from making a terrible mistake, Phil from a knife attack, and then must choose between them: the eligible Phil or the more passionate Con. See also **Romance**; **Sexuality**. McCarthy's characters find themselves in circumstances which are difficult to confront, and for which there may be no happy solution. They are faced with parents who do not support them, friends who do not help them, and a society which is less than caring. Her young characters are confused, even bitter, but full of youthful courage.

McCORMICK, PETER DODDS (?1834–1916), born Glasgow, Scotland, settled in Sydney in 1855. He was a schoolteacher and song-writer, conducting very large choirs — 15 000 children at the laying of the foundation stone of Queen Victoria's statue, and 10 000 at the Robert Raikes Sunday school centenary. 'Advance Australia Fair' is attributed to McCormick. *The Four School Mates, an Australian Tale of Misfortune and Success* (1896) is set at a Sydney school. See **School Stories**; **Religion**.

McCRAE, HUGH RAYMOND (1876–1958), born Melbourne, was a lyric poet, cartoonist and illustrator. He drew cartoons as 'Splash', and created 'Jim and Jam' for the *Comic Australian*, a magazine which appeared from 1911 to 1913. He wrote *The Australian Alphabet* (see **Alphabet Books**) in the 1920s, and illustrated Leigh Bell's *Colin's Story Book* (1924).

McCUAIG, RONALD (1908–93), born Newcastle, NSW, is a poet, short story writer, essayist and journalist. With Isla Stuart, he has written the verses to drawings of animals by Joan Morrison, *You Can Draw a Kangaroo: the Poems Tell You what to Do* (1964). *Gangles* (1972), illustrated by Noela Young, has eight outrageous adventures perpetrated by the exasperating Gangles, a small girl who lives on a fountain in the middle of the lake in Candybar (where there are two Parliament Houses). Gangles's adventures take her to Siddely, where she disrupts a modelling show in a store, and to San Francisco, where she becomes a television star. *Tobolino and the Amazing Football Boots* (1974), illustrated by Lee Whitmore, is also set in Candybar. Toby becomes the star of a football team, the Tantamount Tots.

McCUAIG, SANDRA (1943–) has written the picture-book *Bus Fuss* (1989), illustrated by Cathy Wilcox. Mr Prowley hides his dog, Wombat, in his shopping bag when he is travelling on the bus, and Mrs Martin hides her cat, Tigress, under the knitting in her basket. When they sit next to each other, mayhem ensues. McCuaig's books for older readers include *Blindfold* (1989), in which Sally, with the help of a psychiatrist, must come to terms with the suicide of two boys. In *Spaghetti Connections* (1989) Lucio and Sam become involved in a drug ring, two other boys are murdered and Sam loses an eye. *Shooting Through* (1991) describes Max's adventures when he joins his father in northern NSW, resulting in a confrontation between his parents over logging and wood-chipping.

MACDONALD, ALEXANDER

(1878–1939), born Scotland, wrote accounts of his travels and prospecting experiences in Australia and Papua New Guinea, and adventure stories for boys. In *The Lost Explorers: a Story of the Trackless Desert* (1907), illustrated by Arthur H. Buckland, Bob Wentworth, 18, and Jack Armstrong, 16, leave their work at the Clyde Engineering Works and set off to Australia with Mr Mackay in search of gold. The story moves from the goldfields of WA across the centre of Australia. The character of Mackay is based on Macdonald himself. He is enigmatic, an able fighter, and a sensitive flautist who has a broad general knowledge (which he is not averse to imparting freely) and is moved to tears by music. In *The Quest of the Black Opals: a Story of Adventure in the Heart of Australia* (1908), illustrated by William Rainey, Dick Gordon and Jack Meredith, 18 years old and newly arrived in Australia, explore the opal fields from Victoria to the border between south-west Queensland and north-eastern SA. The boys spend all day cycling to the opal fields of White Cliffs in outback heat, without a trace of sunburn or heat exhaustion. Macdonald includes the complete verses of 'Waltzing Matilda', sightings of bunyips, a grand corroboree, and a voyage down the Darling which borders on the burlesque. See also **Melbourne**. *The Pearl Seekers: a Tale of the Southern Seas* (1908) and *The Island Traders: a Tale of the South Seas* (1909) are adventures in the Pacific. *The Hidden Nugget: a Story of the Australian Goldfields* (1910), also illustrated by Rainey, contains the Macdonald mixture of mystery, adventure, suspense and intricate plot. Frank Brandon is the hero, 'tall and slim of build, but as tough and wiry as most Australians bred on the great back-block plains'. A heavy sense of mystery and foul play centres around a large

nugget hidden somewhere in vast WA. In *The Invisible Island: a Story of the Far North of Queensland* (1910), illustrated by Charles M. Sheldon, Jim Mackay finds a gold button while tracking through the outback. His life is threatened for its possession, and in a series of outrageous adventures, Mackay, Quong Lee, Edmund, Damper Jack, Dandy Charlie, Melbourne Mike, Ginger Bob and others rout their enemies and find their fortunes. *The Mystery of Diamond Creek* (1927) follows the same formula. *In the Land of Pearl and Gold: A Pioneer's Wanderings in the Backblocks and Pearling Grounds of Australia and New Guinea* (1907) is his account of his own experiences, similar to Robert Macdonald's *Opals and Gold* (1928).

MACDONALD, BARBARA, born UK, came to Australia after World War I. She illustrated *A New Book of Old Rhymes* (1920) in an Art Deco style, and *Princess Herminie and the Tapestry Prince and Other Stories* (1922) by Lee Ivatt, both published by the journal *Art in Australia*. The latter is a collection of fairy stories with seventeen colour and black-and-white illustrations, with characters dressed in fine decorative garments in a medieval style. The beautiful red-and-black lettering suggests an illuminated manuscript. See also **Nursery Rhymes**.

MACDONALD, CAROLINE (1948–), born Taranaki, NZ, was an editor with OUP in NZ. Her first novel for children was *Elephant Rock* (1983). Ann's mother is dying, and as she watches her deterioration, Ann finds herself transported to the world of her mother's childhood. *Visitors* (1984), illustrated by Gary Meeson, also touches on the supernatural. Terry's television screen becomes the vehicle for visiting forces from beyond the earth, and he and his friend Maryanne are able to make contact with them. *Yellow Boarding House* (1985) is a psychological thriller. Lyndsay visits a boy who appears to be blind. To this awkward and insecure girl on the verge of adulthood 'nothing looked quite what it was', but her relationship with her mother saves her from disaster. In *Joseph's Boat* (1988), a book for younger readers, Joseph searches for a boat to visit the mainland. *The Lake at the End of the World* (q.v., 1988) showed Macdonald's developing virtuosity. *Speaking to Miranda* (1990) explores issues of race and identity. The mysterious death of Ruby's mother has left many questions unanswered, and her stepfather will not help her. Miranda seems to be an *alter ego*, but the real Miranda emerges through a convincing picture of a Maori family. *The Eye Witness* (1991) is set in Tasmania in 2046. Leo meets a boy with one eye, Jack, who says he is from a Melbourne of 1995. At a time when everyone has a number and an allotted place in society, Jack is identified as a 'feral', or outsider. Only Dove understands Jack's true origins. Leo's own unhappiness, and that of his stepsister Rose and her friend Eva, is worked through as Jack affects everyone's life. A rigidly structured society is also laid bare for Leo, Rose and Eva. *Hostilities* (1991) is a collection of short stories. Macdonald's work attends to central questions affecting our world, not only that of physical survival, but also questions of political or personal tyrannies, race, family and community.

MACDONALD, DONALD ALISTER (1857–1932), born Melbourne, was a journalist and popular writer on natural history. *The Bush Boy's Book* (1911) was based on the column he wrote for the Melbourne *Argus*, and gives advice on living and surviving in the bush. *At the End of the Moonpath* (1922), illustrated by C.E. James and first published in 1900 in *Childhood in Bud and Blossom*, tells how Ita, lost in the bush, is taken to the 'land where the moonpath goes'. She finds playmates, attends a pelican's party and a lyre-bird's concert, and meets the lost Diggers. Macdonald also wrote *The Warrigals' Well: a North Australian Story*

(1901) with John F. Edgar, illustrated by J. Macfarlane, an adventure story for adults. A memorial fountain dedicated to Macdonald was erected in Macdonald Park, Beaumaris, Victoria.

MACDONALD, ROBERT MACLAUCHLAN (1874–?) wrote boys' adventure stories set in Australia and Papua New Guinea, such as *The Great White Chief: a Story of Adventure in Unknown New Guinea* (1908), *The Rival Treasure Hunters: A Tale of the Debatable Frontier of British Guiana* (1909), *Chillagoe Charlie* (1909), *The Secret of the Sargasso* (1909), *The Gold Seekers* (1910), *The Moon God's Secret* (1910), set in the Caroline Islands among the lost idols of the Okapites, and *Danger Mountain: a Story of Adventure in Unexplored New Guinea*

Donald Macdonald

(1911). *The Opal Hunters: or, The Men of Red Creek Camp* (1912) is set in outback Queensland, 'that mystic land where the glamour of hidden treasure still enthralls daring men, and the spirit of the great Never Never calls alluringly to sons of freedom'. Long Tom, Fat Jack, the Shadow, and other redoubtables set off in search of a mysterious opal mine. All the characters make their fortunes, unless they are Aboriginal or Jewish. *The Pearl Lagoons: or, The Lost Chief* (1911) is another adventure about black-hearted scoundrels and British stalwarts. Macdonald's touching faith in the unity of Empire is exemplified in its conclusion: 'From the folds of his kilt the Chief brought forth his strange pipes and "God Save the King" was sounded out erratically on the morning air. The Caledonia's men added their voices, then cheered lustily, and the Adventurers on deck joined. And the flag that braved a Thousand Years floated proudly on a pole above the pearling tables, and Wun Lung and the natives danced around.' *Opals and Gold: Wanderings and Work on the Mining and Gemfields* (1928) describes his prospecting experiences in Queensland, NSW, WA and New Guinea, reminiscent of Alexander Macdonald's *In the Land of Pearl and Gold* (1907).

MACDONNELL, JAMES EDMOND

(1917–), born Mackay, Queensland, writes naval stories for adults. *Colt & Co. in the Valley of Gold* (1960) is an adventure story set in Papua New Guinea. His stories about Captain Mettle were published under the pseudonym 'James Macnell'. See **Mettle**.

McFADYEN, ELLA MAY (1887–

?1976), born Sydney, wrote verse for the *Town and Country Journal*, and published her first collection of poetry, *Outland Born*, around 1912. She worked as 'Cinderella' for the *Sydney Mail*, and contributed to the *Lone Hand* and the *Sydney Morning Herald*. *Here's Fun for You! Children's Verse for Recitation and Group Speaking* (1938), illustrated by Edwina Bell, contained many of the brisk poems previously published in these newspapers. *Little Dragons of the Never Never* (1948), also illustrated by Bell, is the story of Wendy and Marco Polo Junior, horned dragons from the desert. In *The Wishing Star* (1956), illustrated by Ernst Corvus, Tony and Tessie see a falling star, and when they search for it they are transported to Rainbow Castle, where the Goodwillies make toys for lonely children. Her dramas for children appeared in *Kookaburra Comedies: Junior Plays* (?1956). Her inventive stories about Dan and Nobby Pegmen and their mother, Mrs Peg, made by Peter and Joan from clothes pegs, *Pegmen Tales* (1946) and the sequel *Pegmen Go Walkabout* (1947), both illustrated by Edwina Bell, originally appeared as a serial in the *Courier-Mail*. They were taken up by the NSW *School Magazine*, and later dramatised on ABC radio. Dan Pegman says: '"I guess we're only laundry pegs,/With sticks tacked on for arms and legs./The children made us for their play,/But since they loved us day by day,/Something in me begins to glow …/I'm coming to life!" "I guess that's so"', replies Nobby. The Pegmen sail on their ship, the Ark, with their pet monkey, Pongo. *The Big Book of Pegmen Tales* (1959) contains stories from the two adventures in a new format. McFadyen also wrote *Who's Who of Classical Allusion: Containing 500 names of Famous Greek and Roman Myths and Heroes* (n.d.) with pronunciations and relationships from Achates to Zeus.

MACFARLANE, BARBARA RUTH

(1937–), born Melbourne, wrote the Agapanthus books. See ***Naughty Agapanthus***. In *Zop, King of the Fireflitters* (1971) the fireflitters defeat the dragons by joining together to make a fearsome dragon of their own; in *The Mouse Keeper* (1976) Brod's mouse Minny has young, which brings Brod and a school mate, Sunny, together, and gives Brod a stronger link with his family; *Jenny and the Magic Ball* (1974) and *The Birds and Hetty* (1974) are Cheshire 'Cat' books for beginning readers. A wilful ball leads Jenny into mischief, and Hetty flies with the birds. All Macfarlane's simple texts for young readers are illustrated by Margaret Lees.

MACFARLANE, JOHN illustrated the novels of Joseph Bowes, Mary Grant Bruce, Jean Curlewis, Vera Dwyer, Evelyn Goode, Donald MacDonald, Lillian Pyke, and Ethel and Lilian Turner. Macfarlane also painted historical events from descriptions supplied to him by Charles Long (q.v.), who, in turn, based the descriptions on Ernest Favenc's *Geographical Development of Australia*. Six of his pictures are included in *Australian History Pictures* (?1912), a publication for schools depicting scenes such as Stuart planting the Union Jack on Central Stuart and the meeting of Major Mitchell and Henty at Portland, Victoria.

McFARLANE, PETER (1940–), born Adelaide, is a poet and teacher. *The Tin House* (1989) deals with a few months in a boy's life. Bill and his mates have done some shoplifting, and are apprehensive about the consequences; Bill has a budding romance with Heather; Grandpa's trotter looks a likely winner of the Derby. The pressed-tin house on the sandhills is eventually torn down to make way for more conventional houses. The book evokes the feelings of a 12-year-old, his fear of change, and his worries about what his parents do not know. *The Flea and Other Stories* (1992) is a short story collection.

McGowan, Garry, sports journalist for the *Gazette*, is the hero of a series by Allan Aldous: *McGowan Climbs a Mountain* (1945), *McGowan Goes to Sea* (1945), both illustrated by Miguel Mackinlay, *McGowan Goes Motor Racing* (1947), illustrated by Norman Keene, *McGowan Goes Fishing* (1948), illustrated by Harold Ing, and

McGowan Goes to Henley (1949), illustrated by 'Hailstone'. McGowan reports on an attempt on Kinchinga, a formidable Himalayan peak, by rival British and American climbing teams; participates in an ocean race from Sydney to Honolulu; is involved in an invention which will transform motor racing; defeats an unscrupulous sports equipment manufacturer, and reports on the famous regatta. McGowan's capacity to get just what he wants rests on bluff and toughness, and the occasional standover tactics.

McGUIRE, FRANCES MARGARET (1900–), born Glenelg, SA, has written novels for adults, a history of the Royal Australian Nursing Service, and a history of Australian theatre, among other informational books. Her two books for children are *Twelve Tales of the Life and Adventures of Saint Imaginus* (1946), a collection of religious stories, and *Three and Ma Kelpie* (1964), illustrated by Vennetta Brus, an account of life on an outback station. See **Lost in the Bush**.

MACHIN, SUE (1948–), born Sydney, has compiled *Stay Loose, Mother Goose! Stories and Poems to Read Aloud* (1990), illustrated by Jane Disher, a collection of stories and poems from many children's writers. *I Went Walking* (1989), illustrated by Julie Vivas, is a simple repetitive story set in a farmyard. As Sue Williams she worked with the publisher Rigby before founding Omnibus Books (q.v.) with Jane Coverndon.

MACINTYRE, ELISABETH (1916–), born Sydney, worked as an artist and writer for newspapers and journals in Sydney and Melbourne. Her best known character is Ambrose Kangaroo (q.v.). She has used structures which suggest folktales for *The Forgetful Elephant* (1944), in which Alastair's terrible memory is repaired through encountering a crocodile; *The Handsome Duckling* (1944), in

Katherine (1944) by Elisabeth MacIntyre

which the vain Leslie is brought down to earth when he needs rescuing; and *The Willing Donkey* (1944). Dorothy and Lionel stubbornly refuse to co-operate, and have to be tempted with carrots and rests, but Madeline willingly does what is asked of her.

The Black Lamb (1944) is about Leicester, who shakes off his bad reputation by rescuing Mollie the Merino from dingoes. *Katherine* (1946), published in the USA as *Susan Who Lives in Australia* (1944), is a verse story about a country girl's visit to Sydney. 'This is young Katherine, who lives in Australia/With her toys, and her pets, and her paraphernalia.' *Mr Koala Bear* (q.v., 1954) is in the same pattern, a verse story. In *Jane Likes Pictures* (1959), her mother shows Felicity Jane's friends how she draws. *Hugh's Zoo* (q.v., 1964) suggests that animals have rights, and *The Affable Amiable Bulldozer*

Man (1965) proposes that the earth also needs care. *Willie's Woollies: The Story of Australian Wool* (1951) describes the manufacture of woollen clothing from sheep's back to woven garment. MacIntyre also illustrated *Three Cheers for Piggy Grunter* (1959) by Noreen Shelley, and *The Story House* (1960) by Ruth Fenner. *Ninji's Magic* (1966), written by MacIntyre and illustrated by Mamoru Funai, describes the reactions of a village community to the introduction of a school, particularly the clash between Ninji and his grandfather.

In the 1970s MacIntyre turned to novels for older readers. In *The Purple Mouse* (1975) a teenager begins to cope with her impaired hearing. *It Looks Different When You Get There* (1978) describes Jenny's response to a pregnancy, which changes her life and takes her to a commune in Queensland. In *A Wonderful Way to Learn the Language* (1982), Kate becomes an au pair girl to the Montarelli family, in Rome, and copes with the precocious Leonardo.

MacIntyre's books written during the 1940s, 1950s and 1960s, such as *Ambrose Kangaroo* or *Katherine*, were simple and uncluttered picture-books with sprightly characters. Her versatility is demonstrated by the range of her oeuvre.

MACK, AMY ELEANOR (1876–1939), born Adelaide, the sister of Louise Mack, was a journalist and editor of the women's page of the *Sydney Morning Herald* for seven years. Her fairy stories, collected in *Waterside Stories* (1910), *Birdland Stories* (1910) and *Bushland Stories* (1910), illustrated by Joyce Dennys in 1921, use Australian flora and fauna and the Australian environment as their settings. 'The wave', in which a wave lives only for a day, 'The discontented stream', about a stream which learns wisdom, and 'How the flower fairies helped', in which the Queen encourages the fairy Bauera to teach young children to know and love fairies, were republished in *The Flower Fairies and Other Stories of the Australian Bush* (1928). Other collections are *The Gum Leaf that Flew and Other Stories of Australian Bushland* (1928); *The Little Black Duck and Other Stories of Bushland and Sea* (1928); *Why the Spinebill's Beak is Long and Other Stories of Australia's Bushland* (1928); *The Tom-Tit's Nest and Other Stories* (1914); *The Wilderness* (1922) (which first appeared in the *Sydney Morning Herald*); *The Birds' Concert and Other Stories of Australian Bush Birds* (1928); and *The Fantail's House and Other Australian Nature Stories* (1928). *Scribbling Sue and Other Stories* (1913) was illustrated by May Gibbs, and in 1923 by Karna Birmingham. Sue is a small girl who scribbles on everything — the fence palings, the kitchen walls, the wallpaper. When she scribbles on a gum tree, the wood fairy makes her write her name on every leaf in the bush, so that she is cured of the obsession. These child-centred stories are imaginative fantasies, told with panache.

MACK, LOUISE (MARIE LOUISE HAMILTON MACK) (1870–1935), born Hobart, was the older sister of Amy Mack. There were thirteen children in the family of the Rev. Hans Hamilton Mack, and Louise was the first daughter after six sons. She was educated at Sydney Girls' High School where she was a contemporary and close friend of Ethel Turner. Mack's colourful life is described in the biography written by her niece, Nancy Phelan, *The Romantic Lives of Louise Mack* (1991). Mack travelled extensively, living in England, Italy and Belgium, where she reported on the German occupation during World War I. She wrote fifteen adult novels, including *The World is Round* (1896), *An Australian Girl in London* (1902) and *Children of the Sun* (1904). For her *Teens* trilogy about Lennie and Mabel, see **Teens, a Story of Australian Schoolgirls**.

MACKANESS, GEORGE (1882–1968), born Sydney, was a bibliographer, biographer, author and educator. He wrote books on book-collecting and Australian history, and biographies of William Bligh and Arthur Phillip, among others. He collaborated with Bertram Stevens to edit *The Children's Treasury of Australian Verse* (1913) for schools, and with his daughter, **JOAN MACKANESS**, he edited *Frolic Fair: a Book of Australian Verse for Children Under Ten* (1932), illustrated by Pixie O'Harris, containing poems by Ella McFadyen, Ida Rentoul Outhwaite, Madeline Buck, Zora Cross, C.J. Dennis and others. Father and daughter also edited *The Wide Brown Land* (1934), an anthology of Australian poetry.

MACKELLAR, DOROTHEA (1885–1968), born Sydney, wrote the poem familiar to Australian school children, 'My

Country'. The second verse of the poem has inspired book titles and a national myth: 'I love a sunburnt country,/A land of sweeping plains,/Of ragged mountain ranges,/Of droughts and flooding rains./I love her far horizons,/I love her jewel-sea,/Her beauty and her terror — /The wide brown land for me!' *The Little Blue Devil* (1912) and *Two's Company* (1914) were adult novels written in collaboration with Ruth Bedford. *Outlaw's Luck* (1913), another adult novel, was published by Mills & Boon.

McKEOWN, KEITH COLLING-WOOD (1892–1952), born Sydney, was an entomologist specialising in the Australian longicorn beetle, and assistant curator of insects, at the Australian Museum in Sydney from 1929 to his death. He wrote a clever fantasy, *The Magic Seeds: Tessa in Termitaria* (1940), in which Tessa swallows fern seed and is plunged into the world of tiny creatures to learn about the City of the White Ants, Termitaria. She witnesses the terrible battle between the Meat Ants and the White Ants and learns the language of insects. The adventure involves the *Spherodema rusticum*, 'a feminist of the most militant type'. McKeown also wrote popular natural history, including *Insect Wonders of Australia* (1936), and *The Land of Byamee* (1938), legends and facts about Australian nature.

McKIMMIE, CHRISTOPHER. For *Apple to Zoo* (1975) see **Alphabet Books**.

MACKNESS, CONSTANCE (1882–1973), born Tuena, NSW, was a schoolteacher, the first headmistress of Presbyterian Ladies' College, Warwick, Queensland, in 1917. Her family stories began with *Gem of the Flat* (1914), illustrated by May Gibbs, about a 12-year-old schoolgirl with a vivid imagination. The family live by fossicking, rabbit-shooting and subsistence farming in a small holding

on 'Needy Flat', an experience based on Mackness's own childhood. In *Growing Up* (1926) Dr Allen adopts his benefactor's grandchildren when they are left unprovided for, to the wrath of his wife, who imagines herself to be an invalid, and the huge delight of his only daughter, unselfish Midge. The lives of Jim, Dumpy and Blue at school are detailed, and the growing love of two of the boys for Midge. They are both determined to marry her at the end of the book, but we are assured that one will die in uniform. *The Blossom Children* (1927), illustrated by Dewar Mills, are Bob, Billy, Pan, May, Wat, and Peachie, who are taken under the wing of Mrs Goodenough and eventually adopted by her. Pan, one of Mackness's most interesting characters, is a socialist who is unwilling to accept charity from her wealthy benefactor. Mrs Goodenough shows her a family who is suffering real hardship, and Pan is repelled by their dirt and vulgarity. Mrs Goodenough draws the lesson: 'You say they are vulgar people, Pan. If we had their troubles, dear — lack of work and semi-starvation, sickness and sorrow and not a friend to help us face it — we might have been worse. We have no right to judge our brothers by any standard but that of their limited opportunities.' Willa Morton in *Miss Billy* (1928) is the unselfish slave of her mean but wealthy parents and many brothers and sisters. Willa is saved by Mr and Mrs Morton's convenient deaths and a romance with the son of drunken station bookkeeper. *The Young Beachcombers* (1934) is set in North Queensland. The novel describes the love affairs and character conversions occurring in the Walton family, and the experiences of newly orphaned Lilla and timid Mary, with much dutiful gratefulness on the part of the young ones and happy courtships for the older members of the entourage. *Daffy-Down-Dilly* (1937) is about the insecure Daphne, befriended by Alison and her younger brother and sister. Alison has to help Daphne gain confidence and appease Jill's jealousy of Daphne's friendship with Jack. Alison manages both problems and finds romance as well.

Mackness is best known for her school stories. *Miss Pickle: the Story of an Australian Boarding School* (1924), illustrated by M.O. Johnston, describes the ups and downs of school life through the exploits of the irrepressible 'Miss Pickle' (Trixie Carr) and her friend Lola. Lola appeals to Trixie's better nature, and her waywardness is reformed. *The Glad School* (1927), illustrated by Edgar A. Holloway, set in a Presbyterian girls' school in Warwick, Queensland, describes the type of environment which Mackness aimed to create. Although Wattie is fined a penny in the Missionary Box for saying 'Bosker!', teachers are kind but firm, girls are allowed to express their personalities, and there is none of the saccharine Public School Spirit found in many of the school stories of the period. *Di-Double-Di* (1929), also illustrated by Holloway, is set at Brentwood College, where Buzz and Monkey and their pals reform a teacher, Miss Squash. In *Clown of the School* (1935) Mary Trevor is the clown, and the school is Fairview College. In both novels, rebellious schoolgirls with quick wits cannot be subdued by their teachers, who are in the wrong as often as their pupils. Mackness provides insights into the more advanced educational theories of her time, and creates school life with authenticity.

McLEAN, ANDREW (1946–), born Bairnsdale, Victoria, studied art at Prahran Technical School and RMIT. With his wife **JANET** (1946–), born Melbourne, he wrote *The Riverboat Crew* (q.v., 1978). Two other picture-books show the drama of engines and the robust people who work them. In *The Steam Train Crew* (1981) the train escapes when the crew get off to pick blackberries, but George, Alf and Norm climb aboard as it labours up a hill, to arrive on time for Mary's party. In *Fire-Engine Lil* (1990) Lil saves the day, even though she had been put out

of service. Animals crowd in or rush across the page in *Jenny and the Night of the Storm* (1982), when many creatures seek shelter in the family tent. *Hector and Maggie* (q.v., 1990) features a bossy rooster. *Oh, Kipper* (1991) is about a stray dog adopted by Sonja the elderly painter. Kipper goes off with a group of children, but returns to Sonja at last. Andrew has also illustrated Hesba Brinsmead's *Bianca and Roja* (1990).

McLEAN, DONALD JAMES (1905– 75), born Broken Hill, NSW, was an educationist and child welfare worker. His early life was spent in the mining country of western NSW, out of which he wrote *Treasure from the Earth* (1963). See **Great Stories of Australia**. His history books for children include *Finding Out about Australian History* (1962) and *Finding Out about the Ancient World* (1965). He also wrote books for adults, including *The Roaring Days: an Australian Yarn* (1960) which draws on stories of the 1890s told to him by his father.

McLEAN-CARR, CAROL (1948–) has illustrated *Nanna's Magic* (1985), *Crunch the Crocodile* (1986) and *Clackymucky and the Bulldog* (1988) by Josephine Croser; *McGruer and the Goat* (1987) and *The Butcher, the Beagle and the Dog Catcher* (1990) by Christobel Mattingley; *Mr Taddle's Hats* (1987) by Brian Janeen; *Tiny Timothy Turtle* (1989) by Anna Leditschke; and *A Lamb like Alice* (1990) by Eleanor Nilsson. McLean-Carr's generous pictures of animals and people are partial caricatures used to point up humorous situations.

MACLEOD, DOUG (1959–), born Greensborough, Victoria, wrote poetry for the Melbourne *Age* when he was 12, and later compèred the ABC's 'Rage' program. He has edited *Puffinalia* and written scripts for television comedy programs, including 'The Comedy Company'. His poetry for children is humorous, outrageous and irreverent. *Hippopotabus* (1976), written and illustrated when he was only 17, was the first of his verse collections. He wrote and illustrated *The Story of Admiral Sneeze* (1977). *Knees* (1981), illustrated by Jack Larkin, is a poem about a man's enthusiasm for knees which infects the whole town, so that all of Melbourne drops its pants. *In the Garden of Bad Things* (1981), illustrated by Peter Thomson, and *The Fed Up Family Album* (1983), illustrated by Jill Brierley, are poems about people and their absurdities. *Electric Eels and Other Shocking Things* (1987), illustrated by Mark Payne, is a collection of sea poems. *Sister Madge's Book of Nuns* (q.v., 1986) describes the sisters at an unconventional convent.

Tales of Tuttle (1980) contains nine humorous adventures of an absent-minded professor who creates bizarre inventions, such as a parcel-wrapping machine, bionic teeth, and 'Pink Shrink', a shrinking machine. *Frank Boulderbuster — The Last of the Great Swagmen* (1985), illustrated by Michael Atchison, contains six tall tales of outback adventure. In *Ten Monster Islands* (1987), illustrated by Terry Denton, Lord Raymond the hunter meets his match when the monsters he intends to shoot turn on him. In *The Monster* (1988) Doug is made from spare parts from the cemetery and put together by Nurse Frankenstein and Dr Drac to frighten away the inhabitants of Birdsville, but the evildoers do not take Doug's good nature into account. *Whipperginnie: a Radio Play for Young People* (1987), illustrated by Randy Glusac, is set in a crazy school. *Bilge: a Musical Play about Convicts Being Transported from England to Australia in the Year MDCCCXXXVIII* (1988), illustrated by Peter Viska, originally entitled *Soot*, is a melodrama in which Ned Soot is transported from England in 1838 for a crime he did not commit. The handsome villain Douglas Doomface, Soot's mad companion, Flora MacBatty, and his missing sweetheart Nautical Nora all play a part in restoring Soot's fortunes. *Song of the Shearer* (1990), illustrated by Robert Dickins, with music by James Paull, was written for radio. The boastful MacHugh is challenged by the Little Shearer, and has to eat his hat when he is defeated. The singing wakens the Bunyip, and he and the Little Shearer go into partnership as entertainers. *Kissing the Toad and other Stories* (1987), which MacLeod edited, contains stories by young writers. MacLeod has an acute sense of the absurd and merciless insights into pomposity.

'MACNELL, JAMES', see **MACDONNELL, J.E.**

MACPHERSON, PIPPA, born Eaglehawk Neck, Tasmania, has written *Beryl and Bertha at the Beach* (1990) illustrated by Ann James. Two ageing but sprightly hens win the Leghorn Surfing Championships during their quiet day at the beach. In *Caro's Croc Cafe* (1991), illustrated by Leigh Hobbs, Tim and Lucy cure Caro the crocodile of her hunger for humans by introducing her to ice-cream.

McRAE, RODNEY (1958–), born Wellington, NZ, came to Australia in 1984. He trained at the Wellington Polytechnic and the City Art Institute, Sydney. He has illustrated over sixty books, and worked as an animator for television programs, including 'Playschool'. His NZ work includes *The Terrible Taniwha of Timber Ditch* (1982) and *The Haunted House* (1982) by Joy Cowley and *The Spider in the Shower* (1984) by Margaret Mahy. In Australia he has illustrated *Brock and the Dragon* (1984) by Robin Klein; *Raining Cats and Dogs* (1987) by Edel Wignell; *Cockatoo Soup* (1987) by Jean Chapman; *Better Watch Out* (1987), compiled by Maurice Saxby and Glenys Smith; and *A Crazy Alphabet* (1990) by Lyn Cox (see **Alphabet Books**).

McRae has revived interest in nineteenth-century stories with his use of Aboriginal motifs to illustrate *Who Killed*

Cockatoo? (1988), first published in 1860 by W.A. Cawthorne. He uses bright geometric shapes for his interpretations of *The Gaping Wide-Mouthed Waddling Frog: a Counting Book* (1989), based on a nineteenth-century rhyme game. He has also illustrated *Dame Dearlove's Ditties for the Nursery* (1989), a selection from an 1819 collection of rhymes; *The House that Jack Built: a Diverting Story* (1989); *Sixteen Wonderful Old Women: a Book of Limericks* (1989), a selection from an 1820 book of limericks; and *Peter Piper's Practical Principles of Plain and Perfect Pronunciation: a Nonsense Alphabet of Tongue Twisters* (1989); *Who Killed Cock Robin?* (1989), and *Aesop's Fables* (1990).

His picture-books include *Why Doesn't Anyone Like Me?* (1984), in which a small girl wonders why everyone is against her and ponders on what she would like to be — an astronaut, a witch, a rock-singer, or a football-player. A baby observes the kitchen appliances in *My Mother's Kitchen* (1984), imagining what might be inside them. In *The Trouble with Heathrow* (1986) a large and loveable Afghan hound creates chaos, and in *Terrible Tracy: a Cautionary Tale* (1989) Tracy and a particularly horrible plant also wreak havoc. In *The Dragon in the Garden Shed* (1991) a surprise is awaiting when the hero finally summons up the courage to look in the shed. *Cry Me a River* (1991) is a moving account of a river becoming more and more polluted. 'So I cried me a river/And I cared for my river/And I ran with my river to the sea.' McRae blends fantasy and reality in his books, and his illustrations are frequently explorations of pattern. He combines colour with striking designs, often using geometric shapes, and often commenting on art itself.

McROBBIE, DAVID HEWITT

(1934–), born Scotland, works in educational radio. He has contributed to reading schemes, and written material on creative writing for school use. *Flying with Granny and Other Stories* (1989) is a collection about outsiders who learn to deal with their predicaments, with the help of a little magic. *The Wayne Dynasty: Being the Life and Adventures of Wayne Wilson, His Family and Friends* (1989) introduces the adventures of Wayne and his friend Squocka as they babysit, shop, experience work on a building site, and generally create mayhem. The sequel, *Waxing with Wayne: Being More of the Life and Adventures of Wayne Wilson, His Family and Friends* (1991) describes six months in his life, the short time his loveable but irritating grandfather spends with the family before going into care; the engagement and marriage of Wayne's older sister, Patricia; and the blossoming of friendship into love for Violet Pridmore. *The Wages of Wayne* (1992) continues Wayne's adventures.

The shipwreck of the *Loch Ard* is the inspiration for *Mandragora* (1991). Adam and Catriona find five tiny coffins which were aboard the *Dunarling* when it was wrecked off the Victorian coast. The coffins contain dolls, shaped from the root of the mandrake, which call up ancient good and evil. Adam, in the power of the good doll, Tam Dubh, has to avert a tragedy for the town. His relationship with Catriona, his father and the enigmatic Hamish Leckie are all affected by the old Celtic magic. McRobbie's characters are engaging and humorous; they suffer from self-doubt, but are full of energy and courage. The novel is a satisfying blend of history, superstition and modern adolescent culture. *The Fourth Caution* (1991) is a science fiction novel. Danny finds that he has a mysterious link with Louisa, Lena and Idar, and discovers that he is a child from a future time. To return to his own period he must leave the family who have brought him up, a choice which he can hardly bear to make. In *Prices* (1992), the lives of Sara and her mother Pauline are altered when Sara's father dies, and his illicit secrets gradually emerge. McRobbie's work, always compelling reading, encompasses humour, fantasy, science fiction and realism, and in each setting, convincing relationships are brought into sharp focus.

McROBBIE, NARELLE (1965–), born Atherton Tableland, Queensland, is a descendant of the Yidinji people and Pacific Islanders. *Bip, the Snapping Bungaroo* (1990), illustrated by Grace Fielding, is about a turtle whose snap is stolen by Mother Kangaroo.

McSKIMMING, GEOFFREY (1962–), born Sydney, is an actor and novelist. For *Cairo Jim & Doris: In Search of Martenarten: a Tale of Archeology, Adventure and Astonishment* (1991) and *Cairo Jim on the Trail of Chacha Muchos* (1992), both illustrated by Mark Ward, see **Humour**.

McVITTY, WALTER (1934–), born Melbourne, was an academic before he established the publishing company Walter McVitty Books in 1985. His critical work, *Innocence and Experience: Essays on Contemporary Australian Children's Writers* (1981), is a guide to eight major writers of the post-war period. *Authors and Illustrators of Australian Children's Books* (1989) contains biographical and bibliographical information on past and present writers and artists. *Talking to Writers* (1989) and *Australian Children's Authors* (1986) are for classroom use. See also **Criticism of Children's Literature**. *Dorothy Wall, Creator of Blinky Bill: Her Life and Work* (1988) is a two-volume biography and collection of the work of Wall. He collected and edited three books of short stories, *Short Story Favourites* (1977), *Short Story Starters* (1979) and *Short Story Harvest* (1987), and, with Rosalind Price, edited *The Macquarie Bedtime Story Book* (1987), illustrated by Ron Brooks.

Magabala Books, established in 1987 in Broome, WA, was the first Aboriginal publishing house. Sponsored by the National Aboriginal and Torres Strait Islander Bicentennial Program, the Aboriginal Arts Board and the Aboriginal Affairs Planning Authority, it was initially set up by the Kimberley Aboriginal Law and Culture Centre. Its aim is to publish stories and oral histories from the area, and train staff in editing and publishing, so that the preservation and control of their own culture remains with Aboriginal People. 'Magabala' means 'bush banana', a plant which disperses its seeds so that they travel long distances. Titles for children include *The Story of Crow: a Nyul Nyul Story* (1987) by Pat Torres and Magdalene Williams; *Jalygurr: Aussie Animal Rhymes* (1987) by Pat Torres; *Bip, the Snapping Bungaroo* (1990) by Narelle McRobbie, illustrated by Grace Fielding; *Do Not Go Around the Edges* (1990), poems by Daisy Utemorrah, illustrated by Pat Torres; and *The Dream* (1991) by Rae Harris with Beryl Harp. See also **Aboriginal Dreaming Stories**.

'Magic Circle Club' was a children's television program produced by Godfrey Phillip for ATV 0 from 1965 to 1968, a blend of fantasy, storytelling, music and variety segments. The host was Nancy Cato, accompanied by Fredd and Feefee Bear, Mother Hubbard and others; and the stylish sets, costuming and non-patronising approach of Cato lifted the program above its contemporary rivals. In 1966 it won the Veritas Award for the best live show — adult or children's. See also **'Adventure Island'**.

Magic Pudding, The: Being the Adventures of Bunyip Bluegum and His Friends Bill Barnacle and Sam Sawnoff (1918) was written and illustrated by Norman Lindsay. In response to a discussion over what motifs were most popular with children, Lindsay claimed that infantile concepts of happiness are based in the stomach. 'If a kid was offered his choice between food and fairies as delectable reading matter, I was willing to bet he would plump for food.' Lindsay said that 'the sole appeal I have made to childhood in this book is of humour and adventure.

The Magic Pudding (1918) by Norman Lindsay

Sentimental tenderness and prettiness are strictly repudiated.' Justifying his intent, the novel has been a lasting success, with its rollicking verse, robust text and strong black-and-white illustrations. The pudding, Albert, can magically renew himself, 'cut and come again' in different flavours. He is owned by Sam Sawnoff, a penguin and Bill Barnacle, a sailor. Bunyip Bluegum, a koala in waistcoat and porkpie hat, helps Sam and Bill fight off the professional Puddin' Thieves, Possum and Wombat. The Puddin' is rude, irascible and forever trying to escape, but the adventures conclude with the three friends settled in a tree house, with the Puddin' in his own Puddin' paddock. The comic verse from *The Magic Pudding* was reissued in 1977 as *Puddin' Poems*. Lindsay's charac-teristic illustrations and use of Australian speech patterns, slang, and insults have made a permanent contribution to Australian culture.

Magnificent Nose and Other Marvels, The (1991) by Anna Fienberg, illustrated by Kim Gamble, won the 1992 Book of the Year Awards: Younger Readers. Five modern fairy-tales of Lindalou, Andy Umm, Ferdinand, Ignatius and Valentina, all of whom have a special talent, are connected through the beautiful spider, Aristan. The small and intricate illustrations add to the magical quality of the stories.

Magpie Island (1974) by Colin Thiele, illustrated by Roger Haldane, was Commended in the 1975 Book of the

Year Awards. 'A magpie can be happy or sad: sometimes so happy that he sits on a high, high gum tree and rolls the sunrise around in his throat like beads of pink light; and sometimes so sad that you expect the tears to drip off his beak.' Thiele describes the tragic life of a magpie swept from his companions to a lonely island. Despite the efforts of Benny to provide him with a mate, he remains ' ... a symbol. A talisman. Endurance carved into a silhouette.' Haldane's paintings and drawings of seas, cormorants, gulls, bandicoots, and above all, magpies, show the wild beauty of the island.

MAHONY, FRANCIS PROUT (1862–1916), born Melbourne, was an illustrator and watercolourist, who worked for many journals, including the *Bulletin*. His particular speciality was the depiction of horses, but his sympathy with bush life is evident in his illustrations for the work of Henry Lawson, A.B. Paterson, Steele Rudd, and Ethel Pedley's *Dot and the Kangaroo* (q.v., 1899). In Louise Mack's *Teens: a Story of Australian Schoolgirls* (q.v., 1897) he presented a more urban image of Australian life. Mahony went to London in 1904, where he remained until his death.

MAHONY, WILL (FRANCIS WILLIAM) (1907–?86), born London, UK, the son of Francis Prout Mahony (q.v.), came to Australia when he was 9. Mahony was a cartoonist, illustrator, commercial artist and teacher at the National Art School. He illustrated Christobel Mattingley's *The Great Ballagundi Damper Bake* (1975), Graham Jenkin's *The Famous Race for Wombat's Lace* (1977), and Pat Edwards's *Crooked Mick of the Speewah* (1980).

MAHOOD, MARGUERITE (MARGOT) (1901–89), potter, graphic artist and watercolourist, wrote *The Whispering Stone: an Australian Nature Fantasy* (1944). Sandy has a treasure which enables him to talk to the birds and animals of the bush. He learns how badly treated the animals are, how much damage is done to their homes by people and fire, and determines to put understanding before wealth. Mahood contributed an adventure strip to the Melbourne *Age* in 1947, 'The Sandemans', set in bushranging times, and wrote 'Professor Smeebolger' for the fortnightly magazine *Australian Boy* in 1955. She also wrote an account of political cartoons, *The Loaded Line: Australian Political Caricature 1788–1901* (1973).

Makers of the First Hundred Years (1956) by Helen Palmer and Jessie MacLeod, illustrated by Pamela Lindsay, was Highly Commended in the 1957 Book of the Year Awards. Palmer and MacLeod selected people who had made a major contribution to Australian history since 1788, and their choice was unusual at a time when biographies studied in schools were usually limited to Captain Cook, John Macarthur, Arthur Phillip or Joseph Banks. Palmer and MacLeod included George Caley, the first botanist; William Lane, the visionary trade union leader; Patrick Hannan, the discoverer of gold at Kalgoorlie; and Ernest Giles, the explorer. See also *The First Hundred Years* (1954).

MALIN, LIN. For *Stories of Faerieland* (1931) see **Fairies**.

MALONE, JOHN (1945–) is a teacher and poet, and has collected poetry for use in schools. For *First Loves* (1989) see **Collections**.

MALTBY, PEG (1899–1984), born Ashby-de-la-Zouche, UK, arrived in Australia in 1924. She settled in Melbourne, where she studied art at the National Gallery School. In 1943 she had an exhibition which was made into a book by the Melbourne publishers Murfetts. *Peg's Fairy Book* (1944) went into five editions, sold over 180 000 copies, and was reissued in 1975 by Angus & Robertson. See also **Fairies**. *Nursery Rhymes* (1945) appeared a year later. Her fairy folk in bushland settings and Aboriginal children gained popularity over two decades. Other fairy-tales were retold and illustrated in *Little Red Riding Hood* (1950), *Goldilocks and the Three Bears* (1950), *The Sleeping Beauty* (1951), *Winkie's Magic Pepperpot* (1951) and *Little Thumbeline* (1951). Another fairy-like character was Nutchen of *Nutchen of the Forest* (1945), a woman who cares for the forest creatures, who reappeared in *Nutchen and the Golden Key* (1948). Maltby wrote a series about Ben and Bella, collected in *The Adventures of Ben and Bella* (1982), which included *Ben and Bella, Ben and Bella down on the Farm, Ben and Bella in the Hills, Ben and Bella in the Clouds* (all first published 1947), *Ben and Bella at the Beach, Ben and Bella in the Apple Tree* (both first published 1949) and *Ben and Bella in the Gardens* (first published 1951). As 'Agnes Newberry', Maltby wrote *Introducing Pip and Pepita* (1944) and *Pepita's Baby* (1944). Pepita and Pip also featured in *Pepita's Party* (1945) and *Pip and Pepita's New Home* (1945). Other works are *Meet Mr Cobbledick* (1948), *Forever Cuckoo!* (1950) and *Peg Maltby's Birthday Book* (1978). Maltby developed a gallery to exhibit her work at Olinda, outside Melbourne, where her neighbour, William Ricketts, had established a sculpture sanctuary. Her colourful illustrations created a magical and secret world where animals and humans understand each other.

Man from Ironbark, The (1974) by A.B. Paterson, illustrated by Quentin Hole, won the 1975 Picture Book of the Year Awards. The poem was originally published on the front cover of the *Bulletin* in 1892, with illustrations by Lionel Lindsay. A country bumpkin is taken in by a smart city barber and his cronies. In response, he demolishes the shop and returns home where now 'Beards are all the go/way up in Ironbark'. Hole's droll illustrations reinforce the humour in an ever-popular text.

MANLEY, RUTH (1919–86), born Barcaldine, Queensland, was a teacher of German. Her three fantasies, *The Plum-Rain Scroll* (q.v., 1978), *The Dragon Stone* (1982) and *The Peony Lantern* (1987), are set in Japan.

MAPPIN, ALFRED R. (1933–), born Perth, has written curriculum material for schools, and edited two poetry collections. *Sing in Bright Colours: Poetry from Australia* (1975), illustrated by Ingrid Van Dyk, ranges from bush ballads to modern urban themes, with over seventy poets represented. *Taking the Sun: Poetry from Australia* (1981) is a similar collection. Mappin initiated and edits the critical journals *Magpies, Papers* and *The Literature Base*.

MARCHANT, BESSIE (1862–1941), born Kent, UK, wrote over 150 adventures and romances aimed at adolescent girls, many published by the Religious Tract Society. Her novels were often set in lands distant from her home in England, from Argentina to India, and she has been referred to as 'the girls' Henty'. In *A Brave Little Cousin* (1902) Ursula Gifford is sent to 'Bim-Bong' in Queensland after her parents' death, where she restores delicacy to the rough homestead and falls in love with the crippled Ralph, who is restored to health by a trip to Europe. *The Adventurous Seven* (1914) are Nealie Plumstead and her brothers and sisters, who set off to find their father in NSW. They board ship to Australia, camp out and travel by wagon when they arrive, to discover their father after following many false leads. *The Black Cockatoo: a Story of Western Australia* (1910), illustrated by Lancelot Speed, is an adventure story about the Paynter children left to manage on their own when their parents are called away. At one point the children frighten

Ben And Bella Down On The Farm (1947) by Peg Maltby

the Aboriginal People away from 'the plantation' (*sic*) by playing the violin, French horn and a rattle. *The Ferryhouse Girls: an Australian Story* (1912) is about Vic and Lu, courageous girls who run the Blue River Ferry House most capably, row boats across flooded rivers and find true love. In *Sally Makes Good: a Story of Tasmania* (1920), illustrated by Leo Bates, Sally Willet is given a 3-year-old child in Launceston, takes it to Burnie, then to the station her father has been given for service to his country, finds Duckie's mother, and a husband for herself. *Waifs of Woollamoo: a Story for Girls* (1938) is set around Mallacoota, where three orphans and the children of various neighbours manage the farm and the household when their parents go off to find gold. The orphan's guardian, Captain Brandreth, does not find gold, but he does marry Dot's long-lost mother. Other novels by Marchant not set in Australia include *A Girl of the Northland* (1913), *The Girls of Wakenside* (1908) and *Hope's Tryst* (1905).

MARRYAT, AUGUSTA SOPHIA (?–1913) after whom Port Augusta was named, was the niece of the English novelist Frederick Marryat. She lived in Australia from 1848 to 1861, the wife of Sir Henry Edward Fox Young, the Governor of SA. *The Young Lamberts: A Boy's Adventures in Australia* (1878) is dedicated to the boys of England. John and George seek a fortune in NSW when they are deprived of their rightful heritage in England. They have the usual encounters with flood and fire before their fortune is restored. The novel follows the set pattern of colonial adventure, and the boys' hearts remain firmly with 'Home' in England.

MARSDEN, JOHN (1950–), born Melbourne, was a teacher. In his first novel, *So Much to Tell You ...* (q.v., 1987), a girl has been traumatised by her father. In *The Journey* (1988) Argus sets out to collect seven stories which he must tell the Council before he is judged an adult. The stories arise from Argus's experience of life and death during his physical and emotional travels, which include his marriage and fatherhood. Two humorous novels followed. *The Great Gatenby* (1989) explores the relationship between Erle Gatenby and Melanie Tozer, and their escapades at Linley Boarding School, such as hiding in the art room ceiling to smoke, or persuading a fellow pupil to run naked in front of the girls' dormitories. See also **Sexuality**. *Staying Alive in Year 5* (1989), for younger readers, is another school story. See **School Stories**. In *Out of Time* (1990) James finds a machine which transports him to various critical moments in the lives of ordinary people. Personal crises are also taken up in *Letters from the Inside* (1991), which begins as an exchange between pen-friends. Mandy and Tracey swap confidences, and as their inner lives take over, Tracey's criminal past is revealed, and the dark violence in Mandy's 'normal' family.

Marsden is a philosophical and contemplative writer, like his contemporary, Simon French, and his writing makes complex demands on his readers. He does not underestimate his audience, and his perceptions of adolescent tensions have enlarged the portrayal of character in Australian children's books.

MARSHALL, ALAN (1902–84), born Noorat, Victoria, wrote short stories and a novel for adults. *I Can Jump Puddles* (1955), the first part of his autobiography, recalls his rural childhood — his loving relationship with his family and his battle with poliomyelitis. Alan's determination, despite his disability, to walk, ride, fight and play is inspirational. The book has sold over three million copies, been translated into many languages, and made into a film in Czechoslovakia in 1970. Nine fifty-minute television episodes were made in 1980 by the ABC, directed by Kevin Dobson, Keith Wilkes and Douglas Sharp, and written by Sonia Borg, Cliff Green and Roger Simpson. The autobiographical trilogy is completed with *This is the Grass* (1962) and *In Mine Own Heart* (1963).

Whispering in the Wind (1969) is a fantasy. Peter, who lives with Crooked Mick, sets off in search of a beautiful princess with his horse, Moonlight, his marvellous stockwhip, Thunderbolt, and a leather bag containing a magic leaf. He meets Greyfur, a kangaroo with a bottomless pouch from which she can produce food and other useful items, such as starting cords for two-stroke motors and wharfies with cranes. Peter and Greyfur overcome all obstacles before they free Lowana from her tower prison where she has been locked up by her father until she can pass her school examinations. Marshall draws on Australian folklore, bush culture and colloquial idiom for a magical story. See also **Bunyips**; **Fantasy**. *People of the Dreamtime* (1952), illustrated by Lesbia Thorpe and reissued in 1978 with illustrations by Miriam-Rose Ungunmerr, is an interpretation of Aboriginal Dreaming stories. Marshall also wrote *Fight for Life* (1972), illustrated by Rae Dale, for 'Patchwork Paperbacks'. Bill Thompson, lost in the bush, survives a bushfire and hunger to find a billy full of gold in an old miner's camp. Marshall's work is optimistic and direct, and his children are tough-minded survivors. See also **Alan Marshall Prize for Children's Literature.**

MARSHALL, JAMES VANCE (1887–1964), born Casino, NSW, was a union organiser and anti-conscriptionist and an associate of Henry Lawson. He was jailed during World War I for his activities, and as 'Jice Doone' wrote *Jail from Within* (1918) and *The World of the Living Dead* (1919), based on that experience. His adventurous life included working as a reporter in North China, Canada, the USA and London; as a plantation worker in Central America, a fur-trader near the Bering Sea, a timber-cutter in Australia and an administrative officer for the Commonwealth Immigration Department during the 1950s. *Walkabout* (1961), first published as *The Children* (1959), was based on notes derived by Donald Gordon Payne from Marshall's life as a sandalwood-cutter in the NT. It describes how Mary and Peter survive an air crash, and meet an unnamed Aboriginal boy who keeps them alive. Mary's frightened reactions to the boy cause his death. At his death the boy forgives Mary, thus expiating her guilt. The book displays little understanding of Aboriginal culture, and a confused knowledge of the Australian environment. The children range through desert and forest, encountering platypuses and other animals which are not found in such terrain. A film was made in 1971, directed by Nicolas Roeg, with Jenny Agutter as Mary, Lucien Roeg as Peter and David Gulpilil as the 'bush boy'.

Since Marshall's death, his name has been used, with the permission of his family, for other novels, although, with the exception of *A Walk to the Hills of the Dreamtime* (1970), for which his notes were used, 'they are in no way works of collaboration … but are wholly original to their pseudonymous author who helped Mr Marshall in the last years of his life'. *My Boy John That Went to Sea* (1966) follows the emotional maturation of a boy aboard a whaling ship in the Antarctic. John Larsens wants to train as a musician, and when his father's ship seems certain to gain a bonus for a record whaling catch, his hopes appear to be realised. But when a storm threatens the life of the crew, who are his friends, John sacrifices his ambitions for them. *A River Ran Out of Eden* (1962), illustrated by Maurice Wilson, is a survival story set in the Aleutian Islands and is not a children's book. *The Wind at Morning* (1973) is about Magellan's voyage of 1519, told through the eyes of Juan Vizcaya, a 14-year-old cabin boy. In *A Walk to the Hills of the Dreamtime* (1970) Sarah, 14, and Joey, 11, live in outback Australia with the Bindibu people.

MARSHALL, ROBERT HARTLEY (ROCKY) (1924–) has written *Smokey,*

the Bear from Gumeracha (1983), illustrated by Melody Hampton. Smokey the koala and the other bush animals recapture the bunyips who have escaped from the zoo. Smokey's story is told in verse: 'They were tired/and in bad shape/and too exhausted/to escape./They threw in the towel/they wanted to rest/And now knew Smokey/had given them best.' The black-and-white illustrations are more striking than the text. *This Was My Valley* (1983) is an autobiography of Marshall's childhood in the SA bush. In *Hidden Valley* (1983) Davey saves the life of a kangaroo, and in return is given the power of animal speech, and membership of a conservation society which the kangaroos are organising. *Countdown to Sanity* (1984) considers the possibility of a nuclear holocaust. Jenny's growing awareness enables her to realise that it is not inevitable. *King of the Kimberley* (1989) is a biography of Tjandara, a police assistant at Derby who was shot by squatters.

MARSON, CHARLES. For *Faery: Stories* (1891) see **Fairies**.

MARTIN, DAVID (LUDWIG DETSINYI) (1915–), born Budapest, Hungary, began writing in English in the 1940s, after living in Germany, Spain, Holland, Britain, India and Israel. He settled in Australia in 1949. He has written poems and novels including *The Young Wife* (1962), a landmark in modern Australian novels about immigrants. His children's books include poetry, such as *Spiegal the Cat* (1961), illustrated by Roderick Shaw, a sophisticated narrative poem based on a Swiss tale by Gottfried Keller, and *I Rhyme My Time: A Selection of Poems for Young People* (1980), illustrated by Robert Ingpen. The latter includes humorous and serious verse. 'I am a Jew/I carry with me/Through torture vaults/ The spirit of man.' *The Kitten Who Wouldn't Purr* (1987), illustrated by Mark Payne, is a verse story about Catullus, who has to be taught to purr. *Katie* (1974), with Richenda Martin, illustrated with

Noela Young's drawings of a loveable cat, is about a tabby kitten who hides in Mr Dodds's suitcase, and travels with him to Melbourne.

Martin's first novel for young people was *Hughie* (q.v., 1971), about an Aboriginal boy struggling against racism in his home town. He has written many novels about people on the edge of society, including immigrants. *Frank and Francesca* (1972) describes the adventures of the insecure Frank, his girlfriend Francesca Terranova, whose family is involved in a vendetta with the Messinas, and Monty, their mutual friend. It was made into six thirty-minute television episodes by the ABC in 1973, directed by Ric Birch, featuring Peter Cummins, Lenice Reed, Allen Bickford, Gus Mercurio, Alan Wilson, Pauline Charleston and Denny Lawrence. *The Chinese Boy* (1973) recalls the attacks on Chinese miners during the last century. See **Chinese**. Martin captures the longings of the exile for home in *The Man in the Red Turban* (1978), illustrated by Genevieve Rees. Ganda Singh, an Indian hawker, travels along the Murray with Griff and Bron. It is Ganda's last journey before he returns to the Punjab and his wife. For his novels about the young Italian, Peppino, see **Peppino**. *Gary* (1972), illustrated by Con Aslanis, is another outsider. When he arrives at a city school he is not accepted, but through his friendship with a Greek girl, Helen, and the stockman, Lance, he is able to demonstrate his inventive capacities to his school mates. In *Clowning Sim* (1988) Simon runs off with a circus to achieve his ambition. The novel was made into a television mini-series in 1992, 'Clowning Around', with Clayton Williamson as Sim and Ernie Dingo as his friend, Jack. For *Mister P and His Remarkable Flight* (q.v., 1975) see **Animal Stories**.

Martin has also written fantasies. In *The Devilish Mystery of the Flying Mum* (1977) Maisie O'Meara gives her soul to the devil in exchange for a more interesting life and better looks. Her children, Rory and Rosie, and their cat, another Catullus, win back Maisie's soul and their father. Usra becomes a part of the Mermaid Commune in *Mermaid Attack* (1978). She meets Captain Nemo from the Nautilus, and the endangered creatures of the sea. *The Girl Who Didn't Know Kelly* (1985) is a historical novel about Kit, her attraction to two very different boys, and her own changing vision of herself. See also **Kelly, Ned**. In *The Cabby's Daughter* (1974) Bess struggles to cope with the death of her mother and her alcoholic father against the background of Mayhill (Beechworth) at the turn of the century.

Martin's novels for young people are wide-ranging, from fantasies to historical novels to animal stories. He focuses on the outsider, a boy or girl who, through circumstance or inner compulsion, has to follow his or her own direction, despite the pain which may result. Martin says: 'Writing for young people I have no didactic intent, nevertheless when they have read some of my books they may not be quite so likely to look down on people who do not behave or talk as they do.' *Fox on My Door: a Journey Through My Life* (1987) and *My Strange Friend* (1991) are autobiographies.

MARTIN, RODNEY DAVID (1946–), born Adelaide, teacher, writer and publisher, has produced language texts and informational books. *There's a Dinosaur in the Park!* (1980), illustrated by John Siow, shows how a boy's vivid imagination turns a litter bin into a ferocious dinosaur. *Story of a Picture Book* (1981) is an account of the creation of *There's a Dinosaur in the Park*. *Stephen's Useless Design* (1982), illustrated by John Draper, describes the origin of the construction toy, Struts. Martin has retold European stories, such as *The Valley of Mist* (1986) from a story by Arcadio Lobato.

Marty Moves to the Country (1980) by Kate Walker, illustrated by Bruce Treloar, was Highly Commended in the 1981 Picture Book of the Year Awards. When Marty finds that Josie rides a motorbike and catches lizards, he realises that country living can be as much fun as the city, with such an interesting best friend. The story, and Treloar's illustrations, cross gender barriers without preaching.

Mary Grant Bruce Story Award for Children's Literature, sponsored by the City of Sale, Victoria, is administered by the Victorian Fellowship of Australian Writers, and was instituted in 1981, the centenary of the birth of Mary Grant Bruce. The Award is made for a manuscript of short stories for children or young adults. There are two parts to the Award: an open section, and an award to the best Gippsland writer. **1981** S. McCarthy, *The Flood at Spaniard's Creek*. Gippsland writer: Garry Hurle, *The Super-Duper Saddle*. **1982** B. Breen, *Journal* and Robin Klein, *Birk the Berserker*. Gippsland writer: Marie McKenna, *Nell and the Bushranger*. **1983** Robin Klein, *The Blue Denim Ghost* and S. Bursztynski, *My Strange Experience*. Gippsland writer: J. Hodda, *Dancing Waters*. **1984** A. Fusillo, *Talking to the Moon*. Gippsland writer: Garry Hurle, *The Gumnut Reins*. **1985** Edel Wignell, *Catastrophe's Ninth Life*. Gippsland writer: Marie McKenna, *The Trouble with Mitch*. **1986** Lucielle Hanley, *How Casbo Became a Clown*. Gippsland writer: C. Williams, *Holly and the Porpoises*. **1987** S. Bursztynski, *Chris and the Library Ghost* and C. Corbett, *Toad and the Art of Mateship*. Gippsland writer: C. Williams, *The Sewing Contest*. **1988** A. Penniston-Bird, *The Terrible Tale of the Vanishing Library*. Gippsland writer: C. Williams, *Lisa of the Lyre Bird Creek*. **1989** E. Robertson, *Through the Web*. Gippsland writer: Garry Hurle, *The Second-Hand Tongue*. **1990** Errol Broome, *Off the Track*. Gippsland writer: Marie McKenna, *Saturday*. **1991** Helen Manos, *Best and Fairest*. Gippsland writer: Christine Edwards, *Sharron and the Honey Nut Kiss*.

MASON, CYRUS (1830–1915), born UK, was the grandson of Robert and Elizabeth Barrett Browning. He was a draughtsman for the Victorian railways, but his central interest was the art world of Melbourne in the later nineteenth-century. He was a 'respectable Bohemian', founder in the early 1880s of the Buonaretti Club, the first art association in Melbourne. Its members included Sir John Longstaff, Rupert Bunny and Tom Roberts. Mason was also a member of the Victorian Academy of Arts, the precursor of the Victorian Artists' Society. *The Australian Christmas Story Book* (1871), written and illustrated by Mason, contains four stories, 'Sis', 'The Box of Matches', 'The Little Woman' and 'The Conceited Snake'. Sis learns to care for her mother by observing her dog, Rowdy, care for some kittens; Peter is lost in the bush and saved by his box of matches and his dog, Bully; Little Woman is a lost 4-year-old found by Red Dick the limeburner; and the snake is so vain he is rude to everyone, including his mother. When someone remarks that the snake has some good markings, 'he [was] so gratified ... that he curved himself as gracefully as he could, not seeing what was so near him — a huge tom-cat — which seized him across the middle, and spoilt his beauty forever'. Each story has a coloured picture, one of the first Australian books to be so illustrated. The book was republished in 1988 by the Australian Early Childhood Association, with an introduction by Maurice Saxby.

MASON, OLIVE L., born Willoughby, Sydney. *Quippy* (1946), illustrated by Walter Cunningham, is a small duckling whose efforts to find food just miss success, until his mother returns. In *Quippy and Soot* (1953), illustrated by Jimmy Winter, Quippy and his mother swim to the far end of the pond, and meet Soot, a black duck. Soot and Quippy play happily together. Both stories are for 3-year-olds, and were televised as a puppet play in

1958. *Peter Porter* (1952), illustrated by Esme E. Bell, describes the duties of the porter, who averts a disaster at Periwinkle railway station by his calm and conscientious approach. The small-format 'Quippy' books and *Peter Porter* have appeal, adventure, and common sense.

MASON, WALTER G. (1820–66) engraved, selected and arranged *The Australian Picture Pleasure Book: Illustrating the Scenery, Architecture, Historical Events, Natural History, Public Characters, &c. of Australia* (1857), which is regarded as the first Australian illustrated book for children. Published by J.R. Clarke, 205 George Street, it had a preface by Frank Fowler (1833–63), journalist and bookseller, which exhorted the adult reader to send the book 'home to our young friends in England as a reliable picture of Australia, and a faithful portraiture of Australians'. The high-quality engravings are of such fascinations as the new sewer in Pitt Street, Sydney, the arrival of the first railway train at Parramatta, and Madame Lola Montez, among other celebrities of the time. Fowler goes on: 'There are many reasons why this book should be successful; the most powerful, to my thinking, being the extraordinary faith of the publisher in believing there are still girls and boys enough in the colony to make the speculation answer.'

MASS, NURI (1918–), born Melbourne, lived in Argentina for seven years of her childhood. She edited the magazine *Australian Children's World* 1945–46 and has been an editor with Angus & Robertson and with the Sydney *Sun*. She established the Writers Press in 1955, operating from a press in her own home, which published *The Silver Candlestick* (1956), illustrated by Celeste Mass, her daughter; Lydia Pender's first book, *Marbles in My Pocket* (1958), illustrated by Pixie O'Harris; Mary Gilmore's *Verse for Children* (1955), illustrated by Celeste Mass; and Frances Hackney's *Bread-and-Butter Moon* (1956). *The Little Grammar People* (1942), illustrated by Celeste Mass, is a fantasy based on the parts of speech and how to use them. Linda and Barry are taken by Sir Desire to meet King Speech in Grammar Land. Mass has written fairy stories, such as *Magic Australia* (1943), illustrated by Celeste Mass; *Australian Wild-Flower Fairies* (1937) with botanical illustrations by Nuri and fairy illustrations by Celeste Mass; *The Wizard of Jenolan* (1946), illustrated by Celeste Mass; and *Australian Wildflower Magic* (1967). *Many Paths, One Heaven* (1965), illustrated by Nuri and Celeste Mass, is a book on religions for schools. She has written five novels for adults. *The Wonderland of Nature* (q.v., 1964) is non-fiction.

MASSON, SOPHIE (1959–), born Indonesia, is a short story writer and novelist. In her novel *Fire in the Sky* (1990) dreams and a coin link Dominique and Tad to medieval France, where they travel back in time to save their ancestors from a monster. The ensuing battle coincides with the passing of Halley's Comet. In *Sooner or Later* (1991) Scilla arrives at Hogan's Creek to stay with her dying grandmother. During her time there she learns to accept Rosie's impending death, understand her father a little better, and look forward to a romance. See also **Aboriginal People in Children's Fiction**. *A Blaze of Summer* (1992) is set in France, where Brigitte, Marina and Raoul fight a tourist development. Masson has also written *The House in the Rainforest* (1990), a novel for adults.

Master of the Grove (1982) by Victor Kelleher won the 1983 Book of the Year Awards. Derin awakes after being attacked to find that he cannot remember his past. He and Marna, the Witch of Sone, journey to find Ardelan, whom Derin believes to be his father. This is a complex story, and Marna gives Derin many misleading clues on their journey. The truth of his identity is finally revealed, and it is his warm and trusting heart which has enabled him to defeat the forces of darkness. The landscape is peopled by diverse characters, and the plot is full of incident, but Kelleher creates complexity without confusion.

Mathinna's People (1967) by Nan Chauncy, illustrated by Victor G. Ambrus, was Commended in the 1968 Book of the Year Awards. It explores of the life of the Aboriginal People of Tasmania before their first contact with whites, and later how they were taken by George Robinson to Wybalenna, where many died longing to return to their own country. Much of the detail of Aboriginal life which Chauncy provides is now considered to be inaccurate, but the mistreatment of the traditional Tasmanian people by whites is a historical fact. Chauncy's imaginative account of the warrior Wyrum's curiosity and later dread of the white invaders, his son Towterer's reluctance to go with Robinson, and his dignified death, make a powerful story.

MATTHEWS, PENELOPE E. (1945–) is the senior editor of Omnibus Books (q.v.). She has compiled the short story collections *State of the Heart: Stories about Love, Life and Growing Up* (1988), *Bizarre: Ten Wonderfully Weird Stories* (1989), *Amazing* (1989) and *Weird: Twelve Incredible Tales* (1990).

MATTINGLEY, CHRISTOBEL (1931–), born Brighton, SA, has been a librarian in Victoria, ACT and the UK. She was the chairman of the National Book Council in 1979, and has written for radio and television. Mattingley has made a lasting contribution to the novel for 7 to 9-year-olds, her first being *The Picnic Dog* (1970). Piccolo is a miniature fox terrier with an excess of high spirits. Her portrayal of children confronting fear is developed in *Windmill at Magpie Creek*

(q.v., 1971) and *The Long Walk* (1976), illustrated by Helen Sallis, about Michael's fear of the walk home from school. She has used the theme frequently: in *The Big Swim* (1977), illustrated by Elizabeth Honey, Peter learns to swim; in *The Jetty* (1978), illustrated by Gavin Rowe, Brad overcomes his fear of a slippery jetty after his father is lost at sea; and in *Brave with Ben* (1982), also illustrated by Honey, Pete's fear of his grandmother's wild garden is resolved by the appearance of the bold dog, Ben. *Tiger's Milk* (1974), illustrated by Anne Ferguson, is more whimsical. Antony overcomes his despair at his small stature by drinking his grandmother's 'tiger's milk'.

Another concern of Mattingley has been a respect for the natural world and the need to conserve the land. *Worm Weather* (q.v., 1971) has Wendy rescuing stranded worms, and Cathy finds homes for cats in *Queen of the Wheat Castles* (1973), illustrated by Gavin Rowe. *Show and Tell* (1974), illustrated by Helen Sallis, is set in a primary school, and describes what the children bring to show their class. The sensitive Robert takes nothing from the earth. His gift to the class is a walk to see a robin's nest and some spider orchids. *The Battle of the Galah Trees* (1973), illustrated by Gareth Floyd, is another with a direct message of conservation. Matt's campaign to save the gum trees used by the galahs is eventually successful, though not without setbacks. Mattingley often portrays the simple pleasures of family life. In *Emu Kite* (1972), illustrated by Gavin Rowe, Andy spends a long time making a kite for a competition, only to sacrifice it to save his brother from an angry emu. *The Surprise Mouse* (1974), illustrated by Carolyn Dinan, is a birthday present from Nicky to his mother. In *Budgerigar Blue* (1978), illustrated by Tony Oliver, Nicky wins a prize for the mice, and buys a budgerigar for his mother. *Lizard Log* (1975), illustrated by Helen Sallis, is the story of a family holiday, with lizards all around. In *Hide and Seek* (1977)

Janey, Susan, Caroline and Kerry play in the sandhills, and in *The Special Present* (1977), illustrated by Noela Young, the same children appear in a collection of stories about everyday events in their lives.

The plight of the misfit is considered in *New Patches for Old* (1977) and *Rummage* (q.v. 1981). *New Patches for Old* (1977) centres around the selfish Patches (Patricia), from England, who has difficulty adjusting to Australia. She feels different, but her similarity to Australians means that there is no special treatment for her at school. Julie is another difficult personality, in *Southerly Buster* (1983), a novel for older readers. She is angry and ashamed when she is told that her mother, at 40, is pregnant. The novel describes how Julie works through her rage. A more humorous note is struck in *The Great Ballagundi Damper Bake* (1975), illustrated by Will Mahony. Ballagundi has a wheat glut, and the town has a day of baking which brings tourists and solves its economic problems. Other humorous stories are *McGruer and the Goat* (1987), illustrated by Carol McLean-Carr, about an octopus who brings brings warring neighbours together, and *Ghost Sitter* (1984), in which the ghost of a genial headmaster is laid by Imperator Claudius Hobbs.

Her picture-books include *Black Dog* (1979), illustrated by Craig Smith, and *Lexl and the Lion Party* (1982), illustrated by Astra Lacis. Lexl discovers the statues of lions in a German city, and has an imaginative romp with them. In *Duck Boy* (1983), illustrated by Patricia Mullins, Adam helps the ducks protect their eggs from goannas, rats and foxes. *The Butcher, the Beagle and the Dog Catcher* (1990), illustrated by Carol McLean-Carr, describes how Mr Worthy the butcher saves Belle the dog from the dog catcher. In *The Magic Saddle* (1983), also illustrated by Mullins, Jonni rides all over the world on a magic gingerbread rocking-horse.

She has written two books about the effect of war on children and ordinary people, *The Angel With a Mouth-Organ*

(1984), illustrated by Astra Lacis, and *The Miracle Tree* (1985), illustrated by Marianne Yamaguchi. See **War**. Mattingley's young characters confront moral and social issues with courage, humour and resourcefulness.

'MAURICE, FURNLEY' was the pseudonym of **FRANK WILMOT** (1881–1942), poet, who worked at Cole's Book Arcade for over thirty years, before becoming the manager of Melbourne University Press. The thirty-one poems in *The Bay and Padie Book: Kiddie Songs* (1917), illustrated by Vera Hamilton and Cyril Dobbs, were written for his two sons, with a further eleven poems added to the 1926 edition. 'Whisper/Sit up in your beds and hark!/Something said "meow" in the dark!/Was it a gentleman saying some prayers?/Was it a mousie trapped under the stairs?/Was it a manager stealing some shares/Or a newspaper having a lark?/Sit up in your beds and hark!/Something said "meow" in the dark!/Would you your treasures securely keep,/Never turn lamps out and never go sleep.' This lavish production has clever verses and attractive illustrations on every page.

MAYNE, WILLIAM (1928–), born Hull, UK, an English children's author, spent 1974 in Australia, after which he wrote *Salt River Times* (1980), illustrated by Elizabeth Honey. It is set around Footscray, Melbourne, near the Maribyrnong (Salt) River. The river links the lives of Kev, Gwenda, Sophia, Elissa, Joe, Ivan and many others in a mix of cultures. See also **Chinese**. Mayne showed insights into a multicultural suburb when most Australian authors were still centred on the Anglo-Celtic experience.

Me and Jeshua (1984), by Eleanor Spence, illustrated by Shane Conroy, was Commended in the 1985 Book of the Year Awards. The childhood of Jeshua

(Jesus) is told through the eyes of a cousin, Jude, from when Jesus returns to Nazareth to the discussions in the Temple. The special nature of a boy who emanates sweetness and love, but is aware of a grave destiny, is presented without sentimentality.

MEEKS, ARONE RAYMOND (1957–), born Sydney, studied at the Queensland Institute of Technology, Kogarah College of Art and the Alexander Mackie College of Advanced Education. He is a painter, illustrator and printmaker who has illustrated *Pheasant and Kingfisher* (1987), *When the World was New: In Rainbow Snake Land* (1988) and *This is Still Rainbow Snake Country* (1988) by Catherine Berndt. For *Enora and the Black Crane* (1991) Meeks uses the language and traditions of the Kokoimudji people of

Enora and the Black Crane (1991) by Arone Raymond Meeks

northern Queensland. Traditional Aboriginal painting techniques, combined with an individual sense of design, illustrate Enora's transformation into a crane.

MEILLON, CLAIRE (1902–), born Sydney, was editor of the children's page of the *Sydney Morning Herald* Women's Supplement from 1934 to 1939. She wrote serials for the ABC children's session and dramatised classics such as *Oliver Twist* and *Huckleberry Finn*. *Adventure Down Under* (1947) has an American boy, Warren F. Delmar junior, on a station in Australia where he and a group of children are instrumental in revealing a forger. In *The New Surf Club* (1959), illustrated by Jennifer Murray, Hugh and Tony move to Bungala, regretting having to leave the Manly surf lifesaving club. A dramatic rescue from the surf at Bungala convinces them that a club is needed there, and the town's determination to get a surfboat is eventually successful. The novel conveys the drama and excitement of lifesaving on the surf beaches of the east coast. It was made into a film, *Bungala Boys*, in 1961, directed by Jim Jeffrey, and starring Leonard Teale, who acquired a Cockney accent for the part. Meillon and Stuart Glover adapted *The Adventures of Marco Polo Junior* (1973) from the animated feature film. The forty-ninth Polo sets off to rescue Xanadu by returning the golden medallion of friendship.

MEILLON, JILL (FLORENCE BEATRICE) (1905–77), born Sydney, conducted a children's session for the Sydney commercial radio station 2UW, as Aunt Jill. She also worked for 2CH and the ABC, where she ran a women's session. Meillon was the mother of the actor John Meillon. *Robbit Rabbit Finds Out* (1945), *The Ducks who Didn't* (1946), *Percival! Polly! and Pip!* (1946), *The Children's Garden* (1947), with Adye Adams, are books for beginning readers. The royal visit of 1954 is recalled in *The Queen Came By* (1954), illustrated by Noela Young.

Stevie Steam Engine and Billy Boy's dreams come true when the Queen comes to their town. Meillon also wrote *The Jewel Casket: a Play for Eight Girls in Two Acts* (1948).

Melanie and the Night Animal (1988) by Gillian Rubinstein was an Honour Book in the 1989 Book of the Year Awards: Younger Readers. Melanie is shy and timid. She has to go to a new school and walk home with the boys next door. With the help of her new friend Jasmine she learns to depend more on herself than on her parents. When Jaz must go away, Melanie finds she has the courage to sleep outside alone, and discovers the secret of the night animal. Rubinstein presents a perceptive picture of a reticent girl within a supportive family.

Melbourne. From its beginnings as a canvas town in the 1830s, through its heyday in the 1880s, to a modern city of nearly three million inhabitants, Melbourne, on Port Phillip Bay, with its wide streets and Victorian buildings has provided a setting for many children's books. Early Melbourne was unsanitary, overcrowded and rough, as described by George Sargent in *Frank Layton, an Australian Story* (1865): 'In dens nine feet square, in the stifling heat of an Australian summer — half devoured by fleas of the most ferocious character, crawled over by myriads of disgusting cockroaches ... and menaced by bold and angry rats — men, women and children sweltered together by the dozen through the livelong night, to recommence a vain search on the coming day for better accommodation.' Richard Rowe, in 'Fred Leicester' (1889), a story collected in *The Gold Diggers* (1920), describes Fred travelling 'up the winding tawny Yarra Yarra, startling the pelicans ... pitching his tent on Emerald Hill, in foetid Canvas Town in the swampy valley ... along the bush-bordered Sandridge Road'. Fred contracts dysentery, which sends him off to Sydney. James Skipp Borlase, in *Daring Deeds and Tales of Peril and Adventure* (1868), says that 'murders, stabbings and other outrages were of frequent occurrence in the city …'.

Once the city had benefited from the wealth of the gold rushes, novels increasingly emphasised the attractions of Melbourne, and in the latter half of the nineteenth century they frequently enlarge on the grand architectural evidence of 'Marvellous Melbourne', making little acknowledgment of the poverty and squalor behind the wealth. Alexander Macdonald opens *The Quest of the Black Opals: a Story of Adventure in the Heart of Australia* (1908) with a description of 'the noble edifices rearing into the deep blue dome of the sky with a profusion that seemed extravagant … graceful verandahs … well dressed people … majestic thoroughfares. The people who built it were capable indeed of doing almost anything.' Macdonald takes the reader on a walking tour up Swanston Street to Collins Street, through the Block Arcade to Elizabeth Street, through Cole's Book Arcade to Bourke Street and the Post Office, back up to Swanston Street and the 'world famed Museum and Art Galleries'. Jack and Dick then go on to an 'excellent lunch in one of the many really first-class places in Collins Street'. Since the 1950s Melbourne has been a multicultural city. It is its mix of cultures and the working-class side of Melbourne, particularly in the inner suburbs, which has intrigued modern children's writers. Hesba Brinsmead's *Beat of the City* (q.v., 1966) also opens with a description of Melbourne, but this time it is Abbotsford, 'a hugger-mugger of factories, tenements, migrant hostels, and almost brand-new slums …'. David Martin sets *Frank and Francesca* (1972) in the industrial suburbs of Port Melbourne, Brunswick and Footscray, and *Gary* (1972) in Newmarket, where his protagonist becomes a stock-boy at the Saleyards. In Frank Willmott's *Breaking Up* (q.v., 1983) Mark and Andy go to school in a crowded multiracial inner suburb, recognisably Brunswick, and in *Here Comes the Night* (1986) a much darker picture of the suburbs is drawn, as James is caught up in the fast lane of cars, discos and drugs, from Brighton, through Prahran to Fitzroy and Carlton. Jean Holkner's picture of a Carlton which has now disappeared, *Taking the Chook and Other Traumas of Growing Up* (1987), is set in the 1930s. Jean and Lily's parents long for St Kilda or Caulfield, forever hampered by the fluctuating fortunes of their stall at the Victoria Market. In Lee Harding's *Displaced Person* (q.v., 1979), Graeme Drury wanders through the colourful suburb of St Kilda, where he takes fruit off the Fitzroy Street stalls and weeps on the beach front. Edel Wignell in *Escape by Deluge* (1989) connects the Melbourne of 1972 with the Aboriginal spirits of long ago. In all of the late twentieth-century novels, Melbourne is shown as a canvas on which the patterns of life are drawn as on any other city, but with a cosmopolitan character of its own.

MELLOR, DOROTHY was an employee of the Commonwealth Bank in Sydney during the 1930s. She wrote *Mickles and Muckles* (?1939) for the bank, a booklet for schools illustrated by Dorothy Wall. For *Enchanting Isles* (1934), illustrated by Ida Rentoul Outhwaite, see **Adventure Stories**.

MELLOR, KATHLEEN (1906–78) created *Gee Up Bonny* (1945), a novelty counting book for the children of the Lady Gowrie Child Centre, Adelaide. Bonny is saddled up, ready to take the children for a ride. In *The Story of Bim* (1945), written for 'three year old Charlotte', the little white dog, Bim, tries to play with a rooster, a black cat, and a grey mouse. They are all too frightened of him, but a boy comes along and Bim finds his playmate. *Let's Go to the Beach* (1947), *Now I'm Ready* (1947) and *Splish-Splash Rainy Day* (1947), all illustrated by

Marjorie Hann, are flap books featuring Jillian and Jonathan. In these excellent stories for early readers, page sizes were extended to include a cut-out piece which folded over to hide the illustration at the end of the sentence, or pages were cut to make windows. In *Pine Farm* (1952) Auntie and Kay transform the Old House into a holiday farm; in *Over the Hill* (1952) Biffy and John meet the farm animals; and in *Goldy* (1952) a bantam is lost, then found laying an Easter egg for John and Biffy. These three books were illustrated by Harold Freedman. *Stop Look Listen* (1945), with Marjorie Fisher (Marjorie Hann), and *The Traffic Lights* (1945), with Vivienne Morris, are flap books about road safety. All Mellor's books are stories for pre-school children about everyday adventures. *How it Happened: Told to Kindergarten Children in South Australia* (1955) is a history of kindergartens in Adelaide.

MELROSE, GENEVIEVE (1944–) (**GENEVIEVE RAISBECK, GENEVIEVE REES**), born Tanunda, SA, is a designer and illustrator who trained at RMIT. She has illustrated *Baroola and Us* (1973), by Audrey Oldfield; *Striped Wolf: a Bush Adventure* (1969) by Harry Frauca; *The Brown Land was Green* (q.v., 1956), *The Min-Min* (q.v., 1966), *Blue Above the Trees* (q.v., 1967), *Spark of Opal* (1968) and *Nowhere to Hide* (1969) by Mavis Thorpe Clark; *The Bush Bandits* (1966) by Betty Roland; *Snake for Supper* (1968) by Fred Baxter; the six Aboriginal Dreaming stories in Dorothy Carnegie's *Kaka the Cockatoo* (1967); *The Tintookies and Little Fella Bindi* (1966) by Peter Scriven; an edition of *The Wild Oats of Han* (1928) by Katharine Susannah Prichard in 1968 and an edition of Ethel Turner's *The Camp at Wandinong* (1898) in 1978; David Martin's *The Man in the Red Turban* (1978) and Ted Greenwood's *The Boy who Saw God* (1980). Melrose's fine pen-and-ink sketches express the Australian landscape and character.

The Man in the Red Turban (1978) by David Martin. Illustrator: Genevieve Melrose

MERCER, DIANA, born SA, is a writer and journalist. For *Cows Can't Eat Cedar* (1957) see **Historical Novels**.

MEREDITH, LOUISA ANNE (1812–95), born Birmingham, UK, was already an established poet and botanical illustrator when she came to Australia in 1839 to her husband's property in NSW. They settled in Tasmania in 1840. She wrote an account of her impressions of Australia in *Notes and Sketches of New South Wales* and *My Home in Tasmania, During a Residence of Nine Years* (1852), authentic depictions of the society of the times. *Loved and Lost! The True Story of a Short Life* (1860) is a poem about a lorikeet adopted by Meredith's children. Meredith prefaces it with a plea not to cage birds: 'The sight of birds in cages is to me painful ... I should be glad to think that any words of mine might help to deter some of you from keeping birds as pets ... We have no right to subject living creatures of such free and active natures to a cruel incarceration.' In *Grandmamma's Verse Book for Young Australia* (1878) Meredith has written verses about the natural world, e.g. 'Parrots':

'Twas in a fine old garden*
    Where the trees were large and
      high,
And whose ripe and juicy fruit
    Made many a famous pie,

That a pair of pretty white-eyes
Made a dainty little nest,
Wove of grass and hair the finest,
Lined with feathers of the best.

Waratah Rhymes for Young Australia (1891) by Louisa Anne Meredith. Illustrator: E. Minnie Boyd

'"Cushee-cushee, cushee-cushee, cushee-cushee coo!"/We gaze up above, and exclaim "Who are you?"/As the sound goes over us through the air,/Then comes from an old tree, tall and bare,/Where up on the branches, plain to view,/Sits a party of parrots, red, green and blue./You know how a rainbow looks just at its best?/In colours as many these parrots are drest;/No lady, though ever so fine, can compare/With their radiant garb or their elegant air.' *Tasmanian Friends and Foes,*

Feathered, Furred and Finned: a Family Chronicle of Country Life, Natural History, and Veritable Adventure (1880) contained coloured plates from her drawings, with verses from her previous works. The pictures and poems are connected through an account of Lina Merton and her family, whose excursions into the bush are described, and linked to incidents in the history of Tasmania. Appended is a list of algae which Meredith had collected on the east coast of Tasmania. *Waratah Rhymes for Young Australia* (1891) is largely a reprint of *Grandmamma's Verse Book*, illustrated with photo-etched illustrations by Mr R. Andre, the author, and the artist, Emma Minnie Boyd. *Some of My Bush Friends in Tasmania* (1860) and *Bush Friends in Tasmania* (1891) are well-produced large-format books of natural history, with striking colour plates. Meredith wrote 'The Children's Song of Welcome to Prince Alfred' in 1867, with music by F.A. Packer, which was sung by 5000 children on the arrival of the Duke of Edinburgh in Tasmania. She wrote nineteen books, fourteen of them in Australia. In 1884 she was granted a pension by the Tasmanian government for her literary and artistic services to the Colony. The biography of this remarkable woman is *Louisa Anne Meredith: a Tigress in Exile* (1979) by Vivienne Rae Ellis.

Merryll of the Stones (1989) by Brian Caswell was an Honour book in the 1990 Book of the Year Awards: Older Readers. Megan goes to live with her uncle in Wales after her parents have died in an accident. As a descendant of the Old Ones (people with extrasensory powers) she travels back to ancient Wales as Lady Merryll, where she intervenes in a legendary battle to avert the genocide of her people. The novel explores the consequences of having power over others, and proposes peaceful ways of resolving conflict.

Mervyn's Revenge (1990) by Leone Peguero, illustrated by Shirley Peters, was an Honour Book in the 1991 Book of the Year Awards: Younger Readers. Mervyn is a large and egotistic tom-cat who lives for food. When his family leaves him in the care of Elsie, the next-door neighbour, he takes revenge on her by making a mess of her house and pretending to be a night prowler. Elsie's cheerful no-nonsense approach thwarts his intentions, and Mervyn has to swallow his pride.

METHLEY, A.A. For *Bushrangers' Gold* (1930) see **Adventure Stories**.

METHLEY, VIOLET MARY (fl. 1910–40) was a prolific English author who set some of her books in Australia, or used Australian characters in her adventure and school stories. In *The Bunyip Patrol: the Story of an Australian Girls' School* (1926) English Rae falls out with the influential Sheila when she commences at a Sydney boarding school. Through the establishment of a Girl Guide troupe, the two become friends, but only after a brush with sharks, being lost in the bush, fighting bushfires and saving lives, all done with great daring and flair. The novel emphasises the character-building and firm friendships which Guiding encourages. See also **Lost in the Bush**. *The Queer Island* (1934) is another Girl Guide story, in which Dorcas, Carol and Wynne apply their survival skills to existing on an island. *Dragon Island: an Adventure Story for Girls* (1938), illustrated by Stella Schmolle, begins on a 'plantation' in Queensland. Gay and Ann and their English cousin Hilary find themselves on an isolated island, where these daring girls stay for three months. *Cocky and Co. and Their Adventures* (1937) opens in Australia, at 'Bundaburra' Station, where Shelagh is staying with her cousin Coral. What seems to have begun as an animal fantasy where the animals speak to each other soon becomes another adventure story, as the children travel across the Pacific to the Amazon, then on to London. In *Derry Down-Under: a Story of Adventure in Australia* (1943) the Carol family's fortune is restored through the efforts of Derry Joyce. *Two in the Bush* (1945), illustrated by Isabel Veevers, describes the adventures of two silly girls, Betsey and Gillian, and their 'pet', the Aboriginal child Woppity, in Queensland. Methley also wrote children's plays.

Mettle is the hero of three books by 'James McNell' (J.E. Macdonnell): *Captain*

Mettle V.C. (1955), *Mettle at Woomera* (1957), and *Mettle Dives Deep* (1958). Captain Mettle's colleagues aboard the *Scorpion* are the monocled Lieutenant-Commander Cuthbert Crabbe de Courcy, known as 'Crabby', and Chief Petty Officer Hogan, 'Hooky', who has the advantage of a steel hook at the end of his arm. In *Mettle at Woomera* they foil an attempt to steal rocket secrets, and in *Mettle Dives Deep* they tackle gun-runners in the Middle East. The tensions of the Cold War period provide the dramatic impact.

METZENTHEN, DAVID (1958–) has written *Danger Wave* (1990), which traces the relationship between Tommy Callahan and Gerry Kellerman, and their life on the Inlet, where Tommy delights in wind-surfing. In *Lee Spain* (1991) Lee leaves home with his dog Luke and is befriended by Prue who has also left her family, and later, Prue's small daughter Hannah. Prue and Lee work through their problems on Prue's run-down farm.

METZLER, PAUL (1914–), born Sydney, has written books about tennis, and a novel, *A Foreign Father* (1979), illustrated by Sandy Bishop. It depicts what it was like to have a German father, fiercely proud of his cultural heritage, during the prejudiced days of World War I. The children, Dot and Robert, react ambivalently to their father, who behaves very differently from their Australian friends' parents. They are embarrassed by the fun made of him, but defend him because they love and admire him. Paul Gerder eventually wins the lasting respect of the community. The novel is a tender tribute to a man who makes adjustments but does not lose his cultural individuality in the process.

Middy Malone appears in four comic-books by Syd Nicholls: *Middy Malone: a Book of Pirates* (1941), *The Further Adventures of Middy Malone* (1944), *Middy Malone and the South Sea Pirates* (1944) and *Middy Malone and the Lost World* (1943). These popular adventures depict an orphan boy in the company of swash-buckling heroes and pirates, such as the Captain McFlintlock and his evil adversary, Captain Vice — 'as bloodthirsty a rascal as ever slit an honest seaman's gullet'; the charming Mollie, Flintlock's daughter, and the genial wooden-legged Taters, aboard the good ship *Esperance*.

Midnite: the Story of a Wild Colonial Boy (1967) by Randolph Stow, illustrated by Ralph Steadman, was Highly Commended in the 1968 Book of the Year Awards. It is a satire about bushranging, loosely based on the exploits of the WA bushranger, 'Moondyne Joe' and Captain Starlight. The slow-witted Midnite is an endearing 17-year-old, manipulated by an acerbic Siamese, Khat, who engineers Midnite's rise from timorous nonentity to Mayor of Daybrake. Khat pushes Midnite into bushranging, with a gang made up of Khat, the 'rather silly' cow Dora, the horse Red Ned, a cockatoo called Major, and a sheep dog, Gyp. The 'rogue cop', Trooper O'Grady, is the real bushranger, and is bent on undermining Midnite. Midnite's love affair with the beautiful Laura Wellborn is managed by Khat to everyone's advantage, and the story concludes with Midnite changing his name to Daybrake after finding a fortune in gold. The novel alludes comically to events in Australian history, great works of Australian literature and cultural sacred cows.

MILLER, ELLEN (1923–), born Tasmania, wrote the historical novel *Anna Yesterday* (1977) set in 1875 in Oatlands, Tasmania. Eleven-year-old Anna is passed from one home to another. Her past catches up with her when a group of child-thieves comes to enlist her again, but Anna is rescued by her friend Jussy Nyall and given a permanent home with Mrs Finch. In *A Place Called Lantern Light*

(1975) Jane travels from Tasmania to WA, resenting the journey until she is reconciled with her uncle. *Quiet Land* (1979) is a collection of poetry for adults, with photographs by Peter Dombrovskis.

MILLER, ROSALIND has written *The Adventures of Margery Pym* (?1939), illustrated by Jean Elder, and *The Pyms at Yarrambeat* (1940), illustrated by Joan Kiddell-Monroe. They describe episodes in the life of an adventurous girl in Gippsland during the first part of the nineteenth century. Marjory, her brother David and Wilfred Gellibrand become lost, outwit a party of hostile Aboriginal People and bring a gang of cattle-thieves to justice. See also **Lost in the Bush**.

MILLER, SYDNEY LEON (1901–83), born Sydney, was an artist who developed comic-strips for 'Sunbeams' (a supplement to the *Sydney Sun*), the *Bulletin*, the *Daily Telegraph*, the Melbourne *Herald* and *Smith's Weekly*. The cartoon strip 'Chesty Bond' was his creation. His designs for his comics were innovative and often presented mysterious figures in an ominous landscape. Miller drew some of the first animated cartoons made commercially in Australia, and went on to work in film and television until his retirement. He wrote and illustrated *Alphabet Book*, *Penny the Puppy* and *The Four Bears*, all Frank Johnson's Children's Books, published in 1941. *Funny Farmyard: Nursery Rhymes and Painting Book* (1933) contained poems by Kenneth Slessor. He also illustrated *Peggy* (1944) and *Tea Party for Poffinella* (1945) by Amery Paul. Miller is regarded as one of the most talented and versatile commercial artists Australia has produced.

MILTON, MARY (1928–), born Victor Harbour, SA, is a portrait-painter and artist of nature who has illustrated three of Colin Thiele's books, *The Sknuks* (1977), *Pinquo* (1983) and *Farmer Schulz's Ducks* (1986).

Farmer Schultz's Ducks (1986) by Colin Thiele. Illustrator: Mary Milton

Min–Min, The (1966) by Mavis Thorpe Clark was the winner of the 1967 Book of the Year Awards. It is set in a railway siding on the barren desert fringe of the Nullarbor Plain. Sylvie and her brother Reg run away from their parents to an outstation. They are cared for by the Tuckers, who provide Reg with a sense of worth and Sylvie with a determination to set aside the shiftlessness which characterises her parents and make a better life for herself. This account of depressing rural poverty is one of Clark's best novels, and Sylvie is a memorable character.

Minnie (1971) by Annette Macarthur-Onslow was Favourably Mentioned in the 1972 Book of the Year Awards. Minnie is an old white cat who leaves home when strangers stay with her mistress. As Minnie runs through a fierce storm, she travels farther and farther away from the security of her place by the fire. Only her skill at evading predators saves her from being killed by dogs or foxes, until her acute sense of direction leads her to a glade where Jason finds her. Macarthur-Onslow has set the story in the winter landscape of the English Cotswolds.

Mirram (1955) by Margaret Paice was Commended in the 1955 Picture Book of the Year Awards. Mirram is an Aboriginal child, whose life is described from when she first opens her eyes. With her friend Wini she wanders through the bush, but Wini dies from snakebite, and Mirram is encouraged to stay with the owners of the cattle station. She decides, with some regret, to remain with her own people.

Misery Guts (1991) by Maurice Gleitzman was an Honour Book in the 1992 Book of the Year Awards: Younger Readers. Keith's parents are depressed and depressing in their dreary fish shop in perpetually grey London. In an effort to cheer them up Keith precipitates their migration to an idyllic Australian beach resort, which greets them with a tropical cyclone, crocodiles, mosquitoes, flying coconuts and stinging jellyfish. 'Thanks a lot, paradise, ... thanks a bleeding lot', Keith yells. Their story is continued in *Worry Warts* (1991), in which Keith attempts to resuscitate his parents' failing marriage. See also **Humour**.

MISSINGHAM, HAL (1906–), born Claremont, WA, is a graphic artist, designer and watercolour painter. For *Australian Alphabet* (1942) see **Alphabet Books**.

Mister P and His Remarkable Flight (1975) by David Martin, illustrated by Astra Lacis, was considered Worthy of Mention in the 1976 Book of the Year Awards. The lives of Vincent and the pigeon he finds at the Town Hall are juxtaposed. The book is in two halves: the lonely Vincent's efforts to train an unlikely bird to race, and the bird's journey back to its loft over a distance of hundreds of miles. Mr P fights off predators, raises his young for a brief season, and finally returns, battered and barely alive. Martin makes the pigeon's flight exciting and moving without giving the bird human feelings.

MITCHELL, ELYNE (1913–), born Melbourne, has written books for children and adults about the Australian Alps and the wild horses found there. For her Silver Brumby series see ***The Silver Brumby*** (1958). *The Colt at Taparoo* (1976), *The Colt from Snowy River* (1979), *Snowy River Brumby* (1980) and *Brumby Racer* (1981) were illustrated by Victor Ambrus. In *Brumby Racer* the son of Buzz and Yarrawa, a young bay stallion, Nooroo, is enticed by the mare Babilla, despite his love for his mate Honey. He has to choose between the wild herd and the homestead. The action is set in the 1850s, at the time of the first Jindabyne Picnic Races, around the property of Matthew Reid. *Kingfisher Feather* (1962), illustrated by Grace Huxtable, is also set in the Australian Alps. Twins Sally and David and their mother are given a task, to find the dragonfly cave, by an old Aboriginal woman from the past. Their search for the cave involves them in swimming, riding and skiing through the mountains. *Winged Skis* (q.v., 1964) is a skiing adventure. *Jinki, Dingo of the Snows* (1970), illustrated by Michael Cole, is about a dingo named by an Aboriginal boy; throughout his life Jinki is haunted by his contact with human affection. *Light Horse to Damascus* (1971), illustrated by Victor Ambrus, is the story of the Australian regiment in Egypt seen through the eyes of Karloo, a courageous brown horse. *The Man from Snowy River* (1982) is an adaptation of A.B. Paterson's poem, based on the screenplay of the film. Mitchell creates a strong sense of place in her novels, portrays animals without sentimentality, and effectively describes the beauty of the Australian Alps. Her autobiography is *Towong Hill: Fifty Years on an Upper Murray Cattle Station* (1989).

MOFFATT, FRANK (1941–), born Cornwall, UK, writer, artist and illustrator, settled in Australia in 1949. *Pippy: a Day in the Life of the Artist's Dog* (1978) and *Stuffed Parrots* (1979) are cartoon-like satires. In the chalk illustrations for *Neddie Puddin's Book of Things* (1983) the koala swims, draws, plays, and balances. *Farmer Beans and the Pantry Frog* (1985) is a laconic story about a frog which prefers to live in the pantry, and *Farmer Beans and the Baby Wallaby* (1991) describes the friendship between Beans and an orphaned wallaby, Sassy.

Moggie and Her Circus Pony (1967) by Katharine Susannah Prichard, illustrated by Elaine Haxton, was Commended in the 1968 Picture Book of the Year Awards. Moggie rides the foal Frisky in the circus, but only after Frisky has misbehaved and been threatened with having to pull an ice-cream cart for evermore. Striking pictures in brilliant colour sweep across the page, evoking the drama of the circus.

MOLINE, RUTH. For *Money!* (1989) see **Collections**.

MONYPENNY, KATHLEEN (1894–1971), born Riverina district, NSW, has written *The Kites that Flew Into the Moon and Other Chinese Stories* (1938), a collection of folk-tales. *The Children Went Too: Horse and Wagon Days* (1954), illustrated by Irene Maher, is a revised and rewritten version of parts of an earlier factual book, *From Footpath to Bullock Track: Exploration and Settlement in Early Australia* (1938). It traces the early settlement of NSW and Victoria to the discovery of gold. Monypenny also wrote *The Young Traveller in Australia* (1948), which describes the travels of Peter and Anne from Manly to Adelaide.

Monster Who Ate Australia, The (1986), written and illustrated by Michael Salmon, won YABBA Picture Book for 1990. Burra the Boggabri is driven from his home at Ayers Rock (Uluru) by tourists, and travels around Australia, where he swallows the America's Cup in WA, bites into Adelaide's Festival Hall and Hobart's Wrest Point Casino, takes mouthfuls of the muddy Yarra River in Melbourne, and bites out of the painting *Blue Poles* in Canberra, the Big Pineapple in Queensland and the Sydney Harbour Bridge before returning home. The book satirises Australian icons in bold caricatures through a humorous travelogue.

MOODIE HEDDLE, ENID (1904–), born Melbourne, was appointed to assess the reception in Australia of the educational material of Longmans and Collins, and became the education manager of Longmans, Green from 1946 to 1959. She was the editor of a series produced for the SA Education Department, the 'Boomerang Books' (q.v.), such as *The Boomerang Book of Australian Poetry* (q.v., 1956) and *The Boomerang Book of Legendary Tales* (q.v., 1957). Heddle edited *Some Australian Adventurers* (1944), extracts from

Australian writers dealing with discoveries, travel, and exploration, and the collection *Action and Adventure: a Book of Australian Prose* (1954), with fourteen extracts from novels as diverse as *The Getting of Wisdom* (1910) by Henry Handel Richardson and Ray Harris's *The Adventures of Turkey* (1952). Moodie Heddle wrote *How Australian Literature Grew* (1962), illustrated by Iris Millington, and *Boy on a Horse, the Story of Adam Lindsay Gordon* (1957), with Helen Jo Samuel, illustrated by Alison Forbes. *Girdle Round the World* (1952), edited by Moodie Heddle and designed and illustrated by Harold Freedman, contains poems, stories and extracts from Edith Nesbit, Ion Idriess, Rex Ingamells, Henry Williamson and others. She also wrote a history of the winery Chateau Tahbilk, *Story of a Vineyard* (1960).

MOODIE HEDDLE, JOHN FOSTER (1902–73), born Melbourne, the brother of Enid Moodie Heddle, wrote *Seven in the Half-Deck: an Account of the Wreck of the Barque 'John Murray'* (1949). During World War II, the *John Murray*, an old Australian square-rigger, was sent to the USA to bring back car tyres. Moodie Heddle was on board, and kept a diary. The ship was wrecked on the return voyage, and this is the true story of the experiences of seven boys on a small South Pacific coral island where the crew sojourn until help arrives. This astounding story of pluck and endurance is told in a matter-of-fact style. *Son of the Sea Dragon* (1953) follows the adventures of Chan Kwai, and his various sea journeys around Chinese ports and further afield.

MOORE, HENRY BYRON (1839–1925), born UK, was assistant surveyor-general, a fine musician, and secretary of the Victoria Racing Club for forty-four years. Moore, who knew more about roses than horses, was responsible for the beautiful rose display which is a feature of Flemington Race course, Melbourne. *How the Cruel Imp Became a Good Fairy*

(1900), illustrated by Frederick S. Sheldon, George J.S. Ross, T.G. Moore and H. Winkelmann, and published in aid of the Children's Hospital, Melbourne, was based on stories which he had written for his children. The cruel imp is reformed by the Good Fairy. Other stories included are 'Santa Claus' Dolls' House' and 'The Sweetest Country in the World, or, The Fairy Basket'. See **Fairies**. Also written in aid of the Children's Hospital was *Her Royal Highness, Queen Bee: a Story of Fact and Fancy and Other Stories* (1905), 'copiously illustrated by Miss Hope S. Evershed of Launceston'. The life of a beehive is told as a story. Other stories are 'Fidele', about a 5-year-old, her loving father and her dog Masco (only Masco survives) and 'The Strange Adventures of Dick, Tom and Harry, or, A Trip from Carlton to Carpentaria'.

MOORE, INGA (1945–), born UK, writer and illustrator, came to Australia when she was 8. *Aktil's Big Swim* (1980) is about a swim across the English Channel; in *Aktil's Bicycle Ride* (1981) the mice, Aktil and Arnie, deliver the wizard's fireworks on their rocket-powered bikes; and in *Aktil's Rescue* (1982) he saves his favourite Reggae band from kidnappers. In *The Vegetable Thieves* (1983) the thieves steal Des and Hetty's vegetables until they are discovered, and invited in to share the work and the profits. Des and Hetty are mice gardeners, tiny figures among the luscious sprouts, cabbages and beans. In *The Truffle Hunter* (1985) Martine the pig is taught how to search for truffles by Raoul, and finds true love. Moore's sense of place is captured in atmospheric pastels, depicting autumnal forests, and picturesque French towns. *Fifty Red Nightcaps* (1988) is an updated version of the old tale 'Caps for Sale', with the young Nico as the protagonist. *The Sorcerer's Apprentice* (1989) relates the familiar story, with sumptuous medieval illustrations. *Six Dinner Sid* (1991) is a cat whose six households feed him, but also take him to six vets when he becomes ill. In 1980 she created new illustrations for *Barnaby and the Horses* (1961) by Lydia Pender. Moore also illustrated *The Nimbin* (1978) by Jenny Wagner, *Brella: the Story of a Young Fruit Bat* (1976) by Josephine Croser, and *Away in a Manger* (1987) by Sarah Hayes. *Little Dog Lost* (1991) describes Liz and Tom's search for their lost dog Pip, and is set in England, to which Moore returned in the 1980s.

'MORELL, MUSETTE' (MOYRA MARTIN) (1898–1950) wrote for radio, including the ABC children's session and the NSW *School Magazine*. She adapted *Gulliver's Travels* for the session, and the animal fantasies *The Antics of Algy* (1946) and *Bush Cobbers* (q.v., 1948) originated as radio serials. Algy is an ant, and the bush cobbers are Possum, Spiny Anteater, Platypus and others. She wrote plays, collected in *Plays for Children, Book One* (1947), *Presented Without Courtesy, a Comedy* (1948), and *Ten Puppet Plays* (1950).

MORIMOTO, JUNKO (1932–), born Hiroshima, Japan, studied at the Kyoto University of Fine Arts and was art director of the Children's Art Studio in Osaka from 1965 to 1971. She came to Australia in 1982. Her uncluttered designs and dramatic use of colour are seen to great effect in her illustrations to Japanese tales such as *The White Crane* (q.v., 1983), *Inch Boy* (q.v. 1984), *A Piece of Straw* (q.v. 1985), and *Kojuro and the Bears* (q.v. 1986). *The Mouse's Marriage* (1985), an adaptation of a Japanese folk-tale by Anne Ingram, takes a mouse's perspective on the world. An elderly mouse couple searching for a husband for their daughter decide that mice are the most powerful creatures on Earth. For *Kenju's Forest* (1989) see **Conservation**. In *The Twin Stars* (1986), adapted by Anne Ingram from a story by Kenji Miyazawa, two stars are persuaded to leave the Milky Way and are nearly stranded on Earth. *The Night Hawk Star* (1991) was

adapted by Helen Smith from another Miyazawa story. The Night Hawk flies up into the starry sky to shine upon a weary world. Morimoto was present in Hiroshima when it was bombed, and the affecting *My Hiroshima* (1987) recounts her own childhood during that time.

MORRIS, ETHEL JACKSON (1891– 1985) studied at the National Gallery School, Melbourne. *All Among the Fairies* (1909) contains four fairy stories and a poem, but her assured technique is best displayed in her only other book, *The White Butterfly and Other Fairy Tales* (1921), published by C.J. De Garis in an edition which Robert Holden says 'must surely rank as one of the most beautifully produced and illustrated children's books in the whole fairy genre in Australia'. See also **Fairies**.

The White Butterfly and Other Fairy Tales (1921) by Ethel Jackson Morris

MORRIS, JILL (1936–), born Brighton, Queensland, has worked in radio, television and schools, and has written plays and contributed to reading schemes. Her animal stories include *Bobuck the Mountain Possum*, *Harry the Hairy-nosed Wombat*, *Rufus the Red Kangaroo* (all 1970), *Rusty the Nimble Numbat*, *Kolo the Koala* (both 1971), *Percy the Peaceful Platypus* (1972), all illustrated by Rich Richardson, *Animals of Oz* (1986), *Possums on the Roof* (1987) and *Brolga, Ibis and Jabiru* (1985). *Australian Bats* (1992), illustrated by Lynne Tracey, is an outstanding informational account of the species, with detail on the habitat, prey and life cycle of eighteen types of Australian bats. *Adventures at Bangotcher Junction* (1985), with Mary Lancaster, illustrated by Geoff Hocking, are stories originally heard on BBC radio, about Bat Possum and a Norwegian gnome, and include some stories later issued separately. In *Bangotcher Junction: Thrimling* (1988) they travel to Planet Thrim to rescue one of its inhabitants, and in *Bangotcher Junction: Underground Dragon* (1988) they outwit a Norwegian dragon. *Monkey and the White Bone Demon* (1986) and *Monkey Creates Havoc in Heaven* (1987) are adapted from Wu Cheng En's novel. In the picture-book *The Boy Who Painted the Sun* (1983), illustrated by Geoff Hocking, a small boy assuages his homesickness for the country by painting a mural to enliven his drab city neighbourhood.

MORRIS, JULIE (1945–), born Adelaide, artist and graphic designer, studied at the SA Institute of Technology. Her fine animal illustrations appear in *Possums on the Roof* (1987), the story of twin brushtail possums, who are trapped in the roof when their mother goes hunting. Morris has written and illustrated other books about animals, such as *Wolongdilly Bunyip and the Koala* (1990) and *Australian Mammals* (1986).

MORRIS, KATHERINE. For *The Platypus: an Aboriginal Legend Retold and Illustrated for Young Children* (1974) see **Aboriginal Dreaming Stories**.

MORRIS, MYRA (1893–1966), born Boort, Victoria, was a poet, short story writer and novelist. *Us Five* (1922), illustrated by Myrtle Kaighin and the author, was first published in the *Weekly Times* as 'The Other Side of the Hill'. The five are Peter, Cissy, Nancy and twins Beauty and Barbara. When their parents go off to Egypt they are left with Uncle Horace and Cousin Estelle, where they discover a deserted house and garden. The children repair the garden to its original beauty, and when the artist-owner returns he is transformed by the enthusiasm and innocence of the children, so that he is able to paint again. The novel suggests Frances Hodgson Burnett's *The Secret Garden* (1911), although it is more wry and humorous.

MORRIS, RUFUS (1907–82), born NSW, watercolourist, was also a cartoonist, contributing to the *Bulletin* Pink Page, and the series 'It's moments like these …', cartoons developed to advertise the sweet Minties in the 1920s. Morris illustrated *Mother Goose* (1946) by Ennis Josephine Honey. He worked with William Henry Honey on *The Story of Hanky-Panky* (1945), *A Mother Goose Fantasy and Other Stories* (n.d.), *Smookie & Co.* (1947), *Fluff and Floppy* (1947), *The Little Red Hen* (1948), *Three Little Kittens*, *Babes of the Forest*, *Little Animals*, *The Jolly Nursery Rhymes*, *"Oups-a-Daisy" Nursery Rhymes* (all 1949), *Twinkle-Twinkle Nursery Rhymes* (?1940), and *A Book of Fables* (?1945). He illustrated Timothy Kay's *Bobby Rubbernose: a Story about a Little Koala Bear who Lost Himself and Was Found Again* (1944), *The Adventures of Joker Jack* (1944), *Flop the Platypus* (1946) and *Koo-Loo the 'Roo* (1947). All are cheaply produced paperbacks, with simple stories and the humorous edge which Morris displayed in his cartoons.

MORRIS, RUTH (1926–), born Queenscliff, Victoria, wrote *The Runaway* (1961) after a journey through Queensland. Joanne Mitchell, calling herself Joe

Casey, roams through Queensland in a horse-drawn cart, acquiring a puppy, Gabby, living on rice and pumpkin when out of cash, and eventually finding a new family. The novel conveys the variety of outback people and their difficulties and pleasures.

MORT, EIRENE (1879–1977), born Sydney, taught in schools and was active in artists' organisations during the early twentieth century. She was a founder of the NSW Society of Arts and Crafts. Mort was influenced by William Morris and the art of heraldry, and designed many fine bookplates, illustrated for journals, and exhibited. *Country Cousins Presented in Picture and Rhyme* (?1903) is verse about bush animals and birds. *Eirene Mort's Australian Alphabet from the Collection of the Australian National Gallery* (1986), published by the Gallery, was drawn in 1902, when Mort was in London. She illustrated Dame Mary Gilmore's *The Tale of Tiddley Winks* (1917) and wrote and illustrated *The Story of Architecture* (1942) for children. In 1984 the Australian National Gallery purchased a large collection of Mort's work, including designs for craftwork, illustration, examples of her leatherwork, needlework, woodwork and metalwork.

Mother's Offering to Her Children, A (1841), published by George Evans, was the first children's book published in Australia, and represents a unique Australian example of its type. It was by 'A Lady long resident in New South Wales', identified as Charlotte Barton by Marcie Muir. Dedicated to Master Reginald Gipps, son of Governor Gipps, it is written in the form of a catechism, a style of presentation which would have been familiar to its readers, with questions and answers about flora, fauna, and the indigenous inhabitants. Clara, Emma, Julius and Lucy sit around Mrs Saville's knee, and listen with wonder to her stories. 'Mrs S.:

"What are to be the amusements of the evening?" Clara: "Could you favour us with the recital of something entertaining, Mamma?" Julius: "Of shipwreck, please, Mamma". Mrs S.: "You appear to take great interest in shipwrecks, I think." Emma: "We are very, very sorry for the poor people who suffer through them, Mamma, but it is very interesting to hear of so many things that occur in consequence."' And later, Mrs Saville expands the picture even further: 'The heads of the murdered people were arranged in a row.' To which Clara replies, 'What a truly distressing situation for the poor boys.' Mother tells them of the terrors of shipwrecks, including the tragedy of Eliza Fraser (leaving nothing unsaid) the beauty of the Australian countryside, and the domestic detail of the life of pioneers. The book was acclaimed as similar to 'Aitken's *Evenings at Home*, and some of Mrs Barbauld's works', by the critic of the *Sydney Morning Herald*, and was recommended for 'a cordial welcome in the house of every colonist in New South Wales' by the *Sydney Gazette*. Its format and many of the attitudes expressed may not appeal to today's audience, but it is a fascinating social document rich in detail, revealing the author's keen observations of life in the colony. A facsimile edition was published in 1979 by Jacaranda Wiley, with an introduction by Rosemary Wighton examining the importance of the book. Further reading: Muir, *Charlotte Barton*.

Mr Archimedes' Bath (1980) by Pamela Allen was Commended in the 1981 Picture Book of the Year Awards. The book demonstrates the theory of displacement using simple logic and humorous illustrations as an elderly Mr Archimedes takes a bath. When he is joined by Kangaroo, Goat and Wombat, the bath water overflows. As in *Who Sank the Boat?*, the problem is, Who is to blame? But, Eureka! — Mr Archimedes finds the solution.

Mr Koala Bear (1954), written and illustrated by Elisabeth MacIntyre, was Commended in the 1955 Picture Book of the Year Awards. Verse and illustration combine in the story of Albert and James's visit to Mr Koala. They claim to be his nephews, and after they eat the cupboard bare and cause chaos in his garden, their worried mother arrives. They have been in the wrong house! MacIntyre redrew the illustrations for a new edition in 1965.

Mr Squiggle is a television puppet, with a pencil as a nose, who arrives on a rocket. Mr Squiggle originated in 1959 on ABC television as a fill-in on the 'Children's TV Club'. The club collapsed, but the gentle and humble Mr Squiggle, the impatient Blackboard, and Miss Pat (Lovell), succeeded by Miss Jane (Fennell), Roxanne (Kimmorley) and Rebecca (Hetherington) remain to engage children with varied adventures and clever sketches. The operator and voices of the characters is Norman Hetherington, formerly a cartoonist for the *Bulletin*, and the scripts are written by Margaret Hetherington. Books arising from the series include *Mr Squiggle and the Great Moon Robbery* (1980), *The Mr Squiggle Activity Book* (1986), *Mr Squiggle's Australian Activity Book* (1987), *Mr Squiggle and His Rocket Activity Book* (1989) and *Mr Squiggle and the Preposterously Purple Crocodile* (1992), all written by Margaret and Norman Hetherington.

MUDIE, IAN (1911–76), born Hawthorn, SA, poet and passionate nationalist, wrote *The Christmas Kangaroo* (1946). Mirram the kangaroo and her son Joey help Father Christmas deliver presents across Australia. The story is interspersed with Mudie's witty asides: '"Why", said Mr Possum,/"I'm eating my supper,/I'm chewing lovely mistletoe leaves/Between my lower teeth and my upper."' Mudie also wrote informational books for young people.

Muddle-Headed Wombat, The, was created by Ruth Park for the radio program 'The Argonauts' (q.v.), and went into print with *The Muddle-Headed Wombat* (1962). Many further adventures have followed, such as *The Muddle-Headed Wombat on Holiday* (1964) and *The Muddle-Headed Wombat is Very Bad* (1981). Some of the adventures were reissued in paperback format, illustrated by Noela Young. Wombat's endearing stupidity has absorbed young readers as he bumbles his way through his adventures with the very vain Tabby the Cat and the worried and house-proud Mouse.

MUIR, MARCIE (KATHLEEN MAR-CELLE MUIR) (1919–), born Perth, developed the Beck Book Company with her husband. Muir received the first Nan Chauncy Award and the Redmond Barry Award in 1988 in recognition of her major contribution to children's literature and its bibliography. *A Bibliography of Australian Children's Books* (1970, 1976), a two-volume work, listed over 6000 Australian children's books, many in variant editions. A further 2000 were identified for the first volume of *Australian Children's Books: a Bibliography* (1992), edited by Muir. Volume 1 covers the period 1774–1972. Volume 2, edited by Kerry White, covers the period 1973–88. *Australian Children's Book Illustrators* (1977), *A History of Australian Children's Book Illustration* (1982) and *The Fairy World of Ida Rentoul Outhwaite* (1985), with Robert Holden, also opened the study of illustrators. She has traced the identity of 'A Lady Long Resident in New South Wales' in *Charlotte Barton: Australia's First Children's Author* (1980). Muir has edited a collection of stories which presents a panorama of Australian life, in *Strike-a-Light the Bushranger and Other Australian Tales* (1972), containing extracts from Richard Rowe, Louisa Anne Meredith, James Skipp Borlase, Ethel Turner, Katherine Langloh Parker, Louis Becke, W.M. Fleming, Norman Lindsay, Tarlton

Rayment, Mary Grant Bruce, Nan Chauncy, Patricia Wrightson, Henry G. Lamond, Olaf Ruhen and Ivan Southall. *Under the Pepper Trees: a South Australian Anthology of Children's Poetry and Prose* (1987) is a similar compilation of material from SA writers. Muir has also edited the previously unpublished *My Bush Book: K. Langloh Parker's 1890's Story of Outback Station Life* (1982), a story by Parker with a biography by Muir.

MULLEN, SAMUEL (1828–90), born Dublin, Ireland, came to Australia with George Robertson (q.v.) in 1852, and set up the Melbourne bookshop with him. As the result of an argument about the management of the London office in 1857, the two men parted ways, Mullen setting up his own bookshop and lending library at 55 Collins Street Melbourne in 1859, where he operated until 1889. Mullen published James Bonwick's *Astronomy for Young Australians* (1866). His brother William joined with A.G. Melville and Leonard Slade to purchase Samuel Mullen's business, becoming Melville and Mullen in 1900. The firms of George Robertson and Melville and Mullen merged to become Robertson & Mullens in 1921.

MULLINS, PATRICIA (1952–), born Melbourne, is an illustrator and puppet-maker who studied art at RMIT. *The Happy Bush* (1972) by Heather Larsen, *Dolphins are Different* (1972) by Letitia Parr, *Blinky Bill and Nutsy* (1972) by Dorothy Wall, adapted by Carol Odell, *All in Together* (1974) by Vashti Farrer and *Flowers for Samantha* (1975) by Letitia Parr exhibit her skilful line drawing, and her ability to capture the character and charm of animals. A turning-point in her career, 1975, saw her illustrate *Wheels and Things* (1976) by Vedah Hamon Moody et al., a collection of stories about various occupations, using a variety of techniques — crayon resist, pastel, pen-and-ink, and paint. In *Fabulous Beasts* (1976) Mullins used linocuts, photography, collages and oils to create her creatures. In *Rummage* (q.v., 1981) by Christobel Mattingley she continued to use a mixture of media, such as paint, fabric, and paper to suggest the colour and disarray of a busy market. She has used torn tissue-paper to great effect in *Hattie and the Fox* (1986) and *Shoes from Grandpa* (1989), both by Mem Fox. In *Crocodile Beat* (1987) by Gail Jorgensen she uses large sweeps of tissue-paper, and scrap paper such as sweet-wrappers, to provide texture. She illustrated C.J. Dennis's *The Triantiwontigongelope and Other Funny Poems* in 1989. Other books illustrated by Mullins include *Pelican Point* (1977) by Sue Couper, *All Sorts of Poems* (1978), edited by Ann Thwaite, and Christobel Mattingley's *Duck Boy* (1983) and *The Magic Saddle* (1983). She has also written *Rocking Horse: a History of Moving Toy Horses* (1991). Mullins's creative use of paper, fabric and paint gives a depth and texture to her work which is highly atmospheric.

Multicultural Children's Literature Awards were established in 1991 by the Office of Multicultural Affairs, to encourage authors to address the themes of cultural diversity, and are open to authors who have submitted books to the annual awards given by the CBC. The awards are designed for books which have a multicultural theme and express values such as harmonious community relations and social justice. **1991** No award was made in the Junior and Senior categories, but the winner of the Picture Book category was *The Rainbow Serpent* (1990) by Elaine Sharpe, illustrated by Jennifer Inkamala, and published by the Yipirinya School Council, NT. *Scallywag* (1990) by Jeanette Rowe was Highly Commended. **1992** Picture Book: *Big Dog* (1991) by Libby Gleeson, illustrated by Armin Greder. Junior Fiction: *Do Not Go around the Edges* (1990) by Daisy Utemorrah, illustrated by Pat Torres. Senior Fiction: *The China Coin* (1991) by Allan Baillie.

Multiculturalism, see **Immigrants**, and names of national groups, such as **Chinese**, **Germans**, **Greeks**, **Italians**.

Murgatroyd's Garden (1986) by Judy Zavos, illustrated by Drahos Zak, was an Honour Book in the 1987 Picture Book of the Year Awards. Murgatroyd's hair is so long and dirty that a garden grows in it. Only when it becomes too heavy for his head to carry does Murgatroyd agree to wash it. Pictured in colourful detail, Murgatroyd's garden within a head of hair is an absurdist's paradise.

The Magic Saddle (1983) by Christobel Mattingley. Illustrator: Patricia Mullins.

Murray River lies across 'the south-eastern corner of Australia like some old bent tree, the great branches of its tributaries reaching into Southern Queensland and spreading inland over New South Wales and Northern Victoria', as Max Fatchen says in *The River Kings* (1966). 'It rose in the cool Snowy Mountains, it passed through forested gorges, it moved on spilling its silver billabongs on either side of its main channel. It passed through harsh mallee country. It idled by new river settlements where steam pumps sucked up its waters for the vines and orchards. It carried fleets of paddle-steamers on its broad bosom ... [and] at last turned in a leisurely bend above the river port of Morgan in South Australia, finally delivering its waters absentmindedly to the southern ocean below the last river port of Goolwa ...' Many writers have drawn inspiration from this great river and the people who have lived by it. In *The Old Man River of Australia: a Saga of the River Murray* (1945) Leila Pirani traces the Murray's course from the mountains to the sea, interweaving its geography into its history, as a source of life for the traditional people to its exploitation for commercial wealth. John K. Ewers's *Who Rides on the River?* (1956) is a fictional account of the journey of Charles Sturt down the river based on diaries of his two expeditions during 1828–31.

The Murray River paddle steamers which plied their trade along the river from Echuca to Morgan have been a source for writers such as Elizabeth Wilton and Colin Thiele. Wilton's *Riverboat Family* (1967) documents the commerce along the river at the turn of the century and the rivalries between the railways and the river boats, through the fortunes of the Angus family. The crucial role of the river in the lives of the characters is emphasised, although there is no sense of conserving it for the future. *River Murray Mary* (q.v., 1979) by Colin Thiele describes the flooded river and the boatmen and bushmen who have been associated with it. Michael Page's *The Runaway Punt* (1976) describes the bird life and the changing seasons, and follows the journey to Lake Alexandrina. Cliff Green's *The Incredible Steam-Driven Adventures of Riverboat Bill* (1975), *The Further Adventures of Riverboat Bill* (1981) and *Riverboat Bill Steams Again* (1985) are tall tales about the crew of the good ship *Mystery*, with its steam created by Bunyip, the Patent Portable Firebox.

The special attraction to children of life on the river is portrayed in *Riverbend Bricky* (1960) by Ira Nesdale. Bricky lives in a shack near the river with his father, fishing and yabbying through an endless summer, a precursor to Scotty in James Aldridge's *A Sporting Proposition* (1973). Both boys are free spirits, like the river itself. The life of Jock in Colin Thiele's *Yellow-Jacket Jock* (1969) also revolves around the river, where his parents are farmers. In the struggle between those who use the Murray merely for pleasure and those who know its moods and want to keep it safe for its birds and animals, Thiele has the conservationists win out. The book is enhanced by the stylish illustrations of Clifton Pugh. Kerry Kenihan's *Red and the Heron Street Gang* (1985) has Red (Regina) and her gang involved in adventures around the Murray. In *Jess and the River Kids* (1985) by Judith O'Neill, Jess and her friends Kenny and Snowy are told stories of earlier times by Old Lizzie. The pull of the river dominates the book, as the children swim, fish, paint it and live on its boats.

Museum of Australian Childhood, at first called the Australian Museum of Childhood, opened in October 1988. It aimed to conserve and preserve historical objects related to childhood. The collection included illustrated books, mostly from the twentieth century, textbooks, plays, and music for children, games, toys and novelties, and original artwork. The basis was the Thyne Reid Australian Children's Collection, donated to the

National Trust of NSW by James Hardie Industries in 1987. The museum was housed at Juniper Hall, a historic home in Paddington, Sydney, until 1992.

Museum of Childhood, at Edith Cowan University, Claremont Campus, WA, was founded by Mrs Mary Mc–Kenzie, who, showing admirable foresight, developed a large collection between 1969 and 1984. In 1984 she gave the material to the WA College of Advanced Education, now part of Edith Cowan University. The museum organises and runs an educational program for schools, linking its exhibits with the curriculum, and centering on the experience of the Australian child. Home-made and commercial toys and childhood artefacts from the nineteenth and twenti-eth centuries from England, South East Asia, the USA and Australia have been donated and rescued from unlikely sources, such as the rubbish tip. The books in the collection include textbooks, school readers, school and Sunday school prizes, comics, colouring and alphabet books. There are over 18 000 items in this museum.

My Place (1987) by Nadia Wheatley and Donna Rawlins won the 1988 Book of the Year Awards: Younger Readers, and YABBA for Younger Readers in the same year. In an original approach to history, writer and illustrator have presented Australia during 200 years of white occu-pation through a small slice of place. Environment and history are seen through the eyes of working-class children, and social and physical changes are explored. The history of the creek which runs through a Sydney suburb shows how industrialisation has polluted the area,

although the survivors, such as the old Moreton Bay fig tree, also mark the land's resilience. The book begins and ends with two Koori children, who belong to, rather than own, the land. Wheatley and Rawlins show the impact of the rich diversity of immigrants on Australia and Australia's effect on them.

My Place in Space (1988) by Robin and Sally Hirst, illustrated by Roland Harvey and Joe Levine, was an Honour Book in the 1989 Picture Book of the Year Awards. When two children are asked where they live, their reply inspires illus-trations of Earth's place in the universe, and explanations of astronomy. Harvey's humorous asides enhance a story set in a country town, Earth-bound, but with its eyes on the stars.

'MYSTERY, JOHN', 'who lives in Adventure Castle, Sydney' and who intro-duced himself as 'the Nation's Storyteller', produced several hundred popular chil-dren's books before, during and after World War II, published by Publicity Press and Lonsdale & Bartholemew. The many series included the 'Woolly Sisters', who were Pearl and Plain, 'Blinkyland', 'Gypsy Boy', 'Exciting Tales', 'Leisure Hour', such as *John Mystery's Cuddley (sic) Bear Tales* (?1941), 'Tell Tale', 'Story Time', 'Gift Book', 'Exciting Tales', 'Famous', such as *John Mystery's Famous Giants* (1938), 'Get Well', 'Fireside', such as *John Mystery's Teddy Koala's Book* (1939?) and 'Prize Book'. Each book contained a let-ter addressed to his readers — 'Dear Cobber ...' — and an annual appeared irregularly, *'Cobbers': Australian Children's Annual*. Muir (1992) identifies 'John Mystery' as Lester Sinclair.

N

Nan Chauncy Award is a quinquennial award established in 1983 by the CBC, made to individuals for services to Australian children's literature. **1983** Marcie Muir; **1988** Joyce Oldmeadow.

Nancarrow, Clippie is the 'madcap young pilot' who appears in H.F. Brinsmead's *Who Calls from Afar?* (1971), *Echo in the Wilderness* (1972), and *The Sand Forest* (1985). Clippie rescues Lyn Honeyfield, who is working at the Moree tracking station monitoring the Apollo mission. He helps to rescue native animals threatened by the flooding of Lake Tara, and begins a romance with Beverley Rose. Sky Herriot meets Clippie when she is staying with her uncles in Fremantle, and although romance blossoms between Clippie and Sky, Clippie remains faithful to Bev.

NANGAN, JOE. For *Joe Nangan's Dreaming: Aboriginal Legends of the North-West* (1976) see **Aboriginal Dreaming Stories**.

Nargun and the Stars, The (1973) by Patricia Wrightson won the 1974 Book of the Year Awards. When Simon Brent is orphaned he is taken in by Charlie and Edie Waters, at Wongadilla in the Hunter Valley. There he makes contact with Aboriginal spirits, the Potkoorok, Nyols, Turongs, and the ancient and formidable Nargun who is threatening Wongadilla. Wrightson had used some of these Aboriginal spirits in *An Older Kind of Magic* (q.v., 1972), but here they take on a greater tangibility. Simon, Charlie and Edie force the Nargun away from the valley floor, into the Turongs' caves.

Wrightson has created a picture of a creature both fearful and pitiable in the Nargun.

National Children's Literature Award, inaugurated in 1986, is one of the Festival Awards for Literature. It is awarded biennially for a published work of fiction or information, by the SA Government's Department of the Arts, to coincide with the Adelaide Festival. **1986** *The Long Night Watch* by Ivan Southall; **1988** *Space Demons* (q.v., 1986) by Gillian Rubinstein; **1990** *Beyond the Labyrinth* (q.v., 1988) by Gillian Rubinstein; **1992** *The House Guest* (q.v., 1991) by Eleanor Nilsson.

Naughty Agapanthus (1966) by Barbara Macfarlane, illustrated by Margaret Lees, received a Special Mention in the 1967 Picture Book of the Year Awards. Agapanthus is a determined child who is not very obedient, but always imaginative. She will not put on her warm jumper, and plays in the pond in her underclothes. When the doctor is called she bites his finger, but the nasty medicine soon cures her. Her adventures continue in *Queen Agapanthus* (1970) and *Agapanthus is Lost* (1970), also illustrated by Margaret Lees. Agapanthus dresses up in Mother's clothes and eats chocolate cake instead of her spinach, and in the third book she becomes lost, is found by a policeman, and goes to the circus.

Nelson, Thomas was established in Edinburgh in 1798, initially to publish religious tracts and school texts. The Australian branch distributed the UK books until the 1970s, when Nelson developed an important Australian publishing program in children's books under the guidance of Robert Sessions, with authors such as Peter Pavey, Pamela Allen, and Bob Graham.

NESDALE, IRA (Iris) (1919–), born Broken Hill, NSW, has written informational books on ships of the Navy. In *Riverbend Bricky* (1960), illustrated by Charles Keeping, the irrepressible Bricky is responsible for most of the excitement in the peaceful town of Riverbend, on the Murray. Bricky sells his own empty bottles back to the shopkeeper, and catches frogs to send to a professor in Melbourne. He shows his common sense as he saves his goats from the flood, and traces his father when it seems he might be sent into an institution. His adventures are continued in *Bricky and the Hobo* (1964). See also **Murray River**. *The Bay Whalers* (1985) is about whaling in SA. Nesdale has also written a biography of Mrs Aeneas Gunn, *The Little Missus: Mrs Aeneas Gunn* (1977); and a history of primary schools in SA, *Never a Dull Moment* (1988).

New South Wales Bookstall Company, originally owned by Henry Lloyd (1831–97), was a chain of railway and ferry bookstalls, modelled on W.H. Smith & Son, London. It became a publishing company when it was acquired by Alfred Cecil Rowlandson (1865–1922) in 1901. Rowlandson published 200 titles by Australasian writers in cheap paperback editions of 10 000 copies or more, including novels by J.F.M. Abbott and Dale Collins. The first book in the series was Steele Rudd's *On Our Selection* (1899). The 'Bookstall Series' ('1s.1d. posted, written for Australians by Australians') had covers illustrated by Australia's leading artists, including Frank P. Mahony, D.H. Souter, Sydney Ure Smith and the Lindsays. During World War I, the price was increased to fifteen pence. Best-selling authors included Roy and Hilda Bridges, Dale Collins, Louis Becke and Edward Dyson. The company also published comic-books, and *Tom Pagdin, Pirate*

(1911) by E.J. Brady and J. Leslie's *Youth Builds a Monument* (1933). The publishing program of inexpensive and attractive books by local authors captured a readership across Australia and NZ. At the time of his death, Rowlandson had sold around five million copies of his publications.

New South Wales Literary Award: Children's Book Award was inaugurated in 1979 as the Premier's Literary Awards, and renamed in 1987. The Children's Book Award is offered for a work of fiction or non-fiction. **1979** *John Brown, Rose and the Midnight Cat* (q.v., 1977) by Jenny Wagner and Ron Brooks; *The Dark Bright Water* (1978) by Patricia Wrightson. **1980** *Mr Archimedes' Bath* (q.v., 1980) by Pamela Allen; *Land of the Rainbow Snake* (1979) by Catherine Berndt. **1981** *When the Wind Changed* (q.v., 1980) by Ruth Park and Deborah Niland; *The Seventh Pebble* (q.v., 1980) by Eleanor Spence. **1982** *Whistle Up the Chimney* (q.v., 1981) by Nan Hunt and Craig Smith. **1983** *Who Sank the Boat?* (q.v., 1982) by Pamela Allen; *Five Times Dizzy* (q.v., 1982) by Nadia Wheatley. **1984** *Possum Magic* (q.v., 1983) by Mem Fox and Julie Vivas. **1985** *The House that was Eureka* (q.v., 1985) by Nadia Wheatley. **1986** *The True Story of Spit McPhee* (1986) by James Aldridge. **1987** *A Rabbit Named Harris* (1987) by Nan Hunt and Betina Ogden. **1988** *Answers to Brut* (q.v., 1988) by Gillian Rubinstein. **1989** *You Take the High Road* (1988) by Mary Pershall. **1990** *The Blue Chameleon* (1989) by Katherine Scholes. **1991** *Strange Objects* (q.v., 1990) by Gary Crew. **1992** *All in the Blue Unclouded Weather* (1992) by Robin Klein.

NIALL, BRENDA, (1930–), born Melbourne, is a writer and academic. She has written a definitive study of two major authors, *Seven Little Billabongs: the World of Ethel Turner and Mary Grant Bruce* (1979) and a social history of children's fiction, *Australia Through the Looking-Glass:*

Children's Fiction 1830–1980 (1984) with the assistance of Frances O'Neill. Niall has also written the prize-winning biography *Martin Boyd: a Life* (1988).

NICHOLLS, BRONWEN (1944–   ), born Melbourne, teacher, novelist and playwright, wrote *Three Way Street* (1982), illustrated by Dougal Ramsay. Twelve-year-old Aggie Wilson has just completed primary school, and acquired a dog, Bruce, in a picture of a resilient single parent family struggling for survival. Sixteen-year-old Phoebe Mullens, 'Mully', in *Mullaway* (1986) has a mother dying of cancer, her brother Steven is flirting with heroin, her youngest brother has a serious accident, and the family is unable to communicate with their father. Through her diary, Mully looks with candour and love at the family to whom she is the surrogate mother. She finds friendship with Jim, ten years her senior, deaf and unable to speak. In 1988 *Mullaway* was made into a film, *Mull*, directed by Don McLennan, with Nadine Garner, Bill Hunter and Sue Jones.

NICHOLLS, BROOKE (EDWARD DUNHAM BROOKE NICHOLLS) (?1877–1937) was a dentist, lecturer in dentistry, film-maker and naturalist. Dr Nicholls trained the renowned kookaburra Jacko, who appeared on a gramophone record and in films, notably as the bird which introduced Movietone News. *Jacko, the Broadcasting Kookaburra: His Life and Adventures* (1933), illustrated by Dorothy Wall, is told by Dr Nicholls and Jacko himself. It relates his early life and his public appearances throughout Australia. *The Amazing Adventures of Billy Penguin* (1934) also illustrated by Wall, is a similar story about a golden-crested penguin captured at Lorne, Victoria.

NICHOLLS, SYD (SYDNEY WENT-WORTH) (1896–1977), born Port Frederick Bay, Tasmania, was the creator of Fatty Finn (q.v.) and Middy Malone

(q.v.). Nicholls studied at the Royal Art Society, and produced cartoons for the *International Socialist*, the *Bulletin* and *Direct Action*. Because of his political work Nicholls found it difficult to obtain commissions, and moved into designing motion picture posters. He became the senior art editor for the *Evening News*, where he was instrumental in having May Gibbs's 'Bib and Bub' published. Nicholls established *Middy Malone's Magazine*, a comic-book which was an opportunity for himself and other artists to develop their comic art. In the 1940s he wrote *The Magic Boomerang: an Australian Fairy Story* (n.d.), *Sea Adventure* (n.d.), *A Big Book of Australian Adventure* (n.d.). He wrote and illustrated factual books such as *A Book of Planes, Trains and Cars* and *A Book of Famous Ships. About Ships: From the Egyptian Galley to the Queen Elizabeth* (1947) is a careful and accurately illustrated history of ships. Nicholls was a pioneer of Australian comic art.

NICHOLSON, JOYCE (1919–   ), born Melbourne, the daughter of D.W. Thorpe, publisher, was the managing director of D.W. Thorpe Pty Ltd after her father's retirement, and the chief executive of Jayen Press from 1987. She was a founding member of the CBC of Victoria, and of the Women's Electoral Lobby. She has written books for beginning readers, such as *The Little Blue Car* (1950), *The Little Green Tractor* (1950), *The Aeroplane that Could Not Fly* (1951), *An ABC of Ships and the Sea* (1950) and *The Little Red Helicopter* (1954).

Her animal stories include *Kerri and Honey* (1962), the story of two koalas. In *Cranky the Baby Australian Camel* (1963) Jeff lives on a large station. When his dog is killed he tries to make a pet of a baby camel. When Cranky escapes, Jeff and his Aboriginal friend Billy set off to find him, and discover Cranky wants his mother. *Andy's Kangaroo* (1964) is about a joey found on the road, which Andy raises. When the family moves to Sydney, Andy passes Hoppy on to the family who is to live in their house. In *Ringtail the Possum* (1965) Ringtail is threatened by a cat. These three books have photographs by Gordon De'Lisle. In *Sir Charles and the Lyrebird* (1966), with photographs by Brian McArdle, Jane and Tim take their dog Sir Charles to Sherbrooke Forest. In *Yap the Penguin* (1967) Yap is saved by Tony and Susan. In *Woop the Wombat* (1968), with photographs by L.H. Smith, a wombat found by Kathy and Mark is given a home with Libby.

Two holiday adventures for older readers, *Adventure at Gull's Point* (1955) and *Gull's Point and Pineapple* (1957), are set in an area suggesting Port Phillip Bay, Victoria. The Hamilton and McGee children rebuild a boat-house in the first, and solve the mystery of polluted drink bottles in the second. *Freedom for Priscilla* (1974), first published as *A Mortar-Board for Priscilla* in 1963, deals with the 'collision between private and public affairs' as the difficulties faced by a determined girl who wants to become a doctor are seen against the context of nineteenth-century attitudes to such issues as the place of women in medicine, and women's suffrage. *The Convict's Daughter* (1976) is another historical novel. Ellen and her brother Jamie accompany their mother when she is transported to NSW. Ellen's romance with Will Morgan goes through many trials before happiness is achieved.

Nicholson has written informational books. *Our First Overlander* (1956) is the story of the explorer, Hamilton Hume. For *Man Against Mutiny: the Story of Vice-Admiral William Bligh* (1961) see **Bligh**, Sir **William**. *A Goldseeker* (1970), illustrated by Jocelyn Jones, is one of Oxford's 'Early Australians' series. She has written a series on games and competitions, including *Games for the Family* (?1954), illustrated by her four children, and books for adults.

NIEUWENHUIZEN, AGNES (1939–), born Teheran, Iran, of Hungarian parents, a teacher and critic, came to Australia as a child. *No Kidding: Top Writers for Young People Talk about their Work* (1991) has interviews with twelve writers: Allan Baillie, Simon French, Libby Gleeson, Lee Harding, Paul Jennings, John Marsden, David Martin, Joan Phipson, Gillian Rubinstein, Nadia Wheatley, and Patricia Wrightson. *Good Books for Teenagers* (1992) is a critical guide to 200 Australian and overseas books.

NILAND, DEBORAH and **KILMENY** (1952–), born Auckland, NZ, are the twin daughters of Ruth Park (q.v.) and D'Arcy Niland. Both women studied at the Julian Ashton School.

Deborah has illustrated books by Jean Chapman: *The Sugar Plum Christmas Book: a Book for Christmas and All the Days of the Year* (q.v., 1977), *Velvet Paws and Whiskers* (1979), *The Tall Book of Tall Tales* (1985), and *Haunts and Taunts: a Book for Hallowe'en and All the Nights of the Year* (1983); and several other diverse works: *Stuff and Nonsense* (1974) by Michael Dugan is a poetry collection, as is *All Australian Funny and Frightful Verse* (1987) selected by Glenys Smith; *Fairy Strike!* (1980) by Trevor Todd; *The Jacky Dandy Songbook* (1982), with Patrick Niland, a collection of forty folk-songs set to Patrick Niland's music. She has illustrated Hazel Edwards's *There's a Hippopotamus on Our Roof Eating Cake* (1980) and *My Hippopotamus is on Our Caravan Roof Getting Sunburnt* (1989); Nan Hunt's *Families are Funny* (1990); Peita Letchford's *The Very Sniffy Dog* (1990); and Ruth Park's *When the Wind Changed* (q.v., 1980) and *James* (1991). She wrote and illustrated *ABC of Monsters* (q.v., 1976) and *Old MacDonald had an Emu* (1986). The latter begins with the conventional animals, then introduces possums, kookaburras, wombats and other animals in whimsical situations.

Kilmeny has illustrated *The Haunted Castle* (1978) and *Old Witch Boneyleg* (1978) by Ruth Manning-Sanders, the latter a collection of fairy stories from around the world. *Fairy Tale Picture Dictionary* (1979) by Jane Wilton-Smith; *Pancakes and Painted Eggs: A Book for Easter and All the Days of the Year* (1981) by Jean Chapman; *Just Like That* (1986) by Mem Fox; *Fey Mouse* (1988) by Hazel Edwards; and *Grandad Barnett's Beard* (1988) and *My Brother John* (1990) by Kristine Church are all illustrated by Kilmeny. In *Matthew and the New Baby* (1986) by Peita Letchford, Matthew's dancing and singing amuse a baby. Her own texts include *A Bellbird in a Flame Tree* (1989), an Australian version of 'The twelve days of Christmas' with vibrant, festive illustrations; *Bright Eyes and Bushy Tails* (1984), with illustrations and descriptions of some of the world's unusual animals; *Feathers, Furs and Frills* (1980), with illustrations of Australian birds and animals; and *My World* (1981), a collection of short verses in which a nineteenth-century child describes 'My house', 'My father', 'My cat', and other familiar people and things.

Grandad Barnett's Beard (1988) by Kristine Church. Illustrator: Kilmeny Niland

Together they have illustrated *The Little Goat* (1971), *The Farm Alphabet* (1973), *What am I?* (1974) and *The Zoo Alphabet* (1980) by Elizabeth Fletcher; *Riverview Kids* (1971) by Elizabeth Wilton; *Mulga Bill's Bicycle* (1973) and *The Drover's Dream* (1973) by A. B. Paterson; *The Gigantic Balloon* (1975) and *Roger Bandy* (1977) by Ruth Park; and *Tell Me a Tale* (1974), *Tell Me Another Tale* (q.v., 1976) and *Tell Us Tales: Stories, Songs, Verses and Things to Do* (1978) by Jean Chapman. In *Birds on a Bough* (1975), which they both wrote and illustrated, ten silly birds crowd on a bough until it breaks. The Nilands' gawky animals and humans are clever burlesques.

NILSSON, ELEANOR (1939–), born Stirling, Scotland, teacher and academic, came to Australia in 1952. Her first book introduced a fascination with animals and birds which has continued throughout her writing. *Parrot Fashion* (1983), illustrated by Craig Smith, describes the wonderful diversity of Australian parrots when the parrots are housed together in a zoo. Pomily, in *Pomily's Wish* (1987), illustrated by Rae Dale, is a small mouse who is saved from death through her storytelling ability. *Heffalump?* and *Heffalump? and the Toy Hospital* (1989), both illustrated by Rae Dale, are adventures of a toy elephant. *Heffalump?* is teased for his odd appearance, is rescued by the Bengal Tiger, then himself rescues Bengal Tiger from Mr Rupert's toy hospital. In *The 89th Kitten* (1987), illustrated by Linda Arnold, the lonely Miss Berry opens her home to so many cats Sandy realises there will be complaints. With the help of her estranged father, she and Miss Berry advertise for good homes for them. In *Tatty* (1985), illustrated by Leanne Argent, the cat, Charlotte, finds that almost all the coats have gone when she goes to get her adult coat. *A Bush Birthday* (1985), illustrated by Kerry Argent, is a verse story about the native animals who are going to Koala's third birthday party. *Mystery Meals*

(1987), illustrated in soft pastels by Jane Disher, is a collection of short poems about animals. In *A Lamb Like Alice* (1990), illustrated by Carol McLean-Carr, the lamb is saved from the butcher by Sophie and Dan.

Nilsson has used animals to help children confront their difficulties. *There's a Crocodile There Now Too* (1987), illustrated by David Pearson, is about night terrors. Tim's feared tiger eventually saves him from a crocodile. *The Black Duck* (1990), illustrated by Rae Dale, is Tom's pet, and when his parents move from the farm, Squeak Toy is left behind. Tom runs away on his bike to find Squeak Toy. His parents realise that they misunderstood the strength of the bond between the boy and his pet, and Tom and Squeak Toy are reunited. *The Rainbow Stealer* (1984), powerfully illustrated by Leanne Argent, is a fairy-tale about a selfish princess. Ideas of emotional power and extrasensory perception are presented in *The House Guest* (q.v., 1991), her first novel for older readers.

NOEL, ENA (1916–) was the president of the Australian Section of IBBY from its inception to 1992. She has edited *Able to Enjoy: Books and the Young Disabled* (1981) and *Changing Faces: Story and Children in the Electronic Age* (1983), papers presented to Australian IBBY conferences.

NOONAN, MICHAEL JOHN (1921–), born Christchurch, NZ, came to Australia in 1940. He studied art in Melbourne and arts at Sydney University. In the 1950s and 1960s he wrote plays and serials for radio and scripts for films, including *Down in the Forest*, which won the Children's Section of the 1954 Venice Film Festival. *In the Land of the Talking Trees: a Fantasy* (1946), illustrated by D.H. Gilmore, is set in the rainforests, where a soldier wakes up among tiny people. *The Golden Forest, the Story of Oonah the Platypus* (1947), illustrated by Douglas

Albion, is an animal fantasy in which Oonah undergoes many trials before he is admitted into the Golden Forest. For his series about the Flying Doctor, which originated in his radio serials for the BBC, see **Royal Flying Doctor Service**. Noonan lived in England from 1959 to 1980, and wrote radio scripts and books about Australian life. *Air Taxi* (1967), illustrated by Barry Rowe, is a fictional adventure about a flight from Melbourne, in which techniques of flying are combined with an account of the Australian landscape.

His novel about the relationship between Hardy Jamieson and his beloved father, Barney, *The Patchwork Hero* (1958), illustrated by Paul Stanish, is an example of Noonan's ability to bring an era to life. It was not written for children, but Barney's adventurous life, full of exploits with eccentrics, women and booze is seen through Hardy's eyes, and is related to his schoolboy companions with embellishments. Hardy follows in his father's footsteps, but Barney's warm heart, courage, and spirited defence of the boy's misdemeanours make him a hero in his son's eyes. The novel draws the delights of a childhood in the 1930s. It was made into a television series by the ABC in 1981, and reissued by The University of Queensland Press in 1990. *The December Boys* (1963), which was also reissued in 1990, is the second in the 'Patchwork' trilogy. Five country boys from an orphanage spend a holiday by the sea in a boarding house at Captain's Folly. *The Pink Beach* (1969) completes the trilogy. Noonan also wrote *The Invincible Mr Az* (1978). *McKenzie's Boots* (1987) is a poignant story of a 15-year-old fighting an enemy he has grown to care about. See also **War**. Noonan has written a biography, *A Different Drummer: the Story of E.J. Banfield, the Beachcomber of Dunk Island* (1983) and other books for adults, including *Magwitch* (1982) about the Australian years of the character from Dickens's *Great Expectations*.

NOONUCCAL (NUNUKAL), **OOD-GEROO** (1920–), formerly known as KATH WALKER, born Stradbroke Island, Queensland, is a poet, committed to the struggle for equal rights for Aboriginal People, and for the conservation of the environment. *Stradbroke Dreamtime* (1972), illustrated by Dennis Schapel, is an autobiography and collection of stories for young people. Another edition was illustrated by Lorraine Hannay in 1982. *Father Sky and Mother Earth* (1981) and *Rainbow Serpent* (1988) with Kabul Noonuccal express her feeling for the narrative of her people. *Australian Legends of Our Land* (1990), with photographs by Reg Morrison, draws on Dreaming stories from Stradbroke Island, WA and Tasmania. See also **Aboriginal Dreaming Stories**.

NORMAN, LILITH (1927–), born Sydney, worked on the NSW *School Magazine* when Patricia Wrightson was editor, and was editor herself from 1976 to 1978. *Climb a Lonely Hill* (q.v., 1970) describes a family in crisis, and in *The Shape of Three* (1971) one of twins is sent home with the wrong parents, an error not discovered until the boys are much older. Each member of the Malory family loses a special talent in *The Flame Takers* (1973), stolen by a sinister force. For *A Dream of Seas* (1978) see **Death**. In *The Laurel and Hardy Kids* (1989) Emily Laurel is blackmailed by Peter Hardy when she almost drowns him. For younger readers Norman has written *Mocking-Bird Man* (1977), illustrated by Astra Lacis, in Hodder & Stoughton's 'Knight Riders' series. An evil figure, Weedah, from a Dreaming narrative, is defeated by Billy Mullian when it threatens to kill Mike. *My Simple Little Brother* (1979), illustrated by David Rae, contains stories which first appeared in the NSW *School Magazine*. Paddy relates how Fieldsy, aged 5, takes the adult world literally, and the humorous catastrophes which result. *The Paddock* (1992), illustrated by Robert Roennfeldt,

shows the passing of time over ages, as the paddock turns from primeval place to the site of a town, then back to its natural beginnings. *The Hex* (1989) in Methuen's 'Dimensions' series has excerpts from four novels and two stories from the NSW *School Magazine*, with biographical information. *The Brown and the Yellow: Sydney Girls' High 1883–1983* (1983) is a history of the school.

NORMAN, NANCY, see **CATO, NANCY**

NORRIS, EMILIA MARRYAT (1835–75) was the daughter of Captain Frederick Marryat, the British author of adventure stories. *The Early Start in Life* (1867), illustrated by J. Lawson, follows the fortunes of Alexander Stirling, who brings his brothers and sisters (and their servants) to NSW after his parents' death. The young people set about making a farm, and descriptions of the flora and fauna are interspersed with accounts of snakebite, stock theft and bushfires. A younger brother, Hugh, goes off to the Bendigo diggings, is attacked by bushrangers and falls in with bad company. The novel is a romanticised account of pioneering as it was effected by the wealthy. See also **Girls**; **Sydney**. *Jack Stanley: or, The Young Adventurers* (?1882) is set in NZ, although there is a description of an Australian kangaroo-hunt. *The Children's Picnic and what Came of It* (?1880), illustrated by her cousin Augusta Marryat, is a cautionary story of disobedient children, set in England.

NORTON, FRANK CHARLES (1916–83), born NZ, came to Australia in 1919. He was the director of the WA Art Gallery from 1958 to 1979. Norton was a marine painter, and wrote and illustrated *Australian and New Zealand Ships of Today* (q.v., 1958) and *Fighting Ships of Australia and New Zealand* (q.v., 1953). He also illustrated *Meet Simon Black* (1950) by Ivan Southall, *Penguin Road* (q.v., 1955) by Ken

Dalziel, and *Anzac Adventure: the Story of Gallipoli Told for Young Readers* (q.v., 1959) by Dale Collins. Norton was a lieutenant commander and official war artist during World War II and the Korean War, and his detailed pictures, usually black and white, capture the landscape with authenticity.

NOVAK, JIRI TIBOR (1947–), born Prague, Czechoslovakia, is a painter, sculptor, illustrator, book-designer and writer who came to Australia in 1970 and trained at Preston Institute of Technology. In *Fish and Bird* (1981) the fish and bird fall in love and create a flying fish. *One Big Yo to Go* (1980) by Valerie Osborn is a collection of quirky poems, and *The Bear with Bad Eyes* (1987) by Keith Smith is a story about a bear in trouble. For *Frightfully Fearful Tales* (1987) see **Collections**. Novak uses rich and subtle colours to present powerful images.

NTYRBA: Northern Territory Young Readers' Book Award, see **KROC**

NUNN, JUDY (1945–) is an actor and writer. *Eye in the Storm* (1988) and *Eye in the City* (1991) are suspense stories about Jeremy who is blind but is able to see when he becomes an astral traveller. With Patricia Bernard (q.v.) and Fiona Waite, Nunn has written *The Riddle of the Trumpalar* (1981) and *Challenge of the Trumpalar* (1986). Nunn's *Glitter Game* (1991) is an adult novel about the world of television.

Nursery Rhymes. Although their source is in the oral tradition, nursery rhymes have appeared in print since the seventeenth century, and during the eighteenth century there were many collections specifically written for children. Australian collections of nursery rhymes have consistently drawn on European sources, using them often as a vehicle for an artist, such as Barbara Macdonald's lovely portfolio of traditional rhymes, *A New Book of Old*

Rhymes (1920), and Percy Leason's illustrations to Lillian Pyke's *Cole's Happy Time Picture and Nursery Rhyme Book* (1925).

The familiarity of nursery rhymes has made them fair game for commerce. Early advertising material such as *Glaxo Nursery Rhymes* (1919) adapted Mother Goose rhymes to advertise a popular baby food. 'This little pig went to market/This little pig stayed at home/This little pig would have liked some Glaxo/But this little pig looked glum/For this little pig knew 'twas only for baby/So went grumbling all the way home.' Similarly, C.J. De Garis's *"Sun-Raysed" Children's Fairy Book* (1919) contained humorous parodies of nursery rhymes. 'Sing a song of sixpence,/Cost of living's high,/Four and twenty persons/Dined on one big pie;/Yet they rose up nourished/And walked out with a swing;/The pie was filled with Sun-Raysed,/Fit banquet for a king.' Providing music for the rhymes to be sung is equally traditional, and in Australia the music publisher Allans produced *Fifty Nursery Rhymes with Music* (1924) and *A Second Set of Forty Nursery Rhymes* (?1924) by Arthur Adams, containing well-known rhymes, each with a musical accompaniment. Another collection with music is Florence S. Anderson's *Dramatised Fairy Tales and Nursery Rhymes Set to Music* (1928). Anderson's melodies are simpler than Adams's, and there are instructions for making each rhyme into a simple play. Olga Ernst's *Songs from the Dandenongs* (1939) has music by Jean M. Fraser.

Nan Fullarton, Jean Elder, Peg Maltby, Connie Christie and Kay Druce published nursery rhyme collections in the 1940s, Maltby and Christie in the same year, 1945, and with the same title, *Nursery Rhymes*. *Mother Goose* (1946), edited by Ennis Honey, illustrated by Rufus Morris, includes well-known rhymes with sketches in black and white or lurid colour. *A Mother Goose Fantasy and Other Stories* (n.d.), *The Jolly Nursery Rhymes* (1949), *"Oups-a-Daisy" Nursery Rhymes* (1949) and *Twinkle-Twinkle Nursery Rhymes*

(?1940), all by William Henry Honey, were in the same format, all illustrated by Morris. Ida Rentoul Outhwaite's *Nursery Rhymes* (1948, 1984) is a more elegant interpretation of the rhymes. In an attempt to improve on the traditional, F. Oswald Barnett adds a verse to the rhymes (and destroys their dramatic impact) in *Happy Endings to Old Nursery Rhymes* (1945), illustrated by Dorothy Dibdin. '...Wee Willie Winkie runs home at last,/Supper is waiting with all he could ask,/There's plenty of butter, thin slices of bread,/A hot cup of cocoa, then straight off to bed.' Coralie Rees's *What Happened After?* (1972) builds on the stories of Old King Cole, the Queen of Hearts, Humpty Dumpty and others.

Nursery rhymes appeared in the 'Blue Wren' series (q.v. 1951), *Lavender's Blue and Two other Rhymes*, illustrated by Margaret Horder. *Time for a Rhyme* (1982), illustrated by Marjory Gardner, Heather Philpott and Jane Tanner, has each rhyme illustrated by a different artist. Rodney McRae's *Dame Dearlove's Ditties for the Nursery* (1989) is a selection from a nineteenth-century collection. *Ring O' Roses: Nursery Rhymes, Action Rhymes and Lullabies* (1990), compiled and illustrated by Priscilla Lamont, has rhymes enriched by warm, humorous illustrations, and includes music for the lullabies. In *Hickory Dickory Dock* (1991) Carol Jones uses traditional images with a 'peep-through' between picture and text.

Some collections modify traditional rhymes or create new ones with Australian content. Thomas Gunn's collections, written in aid of St George Soldier's Memorial Hospital, *Nursery Rhymes* (1917) and *Bush Nursery Rhymes* (1920), are presented in the style of nursery rhymes, with graphic farmyard verse for young children, such as 'The Crutching': 'The blow flies they sat on the woolly sheep back/And they blew, blew, blew/The wee little maggots found mutton good tack/And they grew, grew, grew.' *Australian Nursery Rimes* (1917), with a preface by Arthur H. Adams, was

compiled in aid of the Children's Hospital, Sydney, from over 1000 poems submitted to the *Bulletin*. Again, these are in the style of Mother Goose rhymes, but their content is local, in one case a reference to World War I: 'Sonny Boy, Sonny Boy, just me and you/Here's a little jacket, here's a little shoe/Daddy's gone to fight for him, far away in France/This year's petticoats, next year's pants.' The illustrations are by such notables as D.H. Souter, David Low, Norman Lindsay and Percy Leason. *Funny Farmyard: Nursery Rhymes and Painting Book* (1932), illustrated by Syd Miller, has large black-and-white illustrations for colouring in, but is distinguished with poetry by Kenneth Slessor. 'Hatty Hen/She's tired of men,/Tired of talking, tired of squawking,/Laying eggs till who knows when./Week by week/She supplies/Eggs of large and noble size.' *Australian Nursery Rhymes and the Playlet 'Friends of the Bush'* (1945), illustrated by Betty and Esther Paterson, and *New Nursery Rhymes* (1956), illustrated by Armstrong, has verse by 'Harold Charles': 'Teddy Koala, you cute little Bear,/So fluffy, so shy, and so easy to scare./You scamper right up to the tops of the trees/While Baby Bear clings to your back with its knees./Teddy Koala, you cute little Bear.' The injection of Australiana continues. *The Australian Nursery Rhyme Book* (1980), illustrated by Charlotte Thodey, contains traditional English rhymes, such as 'London Bridge' or 'Pussy Cat, Pussy Cat', but the illustrations are of Australian icons such as the Black Stump, Arnott's biscuits, Henry Lawson, Kiwi nugget and Ned Kelly in a colonial landscape.

Some writers have used nursery rhyme characters for their stories. In Zora Cross's *The City of Riddle-me-ree* (1918), Boy Blue refuses the Queen's offer of a kingdom, remaining faithful to Bo Peep. The Queen's knights are finally turned into children. *Stories told by 'Little Miss Kookaburra' of 3LO, Melbourne* (1925) were written by 'Idie' (Annie Frost) and illustrated by Guthrie Grant. Originally broadcast by Miss Hazel Maude, 'whose imitation of the kookaburra laugh is acknowledged to be remarkably faithful', they use characters such as the Beast from Beauty and the Beast. Two children are taken to the Moon, which is found to be populated with Mother Goose characters. Evelyn Bartlett wrote *Rosemary in Rhymeland* (1939), weaving Mother Goose characters such as the Three Little Kittens and Jack into the adventures of Rosemary, who has the mumps. Michael Dugan's *Don't Forget Granny* (1991) has a party attended by nursery rhyme characters.

Fractured Fairy Tales and Ruptured Rhymes (1990), compiled by Ann Weld and illustrated by Craig Smith, has parodies of common rhymes. 'Oranges and lemons/Say the bells of St Clements/But no one plays tunes/About prunes' and 'Jack be nimble, Jack be quick/Get the mop/The cat's been sick.' *In the Old Gum Tree* (1989), illustrated by Cathy Wilcox, brings old and new together in a collection of traditional rhymes, including local material, such as 'Kookaburra sits in the old gum tree' and 'Gurrwayi Gurrwayi the rain bird'. Anthropology, folklore, poetry or parody, the nursery rhyme remains a strong thread held by the child, and taken into adulthood to hand on to the next generation. Further reading: Holden, *Twinkle, Twinkle, Southern Cross*.

'Nutcote' was the waterfront house designed by B.J. Waterhouse for May Gibbs (q.v.), at 5 Wallaringa Avenue, Neutral Bay, Sydney. Gibbs lived there for forty-four years. A campaign to save 'Nutcote' from destruction resulted in it being bought by the North Sydney Council in 1990 who then leased it to the Nutcote Trust. The trust's aim is to establish a gallery and museum at 'Nutcote'.

O

OAKLEY, BARRY (1931–), born Melbourne, has been a teacher and lecturer. He has written novels, short stories and plays for adults and two children's books. *A Letter from Hospital* (1975), in the Pergamon 'Kidsbooks' series, is a letter from Warren, who has been burnt in a grass fire lit by his brother during a game. *How They Caught Kevin Farrelly* (1972) is a Cassell 'Patchwork Paperback', an early contribution to the acceptance of ethnic characters in children's books. When his father goes to the country to look for work, Kevin spends a week in hide-outs. His friends make sure that he is fed and warned of any danger, and when the search is on to find him, Kevin realises that his family care about him. Roberto is Kevin's best friend, and there is a glimpse of his Italian family, even a few words in Italian, in a picture of working-class children in a multi-ethnic inner Melbourne suburb.

Oath of Bad Brown Bill, The (1978), a tall tale written and illustrated by Stephen Axelsen, was Commended in the 1979 Picture Book of the Year Awards. Bad Brown Bill the bushranger is so boastful that his horse, Mudpie, challenges him to capture the dead. Bill swears an oath to rob the dead or eat his boots. He meets the dread Pale Jackeroo, robs him, is forced to the Jackeroo's lair, but eats his boots in terror. A chastened Bill sets up a reform school for bushrangers.

O'BRIEN, MAY (1933–) was a superintendent of Aboriginal education in WA. She has written *The Legend of the Seven Sisters* (1990) and *Wunambi the Water Snake* (1991), two picture-books which present Aboriginal Dreaming stories in a storytelling format. See also **Aboriginal Dreaming Stories**.

Obstreperous (1970) by Ted Greenwood was Commended in the 1970 Picture Book of the Year Awards. The Maker constructs a wonderful kite from household objects, but it will not fly. Mr Crinckle names it Obstreperous, and it is given a face to match. When the kite does fly, it has a mind of its own, bent on mischief, until it is set free by a passing parrot. In an imaginative design, illustrations travel across the pages, linking one with the next and capturing Obstreperous's free flight.

'O'CONNOR, ELIZABETH' (BARBARA MCNAMARA) (1913–), born Dunedoo, NSW, wrote *The Chinee Bird* (1966), illustrated by 'Astra' (Astra Lacis). Set on a remote outback station, 'Didgeree', it describes how a bird which Benny shoots down with his catapult changes the lives of the people who care for him. Emma and Sal nurse the bird back to health, Benny runs off with a gypsy circus, taking the bird with him, and Miss Knott, the governess, finds romance with the Flying Doctor who had set the bird's leg. O'Connor draws the world of an outback station realistically. She has also written books for adults, including her two autobiographies, *Steak for Breakfast* (1958) and *A Second Helping* (1969).

October Child, The (1976) by Eleanor Spence, illustrated by Malcolm Green, won the 1977 Book of the Year Awards. Douglas's brother Carl is autistic. His birth disrupts the family, who must leave their calm rural life to obtain help for him in busy Sydney. Spence examines how each member of the family copes with Carl, from Adrienne his sister, who ignores him, to Douglas, who, apart from his mother, shoulders the main burden for his care. Douglas's sense of responsibility is worked through until he is able to love Carl but pursue his own life in music.

O'DEA, MARJORIE COLLARD (1928–), poet and scientist, wrote *Six Days Between a Second* (q.v., 1969) and its sequel, *Of Jade and Amber Caves* (1974).

ODELL, CAROL (CAROL FOOTE) (1925–), born UK, came to Australia in 1956. She has written informational books, including *Fires and Firemen* (q.v., 1963), *A Day at the Zoo* (q.v., 1964), and biographies for children of historical figures, such as *Caroline Chisholm* (1983) and *Thomas Mitchell* (1984). *Let's Call Him Blinky Bill* (1970), based on Dorothy Wall's *Complete Adventures of Blinky Bill*, illustrated by Walter Cunningham, was adapted by Odell. *The Children's Book of Old-Fashioned Singing Games* (1983) is a collection of games which Odell discovered in an old trunk. Her mother, Dorothy Fuller, whose illustrations feature in the book, was a folk-singer early in the century, and the book has songs and instructions for actions to go with them. *The Magic of Verse* (1970), illustrated by Noela Young, was selected by Odell from Joyce Saxby's *Chosen for Children* (1967).

ODGERS, SALLY FARRELL (1957–), born Latrobe, Tasmania, is the sister of Anne Farrell. She began writing for the NSW *School Magazine* as Sally Farrell, and has later written as Sally Farrell Odgers or Sally Odgers. Her stories set in Tasmania, about dairy farming and family life, include *Her Kingdom for a Pony* (1977), illustrated by Noela Young, and *The Day the Cows Slept In* (1979). Rosina and her horse Star appear in *Rosina and her Calf* (1983), *Rosina and the Show* (1985) and

Rosina and Kate (1988), all illustrated by Walter Stackpool. *The Follow Dog* (1990), illustrated by Noela Young, is about the difficulties of a country dog in a city environment.

She has contributed to reading schemes. In *Show Us* (1987), illustrated by Diane Vanderee, in Macmillan's 'Southern Cross' series, Anna Louise's claim that she has a pig is disbelieved by her classmates until she shows them her antique money box. In the same series, Odgers has written short books for beginning readers, including *The Witch*, illustrated by Peter Solomon, *Outside*, illustrated by Shane McGowan, *Maria and the Pocket*, illustrated by Jane Tanner, and *Harry's Ears* and *Amy Claire and the Legs*, both illustrated by David Pearson (all 1987). Her picture-book texts include *Dreadful David* (1984), illustrated by Craig Smith, a verse story about the escapades of a naughty boy who puts the toilet roll in the toilet and jumps in the compost bin. *Emma Jane's Zoo* (1986), illustrated by Janet Ayliffe, using split pages, has a girl creating a zoo by capturing local pets and putting them in containers.

Odgers has introduced the supernatural in *The Ghost Collector* (1988), in which Melinda collects ghosts to haunt a new guest-house; *Ex-spelled* (1989), a series of letters, cuttings, and diary entries about a good witch, Rose, and her human friends Matthew and Stephen, over fifteen years; and *Welcome to the Weirdie Club* (1989) about a ghost and two girls. In the last novel, Julia and Alice learn from a little ghost that it is better to be yourself than try to be like someone else. In *The Magician's Box* (1991) Jessica's calf drinks from the bottle in the box, and shrinks.

Odgers has written family stories for younger children. In *Time Off* (1982) Rosemary learns to relate to her step-family, particularly her new sister Alison, and in *Five Easy Lessons* (1989) Mrs Archer and Justin try to understand the dynamics of family life. *Drummond: The Search for Sarah* (1990), illustrated by Carol

Jones, describes the search for his owner by an elegant and irascible Edwardian bear. When Nicholas, Sarah and Kate help him find the original Sarah, she is so old that she happily returns Drummond to the children. Odgers's informational books include *Tasmania: a Guide* (1989) and *Storytrack: a Practical Guide to Writing for Children in Australia and New Zealand* (1989).

O'FERRALL, ERNEST (1881–1925), born Melbourne, was a short story writer and poet who contributed to the *Lone Hand* and the *Bulletin*, often using the pseudonym 'Kodak'. He wrote *The Adventures of "Chunder Loo"* anonymously, as an advertisement for 'Cobra', *The* Boot Polish, for Blyth & Platt (Australia) Ltd, proprietors of a boot polish company. Advertisements appeared in the *Bulletin* from 1909, and the book was published in 1917. Full-page black-and-white illustrations by Lionel Lindsay, with some by his brother Norman, accompany verses which relate the voyage of Chunder Loo from Sydney to London and back, via the battlefields of World War I. Exploits include Chunder Loo arriving in Melbourne, Adelaide and Perth (or Westralia), bull-fighting in Spain, witnessing a portrait being slashed by a militant suffragette, and on active service. A typical example of the verse is 'At the War': 'Chunder Loo/of Akim Foo,/Drops bombs from/The silent blue./Straight to earth/They flash. "Look out!"/Soldiers raise/a warning shout./But each bomb/A welcome wins,/For they scatter/'Cobra' tins./War or wet/It bears the brunt,/'Cobra's' always/At the front.' O'Ferrall's satiric text and the Lindsays' illustrations combine in these rambunctious adventures of a turbaned Indian, koala and terrier dog.

Offset Printing Company published cheap paperbacks in the 1940s, including the 'Wattle Series', at a time when foreign imports were limited due to wartime restrictions. Titles include *Caught Red-Handed! and Other Stories for Boys*, *The Clever Fox*, *The Secret Tunnel* by Audrey Pederson and others, *Fun for Little Folk*, *ABC and Numbers*, *Adventure Tales for Boys* and *Children on the Farm*.

'O.F.T.', see **TIMINS, OCTAVIUS FREDERIC**

OGDEN, BETINA (1945–), born Adelaide, trained at Caulfield Technical School and RMIT. She has illustrated *When the King Rides By* (1986) by Margaret Mahy, *A Rabbit Named Harris* (1987) and *The Show* (1988) by Nan Hunt, and *Up the Haystack* (1987) by Sally Moss. *Mrs Marbles' Muffins* (1989) is about twins who overeat to the point where they need to be rescued by the fire brigade. *Can I Keep Him?* (1991) is a collection of stories and poems about pets from well-known writers, including Libby Hathorn, Colin Thiele, Kate Walker and Nan Hunt. Ogden designed the 'Domestic Pets' series of postage stamps for Australia Post.

'O'HARRIS, PIXIE' (**RHONA OLIVE HARRIS**, née PRATT) (1903–91), born Wales, settled in Australia at the age of 17, and continued her studies in art at the Julian Ashton School in Sydney. Her first illustrations, stylised black-and-white drawings, appeared in the fairy story *Cinderella's Party* (1923) by Maud Renner Liston. She wrote and illustrated more than forty books and painted many murals in succeeding years, until she was well into her eighties. Her fairy books include *The Pixie O'Harris Fairy Book* (1925), *The Fairy Who Wouldn't Fly* (1947) (retold by David Harris in 1976) and *The Giant's Eiderdown* (1978). Her early work, particularly her illustrations, established her popularity and appeal to children. Such books as *Pearl Pinkie and Sea Greenie, the Story of Two Little Rock Sprites* (1935), about Pearl Pinkie, who is beautiful but vain, and Sea Greenie, who is plain but humble, are lavishly illustrated in her characteristically romantic style.

O'Harris also wrote three novels for older readers about Poppy Treloar (q.v.). Other works include *Goolara* (1943), illustrated by Joyce Abbott, the story of an Aboriginal girl who runs away to avoid marriage to an 'ugly old witch-doctor'. Another story in the book, 'Daughter of the Billabong', is modelled on Andersen's 'The Wild Swans'. She created the possum Marmaduke in *Marmaduke the Possum* (1943), *Marmaduke and Margaret* (1953) and *Marmaduke the Possum in the Cave of the Gnomes* (1977). Marmaduke has magic powers at night, including being able to talk and to shrink Margaret so that she can join him in his bush adventures.

O'Harris has illustrated extensively for other writers, including Frank Dalby Davison's *Children of the Dark People* (q.v. 1936) and Lydia Pender's *Marbles in My Pocket* (1957). She illustrated Kenneth Grahame's *The Wind in the Willows* in 1983, and *The Pixie Alice: Alice's Adventures in Wonderland* (1990) was produced for the 125th Anniversary of the publication of Carroll's masterpiece. Over seventy years, O'Harris wrote and illustrated material which sold in hundreds of thousands of copies. She captured the last of the waning enthusiasm for fairies and wrote formula novels for adolescents just when Nan Chauncy was about to launch a new realism in children's books. *Was it Yesterday?* (1983) and *Our Small, Safe World* (1986) are her autobiographies.

OKTOBER, TRICIA is a surrealist painter. She has illustrated Libby Hathorn's *The Garden of the World* (1989) with elaborate and luxuriant pictures of gardens from England to Japan. In her own story *The Magic Ted and the Moonstones* (1988) Teddy, a toy koala, turns flowers into butterflies. The beautiful illustrations are of Australian wildflowers, such as the coral pea, the bottle-brush and the

flannel flower. *Bush Baby* (1988), illustrated with fine studies of animals, relates how Sugar the glider possum asks the other animals to find a name for her baby. *Bush Party* (1986) is Gecko's birthday party. Delicate Australian wildflowers decorate the pages in *Christmas Bears* (1990), as soft toys create a nativity play. *Bush Song* (1991) is another of her explorations of the natural world on the theme of conservation, as a seed grows into a haven for the creatures of the bush. The flora and fauna illustrated are identified in notes at the end of the book.

Older Kind of Magic, An (1972) by Patricia Wrightson, illustrated by Noela Young, was Highly Commended in the 1973 Book of the Year Awards. The magic is conjured up by the threat to a part of Sydney's Botanical Gardens by Sir Mortimer Wyvern, who wants to extend car parking facilities. Selina, Rupert and Benny, who live in the buildings around the Gardens, learn about the plan. The small spirits who live beneath the earth, the Pot-Koorok, the Nyols and the Net-Nets, have their own ways of thwarting Sir Mortimer, while the children and a modern magician, Ernest Hawke, an advertising man, summon up a protest. When a comet arrives in the sky, the battle for the Gardens is joined. Wrightson appends a call for the magic that has 'been shaped by the land itself' in this urban fantasy. See also **Sydney**.

OLDFIELD, AUDREY (1925–), born Mullumbimby, NSW, teacher and librarian, has written about Aboriginal children in *Daughter of Two Worlds* (1970), illustrated by Jean Elder. Melalla is educated at a mission school, then in Perth, and battles discrimination in an effort to find a place for herself in two societies. In *Baroola and Us* (1973), illustrated by Genevieve Melrose, Tobe McKillop describes the family's first year on a farm. Mr McKillop makes all the mistakes of the new chum, but through determination, organisational ability and the reluctant assistance of Tobe and his brother Ec, the McKillops carve out a living.

OLDMEADOW, COURTNEY (1917– 77) and **JOYCE** (1921–) were awarded the 1975 Eleanor Farjeon Award for service to children's literature. In 1960 they established Oldmeadows, a Melbourne bookshop specialising in children's books and school texts, and bought 'Dromkeen' Homestead (q.v.) in 1973.

OLIVER, TONY (1940–), born Bristol, UK, settled in Australia in 1965. His special interest is the accurate illustration of plant and wildlife. He illustrated Leslie Rees's *Gecko, the Lizard who Lost His Tail* (1970) and *Mokee the White Possum* (1973), *The Swiftlet Isles* (1977) by James Porter, *Budgerigar Blue* (1978) by Christobel Mattingley and *The Gould League Book of Australian Birds* (q.v., 1979) by Don Goodsir, for which he won the Whitley Award. He re-illustrated Lydia Pender's *Sharpur the Carpet Snake* (q.v., 1967) in 1982, and *Dan McDougall and the Bulldozer* (1963) in 1987. Two poetry books illustrated by Oliver are *The Tartan Kangaroo* (1988) by Tom Lewis, a ballad about a bagpipe-playing kangaroo who terrorises the locals, and *More Poems to Read by Young Australians* (1971), edited by Jennifer Rowe. His powerful illustrations to *The Turtle and the Island: Folk Tales from Papua New Guinea* (1978), collected by Donald S. Stokes and retold by Barbara Ker Wilson, reflect traditional art. In *Wunnamurra & Noorengong: How the Animals Came to Australia* (1978) by Peter Davison, he draws on Aboriginal motifs.

Ombley-Gombley, The (1969) by Peter Wesley-Smith, illustrated by David Fielding, was Commended in the 1970 Book of the Year Awards. It is a simple but striking collection of verse, full of witty lines. 'Arbuckle Jones,/When flustered,/Eats custard/With mustard./I'm disgustard.' 'Emily House/is an old, old house,/With cracks in her old, old bones;/And late at night/Her walls delight/In creaking grunts and groans.'

Omnibus Books is the Adelaide publishing house founded by Jane Covernton and Sue Williams (Sue Machin). Williams and Covernton had set up a packaging and freelance design company in 1981, but the company moved into publishing with *One Woolly Wombat* by Rod Trinca and Kerry Argent in 1982. Omnibus was responsible for discovering a number of talented authors and artists, including Mem Fox, Kerry Argent, Gillian Rubinstein and Jeanie Adams. Titles published by Omnibus include *Possum Magic* (q.v., 1983), *Space Demons* (q.v., 1986) and *Pigs and Honey* (q.v., 1989). In 1991 Omnibus was taken over by Ashton Scholastic.

Once There was a Swagman (1979) by Hesba Brinsmead, illustrated by Noela Young, was Commended in the 1980 Book of the Year Awards. When Mr Truelance must leave 'Longtime' during the 1930s Depression, Mungo Brodie, a swagman, helps out around the farm and saves Teddy when she falls into an underground river. Mrs Truelance and her daughters manage the farm with competence, against a background of rural poverty.

One Dragon's Dream (1979) by Peter Pavey won the 1980 Picture Book of the Year Awards. It is an elaborate counting book where the dragon is captured by the frogs and kangaroos, tried and sentenced by the storks, jailed by the seals, and rescued by the elephants, numbats and turtles. The illustrations are highly detailed and fantastic, suggesting strange experiences beyond the text and mirroring the unreality of dreams. See also **Counting Books.**

One Sunday Morning Early (1963) by Irene Gough, illustrated by Noela Young, was Commended in the 1964 Book of the Year Awards. This collection of fifty poems for young children explores the world of play, pets, bush animals, and people, sympathetically illustrated with line drawings.

O'NEILL, JUDITH (1930–), born Melbourne, lives in Edinburgh, Scotland. She wrote a history of convicts transported to Tasmania, *Transported to Van Diemen's Land* (1977). Her novels for children are historical. In *Stringybark Summer* (1985) the great forests are being logged, and the timber taken off by bullocks and horses. *Deepwater* (1988) documents the anti-German prejudice evoked by World War I. See **Germans**. *Jess and the River Kids* (1984), set during World War II, features a strong and independent girl supported by a united family, experiencing the freedom of a rural childhood. See also **Murray River**. *So Far from Skye* (1992) is the story of a group of Skye crofters who emigrate to Victoria in the 1850s. O'Neill's diverse subjects include prejudice, taken up in *Deepwater*, family and community relationships, considered in *Stringybark Summer*, and exclusive communities, in *The Message* (1989) (see **Religion)**. O'Neill avoids sentimentality and creates strong characters, and while her settings are identifiably Australian, specifically Victorian, her concerns are to depict active girls, the variety of family life, and the need for a supportive community.

O'NEILL, TERENCE (1940–) and **FRANCES** compiled *Australian Children's Books to 1980: a Select Bibliography of the Collection Held in the National Library of Australia* (1989), a bibliography of approximately 1000 titles, including many rare items and a large number of foreign language works. Frances is acknowledged as assisting Brenda Niall with her book, *Australia Through the Looking-Glass: Children's Fiction 1830–1980* (1984).

OODGEROO NOONUCCAL (NU-NUKAL), see **NOONUCCAL** (NU-NUKAL), **OODGEROO**

ORD, MARION, born Sydney, has written for radio and television. She wrote *Donovan and the Lost Birthday* (q.v., 1968), *Donovan Saves the Skates* (1970), illustrated by Penelope Janic, and *Ryder's Bend* (1976). In the last Alex and Matt unravel the story of Rose and her last night on the river, laying her ghost. Ord has also written a biography of the nineteenth-century natural science illustrators Harriet and Helena Scott, and selected and introduced books of their drawings from the collections at the Australian Museum, Sydney.

O'REILLY, BERNARD (1903–75), born Hartley, NSW, discovered the survivors of a Stinson aeroplane which had crashed on the Lamington Plateau, Queensland, near where O'Reilly lived, an account of which he gave in *Green Mountains* (1940). His only book for children, *Wild River* (q.v., 1949), is set in the same area.

ORMEROD, JAN (1946–), born Bunbury, WA, studied art and design at the WA Institute of Technology. Her books observe the world of babies and very small children. *Sunshine* (q.v., 1981) and *Moonlight* (1982) are wordless picture-books. Billy and his sister are often frightened in *Be Brave Billy* (1982), which reassures the reader that it is not always easy to be brave. *Rhymes Around the Day* (1983) and *101 Things to Do with a Baby* (1984) illustrate the routine of a busy day in the life of a young family. It has that number of outrageous suggestions for dealing with a baby, featuring Father and the older sister. Some of them are 'Head Banging', 'Letter Eating' 'Bathing' and 'Blowing on his Tummy'. *Just like Me, Silly Goose, Our Ollie* and *Young Joe* (all 1986) are a series, 'Little One'. The first three are comparisons between children, each other, and animals, and the last is a counting book.

The Story of Chicken Licken (1985) uses a clever technique of picturing the audience to a children's performance of the story as silhouettes, and during the final moments, a baby crawls on the stage. Ormerod lives in England, where she has illustrated *Eat up Gemma* (1988), and *Peter Pan* (1988) by J.M. Barrie.

ORR, WENDY (1953–), born Canada, has written *Amanda's Dinosaur* (1988), illustrated by Gillian Campbell. Amanda hatches out a dinosaur to frighten away foxes. In *Bad Martha* (1991) a terrible baby turns out to be a witch, aided and abetted by her grandmother, Matilda. In *The Tin Can Puppy* (1990), illustrated by Brian Kogler, Dylan shows how he is mature enough to own a puppy by rescuing a dog from the local rubbish tip.

OSBORN, ANNIE edited the children's page of the *Leader* newspaper, writing as 'Cinderella'. She wrote *The Willie Winkie Zoo Books* (q.v., 1918). *The Four Bears* (1923) and *Mollie at the Zoo* (?1920) were both issued as Cassells Commonwealth Story Readers. Osborn also wrote a political treatise, *Women and the State* (?1919), and *Almost Human: Reminiscences from the Melbourne Zoo* (1918).

OSWALD, DEBRA (1959–) is a scriptwriter for television, film, radio and theatre. Gina and her eccentric father feature in *Me and Barry Terrific* (1987) and *The Return of the Baked Bean* (1990), illustrated by Mathew Martin. *Dags: the Drama of Gillian's Pursuit of Romance and Happiness* is a play for young people produced in 1986, and Oswald was one of the writers of the 1985 television series 'Dancing Daze'.

OTTLEY, REGINALD (1909–85), born London, UK, came to Australia in 1924. For his trilogy set on an outback station in the 1930s, see *By the Sandhills*

of Yamboorah (1965). *Brumbie Dust: a Selection of Stories* (1969), illustrated by Douglas Phillips, and *A Word About Horses* (1973) are short story collections. *The Bates Family* (q.v., 1969) explores the tensions and dependencies inherent in family life. *Jim Grey of Moonbah* (1970) is set on the Snowy River. Jim leaves his family to work with itinerants, and finds his moral principles continually compromised. In the melancholy *No More Tomorrow* (1971) a swagman wanders through the outback recounting his life story to his beloved dog, Blue. Blue and the swagman are inseparable, even in death. In *Mum's Place* (1974) the orphaned Kim is adopted by Harry, and together they struggle to find enough money to buy a home. In *Black Sorrow* (1980), illustrated by John Van Loon, the disabled Jody rehabilitates a horse. See **Death**. Ottley has a fine command of the harsh and remote settings in which he places his resilient characters, often lonely rural workers. His only urban novel is *The War on William Street* (1971), about young adults and gang warfare in Sydney during the 1930s.

OUTHWAITE, IDA RENTOUL (née IDA SHERBOURNE RENTOUL) (1888–1960), born Melbourne, was the creator of delicate illustrations of fairies and fairyland, and the leading illustrator of the genre during the first part of the twentieth century. She had an international reputation and exhibited in Paris and London as well as in Australia. As Ida Sherbourne Rentoul, Outhwaite began her career with illustrations to a fairy story published in the *New Idea*. Her first books were *Mollie's Bunyip* (1904) by her sister, Annie R. Rentoul, and *Molly's Staircase* (1906) by her mother, Annie I. Rentoul. *Australian Songs for Young and Old* (1907) followed, written by her sister, with music by Georgette Peterson. In *The Lady of the Blue Beads* (1908), again by Annie R. Rentoul, Outhwaite's unique style became apparent, and her illustrations for Tarella Quin Daskein's *Gum Tree Brownie* *and Other Faerie Folk of the Never Never* (1907) confirmed her reputation. She illustrated Daskein's *Before the Lamps are Lit* (1911) and *The Other Side of Nowhere* (1934), and her illustrations of fairies and setting for Daskein's *Chimney Town* (1934) displayed her assured style.

Elves and Fairies (1916) and *The Little Green Road to Fairyland* (1922), with Annie R. Rentoul, and *Fairyland of Ida Rentoul Outhwaite* (1926), again with her sister and Grenbry Outhwaite (her husband), were the first Australian children's picture-books to be produced in high-quality colour printing. Ida also illustrated *The Enchanted Forest* (1921) and *The Little Fairy Sister*, both written by Grenbry Outhwaite (1923), and Madeline Collier's *The Lost Princess* (1937). Outhwaite herself wrote and illustrated *Blossom, a Fairy Story* (1928), *When Winter Comes* (?1920), written for an ice-skating rink in Melbourne, and *Bunny and Brownie, the Adventures of George and Wiggle* (1930). *A Bunch of Wild Flowers* (1933) has illustrations to her own verse: 'I am the fairies' dinner bell/Which summons all the elves/To bring along their mushroom stools/And quickly seat themselves' accompanies a lovely picture of a mauve flax lily. *Sixpence to Spend* (1935) is the story of a koala who wants to buy a present for his mother but cannot resist buying sweets for himself. It is light-hearted and humorous, without the didacticism of many of the other books Outhwaite illustrated. She had a regular comic-strip, 'Benjamin Bear', in the Melbourne *Weekly Times*, and also illustrated *Little Laddie and his Bushland Friends* (1948) by D. MacCormick, and her own *Nursery Rhymes* (1948). In 1984 *Nursery Rhymes* was republished with many colour plates and black-and-white drawings previously unpublished. Her last illustrations appear in Phyllis Power's *Legends of the Outback* (1958). She created stained-glass windows for St Mark's Church, Fitzroy, Melbourne.

Outhwaite's fairy books have continued to attract admiration because of her imaginative depiction of Fairyland. Gauzy-winged fairies in softly falling draperies, curly-haired children posed in water-lilies, butterfly-winged girls standing on blue-bells, or a lithe fairy riding on a bat's back — her realisation of an ethereal magical world remains the high point of fairy-story illustration in Australian children's books.

Over the Bridge (1969) by Deirdre Hill, illustrated by James Hunt, was Commended in the 1970 Book of the Year Awards. Bob Burrow is fascinated by the tram and the suspension bridge which connects the semi-rural suburb of Northbridge with Sydney. His favourite tram, 273, is to be sold for scrap and the route serviced by buses. Bob's resourceful attempts to save up enough money to buy the tram are interwoven with the fluctuating fortunes of his friends, both child and adult.

Oxford University Press established an office in Melbourne in 1908, under E.R. Bartholomew and his son, E.E. Bartholomew. Father and son managed the Australian branch for fifty-nine years. W.H. Wood was appointed as an educational representative, and their first Australian book, Adam Lindsay Gordon's poems, appeared in 1912. A succession of educational material and novels followed, such as Joseph Bowes's *The Young Anzacs* (1918), all published at the London office. From the early 1930s, OUP published educational material in Australia. During World War II when imports from Britain ceased, Oxford expanded its Australian publishing, including books for schools. In 1950 Frank Eyre (q.v.) became editorial manager of the Australian branch. He was succeeded in the children's department by Rosalind Price in 1979 and Rita Scharf in 1982. OUP has published such authors and illustrators as Hesba Brinsmead, Nan Chauncy, Eleanor Spence, Bill Scott, Terry Denton, Alison Lester, Max Dann, Ann James and Robin Klein.

P

Pacific Peoples (1957) by Lyndsay Gardiner, illustrated by Nancy Parker, was Highly Commended in the 1958 Book of the Year Awards. It is a history of the peopling and development of the islands of the Pacific, including Australia and NZ. Part I describes the earliest settlers; Part II deals with the coming of the Europeans, and how this has affected the Pacific. Gardiner's ideas reflect the values of the 1950s, such as her suggestions that whole villages should be moved to less populated islands, and that some islands should be used for nuclear testing. Gardiner casts the best possible light on the European impact on the Pacific, concluding that 'white men and islanders are living and working together, writing in their daily lives ... a new chapter in the story of Pacific Peoples'.

Paddock of Poems, A (1987) by Max Fatchen, illustrated by Kerry Argent, was an Honour Book in the 1988 Book of the Year Awards: Younger Readers. It is a collection of humorous verse on everyday subjects such as gate gossip, cats, the beach and bedtime. 'Here's Albert in his bathers,/There isn't any doubt,/While some of him is in them,/That most of him is out.'

PAGE, MICHAEL FITZGERALD (1922–), born UK, was the publishing manager of Rigby. His partnership with Robert Ingpen began with *The Runaway Punt* (1976). Mr Parrut runs a punt on the Murray River for fifty years until he is set free by the new bridge. See also **Murray River**. In *The Great Bullocky Race* (1984) the race is from Swan Hill, Victoria, to Robe, SA, through Ingpen's autumnal countryside. *Out of This World: a Complete*

Book of Fantasy (1986), also illustrated by Ingpen, is a reference book on fantasy characters, places and events. In *Mr Dohnt's Notice Garden* (1988), illustrated by Michael Atchison, Mr Dohnt puts notices up everywhere: no fishing, no weeds, no creepy-crawlies, no butterflies, but his garden ignores his notices. Mr Dohnt keeps on painting notices, including one on the final page which says, 'NO READING OF THIS BOOK'. Page has also written informational books about cricket, SA and the Murray River.

PAICE, MARGARET (MARGARET D. PAICE HARRISS) (1920–), born Brisbane, studied painting at the Royal Art Society. She has written a history of transport in Australia, *Wheels and Wings* (1979), and over twenty novels for young people. Her two books about Aboriginal children are *Mirram* (q.v., 1955), and *Namitja* (1956). Namitja's broken leg is set at the homestead, where he abandons his ambition to be a great hunter in favour of being a stockman. *Valley in the North* (1957) relates the domestic crises and natural disasters which occur in the Tasman family. For *Blue Ridge Summer* (1979), illustrated by Elizabeth Honey, see **Bushfire**.

The Lucky Fall (1958) introduced Kathy Brown, who lives in a tiny Queensland gold-prospecting settlement. When Kathy's fall leads to a gold rush the close-knit community is invaded, and Kathy is distressed to see the changes which result. Kathy goes to school in *The Secret of Greycliffs: a Sequel to The Lucky Fall* (1960). Paice has written a trilogy set during the 1930s Depression: *Colour in the Creek* (1976), *Shadow of Wings* (1978) and *Applewood* (1986). Alec Fletcher and his family travel through Queensland while his father looks for work. The Fletchers take up goldmining in Coorumbong Creek. Alec wants to fly aeroplanes, and can see some possibility of permanent work, but his father urges the family to move on, and in these early days of flying, with little or no money at his disposal, Alec's ambition is difficult to achieve. In *Applewood* Alec is 17, and the year is 1936. He goes to Applewood to find his sister defying the irascible Mr Fletcher, who is seriously ill. Alec puts his own ambitions aside to help his family but is released through tragedy. Paice has provided an authentic picture of the struggles of a family during hard times, and a likeable group of characters. The novels were made into a television series for the Channel Nine Network, with Judy Morris as Mum, Dennis Miller as Dad, and Ken Talbot as Alec. See also **Historical Novels**.

The relationships within families are also explored in *The Bensens* (1968). Opportunities for Bruce, Kylie and Timmie Bensen are enriched at 'Kyamore', a property in Queensland where their father finds work. *They Drowned a Valley* (1969) follows the fortunes of a group of children when a new dam forces rural families to leave Wambidgee Valley. The novel looks at how a development project alters the lives of those who stand in its way. *The Morning Glory* (1971) is the name of a summer fog which symbolises the cloud which hangs over Sherril Blake when she travels to the outback to re-establish herself with the father she has not seen for ten years. In *Dolan's Roost* (1974) English immigrant Trevor hates Australia and the fact that he is called names, like 'a bloomin' Pom'. Trevor, who is a bookish boy, does not fit in with the extroverted Ocker schoolboys, but ultimately proves himself a hero, establishes friendships and reconciles himself to his new life.

Paice has illustrated Ann Wells's collections of Aboriginal Dreaming stories *Tales from Arnhem Land* (1959), *Rain in Arnhem Land* (1961) and *Skies of Arnhem Land*

(1964), and Stella Sammon's *The Lucky Stone* (1969). Her novels are concerned with children and young people who are trying to realise themselves against a background of difficulty, but their sense of loyalty to family or community and their fundamental decency always see them through.

PALMER, HELEN GWYNNETH (1917–79), born Melbourne, was the daughter of Vance and Nettie Palmer. For *Beneath the Southern Cross: a Story of Eureka* (1954), illustrated by Evelyn Walters, see **Eureka Stockade**. Palmer collaborated with Jessie MacLeod on three history books for children, *The First Hundred Years* (q.v., 1954), *Makers of the First Hundred Years* (q.v., 1956) and *After the First Hundred Years: 1900–1950* (1961). Further reading: Bridges, *Helen Palmer's Outlook*.

Pals was a weekly boys' magazine published in Melbourne from 1920 to 1927 by the Herald and Weekly Times Group of newspapers, and edited by Charles Barrett (q.v.). It had contributions from Conrad Sayce, Vance Palmer, Roy Bridges, Jack McLaren, Bernard Cronin, E.J. Brady, Andrew Walpole and others, and the stories were generally set in the Pacific or Australia. It was lavishly illustrated by well-known artists such as Charles Nuttall, Edgar A. Holloway, Betty and Esther Paterson and Daryl Lindsay. As well as adventure stories and natural history, there were articles on hobbies, Scouting, keeping pets and other interests of young people. Each year the twelve issues were combined into *Pals Annual: for the Boys of Australasia*.

Papa and the Olden Days (1989) by Ian Edwards, illustrated by Rachel Tonkin, was an Honour Book in the 1990 Book of the Year Awards: Younger Readers. It is based on Rachel Tonkin's memories of her father's reminiscences. Papa tells his grandchildren about his childhood in a

Victorian country town where his parents owned a general store. The early twentieth century comes to life in the gentle text and detailed illustrations.

PARK, RUTH (1923–), born Auckland, NZ, began writing early in her life, and was a journalist in NZ before coming to Australia in 1942. In Sydney she married the writer D'Arcy Niland, settling on Norfolk Island some years after Niland's death. Park has the rare ability to write successfully for all age groups. After winning the *Sydney Morning Herald* Prize in 1947 for her first novel, *The Harp in the South* (1948), which was issued for younger readers as *The Puffin Harp in the South* (1988), she created 'The Wide-Awake Bunyip', which became the Muddle-headed Wombat (q.v.) for the ABC Children's Session. Her picturebooks *The Gigantic Balloon* (1975), *Roger Bandy* (1977), *When the Wind Changed* (q.v., 1980) and *James* (1991) reveal Park's humour and vitality, matched by the vigorous artistry of her twin daughters, Deborah and Kilmeny Niland. In *The Gigantic Balloon*, for instance, Messrs Aloysius Hoy and J.J. Jones are rival shopkeepers. In his thirst for publicity, Mr Jones employs a balloonist to advertise his shop, and when the balloonist fails to show up, his place is taken by Peter Thin, Jones's apprentice. Despite the efforts of Mr Hoy to undermine the flight, Peter, now Pierre Maigre, and his quickwitted dog, Belle, take to the skies. The story and pictures recall a Victorian melodrama with its larger-than-life characters and promise of adventure. *The Shaky Island* (1962), a picture-book illustrated by Iris Millington, uses a Polynesian tale of Bobalong, who travels under the island to ask the Giant Turtle to leave so that his home will be still and safe. The same sources have inspired *Nuki and the Sea Serpent: a Maori Story* (1969). Nuki is banished from the village until the Giant Sea Serpent shows the Chief Nuki's worth. *Ring for the Sorcerer* (1967), illustrated by William

Stobbs, is set in Rome, where Mark and Neila lose their cat. Their efforts to find her lead them on a tour which takes in the history, food, markets and culture of the city. In *The Runaway Bus* (1969), illustrated by Peter Tierney, the bus has magical adventures before it finds a new home. *The Big Brass Key* (1983), illustrated by Noela Young, is a time-slip fantasy. Eliza and Paulina discover a key which takes them back in time, causing difficulties when a dog from the past returns to the present with them.

Early works for older readers include books written for NZ schools in the 'Tales of the South' series: *The Ship's Cat* (1961), illustrated by Richard Kennedy, *Uncle Matt's Mountain* (1962), illustrated by Laurence Broderick, and *The Road to Christmas* (1962), illustrated by Noela Young. The first two are set in NZ, the third in Australia. *The Hole in the Hill* (q.v., 1961), set in NZ, is her first longer novel for children. *The Road Under the Sea* (1962), illustrated by Jennifer Murray, is an adventure involving an ancient underwater city off the Cook Islands. Another adventure story, *Airlift for Grandee* (1964), illustrated by Sheila Hawkins, is set on a remote sheep station in NSW. Through their search for Buff, a lost ram, Antonia and Reuben find that life is more exciting than they had previously thought. In *The Sixpenny Island* (1968), illustrated by David Cox, the Swift family members react differently to their upheaval from England and removal to Australia. Donald, for example, is very homesick and upset at having to change his plans for education. When the family wins John Drunkard Island, on the Great Barrier Reef in a lottery, there is even greater uncertainty and dissension. The island is not uninhabited, and they share it with a family of children struggling to survive in the absence of their sick mother. Park's concern for the environment and her understanding of family life can be identified in this early novel. She has gone on to examine the family with affection and humour. In

Callie's Castle (q.v., 1974), for instance, Callie's uneasy relationships in a blended family are resolved when Grandfather Cameron and her stepfather, Laurens, build her a room of her own. In its sequel, *Callie's Family* (1988), the maturing Callie is able to pass on the room to her younger brother, as she grows to understand her brothers and sister better.

Park's two historical novels, *Come Danger, Come Darkness* (q.v., 1978), set on Norfolk Island during its penal days, and *Playing Beatie Bow* (q.v., 1980), evoke a strong sense of place and demonstrate how she incorporates meticulous historical research without allowing the detail to intrude into the progress of her stories. A growing passion for environmental issues directed *My Sister Sif* (1986), about three sisters who are the children of a mermaid and a human. When the pollution of the ocean brings terrible danger to all sea creatures, painful choices must be made by two of the girls. Riko's sister is half sea-creature, and her death serves to emphasise the earth's fragility, and as an inspiration for those who protect it. *Things in Corners* (1989) has five stories with a touch of the supernatural, all revealing elements of family life. Park portrays the rich diversity of life where characters respond to crises with optimism and courage.

PARKER, K. LANGLOH (Mrs CATHERINE LANGLOH SOMER-VILLE STOW) (1856–1940), born Encounter Bay, SA, had been a companion of Aboriginal children as a child on the Darling River. Her two sisters were drowned there, and Catherine (Katie) was herself rescued from the same death. She married Langloh Parker, and lived on the Queensland border at 'Bangate' Station. *Australian Legendary Tales: Folklore of the Noongahburrahs as told to the Piccaninnies* (1896) was dedicated to 'Peter Hippi, King of the Noongahburrahs', with an introduction by Andrew Lang, and illustrated by an Aboriginal artist, Tommy Macrae. Parker spoke the language of the people she was recording and was ahead of her time in her respect for the traditions and culture of Aboriginal People. *More Australian Legendary Tales Collected from Various Tribes* (1898), *The Walkabouts of Wur-run-ah* (1918) and *Woggheeguy: Australian Aboriginal Legends* (1930), the last illustrated by Nora Heysen, followed. Parker says in the last book: 'I need hardly explain that I had no scientific education, nor preparation for research, beyond desultory reading about primitive peoples [*sic*] and an intense interest in the genesis of races and their original mentality. Full of that interest, I seized the time and opportunity of over twenty years' residence in juxtaposition to some of the finest aboriginal tribes [*sic*] in Australia to study them on the spot in an amateur way.' Stories of Dinewan the Emu, the Kamilaroi account of the origin of the Southern Cross, Wahn the crow wizard and many others first appeared in her collections. A selection from these books was made by Henrietta Drake-Brockman and illustrated by Elizabeth Durack, for *Australian Legendary Tales* (q.v., 1953).

PARKER, RICHARD (1915–), born Middlesex, UK, lived in Australia between 1959 and 1961, and drew on his experiences as an immigrant for his novels. In *New Home South* (1961), illustrated by Prudence Seward, Ray travels to Tasmania after his parents' death. The novel follows his journey aboard ship, and his inner journey to an acceptance of his future with his aunt. *The House That Guilda Drew* (1963), also illustrated by Seward, recounts the efforts of the Dutch Rankoops to secure a place in Australia, as Guilda and her parents lead an itinerant life following the fruit seasons from Shepparton to Mildura. The self-reliant Guilda is only able to draw the house she would like. Her experiences at school and adventures with her Aboriginal friend, Carline, are related with verve. *A Valley Full of Pipers* (1962), illustrated by Richard Kennedy, introduced the Pipers, descendants of Jem

Piper and his four sons, who have lived and fought each other in Piper's Creek for over a hundred years. The story is told by Tas, who also feuds with his brother Vince, just as his father feuds with his brother Ross. Feuds are forgotten when Tas and Vince save the valley from a terrible flood. In *Perversity of Pipers* (1964), also illustrated by Kennedy, Tas and Bulldog rescue Bulldog's father and grandfather after an accident in a mine. Parker's slapstick humour, command of the local idiom, and shrewd characterisations provide a down-to-earth picture of country life in a small community. Parker continued to write children's books without an Australian connection after his return to the UK.

'PARLEY, PETER' was the pseudonym of SAMUEL GRISWOLD GOODRICH (1793–1860), born Connecticut, USA. The first 'Peter Parley' book was published in 1827, and from 1828 to 1832 Goodrich wrote five or six books a year. F.J. Harvey Darton identifies six 'pseudo-Parleys' in England, and *Tales about the Sea, and the Islands in the Pacific Ocean* (1837) appears to be a book pirated from Goodrich by one of these, Thomas Tegg. *Tales about America and Australia* (?1840), also by 'Peter Parley' and edited by 'Rev. T. Wilson' (q.v.), was the work of Samuel Clark, who used Wilson as a pseudonym. Many of the 'Peter Parley' books, including the annuals, contained stories about and references to Australia.

PARR, LETITIA (1906–86), born Sydney, wrote stories and poetry for children. Her delight in nature was first expressed in *Green is for Growing* (1968), illustrated by John Watts, which conjures up the atmosphere of the park, and suggests imaginative games to play throughout the year. *Seagull* (1970), with photographs by Geoffrey Parr, and *When Sea and Sky are Blue* (1970), illustrated by John Watts, present a different landscape. In

Grandpa Pearson (1979), illustrated by Sandra Laroche, Grandpa takes his grandchildren Thomas and Lisa down the street on a treasure-hunt. *Getting Well in Hospital* (1976), illustrated by Nyorie Bunguy, is a collection of verses designed to reassure a child going to hospital. *Dolphins are Different* (1972), illustrated by Patricia Mullins, contrasts the world of humans with the environment of the dolphins and the stories which dolphins have inspired. Some of Parr's poetry is collected in *Birds Fly: Poems for the Very Young* (1986), published shortly before her death. One poem, *A Man and His Hat* (1989), was illustrated by Paul Terrett with clay models which were photographed by Bob Peters. *Flowers for Samantha* (1975), illustrated by Patricia Mullins, opens with the happiness which Mr Tidiwell Tompkins feels when he walks in the door of his house, and the sorrow that descends when he learns that the cat Samantha has been killed. The book deals with the grief which the family suffers and their need to support each other.

PARRY, ANNE SPENCER (1931–85) wrote a quartet of novels: *The Land Behind the World* (1976), *The Lost Souls of the Twilight* (1977), *The Crown of Darkness* (1979) and *The Crown of Light* (1980), all illustrated by Kim Gamble. They relate the adventures of Bara, Dov, Eris, Anita and Zaddik the Signbearer, who battle against the Flugs and unite the various peoples of Shemara. One of the most interesting characters in Parry's novels is Fool, a folksy Merlin, all-knowing but removed from action, who enables the others to see a problem in a new way. A further series about 'The Land behind the World' appears as *Zaddik and the Seafarers* (1983) and *Beyond the Outlandish Mountains* (1984). The stories document the boyhood of Zaddik, his life on the ships of Scyld, his admission to manhood in the Northern Mountains, and his betrothal to Ani. Parry contrasts art and materialism in an essentially hopeful outcome as the worlds are united and philistinism dispatched. She also wrote adult novels and informational books.

Pastures of the Blue Crane (1964) by H.F. Brinsmead, illustrated by Annette Macarthur-Onslow, won the 1965 Book of the Year Awards. Sixteen-year-old Ryl discovers that she has been left part of a property in northern NSW, an area atmospherically captured in the novel. When Ryl goes there with her grandfather, Dusty, she discovers her origins and finds her brother, Perry. Brinsmead contrasts two temperaments: Ryl is impulsive and adventurous: Dusty is tied to routine, but resourceful and wise. Ryl's emergence into a responsible young woman is the central theme, but the novel also touches on race relations. *Pastures of the Blue Crane* was made into a television serial in 1969, with Jeanie Drynan as Ryl. Its five thirty-minute episodes were directed by Tom Jeffrey, with a script adapted by Eleanor Witcombe. See also **Girls**; **Melbourne**.

PATCHETT, MARY ELWYN (1897–1989), born Sydney, lived in London from the late 1940s, although much of her childhood was spent on a cattle station, 'Gunyan', in northern NSW. She wrote over fifty novels, not all of them for children, and not all located in Australia. Her animal stories set overseas include *Roar of the Lion* (1973), illustrated by Douglas Phillips, about the friendship between the white African boy Cam Conway and a lioness, Taw, and *Hunting Cat* (1976), about an independent cat who travels from Trinidad to England. *The Lee Twins, Beauty Students* (1953) and *"Your Call, Miss Gaynor"* (1955), illustrated by Bill Martin, are career novels based on her experience as the proprietor of a beauty salon. *Undersea Treasure Hunters* (1955), illustrated by William Stobbs, *Caribbean Adventure* (1957), illustrated by Joan Kiddell-Monroe, and *The Quest of Ati Manu* (1960), illustrated by Stuart

Tresilian, is a trilogy about the Brevitt family whose adventures include diving on the Great Barrier Reef, Trinidad and north of Cooktown. *Summer on Wild Horse Island* (1965) and its sequel, *Summer on Boomerang Beach* (1967), both illustrated by Roger Payne, are also set on the Reef.

Most of her novels are adventure stories, often set locally, and often exploring the life of animals. *Ajax the Warrior* (1953), illustrated by Eric Tansley, was the first of these. Ajax is a huge dog, part dingo part kangaroo dog, who is found in a log after a flood. The girl who tells his story raises him to be the courageous and loyal dog Ajax becomes in maturity. In *Tam the Untamed* (1954), illustrated by Kiddell-Monroe, the proud silver horse becomes loyal only to Mary, who relates Tam's story. The novel includes Ajax as Tam's companion. The many animals which surround the young heroine join her on various adventures in *Treasure of the Reef: an Ajax Book* (1955), *Return to the Reef* (1956), *Outback Adventure* (1957), *The Call of the Bush* (1959), *The Golden Wolf* (1962), *Ajax and the Haunted Mountain* (1963) and *Ajax and the Drovers* (1964). In *The End of the Outlaws* (1961) Mary returns to her early childhood, acquires a large cat, Bundy Thomas, and foils an attempt by thieves to steal her father's brood-mares. Another animal book is *The Mysterious Pool* (1958), illustrated by Pat Marriot, and written for younger readers, about twins Anabel and John who find a seal in a pool. Patchett's interest in the animals of the bush runs away with her as she introduces koalas, emus, kangaroos, a plethora of birds and a seal in the one habitat. *Wild Brother* (q.v., 1954) is an accurate and sympathetic novel about dingoes.

The life on 'Gunyan' must have involved much contact with Aboriginal People, and Patchett has used many Aboriginal characters. The early books in the Ajax series display patronising attitudes to an Aboriginal girl, Mitta, and her family. In *Quarter Horse Boy* (1970), however,

Tod, an Aboriginal stable-hand, cares for the horses belonging to Nakimer, the owner of 'Booramby'. Nakimer is finally forced to acknowledge Tod's value by a niece, Perina, and to accept that Tod and he are related to each other. Patchett pursued her interest in Aboriginal People in such adult books as *The Last Warrior* (1965), illustrated by Maurice Wilson, about the education of Eechairri into white civilisation, *The Proud Eagles* (1960) and *In a Wilderness* (1962). See also **Aboriginal People in Children's Fiction**.

Another successful series began with *The Brumby* (1958), illustrated by Juliet McLeod, in which she introduced a bush boy, Joey Meehan, and his father Jim, who eke out a living at the foot of the Snowy Mountains. Joey's determination to have his own herd of silver horses is continued in *Come Home, Brumby* (1961), illustrated by Stuart Tresilian, *Circus Brumby* (1962), *Stranger in the Herd: a Brumby Book* (1964), *Brumby Foal* (1965), illustrated by Victor Ambrus, and *Rebel Brumby* (1972). In *The Long Ride* (1970), illustrated by Mike Charlton, Joey follows the trail of the explorer John McDouall Stuart to win the prize offered by a newspaper. *Warrimoo* (1961), *Dangerous Assignment* (1962), and *The Venus Project* (1963), all illustrated by Roger Payne, have Jeff James adventuring through the outback and South America. Warrimoo is the name the Aboriginal People give Jeff when he lives with them in Arnhem Land.

For her science fiction, *Kidnappers of Space, the Story of Two Boys in a Spaceship Abducted by the Golden Men of Mars* (1953), *Adam Troy, Astroman, the Exciting Story of How a Great Space-Pilot Saved the World from Radiation Beasts* (1954), *Lost on Venus, the Thrilling Story of Two Boys Who Land on the Planet and Explore a Fantastic World* (1954), *Send for Johnny Danger, the Amazing Adventures of the Ace Pilot, Captain Danger and his Crew on the Moon* (1956) and *Farm Beneath the Sea* (1969) see **Science Fiction**.

Patchett's work is at its best when she is writing about animals and describing the countryside where she spent her childhood.

Patchwork Grandmother (1975) by Nance Donkin, illustrated by Mary Dinsdale, was considered Worthy of Mention in the 1976 Book of the Year Awards. Joe's grandmother disappears on a trip to Melbourne from Sydney. When the family moves to Melbourne some years later Joe traces her through a patchwork toy, discovering that the old lady had fallen and lost her memory.

'Patchwork Paperbacks' were a series of simple language texts published by Cassell. They included *Bottle-O!* (1973) by Judah Waten, *Fight for Life* (1972) by Allan Marshall, *Gary* (1972) by David Martin, *The Greatest Juggler in the World* (1972) by Barry Carozzi, *How They Caught Kevin Farrelly* (1973) by Barry Oakley and *The Silver Fish* (1972) by Joan Wise.

PATERSON, A. B. (ANDREW BARTON), known as 'Banjo' Paterson, (1864–1941), born 'Narambla' Station, near Orange, NSW, was a poet and short story writer, the creator of such folk legends as the 'Man from Snowy River' and 'Clancy of the Overflow'. *The Animals Noah Forgot* (1933), illustrated by Norman Lindsay, is a collection of twenty-six poems, including 'Frogs', 'Weary Will', 'Old Man Platypus', 'Black Harry's Team' and other rollicking verse, such as 'No soft-skinned Durham steers are they,/No Devons plump and red,/But brindled, black, and iron-grey/That mark the mountain-bred;/For mountain-bred and mountain-broke,/With sullen eyes agleam,/No stranger's hand could put a yoke/On old Black Harry's team.' Paterson's poems have inspired Australian illustrators. Examples are Walter Stackpool's *Banjo's Bush Ballads: The Man From*

Mulga Bill's Bicycle by A.B. Paterson (1973 edition). Illustrator: Kilmeny and Deborah Niland

Snowy River, Father Riley's Horse, Story of Mongrel Grey (1980), first published as *Banjo Paterson's Horses* in 1970; Desmond Digby's *Waltzing Matilda* (q.v., 1970); Rich Richardson's *Benjamin Bandicoot* (1971) and *Weary Will the Wombat* (1971); Kilmeny and Deborah Niland's *Mulga Bill's Bicycle* (1973); Quentin Hole's *The Man from Ironbark* (1974) and *A Bush Christening* (1974); Annette Macarthur-Onslow's *The Man from Snowy River* (1977); Robert Ingpen's *Clancy of the Overflow* (1982); Ninon Phillips's *The Geebung Polo Club* (1984); and Dee Huxley's *Banjo Paterson, A Children's Treasury* (1984).

PATERSON, ESTHER (1892–1971) and **BETTY** (1895–1970) (Mrs K. NEWMAN), born Melbourne, were sisters who studied at the Gallery School under Bernard Hall and Frederick McCubbin. They contributed to the *Bulletin*, and individually and together illustrated many cartoons, comic-strips and children's books, such as Mary Grant Bruce's *The Cousin from Town* and *Rossiter's Farm* in the Whitcombe Story books, Leslie Deans's *The Imp and the Fairy* (1945) and Leila Pirani's *The Princess of the Water-lilies* (1946). Betty wrote a cartoon-strip

for the Melbourne *Argus* in 1933, 'The Softfurs'. Her be-ribboned and plump children, dressed as sophisticates, were used to make sardonic remarks in her *Bulletin* cartoons. Esther completed a series of portraits of Australian authors, including Mary Grant Bruce and Gertrude Hart, for the *Australasian* in 1939.

PAUSACKER, JENNY (1948–), born Adelaide, began writing for the Women's Movement Children's Literature Co-operative (q.v.). Her early books suggest to younger readers that they could accept their own feelings and appearance rather than stereotyped gender roles, issues considered in *The Three Dragons* (1975), *Marty Hollitt & the Amazing Game Machine* (1979) and *Fat & Skinny* (1981). Pausacker's involvement with youth in the western suburbs of Melbourne led her to edit *Friday Night and Other Stories from the West* (1983), with J. Elliot, a collection of stories by young people.

Her novels for adolescents explore sex, politics and responsibility. *What are Ya?* (1987) is a series of encounters between a group of high school students, in which they explore their sense of self and the restrictions and opportunities afforded to them. Pausacker pursues some unstereo-typed choices. See also **Sexuality**. *Can You Keep a Secret?* (1989) looks at the eviction battles in Richmond during the 1930s Depression and Graham's involvement in the secret League of National Security and the Unemployed Workers' Union. In *Fast Forward* (1989), illustrated by Donna Rawlins, Kieran tampers with time to avoid confrontation, with humorous outcomes. Pausacker wrote *Melissa* (1991) and *Rebecca* (1991) in the 'Hot Pursuit' romantic thrillers, as 'Jaye Francis', and *Love or Money* (1990) and *Nobody's Perfect* (1989) in 'Dolly' fiction.

PAVEY, PETER (1948–), born Melbourne, trained as a graphic designer at Swinburne Institute of Technology. His first illustrations were in black and white for Olaf Ruhen's *The Day of the Diprotodon* (1976). Since then he has written and illustrated his own material. *One Dragon's Dream* (q.v., 1979) is a counting book. In *I'm Taggarty Toad* (1980) a boastful toad adventures through jungle, magical forests, the seven seas and a night landscape until a tiger proves his nemesis. *Battles in the Bath* (1982) depicts a girl and the strange, dreamlike creatures who swamp her at bath-time. Her bath toys become a cat with a bird's body, a frog with a pig's head, and a bird with a dog's head, changing each page into even more bizarre combinations. *Is Anyone Hungry?* (1987) is set in a watery landscape, as Alfred searches for the twittering grimbix. From the understatement of *The Day of the Diprotodon* to the exuberant monsters in *Battles in the Bath* Pavey pursues his fantasies to 'encourage kids to use their imaginations to … invent and solve … problems that we haven't even faced'.

Paw Thing, The (1989) by Paul Jennings, illustrated by Keith McEwan, won YABBA for Younger Readers in 1990 and the WAYRBA Hoffman award in 1991. The cat, Singenpoo, earns her name by swallowing and defecating a transistor while the tune being played is 'Please release me, let me go'. Major Mac's fried chicken business is threatened by another take-away food shop, 'The Dead Rooster', and a plague of mice. Mac blames the cat for revealing his secret recipe to the opposition, but Singenpoo redeems herself in a surprise ending.

PAYNE, DONALD GORDON, see **MARSHALL, JAMES VANCE**

PEARCE, FRANCES, see **'FRANCES, HELEN'**

PEARCE, MARGARET LORRAINE (1940–), born Melbourne, has written science fiction, romance and books for young readers. *The Circus Runaways* (1978), illustrated by Lauren Murray, and *Wanted! A Horse* (1983) are stories about John Phillips's family and his animals, including John's adventures with a circus. *The Misfit* (1984), illustrated by Astra Lacis, is another family story. The exasperating 11-year-old Jennifer smashes her brother's bike, disobeys her mother, is involved in shoplifting and dyes her hair bright orange. *When Doggo Went Purple* (1989) describes the mayhem which results when the disreputable Morris family moves next door to the conventional Hildersens. In *The Secret in the Compost Bin* (1990), illustrated by Sharon Thompson, Jeremy hatches a turtle in the compost which must remain a secret because his parents have forbidden him a pet. *The Convertible Couch* (1991) explores Beebie's adjustment when his father leaves the family for a new relationship. Historical stories in Macmillan's 'Southern Cross' series for young readers are *One Day in the Life of a Maidservant* (1987), illustrated by Kay Stewart, about a currency lass; *The Castle Hill Uprising* (1987), also illustrated by Stewart, about the Irish revolt of 1804; and *The Weekend of Herman John* (1987). *Altar of Shulaani* (1981) is a science fiction story. Mike and his father travel to an ancient civilisation where

Mike can communicate telepathically with Alinea, who returns with them. *Three's a Crowd* (1991) is one of Bantam's 'Wildfire' series.

As 'Jacquelyn Webb' Pearce has written *The Look of Love* (1988), *Lonely Heart* (1990), and *Roses are for Romance* (1991) in the 'Dolly' fiction series. *Bobby and Frank* (1989) is from the television series 'Home and Away'.

PEARSON, DAVID (1949–), born UK, has illustrated *Festivals* (1984) by Dorothy Rickards; *Ernest Pickle's Remarkable Robot* (1984) and *One Night at Lottie's House* (1985) by Max Dann; *There's a Crocodile There Now Too* (1987) by Eleanor Nilsson; *Amy Claire and the Legs* (1987) by Sally Farrell Odgers; *The Archer and Her Enemy: a Korean Folk Tale* (1989) by David Lander; *Laurence's Water Wings* (1990) by Leone Peguero; and books in Macmillan's 'Southern Cross' series, including *The Umbrella* (1987).

PECK, JEFF (1946–) wrote the screenplay and the novel *Bushfire Moon* (1989). In the year of 1891 Ned O'Day mistakes a swagman for Father Christmas. The film was directed by George Miller and starred Dee Wallace Stone as Elizabeth O'Dea and John Waters as Patrick O'Dea, with Charles Tingwell as Max Bell. Peck collaborated with Paul Cox on the screenplay for *The Gift*, which also appeared as a novel by Roger Dunn in 1988. *The Secret Life of Trees* (1987), illustrated by Jenny Rendall, is based on Paul Cox's screenplay for the 'Kaboodle' series, and *The Wizards of Solmar and other Stories* (1988) is based on a screenplay by Gary Davis. Peck has also written critical material on film and theatre.

PEDLEY, ETHEL (?1860–98), born London, UK, came to Australia with her parents. Pedley was a violinist and music-teacher and conducted the first all-female orchestra in Sydney in 1888. She wrote the libretto of a cantata 'The Captive

Soul', in 1895, and the novel, *Dot and the Kangaroo* (q.v., 1899), which was published posthumously.

Ethel Pedley

Pegmen were characters made from wooden clothes pegs created by Ella May McFadyen.

PEGUERO, LEONE born Grafton, NSW, has written the picture-book *The Rainbow Umbrella* (1987), illustrated by Jan Neil and Gerard Peguero. When Numbat cannot buy an umbrella as beautiful as Honey-Possum's, the two agree to share it. *Mervyn's Revenge* (q.v., 1990) is about a jealous cat. In *Laurence's Water Wings* (1991), illustrated by David Pearson, Laurence wears his water wings wherever he goes. They prove their usefulness when Laurence is first in the new swimming pool. Peguero has written language texts for secondary schools, a book of names for pets, a book on road sense and a poetry anthology, *Poetry Speaks* (1982).

PENDER, LYDIA (1907–), born London, UK, came to Australia in 1920. In 1943 she began writing for the NSW *School Magazine. Marbles in My Pocket*

Big Book of Pegmen Tales (1959) by Ella McFadyen. Illustrator: Edwina Bell

(1957), illustrated by Pixie O'Harris, was her first book of verse, and she collaborated with Mary Gilmore on *Poems to Read to Young Australians* (1968), illustrated by June Gulloch. Her two books about Barnaby are *Barnaby and the Horses* (1961), illustrated by Alie Evers, and *Barnaby and the Rocket* (q.v., 1972). In an innovative style, Pender uses prose interspersed with verse and repeated phrases. *Sharpur the Carpet Snake* (q.v., 1967) is equally successful. In *Dan McDougall and the Bulldozer* (1963), first illustrated by Gerald Rose, and then by Tony Oliver in 1987, Dan drives his bulldozer to Sydney, where it creates havoc in the city streets. *The Useless Donkeys* (q.v., 1979) is about loveable but very silly donkeys. *Morning Magpie: Favourite Verse* (1984), illustrated by Noela Young, contains new poems and poems previously published in *Marbles in My Pocket* (1957), *Brown Paper Leaves* (1971) and the NSW *School Magazine*. *The Land and the Spirit: an Australian Alphabet* (1991), illustrated by Kilmeny Niland, celebrates Australian animals.

Penguin Books was established by Allen Lane in 1935, and the first four Puffins appeared in 1940. The company commenced in Melbourne in 1946 under the direction of Brian Stonier, Max Harris and Geoffrey Dutton. The first Australian Puffins appeared in 1963, and included Rosemary Wighton's *Kangaroo Tales*. Penguin Australia has become the largest single publisher of Australian titles. The Australian Puffin Club was formed in 1977, generating the magazine *Puffinalia*. Penguin has produced guides to reading for children, such as *Puffins for Parents* and *Good Book Guide to Children's Books*, both edited by Moira Robinson.

Penguin Road (1955) by Ken Dalziel, illustrated by Frank Norton, was Highly Commended in the 1956 Book of the Year Awards. Using the letters he had written to his children while on an expedition to Antarctica, in a simple and conversational style Dalziel captures the thrill of seeing an iceberg for the first time, the magnificence of the Aurora Australis, being caught in a blizzard, and sliding down a mountain for 1000 feet. The book has fascinating information on Antarctic life — the huskies, penguins, elephant seals, the natural beauty of the glaciers, the important explorers, all interwoven with anecdotes of the author's own experiences. It includes photographs supplied by the Antarctic Division.

Penny Pollard's Diary (1983) by Robin Klein, illustrated by Ann James, was Highly Commended in the 1984 Book of the Year Awards. Penny's individualism and spontaneity lead her into various difficulties, but her strong sense of justice and her imagination see her through. Despite her reservations, Penny befriends the elderly Mrs Bettany, a kindred spirit. The novel was adapted for television as part of the 'Kaboodle' series. In *Penny Pollard's Letters* (1984) Penny conducts a correspondence when her mother is in hospital and learns to stop hating babies and boys. The reluctant Penny is forced to be a flower-girl at a wedding in *Penny Pollard in Print* (1986), but later wins a prize for a story about the experience. *Penny Pollard's Passport* (1988) contains her diary and her letters back to Mrs Bethany when Penny and her friend Alistair travel to London. In *Penny Pollard's Guide to Modern Manners* (1989), Penny's project is on manners, and despite sabotage by Jason Taylor, her work is completed successfully. Ann James's original use of photographs, drawings and collages in an exercise-book format, convey Penny's character, with all its humour and eccentricity. See also **Girls**.

People Might Hear You (1983) by Robin Klein won the COOL Awards for 1991. Frances's timid aunt and guardian, Loris, marries Finley Tyrell, who is a member of a repressive Christian sect. Frances is a prisoner in a joyless household, with Helen, Claire and Rosgrana Tyrell. In a struggle to maintain her identity, she finds that her confidence is gradually being eroded, and the zeal, hellfire and damnation of the members of the temple is closing in on her. The climax comes when Claire is taken ill and Frances tries to escape, taking with her the one person who has registered any doubts about the strange lifestyle. This is a frightening account of religious fanaticism and the courage of a girl determined to survive. See also **Religion**.

Peppino appears in David Martin's *Peppino Says Goodbye* (1980), *Peppino Turns His Luck* (1982), *Peppino in the Tobacco War* (1983), collected in *Peppino* (1983), illustrated by Guy Mirabella. These books for younger readers describe the homesickness and disorientation experienced by a boy from Italy as he leaves his home and adjusts to a new country. Peppino does not allow setbacks to defeat him, and his opinions are held with such conviction that in *Peppino and the Tobacco War*, for instance, he questions the morality of his father's livelihood. Martin's understanding of the emotions of the outsider enrich his narrative.

PERSHALL, MARY (1951–), born USA, came to Australia in 1974 as a teacher, an experience recalled in an adult novel, *A Long Way Home* (1992). She has edited *Pursuit* for the Victorian Ministry of Education. She wrote *The Shopkeeper* (1980) for the Women's Movement Children's Literature Co-operative's 'Sugar and Snails Work' series, and a book on music for Macmillan's 'Southern Cross' reading series, *Oz Rock* (1987). She has contributed short stories to collections. Pershall has treated grief and loss with sensitivity from two viewpoints. In *You Take the High Road* (1988) the tragic death of a beloved baby brother devastates Sam. See also **Death**. *Hello, Barney!* (1988), illustrated by Mark Wilson, is a picture-book about a sulphur-crested cockatoo, William Jackson's lifelong pet. When William is about to die he lets Barney go.

Perth, on the Swan River, is the capital city of WA. In Roger Burns's *Two Boys in Australia* (1936) Pat and Sandy see Perth as 'roomy and well planned, with plenty of open spaces'. They admire 'St George's Terrace, where the government and Parliament buildings are'. The same street appears in *The Cattle Duffers: Adventures in the Kimberleys* (1948) by Stanley Brogden, when its hero John Hamilton and friend walk 'in the broiling sun along St George's Terrace ... '. In Allan Aldous's *The New Australians* (1956) the Gail family on arrival 'saw glorious, wide, silvery beaches; the Swan River ... sparkling blue and spattered with yachts ... the great University of creamy sandstone — "the only free university in the world"'. Carolyn Bear's *Under Different Stars* (1988) is set in Perth. Julia leaves the university and wanders towards the city along the Swan River. Her romance with Zig is explored in the zoo and through the suburbs of Floreat Park and its surrounds. There is no novel which depicts the zest and beauty of Perth or its unique character.

Peter (1991) by Kate Walker was an Honour Book in the 1992 Book of the Year Awards: Older Readers. Peter finds that he is attracted to his brother's gay friend, David. David tells him that he is too young at 15 to make a definite sexual commitment. Despite the sneers of his father, his school friends and his trail-bike companions, Peter will not deny his feelings. Walker presents no easy solution to Peter's search for identity, and treats a sensitive subject with honesty.

Peters, Shelley appears in Ellen Bosworth's *Shelley and the Pony of the Year* (1972), *Shelley and the Bushfire Mystery* (1972) and *Shelley and the Problem Pony* (1974). Shelley, aged 14, and her sister Anne solve unlikely coincidences and mysteries, with Shelley always ready to display her superb horsewomanship. Shelley comes recommended by the more famous 'Trixie Belden', an invention of the American Western Publishing Company and Golden Press, Australia and NZ. See also **Gordon, Julie**.

PETERS, SHIRLEY (1953–), born Sydney, has worked in advertising and as production manager for Hodder & Stoughton. She is president of the Society of Book Illustrators (NSW). Peters has illustrated *The Moon is Shining* (1988) by Edwin A. Schurmann; Mary White's *Martha Thompson, Wondercook!* (1988); *The Diary of Megan Moon (Soon to be Rich and Famous)* (1988) by Margaret Wild; *The Rainy Day Fun Book* (1988) by Anne Ingram and Peggy O'Donnell; *The Christmas Fun Book* (1988) and *Mostly Me* (1990) by Jean Chapman; *Mervyn's Revenge* (q.v., 1990) by Leone Peguero; *The Horribubble* (1990) by Alicia Braithwaite; and *Amy's Bath* (1991) by Susan King.

PHIPSON, JOAN (1912–), born Sydney, spent part of her childhood in England and India. Her early works were straightforward rural adventures, such as *Christmas in the Sun* (1951), which was rewritten as *It Happened One Summer* (q.v., 1957), *Good Luck to the Rider* (q.v., 1953), *Six and Silver* (1954), *The Boundary Riders* (1962), *The Family Conspiracy* (q.v., 1962) and its sequel *Threat to the Barkers* (q.v., 1963), all illustrated by Margaret Horder. These early books presented small adventures against a strongly realised landscape. The experiences of Jack and Pat Steadman and Tess Moorland are set at the beach and in the bush in *Six and Silver*. Tess's swimming skills save the Steadmans from danger in the water, and when she visits the Steadman property they teach her to ride. In *The Boundary Riders*, three children become lost in the bush when they search for a waterfall glimpsed from afar. As the incident becomes more and more life-threatening, the reader observes the increasing assurance of Bobby, the taciturn younger boy, the hesitations which emerge in his confident older cousin Vincent, and the growing resolve of Bobby's sister, Jane. Phipson has created many sensitive male characters, such as Tony in *Birkin* (1965), also illustrated by Horder, about a calf, named after the explorers Burke and Wills, who is cared for by Frances, Tony and Angus. His various adventures include precipitating a car accident, being washed away in a flooded river, and assisting in the rescue of a pilot. Again, Phipson's capacity to create character can be identified in her pictures of Frances under duress, and Tony, who is irascible to outsiders, but his family's stalwart. A book for younger readers followed, *A Lamb in the Family* (1966), illustrated by Lynette Hemmant. For his eighth birthday, Charlie is given a pet lamb which proves to have a heroic nature. *Helping Horse* (1974) is a domestic story of children overcoming minor obstacles. See also **Germans**.

Phipson then pursued an interest in the psychology of fear. In *Hide Till Daytime* (1977), illustrated by Mary Dinsdale, two children are locked overnight in a large department store. *Mr Pringle and the Prince* (1979), illustrated by Michael Charlton, describes the hijacking of a school bus with a Malaysian prince on board. The girl in *Polly's Tiger* (1973), illustrated by Gavin Rowe, has to overcome her fears before she can do away with an imaginary protector. In *The Haunted Night* (1970) Patricia and her three teenage friends spend the night alone in a supposedly haunted house. The night is described from hour to hour until daylight. Shut doors open by themselves, lights go on and off without warning, strange noises are heard, and eventually voices. The ingredients of the classic primitive thriller make a suspenseful story, combined with an examination of the reactions of the girls to each other and their fears. In *The Bird Smugglers* (1977), for younger readers, Margaret disturbs a group of bird-smugglers when she is admiring a flight of beautiful parrots, and later, on a plane to

England, recognises an elderly couple as their agents. The graphic description of the cruelty used to smuggle the parrots, Margaret's desperate struggle to be taken seriously, and the confined space of an aircraft create a high level of tension. *The Cats* (q.v., 1976) is the most compelling of these suspense novels. *Keep Calm* (1978) is a survival story in which Sydney is paralysed. In *Hit and Run* (1986) a boy faces the consequences of running away from an accident, and *Bianca* (1988) is about the trauma of a girl who believes she has been rejected by her mother.

The relationship between humanity and the environment inspired *The Way Home* (1973), about a mystical journey in which the children explore the need to recognise the spirituality of nature. After a road accident, a group of children wander through time and space until they are brought back from a vast dreamlike world to contemporary reality by 'the Protector'. Phipson returned to the theme in *The Watcher in the Garden* (1982), where Catherine and Terry's affinity with the garden converts them from anger into a new peace. *Bass & Billy Martin* (1972), illustrated by Ron Brooks, recounts the explorations of Bass and Flinders in the *Tom Thumb* through the eyes of Bass's servant boy, and the effect of white settlement on the natural world. Phipson's environmental awareness has also led to *No Escape* (1979), another novel concerned with the protection of rare Australian birds. See also **Conservation**. *Peter and Butch* (1969) confronts notions of manliness. Sixteen years later, *The Grannie Season* (1985), illustrated by Sally Holmes, takes up the same issue, but here Phipson challenges stereotyping more openly. Grannie is tall and thin, and at first disappoints her grandson because she is not pink, plump and fluttery. But when he discovers that she has played cricket for Australia and is prepared to save his team from defeat, his discomfort turns to admiration. See also **Sport**. In *The Crew of the Merlin* (1966), illustrated by Janet Duchesne, *A Tide*

Flowing (1981) and *Dinko* (1985) (see **Science Fiction**) Phipson examines family and identity. In *The Crew of the Merlin* Charlie is inadvertently left aboard the *Merlin*, and when his older cousin, Jim, has a falling-out with his parents, and takes the *Merlin* north, the two boys must rub along together. The outcome strengthens both and ensures a lifelong friendship. See also **Sydney**. In *A Tide Flowing* Phipson examines Mark's grief at his mother's sudden death, and offers some consolation through a friendship with Connie. See also **Death**.

Beryl the Rainmaker (1984), illustrated by Laszlo Acs, for younger children, shows the dilemma of a small girl who finds a stone which is able to bring rain. Beryl uses the stone to help the local farmers, but when her anger intervenes, the stone's power causes a near tragedy. *The Shadow* (1989), illustrated by Stephen Campbell, is in Methuen's 'Dimensions' series, containing two short stories and excerpts from her suspense novels, with biographical material.

Phipson's simple adventure stories of the 1950s and 1960s are a far cry from the intricate explorations of character, motivation, and relationships which typify her later work. These are marked by the creation of tension, empathy for the natural world, and a recognition of the complexities of adolescent experience. She was awarded the Dromkeen Medal in 1987.

Piccaninny Walkabout: a Story of Two Aboriginal Children (1957), written and photographed by Axel Poignant, won the 1958 Picture Book of the Year Awards. It was redesigned and retitled *Bush Walkabout* in 1972. After staying for some months at Milingimbi, on the Arnhem Land coast, Poignant developed a story about the adventures of two children on the mainland. He acknowledged the influence of Raiwalla, his interpreter, who altered the story for the present version. Nullagundi and Rikili hunt for fish and lizards, become lost, are found by their parents

and celebrate their return with a corroboree. The story is a vehicle for Poignant's fine black-and-white photographs.

Picture Book of the Year Awards, see **Book of the Year Awards**

Picture-Books. The origins of the contemporary Australian picture-book can be found in the work of illustrators such as Dorothy Wall and May Gibbs. The refinements in offset lithography, involving colour separation, overprinting and other advances, and a greater recognition of the significance of visual images to the child saw the emergence of a book which was shaped as a whole, where picture and text worked together to tell the story. During the late 1960s and early 1970s, books such as *Uhu* (q.v., 1969), illustrated and written by Annette Macarthur-Onslow, integrated text and picture in the design of the page. Desmond Digby's sweeping scenes, Ted Greenwood's architectural structures, Noela Young's spontaneity, Dick Roughsey's Aboriginal landscapes, Ron Brooks's dark symbolism, and the exuberant Niland sisters, the energetic Armitages and the gentler McLeans have produced individual and stylish picture-books.

Peter Pavey's surrealist detail, first identified in *One Dragon's Dream* (q.v., 1979), has undertones of the earlier illustrator Harold Gaze, but in Pavey's work the illustrations need to be read as closely as the text. Pamela Allen's witty books deal with simple and universal ideas pared down to a minimum in both text and picture, but suggest character and incident in a non-verbal way through a curving line or raised eyebrow, exemplified in *Who Sank the Boat?* (q.v., 1982). Since the 1970s the Australian picture-book has established an international reputation, moving beyond local images, in the works of such author-illustrators as Jeannie Baker, Graeme Base, Terry Denton, Bob Graham, Ann James, Alison Lester, Rodney McRae, and Junko Morimoto.

These artists use varied techniques, such as collage, detailed and precise paintings, casual cartoon-like images, abstraction and realism to create mood, emotion and reaction.

Outstanding partnerships between author and artist are also evident, such as Jenny Wagner and Ron Brooks in *John Brown, Rose and the Midnight Cat* (q.v., 1977), Margaret Wild and Julie Vivas in *The Very Best of Friends* (q.v., 1989), Mem Fox and Vivas in *Possum Magic* (q.v., 1983), and Allan Baillie and Jane Tanner in *Drac and the Gremlin* (q.v., 1988). Jane Tanner's work, for example, uses patterns of light and shade, and a symbolic subtext. Like her contemporaries, Tanner takes a text beyond the words, offering the reader another level of story. In *The Wolf* (1991) by Margaret Barbalet, the leaves on the page which indicate changing seasons and emotional climate, the barely comforting caress of the mother, and a photograph turned down on the table, suggest overtones to the reader without imposing an interpretation.

The sophistication in presentation and ideas represented in modern picture-books reveal a range from the domestic delight of Bob Graham's happy families to the survival of the human spirit under extreme adversity, in Wild and Vivas's *Let the Celebrations Begin!* (1991). See also **Illustration**.

Picture History of Australia, A (1962) by R.M. Crawford, illustrated by Clarke Hutton, was Commended in the 1963 Book of the Year Awards. Opening with the dinosaurs, the book has six pages describing the Aboriginal People, and the next fifty pages deal with the history of Australia since Abel Tasman's voyage of 1642. The illustrations are colourful and enlightening. Despite the shortcomings typical of Australian history books of the period, this is a clear and interesting account of Australia's settlement by white people.

Piece of Straw, A (1985), illustrated by Junko Morimoto, with a text adapted by Helen Smith, was Highly Commended in the 1986 Picture Book of the Year Awards. Through a series of exaggerated exchanges beginning with a straw, and his own unselfishness and generosity, Yohei's fortunes are transformed. Morimoto's illustrations recall old Japanese watercolours.

Pigs and Honey (1989), written and illustrated by Jeanie Adams, won the 1990 Book of the Year Awards: Younger Readers. A group of children and their parents catch a wild pig to eat, discover a wild bees' nest, and combine the two into a delicious evening meal. The narrative style follows the voice of the Aurukun storytellers, and is based on the author's knowledge of their life. The sunny watercolour and crayon sketches depict the traditional activities of a bush outing. It is endorsed as an authentic picture of their lifestyle by the people themselves, and has been published in Wik-Mungkan, the language of the Aurukun, and translated into the languages of the people of the Kimberleys. See also **Aboriginal People in Children's Fiction**.

Pigs Might Fly (1986) by 'Emily Rodda', illustrated by Noela Young, won the 1987 Junior Book of the Year Awards. A bored Rachel is unexpectedly transported to a bizarre place where the state of the weather is assessed by the number of flying pigs. Although she is welcomed by the elderly Bert and Enid, Rachel is desperate to return to the comfortable familiarity of her own family. When Rachel returns home she keeps a little UEF (Unlikely Events Factor) to relieve any future boredom, only to find that she is not the only Outsider to return. Rodda has developed an original idea with consistency and humour.

PIRANI, LEILA (1892–1963), born Melbourne, was a journalist, poet and novelist. She wrote the libretto for *Old Mr Sundown in Fairyland* (1935), a children's cantata with music by Mirrie Hill; *Cowboys and Indians: or the Story of Grey Eagle and Paleface, a Juvenile Operetta* (1937), with music by Alfred Wheeler; and *Play Day in Happy Holland: a Juvenile Operetta* (1937), with music by Ethel Harrhy, the musical director of the National Theatre. *I Met Them in China* (1944), illustrated by Ruth Shackel, is a collection of verse. *The Old Man River of Australia: a Saga of the River Murray* (1945), illustrated by Walter Cunningham, tells the story of a humanised Murray from his origin as a baby 'creeping out from the mountain snows', his observation of the Aboriginal People, the coming of Hovell and Hume, Sturt, Mitchell, a lost child, the farmers who live along the river, and so on, until he reaches the sea. *Lazy the Pig and His Chinese Adventures* (1945), illustrated by Joyce Janes, is a fantasy. In *Little Hans of Holland* (1945) Hans talks to the garden creatures such as Goldenwing the Butterfly and Septimus Spider. Princess Sadeyes, in *The Princess of the Water-Lilies* (1946), illustrated by Betty and Esther Paterson, finds her Prince Goldenheart after she has been given the gift of Hope by the fairy Cloud-of-Love. *Mrs Hen Counts her Chickens* (1949), illustrated by Norman Davis, is a counting book, in which Mrs Hen numbers and names her chickens as they hatch. See also **Counting Books**. Pirani also wrote adult romances. An account of her life can be found in Barbara Falk's *No Other Home: an Anglo-Jewish Story 1833–1987* (1988).

'Play School' is a television program, based on a British production with the same name, for 2 to 5-year-old children. The program began in 1966 on the ABC, with Lorraine Bayley and Anne Haddy as compères. Its combination of music, stories and activities and its consistently high level of presentation has attracted wide audiences. Many major actors have participated, including Benita Collings, Simon Burke, George Spartels, John Waters, Peter Sumner and Noni Hazlehurst. Forty-five new programs are made each year in Sydney, and are shown twice daily each weekday. Publications from the program include *The Blue Book* (1974), *The Green Book* (1976), and *The Useful Book* (1979) compiled by Henrietta Clark, and *The Yellow Book* (1986) compiled by Claire Henderson.

Playground Rhymes, see **Folklore**

Playing Beatie Bow (1980) by Ruth Park won the 1981 Book of the Year Awards. Through a piece of lace which she finds at her mother's shop, Abigail is transported back to the Rocks in 1873, called there by Beatie Bow who has been summoned up by a group of children playing a game named after her. Abigail is taken in by the Bow family who believe that someone in the family will be saved by a stranger. With great realism, the novel recreates the sights, smells and dangers of the period. Park does not flinch from the harshness and depravity of day-to-day life without twentieth-century conveniences, neither does she paint modern society as a better place. The warmth and sense of community of the working-class Bows contrasts with the more affluent but also more selfish twentieth-century Kirk family. The romance between Judah and Abigail, and her sacrifice for the sake of Dovey, enables Abigail to understand her mother's love for her estranged father. It was filmed by the SA Film Corporation in 1985, scripted by Peter Gawler, with Imogen Annesley as Abigail, Mouche Phillips as Beatie, and Peter Phelps as Judah. See also **Fantasy**; **Girls**; **Historical Novels**; **Sydney**.

Plum-Rain Scroll, The (1978) by Ruth Manley, illustrated by Marianne Yamuguchi, won the 1979 Book of the Year Awards. The resourceful, clever and brave Taro searches for the missing scroll which contains the secret of immortality, the secret of turning metals into gold and the Word of power. His quest sets him against Marishoten, the Black Iris Lord, but he is assisted by Aunt Piety and others. Manley creates a rich tapestry of Japanese folklore and adventure. *The Dragon Stone* (1982) and *The Peony Lantern* (1987) complete a trilogy which is based on values of bravery, honesty and morality.

Pochetto Coat, The (1978) by Ted Greenwood, illustrated by Ron Brooks, was Commended in the 1979 Book of the Year Awards. Patrick the juggler inherits a magical coat with a 1000 pockets. The novel is a dialogue between Sam and Patrick. Patrick tells Sam stories about the coat's previous owners, and passes it on to her when he is about to die.

Poetry. From nursery rhymes, playground chants, counting-out rhymes, finger-plays and children's taunts to the formal poetry of the classroom, the rhythm and dexterity of words engage children. Poetry is their natural province, and a spontaneous activity. Poets for adults have often included children in their audience. During the nineteenth and early twentieth centuries poets who wrote for children include Emily Barton, C.J. Dennis, 'Arthur Ferres', Mary Gilmore, Ernestine Hill, Norman Lindsay, Agnes Littlejohn, 'Furnley Maurice', Louisa Anne Meredith, and 'Banjo' Paterson. In the later twentieth century, Michael Dugan, Geoffrey Dutton, June Factor, Max Fatchen, Barbara Giles, Irene Gough, Robin Klein, Doug MacLeod, David Martin, Oodgeroo Noonuccal, Letitia Parr, Lydia Pender, Eric Rolls, Bill Scott, Colin Thiele, and Daisy Utemorrah have all contributed volumes of poetry for young readers.

There have been many anthologies of Australian poetry produced for children, an early collection being Rex Ingamells's *New Song in an Old Land* (1943). Joyce Saxby edited *One Hundred Poems Chosen for Children* (1967), illustrated by Astra Lacis, which included such poets as D.H. Souter, Mary Gilmore, Rex Ingamells, Will Lawson, J.K. Ewers, Ella McFadyen and A.B. Paterson in a well-organised production. A companion volume was Rosemary Dobson's *Songs for All Seasons: 100 Poems for Young People* (1967), illustrated by Margaret Horder, aimed at 9 to 14-year-olds, which includes poems which were not written specifically for children by David Campbell, Mary Gilmore, Kenneth Slessor, Judith Wright and many others. Many collections represent the variety of Australian poetry from the bush ballad to lyric verse. Celia Jellet and Jill Heylen have collected traditional and contemporary poetry, from Paterson to Doug MacLeod, in *Someone is Flying Balloons* (1983), illustrated by Kerry Argent, *Rattling in the Wind: Australian Poems for Children* (1987) and *It Must Have Been Summer* (1990), illustrated by Maire Smith. Clare Scott-Mitchell's *When a Goose Meets a Moose* (1980) is a collection for pre-schoolers, and *Apples from Hurricane Street* (1985) for children aged from 6 to 10. Neither is exclusively Australian. Jane Covernton has edited a series of humorous collections in *Putrid Poems* (1985), *Petrifying Poems* (1986), *Vile Verse* (1988), all illustrated by Craig Smith, and *Four and Twenty Lamingtons* (1988), illustrated by Jenny Rendall. Two comprehensive collections are *A First Australian Poetry Book* (1983) by June Factor, illustrated by Bob Graham, Rolf Heimann, Ann James and others, and *A Second Australian Poetry Book* (1983) compiled by Barbara Giles, illustrated by Brett Colquhoun, Terry Denton and others. *Stay Loose, Mother Goose: Stories and Poems to Read Aloud* (1990) compiled by Sue Machin, illustrated by Jane Disher, includes poems by Bill Scott, Jean Chapman, Barbara Giles and Max Fatchen. *All Australian Funny and Frightful Verse* (1987), selected by Glenys Smith, with cheeky illustrations by Deborah Niland, has verse by C.J. Dennis, Norman Lindsay, Max Fatchen and Doug

MacLeod. The inclusion of the Aboriginal and immigrant voice in many of these later collections distinguishes them from earlier works.

POIGNANT, AXEL (1906–86), born England, was a photographer. He wrote and photographed *Piccaninny Walkabout: a Story of Two Aboriginal Children* (q.v., 1957). With his wife Roslyn Poignant, an anthropologist, he also wrote and photographed *Kaleku* (1972), an adventure in the Chimbu district of Papua New Guinea, *Children of Oropiro* (1976), set on a Pacific island, and *Tama's Quest*, about a boy seeking his Maori identity.

Ponny the Penguin (1948) by Veronica Basser, illustrated by Edwina Bell, was Highly Commended in the 1948 Book of the Year Awards. The story follows the life of an Adelie penguin from birth, through migration, and mating, until she has a chick of her own. Ponny remains cheerful and sturdy, despite attacks by skuas and a sea leopard, reacting to her situation in a human way. The book is enriched by Bell's dramatic black-and-white illustrations of sea vistas and personable birds.

POPLE, MAUREEN (1928–) has written *The Other Side of the Family* (1986). Katharine, an English evacuee, meets her father's eccentric mother, who is careless of convention, but sticks to what she believes is right. See **Italians**. In *Pelican Creek* (1988) Sally discovers a romance of long ago between Ann and Jem. Enduring love is contrasted with transient relationships. *The Road to Summering* (1990) traces Rachel's attempts to solve an old mystery after her parents have separated. *Relative Strangers* (1992) is another mystery. Henry wants to know who has attacked Linda, suspecting Barney Dooley, who claims to be Henry's uncle. Henry pursues his investigations despite the town's silence, until the truth is finally revealed. Henry's own social life is much enriched in the process.

PORTEOUS, RICHARD SYDNEY (1897–1963), born Melbourne, wrote short stories and novels. In *Tambai Island* (1955), set on a lonely Pacific island, the search is for sunken treasure. Ken and Steve Gellatly sail to Rabaul in a schooner with a gang of ruthless killers battened below deck. In its sequel, *The Tambai Treasure* (1958), illustrated by Walter Stackpool, Ken has to take over the responsibility of sailing a cruiser from Sydney to Tambai when the crew's ignorance of the sea becomes apparent. *The Silent Isles* (1963), also illustrated by Stackpool, is a further adventure of the brothers Gellatly, in which they save Steve's sweetheart, Nina, and her father from Indonesian pirates. Porteous's experience and knowledge of seamanship give veracity to these Pacific adventures.

PORTER, JAMES (1929–), born Adelaide, has lived in Ethiopia, Papua New Guinea and NZ. In *The Swiftlet Isles* (1977), illustrated by Tony Oliver, Erik Douglas runs away to a tiny island on the Great Barrier Reef. The novel details Erik's observations of the natural life on the island, and his Thoreau-like existence as he strives to live off the land. *Warri of the Wind* (1977), also illustrated by Oliver, is a sailing story about a catamaran taken to Papua New Guinea by Alan Lonsdale and his son Pete. In *The Edge of the Rainforest* (1991) Karen and her mother fight off attempts to ruin their small farm. *The Kumul Feathers* (1979), illustrated by Jenny Elliott, and *Hapkas Girl* (1980) are set in Papua New Guinea and represent the conflicts caused by the tension between traditional ways and western cultural influences. *The Sacred Tree* (1982), illustrated by Steve Hederics, describes the catastrophes which occur when a noble tree is destroyed by a pioneering family in NZ. *The Sacred Tree*, *The Kumul Feathers* and *White Water Crossing* (1984) are in Rigby's 'Australian Magpie' series. *Long White Cloud* (1989) is set in NZ. Gil's impatience with his father drives him away from the farm, but he eventually returns and rescues his father from drowning. Gil's time away brings a new tolerance to father and son, and his friendship with Hemi and Kiri contributes to his maturing. *Piya* (1991) is about an Aboriginal girl who forsakes her own people for the freedom to live with her friends. Porter's novels promote a simpler set of values, based on the preservation of indigenous culture and the natural world.

Possum Magic (1983) by Mem Fox, illustrated by Julie Vivas, was Highly Commended in the 1984 Picture Book of the Year Awards and was the Primary Winner of KOALA in 1987. Fox rewrote the book over a period of five years before it was accepted for publication. The resourceful Grandma Poss protects Hush by making her invisible, but trouble arises when Hush wants to be visible again and Grandma Poss has forgotten what food will restore her. Together the two travel Australia, trying Vegemite sandwiches, lamingtons, Minties and other Australian delicacies until Hush is seen again. Its appealing illustrations and use of national images have made *Possum Magic* much loved, and its popularity has generated a small industry of related items, such as handkerchiefs, badges and ceramics.

POTTER, DORA JOAN (d.1987) wrote serious school stories with unintentionally funny plots. The school is Winterton, 'the school chosen by all the society people for their daughters'. *With Wendy at Winterton School* (1945) introduced Wendy Murphy, the daughter of a butcher. She is reluctant to obey the orders of 'snobs' like Felicity Filmore-Danvers, the head prefect, but is redeemed by exposing two Japanese spies and saving the life of the daughter of the headmistress. Wendy is rewarded with a stained-glass window in her honour. *Wendy Moves Up* (1947) concludes with her friend Mary Mornington winning a scholarship to Winterton, Wendy elected

as head prefect and Peggy Trethewey found to be the long-lost niece of a teacher, an English aristocrat. *Wendy in Charge* (1947) describes Wendy's dislike of Venetia Kirby, a new girl who is appointed as a prefect by the headmistress. Their troubles are resolved when Venetia has a party to which she invites a blind man, a child suffering from infantile paralysis, a deaf boy who wanted to be a musician, a girl who cannot speak, a child suffering from an obscure blood disease, a drunkard, an old lady whose son is in jail, and a victim of child abuse. All guests have difficulty restraining their desires to kiss the girls' hands, which reduces Wendy and Venetia to tears. *Althea's Term at Winterton* (1949) describes how Lady Althea St George wins over the girls. *Winterton Holiday Cruise* (1949) has men overboard, stolen heirlooms and writers in disguise. In *A New Girl at Winterton* (1950) Jill Bentley brings two people together, this time the headmistress and her long-lost husband. In *Pam Pays her Debt* (1945) Pam restores a lost child to her parents. *Those Summer Holidays* (1946) is set in Port Lincoln, SA. Celia Steele, mother of five, has been injured in a car accident. One of the girls, Ashley, wants to be a doctor, but her father says he needs her at home, not just to keep the household running but also for 'companionship'. After many miraculous meetings and transformations, including loyal British subjects being mistaken for Nazis, Mrs Steele is restored to health by Dr Von Stein, assisted by Ashley, who performs 'one of the Rarest Operations Known to Medical Science'.

Helen's Inheritance (1950) speaks of the courage which Helen's mother displayed before she was killed in France during the war as a secret service agent. Helen attends a girls' school, where she is at first despised as a coward, but her discovery of a secret tunnel and the true identity of the school gardener reveal her as her mother's true inheritor. Perhaps the most action-packed of Potter's novels is *Margaret's Decision* (1947). Margaret must choose between Wirra-Warra, a private school, or attending high school. If she chooses the latter, then her brother will be able to continue at the university. She chooses to stay at Wirra-Warra, her brother is believed killed in the war, she falls into the hold while visiting a ship, floats in a lifeboat after the ship is sunk, finds her brother on a deserted island, and returns home perfectly happy again. Margaret restores the spirits of the survivors by teaching them the ringing verses of the school song. 'It is here that they learn/To be moderate too,/And to do what is honourable/Gracious and true./To love next to God/Australia their own/In conjunction with Britain — /Little grey island Home!'

'POWELL, ELIZABETH' was the pseudonym of **EFFIE SANDERY** (1895–1986), born Adelaide, who as 'Kirkcaldy' edited the children's column in the Adelaide *Register*. In *The Beehive* (1928) the Campbell children, Barbara, Bob, Brenda and Bubbles, transform Beryl through a series of domestic crises. *Sunset Hill* (1929) continues the Campbell saga, and introduces the Loftus family, all musical, but all thwarted until the Campbells sort them out. Brenda becomes a writer and Beryl, 'who has no ambition', gets her man. *The Old Brown House* (1942) is another romance, this time about Christine, who is staying with an unpleasant aunt and cousin while Dad is a war correspondent. Christine moves to another household, where she also encounters some hostility, but she consoles herself with writing, is eventually published, and gains a stepmother. Sandery's *Mr Jigsaw* (1928) is a witty story for younger readers. When his wife scolds him, Mr Jigsaw literally falls to pieces, which Mrs Jigsaw finds very annoying. She sends him away with threepence, a new toothbrush and a clean handkerchief. Mr Jigsaw meets a boy with his feet back to front, and takes him home with him after Mr Jigsaw has been stuck together by the Glue Man.

POWER, MARGARET (1945–   ), born Melbourne, studied illustration at RMIT. Power lived in London for ten years and returned to Australia in 1976. She has illustrated *Running Away* (1977) by Roger Vaughan Carr; *Honoured Guest* (1979), *Sprung!* (1982) and *The Ghost in Abigail Terrace* (1989), by Robin Klein; *A Mirror for Midnight* (1985) by Barbara Mitchelhill; *Creatures in the Beard* (1986) by Margaret Wild; *The Long Red Scarf* (q.v., 1987) by Nette Hilton; *Senka's New Coat* (1987) by Keith Pigdon; and *Spider in the Toilet* (1988) by Edel Wignell. Power was commissioned to paint a series of watercolours for the National Australia Bank to commemorate 150 years of white settlement in Victoria.

POWER, PHYLLIS MARY (1887–1977), born Brighton, UK, spent her early childhood in Australia, travelled to Europe, and returned to Melbourne in 1934. Her first book, *Two Stories* (1906), was for adults. Her books for younger readers include *The Tale of Billy Flea's Experiences* (1912), *Five Stories for Margrette Anne* (1945), written in aid of the Children's Hospital, *Fairy Chatter Book* (1951), eleven stories (including 'The Three Wishes — Australian Style'), *The Story of a Carpet Bag* (1952) and *Michael Flannigan and His Cow* (1952), both Mullens's Stories for Children, illustrated by Marjorie Howden, and *The Sammy Stories, Being the Adventures of a Black Doll* (1960), about a doll who is an adviser to the Fairy Queen. Sammy relates his adventures to his small owner each morning. *Something to Read for Teenagers* (1951) is a collection of thirteen short stories, from 'Clare's Easter Bonnet' to 'Granny's Ear Trumpet'.

Power has written adventure stories set in the outback. *Lost in the Outback* (1954) introduces Hannah Maine and her friend Mary Frazer, who also appear in *Nursing in the Outback* (1959). In both books Hannah and Mary become lost, and meet Aboriginal People who help them survive.

Nicholas's father had the biggest, bushiest beard in the world.

It was so big and bushy that Nicholas said, "There are creatures living in your beard. There is a robin, a field mouse and a baby possum."

"Rubbish," said Nicholas's father. "There are no creatures in my beard. Not one."

Creatures in the Beard (1986) by Margaret Wild. Illustrator: Margaret Power

Legends from the Outback (1965), illustrated by Ida Outhwaite, is a collection of quasi-Aboriginal stories. *Under Australian Skies* (1955) describes an outback station before the Royal Flying Doctor Service and pedal wireless. The seven Clarke daughters help their mother and father run a large household, muster the cattle, ride horses brilliantly, and show enormous resource. See also **Aboriginal People in Children's Fiction**. In *Adventure in the Outback* (1957), illustrated by Helen Harvie, the British Bert becomes an expert stockman at his uncle's station, 'Princes Soak', where he also helps track down a group of cattle-duffers. *Kangaroo Country* (1961) is an account of everyday life on a large station, 'Emily Downs', with plentiful explanations of the daily routine and many descriptions of Australian animals. The Blake daughters, Agatha, Julie and Mary, deal with brumbies, snake bite, injured travellers, aggressive shearers and a large family of Dutch people who come to stay. Power's outback novels present assertive and

courageous girls, who are as proficient as their male friends. In contrast, Celestine and her mother are less capable than Jean-Marie in *Sabotage in the Snowy Mountains* (1961). The Froust family travel from Paris to Cooma to work for the Snowy Mountains Authority, where Jean-Marie reveals a saboteur. The novel is liberally dotted with lectures on the Snowy Mountains Scheme, its value to Australia and its interesting people. The Froust family are easily assimilated into the Australian Way of Life by taking the wise advice of helpful locals and marrying into the right families — the local squattocracy. *From the Fig Tree: the Adventures of Two Boys from the Swan River in Western Australia One Hundred Years Ago* (1968) is a historical novel.

POWNALL, EVE (MARJORIE EVE-LYN POWNALL) (1901–82), born Sydney, was an editor, radio scriptwriter, reviewer and novelist. She was the children's editor of the monthly *Australian Book News and Library Journal* from 1946 to 1948. Pownall has written books for young readers, such as *Squik the Squirrel Possum* (1949), illustrated by Raymond Johnson, *Nursery Rhymes Told Anew* (1945), *Five Busy Merry-Makers* (1953) and *Binty the Bandicoot* (1957), illustrated by Bob Booth. *The Story of a Baby* (1948), illustrated by Dorothea Johnston, is an album for parents. Her interest in history led her to write *The Australia Book* (q.v., 1952), *Cousins-Come-Lately: Adventures in Old Sydney Town* (q.v., 1952) and factual books about Australia, such as *Exploring Australia* (q.v., 1958), illustrated by Noela Young, and both *A Pioneer Daughter* (1968), illustrated by Joan Walker, and *A Drover* (1970), illustrated by Anne Culvenor, for Oxford's 'Early Australians' series. Pownall was a founding member of the CBC, of which she has written a history, *The CBC in Australia 1945 to 1980* (1981). See also **Eve Pownall Award**.

Premier's Literary Awards, see **Alan Marshall Awards**; **New South Wales Literary Awards: Children's Book Award**.

PRESTON, JAMES (1913–), born Ballarat, Victoria, has written *Paper Boy* (1974), in which Mike Grant sells papers to save up the money to buy his mother a washing machine. *Jeedarra Country* (1971), illustrated by Helen Sallis, is a description of the experiences of Greg and Janie when they become lost on the Nullarbor. See also **Lost in the Bush**. Both *The Ring of the Axe* (1968) and *The Sky Between the Trees* (1986) deal with axemanship, the latter based on the real story of Peter McLaren, a champion axeman. Peter's determination to achieve excellence is opposed by his father, who is embittered by the struggle to survive. Besides his prowess as axeman, Peter has literary skills. He writes a story, entitled 'Retribution', for the *Bulletin* about how bushfires destroy a hard-won livelihood after his family has fought a bushfire. The novel is set in the same area as Mavis Thorpe

Clark's *The Blue Above the Trees* (1967), McDonald's Track, with its great canopied forests. Preston has also written for adults.

PRICE, PAT PEATFIELD (PATRICIA RYCROFT) (1929–), born Kent, UK, came to Australia in 1966. *Jobs for the Boys* (1977) was written for Macmillan's 'Orbit' reading scheme. *The Hills of the Black Cockatoo* (1981), illustrated by Betty Greenhatch, tells how Tingali and her brothers Rineka and Koonya return from their first glimpse of white men to discover that their people have fled. With a toddler who has been left behind, Lowanna, they search for their family, finding refuge with others when they learn that their own people have been murdered. See also **Aboriginal People in Children's Fiction**. In *Brett and Boo and the BMX Bike* (1986) young people co-operate to set up a practice BMX track. Price has also written informational books.

PRICE, ROSALIND (1952–) became the editor of children's books at OUP when Frank Eyre retired in 1979. In 1982 she became the children's publisher at Allen & Unwin, developing their 'Little Ark' books. Price has written the book based on the film *BMX Bandits* (1984), and co-edited *The Macquarie Bedtime Story Book* (1987) with Walter McVitty.

PRICHARD, KATHARINE SUSANNAH (1883–1969), born Levuka, Fiji, came to Australia as an infant. *The Wild Oats of Han* (1928) recreates her childhood around Launceston on the Tamar River, stealing apples, playing on the hills, and on the river. *Moggie and Her Circus Pony* (q.v., 1967) was written for children. Prichard wrote many books for adults, including *Coonardoo* (1929) and a trilogy of novels about the WA goldfields.

PRIOR, TED (1945–), born Sydney, wrote the Grug (q.v.) series.

Puberty Blues: a Surfie Saga (1979) by Kathy Lette and Gabrielle Carey is about the Sydney adolescent subculture of the 1970s. Surfing, sexual exploits in panel vans, and experimenting with drugs are described frankly in the language of youth. The enthusiasm of young people for the novel initiated a greater realism in books for adolescents. It was filmed in 1981 under the direction of Bruce Beresford, with Nell Schofield as Debbie and Jad Capelja as Sue.

Puffing Billy: A Story for Children (1967) by Esta de Fossard, illustrated by John Mason, was Commended in the 1968 Picture Book of the Year Awards. It describes the rebuilding of the line for the narrow-gauge steam train which runs from Belgrave to Emerald in the Dandenong Ranges, Victoria. Another edition was produced in 1978, with photographs by Haworth Bartram. In 1984 it was updated to remove any sexist material, illustrated by Lyn Stocks and retitled *Here Comes Puffing Billy*.

PUGH, CLIFTON (1924–90), born Melbourne, was a figurative painter. He illustrated *Yellow Jacket Jock* (1969) by Colin Thiele; *Death of a Wombat* (1972) and *Dingo King* (1977) by Ivan Smith; and *Chai the Kangaroo* (1985) and *A Sometime River* (1986) by Pam Blashki. See also **Animal Stories**. His last illustrations were for *Digger's Mate* (1991) by Helen Lunn, which tells the story of a wombat, Myrtle, and her friend the dog, Digger. Pugh's oils, line drawings, water colours, etchings and gouaches of the Australian landscape and its animals reveal the rawness and beauty of the Australian bush.

PUGH, JUDITH. For *Wombalong* (1985) see **Animal Stories**.

Pugwall, Peter Unwin George Wall, is the central character in M.D. Clark's *Pugwall* (1987) and *Pugwall's Summer* (1989). The two books were made into a television series, 'Pugwall', in 1989, with a sequel in 1990.

PYKE, LILLIAN (?1881–1927), born Victoria, wrote *Cole's Happy Time Picture and Nursery Rhyme Book* (1920), illustrated by Percy Leason, which has forty-five nursery rhymes. *Saturday Island* (1922) is a fantasy, published in Cassell's Commonwealth Story Readers. For *Brothers of the Fleet* (1924) see **First Fleet**. Pyke also wrote novels for adults, sometimes using the pseudonym 'Erica Maxwell', and *Australian Etiquette* (1916).

She wrote many school stories. Her fictional school, St Virgil's, was based on Melbourne's Wesley College, the school attended by her son, Lawrence Pyke, who was a Rhodes scholar and later headmaster of Newington College, Sydney. *Max the Sport* (1916) set the tone for Pyke's school stories, with its model hero, Max, a fine sport and perfect gentleman, the obvious choice for Captain of the First Eleven and Senior Prefect. *Jack of St. Virgil's* (1917) takes up the unknown parentage of another thoroughly admirable sporting schoolboy who turns out to be the son of a wartime hero. It includes a scene where Jack's sex education is provided by one of the older boys, who points him towards healthy activities rather than unsavoury novels, and a picture of an opium den in Townsville, run by 'yellow wretches' who rob their customers and knife anyone who interferes. Both books were illustrated by J. Macfarlane. In *A Prince at School* (1919) Lester, the headmaster of Whitefield, is bequeathed the guardianship of two 'children' Lola, 20, and Arnold, 16, after their mother's death. They live on Vilatonga where Lola is courted by Mr Bernstein who was 'tall and good-looking with a blond handsomeness which betrayed his Teutonic origin'. Arnold is not fooled by his good looks, because although he is charming to Lola he reveals a streak of cruelty when he hits young Andi, 'a common islander'. Vilatonga is an important

British naval base and Bernstein has designs on it for his country. However, the reader is assured at the end of the book that 'Vilatonga was fairly in the way of becoming a loyal British possession'. The footballer Smith, hero of the *The Best School of All* (1921), also illustrated by Macfarlane, has a conflict of loyalties between his old school, Mervale, and St Virgil's.

For girls, Pyke wrote *Squirmy and Bubbles, a School Story for Girls* (1924), illustrated by Perce Clark, set at Riverside College, Victoria, where the twins Theodora (Bubbles) and Dorothea (Squirmy) Bonney confuse their teachers by impersonating each other. (The sister of *A Prince at School*, Princess Lala, attended Riverside.) In *The Lone Guide of Merfield* (1925), illustrated by J. Dewar Mills, Mary Grey displays her initiative and Girl Guide training during a shipwreck. Other school stories are *Sheila at Happy Hills* (1922), illustrated by J. Macfarlane, and *Sheila the Prefect* (1923), illustrated by J. Dewar Mills. Sheila is also featured in *Three Bachelor Girls* (1926), as an Old Girl of Pyke's other school creation, Riverview. Sheila's chosen future is marriage, despite her talent as a singer and the prospect of a concert tour. For boys, Pyke's schools offer a future as heroes: for girls, they offer marriage and children.

Pyke's novels about railway construction camps in Queensland are realistic insights into the life of construction workers and their families. *Camp Kiddies: a Story of Life on Railway Construction* (1919) describes the daily life of the family of the accountant Mr Clifford when they move from the comforts of Melbourne to the Spartan camping life. In *Phyl of the Camp* (1918) Phyl Langton wins her dour father over with her refinement, good cooking and skilful bridge-playing, and patches up a vendetta between her father and another engineer. *Bruce at Boonderong Camp* (1920) also features Phyllis and her father. Bruce Henshaw is sent to stay with them after a particularly hair-raising escapade. Bruce is reconstructed into a model boy and Phyllis falls in love with a young engineer. There is a conventional melodrama about a schoolteacher, Peter Bright, with a deranged wife in the background, but Peter Bright provides Pyke with a vehicle for her educational ideas, which are notably enlightened and ahead of her time.

Q

Quest for Golden Dan, The (1962) by Frank Kellaway, illustrated by Deborah White, was Commended in the 1963 Book of the Year Awards. The novel opens in 1855 as the *Sealion* berths in Melbourne. Dan Jones is kidnapped by Blowfly Joe (Joseph Alaric Blough) to be his singing apprentice. Dan's escape into the arms of the gentle Caro family, his attachment to Arne Sturluson, and his journey to find his parents, provides a tale full of adventure and excitement. The goldfields of Victoria make a colourful background for Dan's transition from boy to young man. The inclusion of the songs of the people Dan meets, and the fantasies of Ruth Caro, who has an imaginary friend, Pym, add a magical dimension to the novel.

QUIN, TARELLA, see **DASKEIN, TARELLA QUIN**

Quinkins, The (1978) by Percy Trezise and Dick Roughsey won the 1979 Picture Book of the Year Awards. Mother and Father are out hunting when the children, Moonbi and Leealin, are lured away from camp by the bad Imjim. They are saved by the tall and whimsical Timara. The Imjim and Timara are two groups of spirit people, pictured on the sacred sites of Cape York, and the vibrant illustrations draw on these traditional figures. A film of the book was made in 1982. *Turramulli the Giant Quinkin* (q.v., 1982) is another Quinkin story.

QUIRK, LORNA produced board books for Georgian House, including *A Day at the Beach, Play Time, Our Pets, Planes, Trains and Boats, Speed,* (all 1946) and a picture-book, *Poohbah the Pekinese Pup* (1947). Poohbah is frightened by a wolf and retreats to a rabbit warren where he finds new friends. The stylish, geometric illustrations exhibit her gift for colour and design.

R

Racketty Street Gang, The (1961) by L.H. Evers was a joint winner of the 1962 Book of the Year Awards. It is one of the first Australian children's books which has an immigrant child as the main character, and also one of the first of the post-war urban novels. Anton Smertzer and his parents have emigrated from Germany after World War II. In Racquetier Street, by Sydney Harbour, Anton and his friends uncover a gang of bank-robbers, stop the robbery, collect a reward, and save Mr Smertzer from the consequences of a family secret. The novel has an assimilationist approach to immigration, but its call for tolerance is notable. The boys' enthusiasm for technology, their eagerness for Do-It-Yourself activities, and their confidence in Australia's future, together with the novel's immigrant characters, makes *The Racketty Street Gang* an example of how a writer has integrated contemporary attitudes into an adventure story.

RAE ELLIS, VIVIENNE, see **ELLIS, VIVIENNE RAE**

Rafferty Rides a Winner (1961), written and illustrated by Joan Woodberry, was a joint winner of the 1962 Book of the Year Awards. It is the third book in a series about Rafferty, a Yorkshire immigrant. In this book, Rafferty and his friends, Bob, Paul, Happy and Billie set out to earn £60, which will enable them to buy a boat, the *Gay Adventure*. These lifelike outdoor boys ride, swim, fish, do odd jobs, enter their undisciplined pets in the local pet show, and live out summer in a small fishing township, Bo-ambee, on the coast of NSW. Rafferty's adventures began with *Rafferty Takes to Fishing* (1959), in which Rafferty is initiated into Australian ways during a fishing trip. *Floodtide for Rafferty* (1960) followed, with Rafferty involved in a rescue operation. The final novel about Rafferty is *Rafferty Makes a Landfall* (1962), in which Rafferty and his mates go shopping in Sydney before an adventure at sea. Rafferty, his mates, and his adventurous grandfather, present a happy picture of rural Australia, with days full of sailing and adventure.

Rainbow Serpent, The (1975) written and illustrated by Dick Roughsey, won the 1976 Picture Book of the Year Awards. As Goorialla the serpent travels throughout the land he makes mountains and lagoons and teaches the people to dance and decorate themselves. He swallows the Bil-bil brothers, but they are cut from his stomach, and in his rage he throws a huge mountain of rocks around the land. He now lives in the sea, and his eye, the shooting star, watches everybody. The traditional account of Goorialla, the great Creator, is powerfully retold with dramatic illustrations set in the landscape of northern Queensland.

RAISBECK, GENEVIEVE, see **MELROSE, GENEVIEVE**

RANDELL, BEVERLEY (1931–), born NZ, wrote *John the Mouse who Learned to Read* (q.v., 1969).

Rangatira (The High Born): a Polynesian Saga (1959) by Norman Tindale and Harold Lindsay, illustrated by Douglas Maxted, was Commended in the 1960 Book of the Year Awards. It is an account of the migration to NZ of a group of Polynesians around the twelfth century. When Rehua arrives at an overcrowded island in Hawaiki, he tells the people about the great land of Aotearoa, to the south. A boat is built to take some of the young people, led by Rehua, to a new home. After a long and dangerous voyage and a search for a secure place for their village, Maui, Kura and the others overcome their troublesome neighbours and create a permanent settlement. The next generation is represented by their son, Perere, who travels as far as the shores of Australia before he marries. The novel is a rich mixture of Polynesian culture and legends, with sources, notes and a pronunciation guide.

Rankin, Ann features in the series by Paul Buddee. In *Ann Rankin and the Boy Who Painted Horses* (1973) Ann persuades James Read, a boy artist, to decorate the Junior Club Room with murals. In *Ann Rankin and the House on Coolabah Hill* (1973), Ann and the Murra Wanda Pony Club members save the El Shariff family from being kidnapped by terrorists. Ann and her friends need to raise thousands of dollars in *Ann Rankin and the Lost Valley* (1973) to establish a camp school in the hills. They rediscover Moola Valley, already set up with buildings, and lease it for their camp, and for the mining of its kaolin and tin deposits. Ann's feud with Chris Hales is resolved in *Ann Rankin and the Great Flood* (1973) when they work together to save the passengers of an express train derailed during a flood.

RAWLINS, DONNA (1956–   ), born Melbourne, is a community artist, designer, illustrator and print-maker, and an associate editor with Ashton Scholastic. She illustrated *Miranda Going Home* (1985) by Eleanor Spence; *Time for a Number Rhyme* (1983); *The Kinder Hat* (1985) and *Tucking Mummy In* (1987) by Morag Loh; *My Place* (q.v., 1987) by Nadia Wheatley; *Fast Forward* (1989) by Jenny Pausacker;

Jeremy's Tail (1990) by Duncan Ball; and *Jezza Says* (1990) by Libby Hathorn. In *Digging to China* (1988) Alexis digs through the Earth to get a Chinese birthday present for Marj. The hole made is used by two Chinese children, who appear on the last page of the book. Rawlins presents unstereotyped and multicultural families. Her colourful and vigorous illustrations show children undertaking imaginative pursuits, with an unselfconscious delight in their individuality.

RAY, N. L., see **HUNT, NAN**

RAYMENT, TARLTON (1882–1964), born Reading, UK, came to Australia around the turn of the century and worked as a commercial artist and apiarist, becoming a world authority on bees, wasps and ants. He was president of the Entomological Society and a contributor to the magazine *Walkabout*. He wrote textbooks on his speciality, such as *Bees in Australia* (1916), which he illustrated himself. Rayment was also a broadcaster, and *The Prince of the Totem: a Simple Black Tale for Clever White Children* (1933), illustrated from crayon drawings by the author, in which the Aboriginal Gor-ree learns to be a great artist and the saviour of his people, was first broadcast on the ABC's Children's Session in 1932. The novel was republished in *The Australian Wonder Book* (q.v., 1935). See also **Aboriginal People in Children's Fiction**. Rayment also wrote *Golden City of the Bees* (1921) and *Goldwing: the Life Story of the Queen Bee* (1922), an Australian Nature Story Reader for Whitcombe & Tombs. *The Valley of the Sky* (1942), another Whitcombe & Tombs production, is an abridgement of his adult novel of the same name based on the settlement of Gippsland and the life of Angus McMillan. His biography is *The Melody Lingers On: Biography of Tarlton Rayment FRZS* (1967) by Lynette Young.

RAYMOND, MOORE, see **'Smiley'**

Digging to China (1988) by Donna Rawlins

REED, ALEXANDER WYCLIF
(1908–79), born Auckland, NZ, was the
chairman of A.H. & A.W. Reed, publishers. He has rewritten Aboriginal Dreaming stories such as *Aboriginal Fables and
Legendary Tales* (1965) (see **Aboriginal
Dreaming Stories**), *Myths and Legends of
Australia* (1965), illustrated by Roger Hart,
The Mischievous Crow: Stories of the

Aborigines (1969), illustrated by Max
Tilley, and *The Wonder Book of Australian
Animals* (1970), illustrated by Colin
Archer.

REES, CORALIE CLARKE (1909–
72), born Perth, was a journalist for the
West Australian, wrote travel books with
her husband, Leslie Rees, and children's

plays. One of her plays, 'Wait till we grow up' is included in *Australian Youth Plays* (1948), edited by Leslie Rees. *What Happened After?* (1972) extends the stories of some well-known nursery rhymes, such as Old King Cole, The Queen of Hearts, Humpty Dumpty and others. See also **Nursery Rhymes**.

REES, GENEVIEVE, see **MELROSE, GENEVIEVE**

REES, LESLIE (1905–), born Perth, has been a journalist, editor and drama critic, and written over forty books, including plays, travel books and novels. His books for children began with the first of his Digit Dick (q.v.) series. He then turned to Australian animals, with *The Story of Shy the Platypus* (1944), illustrated by Walter Cunningham, the first of his animal picture story-books. In *Gecko the Lizard Who Lost His Tail* (1944), also illustrated by Cunningham, Gecko is invited to Jack Kookaburra's parties, where each of the animals must perform. When Gecko walks on the ceiling, a jealous Jack threatens to eat Gecko, but when the lizard drops his tail, Jack is satisfied to eat that. *The Story of Karrawingi the Emu* (q.v., 1946), *The Story of Sarli the Barrier Reef Turtle* (1947), *The Story of Shadow the Rock Wallaby* (q.v., 1948), *Bluecap and Bimbi* (q.v., 1948), *The Story of Wy-lah the Cockatoo* (1959), *The Story of Russ the Australian Tree Kangaroo* (1964), set in the jungles of northern Queensland, were all illustrated by Walter Cunningham. *The Story of Aroora the Red Kangaroo* (1952) was illustrated by John Singleton. *The Story of Kurri Kurri the Kookaburra* (q.v., 1950), *Two-Thumbs: the Story of a Koala* (1953) and *The Story of Koonaworra the Black Swan* (1957) were illustrated by Margaret Senior. *Mokee the White Possum* (1971) was illustrated by Tony Oliver and *Billa, the Wombat who Had a Bad Dream* (1988) was illustrated by Penny Walton. The fauna in stories is often humanised, but there is also much information about the life of the bird or animal. For instance, in *Billa*, the orphaned Billa is taken home by Julie and Max. The wombat's fear of the boxer dog, Bob, is overcome when she dreams she is surrounded by the much more fearsome giant wombats of antiquity. Rees's animal stories have been widely translated, and have sold over a quarter of a million copies. *Mates of the Kurlalong* (1948), illustrated by Alfred Wood, is a light-hearted story about Wombat, Chimp, Wiggy and Snooty aboard a Sydney Harbour ferry. *A Treasury of Australian Nature Stories* (1974) includes previously published stories.

Rees's realistic novels for older readers are adventure stories. *Quokka Island* (1951), illustrated by Arthur Horrowicz, in a setting suggesting Rottnest Island, off Perth, conceals an experiment to make artificial diamonds being conducted by a mad scientist, M. Crystal. Showing endurance and courage beyond their years, Jack, Ric and Jim join forces with a group of Italian fishermen and a policeman to foil the foreigners who want the secret. In *Danger Patrol: a Young Patrol Officer's Adventures in New Guinea* (1954), Bruce James saves his superior officer after an arrow attack, subdues a group of restive axe-wielders, and experiences a volcano erupting. The novel provides an interesting account of Australian colonialism at work, and the hazards of life in Papua New Guinea. *Boy Lost on Tropic Coast: Adventure with Dexter Hardy* (1968), illustrated by Frank Beck, describes how Dexter Hardy, a bush pilot, finds Brace Edwards, who has run away from his home in north Queensland. Much of the action is set in Torres Strait. See also **Aboriginal People in Children's Fiction**. *Panic in the Cattle Country* (1974) also features Dexter Hardy. When Tom's cattle are mysteriously savaged, Dexter agrees to help Tom and his sister Robbie find the culprit. After various outback experiences, including witnessing a corroboree and tangling with a gold-prospector, they find a pride of lions, which they either shoot or take into captivity. *Here's to*

Shane (1977) is the case history of a severely hearing-impaired boy who became an expert on the birds of the Ord River. An account of how Rees wrote his natural history and his Digit Dick series may be found in his autobiography, *Hold Fast to Dreams: Fifty Years in the Theatre, Radio, T.V. and Books* (1982). Rees provided life histories of Australian fauna within appealing adventure stories. Their excellent illustrations and accurate details made an important contribution towards lifting the standard of children's publishing at the end of World War II, when it was at a low ebb.

REES, LU (LUCY FRANCES HARVEY WAUGH) (1900–83), born New England, NSW, was the manager of the Canberra branch of F.W. Cheshire. She was the first president of the Canberra Branch of the CBC, and was active in setting up school libraries for Canberra children. She was awarded the Dromkeen Medal in 1982. See also **Lu Rees Archives**.

REEVES, WILF. For *The Legends of Moonie Jarl* (1964) see **Aboriginal Dreaming Stories**.

REID, Captain **MAYNE** (1818–83), born Ballyroney, Ireland, was a prolific writer of adventure stories. For *Lost Lenore: or, The Adventures of a Rolling Stone* (1864) see **Eureka Stockade**.

REILLY, PAULINE NEURA (1918–), born Adelaide, ornithologist and writer, has written three books in the Macmillan 'Orbit' series for reluctant readers: *Liz* (1976), *Liz Goes West* (1977), and *Barry* (1977). *The Penguin That Walks at Night* (1985), illustrated by Will Roland, provides facts and an imaginary life story of a female penguin and is in a similar format to *The Emu that Walks Towards the Rain* (1986), also illustrated by Roland, *The Lyrebird That is Always Too Busy to Dance* (1986), *The Kookaburra That Helps at the*

Nest (1987), *The Wombat* (1987), *The Tasmanian Devil* (1988), also illustrated by Roland, *The Koala* (1989), *The Echidna* (1990), and *Malleefowl, the Incubator Bird* (1990). She has also written informational books about animals, and worked on the research which identified the life cycle of the fairy penguin.

Religion. The predominant religion treated in Australian children's books is Christianity. Nineteenth-century authors enthusiastically included conversions or reformation through religion. In Maud Jean Franc's *Emily's Choice* (1867) the choice is between the Bible and the devil; Sophia Tandy's *The Children in the Scrub: a Story of Tasmania* (1878) concludes with the conversion of the parents of the lost children; Marion Downes, Agatha Le Breton, Bessie Marchant, and Mary Agnes Finn wrote accounts of girls struggling to keep up their faith. P.D. McCormick's *The Four School Mates, an Australian Tale of Misfortune and Success* (1896) has many debates about the need for a religious life. Tasman's *A Little Aversion* (1910) includes a missionary, Conscie. Lydia Eliott's *Kangaroo Country* (1955) is built around overt Christian moral lessons. Barry Chant has written a series about Spindles which illustrates biblical lessons. For instance, in *Spindles and the Wombat* (1978), the story 'Spindles and the Fossils' supports Creationist theory. Corrie Doedens's *Cyclone Ruth* (1984), *Bonnie* (1986) and *Tanzi's Search* (1986) describe a crisis of faith in three girls. More subtle than these, Eleanor Spence's *Me and Jeshua* (q.v., 1984) recounts the boyhood of Jesus. In *Miranda Going Home* (1985), also by Spence, Miranda discovers her Jewish origins at the time of Jesus. These are historical novels which examine the origins of spirituality. Spence imagines the childhood of Jesus with originality. His benignity and mystical presence are drawn, yet he emerges as a believable child. In *The Nativity* (1986) Julie Vivas has taken the King James version of the birth of Christ.

Her powerful illustrations show a pregnant peasant girl and a tattered Angel Gabriel, evoking the earthy impact of the story.

Ted Greenwood's *The Boy Who Saw God* (1980) looks at the impact of religious fervour on an impressionable boy. Greenwood describes how Leo's unhappy home life forces him into self-examination. Like Abraham, Leo sacrifices a sheep at what he believes is God's bidding. Misunderstood and outcast, only his artistic dioramas secure his link with humanity. Gary Crew's *The House of Tomorrow* (1988) and *No Such Country: a Book of Antipodean Hours* (1991) also examine the effect of fundamentalist religion, as does Bron Nicholls's *Mullaway* (1986). Robin Klein's *People Might Hear You* (1983), Judith O'Neill's *The Message* (1989) and Nan Hunt's *Never Tomorrow* (1989) look at closed communities. In Klein's novel, Frances's efforts are directed towards escaping from the suffocating repression of the temple. O'Neill's book deals with the power struggles within Arcady, and its disintegration under stress. Here the cult is not specifically religious, but the rules which are imposed on the cult's members, and the ritualistic practices suggest a pseudo-religion. Nan Hunt's *Never Tomorrow* (1989) also deals with a cult, the Children of Today, run by the Total Omega. 'Virginia Whatshername' runs away from the bombing of a church, and the hunt for her real identity exposes the cult.

My Brother Tom (1966), *The True Story of Spit MacPhee* (1986) and *The Untouchable Juli* (1975) by James Aldridge, look at religious bigotry in a small town. Hazel Edwards's *So Who's the Misfit* (1989) examines Crystal's response to Jewish rituals. Eleanor Spence also looks at bigotry in *The Seventh Pebble* (q.v., 1980). David Martin in *The Man in the Red Turban* (1978) and *The Chinese Boy* (1973) touches on eastern religions. Islam appears in Maureen McCarthy's *Fatima* (1987) (which considers culture rather than religion) and Katherine Scholes's *The Blue*

Chameleon (1989). The impact of religious prejudice has been well documented in the novels of Aldridge, Martin and Spence, and the transforming power of religious experience has been raised in the books of Spence and Tim Winton. See also **Aboriginal Dreaming Stories**.

RENTOUL, ANNIE ISOBEL (?1860–1928), born Valparaiso, Chile, was the mother of Ida Sherbourne Rentoul (Outhwaite) and Annie Rattray Rentoul, and wife of the poet John Laurence Rentoul (1846–1926), Moderator of the Presbyterian Church 1912–14. *Mollie's Staircase* (1906), with Ida Sherbourne Rentoul, is a collection of verses of childhood reminiscences, with the motif of a staircase on which the children play, symbolising the separation of childhood and adulthood. Childhood is farewelled in the last poem, on Mollie's wedding day.

RENTOUL, ANNIE RATTRAY (1883–1978), born Melbourne, taught at Presbyterian Ladies' College, Melbourne, from 1913 after graduating from the University of Melbourne. Rentoul was the first female to win the Exhibition in Classics, in 1902. She was the sister of Ida Rentoul Outhwaite, and her books were illustrated by Ida. She wrote *Mollie's Bunyip* (1904), *The Lady of the Blue Beads: Her Book, Being an Account of Her First Blue Moon Spent on Sun Island* (1908), *The Little Green Road to Fairyland* (1922) and *The Fairyland of Ida Rentoul Outhwaite: verses by Annie S. Rentoul: stories by Grenbry Outhwaite and Annie R. Rentoul* (1926). See also **Bunyips**; **Fairies**. The material which accompanied the Christmas pantomime productions of J.C. Williamson, *The Story of the Pantomime Humpty Dumpty: Specially Written for Little Ones* (1907) and *The Story of Peter Pan* (1908), illustrated with photographs from the stage production and her sister's illustrations, were developed by Annie Rentoul. She collaborated with the musician Georgette Peterson to produce *Bush Songs of Australia* *for Young and Old* (1910), which contains 'Kookaburra, kookaburra, sitting on a gumtree/High among the branches, up tip-top ...', the Kangaroo song, 'Old Bumpety Jumpety Hop and Go One/Was lying at ease on his side in the sun ...', both still familiar to many pre-school Australians. *More Australian Songs for Young and Old* (1913) and *Australia's Song of Empire* (1910) were also written in collaboration with Peterson. With Alfred Wheeler she wrote a children's cantata, *The Rose of Joy* (n.d.).

Research Collections in Australian Children's Literature can be found in the CBC: Victorian Branch collection, which includes almost all of the winners and Honour books of the Book of the Year Award; the Dromkeen Collection (q.v.); the Kapper Collection (q.v.); the Lindsay Shaw Collection (q.v.), the Lu Rees Archives (q.v.); the Museum of Australian Childhood (q.v.); the McLaren Collection at the University of Melbourne; the National Library of Australia and the various state libraries. There are also private collections, such as those of Judy Bensemann and Ken Pound in Melbourne, Ron Maria in Sydney, Maxine Walker in Perth, and Marcie Muir in Adelaide.

RICE, ESMÉE wrote *Quackleduck* (1947), illustrated by Elizabeth Paterson, a book for pre-school children about a charming duck which eats Grandpa's cabbage, wears a coat knitted by Auntie Bon, rides a bike and visits school. She also wrote *The Secret Family* (q.v., 1948) for older readers.

RICHARDSON, ROBERT (1850–1904), born Armidale, NSW, is regarded as the first Australian-born children's novelist. *The Boys of Springdale* (1875), *The Cold Shoulder* (1876), *Our Junior Mathematical Master* (1876) and *The Boys of Willoughby School* (1877) are early school stories with Australian settings. *Black Harry: or, Lost in the Bush* (1877) is set in the Blue Mountains of NSW. Jack dislikes Harry because Harry is a friend of Jack's sister, Anna. When Jack and Will become lost 'in the forest primeval', and must drink bird's blood for sustenance, they are found by Black Harry. The moral lesson is driven home: 'My feelings of gratitude and thankfulness were mingled with a keen sense of shame and remorse for the way in which I had acted towards him.' *A Little Australian Girl: or, The Babes in the Bush* (1881) draws on the same motif, in this case, the incident of the Duff children. See **Lost in the Bush**. *The Hut in the Bush: a Tale of Australian Adventure and other Stories* (1882), dedicated to Richardson's 'brother Alexander, in memory of our boyhood', begins with a story about the robbery of a store by bushrangers, told by Will Frankland. The hiding place of the bushrangers is revealed by the Chinese gardener, and they are captured by Will and Ralph Halloran. In another story, 'Tom Cuthbert's Chum', Joe is maligned by the schoolmaster until he redeems himself by rescuing Tom Cuthbert from drowning, and dies himself in the same accident. Richardson lived in London and Edinburgh during the 1870s and contributed to boys' magazines, including *Chums* and the *Boys' Own Paper*. His vigorous stories deal with school life, bush adventures, and rural life in general.

RICKARDS, DOROTHY (1919–), born Melbourne, has written poetry, plays, informational books and radio scripts. She worked with June Epstein, June Factor and Gwenda McKay on *Big Dipper: Stories, Poems, Songs and Activities for Young Children* (1980), *Big Dipper Rides Again: Stories, Poems, Songs and Activities for Young Children* (1982) and *Big Dipper Returns: Stories, Poems, Songs and Activities for Young Children* (1985), all illustrated by Alison Lester. She has written novels for younger readers, such as *A Kick in Time* (1991), which deals with drugs and domestic violence. Rickards has also contributed to reading schemes, such as Nelson's 'Australia File' series, for which she wrote *Festivals* (1984), illustrated by David Pearson, Rolf Heimann and John Nicholson.

RIDYARD, DAVID (1942–) has written *Our Grandfather* (1983), *Eat Your Carrots* (1983), *Australian Wildlife with Their Babies* (1984) and *Christmas* (1985). For *Koalas, Kites and Kangaroos* (1985) see **Alphabet Books**.

RISH, DAVID (1955–), born UK, has written *Sophie's Island* (1990), illustrated by Wendy Corbett. Sophie is 10 when her brother is stillborn, and grows to accept the tragedy in the chaotic household of her cousin Mike. See also **Death**. In *Detective Paste* (1991) Melissa, who has a hectic imagination, pursues Mr Williams. She believes he has killed someone, but the outcome is not what she expected.

River Kings, The (1966) by Max Fatchen, illustrated by Clyde Pearson, was Commended in the 1967 Book of the Year Awards. Shawn runs away from the farm he hates, to the Murray River, where he works on the *Lazy Jane*, a cargo riverboat. Its crew — Cap'n Elijah Wilson, Charlee the Chinese cook, Lord Eric Angus, Silent Sam and Praying Jack — are hard-working, but good company. In a series of amusing and exaggerated incidents, Shawn experiences near drowning, exciting races, and a hijacking, until the *Lazy Jane* is burnt by rivals and the crew go their separate ways. The riverboat trade is under threat from the railways, and Shawn is persuaded to stay on with the Thompsons, parents of his friend Mary. Fatchen's evocation of the times when the river served as a vital link between Australian States is impressive, leavened with a sense of fun. *Conquest of the River* (1970), also illustrated by Pearson, is its sequel. Once again Shawn has joined Cap'n Elijah, this time on the *River Queen*, where the crew has lost Angus, but gained Tiny the bargemaster. Shawn and the others fight off sharks, rout fish-thieves, rescue an old woman and her rocking chair and save a town from the flooding river. See also **Murray River**. The two novels were made into a four-part television series in 1991, written and produced by Rob George, directed by Donald Crombie, with Tamblyn Lord as Shawn and Bill Kerr as Cap'n Elijah.

River Murray Mary (1979) by Colin Thiele, illustrated by Robert Ingpen, was Commended in the 1980 Book of the Year Awards. Mary Baker's father is a soldier settler after World War I. Eleven-year-old Mary helps on the small vineyard, rows across the river for stores, make friends with Abel Stenross, captain of the paddle steamer, and observes nature with a sympathetic eye. When her reluctance to report a snake to her father leads to her mother's accident, the resourceful Mary must cross the dangerously flooded Murray River for help. See also **Murray River**.

Riverboat Crew, The (1978) by Andrew and Janet McLean was Commended in the 1979 Picture Book of the Year Awards. Aboard the *Alice*, Captain Bill and Gus the stoker argue about who is the most important person. Sam the cook merely smiles, but when Bill and Gus exchange roles, and bring on disaster, Sam is proved to be indispensable.

Roan Colt of Yamboorah, The (1966) by Reginald Ottley, illustrated by David Parry, was Commended in the 1967 Book of the Year Awards. See **By the Sandhills of Yamboorah** (1965).

Roaring 40, The (1963) by Nan Chauncy, illustrated by Annette Macarthur-Onslow, was Highly Commended in the 1964 Book of the Year Awards. It is the final book in the trilogy about the Lorenny family. Badge, Dad and an old mate of

Dad's, Vik Viking, set off for Port Davey to search for gold. They discover a wild boy, Ned, who has been abandoned on a lonely beach for some years. He is finally identified as a long-lost nephew of Old Harry, the hermit who appears in *Tiger in the Bush* (q.v., 1957). Ned is taken back to the valley to live with his uncle and go to school with Badge. The plot is unlikely, held together with a series of coincidences, although Chauncy's depiction of the wild child is poignant, and the misery which Badge experiences on his Uncle Link's farm and at school is vividly conveyed.

ROBERTS, BETH (1924–), born Tasmania, has written *The Little Lake Who Cried* (1976) illustrated by Max Angus, a parable of the history of the world, set around a lake. When the white man arrives he pollutes the lake, and the story ends with warning of ecological disaster. *The Wombat Who Couldn't See in the Dark* (1987), *The Upside-Down Bird* (1987) and *The Tasmanian Devil Who Couldn't Eat Meat* (1988) are about young animals suffering identity crises. *Flowers for Mother Mouse* (1989), illustrated by Carolyn Daly, describes the adventures of a mouse looking for a new home. In *The Magic Waterfall: a Tasmanian Tale of an Invisible Thylacine* (1990), illustrated by Jane Fenton, Winnie the Wombat helps Nenner become invisible so that he can find his way home without danger. See also **Animal Stories**. A novel for older readers, *Magpie Boy* (1989), is set in the early nineteenth century. Dreenee is an Aboriginal boy who is captured by a white family, learns their customs, and escapes with the help of the magpies, taking a servant girl with him. In *Manganinnie* (1979), illustrated by Joanne Roberts, Manganinnie is an elderly Tasmanian Aboriginal woman who is separated from her people during an attack by white settlers. She steals a white child, Tonytah (Joanna), as a companion, and wanders throughout her traditional territory.

Manganinnie portrays Tasmanian Aboriginal life with authenticity. It was made into a film in 1979 directed by John Honey.

ROBERTS, BETTY, see **Horse Stories**

ROBERTS, MARY (1914–), born UK, is the mother of the publisher Hilary McPhee. In *What a Birthday!* (1987), illustrated by Sue O'Loughlin for Macmillan's 'Southern Cross' series, Tina gets a baby sister for her present. Jacky's estranged father invites her to visit him for a beach holiday in *A Kind of Magic* (1989). Her unhappiness is relieved by a friendship with the dolphins Mummah and Sam. When there is a possibility that they will be kept in a marine park, Jacky's actions also resolve her antagonisms towards her new family. Detail on the life of the dolphin is well integrated into the novel. *Anna the Vanner* (1990) follows the fortunes of the Pickering family, who live in a caravan park after their business fails. At school, Anna confronts prejudice against itinerant families by teachers, librarians and the other students. Roberts creates multi-faceted characters, such as Anna herself, the eccentric Miss Lauderdale, and Anna's supportive mother.

ROBERTSON, GEORGE (1) (1825–98), born Glasgow, Scotland, and Samuel Mullen (q.v.), who had worked together in Dublin, emigrated to Australia in 1852. (E.W. Cole (q.v.) arrived the same day.) Robertson sold a case of books on the wharf to finance his bookselling ventures, which soon prospered. He became a leading bookseller, and in 1860 set up a shop at 69 (now 107) Elizabeth Street, Melbourne, and established branches in other states. The site later became Robertson & Mullens, and Angus & Robertson in 1960. The firm, George Robertson & Co., under Robertson's two sons, published over 600 titles, including many textbooks. *Santa Claus and a Sun-Dial: an Australian Christmas Fantasy* (1909) by E.S. Emerson, 'Arthur Ferres's' *His Cousin the Wallaby* (1896), and books by Tarella Quin Daskein were published by Geo. Robertson & Co.

ROBERTSON, GEORGE (2) (1860–1933), born Halstead, UK, came to Australia in 1882, where he was employed in the Sydney Branch of George Robertson (1), working with David Mackenzie Angus. The two set up Angus & Robertson (q.v.), publishers, in 1885.

Robertson & Mullens was set up in 1921 through the merger of George Robertson & Co. and Melville & Mullen, with C.H. Peters as general manager. 'Mullens stories for children' were paperbacks offered for children 'aged seven to eight' and 'ten to twelve' published by Robertson & Mullens. The firm was merged with Angus & Robertson in 1960, when, although adult publications continued to bear the Robertson & Mullens imprint, children's books were published by Angus & Robertson. In 1924 Robertson & Mullens organised the first children's book week in Melbourne.

ROBINSON, MOIRA (1933–), born Isleham, UK, bookseller, reviewer, and publisher's reader, edited *Readings in Children's Literature: Proceedings of the National Seminar on Children's Literature at Frankston State College 1975* (1977). *Make My Toenails Twinkle: The Complete Resource Book for Sharing Poetry with Children* (1989) contains poems and ideas for their use in the classroom. Robinson adapted Jim Trelease's *Read-Aloud Handbook* (1986) for Australian readers, and edited *Puffins for Parents* (1983) and *Good Book Guide to Children's Books* (1983) for Penguin.

ROBINSON, ROLAND (1913–), born County Clare, Ireland, poet and critic, came to Australia at the age of 9. He has had a close association with Aboriginal

People, and selected their stories for *Wandjina: Children of the Dreamtime; Aboriginal Myths & Legends* (q.v., 1968) and *The Nearest the White Man Gets: Aboriginal Narratives and Poems of New South Wales* (1989). See also **Aboriginal Dreaming Stories**.

ROC, MARGARET (1945–), born Stirling, Scotland, has written *Little Koala* (1989), illustrated by Deborah Brown, which has a koala drawing bizarre animals, as each bush animal says it is the most beautiful. See also **Animal Stories**. In *Oodles of Noodles* (1987), illustrated by Allan Stomann, a noodle freak discovers all the things he can do with noodles, such as knit them, create art with them, use them as fangs, and eat them.

'RODDA, EMILY' **(JENNIFER ROWE)** (1948–), born Sydney, has been an editor for Angus & Robertson and the *Australian Women's Weekly* and has written adult detective stories. She selected *More Poems to Read to Young Australians* (1971), illustrated by Tony Oliver, as Jennifer Rowe. Her novels for younger readers are fantasies. In *Something Special* (q.v., 1984), old clothes summon up their previous owners for Sam; *Pigs Might Fly* (q.v., 1986) is a fantasy about Rachel's quest to return to her own world; *The Best-Kept Secret* (q.v., 1988) takes Jo into her future. Another dimension is also explored in *Finders Keepers* (q.v., 1990). All are illustrated by Noela Young. *Crumbs!* (1990), illustrated by Kerry Argent, is told by Pete. When his 4-month-old sister, Ellie, eats a special biscuit she takes on the evil character of Kraak. Pete is blamed, and despite his efforts to tell his parents about the danger of the biscuits, he is not believed. The dilemma is resolved when the biscuit company itself changes the formula. 'Emily Rodda's' novels suggest that there are patterns in our lives, and her characters seek to find the whole behind the disparate parts of their universe.

Pigs Might Fly (1986) by Emily Rodda.
Illustrator: Noela Young

ROENNFELDT, ROBERT (1953–), born USA, came to Australia in 1955. Roennfeldt studied graphic design at the Gordon Institute, Geelong. He has illustrated *Tiddalick the Frog who Caused a Flood* (1980), an adaptation of the Aboriginal Dreaming story; *The Tie Olympics* (1987) by Edel Wignell; *Let's Go!* (1987) by Josephine Croser; *Ten Times Funny: 100 Hilarious Poems* (1990) by Michael Dugan; and *Good Morning, Isabel* (1990) by Nette Hilton. *A Day on the Avenue* (1983) is a wordless picture-book which chronicles the life of an Australian street, from dawn to dusk. In *What's that Noise?* (1987), written by his sister-in-law Mary Roennfeldt, George wakes at a strange noise. He searches the garden, and although he sees nothing, the reader identifies animals hidden on the page amid the dark greens and blues which provide an air of mystery. He has illustrated a humorous

religious series by Peter Thamm: *The Bald-headed, Bashful, Bow-legged, Baggy-Pantsed Brain Bug, The Legless, Egghead, Green Fluffy-Haired Monster, The Low-Drag, Single-Side-Band, Twin-Whiskered, Fleecy-Feathered Homing Duck* and *The Raucous, Underhand, Smooth-backed, Yellow Spotted Been-Beetle* (all 1988), published by Lutheran Publishing House. In *The Marmalade Cat* (1991) Maria and Paolo search for their cat, while the reader glimpses him in the background. In Lilith Norman's *The Paddock* (1992) he shows the transformations to the land as the ages pass.

'ROLAND, BETTY' (ELIZABETH MCLEAN) (1903–), born Kaniva, Victoria, has worked as a journalist and written novels and plays for stage and radio for adults and children. She wrote adaptations of classic stories for the ABC, including a serial based on the *Odyssey* for 'The Argonauts' (q.v.). Roland also contributed to the English magazine *Girl*. For her novels about Jamie, *The Forbidden Bridge* (1961), *Jamie's Discovery* (1963), *Jamie's Summer Visitor* (1964) and *Jamie's Other Grandmother* (1970), see **The Forbidden Bridge**. In *The Bush Bandits* (1966), illustrated by Genevieve Melrose, Ruth is kidnapped by animal-smugglers, and Martin and Geoff set out to rescue her, a task which involves braving a bushfire and an exciting chase across Sydney Harbour.

ROLAND, Mrs S. A. For *Rosalie's Reward: or, The Fairy Treasure* (1870) see **Fairies**.

ROLLS, ERIC C. (1923–), born Grenfell, NSW, poet and farmer, is the author of several books including the prize-winning *They All Ran Wild* (1969), and *A Million Wild Acres: 200 Years of Man and an Australian Forest* (1982). *Miss Strawberry Verses* (1978), illustrated by

Deborah Niland and originally published in the *Bulletin* and anthologies, contains humorous poems about the dreadful Miss Strawberry. Miss Strawberry's purse is a crocodile, and when she invites the shop-keepers to take their money 'The shop-keeper usually says, "No worry./Pay next month. I'm in no hurry."'

Romance. 'Now she was experiencing something else: her whole body was suf-fused with an ache, a kind of physical longing, so deep and strong that she couldn't quite believe is wasn't tactile or at least visible to the others. A great orange and yellow flame had burst alight inside her, eating her up, burning her alive. Why didn't he turn around and face her?' thinks Kelly, in Maureen McCarthy's *Ganglands* (1992). One hundred years before *Ganglands*, in *Seven Little Australians* (1894), Meg's passion is expressed in a sigh. When Meg sees Andrew Courtney, 'a handsome lad of eighteen', she 'blushed right up to her soft, pretty fringe every time he spoke to her and looked painfully conscious and guilty if he said anything at all complimentary to her'. Her greatest fear is the threat of a kiss: 'I do not like kissing at all', she writes to Courtney. In Leigh Bell's *Breakers on the Beach* (1926) Iris and Tom are in love: 'And the hands were raised from her lap until their palms felt the warm pressure of Tom's lips on them. "'Tom, you mustn't!" cried Iris, snatching them away. "Why? Don't you like it?" "Yes — no — I mean, it's not a question of liking", said Iris. "You ought not to do such things unless we were engaged." "Well, let's get engaged, and then I can do them and lots more besides."'

The romance has been considered suit-able reading material for adolescent girls since Samuel Richardson's *Pamela* (1740). Nineteenth-century Australian novels fol-lowed the pattern of courtship as the ful-filment of a girl's longings. The romance rather than its consummation is the focus of these novels. Richard Ernest Churchill Shann, as 'John Curfew', wrote *Lights Burning Bright, and All's Well: an Australian Idyll* (1894), a typical example. Mary Tempest is a poor girl who lives with her drunken father. Her honour is saved by the handsome sailor Tom Bowling, who comes home to promise her marriage just as she is dying. *A Little Aversion* (1910) by 'Tasman' describes the ups and downs of a romance set in Tasmania, between Jeannie Lascelles, who suffers from excessive good taste, and her cousin from England, Keith Cordey.

The impediments to the straightforward course of love are varied. In Marion Downes's *Flower o' the Bush* (1914) Dora rejects a faithful childhood sweetheart for a less worthy husband, by whom she has a child, before the true lovers are recon-ciled. Agatha Le Breton's *Dolour D'Arcy* (1915) is a romance where the problem is differing religions. Ethel and Lilian Turner, Vera Dwyer, Lillian Pyke, Constance Mackness and Louise Mack wrote romances where girls may have chosen unworthy suitors, but always came to their senses in time to save their hon-our. Nourma Handford's 'Carcoola' novels (1950–56) and Pixie O'Harris's later Poppy Treloar novels (1947–69) are romances where a predictable course is followed — boy meets girl, another boy or girl upsets the romance, and a reconcil-iation ends in the promise of marriage. Sexuality does not intrude into courtship.

Hesba Brinsmead and Ivan Southall kept the flame of romance alight. Clippie Nancarrow's modest affair with Bev in *Who Calls from Afar?* (1971) and *Echo in the Wilderness* (1972) and Matt's passion for Jo in *Matt and Jo* (q.v., 1973) or Sam's con-fusion in *What About Tomorrow?* (1977) are the most overt of the boy-meets-girl plots. Joyce Nicholson's *The Convict's Daughter* (1976) sets a romance against the difficul-ties of early settlement. A more complex analysis of the role of love is pursued by Ruth Park. The love that Abigail has for Judah in *Playing Beatie Bow* (q.v., 1980) teaches her to understand what love is about, enabling her to see her mother's point of view. Other writers such as Elisabeth MacIntyre in *It Looks Different when You Get There* (1978) and Max Fatchen in *Closer to the Stars* (1981) have a romance, but it is not the romance but the aftermath, the birth of a child, which dominates their novels.

In the late 1980s and early 1990s every writer was trying his or her hand at the short story romance. *State of the Heart: Stories about Love, Life and Growing Up* (1988), edited by Penny Matthews; *First Loves* (1989), edited by John Malone; *Absolutely Rapt* (1990); *The Blue Dress* (1991), edited by Libby Hathorn; *Bittersweet* (1992), edited by Toss Gascoigne, all have stories by well-known writers such as Gillian Barnett, Michael Dugan, Barbara Hanrahan, Nette Hilton, Tony Lintermans, Bron Nicholls, Debra Oswald, Jenny Pausacker, Mary Pershall, Gillian Rubinstein, Colin Thiele, Nadia Wheatley, Tim Winton and many others. Robin Klein looks at the effect of a romance on the friendship between two girls in *Laurie Loved Me Best*. Nigel and Caron Krauth's *Sin Can Can* (1987) traces the romance of Ashlie Fallowfield and Rai.

The advent of 'Dolly' fiction in the early 1990s brought nearly sixty titles dealing with romance. The series arose from the success of *Dolly* magazine, a periodical for teenage readers, and was modelled on the 'Sweet Dreams' and 'Sweet Valley High' series popular in the USA. 'Dolly' romances were written by leading writers, sometimes using pseudonyms. The titles frankly appeal to the thirst for romance: *Who do You Love?*, *Boys Next Door*, *My Sister's Boyfriend*, *Hungry for Love*, *Who Said Love was Easy?*, *Too Much Love*, *Loving Pen Pals*, and the plots generally follow the accepted pattern of the romance, although there is the occasional departure from formula. 'Jaye Francis's' *Love or Money* (1990) has a lesbian romance, *Bigger and Better* (1990) by Mary Forrest has a fat heroine,

and Amanda Graham's *Who Said Love was Easy?* (1989) has a Japanese hero. 'Hot Pursuit' is a series of novels which combine romance and thriller. *Melissa* and *Rebecca* (both 1991) by 'Jaye Francis', and *Louise* and *Franca* (both 1991) by Merrilee Moss, are about friends who become involved in such episodes as a stolen painting, a burglary or a missing person.

The mainstream romance has become more openly concerned with sexual aspects of romance, and is less linked to courtship and marriage. David McRobbie's *Mandragora* (1991) is an example. Adam's response to Catriona is physical as well as emotional, but their relationship is based on common interests and concern for each other, and there is no suggestion that it will be the map of their futures.

ROSE, MADELINE (1932–), born Swinton, UK, came to Australia in 1960. She has written *The Secret of Shelter Bay* (1982) and *Dragon on the Mountain* (1987), illustrated by Mary Davy, in which the Blair children discover a dragon's egg. The magical Granny Enders in *Witch Over the Water* (1980) and *Witch in the Bush* (1985), both illustrated by Trevor Weekes, travels with the Pitt family to Australia, and teaches the children water-divining, rainmaking and other magic.

ROSE, RONALD (1920–), born Sydney, has written two historical novels for children. *Drummer Crispin* (1980) is set in the very early days of the colony. See **First Fleet**. *Five Honest Guineas* (1982) takes a year in the life of Meg O'Brien. It is 1852, and Meg and her drunken father Paddy, his friend Tuppeny Burden, and the enigmatic Foxcroft Grubscrew, alias 'Urchin', leave Sydney in search of gold in the Araluen Valley. Over the year Meg comes to the painful realisation that Paddy is a hopeless drunk, that gold cannot be found in every pan washed from the creek, and that Urchin prefers to live a gypsy life. *Inoke Sails the South Seas* (1966) and *Ngari the Hunter* (1968) are books for younger children describing the lifestyle of children in the Pacific.

ROUGHLEY, EDNA, poet and novelist, wrote *Ellice of Ainslie* (1947). It describes the experiences of Ellice at school, on holiday and at home, and her affection for her beautiful school friend Madelon, which suggests a passion rarely touched on. See also **Girls**. *Our Songs* (1952) has eighteen songs with music by Mary Moulton, including 'The Kangaroo', 'Golden Wattle', 'Dew Frock' and 'In the Toy Shop'. 'Captain Toothbrush' promotes dental hygiene: 'Teeth are ivory castles/So I must keep mine white./Captain Toothbrush helps me brush/Each morning and at night./I defend my castles/Against the enemy./Bristles are the army/They're fighting just for me.' *The Locked Door* (1948) is an adult novel about a mission in New Guinea, and *Remembered Joys* (1948) a collection of her adult poetry.

ROUGHSEY, DICK (1924–85), born near Mornington Island, whose skin name, Goobalathaldin, is translated as 'rough sea', was a hunter, fisherman, cattleman, sailor and handyman, and the first chairman of the Aboriginal Arts Board, in 1976. Roughsey was assisted in his painting career by Percy Trezise with whom he

Gidja (1984) by Dick Roughsey and Percy Trezise

collaborated for twenty-four years. Roughsey's first books were *The Giant Devil Dingo* (q.v., 1973) and *The Rainbow Serpent* (q.v., 1975). Moonbi and his sister Leealin, and their parents Warrenby and Margara, appear in two stories from the Yalanji people of Cape York, *The Quinkins* (q.v., 1978) and *Turramulli the Giant Quinkin* (q.v., 1982), by Roughsey and Percy Trezise. Further collaborations with Trezise produced *Banana Bird and the Snake Men* (1980), about how the birds outwitted the snakes; *The Magic Firesticks* (1983), a story from the Yalanji people which tells how Bandicoot and Curlew learnt the secret of making fire by twirling sticks; *Gidja* (1984), a legend from Cape York Peninsula about the origins of the moon and the morning and evening stars; and *The Flying Fox Warriors* (1985), about how the Bird people defeat the Joonging, or Flying Fox people, with the help of the friendly Quinkins. *The Turkey and the Emu* (1978) was a story told by Roughsey's wife Labamu and recounted by Ted Egan, about why the Turkey has a small family and the Emu cannot fly. Roughsey and Trezise's retellings of traditional stories were among the first picture-books to present Aboriginal culture to children. The graphic storytelling and pictures, which depict a wide range of Australian landscapes, ensure an enduring appeal. A video, one of the 'Storymakers' series, has been produced on Roughsey's collaboration with Percy Trezise. His autobiography is *Moon and Rainbow: the Autobiography of an Aboriginal* (1971).

'Round the Twist' is a series of half-hour videotapes produced in 1989 by the Australian Children's Television Foundation, and written by Paul Jennings. Volume 1 contains 'Skeleton on the Dunny', 'Birdsdo', 'A Good Tip for Ghosts', 'The Cabbage Patch Fib', and 'Spaghetti Pig Out'. Volume 2 contains 'The Gum Leaf War', 'Santa Claws', 'Wunderpants' and 'Lucky Lips'. Volume 3 contains 'Know All', 'The Copy', 'Without My Pants' and 'Lighthouse Blues'. The series was in thirteen parts, directed by Esben Storm, Steve Jodrell and Mark Lewis. The book of the series, *Round the Twist* (1990), won YABBA for Older Readers, the COOL Award and the KROC Award in 1991. It has stories, biographies, interviews with the actors, scripts, comments and anecdotes by the author.

ROWAN, ELLIS (MARIAN ELLIS ROWAN) (1848–1922), born Melbourne, was a painter of flowers, birds and butterflies, for which she won a gold medal at the 1880 Melbourne Exhibition, and first prize at the 1888 Centennial Exhibition. Rowan travelled extensively throughout Australia and Papua New Guinea, and completed over 3000 paintings during her lifetime, 900 of which are held at the National Library of Australia. Her only children's book was *Bill Baillie; his Life and Adventures* (1908), also published as *Bill Baillie: the Story of a Pet Bilboa*. Bill the bilboa is found by Tom on his way to Laverton, WA, and the small animal is raised by a painter, Tabitha, who takes him to Melbourne. It is decorated with Rowan's delicate and accurate pictures of the bilboa, and WA flora. Rowan also illustrated the cover of Dorothea Vautier's *The Story of Teddy Koala* (?1931).

ROWE, JEANNETTE (1954–), illustrated *Scallywag* (1990), about a cat who is 'Orlando' to Louis and Marcella, 'Darryl' to Winsome, 'Tubby' to Bert, and 'Brutus' to Sylvia and her children. One day he fails to arrive for his meals, and his searchers discover the trick the cat has been playing. Although he has been exposed, Scallywag has yet another trick up his sleeve. Rowe's design uses the white of the page to advantage, with effective characterisations of both the cat and his 'owners'. *Teacher-Eater* (1991) by Paul Jennings is illustrated with richly coloured dragons with fiery breaths and kindly expressions.

ROWE, JENNIFER, see **'RODDA, EMILY'**

ROWE, RICHARD (1828–79), born Doncaster, UK, came to Australia in 1853 where he lived for fourteen years, working as a journalist with the *Sydney Morning Herald* during the 1850s. Rowe was a member of the circle surrounding the literary patron Nicol Drysdale Stenhouse. He contributed to Frank Fowler's literary journal, the *Month*, and some of the material he wrote for it is included in *Peter Possum's Portfolio* (1858), dedicated to Stenhouse. As 'Edward Howe' he wrote *The Boy in the Bush* (1869), first published as a serial in *Good Words*. Each chapter describes an incident in the life of Harry and Sydney Lawson. The Lawsons deal with bushrangers, snakes, and lost children with courage and humour, and details such as life on the goldfields and the influence of and attitudes to the Chinese are presented in a direct, often ironic style. Rowe subscribes to the superiority of the native-born Australian over the immigrant: 'They're a queer lot the blackfellows … but they're a long sight better than the new chums — they were born in the colony just like us. A blackfellow can ride like a native but those Englishmen look so scared when a horse begins to buck.' He enlarges on his views later: 'If Englishmen can't stand our climate they oughtn't to come to it and then expect us to pay them wages for shirking their work … your English officers that you think such heavy swells at home are glad to get us to employ them as mailguards and milkmen and things like that.' Harry is aggressively nationalistic: 'Anyhow we're a deal better than the English … We shouldn't have any scamps in the colony if it wasn't for the lot they sent us out from home …'

Roughing it in Van Diemen's Land (1880) by 'Edward Howe' is an account of wealthy pioneers, the Normans, who fight off the bushranger Strike-a-Light, interspersing their battles with kangaroo-hunts and exploring. Two chapters deal with William Buckley and his escape from the Collins settlement in Victoria, and the Black War in Tasmania. Rowe is often critical of the colonial role of Britain, and gives his characters some ethical predicaments in their treatment of the Aboriginal People. See also **Hobart**.

The Gold Diggers (1920) is a collection of three stories by Rowe. The first, *Fred Leicester: or, The Southern Cross and Charles's Wain* originally published in 1889, is set in Australia. Fred, a young Englishman, acquires 'colonial experience', finds a fortune on the diggings, and returns with it to England to marry 'his Helen'. See also **Melbourne**; **Sydney**.

ROY, THOMAS ALBERT (1909–), born Durham, UK, emigrated to Australia in 1925. For his two books about Jimmy Brent and his family, *The Curse of the Turtle* (1977) and *The Vengeance of the Dolphin* (1980) see **The Curse of the Turtle**.

Royal Flying Doctor Service, which was first developed by John Flynn, then superintendent of the NT Mission area, to provide medical assistance to remote communities, has provided much copy for children's books. John Flynn appears as a character in Phyllis Power's *Under Australian Skies* (1955) and *Nursing in the Outback* (1959), as a saintly figure doing 'the Lord's work' at a remote station, or as an old man pleading at Scots Church, Collins Street, Melbourne, for money for the 'Mantle of Safety'. Barry Brown's *The Flying Doctor: John Flynn and the Flying Doctor Service* (1960) is a factual account written as a narrative, with much sensible information and recognition of the often mundane medical cases which the doctors must attend.

The romance of flying and the glamour of the medical profession are a heady mix. In *The Flying Doctor Mystery* (1954) by James Downie, Dr Stephen Rowe is misled by phoney radio calls, and holed up for days with a wrong-headed patient. Elisabeth Beresford wrote two books about the service, *The Flying Doctor Mystery* (1958) and *The Flying Doctor to the Rescue* (1964), part of a series of adventures featuring Vicky and Peter Lofts. The first title takes them to Australia where they are responsible for revealing a spy who hides rolls of film in chocolates and confuses his pursuers by using an aeroplane similar to the Flying Doctor's. In *Doctor with Wings* (q.v., 1960) by Allan Aldous, there is a chapter on John Flynn, and the dependence of remote communities on the service is made clear. Dr Locke has come to Australia to join the service. Michael Noonan's *Flying Doctor* (1961), illustrated by R.E. Hicks, introduced a series which used the service as a background to adventure. The books are set in the fictitious Mustard Creek, and Drs Jeremy Janes and Saxon, Nurse Barbara Wright, Monty Marsh the radio operator, Stefan the mechanic and Copper Kennedy, the pilot, rescue stockmen, cure laryngitis, save injured prospectors from underground tunnels, and generally protect the outback inhabitants from berserk opal-diggers and spies, often enlisting the help of local boys and girls. Other titles include *Flying Doctor and the Secret of the Pearls* (1962), *Flying Doctor on the Great Barrier Reef* (1962), *Flying Doctor Shadows the Mob* (1964), *Flying Doctor Hits the Headlines* (1965) and *Flying Doctor Under the Desert* (1969). Noonan developed the original 'Flying Doctor' television series in Australia and Britain.

Royal Readers, published by Nelson, were used in Victorian schools from 1877, supplanting the *Irish Readers* (q.v.), and supplied to Victorian schools on the basis of one book for each three pupils. They were graded by age and interest level and were less religious in emphasis than their predecessors, although still pious in tone. Australian editions began to appear from 1879 and in 1886 new and enlarged editions were produced to match the widening of the school curriculum.

RUBINSTEIN, GILLIAN (1942–), born Potten End, UK, came to Australia in 1973. In her novels for older readers she has looked at alienation. The children in *Space Demons* (q.v., 1986) and its sequel *Skymaze* (1989) are drawn into the centre of a computer game. There are demons within and without in these novels — Andrew and Mario are at odds with their families; Elaine and Ben have difficulties but are much more at peace with themselves. Similarly, in *Answers to Brut* (q.v., 1988) and *Melanie and the Night Animal* (q.v., 1988), fears and insecurities must be confronted before they can be defeated. *Beyond the Labyrinth* (q.v., 1988) uses the alien, Cal, to show Brenton and Victoria how to cope with their solitariness. See also **Death**; **Families**; **Science Fiction**. *At Ardilla* (1991) is a portrait of an emotional girl caught between primary and secondary school. She finds that she must share her summer holiday at the beloved 'Ardilla' with a family to whom she takes an instant dislike. Jen's melancholy is associated with the house itself, as her intense hatred of Sally pushes her towards tragedy. In *Galax-Arena* (1992) Joella, Peter and Liane are apparently kidnapped and taken to another planet to perform as slave-acrobats for the Vexa.

Flashback: the Amazing Adventures of a Film Horse (1990) is a comedy and adventure story. Antony and a group of stunt men — and the remarkable horse — foil a vain (and shady) movie star. Rubinstein has also compiled two collections, *After Dark: Seven Tales to Read at Night* (1988) and *Before Dawn: More Tales to Read at Night* (1988), mystery and adventure stories from notable writers. Her picture-book *Dog In, Cat Out* (1991), illustrated by Ann James, chronicles a family's busy day. *Squawk and Screech* (1991), illustrated by Craig Smith, are two lorikeets cared for by the local bird-woman, who become heroes when a burglar breaks into the house. Rubinstein has a capacity to capture some of the terrors and miseries of childhood, such as Melanie's fear of the unknown, Brenton's fear of the nuclear holocaust, or Jen's turmoil as she moves beyond childhood. Her books carry her vision of the world, its possibilities and its dangers.

RUHEN, OLAF (1911–89), born Dunedin, NZ, was a farmer, gold-prospector, sailor, airman, journalist and explorer. He came to Australia in 1947. Ruhen has written novels, short stories and documentary pieces for adults, and two books for young people. *Corcoran's the Name* (1956), illustrated by Jennifer Tuckwell, is a series of episodes in the life of Bob Corcoran, who leaves the care of his brother when he turns 16 to make his own way, travelling through the Centre with his horses, sleeping under the stars, and learning from anyone who has the skill to teach him. Sometimes he is at hand to help someone in trouble, often he is alone. The limitless horizons of the dry country are evoked in laconic prose, and the excitement of droving cattle through an unforgiving environment is caught. *The Day of the Diprotodon* (1976), illustrated by Peter Pavey, is an imaginative account of the life of a family of diprotodons, the ancient beasts which inhabited Lake Callabonna. Ruhen relates their demise at the end of the Ice Age, brought into focus by Pavey's powerful grey illustrations.

Rummage (1981) by Christobel Mattingley, illustrated by Patricia Mullins, was Commended in the Book of the Year Awards and won the Junior Book of the Year Awards in 1982. Septimus Portwine runs a second-hand stall at a market. The other stall-holders complain about his mess, but when he is bullied into tidying it up nobody will buy his goods and he is unhappy. When Mr Portwine asserts himself, business, friends and happiness return. Mullins's combination of collage and humorous caricature appears against the busy background of an inner-London market.

'RUSSELL, ARTHUR', see **GOODE, ARTHUR RUSSELL**

RUSSELL, HEATHER (1955–) has written a study of the folklore of children, *Play and Friendships in a Multicultural Playground* (1986). *Carmen Out to Play!: a Collection of Children's Playground Games* (1989), illustrated by Peter Viska, describes how to play Chasey, Skippy, Hopscotch, Pencil and Paper Games, Ball Games, and their many variants. *Toodaloo Kangaroo* (1991) is a record and a book illustrated by Ewan Cameron, another collection of playground songs and rhymes.

RUSSELL, MARY ANNETTE VON ARNHIM, Countess (1866–1941), born Sydney, used the pseudonym 'Elizabeth'. When her first husband Count Von Arnhim died she supported their five children with her writing. She later married the second Earl Russell. *The April Baby's Book of Tunes: With the Story of How They Came to be Written* (1900) is set in Germany, and is the last book which Kate Greenaway illustrated.

RYAN, LAWRIE (1928–), born North Adelaide, was the Queensland State Librarian from 1970 to 1988. In *A Boy Called Tully* (1977), illustrated by Genevieve Melrose, Tully, lonely and cruelly treated, is saved by a horse-breaker, McCabe, who writes him a letter. The Gunner refuses to read him the letter, so Tully runs away, breaking the control which the Gunner has over him. For *Toog's Island* (1979) see **Adventure Stories**. In *The Hole in the Forest* (1981), illustrated by Bron Nicholls, Little Nose the wombat finds her missing father. Ryan also edited *Turns of Phrase: Young Queensland Writers* (1988) with Ross Clark.

S

SALLIS, HELEN has illustrated *Show and Tell* (1974), *Lizard Log* (1975) and *The Long Walk* (1976) by Christobel Mattingley; a new edition of *Gloop the Bunyip* (1962) in 1970 and *Thiele Tales: Three Long Stories for Children* (1980) by Colin Thiele; *Jeedarra Country* (1971) by James Preston; and *North to the Isa* (1971) by Una Rothwell.

SALMON, MICHAEL (1949–), born Wellington, NZ, came to Australia in 1966. He is a naive painter, stage designer and author. He has written over eighty children's books, including the Alexander Bunyip books after a program he created for ABC television, 'Alexander's Afternoon'. In *Brother Bert Comes to Stay* (1981), Bert is Alexander Bunyip's younger brother from Queensland. He constantly compares Alexander's billabong to his own more salubrious home, but when he tries to steal Kevin the Koala's opals, Eric the Cockatoo and Bruce the Platypus foil his plans. In *The Monster That Ate Canberra: a Book for the Younger Generations of Canberra* (1972), with photographs by Peter McKee, Alexander eats the National Library, the old Parliament House and other landmarks until he is sentenced to life in the zoo. *The Monster Who Ate Australia* (q.v., 1986) is about Borra the Boggabri, who also has a terrible appetite. Other monster books include *Son of the Monster: a Story of Canberra in the Year 2022* (1973), in which Ralph returns to Canberra, a polluted space-age city, and saves it by eating the smog; *The Little Monster Book: Rhymes for all Monsters* (1989), which has simple verses about monsters in various occupations, from playing netball to space-travelling; and

Grunt Goes to School (1988). Grunt is a small monster who anticipates school with misgiving, but enjoys himself when he gets there. *The Great Tasmanian Tiger Hunt* (1986) has Colonel Housfield-Smythe in search of a thylacine, and although there is one hidden on each page, his efforts fail. In *The Dream Machine* (1987) Jonathan and Bear nearly cause disaster with Grandfather's magical machine. *Where Elephants Go at Night: a Book for Bedtime* (1987) describes how elephants eat curry, go to the movies and nightclubs, or, if they are babies, go to bed. Other series by Salmon are his 'Animal Antics' series, his series about dinosaurs, such as *Glub the Baby Dinosaur* (1989) and *Under the Volcano* (1989), and his 'Junior Detective' series. Salmon uses satire and exaggerated characters in his popular books for younger readers.

SAMMON, STELLA, born Sydney, has written *The Lucky Stone* (1969), which explores the life of an Aboriginal girl, Quei, who decides to stay on with her white benefactors. See also **Aboriginal People in Children's Fiction**. In *Call Him Muddy* (1980) Robert finds a troublesome brumby foal, which reprieves itself by saving the family from a fire. In *Nifty the Sugar Glider* (1981) Nifty overcomes James's fear of animals.

SAMUEL, HELEN JO (1909–81), born Adelaide, edited the children's page of the Adelaide *Advertiser* and wrote for the ABC. *A Saddle at Bontharambo* (1950), illustrated by Cordelle Samuel, relates the journey of the Docker family from NSW to Victoria, in the steps of Major Mitchell.

Mary Docker's account of her childhood and her Aunt Spencer's diary provided the framework, characters and main incidents in the book. She also wrote *The New Australians* (1958) and the biographies *Wild Flower Hunter, the Story of Ellis Rowan* (1961) and, with Enid Moodie Heddle, *Boy on a Horse: the Story of Adam Lindsay Gordon* (1957).

SANDS, JOHN (1818–73), born Sandhurst, England, arrived in Sydney in 1837 where he established a retail stationery business. He moved into publishing and produced almanacs, directories, gazetteers, greeting cards and children's books. He went into partnership with Dougal McDougall in Melbourne in 1862, a partnership which was disbanded at his death, with the Sands family operating the Sydney branch and the McDougall family operating in Melbourne. Sands's son, Robert, assumed the business, which remained in the family until the 1950s. Sands published games, such as Snakes and Ladders, and the Ginger Meggs annuals from 1924, and in 1931 an early series of alphabet and nursery rhyme and novelty shape books, 'The Sunny South Series of Australian Children's Books', which included *Tiny Toddlers' A.B.C.* by Edgar A. Holloway and *The Magic Billabong* by Thomas E. Grattan-Smith. Sands's high-quality production and design of Leslie Rees's animal stories, under the guidance of the manager, Maurice Cadsky, showed to advantage the illustrations of Walter Cunningham. *The Australia Book* (q.v., 1952) by Eve Pownall exemplifies the publisher's attention to quality. Other authors and illustrators published by Sands were Margaret Senior, Peggy Barnard, Kathleen Basser, Jane Ada Fletcher, Leila Pirani, Ina Watson, Olive Mason, Noreen Shelley and Elaine Haxton.

SARGENT, GEORGE ETELL (?1808–83) wrote *Frank Layton, an Australian Story* (1865) which was published by the Religious Tract Society, and first appeared in the *Leisure Hour* in 1854. Frank's father has died, leaving no inheritance, so he and a farm labourer, Simeon Barnes, decide to emigrate. They travel from Sydney, making their way to a station where they each find work. Frank brings a whiff of civilisation to the bush, accomplished through washing the blankets in the rough hut he is forced to share, making the chimney draw properly and having his hair cut. Bush conveniences are compared with the 'cultivated taste of a highly polished life'. Sargent states that the novel was designed to describe faithfully 'the lights and shadows of emigrant life in that country at the most eventful period in its history', and 'lift up a warning voice concerning the dire temptations and miseries to which young and friendless women are exposed ... and to show the profligacy ... by which young men of uncertain principles may speedily be hurried on to ruin'. Frank and Simeon are made of stern stuff, and far from ruin, they find their fortunes on the goldfields, and settle on the land. Sargent never visited Australia. See also **Melbourne**.

SAXBY, HENRY MAURICE (1924–) teacher, library advisor and academic, wrote *A History of Australian Children's Literature: 1841–1941* (1969) and *A History of Australian Children's Literature: 1941–1970* (1971), which began as an academic thesis. The history is continued in *The Proof of the Puddin': Australian Children's Literature 1970–1990* (1993). He was the first national president of the CBC, and has promoted the introduction of courses in children's literature in academic institutions. He has edited *Through Folklore to Literature* (1979), papers from an IBBY conference, and *Growth Through Literature* (1980), papers presented at a one-day seminar held at the Kuring-gai College of Advanced Education (University of Technology, Sydney). *Give Them Wings: the Experience of Children's Literature* (1987), edited with Gordon

Winch, is a further collection of papers on children's books. He has produced two books about heroes. In *The Great Deeds of Superheroes* (1989), illustrated by Robert Ingpen, Saxby retells Greek, Sumerian, Scandinavian, biblical, Anglo-Saxon, French and Spanish hero tales for young readers. The deeds of Perseus, Heracles, Jason, Gilgamesh, Sigurd, Moses, Beowulf, Roland, Cuchulain and others are recreated to remind the young reader of the need for courage as well as intelligence. Saxby's introduction points out the many common characteristics of the tales, such as the quest, the talisman and the reward. Its companion volume, *The Great Deeds of Heroic Women* (1990), also illustrated by Ingpen, has accounts of women from a diversity of cultures, including Athena, Judith, Scheherazade, Boadicea, Lady Godiva, and Mary Bryant. He compiled *The All Over Australia Joke Book* (1989) and *The All Over Australia Riddle Book* (1989), illustrated by Randy Glusac, and has contributed titles to Methuen's 'Dimensions' reading scheme, many with Glenys Smith. *Challenges* (1986), compiled by Saxby and Smith and illustrated by David Pearson, has excerpts from well-known overseas and Australian children's novels. *If Pigs Could Fly* (1987), illustrated by Terry Denton, is a collection of stories compiled with Glenys Smith. He wrote *Teaching Literature to Adolescents* (1988) with Valerie Hoogstad, and with Glenys Smith he has compiled *First Choice: a Guide to the Best Books for Australian Children* (1991). *Russell and the Star Shell* (1990), illustrated by Astra Lacis, is a picture-book in which Russell and his grandfather search for a perfectly shaped star shell as a secret present for Grandma.

Maurice Saxby has exerted a major influence over children's books in Australia. His account of the genre involved primary research, and its publication broke new ground in literary history. His dedication and commitment to Australian children's authors and illustrators has been an important influence on community attitudes to books for children. He was awarded the Dromkeen Medal in 1983.

SAXBY, JOYCE BONIWELL (1923–64), born Tasmania, was a librarian in Tasmania, NZ, at the Toronto Boys' and Girls' House, and at the National Library in Canberra. In 1963 she became the first children's book editor appointed in Australia, to Angus & Robertson. For *One Hundred Poems Chosen for Children* (1967) see **Poetry**. *The Magic of Verse* (1970) is a selection from this work made by Carol Odell.

SAYCE, CONRAD HARVEY (1888–1935), born Hereford, UK, was an architect by profession but also wrote adventure stories, sometimes using the pseudonym 'Jim Bushman'. *In the Musgrave Ranges* (1922), illustrated by Fred Leist, is an account of the adventures of Saxon Stobart and Rodger Vaughan, who travel to Oodnadatta (partly by camel), are attacked by 'wild savages', and discover a valuable goldmine. Similar plots are found in *The Golden Valley* (1924), illustrated by M. Coller, set at 'Mentone Downs' cattle station, and *The Valley of a Thousand Deaths* (1925), illustrated by W.E. Wightman, set at 'Narrawingi' Station. *The Splendid Savage: a Tale of the North Coast of Australia* (1927), illustrated by Victor Cooley, is a Robinsonade, in which Duncan and Ballanda exist on the shores of the Gulf of Carpentaria. Other titles include *Golden Buckles* (1920) and *Comboman* (1934). Sayce's stories are Australian 'Westerns', full of near-death escapes, fine horsemanship, submissive or threatening Aboriginal People and treasure for the white men.

SCHOLES, KATHERINE (1959–), born Tanzania, moved to Tasmania when she was 10, where she lived until 1981. She has been a teacher, and for a time worked at the Flinders Island school. Her concern for the environment pervades her three novels, *The Boy and the Whale* (1985), *The Landing: a Night of Birds* (1987) and *The Blue Chameleon* (1989), all illustrated by David Wong. In *The Boy and the Whale* Sam fights for the life of a stranded Pygmy Sperm Whale, against two men who want its teeth. Bass Strait is again the setting for the mystical story, *The Landing: a Night of Birds*. A flight of mutton birds, or shearwaters, take shelter in Old Joe's boat shed, where the birds speak to Annie, his granddaughter, recalling their legendary past. The story is interspersed with descriptions of their experiences during their flight from the Aleutians, with references to the birds of poetry and drama. In *The Blue Chameleon* Beni, from the ancient tribe of Ish-Mahel, longs to search for his lost twin, Ziad, but has been sent to Australia to avoid capture. When he stows away, he finds himself in Antarctic waters, where he is befriended by a scientist who discovers a plant which will survive in the desert. Scholes's picture of a confused boy with little English is convincing. As her themes become more complex, Scholes retains her passion for conservation, and her ability to create tangible settings, enhanced by the atmospheric illustrations of David Wong. *Peacetimes* (1989), illustrated by Robert Ingpen, suggests the necessities for peace, such as food, freedom from fear and prejudice, and the ways we can learn to get along with others. 'Peace is something that lives, grows, spreads. And needs to be looked after.' Scholes looks at the relationship between 'humankind and wild life' and how the changing moods of land, sea and sky are reflected in character.

School Magazine was established by the NSW Education Department in 1916, edited by Stephen Henry Smith. Doris Chadwick began working on the magazine in 1922, and was the editor from 1950 to 1959. The early work of writers such as Ella McFadyen, Doris Chadwick, Lilith Norman, Lydia Pender and Patricia Wrightson first appeared in the *School Magazine*. It has had a distinguished editorial succession. Chadwick was followed by Noreen Shelley, Patricia Wrightson, Lilith Norman, Duncan Ball, Kath Hawke, Anna Fienberg and Jonathan Shaw. *School Magazine Stories* (1967) and *A Puddin' Rich and Rare* (1992) contain reprints of stories and illustrations from the magazine. In the 1980s it was issued in four parts: 'Countdown', 'Blast Off', 'Orbit' and 'Touchdown'.

School Paper was established by Charles Long in Victoria in 1896, the name also given to the Tasmanian and Queensland magazines for schoolchildren. The Queensland version adapted the *School Paper* by adding local material. WA also used the Victorian *School Paper*, and later developed its own version. The magazine presented excerpts from Australian and overseas literature, poetry, history and geography, and advice on things to do and make. Every festival was taken up with enthusiasm, from Christmas to the Queen's Birthday, frequently accompanied by the words and music of an appropriate song. Each month every child in the State system received a copy of the magazine, the mainstay of reading before the advent of school libraries. The Victorian *School Paper* ceased publication in the 1970s, and *Comet*, *Explore*, *Challenge* and *Pursuit* were produced by the Victorian Ministry of Education.

School Stories. The imaginary landscape of school, a microcosm of real life, has featured in children's books since Tom won his victory over Flashman, and was himself reformed by the morally pure George Arthur in Thomas Hughes's *Tom Brown's Schooldays* (1857). Twenty years later, between 1875 and 1877, Robert Richardson's stories about boys' schools in Australia appeared, *The Boys of Springdale* (1875), *The Cold Shoulder* (1876), *Our Junior Mathematical Master* (1876) and *The*

Boys of Willoughby School (1877), the first of a long line of local additions to the genre. Hughes's novel was set at Rugby, the famous English 'public' school, and following the tradition of the English school story, P.D. McCormick's *The Four School Mates, an Australian Tale of Misfortune and Success* (1896) is set in a Sydney private school. Their education is hardly the issue, however, as the boys spend much of their time arguing about the characteristics of specific races and the need for temperance, abstinence, church attendance and religion. By contrast, Louise Mack's *Teens: a Story of Australian Schoolgirls* (q.v., 1897) is set in a state high school.

The remote nature of much of the Australian inland, however, required the institution of the boarding school. 'Miriam Agatha' looks at a convent boarding school in *Nellie Doran: a Story of Australian Home and School Life* (1915), and Mary Grant Bruce's *Dick* (1918) describes Dick Lester's first days at Melbourne Church of England Boys' Grammar School, complete with bullying, fags, fights, midnight feasts, schoolboy slang and endless sport. Eustace Boylan's *The Heart of the School* (1919) is based on Xavier College, Melbourne, and Alice Guerin Crist's *Go It! Brothers!!* (1929) is set in St Mary's Christian Brothers College. In the boys' school stories, school spirit takes precedence over academic success, and being a 'sport' is the touchstone of a true 'white' man.

Constance Mackness pays greater attention to the philosophy of education, so that her novels are less about sport and the school spirit and more about how school should develop the whole individual, a philosophy put forward in *Miss Pickle: the Story of an Australian Boarding School* (1924) and *The Glad School* (1927). Mary Grant Bruce considers the reforming role of good teachers in *Gray's Hollow* (1914), as Horace and Thelma Densham are confronted with their own superficiality at a small bush day school. Writing in the same period, Lillian Pyke based a series of

school stories on Wesley College, Melbourne, including *Max the Sport* (1916), *Jack of St. Virgil's* (1917), *A Prince at School* (1919) and *The Best School of All* (1921). Pyke's novels show school as a place where boys of good breeding are shaped to take their place as possible members of the Melbourne Club. D. Lindsay Thompson's two novels set at Sydney Grammar, *Blue Brander* (1927) and *The Gang on Wheels* (1930), are not at all concerned with breeding. Blue and his mates have no snobbery, lots of rough and tumble, and a dry humour.

During the 1940s Dora Joan Potter had girls who unmasked spies and saved younger children from early deaths in a series about 'Winterton', a girls' version of Pyke's boys' school, providing all the accoutrements of an English Public School story — Prefects, Senior Girls, Removes, Houses, sport, and much non-Catholic Christianity. Keane Wilson used the same

Dick (1918) by Mary Grant Bruce. Illustrator: J. Macfarlane

formula for her stories about 'Brooklands'. Mavis Thorpe Clark continued the tradition in her early novels, beginning with *Hatherley's First Fifteen* (1930).

For the next three decades the school story went into decline, and school appears only marginally in the novels of Chauncy, Phipson, Southall, Spence, Thiele, Wrightson, and other writers of the period, a rare example being Simon French's *Hey, Phantom Singlet* (q.v., 1975). French showed a more relaxed, child-centred environment, where social conditioning has been set aside in favour of a subtler depiction of the interaction between student and student, student and teacher, and teacher and teacher. Robin Klein's *Hating Alison Ashley* (q.v., 1984) depicts a primary school where teachers are as vulnerable as children. Klein shows the humour and frustration of teacher and pupil in a modern classroom. 'Barry Hollis's project, written on the back of an old envelope, had only two sentences saying, "I never been to a theaer in my hole life and I dont wantto, and if I knew any guy lerning ballay I would bash him." Miss Belmont was waving it around angrily while she was telling Barry off ...'

School took a higher profile in the 1980s. In *Cannily, Cannily* (q.v., 1981) by Simon French, unlike his early twentieth-century counterparts, Trevor Huon does not have a natural sporting ability, and therefore fails to earn a place in the classroom heirarchy. It is the sport-mad and conformist teacher who is at fault, however, not Trevor. The other side of school life appears in Lowell Tarling's funny *Taylor's Troubles* (1982). Tommy Taylor is in his first year at secondary school, in the middle of every misfortune in his class, forever hoping for the best, but fearing the worst. *The Split Creek Kids* (1988) by Roger Vaughan Carr shows the intimacy of a single-teacher rural school in the mid-twentieth century, where community and school are so connected that when Nipper runs away from school he must run the gauntlet of the whole town.

The diversity of school environments has been a feature of the late twentieth-century school story. *So Much to Tell You ...* (q.v., 1988) and *The Great Gatenby* (1989) by John Marsden are set in boarding schools, *Breaking Up* (q.v., 1983) by Frank Willmott in an inner-city multicultural state secondary school, and Margaret Sharpe's *The Traeger Kid* (1983) in an Aboriginal school. Marsden introduced fantasy, with *Staying Alive in Year 5* (1989), in which a magical new teacher transforms attitudes. Judith Clarke's *The Heroic Life of Al Capsella* (1988) and *Al Capsella and the Watchdogs* (1990) provide humorous descriptions of teachers and students, as does David McRobbie's *The Wayne Dynasty* (1989).

Although the development from the strict code of obedience in the late nineteenth and early twentieth century school to the freer atmosphere of the modern classroom is well chronicled, none of these school stories shows the real rebelliousness and anger found in modern schools. In Australian children's books, school is generally regarded as a benign influence, and there is nothing to compare with the dark picture of American or English schools seen in Robert Cormier's *The Chocolate War* or Robert Westall's *The Scarecrows*. Perhaps the most chilling picture of an Australian school can be found in a real-life account, *Tom: a Child's Life Regained* (1978) by John Embling, in which schools are seen as failing 'illiterate, inarticulate and deprived children', and providing only 'directionless boredom'.

SCHURMANN, EDWIN A. (1917–), born Nattimuk, Victoria, has written short stories and natural history for adults. *No Trains on Sunday* (1967) is a series of anecdotes about the experiences of 11-year-old Willie Kohlmann, living in a small country town, Bullawollock, after World War I. Both *Charlie up a Gum Tree* (1985) and *The Moon is Shining* (1988) draw on the same setting. In *Charlie Up a Gum Tree*, illustrated by Bruce Treloar, the year is 1929. Charlie is a magpie who terrorises the locals, and when Johnnie's football becomes stuck in Charlie's tree, a tragedy is only just averted. *The Moon is Shining* (1988), illustrated by Shirley Peters, is set in a railway town during the 1920s. Willie and his friend lose a pet echidna, and are themselves lost while searching for it. Schurmann captures the innocence of a pre-war childhood.

Science Fiction, as well as speculating about possible futures, takes up the major themes of all writing for children, such as illuminating the difficulties of the individual in an increasingly complex society, the emotional links between family and friends, or the development of courage and initiative.

The fascination with technology, often described with questionable scientific accuracy, was a feature of the early years of science fiction. In Winifred Law's two novels about the Hannon boys, Tom, Ralph and Allister, *Through Space to the Planets* (1944) and *Rangers of the Universe* (1945), both illustrated by Dick Alderton, the spaceship Flame has been built by Ralph in his spare time; when Allister twiddles with one of the knobs, Flame roars off into space. Fortunately, the boys are wearing overcoats and have rugs to wrap themselves in. On the planet Aureela they meet 'weird, squat men, with eyes abnormally large and blue', and are able to persuade the Aureelians to built a fleet of spaceships for their return to Earth. In Leslie Greener's *Moon Ahead* (1951) Brock and Frank are able to stow away on the rocket, and William Pene du Bois's illustrations have the space men in spacesuits which resemble tomato soup cans made of chain mail.

The 1950s saw a proliferation of novels about space travel, drawing on the Woomera Rocket Range, the Blue Streak Rocket, and Sputnik. In Ivan Southall's *Simon Black in Space* (1952) Simon and Alan and their dog Rex investigate mysterious flying saucers from Mars. The trio travel to Mars and negotiate peace between the planets. The same author's *Simon Black and the Spacemen* (1955), later published as *Simon Black on Venus* (1974), shows only a little more respect for reality. 'Into Firefly I was built the manoeuvrability of a helicopter and the speed of a rocket.' Simon and his friends chase three Venusian scientists to their planet, only to discover that there are two dimensions on Venus, and Venusians live mostly in the invisible one. In Mary Elwyn Patchett's *Kidnappers of Space* (1953) two boys are abducted by the golden men of Mars, and in *Adam Troy, Astroman* (1954) the hero saves the world from radiation beasts. In the same author's *Lost on Venus* (1954) the planet is explored for the first time. The adventures of Johnny Danger and his crew in Patchett's *Send for Johnny Danger* (1956) take place on the Moon. 'Hugh Walters', the author of *Blast off at Woomera* (1957) has the unusually small schoolboy, Chris Godfrey ('well under five feet tall') blasted off in a rocket in an attempt to pre-empt Russian experiments. The discovery of buildings on the moon, near the area of Pico, is such a shock to the people of Earth that they take the unlikely step of joining together against the common enemy. *The Domes of Pico* (1958) followed. 'Walters' uses state-of-the-art information for his technological detail. *The Gravity Stealers* (1965) was 'written by the boys and girls of Australia', and edited by John Gunn. In the year 2046 Earth is controlled by three groups, Democrats, Communists and Anarchists, and the inventor of the powerful anti-gravity ray is kidnapped, then rescued by John, Peter and Vivian. In Mary Elwyn Patchett's *Farm Beneath the Sea* (1969) the Dexter family have a false lung of fine silicone membrane implanted in their bodies so that they are able to breathe under water. Showing enviable powers of recovery, they are out of hospital after a couple of days. The Dexters have a pet dolphin, Kooky, who saves the family from the sabotage attempts of rival undersea farmers.

As fascination with technology lessened, writers for children examined more human problems. Contact with other life forms became the favoured speculation. Cathy, George and David discover Martin, a visitor from another planet, in Patricia Wrightson's *Down to Earth* (1965). Martin's responses to Sydney provide a commentary on twentieth-century life. In Lee Harding's *The Fallen Spaceman* (1973), illustrated by Lee Walsh, an adventure is shared by an alien and a boy. Tyro saves Erik's life when he becomes trapped in Tyro's spacesuit. In the same author's *Return to Tomorrow* (1976), illustrated by Irene Pagram, an exploding spaceship apparently obliterates the town of Alderson in 1982. Then, in 2032, something stirs in the crater, and the town emerges again — it has been 'hurled forward in time'. *Children of Atlantis* (1976), illustrated by Murray Frederick, also by Harding, is based on the myth of Atlantis. As the Earth shifts, the people of Atlantis realise that their island will disappear, so they move to a continent, where they intermarry with prehistoric people. *The Luck of Brin's Five* (1977) by Cherry Wilder is the first of a trilogy about the land of Torin. The family life, language, customs and social order of the Moruia on Torin are intricately realised. The others in the trilogy are *The Nearest Fire* (1977) and *The Tapestry Warriors* (1983). A modern folk-tale is used in Victor Kelleher's *The Green Piper* (1984), which recalls Robert Browning's Pied Piper. Ross, Angie and Mad Jack fight off the attempts of a Pied Piper figure, a sinister plant-like alien, who is cloning people, mainly children, in order to inhabit them and spread all over the world.

Lee Harding's *Displaced Person* (q.v., 1979) was an early study of emotional alienation. Graeme Drury disappears through an interface between reality and a grey world inhabited by the dislocated Marion and Jamie. Nine years later, Allan Baillie's *Megan's Star* (1988) uses a similar theme, with Kel rejecting society. One

possibility, in Gillian Rubinstein's *Beyond the Labyrinth* (q.v., 1988), is for Brenton to take the same path. *Visitors* (1984) by Caroline Macdonald has aliens contacting the neglected Terry and the misunderstood Maryanne in order to obtain a particular sort of spectrum which contains the energy they need to return home. Gillian Rubinstein's *Space Demons* (q.v., 1986) and its sequel *Skymaze* (1989) use a computer game to work through the strong emotions felt by the participants, who must learn to co-operate and care for each other.

Conservation is the problem in *Quickhoney* (1979) by Garry Hurle. Jamie and Anne decode the dance of the bees, and are able to save the forest from the developers. A more sombre note is struck in Sheryn Dee's *Tarin of the Ice* (1987), which has a race of people who are extraordinarily skilful swimmers living deep in Antarctica. When the Norwegian whalers intrude into their territory, many of the Ice People prefer to ignore the threats to their lifestyle, but Tarin ventures out of the safe waters to find out the truth. There are no promises made for the survival of this vulnerable group. Caroline Macdonald's *The Lake at the End of the World* (1988) also considers the results of dramatic pollution. Diana and her parents believe they are the sole survivors until they meet Hector, from another underground enclave. Mike, in *Quest Beyond Time* (1985) by Tony Morphett, one of the 'Winners' series, falls through time to an Australia of the future where clans, tree-dwellers and cannibals exist beside feral animals such as lions and 'Chagwars'.

Other science fiction novels pursue areas such as telepathy, or time as a dimension. In Lee Harding's *The Web of Time* (1980) time is not linear but in the form of a net. Gordon Anderson and his grandson Tony travel in their 'trans-temporal precessor', or time machine. With the assistance of Miranda, whom they meet on their journey, they are able to retrace their passage across the web. *Shields of Trell* (1986) by

Jenny Summerville has three children from the future, Rex (RE-EX 781), Peaty (PE-TE 611) and Lira (LI-RA 354) who become lost in space. Lira discovers that she is able to communicate through thought transference, and is taught to control the gift by a chimpanzee, Radar. Summerville suggests the enormous possibilities of technology while pointing out the likely losses to the natural world in the future. Roger Dunn's *Matty Tracker and the UFO* (1985) combines the future and the past in an adventure set on the Greek island of Thera. In *The Girl from Tomorrow* (1990) and *Tomorrow's End* (1991) by Mark Shirrefs and John Thomson, Alana is kidnapped from the year 3000 and brought to the present day in a stolen time capsule.

The possible reconstruction of society after a holocaust is another scenario for science fiction writers. In Lee Harding's *Waiting for the End of the World* (1983) a community of exiles living in the hills is increasingly besieged by a totalitarian urban force. Manfred has a vision of a freer life, and at the conclusion of the novel he and the younger members of the commune leave to form a new community. *Dinko* (1985) by Joan Phipson, set in Sydney in 1999 and on the shores of the Adriatic in the seventh century, describes the experiences of Tom and Dinko, who both have the ability to predict the future. The human spirit survives the cataclysms facing both boys and their families. *Taronga* (q.v., 1986) by Victor Kelleher is another post-holocaust novel. The same author has the young warriors, Jeth and Rae, under the control of mutant masters in *The Makers* (1987). Through refusing to kill each other, they are exiled from the Keep, but are able to provide hope for a new generation opposed to violence. In Isobelle Carmody's *Obernewtyn* (1987) a 'Great White' holocaust has left mutants who are persecuted by the powerful Council. Through her premonitions and her strong psychic capacities, called 'farseeking', Elspeth is able to break the power of the Council. *The Farseekers* (q.v.,

1990), its sequel, concludes with the promise of a further adventure.

The role of education in a future society is examined in Penny Hall's *The Paperchaser* (1987). Hinton joins the Miners, an underground movement opposed to the totalitarian government, and eventually qualifies for the select group who enter university. By doing this he will effect a change in the social order. Hinton and the Miners also appear in the sequel, *The Catalyst* (1989), in which the Miners are cleared out, and some of them join the ganglads. Claudia and her friends are children of the survivors of nuclear war in Jill Dobson's *The Inheritors* (1988). The repressive nature of the society within the Dome leads them to rebellion. The novel looks at aspects of twentieth-century life — the casual approach to sex and drugs and the menace of gangs. *The Adonis Strategy* (1989) by Alex Fazakas examines the power of youth culture. Adonis (Matt Cooper) is the current idol, a gifted singer in a band which is used to manipulate, even kill, its audience. Adonis is kept a virtual prisoner until he decides to break away from his captors. In Caroline Macdonald's *The Eye Witness* (1991) the future may seem environmentally attractive, but the price is totalitarian control.

Some novels extract humour from science fiction. In Robin Klein's *Halfway Across the Galaxy and Turn Left* (1985) Dovis, X, Qwrk and their parents from the planet Zyrgon view daily life through alien eyes. Klein's aliens visit the supermarket, experience an earth school, and are wildly confused in their contact with others. In Joan Flanagan's humorous collection of stories, *The Squealies and Other Extraordinary Stories* (1987), extraterrestrials from planet Helioz come to live with the Furley family. In Jenny Pausacker's *Fast Forward* (1989) the Anti-Boredom Machine enables Kieran to avoid his boring family. Ann Grocott's *Danni's Desperate Journey* (1987) is about a girl who is threatened by a smelly mould which grows on her after she has kicked a Moldy

Flizzard's egg. The search for a cure sends her to bizarre worlds inhabited by equally bizarre creatures, on the back of Webbers, a vain flying man.

The early enthusiasm for warding off aggressive aliens and the unlimited possibilities of space flight has paled before the more pressing problems which face today's world: the likelihood of a nuclear holocaust or environmental disaster on the one hand, and the alienation from society experienced by many people on the other. In common with other contemporary children's books, the science fiction novel frequently takes a pessimistic view of the capacity of adults to create a worthwhile future.

SCOTT, BILL (1923–   ), born Bundaberg, Queensland, is a folklorist and writer about Australian life. *Following the Gold* (1989) is a collection of his poetry, and *Many Kinds of Magic* (1990) is a collection of stories based on traditional themes drawn from Australia, Japan, Ireland, Central Europe and South America. His knowledge of Aboriginal life is the source of *Boori* (q.v., 1978), *Darkness Under the Hills* (1980 see *Boori*) and *Shadow Among the Leaves* (1984). Aboriginal spirits are aroused to protect the forest from developers in *Shadow Among the Leaves*. Scott has also written books for adults about Australia and its characters, such as *Australian Bushrangers* (1987) and *My Uncle Arch and Other People* (1977).

SCOTT, MAVIS (1924–   ), born Brisbane, the wife of Bill Scott, has written for radio and theatre. *The Captain and the Kids* (1980), illustrated by Brian Dean, is set in Coolangatta, Queensland. Fiona and Freddie solve an old mystery by finding a ring which the Captain's ghost returns to its owner. *A Gift from the Past* (1984), illustrated by Sandra Laroche, is in Jacaranda's 'Expressway' reading series. Other books by Scott include *Little Ho and the Golden Kites* (1990) and *Bunyip in the Billycan* (1991).

SCOTT, PATRICIA (1926–   ), born Oatlands, Tasmania, is a storyteller. In 1981 she established a publishing company, Storytellers' Press, with a collection of traditional and original poems about hens, *I Had a Little Hen: Rhymes and Stories Old and New* (1981), illustrated by Marjorie Lovelock, as a first production. *Pigs Everywhere: Rhymes and Stories Old and New* (1982), also illustrated by Lovelock, is a similar collection. Scott was awarded the Dromkeen Medal in 1988.

SCOTT-MITCHELL, CLARE has lectured in children's literature at academic institutions in Sydney. *When a Goose Meets a Moose: Poems for Young Children* (1980) and *Apples from Hurricane Street: Poems for Children* (1985), both illustrated by Louise Hogan, are poetry anthologies. See **Poetry**. She has retold folk stories in *The Singing Drum: a Traditional Collection* (1987) and *The Fabulous Spotted Egg: a Traditional Collection* (1987).

SCRIVEN, PETER (1930–   ), born Melbourne, established the Marionette Theatre of Australia. He produced many puppet plays, including *The Tintookies*, which first appeared in 1956. *Little Fella Bindi* and *The Magic Pudding* followed. *The Tintookies and Little Fella Bindi* (1966), illustrated by Genevieve Melrose, arose from the puppet plays. Scriven worked in ABC television on the 'Sebastian and the Fox' series, filmed by Tim Burstall.

Sea Menace (1958) by John Gunn, illustrated by Brian Keogh, was Joint winner of the 1959 Book of the Year Awards. Paul Harris, his uncle Charles Britton and cousin Ian are travelling to Sydney to begin a new life in the infant settlement. When their ship is wrecked, they are taken aboard a whaler, really a pirate ship in disguise. After attempted escapes, they enlist the help of the evil Captain Kendrick's nephew Patrick, and foil the Captain's plans to attack Sydney. Through the many twists of fortune in this adventure story, the hazards of sea life during the early nineteenth century are well drawn.

'Search for the Golden Boomerang, The' was a radio serial broadcast over twenty-eight commercial stations in the early 1940s. It was produced by George Edwards, and written by Laura Bingham, who also wrote books based on the serial: *The Search for the Golden Boomerang* (1941), *Further Adventures of Tuckonie: From the Golden Boomerang Serial* (1942), *The Lost Tribe* (1943) and *Tuckonie's Warrior Friend* (1944). *Tuckonie on Tour* (1946) was adapted from the serial by Marianne Martin. Another book drawn from the serial, without a named author, was *Boomerang Stories for the Children* (1942). The serial was built around the surprising adventures of an Aboriginal boy, Tuckonie, who had first appeared in an earlier Edwards's serial, 'David and Dawn'. In the Land of the Female Warriors there are medicine men perpetrating human sacrifices who use hypodermic needles filled with drugs. Luckily, a 'witch woman' has another hypodermic filled with the drug's antidote.

Secret Family, The (1948) by Esmée Rice, illustrated by Pixie O'Harris, was Highly Commended in the 1950 Book of the Year Awards. Ariel Strong has a secret group of marionettes which she has made herself. When her father remarries, and Ariel's new aunt introduces her to the Steleviskis and their puppets, Ariel's parents discover her secret, and Ariel finds her niche.

Selby's Secret (1985) won WAYRBA in the Primary category in 1987. Selby is a talking dog originally created by Duncan Ball for *Family Circle Magazine*. *Selby's Secret* (1985), *Selby Speaks* (1988), which won the same award in 1990, and *Selby Screams* (1989), which won WAYRBA in 1991, are all illustrated by Allan Stomann. Selby teaches himself people-speech by watching television, but is reluctant to reveal his secret to his owners, the Trifles, for fear of being given the role of a domestic servant. Each book has a series of amusing episodes for younger readers.

SENIOR, MARGARET (1917–), born London, UK, came to Australia after World War II. She was a contributor to the NSW *School Magazine*. As 'Piers', with Anne Bracken she produced *The Lost Toy Shop* (1946) and *Meg & Peg: Adventures of Two Peg Dolls* (1946). She illustrated *The Story of Kurri Kurri the Kookaburra* (q.v., 1950), *Two-Thumbs, the Story of a Koala* (1953) and *The Story of Koonawarra the Black Swan* (1957) by Leslie Rees; *Little Brown Piccaninnies of Tasmania* (q.v., 1950) by Jane Ada Fletcher; *The Australia Book* (q.v., 1952) and *Cousins-Come-Lately: Adventures in Old Sydney Town* (q.v., 1952) by Eve Pownall; *John of the Sirius* (1955) and *John and Nanbaree* (1962) by Doris Chadwick; *Snow Boy* (1958) by Noreen Shelley; *Larry the Story of an Australian Seagull* (1961) by Ina Watson; *Two at Sullivan Bay* (1985) by Nance Donkin; and *Nunga* (1985) by Rus Center. *Bush Haven Animals: an Australian Picture Story* (1954), which she wrote and illustrated, is an authentic account of local fauna in an animal hospital, enriched with her delicate pictures.

SERVENTY, VINCENT (1925–), born Bickley, WA, is a naturalist, lecturer and film-maker. He has written over forty books, and contributed to over fifty films. In *Turtle Bay Adventure* (1969), illustrated by Faye Owner, Joan and Jim discover the diversity of wildlife on land and sea when the family moves to Turtle Bay, in north-west WA.

SESSIONS, ROBERT (1942–), editor and publisher, born Gloucester, UK, came to Australia in 1964 as Australian editor for Cassells. In 1971 he transferred to Penguin, where he became managing editor, and in charge of Puffin books in Australia. The early books of Ivan Southall, Nance Donkin and H.F. Brinsmead appeared under his aegis. In 1976 he moved to Nelson, where for ten years he developed a program which included the work of Graeme Base, Bob Graham, and Elizabeth Honey. In 1987 he returned to the senior management of Penguin. For nearly thirty years Sessions has influenced the development of children's books in Australia, through publishing books of quality and encouraging authors with potential.

Seven Little Australians (1894) was Ethel Turner's first novel, written when she was 24. When William Steele, manager of Ward, Lock in Australia read the manuscript, he wrote: 'I hurried through my meal and resumed the story as quickly as possible, and when I had finished it in the afternoon, I felt certain that I had *a very good thing*.' Steele's judgement was vindicated. The novel has sold many more than a million copies, has been translated, made into a play in 1915, filmed in 1939, televised by the BBC in 1953, by the ABC in 1973, and made into a musical in 1988. The 1939 film was directed by Arthur Collins, with Charles McCallum as Captain Woolcot and Mary McGowan as Judy. The ABC's ten-episode television series in 1973, directed by Ron Wray, adapted by Eleanor Witcombe, starred Leonard Teale as Captain Woolcot and Jennifer Cluff as Judy. A.J. Johnson illustrated the first edition. Later editions were illustrated by J. Macfarlane and Sandra Laroche.

The novel is a watershed in Australian children's books. It is urban, nationalistic and full of memorable characters. Captain Woolcot is something of a martinet, a refreshing change from the understanding and patient parents who peopled other books of the times. With his family, Esther (his second wife), Meg, Pip, Judy, Nell,

Bunty, Baby and the General, he lives on the Parramatta River in a house they have aptly called 'Misrule'. The escapades of the children and the adolescent love affairs of Meg conclude with the accidental death of Judy, who dies saving her half-brother, the General. Judy is drawn with imagination and colour, and she initiated a tradition of strong and independent girls. See also **Girls**.

Judy's time in boarding school, where she is sent by Captain Woolcot as a punishment for her misdemeanours, and her journey back to 'Misrule' during the school holidays, is related in *Judy and Punch* (1928), although Turner's picture of Judy is less dynamic than in *Seven Little Australians*.

Turner wrote *The Family at Misrule* a year after *Seven Little Australians*, in 1895, but set it after five years have elapsed. Meg becomes engaged to Alan Courtney, Nell and Pip are cured of the desire to mix with 'unsuitable' people (the nouveau riche and a dressmaker, no less) and Bunty's character is redeemed through the loyalty of Baby, now called Poppet. The General, now Peter, is 6, speaking with a lisp which requires the reader to make constant mental translations, and there is a new baby, Essie, to make up the seven. *Little Mother Meg* (1902), illustrated by A.J. Johnson, takes place three years after Meg's marriage to Alan Courtney. Captain Woolcot has become Major Woolcot, and Bunty is thoroughly reformed. The novel is mainly concerned with Nell, who falls in love with a 'bounder', who 'had treated her as a plaything, and she had not had sense enough or dignity enough to see it: instead she had given away unasked — what?' In fact the worst Nellie had done was hold his hand. There is a theatrical account of mysterious neighbours, and in a final desperate attempt to enliven the novel Turner resuscitates the death of Judy with a visit to her grave at 'Yarrahappini', where, we are told, Esther comes to the surprising conclusion that Judy's death 'had been for the best'.

Seventh Pebble, The (1980) by Eleanor Spence, illustrated by Sisca Verwoert, was Commended in the 1981 Book of the Year Awards. Rachel's life is changed when the Connells come to Hollybush Flat. The imaginative Bridget and her interesting brothers and sisters fascinate Rachel, despite the town's disapproval of their Catholicism. Rachel takes the Connells for what they are — generous, loving and poor — but bigotry and small-town meanness finally drive them out. As World War II threatens, Rachel learns about her own ancestors. Spence presents the ugly face of intolerance against a girl's loss of innocence.

Sexuality. In a revealing and unmoralistic exploration of teenage sexuality, Debbie and Sue lose their virginity in the back of their boyfriends' vans, and discuss their feelings openly in *Puberty Blues: a Surfie Saga* (q.v., 1979) by Kathy Lette and Gabrielle Carey, which introduced a new frankness into books for young people in Australia. The writers of the 1970s had ignored adolescent sexuality, although Ivan Southall recognised its power, in *Matt and Jo* (1973) and *What About Tomorrow?* (1977). Frank Willmott's *Breaking Up* (1983) took up from *Puberty Blues*. He includes a scene in which Mark masturbates, and the boys observe their parents having sexual intercourse. John Marsden writes frankly about adolescent sexual encounters. In *The Great Gatenby* (1989) Melanie and Erle explore each other's bodies with delight and humour. In *The Journey* (1988) Argus is present at the birth of Adious's daughter Jessie, and his sexual experiences with Temora and Adious form part of his maturation. In Nigel and Caron Krauth's *I Thought You Kissed with Your Lips* (1990) Zoe is educated in seduction when she holidays in Surfers Paradise. Maureen McCarthy's *Ganglands* (1992) describes Kelly's first experience of sex. *Lockie Leonard, Human Torpedo* (q.v., 1990) by Tim Winton, reflects on the nature of sex and love, and Lockie decides that he is

'not in a hurry for all this stuff'. It is not until Jenny Pausacker's *What Are Ya?* (1987) that there is an exploration of lesbian sexual relationships. In a group of students in their final year at a secondary school, Leith recognises her preference for females, and Barb finally finds sexual expression with her friend Paul. *Peter* (1991) by Kate Walker is about a 15-year-old boy who falls in love with his brother's best friend, who is gay. Post-war novels opened the way for an examination of the individual's sexual choice in a context of a maturing view of self.

Shackleton's Argonauts: a Saga of the Antarctic Ice-Packs (1948), written by Frank Hurley and illustrated with his photographs, won the 1948 Book of the Year Awards. In 1914 Sir Ernest Shackleton led an expedition which aimed to cross the Antarctic continent. The ship, aptly called the *Endurance*, was gripped for six months in the pack-ice, and finally crushed. The party then set up camp on an ice-raft, which drifted at the mercy of winds and weather. When it became clear that the floe was about to disintegrate, they took to the boats they had salvaged, and while twenty-two of the men waited on Elephant Island, Shackleton and five others set off to find help. How they survived these terrible journeys, suffering from the awful weather and severe shortages of food, is told in the bare prose and beautiful photographs of the official photographer of the expedition.

Shadow the Rock Wallaby, see ***The Story of Shadow the Rock Wallaby***

SHAPCOTT, THOMAS (1935–), born Ipswich, Queensland, is a poet and novelist. *Flood Children* (1981), illustrated by James Phillips, was Shapcott's first novel, and is set in the 1974 Queensland floods. Peter and Michelle Griffith are left in the charge of their 16-year-old sister Janni. Together with Janni's boyfriend Don they survive the floods and solve a mystery, earning themselves a reward in the process. In *Holiday of the Ikon* (1984) four children search for a lost Polish ikon on Stradbroke Island. For the 'More Winners' series, Shapcott wrote *His Master's Voice* (1990) with Roger Simpson, about a haunted music camp at Montsalvat, Melbourne, and *Mr Edmund* (1990) with Steve Spears. Mr Edmund creates miracles out of wishes.

SHARP, DONNA (1956–), born Brisbane. For *Blue Days* (1986) see **Death**.

SHARPE, MARGARET (1934–) wrote *The Traeger Kid* (1983), a picture of Aboriginal schooling set at Traeger Park Primary School, Alice Springs. Patricia visits an outstation school under a gum tree, and finds friends in Brisbane. A guide to the spelling and pronunciation of Arunta and Bundjalung languages is included.

Sharpur the Carpet Snake (1967) by Lydia Pender, illustrated by Virginia Smith, was Commended in the 1968 Picture Book of the Year Awards. In his efforts to get rid of the rats who are a pest in a Sydney market, Benjamin Colley (who loves the resonances of multi-syllabled words) buys a snake. The plan works well until Sharpur escapes, causing pandemonium. Smith's unusual perspectives and page design enhance an attractive picture-book. It was reissued in 1976, illustrated by Allan Stomann, and again in 1982 with illustrations by Tony Oliver.

SHEAD, ISOBEL ANN, born Adelaide, directed the ABC children's session in Victoria from 1933 to 1937 as 'Isobel Ann'. She left Australia for England in 1937, where she married the pianist Charles Zwar, and remained to develop her own radio program at the BBC. Shead's connection with radio and journalism is used in some of her early novels. In *Sandy* (1935), originally a radio serial, Sandy Rainer runs away from a harsh father and becomes a cadet journalist. In *Mike* (1936) Mike makes his career in radio. *This Way Please!* (1939) has a similar plot to *Sandy*, but is set in England at the BBC. A departure from these career novels was *Clancy* (1937). Clancy Collins leaves the Mallee and joins Bunny Shepherd in Melbourne. They have a series of adventures, and Clancy's lameness is cured after a car accident. *The Flying Kangaroo* (1940) is another boys' adventure story. Chips Warner is trained as an intelligence officer, flies the plane *Flying Kangaroo* to Maralinga, and is able to shoot down German spies in an aerial dogfight. *They Sailed by Night* (1943) is the story of three English evacuees in Australia. Class distinctions are made very clear in *To See the Queen* (1953). Patsy, Cherry, Roger and Christine are from families where wrist-watches, ponies and large properties are the order of the day, while the Fords live in a wretched shack, which they do not seem able to keep tidy. Fortunately, breeding wins through, and the girls soon straighten things up. In *The Jago Secret* (1966) the Australian Jagos search for their ancestors in Cornwall, and discover that an earlier-generation Jago was sent to Australia as a convict, and that a modern relative is also involved in illegal activities. *The Canary Jacket* (1968) tells the story of this first Richard Jago, caught smuggling, who endures the hardships of life in the colonies. *Off the Chain, Telling of the Exciting Adventures that Befell Beetle when He Ran Away* (1938) is set in London. Beetle the cocker spaniel puppy leaves his happy life with Elizabeth and David, tramps the streets, and returns. Shead also wrote *Kooboor the Koala* with Charles Barrett (1941), as well as books for adults.

SHEARER, J. D. For *Bound for Botany Bay: Impressions of Transportation and Convict Life* (1976) see **First Fleet**.

SHELDRAKE, PAMELA (1944–), born UK, has written a series about the animals who inhabit Mulga Creek,

Welcome to Mulga Creek (1988), *A False Alarm* (1988), *Beach Holiday* (1990) and *A Day at the Show* (1990). Koalas Murray and Bliss go to school with Miss Pindrop the platypus, and their busy lives include adventures with other Australian animals. *Thomas Bull, Walter Roo and the Stringbark Cockatoo* (1987) is in Macmillan's 'Southern Cross' series. Sheldrake has also written *The Frog and the Wild Rope* (1990).

SHELLEY, NOREEN (1920–85), born Lithgow, NSW, wrote scripts for the ABC children's session and 'Kindergarten of the Air', and was editor of the NSW *School Magazine* from 1960 to 1970. Shelley contributed nine titles to Longman's 'Australian People' series, including *The Baker* (1963), *The Dentist* (1963), *The Life Savers* (1963) and *The Postman* (1963). She wrote about a small pig, Piggy Grunter, some of whose adventures first appeared in the *School Magazine*: *Piggy Grunter's Red Umbrella* (1944), *Piggy Grunter's Nursery Rhymes* (1944), *Piggy Grunter at the Fire* (1944), *Piggy Grunter at the Circus* (1944), all illustrated by Ralph Shelley and gathered in *Piggy Grunter Stories* (1954). Piggy goes camping and gets wet, saves the cow from the flood, goes fishing, makes a cake, and so on. He invariably gets into trouble. 'Three cheers for Piggy Grunter' is the concluding line of Piggy's tales, and *Three Cheers for Piggy Grunter* (1959), illustrated by Elisabeth MacIntyre, was the last story bringing together Piggy and his family and friends at the town of Snorter Pigwhistle. Other stories from the *School Magazine* are gathered in *Roundabout: Book One* (1967), illustrated by Astra Lacis, *Animals of the World* (1952), *King of Spain and Other Plays* (1953) and *The Runaway Scooter* (1953). *Snow Boy* (1958), illustrated by Margaret Senior, is about a Dalmatian puppy which wins first prize for tail-wagging.

Shelley's novels for older readers began with *Family at the Lookout* (q.v., 1972) and *Faces in a Looking-Glass* (q.v., 1974). *Cat on Hot Bricks* (1975), illustrated by Robert

Gibson, is about the small adventures of the Newcombe family in England, Spain and France, where they visit a sister and family friend. In *The Other Side of the World* (1977), Ben is brought to Australia by his grandmother when his parents go to Ethiopia. He shows his anger through antagonism to his grandmother and constant sulkiness. When he runs away with the boy next door, Fergus, who is soon revealed as an unreliable friend, Ben has a change of heart. Shelley adapted folk-tales for *Legends of the Gods: Strange and Fascinating Tales from Around the World* (1976), illustrated by Astra Lacis.

SHEPPARD, NANCY (1933–), born Sydney. See *Alitjinya Ngura Tjukurt-jarangka/Alitji in the Dreamtime* (1975).

Short List, see **Book of the Year Awards**

SHIRREFS, MARK and **JOHN THOMSON** wrote *The Girl from Tomorrow* (1990) and *Tomorrow's End* (1991). See **Science Fiction**. The novels were originally a television serial of twelve thirty-minute episodes made by Film Australia in 1990 and 1991, directed by Kathy Mueller and scripted by the authors.

SHRAPNEL, PAMELA (1947–), born Boonah, Queensland, writes for younger readers. Hermione Prickleburr, in *Meanie and the Min Min* (1987), illustrated by Terry Denton, is a witch who hurtles across the desert in a billy-cart drawn by a team of thirteen specially trained goannas. No 'sooky cat' for her, but a big black crow as a companion. Bindii and Mike have to use guile and the special magic of Mike's grandfather to save Bindii's pet Thorny Devil lizard from her dreadful clutches. In *Freddie the Frightened and the Wondrous Ms Wardrobe* (1988), also illustrated by Denton, Freddie is terrified of the terrors of the night until cousin

Penelope Wardrobe conquers each monster but one in original ways. Barbara and Brian have a bubble-blowing contest in *B is for Bubbles* (1983), illustrated by Noela Young, until they both lose their front teeth. *The Shy Giant* (1982), illustrated by Allan Stomann, is in Jacaranda's 'Expressways' series.

SIBLEY, IRENA (1944–   ), born

Kaunas, Lithuania, artist and writer, settled in Australia in 1949. She is married to the artist Andrew Sibley. Sibley studied at the National Art School in Sydney, and has taught art in schools. She has published some of her books in limited editions, such as *Rainbow* (1980), *William, the Wizard who Wasn't* (1986), *When the Sun Took the Colour Away* (1987) and *Australian Wildflowers: an Alphabet* (1988), using the original linocuts. *Rainbow* celebrates the multicultural nature of Australian society. Amanda and her dolls welcome a gypsy doll from Lithuania, prompting a discussion of the various origins of Golli, Teddy, Jack-in-the-Box and others. *William, the Wizard who Wasn't* is about a reluctant wizard who lives at Waiting Dog Creek. While most of his spells are bungled, he is able to bring about a meeting of the world powers when a war threatens. *The Other Tansy* (1985) was produced for Sugar and Snails Press. In *When Herb's Mess Grew* (1990) Herb's messy habits lead to near disaster. She has also illustrated *The Trouble with Peggetty* (1984) by Mary Small and *The Last Voyage of the Araminta* (1985) by Lynne Duncan. Sibley's bouyant linocuts of birds, animals and people express a joy in the natural world, and a pleasure in Australian motifs.

Silver Brumby, The (1958) by Elyne Mitchell, illustrated by Ralph Thompson, was Highly Commended in the 1959 Book of the Year Awards, and *Silver Brumby's Daughter* (1960), illustrated by Grace Huxtable, was Commended in the 1961 Book of the Year Awards. *The Silver Brumby* was written for the writer's 9-year-old daughter and has remained in print since its publication. The books are set on the Crackenback River in the Snowy Mountains area of south-eastern Australia, around Mount Kosiusko. Bel Bel gives birth to a silver foal, Thowra, and together they join Yarraman's herd. Thowra quickly learns that Man is his most feared enemy, but his rivalry with Arrow, another colt, leads him to leave the herd until he defeats its new leader after Yarraman's death. Kunama is Thowra's daughter in *Silver Brumby's Daughter* and Baringa is Thowra's grandson in *Silver Brumbies of the South* (1965), illustrated by Annette Macarthur-Onslow. *Silver Brumby Kingdom* (1966), also illustrated by Macarthur-Onslow, again features Baringa, and his rivalry with Thowra's son, Lightning. *Moon Filly* (1968), illustrated by Robert Hales, is the story of a filly, Ilinga, and her foster-brother

The Trouble with Peggetty (1984) by Mary Small. Illustrator: Irene Sibley

Wurring. Ilinga is stolen by a stallion, but escapes to find Wurring again. In *Silver Brumby Whirlwind* (1973), illustrated by Victor Ambrus, Thowra travels to the north to meet the beautiful filly Yuri. *Son of the Whirlwind* (1976), illustrated by Victor Ambrus, is the story of Wirramirra, son of Thowra and Yuri, who searches for his sire. Although the animals are personified, and converse as humans, Mitchell has captured the powerful, wild, even brutal nature of their existence among the high country of the southern Australian Alps, during changing seasons.

SILVESTRO, LOUIS. For *The Australian ABC Book* (1984) see **Alphabet Books**.

Sinabouda Lily; a Folk Tale from Papua New Guinea (1979) by Robin Anderson, illustrated by Jennifer Allen, was Commended in the 1980 Picture Book of the Year Awards. Sinabouda Lily is snatched from her swing by the wicked witch Sinawakelakela, but saved by her father and his magic bananas. The brightly coloured and stylised illustrations give a tropical flavour to the story.

SIOW, JOHN (1948–), born Malaysia, is a graphic designer and illustrator. He has illustrated *There's a Dinosaur in the Park!* (1980) and *The Story of a Picture Book* (1986) by Rodney Martin, and *Picasso the Green Tree Frog* (1985) by Amanda Graham.

'SISTER AGNES'. For *Fairy Tales Told in the Bush* (1912) see **Fairies**.

Sister Madge's Book of Nuns (1986) by Doug MacLeod, illustrated by Craig Smith, was an Honour Book in the 1987 Junior Book of the Year Awards, won YABBA for Younger Readers in 1987 and was the Primary Winner of KOALA in 1988. Set in the Convent of Our Lady of Immense Proportions, it is a collection of funny and irreverent verses about Sister Bossy, Sister Flo, Sister Stephanie and others, who ride motorbikes, take snuff, grow antlers, and have other bizarre experiences.

Six Days Between a Second (1969) by Marjory O'Dea, illustrated by Jonathan Waud, was Commended in the 1970 Book of the Year Awards. In a fantasy set in Canberra, the four Collard children go through a layer of the world into another reality, where they join a battle between good and evil being fought out between Basilisks, Gryphons, Unicorns, Dryads, Ermines, Dolphins, and Bees. The Basilisks are poised to pollute the Canberra water supply. The Collard's adventures are continued in *Of Jade and Amber Caves* (1974), illustrated by Tim Bass. The children are two years older, and are taken prisoner by the Basilisks, but return to reality over the Rainbow Sea. O'Dea draws on classical myths and real creatures, using names such as Imhotep and Pythoban to invoke a sense of fable.

SKIPPER, MERVYN G. (1886–1959) spent some years in Malaysia, and was the art and drama critic for the *Bulletin* from 1956 to his death. In *The Meeting Pool: a Tale of Borneo* (1929), illustrated by R.W. Coulter, the insects and animals of the jungle try to prevent the White Man from destroying their habitat. *The White Man's Garden: a Tale of Borneo* (1930) is a collection of folk-tales told by the plants in a garden. The author acknowledges his indebtedness to the people of Malaysia in his notes at the beginning of this interesting and stylishly illustrated book. One of the stories, 'Lazy Tok', appeared in the Victorian Education Department's third reading book, *Among Friends* (1954). Another story from *The White Man's Garden* , 'The Fooling of King Alexander', illustrated by Gaynor Chapman, was published as a picture-book in 1967.

Skippy began her life as a pet kangaroo in over ninety episodes on Australian television, and the picture-books are outlines of the stories with plentiful illustrations. In *Skippy the Bush Kangaroo* (1968) by Victor Barnes, illustrated by Walter Stackpool, Skippy is orphaned, and taken home by Sonny Hammond. Skippy and Sonny become firm friends, and the kangaroo comes when Sonny calls her on his gumleaf. Skippy saves Sonny when he is stuck in a tree, and with Sonny's family and other visitors to the National Park Skippy outwits all evildoers. In *Skippy to the Rescue* (1969), also illustrated by Stackpool, Skippy saves her bush friends from a hunter and a bushfire. Skippy helps rout the gold-stealers in *Skippy and the Intruders* (1970), again illustrated by Stackpool. This book was based on the 1969 film *The Intruders*, directed by Lee Robinson and using the same actors as the television series: Garry Pankhurst as Sonny, Ed Devereaux as Matt, and Lisa Goddard as Sonny's friend Clancy. See also **Barnes, Victor Dominic Suthers**.

'SLADE, GURNEY' was the pseudonym of **STEPHEN BARTLETT** (?–1956). In *Pleasure Island* (1924), illustrated by Frances Hilley, and *The Fifteen Men* (1925) Richard reads 'Aladdin and his wonderful lamp', and conjures up the Seahopper, who takes him to meet Guy Fawkes, Colonel Bogey and other literary and historical figures. 'Slade' also wrote adventure stories, such as *The Pearlers of Lorne: a Story for Boys* (1925) set in a town like Broome, and *Marling Ranges* (1926), illustrated by W.H. Holloway, which describes how Roy Lavington finds his fortune in WA. Two books featured the dauntless *Captain Quid* (1937). In *Quid's Quest* (1939) Chris Santrey sets off for Australia in search of a friend's brother. Australian characters appear in many of 'Slade's' books, such as *In Lawrence's Bodyguard* (1931), *Led by Lawrence* (1933), *The Black Pyramid* (1926), *The Delta Patrol*

(1934) and *The Treasure of the Pass* (1941), all set in the Middle East. Other books by 'Slade' include *Gentlemen o' Fortune* (1935) and *A North Sea Quest* (1935). *The League of Guy Varenne* (1954) is set in France. Animal books include *Kharga the Camel* (1949), *Pingoo the Penguin* (1949), *Tamba the Lion* (1949) and *Bawse the Badger* (1950). *Through the Never-Never* (1935) is a travel book.

SLESSOR, KENNETH (1901–71), born Orange, NSW, poet, provided the verses for Frank Johnson's cheap publication *Funny Farmyard: Nursery Rhymes and Painting Book* (1933), illustrated by Syd Miller. See **Nursery Rhymes**.

Sly Old Wardrobe (1968) by Ivan Southall, illustrated by Ted Greenwood, won the 1969 Picture Book of the Year Awards. When Tom buys an old wardrobe for the dollar which Grandma has given him, no one can think of a use for it. It is only when Grandma sees it that the wardrobe finds a home. Greenwood's challenging illustrations depict the ambivalence of Tom's feelings towards the wardrobe — fearful or playful.

SMALL, MARY (1932–), born Plymouth, UK, writer and speech therapist, came to Australia in 1962. In her first children's book, *A Bear in My Bedroom* (1976), illustrated by Ingrid Van Dyk, Great Aunt Philomena sends Andrew, an English boy, a magical koala bear (*sic*) who takes his new owner on tours around Australia. Her work with Riding for the Disabled inspired *And Alice Did the Walking* (1978), with photographs by Lionel Jensen, which describes the relationship which develops between Scott, who cannot walk and Alice, the pony on which he learns to ride. *Rattletrap Rosie* (1984), illustrated with photographs by Ron Ryan, is a study of a Shetland pony which Jeremy and Susan share with disabled children. *Jodie's BMX Wheelchair*

(1985) is another book about a disabled boy. Small edited *Riding Free*, the journal of the Riding for the Disabled Association of Australia.

In *Night of the Mutton Birds* (1981), illustrated by Robert Ingpen, Matthew wants to be a pilot. He leaves Cape Barren Island for high school in Launceston, but racist jokes and his own homesickness force him to return to help his family catch the shearwaters on Big Dog Island. He meets a scientist who befriends him and encourages him to continue his education. See also **Aboriginal People in Children's Fiction**. *Broome Dog* (1989), illustrated by Arthur Boothroyd, relates the adventures of Knuckles the dog when he sets off from Katherine to Broome.

Small has written books for younger readers, such as *Peter Moss* (1985). In *Thack's Army* (1987) a group of children set out to frighten Mrs Thackeray until they realise that what they are doing could seriously hurt her. In *The Trouble with Peggetty* (1984), illustrated by Irena Sibley, the problem is that Emma's horse was bought without her parents' approval. For *Grandfather's Tiger* (1985) see **Animal Stories**. Her picture-books include *The Sea Dog* (1978), illustrated by I. Putu Santosa. In *The Lizard of Oz* (1986), illustrated by Julia McLeish, a frill-necked lizard terrorises the animals who come to the billabong to drink. Simon and Lucy search for Easter eggs in *Muddy Footprints* (1987), which has photographs by Sue McKinnon. *The Enormous Hole* (1988), illustrated by Hal Slatter, is a clever exploration of the uses of a hole and its parts. Santa and a house-wrecking possum visit on Christmas Day in *Santa Claws* (1989), illustrated by Vicky Kitanov. *Tracey McBean's Stretching Machine* (1989), illustrated by Arthur Filloy, relates in text and cartoons the disastrous attempts which Tracey the inventor makes to stretch people. In *Country Cousin* (1991), illustrated by Dee Huxley, Edith comes to Sydney during the Centennial, and is amazed at such urban delights as the steam trams, omnibuses, and the Manly Aquarium. Small has also contributed to reading schemes.

SMEATON, WILLIAM HENRY OLIPHANT (1856–1914), born Scotland, poet, novelist and editor, spent some time in Australia. After his return to Edinburgh, he was associated with Dent, the publishers, and worked with J.M. Dent on the editorial work required for the Temple Classics from 1901, and for the Everyman Library. Smeaton edited the *Temple Bible* (1901), books of ballads and a life of Shakespeare. His adventure story *The Treasure Cave of the Blue Mountains* (1898) begins in Balmain, Sydney. A search for gold is undertaken by John Cameron, Billy Arbuthnot, Arthur Roberts and the resourceful Leila Cardiff, who defies convention. 'I quarrelled with [Mrs Grundy] long ago', she says. Leila shoots straight, and is unfazed by the brutal Black Bob the Bushranger, Lanky Larry or Slippery Sam, his accomplices. See also **Adventure Stories**. When the crew of the *Fitzroy* are searching for castaways, in *A Mystery of the Pacific* (1899), a Roman trireme emerges from the mist, and leads them to an island inhabited by the descendants of Brutus. Their perfectly constructed marble city, Nova Messana, is fully equipped with the accoutrements of Rome. Fortunately, some of the crew speak Latin.

'Smiley' is the nickname of William Thomas Greevins, the character created by Moore Raymond in three books, *Smiley* (1945), *Smiley Gets a Gun* (1947) and *Smiley Roams the Road* (1959), illustrated by Pat Nevin. High-spirited Smiley romps through larger-than-life adventures in the country during the 1940s. The first two novels were made into films, in 1956 and 1958 respectively. Anthony Kimmins directed both, with Colin Petersen as Smiley in *Smiley* and Keith Calvert playing the role in *Smiley Gets a Gun*. Chips

Rafferty appeared in both films, and in the second film Leonard Teale, Ruth Cracknell and Dame Sybil Thorndike played major roles. See also **Boys**.

SMITH, CRAIG (1955–), born Woodside, SA, studied at the SA Institute of Art. He has illustrated *The Room Upstairs* (1978) and *Dreadful David* (1984) by Sally Farrell Odgers; *High Dive and Free is Lonely* (1979) by Hesba Brinsmead; *Black Dog* (1979) by Christobel Mattingley; *The Prowler* (1982) by Geoffrey Dutton; *Parrot Fashion* (1983) by Eleanor Nilsson; *Elizabeth's Red Rooster* (1986) by Heather Fidge; *Sister Madge's Book of Nuns* (q.v., 1986) by Doug MacLeod; *Putrid Poems* (1985), *Petrifying Poems* (1986), *Vile Verse* (1988) and *Four and Twenty Lamingtons* (1988), edited by Jane Covernton; *The Cabbage Patch Fib* (q.v., 1988) by Paul Jennings; *Beware!* (1988) and *On a Dark and Scary Night* (1988) by Gail Jorgensen; *My Dog's a Scaredy Cat* (1987) and *Comedies for Kids: Preposterous Plays, Silly Skits, Daft Dramas* (1988) by Duncan Ball; *Still Room for More* (1989) by Marcia Vaughan; *Goodness Gracious!* (1990) by Phil Cummings, a book of rhymes for the very young; and *Squawk and Screech* (1991) by Gillian Rubinstein. In *A Strange Visitor: an Old Story Retold* (1987) by Mary O'Toole, as the old woman sits and spins, a skeleton builds up before her eyes, menacing her existence. *I Hate Fridays: Stories from Koala Hills Primary School* (1990) by Rachel Flynn is a collection of stories from an imaginary school, based on the author's teaching experiences. *Where's Mum?* (1992) by Libby Gleeson is a response to the rich imagination of the children who see their mother as a character in fairytales. Smith illustrated Nan Hunt's books about the enterprising Mrs Millie Mack, *Whistle Up the Chimney* (q.v., 1981), *An Eye Full of Soot and an Ear Full of Steam* (1983), *Rain, Hail or Shine* (1984) and *The Whistle Stop Party* (1990). His sense of the absurd and eye for detail ranges from the homely interiors of *Whistle Up the Chimney* to the fantastic adventures of *Where's Mum?*.

SMITH, GLENYS (1928–) has worked with Maurice Saxby on reading schemes. She selected the poetry for *All Australian Funny and Frightful Verse* (1987), illustrated by Deborah Niland.

SMITH, IVAN (1931–), born Perth, was radio features editor for the ABC, and author of the radio documentary *The Death of a Wombat*, which was produced in 1959, with music by George English. The drama won the Italia Prize. It was published as a book in 1972, illustrated by Clifton Pugh. For this, and *Dingo King* (1977), also illustrated by Pugh, see **Animal Stories**.

SMITH, KEITH R.A. left school to start work in a foundry when he was 13 years old during the 1930s Depression. He served an apprenticeship as a signwriter, recalled in his autobiography, *The Palace of Signs: Memories of Hard Times and High Times in the Great Depression* (1991). In the later years of his apprenticeship he began to write comedy sketches and to act in radio plays. After World War II he was a journalist with the ABC. His programs included two about children, begun in 1950, 'A Word from Children' and 'The Pied Piper'. *A Word from Children* (1960) and a series of riddle books, including *The Pied Piper: Keith Smith's Riddle Book for Children* (1960) and *Riddle Roundup* (1977), are drawn from these radio shows. The first is a series of interviews of children which aimed to give insights into child behaviour and psychology. Smith's work for television generated *Keith Smith's T.V. Jokes for Children* (1972) and *T.V. Cook Book for Kids* (1972).

In *The Pig That was Different* (1988), illustrated by Mary Ferguson, Thomas has a straight tail. When Thomas saves the other pigs, their tails are also straightened. In *The Bear with Bad Eyes* (1987), with illustrations by Jiri Tibor Novak, the biggest but gentlest bear in the forest is hunted for twenty years; when his eyesight fails he is in danger of being shot, until he saves Jake's life and is rewarded with a pair of spectacles. *The Migrant Mouse* (1988), illustrated in cartoon style by Bruno Jean Grasswill, is about Tess, a resourceful mouse who stows away on the *Scarborough*, a ship of the First Fleet. When her companion is eaten by the ship's cat, Tess and her children use ship's biscuits as life-rafts to reach the shore.

SMITH, MAIRE (1952–   ), born Woodside, SA, the sister of Craig Smith, trained at the SA School of Art. She has illustrated *The Princess Who Hated It* (1986) by Robin Klein; *Rattling in the Wind, Australian Poems for Children* (1987), selected by Jill Heylen and Celia Jellett; and *It Must Have Been Summer: an Australian Poetry Anthology for Children* (1990), selected by Sarah Keane.

SMITH, SYDNEY URE (1887–1949), born London, UK, came to Australia as a child. He founded and edited the journal *Art in Australia*, and later established the publishing company Ure Smith. He illustrated Agnes Littlejohn's fairy story *Star Dust and Sea Spray* (1918) with Percy Leason, and covers for the 'Bookstall Series' published by the NSW Bookstall Company (q.v.).

SMYTH, GWENDA (1928–   ), born Melbourne, is a teacher, writer and editor. She has written two books about the determined Mrs Arbuckle: *A Pet for Mrs Arbuckle* (1981), in which Mrs Arbuckle searches for an appropriate pet, with the cat commenting on each of them; and *A Hobby for Mrs Arbuckle* (1987), in which she tries ballooning, worm farms, mobiles and other hobbies. Both are illustrated by Ann James. *Orlando* (1987), illustrated by Mervyn Pywell, is about a conductor who has a tendency to conduct everything. He finds, to his surprise, that life goes on whether he conducts it or not, but is relieved that his orchestra always needs him.

Snugglepot and Cuddlepie are characters created by May Gibbs in *Snugglepot and Cuddlepie: Their Adventures Wonderful* (1918), *Little Ragged Blossom* (1920) and *Little Obelia* (1921), collected in *The Complete Adventures of Snugglepot and Cuddlepie* (1942). These cherubic babies, with their gumnut caps and blossom skirts or gumleaf sporrans, have engaged readers since their creation. Gibbs made the pleasures and dangers of the Australian bush every child's land of adventure and fantasy, with her evil snakes and Banksia men, pet ants and kindly kookaburras and lizards. *Snugglepot and Cuddlepie* was adapted by the ABC for radio in the mid-1930s, and a ballet was produced in 1988 by the Australian Ballet, with music by Richard Mills and choreography by Petal Miller-Ashmole.

So Much to Tell You … (1987) by John Marsden won the 1988 Book of the Year Awards: Older Readers and was Secondary Winner of KOALA in 1989. Fourteen-year-old Marina has been physically abused by her father in a domestic argument, and as a result refuses to speak. The support and understanding of her teacher, Mr Lindell, and a friend, Cathy, enable Marina to reveal her story through her diary entries, both how she came to be what she is, and what she hopes will happen in the future.

Something Special (1984) by 'Emily Rodda', illustrated by Noela Young, won the 1985 Junior Book of the Year Awards. Sam's mother has a stall of second-hand clothes at the school fête. The observant and sympathetic Sam watches as dresses, dressing-gowns, and other articles of clothing conjure up the original owners. Each piece becomes important to her, and as it finds a new owner, Sam meets the true inheritors of the clothes' special characteristics, and understands that the experiences of people who may never meet are mingled or run parallel in the jigsaw of life. Noela Young's soft pencil drawings of Sam's happy and active family underline the warmth of the story.

SORENSON, EDWARD S. For *Spotty, the Bower Bird and Other Nature Stories: Life Histories of Australian Birds and Animals* (1921) see **Animal Stories**.

SOUTER, DAVID HENRY (1862–1935), painter, cartoonist, designer, short story writer and novelist was born in Aberdeen, Scotland, and settled in Australia in 1887. He worked for John Sands for twelve years, then was the manager of the art department of William Brooks & Co. He edited *Art and Architecture* from 1904 to 1911. Souter was employed as a cartoonist for the *Bulletin*, and his drawings appeared in every issue of the *Bulletin* for forty years. He illustrated magazines for children and worked as a cartoonist for the 'Sunbeams Page' of the *Sunday Sun*, a children's page edited by Ethel Turner. Some of his finest work is found in *Bubbles his Book* (1899) by R.F. Irvine and the five books he illustrated for Ethel Turner, *Gum Leaves* (1900), *Happy Hearts* (1908), *The Raft in the Bush* (1910), *An Ogre Up-to-Date* (1911) and *The Sunshine Family* (1932). He contributed to *Australian Nursery Rimes* (1917). With Percy Spence he illustrated *Tales for Young Australia* (1900), edited by Ernest Favenc and others. When he was 70 he wrote a series of simple verses under the title *Bush Babs* (1933). 'Birthdays come but once a year,/But when they do, we're glad they're here.' Souter provided three illustrations for Emily Coungeau's adult play *Princess Mona: a Romantic Poetical Drama* (1916), written as an 'operatic romance', later set to music by Alfred Hill, and re-named *Auster*. He also wrote his own operetta, *The Gray Kimona*. His adult novel *The Ticket in Tatts* (first published 1988) is set

in Redfern. He had a talent for drawing haughty cats, which became his trade mark, and one of his drawings was reproduced on Royal Doulton ware. He was an admirer of the work of Aubrey Beardsley; his dramatic, fluid lines and stylish black-and-white illustrations draw on art nouveau and art deco styles. See also **Illustration**.

SOUTHALL, IVAN (1921–), born Melbourne, served in the RAAF during World War II, where he won the Distinguished Flying Cross. Southall's first books for children were a series on a larger-than-life flying ace, Simon Black (q.v.), written between 1950 and 1961. In 1954 he provided the storyline for a cartoon strip published in *Woman's Day*, 'Mike Manly — Miracle Man', illustrated by Peter James. His informational books are *Journey into Mystery: a Story of the Explorers Burke and Wills* (1961) and *Lawrence Hargrave* (1964) for Oxford's 'Great Australians' series, *Rockets in the Desert: the Story of Woomera* (1964), *Indonesian Journey* (q.v., 1965), *Seventeen Seconds* (1973), a version for children of his adult book *Softly Tread the Brave* (1960) and *Fly West* (q.v., 1974). He has retold two volumes of Bible stories, *The Sword of Esau* (1967) and *The Curse of Cain* (1968), both illustrated by Joan Kiddell-Monroe, and he wrote the picture-book *Sly Old Wardrobe* (1968), illustrated by Ted Greenwood.

With his novel *Hills End* (1962), Southall changed his direction. The novel presents a group of children isolated from adult help during a flood. How they survive against the river, an escaped bull and a shortage of food offers an analysis of the process of development each child undergoes through the experience. In 1987 it was made into a television series of six half-hour episodes directed by Di Drew, with a script by Noel Robinson. *Ash Road* (q.v., 1965) takes up the same theme, this time during a bushfire, and *The Fox Hole* (q.v., 1967) deals with a boy trapped in a mine. In *To the Wild Sky* (q.v., 1967) and its sequel, *A City Out of Sight* (1984), six children survive when their aircraft crashes on a deserted island. Southall continued his exploration of the need of children to assert themselves with *Let the Balloon Go* (q.v., 1968). *Finn's Folly* (q.v., 1969) was criticised when it appeared for undermining 'cultural trust' by the English critic, David Holbrook, a criticism which now appears very dated. *Bread and Honey* (q.v., 1970) followed, again examining the inner turmoil of childhood. In *Chinaman's Reef is Ours* (1970) a group of children unite to save a small town threatened by a mining company.

Josh (1971) won the Carnegie Medal in 1971. Josh is an outsider, sensitive and misunderstood. When he visits his forbidding Aunt Clara, he antagonises the local children, and Josh decides to walk home to Melbourne rather than continually confront their hostility. This novel touches on many of the themes which absorb Southall: the desire for recognition by the unappreciated adolescent, the burden of a well-thought-of family, the difference between the extroverted and the more vulnerable and susceptible.

Head in the Clouds (1972), illustrated by Richard Kennedy, is about the disabled Ray Plumtree who works magic to turn his neighbours upside down, and *Over the Top* (1972), illustrated by Ian Ribbons, has Perry Benson frantically trying to seek help for his mother, about to give birth. In *Christmas in the Tree* (1985), illustrated by Kay Dattner, Jonathan and Zoe put a spell on Father Christmas so that he grants their wishes, with unexpected results. These three novels are for younger readers, and show Southall's capacity for humour.

Matt and Jo (1973) explores a love affair between two young people on a train on their way to school. In *What About Tomorrow?* (1977), set in Depression times, Sam runs away when he believes that his job as a paper boy is at risk. The novel describes Sam's experiences with three girls, and prefigures his future, in a sometimes awkward time sequence. *King of the Sticks* (1979) features the fey and lonely Custard, bullied by a group of rough and insensitive cowards. *The Golden Goose* (1981) continues Custard's story when he is kidnapped by Preacher Tom.

The action of *The Long Night Watch* (1983) takes place on a remote Pacific island, Tangu Tangu, where the members of the Society for World Order under Divine Rule, led by the charismatic Brigadier Palmer, await deliverance from the chaos of a world at war. Complex relationships develop between the young people who are thrown together under stress. *Rachel* (1986), set on the goldfields in the late nineteenth century, is based on an experience of Southall's mother. Rachel becomes lost when she tries to escape from teasing boys, and is saved by Eddie. This portrait reveals a warmer, more tender side to this controversial and perceptive writer, and Rachel is his most successful female character. *Blackbird* (1988) is set during World War II, in a house in the mountains, where Will, Geoffrey and Patricia Houghton undergo the trials which are necessary to steel their characters for the future. The novel concludes with a speech which sums up Southall's philosophy: 'Better, I think, to go out saying Help me please, to be the man I'll need to be if I'm to cope with the world that others have made. Help me to meet it with courage and dignity. Help me afterwards to make it new.' In *The Mysterious World of Marcus Leadbeater* (1990) Southall's hero journeys to see his grandmother after the death of his beloved grandfather, but she is not to be found, and the certainties of Marcus's world are shaken. The boy's ancestors, his strong links with his family, and his confused grief are evoked.

Southall's tense and dramatic plots, his absorption with the inner life and his style, which shapes language in an unusual way, make his work challenging and intricate. He was the first of the contemporary writers to take up the fallibility, even untrustworthiness, of parents. While he overlaid adolescents with guilt and some primness, he freely admitted their sexual feelings. His characters may be often self-centred and arrogant, but they are also full of self-doubt and a determination to make the best moral choice, unusual touches in the late 1960s. Southall's preoccupation with the psychological pain of his characters set a new course for children's writers, taken up by many who followed him, such as Simon French, Gillian Rubinstein and John Marsden. He has written about his development as a writer in *A Journey of Discovery: on Writing for Children* (1975).

Southward Ho with the Hentys: the Adventures of a Pioneer Family who Sailed from Sussex, England, Aboard the Barque 'Caroline' in the Spring of the Year 1829 and with Edward Henty established the First Permanent Settlement in Victoria at Portland Bay 19th Nov., 1834 (1953) by Fitzmaurice Hill was Highly Commended in the 1954 Book of the Year Awards. The story is told through the eyes of Judy and Jim Hall, 10-year-old twins, who have a pet sheep, Captain Tuffems. Mr Hall is one of Henty's shepherds who is promised a farm when the family reach New Holland. They settle temporarily in Launceston when Jim becomes a ship's boy, and then join Henty again at Portland. This straightforward account of early settlement also won first prize in the Children's Story Section of the Victorian State Government's Centenary Literary and Historical Competition.

Space Demons (1986) by Gillian Rubinstein was an Honour Book in the 1987 Book of the Year Awards: Older Readers, and won YABBA for Older Readers in 1990. Andrew, Elaine, Ben and Mario become involved in the heart of a computer game in which they must carry out a desperate struggle with the sinister demons who feed on the children's own hatreds. It is only by the power of love

that Andrew, Elaine, Ben and Mario are able to survive. Its sequel, *Skymaze* (1989) takes the same characters into a similar situation, carrying with them the knowledge gained from the previous adventure. This time only co-operation saves them from being trapped forever in the maze. The novels present exciting plots and strong themes in a winning mixture.

Spear and Stockwhip: a Tale of the Territory (1950) by Richard Harry Graves was Commended in the 1951 Book of the Year Awards. Stones, Tom, Darkie, Snowy and Joker, join Chikker Jackson on a 1000-mile drive of 2000 cattle from a property near Proserpine, Queensland, to a station on the Roper River. On the way Jackson is killed by a spear. With his last breath, Chikker wills his money and property to the boys. A sinister cattle-thief is found to be involved in gold, opium and hashish-smuggling. The young adventurers are joined by Baroopa, an Aboriginal boy. *Tidinbilla Adventure: a Sequel to Spear and Stockwhip* (1951) opens with the boys at agricultural college, from which they move on to deal with a gang of international spies. See also **Adventure Stories**.

SPENCE, ELEANOR (1928–   ), born Sydney, wrote two of OUP's 'Early Australians' series: *A Schoolmaster* (1969), illustrated by Jane Walker, an account of the career of William Cape, a pioneer educator in NSW, and *A Cedar Cutter* (1971), illustrated by Barbara Taylor, the history of the timber-worker Basil Kendall, father of the poet Henry Kendall. A longer biography is *Mary and Francis: a Story about Mary MacKillop and the Sisters of St Joseph* (1986), illustrated by Heather Potter.

Her first two novels, *Patterson's Track* (1958), illustrated by Alison Forbes, and *The Summer in Between* (q.v., 1959), are both seaside adventures which occur during the Christmas holidays. Her historical novels began with *Lillypilly Hill* (q.v., 1960), set late in the nineteenth century.

The Switherby Pilgrims (1967), illustrated by Corinna Gray, and its sequel, *Jamberoo Road* (1969), illustrated by Doreen Roberts, follow the fortunes of Cassie and a group of orphans who arrive in Australia in the 1820s. Spence has combined her interest in Australian history and her perceptions of childhood in *The Family Book of Mary-Claire* (q.v., 1990).

Spence has fearlessly examined difficult social questions in many of her novels. The events in *The Seventh Pebble* (q.v., 1980) occur just before World War II, but the issue is religious bigotry. The reader is aware that the prejudice which the Irish Connells have suffered in Hollybush Flat will be more than matched in Europe under Hitler's dominance. Religion and history are themes in her two novels about the boyhood of Jesus, *Me and Jeshua* (q.v., 1984) and *Miranda Going Home* (1985), illustrated by Donna Rawlins. See also **Religion**. The latter novel also looks at displacement, which has absorbed Spence since *The Green Laurel* (q.v., 1963) and *The Year of the Currawong* (q.v., 1965). The issue is taken further, to a study of children who are in some way different from their friends, in *The Nothing Place* (1972), illustrated by Geraldine Spence, about Glen, a hearing-impaired boy; *The October Child* (q.v., 1976), *A Candle for Saint Antony* (q.v., 1977), *The Left Overs* (q.v., 1982) and *Deezle Boy* (q.v., 1987). *The Travels of Hermann* (1973), illustrated by Noela Young, recounts the adventures of a white mouse and his search for his destiny. In *Time to Go Home* (1973), illustrated by Fermin Rocker, Rowan suffers some of the everyday trials of adolescence: a passion for football, some heavy bullying, and a growth in maturity.

Spence is critical of materialism and bigotry, and the smugness of middle-class values. Bridget in *The Seventh Pebble* has a raw courage which the more affluent girls at her school lack. At first a wealthy hedonist, Justin in *A Candle for Saint Antony* learns to value the culture of Rudi. Both books explore a loss of innocence: for Rachel in *The Seventh Pebble*, and for Justin in *A Candle for Saint Antony*. *Another Sparrow Singing* (1991) examines the process of adjustment undergone by Courtney and Keith when their father leaves. Courtney regrets the comfort of 'normality'; Keith is traumatised by his father's violence towards him. Both children find some peace within a small community. Never afraid to tackle difficult issues such as class, culture and religion, Spence has shown the Australian child outside the mainstream. Her autobiography is *Another October Child* (1988).

SPENCE, PERCY (PERCIVAL FREDERICK SEATON SPENCE) (1868–1933), born Sydney, lived in Fiji and the UK. He was a cartoonist for the *Bulletin*, but also illustrated with realistic black-and-white sketches adventure stories and children's books, such as *Marooned in Australia* (1897) by Ernest Favenc, *His First Kangaroo* (1898) by 'Arthur Ferres' and "L.E.M."'s *Stories told to Baba and Billy* (1902). In 1890 he illustrated 'Gnomes and Nails', a story by Mary Feld (Whitfeld), for the *Illustrated Sydney News*.

Spirit Wind, The (1973) by Max Fatchen, illustrated by Trevor Stubley, was Highly Commended in the 1974 Book of the Year Awards. For Jarl Hansen the only escape from the brutal first mate, Heinrich the Bull, is to jump ship when the *Hootzen* reaches port in SA. During his desperate swim he saves the life of Nunganee, who was himself a fugitive from his people a long time ago. Jarl is taken in by a welcoming family, but the vicious mate pursues him until Nunganee uses the old magic to conjure up a dreadful wind. Fatchen writes about the tough stoicism of the sailors aboard the old sailing ships, their battle with an unforgiving sea, and the excitement of the chase.

Sport. As a strong feature of Australian life, sport is often included as a part of the adventure (q.v.) or school story (q.v.). In a typical early adventure story, Joseph Bowes devotes a chapter of *Pals: Young Australians in Sport and Adventure* (?1910) to a school cricket match between Dingdongla and Tareela. The pals of the title, Joe Blain, Sandy McIntyre, Jimmy Flynn and Yellow Billy, save the day for Tareela, despite the primitive nature of the equipment: 'The stumps, like much of the material, were home made. The Dingdonglas had only one "spring handle"; the others were chopped out of beech boards. The Tareelans were not much better off for material. They ... were like their opponents, sans leggings and gloves.' The cricket match between Cungee and Mulgoa in *Mates at Billabong* (1911) by Mary Grant Bruce, while not as primitive, serves to show the moral fibre of Jim and Wally. Wally is able to rally Jim's bowling by calling 'Play up, School!' In Lillian Pyke's school story *A Prince at School* (1919) the prince, Andi of Vilatonga, earns acceptance by the other boys through his prowess at cricket. Joan Phipson has girls in the cricket team in *The Grannie Season* (1985) in a school cricket match in which grown-up relatives are asked to play with the children selected as the best in the school. When Timothy White's mother comes into labour at the critical moment, his grandmother steps in to take his father's place, producing an 'electrifying innings'. In Marilyn Cosgrove's *The Cricket Kid* (1989) Rick learns new skills as a spin bowler from his grandfather.

Noel Bennett in James Preston's *The Ring of the Axe* (1968) wants to be a champion axeman, despite his mother's opposition. He overcomes her objections by using his skill to save the life of a mysterious old man. The same author's *The Sky Between the Trees* (1986) also deals with wood-chopping. The story is loosely based on the childhood of a champion wood-chopper, Peter McLaren, and this time it is Peter's father who opposes Peter's ambition. *Olympic Kayak* (1968) by Allan Aldous shows the rigorous training and desire to win required to be selected for an Olympic team. By contrast, in *Cannily,*

Cannily (q.v., 1981) Simon French makes a football match the issue which identifies Trevor Huon's difficulties to his parents. His need to fit in with the other boys at his school leads him to lie about his prowess as a player, and the relaxed and amused tolerance of his parents to sport is contrasted with the intensity which drives the coach. Trevor's last day at school concludes with a game of soccer without competitiveness. In Thurley Fowler's *Wait for Me! Wait for Me!* (1981) Robert's feelings of inferiority towards his sporting brothers prove to be unimportant compared to his courage and resourcefulness when the boys are held captive. Tennis is the pivot of the plot in *Playing for Keeps* (1989) by Damian Morgan. Two of the Quill family members pursue their own goals to the point of family breakdown.

Paint a Dream (1980) by Mary White is about Craig's inability to read, a problem which he overcomes when his teacher gives him a book about famous swimmers. Craig's passion for the sport drives him to master the text. The delights of surfing are treated in *Dead Man's Float* (1973) by Roger Vaughan Carr; *Puberty Blues* (q.v., 1979) by Gabrielle Carey and Kathy Lette; *The Surfing Kid* (1987) by Marilyn Cosgrove, with photographs by Jacqueline Lampe; and Tim Winton's *Lockie Leonard, Human Torpedo* (q.v., 1990). *Puberty Blues* is more about the subculture than the sport itself, *The Surfing Kid* is the story of a champion surfer, and *Lockie Leonard, Human Torpedo* captures the exhilaration of riding the waves. Eleanor Stodart's *When the Mountains Changed Their Tune* (1985) is a novel containing much detail about the techniques of skiing. Elyne Mitchell's *Winged Skis* (q.v., 1964) is a more integrated account of skiing in the Australian Alps, particularly the Snowy Mountains area, and captures the pleasure of the sport.

A match or sporting event may be the turning-point of the plot, or an indicator of character. Occasionally, sport is also seen as fun.

'**St Helen**' is the setting for *The True Story of Lilli Stubeck* (q.v., 1984) and other novels by James Aldridge.

STABLES, WILLIAM GORDON (1840–1910), born Scotland, led an adventurous life, including crewing on two whaling expeditions to Greenland. He was a prolific contributor to the *Boy's Own Paper*, where he also conducted a 'Dorothy Dix' column. He wrote around five books a year for thirty years. *From Squire to Squatter* (1888) promotes the idea of settlement in Australia, even to detail on the cost of selections. 'The youth who finds an undoubted pleasure in working is sure to get on in Australia. There is that in the clear, pure, dry air of the back Bush which renders inactivity an impossibility to anyone except ne'er-do-wells and born idiots.' Proving himself neither, Archie returns to England with a wife and a fortune. See also **Sydney**. Stables wrote other novels which refer to, or are partly set in, Australia, such as *From Pole to Pole* (1886), *The Naval Cadet* (1897) and *Wild Life in Sunny Lands* (1906). In *Kidnapped by Cannibals* (1899), Willie Stuart, aboard the *Ornithorhynchus*, assists in some 'blackberrying', i.e. kidnapping of South Sea Islanders, east of New Caledonia. *Frank Hardinge: From Torrid Zones to Regions of Perpetual Snow* (1908), originally serialised in the *Boy's Own Annual*, opens in Brisbane, where Frank is awaiting the return of his father. With the naturalist Jansen Skoolberg and a motley company, Frank sets off to collect specimens for the museum Jansen intends to establish in Castle Skoolberg. There is much comment on the unique plants and animals, which are preferred to the traditional human inhabitants. See also **Aboriginal People in Children's Literature**; **Animal Stories**; **Brisbane**.

STACKPOOL, WALTER (1915–89), born Corowa, NSW, first illustrated the book of the film, *Bush Christmas* (1947) by Mary Cathcart Borer. He illustrated nearly a hundred children's books, including some of the 'Australians in History' series published by Collins in the 1970s; Victor Barnes's 'Skippy' and 'Minus Five' books; books by Joan Dalgleish, Pat Edwards, George Finkel, N.L. Ray, Nancy Keesing, Melva Lear, Sally Farrell Odgers, and R.S. Porteous. *Nonsense Places, an Absurd Australian Alphabet* (1976) by Michael Dugan is illustrated in Stackpool's typical style — free, assured and accurate, with a humorous edge. His conscientious research and his sensitive drawings of animals and places extend the narrative and develop atmosphere.

Starland of the South (1950) by William Allan McNair, illustrated by William R. Taplin, was Highly Commended in the 1951 Book of the Year Awards. In a series of bedtime stories, Uncle Michael tells David and Beth, who live on a farm in NZ, about the stars. Before each story is told, the children are shown how to find the constellation or star in the night sky, so that the fabulous accounts of creatures such as the Centaur, Pegasus or Orion are accompanied by facts about the southern sky. The text is integrated with star maps, pronunciation guides, and the monthly journeys of the stars, in an excellent introduction to the science and romance of astronomy.

State Library of South Australia: Children's Literature Research Collection was established in 1959. It consists of over 45 000 children's books, with an emphasis on local material, but there are also many other early children's books in English. Two private collections of 300 books, and 110 toys and games from the 1820s to 1910 are also included.

State Library of Tasmania: Children's Literature Research Collection contains early children's books from 1900 to the late 1930s, and a representative collection of Australian children's titles, some rare. There is a complete collection of Book of the Year Awards, a comprehensive collection of recent works, and a collection of folk-tales.

State Library of Victoria: Children's Literature Research Collection is a comprehensive, historical and current collection of more than 20 000 volumes which was assembled from the library's general holdings by Mrs Margaret Ingham between 1975 and 1980. The major collecting emphasis is Australian material, particularly titles published in Victoria. Books from the nineteenth century to the present, including first editions and rare items, are arranged in two sequences, Australian and overseas material.

State Library of Western Australia: Research Collection of Children's Literature contains material by Australian authors and illustrators, or with an Australian setting, collected and arranged chronologically to provide the researcher with an overview of the attitudes, range of writing, changing formats and presentation of children's books over two centuries. Annuals, periodicals, comics, biographies, audio cassettes and critical works are included in a collection with many rare and ephemeral items.

STEELE, MARY (1930–), born Newcastle, NSW, writer and reviewer, has written two books about an aardvark, *Arkwright* (q.v., 1985) and *Citizen Arkwright* (1990). In *Mallyroots' Pub at Misery Ponds* (1988) the destitute Mallyroots inherit the pub at Misery Ponds and make it a tourist attraction with the help of two American tourists, Bluebird and Hiram B. Rumbleburger. Exaggerated national stereotypes and the legendary outback provide a humorous story.

STEPHENS, J. BRUNTON (1835– 1902), born Borrowstounness, Scotland, came to Australia in 1866. He was a leading literary figure in his time, contributing poetry to the *Bulletin* and to anthologies. H.M. Green calls him 'Australia's first scholar-poet … the first to introduce wit and humour into Australian poetry'. *Marsupial Bill, or, The Bad Boy, the Good Dog and the Old Man Kangaroo* (1879), illustrated by J.A. Clarke, first appeared in the *Queenslander*. 'A little boy, whose moral tone/Was lamentably low,/A shocking scamp, with just a speck/Of good in embryo/His name was Bill; to wallabies/He bore an evil will;/All things that hop on hinder legs/His function was to kill,/And from his show of scalps he won/The name, Marsupial Bill.' While illicitly smoking his father's meerschaum, Bill is grabbed by a kangaroo who takes him to court, where he is saved from execution through the intervention of the boss kangaroo's daughter and his own faithful dog. The poem is illustrated with masterly drawings of climactic moments in the story. Often Stephens is lost for words to describe Bill's misdemeanours, and exhorts the artist to reveal the events with his pen.

STEVENS, FAE HEWSTON (1907–), born Wedderburn, Victoria, has written local histories of Victorian areas. Her 'Koronglea' series was inspired by Mary Grant Bruce's Billabong books. The first was *Koronglea Cobbers* (1961). The Dixons have a large sheep property in Diggora West, Victoria, where their idyllic lifestyle is further enriched by a visit from the eldest daughter Helen and her small son Paul, who have been living in America. *Koronglea Ponies* (1962) describes the visit of Anne and Noelle, and their journey by ship from Perth to Melbourne. *Koronglea Holidays* (1963) also means summer visitors for 'Koronglea', where it is shearing time. There is the additional excitement of an escaped prisoner hiding in the barn, and an impending marriage. In *Koronglea Adventures* (1965) John and Max visit their cousins in WA, journeying by car across the Nullarbor. The *Koronglea Twins* (1967) are Rex and Peggy-Sue, Helen's children, who are staying at 'Koronglea'. They rescue Tessa from her awful relatives, survive a flood and visit Coober Pedy. The 'Koronglea' series were all illustrated by Ian Nimmo Forrest. In *The Mallee Riders* (1965) Mark Holden suffers from a snobbish mother and the Hamilton twins from a farm threatened by drought. Both problems are solved, or at least moderated, at the end of the novel. See also **Aboriginal People in Children's Fiction**.

STEVENS, THOMAS, see **TJAPAN-GATI, THOMAS STEVENS**

STEWART, MAUREEN (1939–), born Brisbane, has written over forty novels and informational books. She was one of the few Australians to write for 'Topliners', the Macmillan series for reluctant readers, for which she wrote *Orange Wendy* (1974). She has also contributed to Australian reading schemes, such as 'Flag', 'Trend', and 'Orbit'.

Stewart often uses a humorous style and format, such as letters or a diary, which establishes an immediate interest. In *Dear Emily* (1986), *Love from Greg* (1987), *Maria's Diary* (1988) and *Maria in Love* (1990) Emily is a well-spoken young lady who lives in the country and Greg is a surfie drop-out. He and his sister Maria live in Richmond, an inner suburb of Melbourne. Maria writes to Emily in the first book, Greg continues the correspondence in the second, and we learn more about Maria in the last two. In *Henry and Voula: an Off-Beat Love Story* (1989) and *Please Write Back: More Letters from Henry and Voula* (1990), a developing romance has its ups and downs. See also **Greeks**. The romance is continued in *Henry Goes Green* (1990), when he moves to the country.

Stewart has dealt with issues such as alcoholism in *Vicki's Habit* (1986), a correspondence between two alcoholic girls, Vicki and Sharon; shoplifting in *Orange Wendy*; and teenage death in *Miranda's Story* (1988), where Miranda has a life-threatening disease. She is hospitalised for long periods for a treatment which makes her ill, and encouraged by a nurse to write down her feelings and reactions.

She has edited short story collections, such as *Tall Tales from the Speewah: Australian Stories that are Bigger and Better* (1988), illustrated by Jeff Hook, a collection of stories about Crooked Mick; *Trees Can Speak and Other Stories* (1984), with short stories by Australians and overseas writers; and *Creation Myths* (1987), illustrated by Graeme Base, legends from many cultures about the creation of the world.

Stewart confronts stereotypes, and has done so since the early 1970s. Wendy, in *Orange Wendy* is short and fat and clever, unlike her counterparts in prize-winning books of the time. Her adolescents can be self-destructive, such as Vicki in *Vicki's Habit* or Frank in *Orange Wendy*, and are frequently caught up in situations which threaten respectability. Stewart presents in accessible narratives the social context of adolescence and the pressures placed on young people.

STIVENS, DAL (1911–), born Blayney, NSW. For *The Bushranger* (1978) see **Bushrangers**.

STODART, ELEANOR MARY (1940–) was editor of *Reading Time* from 1977 to 1981, and has written many informational books for young readers, including titles in Angus & Robertson's 'Young Nature' series, such as *Trees* (1980). Her novel *When the Mountains Change Their Tune* (1985) is set in the Snowy Mountains. Karl, Andrew, Ian and Jason are lost in a blizzard while skiing, and the author describes what is required for survival. She also edited *Writing and Illustrating for Children: CBC ACT Seminars 1975–1980* (1985), a collection of papers by authors, illustrators and critics.

STOMANN, ALLAN (1943–), born Melbourne, illustrated Coralie Rees's

What Happened After? Nursery Rhyme Sequels (1972); *Oodles of Noodles* (1987) by Margaret Roc; and re-illustrated *Sharpur the Carpet Snake* (1967) by Lydia Pender in 1976. His illustrations to Duncan Ball's *Selby's Secret* (q.v., 1985), *Selby Speaks* (1988) and *Selby Screams* (1989) have contributed to the success of these books. Stomann has illustrated for reading schemes, with titles such as *The Shy Giant* (1982) by Pamela Shrapnel, in the 'Expressways' series; the *Say What You Like* (1979) series by Margaret Roc and Kathleen Hawke; and *Loads and Loads of Limericks* (1985) collected by David Harris for Angus & Robertson's 'Young Australia' series. He has illustrated a series of Junior Field Guides by Eleanor Stodart, and the 'Sing' books produced by the ABC for ten years.

Storm Boy (1963) by Colin Thiele, illustrated by John Baily, was Commended in the 1964 Book of the Year Awards. Storm Boy lives on the Coorong with his reclusive father, Hideaway Tom. His only friend is Fingerbone Bill. Storm Boy finds three baby pelicans and raises them to maturity. One, Mr Percival, remains with him when Storm Boy releases the birds into the wild. The bird gives the boy the companionship he longs for, strengthened when Mr Percival helps in the rescue of the crew of a stricken tugboat during a storm. The tragic death of the pelican precipitates a major change in Storm Boy's life, and he agrees to go to school. This widely read and much-loved novel has been reprinted over many editions, with a particularly fine one published in 1974, illustrated by Robert Ingpen. See also **Aboriginal People in Children's Fiction**. It was made into a film by the SA Film Corporation in 1976, directed by Henri Safran, with a script by Sonia Borg. Greg Rowe played Storm Boy, David Gulpilil was Fingerbone Bill and Peter Cummins was Hideaway Tom. The film was voted the best film at the 1977 Australian Film Awards.

Story of China, The (1970) by Lo Hui-Min, illustrated by Elaine Haxton, was Highly Commended in the 1971 Book of the Year Awards. The author was a senior fellow in the Department of Far Eastern History at the Australian National University, and wrote the book for his son, providing a simple, sympathetic and accurate picture of China's long and fascinating history. The account takes the reader to the establishment of the People's Republic of China. The book is illustrated by Haxton in full colour, with maps and pictures which evoke the culture of a great nation.

Story of Karrawingi the Emu, The (1946) by Leslie Rees, illustrated by Walter Cunningham, was the first winner of the Book of the Year Awards, in 1946. Karrawingi's life begins near the sea, hatched out by his father, old Baramool. Growing up brings encounters with eagles, escape from Aboriginal hunters, and pairing with Warree. Karrawingi hatches his own eggs, although he loses some to white men, until the settlers decide to hunt the emus off the land. Karrawingi is such a fine bird that he is captured and taken to a zoo, where he languishes for nearly a year, only to escape from a truck which is transporting him to the city. Karrawingi is free again to 'gulp the rushing air'. The life cycle of the emu is told with flair, with Cunningham's illustrations adding interest to each page.

Story of Kurri Kurri the Kookaburra, The (1950) by Leslie Rees, illustrated by Margaret Senior, was Highly Commended in the 1950 Book of the Year Awards. It is a fictional account of how the kookaburra was introduced into WA. Kurri Kurri and his friend Karloo are taken from NSW to 'Blackswanland' by Mr Hensman to become family pets. Karloo escapes, but Kurri Kurri's wings are clipped, and he learns to live with humans, until he is able to join Karloo in the wild and father his own chicks. The book includes information about the habits of the kookaburra and full-page coloured illustrations. It was reissued in 1978 and 1988, the latter with illustrations by Patrick Watson.

Story of Shadow the Rock Wallaby, The (1948) by Leslie Rees, illustrated by Walter Cunningham, was Highly Commended in the 1948 Book of the Year Awards. Shadow's life is traced. He learns to survive in the wild, sees his friend Tuft killed by a carpet snake, is threatened by a fox, comes to a house where he is caught, but escapes to tell the other wallabies of his journey. His sister is born, and he mates with Lillypilly after fighting another wallaby for her. The life cycle of the animal is told in series of graphic adventures, and the dangers of life in the wild are not glossed over.

'Storymakers' was a series of four television studies of Australian writers and artists for children, made by the Australian Film Institute. The programs aimed to develop children's awareness of how books are conceived and created, and included dramatisations of scenes from the books. Authors include Robin Klein, Dick Roughsey and Percy Trezise, and Colin Thiele. A further study, 'The Illustrators', presents Jeannie Baker, Roland Harvey and Julie Vivas.

STOW, CATHERINE SOMMER-VILLE, née FIELD, see **PARKER, KATHERINE LANGLOH**

STOW, JULIAN **RANDOLPH** (1935–), born Geraldton, WA, is a writer for adults. He has written novels, poems, libretti and the children's novel, *Midnite: the Story of a Wild Colonial Boy* (q.v., 1967).

'STRANG, HERBERT' was the pseudonym used by GEORGE HERBERT ELY (1866–1958) and CHARLES JAMES L'ESTRANGE (1867–1947), members of staff at OUP in England. They wrote and edited many adventure stories and collections, as 'Herbert Strang' and 'Mrs Herbert Strang', including *Adventures in the Bush: Australia's Story* (1915). One of Oxford's 'Romance of the World' series, it contains extracts from E.W. Landor's *The Bushman*; John Henderson's *Excursions and Adventures in N.S.W.*; and, from the anonymous work *Adventures Ashore and Afloat* (1866), 'A ride through the Mallee' and 'Fighting in the Bush'.

Strange Objects (1990) by Gary Crew won the 1991 Book of the Year Awards: Older Readers. The novel is built around the incidents which occurred when the Dutch vessel *Batavia*, was wrecked off the WA coast. Steven Messenger finds a mummified hand, a diary, and a cannibal pot in a cave. They are identified as relics of the wreck, or from that time. The diary belongs to Wouter Loos, a survivor of the *Batavia* (q.v.), and relates his experiences in the company of Jan Pelgrom, their lives linked to Messenger's through a ring he found with the mummified hand. Crew depicts the historical period, 1629, and the characters of Pelgrom and Loos, with the modern Steven Messenger reliving the terrors of the psychotic Pelgrom. Newspaper articles, diaries, letters, extracts from historical texts, and scientific reports are used to build an intriguing mystery with psychological nuances. See also *Batavia*.

STREDDER, ELEANOR, born Royston, UK, wrote *Archie's Find, a Story of Australian Life* (1890). Gold is found in an underground cave. It saves from impoverishment Archie's family and their friends, Zachary Fenn and his long-lost niece. The novel opens with three children hiding in the base of a tree from a huge eagle which they fear will attack them, as it has already carried off a calf. Stredder describes the countryside: 'The river by which the boys were standing found an outlet through a dark and perilous ravine, where the hyena-opossum made its lair ... Far stretching plains and rising downs were interspersed with stately forests, where tree-like ferns mingled with graceful palms, and dark shadowy cedars contrasted with the tall, straight stems of the grass gum-tree.' Not surprisingly, the location, the 'Zabba valley', is unclear.

STRUTT, WILLIAM (1825–1915), painter, came to Australia in 1850 and remained until 1962. Strutt painted landscapes and portraits from Australian life, such as the aftermath of the 1851 bushfires which ravaged Victoria, and incidents in the Burke and Wills expedition. For *Cooey: or, The Trackers of Glenferry* (1989) see **Lost in the Bush**.

STURGESS, REGINALD WARD (1892–1932), born Melbourne, began his studies at the Melbourne National Gallery under Fred McCubbin and Bernard Hall when he was only 13. He was a friend of Percy Leason, and often went with him to the Melbourne Zoo, where they would sketch the animals. Out of this experience, Sturgess illustrated W.M. Fleming's *Bunyip Says So: a Tale of the Australian Bush* (1922).

Sugar and Snails Press was set up to publish counter-sexist books for children, after a short period publishing as the Women's Movement Children's Literature Co-operative (q.v.), established in 1972. The original counter-sexist position has changed to a non-sexist one. *The Sugar and Snails Guide to Non-sexist Books for Children* was first edited by Jenny Pausacker in 1975. Another edition, edited by Annette Rubenstein, appeared in 1977. The 1985 edition was edited by Irene McGinnigle. Selection criteria for this edition were 'That main characters were not stereotyped on the basis of gender', that 'background characters offered

... the reader a positive role model', despite stereotyped main characters, and that 'books of questionable literary and artistic value were only included if they dealt with an aspect of non-sexism otherwise poorly covered'. The list is limited to fiction, with some traditional stories and poetry. The organisation ceased in 1992.

Sugar-Plum Christmas Book: a Book for Christmas and All the Days of the Year, The (1977) by Jean Chapman, illustrated by Deborah Niland, was Commended in the 1978 Picture Book of the Year Awards. It is a collection of stories, carols, poems and activities associated with Christmas customs. Humorous black-and-white or coloured illustrations decorate each page. A companion volume was *The Sugar Plum Song Book* (1977), with song settings by Margaret Moore, and also illustrated by Deborah Niland.

Summer In Between, The (1959) by Eleanor Spence, illustrated by Marcia Lane-Foster, was Commended in the 1960 Book of the Year Awards. The Christmas holidays between Faith Melville's last year at primary school and first year at secondary school are taken up with the production of her own play. Faith's confidence is shattered when Colleen, a girl she has never liked, is a better actor than she is, but Faith's new friend Pauline and her Aunt Elizabeth teach Faith that what is best for the drama is the most important consideration in the theatre. In the process of the production, other of Faith's certainties are questioned and she begins to understand the richness of individual differences. This gentle analysis of how maturity is developed was Spence's second book.

SUMMERVILLE, JENNY. For *Shields of Trell* (1986) see **Science Fiction**.

Sun on the Stubble (1961) by Colin Thiele was Commended in the 1962 Book of the

Year Awards. In an evocation of a child-hood before World War I, the observant Bruno is depicted as he is about to go to secondary school in Adelaide. The free-dom of a rural childhood in a colourful German settlement, with its eccentric characters and rich traditions, is thrown into sharp focus as Bruno feels the pain of leaving it all behind, 'coming down from the sunny uplands of his boyhood, to the great grey plains of adult life ahead'.

Sunlight Australian ABC, see **Alphabet Books**

Sunshine (1981) by Jan Ormerod won the 1982 Picture Book of the Year Awards. A small girl goes through the morning ritual of getting up, having breakfast and rushing off to kindergarten in a wordless picture-book. Each page provides homely details to entertain the youngest readers.

Sydney, largest city in Australia, set on a magnificent harbour spanned by the Harbour Bridge, has inspired writers for children from the earliest times. When Captain Spencer arrives in Sydney, after traversing the continent, in *Adventures in Australia; or the Wanderings of Captain Spencer in the Bush and the Wilds. Containing Accurate Descriptions of the Habits of the Natives, and the Natural Productions and Features of the Country* (1851), by Mrs Robert Lee, the scene strikes him as 'per-haps the finest which he had ever beheld … a noble estuary presented itself, decked with the loveliest bays, inlets, islands, vil-las, cottages, and gardens; and the silvery sand of the beach formed a glittering bor-der'. Richard Rowe's *Fred Leicester* (1889) makes an early comparison between 'pic-turesque Port Jackson' and 'dreary-looking Port Phillip', and presents the same vista. 'As soon as you run in between the frowning Heads and see the lovely expanse of inosculating bays, bordered by silvery sands and rocky villa-dotted shores … you take a fancy to the place. And after the raw look and mad rush of Melbourne,

Fred found refreshment in the time-mellowed buildings and more leisurely pace of life in Sydney.' However, in *The Early Start in Life* (1867) by Emilia Marryat Norris, the Stirling family arrive from England and are at first shocked by what they see. 'At the time I write of, Sydney was not a prepossessing town. It may be improved now. The houses were badly built, partly of brick and partly of wood. The streets were dirty and unpaved, or only partially so. The townspeople, in dirt, seemed to match the streets.' They are more impressed as they walk to more affluent parts. A year later James Skipp Borlase, in *Daring Deeds* (1868), describes Sydney as having 'an English street, a French street, a Chinese street, and a colo-nial street, with a dash of German, Irish and native peculiarity in each'. Nine suc-cessive houses in George Street are then described: 'Number one a bank (architec-ture pure Italian), secondly a French cafe, next a German divan, then a Chinese merchant's, followed by a colonial wooden shanty; then an English draper's; then a pension Suisse, next a Turkish bath and lastly an American rifle gallery and bowl-ing saloon.' Gordon Stables is also enthusi-astic, in *From Squire to Squatter* (1888): 'There is an air of luxury and refinement about many of the buildings that quite impresses the young man; but he cannot help noticing that there is also a sort of business air about the streets which he hardly expected to find, and which reminds him forcibly of Glasgow and Manchester.'

In its role as the first point of settlement after the arrival of the First Fleet, Sydney is the setting for Doris Chadwick's *John of the Sirius* (q.v., 1955), *John of Sydney Cove* (1957) and *John and Nanbaree* (1962), and also Eve Pownall's *Cousins-Come-Lately: Adventures in Old Sydney Town* (q.v., 1952) set during the time of Governor Bourke. Uncle John's home in Castlereagh Street is described, and as the children explore the town, they see Hyde Park, the Rocks, glimpse Darling Harbour and watch the cedar-cutters in the bush on the North Shore. *Johnny Neptune* (1971), *The Best of the Bunch* (1978) and *A House by the Water* (1970) by Nance Donkin are also set in Sydney in the early nineteenth century. Joyce Nicholson's *The Convict's Daughter* (1976) begins in 1814, and describes the Harbour and town of the period from the point of view of a convict. A powerful picture of early Sydney is found in Ruth Park's fantasy *Playing Beatie Bow* (q.v., 1980). In 1873 Abigail walks around the Rocks, noting the Garrison Church, the shops on the corner of Cambridge and Argyle Streets, with Circular Quay and George Street close by. 'Stone steps ran up one side and on the other two tottering stairways curled upon themselves, over-hung with vines and dishevelled trees, and running amongst and even across the roofs of indescribable shanties like broken down farm sheds. These dwellings were propped up with tree trunks and railway sleepers; goats grazed on their roofs; and over all was the smell of rotting seaweed, ships, wood smoke, human ordure, and horses and harness.'

Ethel and Lilian Turner, Louise Mack and Jean Curlewis set many of their novels in their home city. Louise Mack's three books about Lennie and Mabel begin at a school like Sydney Girls' High School, and include their journeying around the city. Curlewis's *The Ship that Never Set Sail* (1921) has descriptions of Circular Quay, Market Street, Pyrmont Bridge, Darling Harbour and the Rocks which recall these places before the erection of the Harbour Bridge.

Libby Hathorn's *The Tram to Bondi Beach* (q.v., 1981) shows a later Sydney, featuring the now defunct trams. Sydney during the 1930s is also the setting for *The Boys from Bondi* (1987) by Alan Collins, as Jacob and Solly ride on the Gladesville ferry, walk from Darlinghurst to Bondi Junction and window-shop in George Street. Pre-war Sydney appears in Michael Noonan's *McKenzie's Boots* (1987) as Rod works as a milkman travelling around the Sydney

suburbs. Also recalling the 1930s, Nadia Wheatley's *The House that was Eureka* (q.v., 1984), set in the inner-city suburb of Newtown, recounts the clashes between the unemployed and the police over the evictions of the Depression. In a recon-struction of an important moment in Sydney's development, Deirdre Hill's *A Bridge of Dreams* (1982) observes the Sydney Harbour Bridge being built, rivet by rivet. The difficulties of its engineer-ing, accidents which occurred, and its opening drama are described in detail, and in her *Flight from Fear* (1988) the threat from Japanese submarines during World War II is seen through the eyes of Harbour-dwellers. Thomas Shapcott and Steve Spears's *Mister Edmund* (1990) is also set around the Harbour Bridge and Opera House.

Gabrielle Carey and Kathy Lette's *Puberty Blues* (q.v., 1979) is a powerful evocation of Sydney's surfing culture, set around Cronulla, an earlier view of which can be found in Claire Meillon's *The New Surf Club* (1959). Enid Conley's *The Dangerous Bombora* (1968) describes boat-ing in Middle Harbour, at Manly, and the Bluff. A vivid picture of the busy life of the Harbour is provided by Joan Phipson, in *The Crew of the Merlin* (1966). 'From the grim little turret of Fort Denison and the etched curve of the bridge to the dis-tant and barely visible bastion of South Head there were ships moored every-where. Some were naval craft and some were weathered old merchantmen swing-ing on buoys that looked as big as houses when they passed them close. Up and down the fairway the squat yellow and black ferries bustled to their timetables and motor-boats and tugs wove their way among the bigger ships. Once a deep, hoarse boom heralded the approach of a liner on its way to the passenger dock at Circular Quay.'

Anne Brooksbank's *On Loan* (1985) pic-tures the multicultural aspects of Sydney, particularly the Vietnamese in the western suburbs. *Five Times Dizzy* (q.v., 1982) and

Dancing in the Anzac Deli (1984) by Nadia Wheatley are set in Newtown, evoking its rich mixture of cultures. Patricia Wrightson's *An Older Kind of Magic* (q.v., 1972) presents a modern and bustling city as the children play in its streets and lanes, and conjure up the ancient spirits who live beneath the parks. Jeannie Baker's *Millicent* (1980) is set in Hyde Park, where we see the statue of William Bede Dalley, the Archibald fountain and the characters who are to be found there. In Penny Hall's *Nim's Time* (1991) Nim wind-rides to the 'biggest stegosaurus spike of the Sydney Opera House, [and from there] he sees the harbour below, the Harbour Bridge, the Lego set that was North Sydney, the castle that was Government House, and the mansion that was the State Library'.

A modern history of Sydney is to be found in *My Place* (q.v., 1987) by Nadia Wheatley, which shows the changes occurring since and before white settlement. Barbara Ker Wilson has used a similar approach in *Acacia Terrace* (1988), which reflects the alterations in a row of terrace houses from 1860 to the present. Other writers who have used Sydney as a setting include Lilith Norman, Reginald Ottley, Eve Pownall, Noreen Shelley, Eleanor Spence, Celia Syred, and Valerie Thompson. The dramatic beauty of Sydney, its history and the bustle of its harbourside setting is brought to life in these stories of those who live and work in a city of great diversity.

Sydney Gazette, Australia's first newspaper, established in 1803, published the first Australian book for children, *A Mother's Offering to Her Children* (q.v., 1841), later republished as a single work by George William Evans (q.v.).

SYRED, CELIA MARY (1911–), born Gloucestershire, UK, came to Australia in 1955. She studied at the Royal College of Arts, London, and was a lecturer in art. *Cocky's Castle* (q.v., 1966) is a story of a girl's attachment to an old house. *Baker's Dozen* (1969), illustrated by Astra Lacis, relates the fortunes of the large Cotgrove family who come to Sydney in the 1860s and struggle to find a place in the colony. Syred also wrote *Hebe's Daughter* (q.v., 1976), and *Melissa Woodruff* (1981), neither set in Australia. *The Shop in Woolloomooloo* (1983), illustrated by Deborah Crooks, set in the nineteenth century, is a haven for Vicky Collicott and her mother, where they are joined by a forlorn boy, Daniel Warner, whom they teach to read. Syred's informational books include *An Innkeeper* (1970), illustrated by Dinny McKay, and *A Printer* (1971), illustrated by Joan Walker, for OUP's 'Early Australians' series.

T

'TAGG, TIMOTHY' (ALFRED BURKE) produced colourful, board-covered books at the end of World War II. *When I Grow Up ...* (1945), illustrated by Alan Rigby and Laurie Greenacre, an 'Uncle Peter Playbook', is verse: 'I'd like to be a hot dog man,/Now that must be grand fun,/Selling little frankfurters,/With mustard, in a bun.' *I'm a Captain* (1945), *Jeep: a Story of Four Dogs* (1945), and *Pot and Pan* (1945) are in similar format.

TANDY, SOPHIA. For *The Children in the Scrub: a Story of Tasmania* (1878) see **Lost in the Bush; Religion.**

Tangara: 'Let Us set off Again' (1960) by Nan Chauncy, illustrated by Brian Wildsmith, won the 1961 Book of the Year Awards. Lexie, with a shell necklace as the key, enters the world of her great-aunt Rita, where she meets Merrina, a Tasmanian Aboriginal child. The two children play happily together until Lexie, called 'Weetah' by Merrina, has to go home. Just before she leaves, Lexie witnesses a massacre of Merrina's people, and later learns that all of the Aboriginal People she had met in Merrina's company had died long ago, in Rita's time. See also **Aboriginal People in Children's Fiction.**

TANNER, JANE (1946–), born Melbourne, studied at the National Gallery School. She resigned from teaching to become a full-time illustrator. Her first illustrations appeared in *Time for a Rhyme* (1982) and *Time for a Number Rhyme* (1983), which are collections of traditional nursery rhymes. She has contributed illustrations to reading schemes. *There's a Sea in my Bedroom* (1984) by Margaret Wild revealed her unusual approach to perspective, offering a view of the world through a child's eye. In *Niki's Walk* (1987), a wordless picture-book, Niki wanders through the rich life of an untidy, busy, multicultural suburb. Her pictures for *Drac and the Gremlin* (q.v., 1988) by Allan Baillie present a paradox between fantastic story and children at play in a garden. *The Wolf* (1991) by Margaret Barbalet is a much darker book, in which the arresting illustrations capture the uncertainty and threat of the story. Tanner's illustrations are lustrous and emotional, reflecting her admiration for the great painters of the past. Her unconventional angles involve the reader in the text, and her intense response to character adds complexity.

TANTON, BRUCE (1946–), born England, came to Australia when he was 9 years old. *Time's Lost Hero* (1990) is about Ginger Tom, falsely accused of cowardice during the Boer War. When Roger Thomas discovers an old photograph of a group of soldiers, and one of the boys in it is himself, he is drawn back to the times, so that he is able to prove Ginger's bravery. See also **War.**

TARLING, LOWELL (1949–), born London, UK, came to Australia in 1959. For *Taylor's Troubles* (1982) see **School Stories.** In *The Secret Gang of OomLau* (1988), illustrated by Brett Colquhoun, Ivan, a comic fanatic, joins the OomLau, a gang of boys who help to expose bird-smugglers. In a complex adventure, Ivan develops a new friendship and retains his fantasy world, despite his rejection by the gang. Ivan is imaginative, scatty, cowardly and disaster-prone, but irrepressible.

Drac and the Gremlin (1988) by Allan Baillie. Illustrator: Jane Tanner

Tarling has written *Thank God for the Salvos: The Salvation Army in Australia 1880–1980* (1980).

Taronga (1986) by Victor Kelleher was an Honour Book in the 1987 Book of the Year Awards: Older Readers. In a post-holocaust setting, Ben is able to communicate telepathically with animals. He is involved, against his will, in calling to them so that they can be killed. His guilt is expiated by helping Ellie with her plans for the animals at Taronga Zoo, which are being used by an autocratic group to guard a fortress against an insurrection. See also **Science Fiction**.

'TASMAN'. For *A Little Aversion* (1910) see **Immigrants**; **Religion**.

TAYLOR, ANDREW. For *The Day we Lost Forever* (1988) see **Aboriginal People in Children's Fiction**.

Taylor, Arnold is the ghost who inhabits 40 Wattle Street in Duncan Ball's *The Ghost and the Gogglebox* (1984), illustrated by Noela Young, *The Ghost and the Gory Story* (1987), and *The Ghost and the Shutterbug* (1989). Arnold falls into the television set at the moment of his death, and in each novel he causes trouble for the new tenants. His efforts are in vain as practical and resourceful children defeat him by engaging the help of their neighbours or photographing him when his back is turned.

TAYLOR, KAY (née KATHERINE GLASSON) (1893–?), born Kywanna, Queensland, wrote *Ginger for Pluck* (1929) using the pseudonym 'Daniel Hamline'. In *Pick and the Duffers* (1930), Gaynor from England marries Neil, Pick's brother, after initial opposition from Pick. *Bim* (1947) was first published as a serial in the *Sydney Morning Herald* in 1946. Beatrice

Iphigenia Merryweather lives with her guardian, Professor McNair. The high-spirited Bim dresses as a boy, and when her aunt is due to arrive from England, Bim blackens her face and pretends to be an Aboriginal child, like her friend Lundi. Bim wins over her aunt, who marries the professor. Taylor's larrikin girls are the antecedents of Robin Klein's Penny Pollard.

Teens: a Story of Australian Schoolgirls (1897) by Louise Mack, illustrated by Frank P. Mahony, introduced Lennie Leighton and her best friend, Mabel James, who attend a Sydney high school. Lennie and Mabel's pleasure in each other's company, their differing family lives, and their schoolgirl enthusiasms, including founding a magazine, are shrewdly explored. In *Girls Together* (1898), illustrated by G.W. Lambert, set two years later, Mabel falls in love with Lennie's brother Bert, much to Lennie's chagrin. Lennie feels out of kilter with the more mature interests of Mabel, recently returned from studying art in Paris. *Teens Triumphant* (1933) takes up Lennie's life in London, where she, too, is studying art. Her changing fortunes and spiritual life are detailed, until she decides to return to Australia. Mack denied that *Teens* was about Sydney Girls' High School, and demanded that Angus & Robertson cease advertising it as 'a story of Sydney Girls' High'. Unlike Lillian Pyke, or Eustace Boylan, who wrote about the virtues of the Greater Public Schools, Mack used an urban high school as the milieu in which Lennie and Mabel played out their small but realistic dramas.

Tell Me Another Tale: Stories, Verses, Songs and Things to Do (1976) by Jean Chapman, illustrated by Deborah and Kilmeny Niland, with song settings by Margaret Moore, was Commended in the 1977 Picture Book of the Year Awards. It continued the format of *Tell Me a Tale*

(1974), also illustrated by the Nilands. Stories, songs and activities for young children are presented in simple language, with plenty of the Nilands's comical characters on each page.

TENNANT, KYLIE (KATHLEEN) (1912–88), born Manly, Sydney, wrote novels for adults and the children's novel *All the Proud Tribesmen* (q.v., 1959). For *Trail Blazers of the Air* (1965) see **'Great Stories of Australia'**. Tennant has also written plays for children: *John o' the Forest and Other Plays* (1950), *The Bells of the City and Other Plays* (1955) and *The Bushranger's Christmas Eve and Other Plays* (1959). She adapted *Long John Silver: the Story of the Film* (1954) from Martin Rackin's screenplay for the film. *The Missing Heir* (1986) is Tennant's autobiography, and contains a bibliography of her works compiled by Jeanne Rudd.

Terry's Brrrmmm GT (1974), written and illustrated by Ted Greenwood, was Commended in the 1976 Picture Book of the Year Awards. Terry, George and Little Mary build a billy-cart out of Mary's old pram. Pieces fall off it as they race in the Billy Cart Derby, but they finish with honour. The story considers trust and friendship, and Greenwood's unusual line drawings have a deceptive simplicity.

TETLOW, GEORGE (1934–), born Manchester, UK, came to Australia in 1959. He has illustrated Joan Woodberry's *Come Back Peter* (1968), Eugene Lumbers's *A Taste for Blue Ribbons* (1969), George Finkel's *Twilight Province* (1967) and *The Long Pilgrimage* (1967), and Ruth Hawker's *An Emu in the Fowl Pen* (1967).

THIELE, COLIN (1920–), born Eudunda, SA, has written over forty novels for children and young people, published poetry for adults and children and written for radio. *Songs for My Thongs*

(1982), illustrated by Sandy Burrows, and *Poems in My Luggage* (1989), illustrated by Robert Cousins, are collections of his poetry for children. Thiele has drawn on his childhood in the German farming settlements of the Barossa Valley for *The Sun on the Stubble* (q.v., 1961), *Uncle Gustav's Ghosts* (q.v., 1974), *The Shadow on the Hills* (1977), *The Valley Between* (q.v., 1981), *Farmer Schulz's Ducks* (1986), illustrated by Mary Milton, *Farmer Pelz's Pumpkins* (1991), illustrated by Lucinda Hunnam, and *Emma Keppler* (1991). Thiele evokes the community with humour and sympathetic warmth, using its people as a fertile source of character, and its traditions of frugality, honesty and neighbourliness as a background.

His books and verse for young readers include *Gloop the Gloomy Bunyip* (1962), illustrated by John Bailey, *Flip-Flop and Tiger Snake* (1970), illustrated by Jean Elder, and *The Sknuks* (1977), illustrated by Mary Milton. *Gloop the Bunyip* (1970) is a revised edition, illustrated by Helen Sallis, with an additional story added, 'Gloop the Happy Bunyip'. *The Sknuks* are greedy animals who destroy their planet, Htrae, and attack those who want to help them. Eventually they become almost extinct, without having learnt the lesson of caring for their environment. Other novels for young readers are *Mrs Munch and Puffing Billy* (1967), illustrated by Nyorie Bungey, *Yellow Jacket Jock* (1969), illustrated by Clifton Pugh, *Albatross Two* (1974), *Magpie Island* (q.v., 1974), *River Murray Mary* (q.v., 1979), *Patch Comes Home* (1982), illustrated by Tony Oliver, *Potch Goes Down the Drain* and *Pitch the Pony* (both 1984), both illustrated by David Pearson, *Tanya and Trixie* (1980), with photographs by David Simpson, *The Ab Diver* (1988) and *Speedy* (1991), illustrated by Coral Tulloch.

In many of these stories for younger readers, and in his most famous work, *Storm Boy* (q.v., 1963), there is a close affinity with nature. In *Little Tom Little* (1981), with photographs by David Simpson, Tom learns about survival in a national park in the NT and saves his father after he has been attacked by a wild pig, but the message of the novel is that humans have a responsibility to preserve the environment. The despoliation of nature is further explored in *Albatross Two* (1974), which describes the effect of an oil rig on a small fishing village, Ripple Bay, and an accidental oil spillage. Thiele has linked the theme with the preservation of Australia's past in *The Hammerhead Light* (1976). The townspeople of Snapper Bay, on the windswept southern coast, do not want the old lighthouse demolished, and although time and weather defeat them, that is not before the old light averts a tragedy. In a sad conclusion, Tessa weeps for loneliness and loss, as her ageing friend, Uncle Axel, is sent to a nursing home.

Thiele's love for the wilder places of his homeland is expressed in his settings. The Coorong, a narrow stretch of land in SA, bounded on one side by the Southern Ocean, which 'curves away southeastwards from the Murray mouth', is the home of *Storm Boy*. *Coorong Captive* (1985) takes up the violation of this wilderness in an account of bird-smuggling, but there is a stronger place given to the traditional people. Thiele successfully evokes the character of the area before the white invasion. *Pinquo* (1983), illustrated by Mary Milton, is about a Fairy penguin, found hurt by Kirsty and Tim. Five years pass, and the life cycle of the penguin and his offspring is traced. When an earthquake and tidal wave endanger Sickle Bay, the penguins warn the people of their danger, and after Pinquo's death the inhabitants erect a monument to a very special penguin. The novel shows that a positive interaction between humans and animals is possible.

Thiele writes contemporary realistic fiction in which his characters struggle to achieve adulthood in a difficult world. Often the difficulties are natural — bushfire in *February Dragon* (q.v., 1965) and

Jodie's Journey (1988) (see **Bushfire**), flood in *Flash Flood* (1970), or earthquake in *Shatterbelt* (1987). Often they are caused by other people in the family, such as a father as in *The Fire in the Stone* (q.v., 1973) or *Blue Fin* (q.v., 1969). In *Chadwick's Chimney* (1980), illustrated by Robert Ingpen, Ket dives into a treacherous underground cave to rescue his two friends and finds that to get back to the surface he must lead them deeper into the water than he has ever gone before. The resourcefulness of Ket in the face of his own and the other boys' fear is drawn realistically, and the characterisation of a stern father is memorable. A constant theme in Thiele's novels is the importance of the family network, but also the need to strike out from it — to stand on the rim of life, a metaphor Thiele employed for the title of an early collection of stories, *The Rim of the Morning: Six Stories* (1966), and at the conclusion of many of his novels. From Ernie in *The Fire in the Stone* through Snook in *Blue Fin* to Joe in *Seashores and Shadows* (1985) and Jodie in *Jodie's Journey*, boys and girls have shown their courage and resourcefulness. *Jodie's Journey* traces the onset of arthritis in an active 11-year-old girl who is a champion equestrian. Her progress through refusal, misery and eventual acceptance of her illness is drawn.

Many of Thiele's major themes can be identified in the collection *Stories Short and Tall* (1989). Thiele's respect for his young readers, his admiration for the hardworking characters who people his books, his strong sense of justice and his powerful creation of setting has provided a yardstick for other writers. For over thirty years he has made a major contribution to Australian children's books, writing for all ages. His many books have been eagerly read and much loved by Australian children.

Thing (1982), which won the 1983 Junior Book of the Year Awards, and *Thingnapped* (1984) by Robin Klein are humorous novels for young readers about a pet dinosaur, both illustrated by Alison Lester. In *Thing* Emily finds a rock in the park opposite her flat, where she is not allowed to have pets. The rock hatches into a dinosaur with winning ways, and the landlady is soon charmed. In *Thingnapped* (1984) Thing is kidnapped by the jealous Stephanie Strobe.

Things My Family Make (1954) by Sue Lightfoot, illustrated by Peter Clark, was Highly Commended in the 1955 Picture Book of the Year Awards. It describes how to make simple toys, and was produced when the author and illustrator were 11 and 16 respectively.

THODEY, CHARLOTTE (1951–), born NZ, illustrated *Behind the Blue* (1984) by Edina Thomson. For *The Australian Nursery Rhyme Book* (1980) see **Nursery Rhymes**.

THOMAS, MAY, born Cottesloe, WA, has written and illustrated fantasies for young children about an Aboriginal child, his sister and their kangaroo in *Gundy* (1944) and *Warraninni* (1945). Both books are illustrated with linocuts by S.H. Fisher. *Wandi* (1968) is a book of verse.

THOMPSON, CHARLES KEN-NETH (?1905–80), born Maitland, NSW, was a journalist and amateur naturalist. He was a crime reporter for over twenty years, and wrote novels and short stories for the Sydney book and magazine publisher Frank Johnson (q.v.). Thompson was a prolific author of crime novels, Australian 'westerns', and animal books for children. *King of the Ranges, the Saga of a Grey Kangaroo* (1945) first appeared as a serial in the *Newcastle Sun*. It traces the life story of a large grey kangaroo, Joey, who remains for most of his life in the Great Dividing Range, rather than the plains which are his natural home. Though attacked by men and dogs, captured and shot at, Joey survives to become a leader of his own mob. *Red Emperor* (1950), illustrated by Ron Madden, is another kangaroo story, this time about the red kangaroo Arunga. Other titles which describe the life histories of birds and animals are *Monarch of the Western Skies: the Story of a Wedge-tailed Eagle* (1946), *Warrigal the Warrior* (1948), *Maggie the Magnificent* (1949), illustrated by Ron Madden, *Blackie the Brumby* (1951), illustrated by Carl Lyon, *Wombat* (1953), illustrated by Alan Rigby, and *Willy Wagtail* (1957). Dasyure in *Tiger Cat* (1952) is a 'brave and useful' animal from birth to adulthood; *Thunderbolt the Falcon* (1954), illustrated by Frank Hodgkinson, describes how two boys and an old man train a peregrine falcon. Boofie in *Wild Canary* (1956) is a domesticated bird set free during a flood. *Old Bob's Birds* (1950), also illustrated by Madden, has stories about birds told by Old Bob the Sundowner to his young friends Roddy and Susan. Thompson acknowledges Will Lawson as the source of much of the material.

THOMPSON, DOUGLAS LINDSAY (1899–1975), known as 'Duncan', was the son of Lilian Turner. He was a journalist with the Adelaide *Advertiser*, the Melbourne *Herald* and was chief of staff and a feature-writer with the *Sydney Morning Herald*, where his work as an investigative journalist prompted an inquiry into health service in NSW. Thompson wrote a history of the charitable organisation the Smith Family. His novels were based on his schooldays at Sydney Grammar. *Blue Brander: a Story of Adventure and Australian School Life* (1927), illustrated by W.F. Wightman, opens with a sporting hero being debarred from the rowing team for a misdemeanour. The boys, led by 'Blue' Brander, set off to extract a revenge on the master, Michael Doohan, and become involved in a robbery in the Jenolan Caves area. All's well at the end, as Grantham School wins the boat race and Doohan is engaged to 'Blue's' sister Daphne. *The Gang on Wheels* (1930), illustrated by W.E. Wigtall, continues the adventures of 'Big' Johnson, 'Possum' Burton, Walter Weatherstone Warnecke, 'Jeckyll' Hyde and 'Blue' Brander, and their rival Kidman, in pursuit of forgers. The boys are now in the Upper Sixth, and an influenza epidemic forces the school to close, providing a free week for the gang's adventure. These funny, robust boys are handy with their fists, sometimes moody, forever in trouble from parents or schoolmasters, overwhelmed in the presence of good-looking girls, and rely on each other to stick together in adversity. Thompson's stories were in the tradition of the British Public School novels of the time, but they use Australian idiom and character, and have a clever, sardonic tone.

THOMPSON, VALERIE (1919–   ), born Sydney, has written a series of historical novels, set in the nineteenth century, during the adventurous days of gold. In *Rough Road South* (1975), illustrated by Edwina Bell, Rob Howell journeys from Sydney to Melbourne during the 1850s, and in *Gold on the Wind* (1977) he has an enforced stay there when his ship leaves without him. See also **Death**. In *The Mountain Between* (1980), which concludes the trilogy, Rob has to adjust to life back with his family. *A Girl Like Alice: the Story of the Australian Helen Keller* (1990) is a biography of Alice Betteridge. *Colour of Courage* (1978), also illustrated by Bell, recounts the real-life stories of fifteen girls and boys who displayed courage — from Narrabeen, who saved a family from a massacre, to the 13-year-old Sidney Kidman's brush with death near Menindee.

Threat to the Barkers (1963) by Joan Phipson, illustrated by Margaret Horder, was Commended in the 1964 Book of the Year Awards. See *The Family Conspiracy*.

Thunderwith (1989) by Libby Hathorn was an Honour Book in the 1990 Book of the Year Awards: Older Readers. When her mother dies, Lara joins her father's wife and children in a remote area of northern NSW. Her stepmother, Gladwyn, is hard and unwelcoming. Lara meets a secret and 'mystical' dog during a thunderstorm, to whom she expresses all her grief and misery. A tragedy precipitates Gladwyn's change of heart and Lara's acceptance. This touching novel has vigorous characters and a palpable setting. See also **Families**.

Thyne Reid Collection of Australian Children's Books and Juvenalia began in 1982 as a part of the James Hardie Library. The genesis of the collection was the purchase of around 600 Australian children's books, from *A Mother's Offering to Her Children* (1841) to Mary and Elizabeth Durack's *Way of the Whirlwind* (1941). An additional purchase was a collection of a hundred boys' adventure stories and some significant individual titles. The bulk of the collection was of twentieth-century material and ephemera of such authors as Gibbs, Outhwaite, Wall, the Lindsays, and O'Harris. It includes 250 illustrations from the first half of the twentieth century, nineteenth-century Australian school-books and other educational material, board games, and children's plays.

Tiger in the Bush (1957) by Nan Chauncy, illustrated by Margaret Horder, won the 1958 Book of the Year Awards. It is set in a Tasmanian valley where the Lorenny family live in a small split-log house which Dad built himself. The novel centres on the youngest child, Badge (q.v.). Lance, his brother, is at school in Hobart with Iggy, his sister, set to join him soon. The adults want the valley's location to remain secret from 'Outside'. But two scientists, Russ and 'Doc', persuade Badge to show them a Tasmanian tiger which Old Harry, a hermit, has revealed to Badge and Iggy. At first seduced by their knowledge and friendliness, Badge realises at the last moment that the valley will no longer be a wild sanctuary if 'Outside' is allowed to invade it. *Tiger in the Bush* remains one of Chauncy's best novels, with the characters emerging strongly, a complex dilemma explored for Badge, and an impressively drawn setting.

TIMINS, OCTAVIUS FREDERIC (1816– ?) was secretary to the Governor of Victoria, Sir Henry Barkly, from 1856 to 1863, and remained in Australia when the governor left for Mauritius. For his novel *Station Dangerous: or, The Settlers in Central Australia, a Tale Founded on Fact* (1866) he used the pseudonym 'O.F.T.' The novel describes with some relish how the Ames family and their employers overcome the local Aboriginal People to take up land. 'The savages, with their clubs and spears, were as no match for their enemies, armed as they were with swords, and the more deadly revolver.' See also **Lost in the Bush**.

TIMMS, EDWARD VIVIAN (1895–1960), born Charters Towers, Queensland, was a popular writer of adult historical romances. *Red Mask: a Story of the Early Victorian Goldfields* (1927) has a 'Scarlet Pimpernel' hero, Rex Neville, who dons a red mask and brings retribution to evildoers: 'He did not kill, but only wounded … A sharp command and the cornered ruffian would raise his right hand. A report would ring out and the outlaw's hand would drop helpless and shattered.' Neville's victims are Jews and foreigners. See also **Eureka Stockade**. *The Valley of Adventure: a Story for Boys* (1926), illustrated by Edgar A. Holloway, is set in the north of Australia, and features Aboriginal People, snakes, crocodiles, and other standard fare.

TIMPERLEY, WILLIAM HENRY (1833–1909), born Warwickshire, UK, arrived in WA in 1851, later joining the police force. In 1885 he became the superintendent of the Aboriginal prison on Rottnest Island, WA. *Harry Treverton, His Tramps and Troubles* (1889) is his autobiography in the form of a novel, originally serialised in the *Boy's Own Paper*. He was encouraged to write his story by Lady Broome (q.v.). Harry arrives in WA, aged 17, and his experiences in the outback conclude with the acquisition of a property, and marriage to Lily. *Bush Luck: an Australian Story* (1892), illustrated by W.S. Stacey, was also serialised in the *Boy's Own Paper* from 1887 to 1890. It has the curious image of Hugh and Jack's uncle setting himself up in England as though he were camping out in Australia, bush hut, camp fire, damper, mutton chops and all. Hugh makes his fortune in Australia, and finds his true love, Lucy. There are many comparisons between English and Australian ways, such as kangaroo-hunting, women who work in the bush, and the Australian country habit of travelling fifty miles to a party. The novel concludes with propaganda for settlement: 'I can assure my friends that, if they wish to come out and try their "bush luck", there is still plenty of room for those who possess the pluck to brave the hardships of bush life and the spears of the savage. Yet they should bear in mind that enterprise must be backed up with money, and courage tempered with judgement and mercy.'

Tin Lizzie and Little Nell (1982), written and illustrated by David Cox, was Commended in the 1983 Picture Book of the Year Awards. Tin Lizzie is William Winterbottom's old blue motor car, and Little Nell is Billy Benson's old grey mare. Every Saturday the race is on to see which family will reach Budgiwogerai first. Like the hare and the tortoise, the Winterbottoms stop along the way while the Bensons keep trotting on, although who wins is left unresolved. Cox's detailed illustrations add zest to the story.

TINDALE, NORMAN BARNETT (1900–), born Perth, collaborated with Harold A. Lindsay on a series of books on anthropological themes. Tindale is an anthropologist and ethnologist, a curator of anthropology at the SA Museum, who carried out field-work with the Pitjantjatjara in the 1930s. *The First Walkabout* (q.v., 1954) and *Rangatira (The High Born): a Polynesian Saga* (q.v., 1959) look at early migrations to Australia and NZ. *Aboriginal Australians* (1963) is an anthropological work.

'Tintookies', see **SCRIVEN, PETER**

TJAPANGATI, THOMAS STEVENS. For *The Lost Boomerang* (1983) see **Aboriginal Dreaming Stories**.

To the Wild Sky (1967) by Ivan Southall, illustrated by Jennifer Tuckwell, won the 1968 Book of the Year Awards. In a novel which is reminiscent of Golding's *Lord of the Flies*, six children manage to get the aircraft down on a deserted island after a flight where the pilot dies. At first in despair, they regroup in order to survive. They are unco-operative and unwilling to support each other until a leader emerges. *A City Out of Sight: To the Wild Sky: Book Two* (1984) takes the characters on another eleven years, concluding with the promise of their rescue. The author's interest in the passage from timidity to authority figure is explored in these tense and closely plotted stories.

TOBIAS, LIN (1955–) has illustrated *Flying Backwards* (1985) by Barbara Giles, *Balancing Act* (1985) by Marysia Murray and *Tina Tuff* (1991) by Margaret Clark. She uses a lively cartoon style.

Toby's Millions (1982) by Morris Lurie, illustrated by Arthur Horner, was Commended in the 1983 Book of the

Year Awards. When the level-headed Toby finds buried treasure in his vegetable patch, his father is thrilled. But Toby insists that it is his treasure, a matter soon settled by the local judge. Toby is very generous, and the family have a great deal of fun, but the marvels which he provides for his banker father, such as his own train to work, or a helicopter, do not help their relationship until a real emergency shows Toby's father just what is important. The story of a boy who is wiser than his parents is told with Lurie's customary humour.

TODD, GEOFF (1950–) has illustrated *The Inside Hedge Story* (1981) by Gillian Barnett, *When Tracy Came for Christmas* (1982) by June Epstein and *Ganglehoff* (1986) by Brian Murphy. He contributed illustrations to *The Book of Melbourne: the Story of a City* (1983), by Carolyn Dowling and Noelle McCracken.

TODD, TREVOR (1947–), born UK, came to Australia in 1952. In *The Cockroach that Wrote a Symphony* (1979), illustrated by Thomas Trahair, Cockroach is Benjy's pet. He writes beautiful music, but his career is cut short by a zealous cleaning lady, although his music is preserved through the efforts of the conductor, Sir Peregrine Ample. In *Fairy Strike!* (1980), illustrated by Deborah Niland, the fairies go on strike when children stop believing in magic, a problem overcome by Mr Magic. *Kneedeep* (1981), also illustrated by Niland, is about an adventurous frog who learns to speak. He helps Howard keep his job as Court Magician, but finds the pace is too much when the princesses want him to solve their romantic problems. *Mason Judy* (1977), illustrated by Robert Juniper, is a verse story. In *The Racing-Car Driver's Moustache* (1984), illustrated by Stephen Axelsen, Phinneas Bertram McGhee's moustache is invaded by a flea, which bites him during a motor race. Phinneas's moustache is 'handle-bar bristley, end-twirled and twistelly,/Full-

formed, magnificent...' In *Old Sam Jasper and Mr Frank* (1985), illustrated by Betty Greenhatch, Jasper befriends Old Sam who helps him train Mr Frank the pigeon.

TONKIN, RACHEL (1945–), born Melbourne, studied illustration at RMIT, and has worked as a freelance illustrator since her graduation. She illustrated *Gems of the Australian Bush and Other Poems* (1968) by R.W. Barclay. 'I am a jolly platypus,/And over me, oh, what a fuss/The people make who visit me,/At my platypussery/I love to roam the whole day long,/In rivers, lakes and billabong,/Or play among the rushes tall/That grow beside the waterfall.' The verse is not exciting, but Tonkin's illustrations are appealing. She illustrated the 1971 edition of Judith Wright's *The River and the Road* (1966), *Hustler's Gold* (1969) by Pat Spencer, and Mavis Thorpe Clark's *Gully of Gold* (1969) and *Pony from Tarella* (1969). She has also illustrated books for the Joint Board of Christian Education, such as *Conversations with God* (1971) by Joy Merritt, and some of the Clare Carson books by Mary Elliott published by Golden Press. *Great Grandma Remembers* (1987) by Judith Smith and *Papa and the Olden Days* (q.v., 1989) by Ian Edwards draw on Tonkin's remembrance of her ancestors. *The Money Eaters* (1988) was also written by Ian Edwards, as was *Little Chicken's Big Trouble* (1992). *Trouble with Rainbows* (1991) by Tess Brady describes a broken rainbow which Abi and Charlie unsuccessfully try to clean up. *That's Another Story* (1990), *In a Picture* (1991) and *Lifelines* (1992) were written by Jo Denver and Linda Rossi for the Queensland education system to introduce an approach to English through social issues. She wrote and illustrated *Willy and the Ogre* (1991) which has hidden animals the reader must discover on each page. *Bridget was Bored* (1992) by Anne Moorehead and Peter Hillary describes Bridget's explorations of an inner Melbourne street.

TORRES, PAT (1956–), born Broome, WA, is a Yawuru woman who is a traditional storyteller and artist. She has written and illustrated *The Story of Crow* (1987) in collaboration with Magdalene Williams, who is one of the only surviving fully versed speakers of Nyul Nyul. *Jalygurr: Aussie Animal Rhymes* (1987) is also bilingual, with English and Yawuru texts. ('Jalygurr' means 'children'.) She also illustrated Daisy Utemorrah's *Do Not Go Around the Edges* (1990). See **Aboriginal Dreaming Stories**.

'Touch the Sun' was a series of tele-movies produced in 1988 by the Australian Children's Television Foundation for the Bicentennial year. Books were written from the scripts, so that reading and watching could be linked. In *Top-Enders* by Jennifer Dabbs, based on a script by Michael Aitkens and Jackie McKimmie, Mick runs away with Alice in her mother's car to escape from her father and to join Mick's uncle. *Princess Kate* by Kristin Williamson, based on the screen-play by David Williamson, examines the trauma of a girl who discovers that she has been adopted. *Devil's Hill* (*sic*) by David Phillips is based on Nan Chauncy's novel *Devils' Hill* (q.v., 1958). In *Peter and Pompey* by John Misto, three children uncover a Roman boat which hides a secret. *Captain Johnno* by Rob George is about a hearing-impaired boy who runs away when he learns that his sister is leaving for school. A Greek family win a valu-able block of bushland in a lottery in *The Gift* by Roger Dunn, based on the screen-play by Paul Cox and Jeff Peck.

Train, The: the Amazing Train Chase that Unfolds into one of the Longest Books in the World (1982) by Witold Generowicz was Highly Commended in the 1983 Picture Book of the Year Awards. In this wordless frieze, robbers chased by police run along the roof of the train, which is carrying everything from a milking machine to a Krollsnork.

Tram to Bondi Beach, The (1981) by Elizabeth (Libby) Hathorn, illustrated by Julie Vivas, was Highly Commended in the 1982 Picture Book of the Year Awards. Keiran becomes a paper boy so that he can sell papers on the Sydney trams, but after an accident he sells them at the beach, satisfying his fascination with trams by travelling on them to work. Vivas's delicate and sweeping watercolours recapture the 1930s.

TRAVERS, PAMELA LYNDON (1906–) spent her youth in Queensland, and went to England in the 1920s, writing the first of her popular 'Mary Poppins' series in 1934.

TRELOAR, BRUCE (1946–), born Hamilton, NZ, came to Australia in 1977. He is a painter and illustrator, often of marine subjects. *Kim* (1978) is set on Norfolk Island, where Kim and her dog explore the sweeping beachscape. *Mystery Surf-Rider* (1978) by Lance Loughrey and *Sea* (1981) by Ned Ward are also seascapes. Treloar has illustrated *The Maidens of Pefka* (1979) by Nance Donkin, *Marty Moves to the Country* (q.v., 1980) by Kate Walker, *The Ghostly Jigsaw* (1985) by Edel Wignell, *Charlie up a Gum Tree* (1985) by E.A. Schurmann, *Winkie* (1986) by Jean Chapman and *The Bushranger* (1978) by Dal Stivens. For his books about Bumble and Timothy, see **Bumble's Dream**. Other picture-books are *Cake I Hate* (1984), in which two exuberant chil-dren romp through their likes and dislikes; in *Toby Jug and It* Toby searches for 'IT', but joins a family of wombats when his sceptical friends desert him. *Beware, Take Care: Baggable Tales* (1987) and *Only Me from Over the Sea: Baggable Tales* (1988) introduce Baggables, human-like creatures who live in the trees. *Benjamin Goes to Hospital, an Introduction to Hospital for Children and Parents* (1978) by Tony Lipson is an informational book. Treloar develops

Marty moves to the country (1980) by Kate Walker. Illustrator: Bruce Treloar

strong characters like Mr Bumble and Josie, who bring their energy to his closely focused double-page illustrations.

Treloar, Poppy appears in four novels by Pixie O'Harris, set around the Sydney beaches, Camp Cove and Watsons Bay. In *The Fortunes of Poppy Treloar* (1941), Poppy learns that she is a foundling, runs away from her adoptive family, finds her way to 'Wildacres', owned by her grandmother, and discovers that she is really Percita Rodriques, the daughter of a Spanish count! *Poppy and the Gems* (1944) tells how Poppy and Pearl, Opal, Beryl and Garnet Jasper rescue Bryony Blake from a cruel aunt. Poppy becomes an art student in *Poppy Faces the World* (1947). When her foster-father dies, and there are money troubles, Poppy works as a fashion artist for a department store. She has an unrequited love affair with a teacher at the art school, is reunited with her father Carlo, and finds true love and friendship with Phillip Brooks. In *Poppy at Wildacres* (1969), written for the collection *The Fortunes of Poppy Treloar* (1969), Poppy's romance with Phillip becomes stale, and when Phillip becomes engaged to another girl, Poppy finds that she really loves Robert Treloar, but she thinks Robert is her cousin. He assures her that he was an adopted child, and they live happily ever after.

'Trend' was a series of books for reluctant readers first produced by Cheshire in 1968. The first six books were written by Bettina Bird and Tony Scanlon, after their experiences as teachers of young people with reading difficulties. Early titles by Bird included *Coffee at Charlie's*, *Crash Landing*, *Robbie* (all 1968) and *A Real Hero* (1969). Different reading age groups were provided for in 'Approach Trend', 'Trend' and 'Trendset'. The series was criticised for its simplistic approach to reading difficulties and its superficiality. But its approach to literacy set a pattern which was followed by numerous series for young readers, such as Macmillan's 'Flag', Cassell's 'Patchwork' and Ashton's 'Bookshelf'.

TREZISE, PERCY (1923–), born Tallangatta, Victoria, was a pilot when he met Dick Roughsey, with whom he collaborated for many years. After Roughsey's death, Trezise wrote and illustrated *Ngalculli, the Red Kangaroo* (1986), told to him by Joogamoo and Toomalcalin of the Olcoola People, which is dedicated to Roughsey. *The Owl People* (1987) is a story from the Palmer River people, about how Jimbal and Andidjeri defeated the cannibalistic owl people. *The Peopling of Australia* (1987) is a pictorial history of Australia from the age of the dinosaurs to white invasion. *The Cave Painters* (1988) recalls his work with Roughsey, as children from the rainforest look at rock art in Quinkin country and listen to stories about Goorialla, the Rainbow Serpent, the Giant Devil Dingo, Turramulli the Quinkin and other Dreaming stories. In *Lasca and Her Pups* (1990) the dingo saves her offspring from an eagle. In *Black Duck and Water Rat* (1988), written with Mary Haginikitas, the beautiful duck, Mara, is captured by Goomai, the water rat, and Mara's children are born as platypuses. *The Platypus: an Aboriginal Legend Retold and Illustrated for Young Children* (1974) by Katherine Morris tells the same story. With Mary Haginikitas, Trezise illustrated Henry Kendall's nineteenth-century poem *The Last of His Tribe* (1989). *Mungoon-Gali the Giant Goanna* (1991) is set in the days of the diprotodons, 'kadimakaras' to the Aboriginal People. Ngali and Mayli are trapped by Mungoon-Gali the giant goanna, but drive him away with fire. For works with Roughsey see **Roughsey, Dick**. Trezise's work has engaged a large audience for the artistic traditions, stories and customs of the Aboriginal People of northern Queensland.

TRINCA, ROD (1954–) wrote *One Woolly Wombat* (1982), illustrated by Kerry Argent, a counting book in rhyme. Australian symbols and culture appear on each page — lamingtons, flowering gums, Australian Rules football.

TRIST, MARGARET (1914–86), born Dalby, Queensland, wrote short stories and novels. *Morning in Queensland* (1958), published as *Tansy* (1991), follows the life of a girl from her first memories to when she leaves the small country town where she was born for Sydney. Meredith, Cuthie, Great Aunt Ruby, Janet — all the neighbours, aunts, grandmothers and great-grandmothers watch over her, as she observes and participates in a large family: the mysterious secrets of adults, their complicated relationships, and their memories of the past, often more vivid than the present lives they are leading. Trist sees the small town of Goombudgerie through the eyes of a child gradually awakening to her own capabilities in this gently humorous evocation of community life.

Trouble with Mr Harris, The (1978) by Ronda Armitage, illustrated by David Armitage, was Highly Commended in the 1979 Picture Book of the Year Awards. Mr Harris's brusqueness hides his shyness, and only little Effie can see the golden heart beneath the cold exterior of the new postmaster of Hodgeton. When Effie's baby brother's pram runs away, Mr Harris rescues him. The village then realises his worth, and accepts him wholeheartedly.

True Story of Lilli Stubeck, The (1984) by James Aldridge won the 1985 Book of the Year Awards. It is one of the 'St Helen' novels, set during the Depression, and told by Kit Quayle. Aldridge's novel traces the relationship between two strong characters, Lilli and Miss Dalgleish, who acquired Lilli for £30 from her itinerant family. When Lilli arrives in the household, she is 11. By the time she is grown up, she is as cultured and as strong as Miss Dalgleish, the authority roles are reversed, and she is no longer Miss Dalgleish's creation. The skilfully crafted transformation of Lilli from child to woman is pursued within a philosophical tenet — 'to thine own self be true'. See also **Girls**.

TULLOCH, CORAL has illustrated *Being Bad for the Babysitter* (1991) by Richard Tulloch, and *Adam's Apple* (1989) by Richard and Marcia Vaughan.

TULLOCH, RICHARD GEORGE (1949–), born Melbourne, is a story-teller, writer and director for stage and radio, and was the artistic director of a Theatre in Education company in the 1980s. He has written stories for the ABC's 'Playschool' program, published as *Stories from Our House* (1987) and *Stories from Our Street* (1989), both illustrated by Julie Vivas. These are domestic tales for pre-school children. He has created stage versions of Gillian Rubinstein's *Space Demons* (q.v., 1986), performed in Adelaide in 1989, Robin Klein's *Hating Alison Ashley* (q.v., 1984), Randolph Stow's *Midnite* (q.v., 1967) and other novels and stories. In *The Strongest Man in Gundiwallanup* (1990), illustrated by Sue O'Loughlin, Dan Drummond, a strong-man, is taught a lesson in humility. In *Rain for Christmas* (1989), illustrated by Wayne Harris, Sally persuades Santa to bring rain to a drought-stricken area. *The Brown Felt Hat* (1990), illustrated by Craig Smith, traces the rise and fall of a race-goer's dec-orated hat. Danny will not come out of his toybox in *Danny in the Toybox: a Story* (1990), illustrated by Armin Greder. Jane hates being baby-sat, so in *Being Bad for the Babysitter* (1991), illustrated by Coral Tulloch, she devises a devilish plan of behaviour.

TURNER, ETHEL MARY (1870–1958), born Doncaster, UK, settled in Australia in 1881. She edited a schoolgirls' magazine, *Iris*, and later *Parthenon* with her sister, Lilian, and wrote the children's pages for the *Illustrated Sydney News*, Sydney *Daily Telegraph* and the *Bulletin*. There are strong autobiographical ele-ments in her novel *Three Little Maids* (1900), illustrated by A.J. Johnson, which opens with the death of Phyl's and Dolly's stepfather. The children and their step-sister, Weenie, emigrate to NSW, where the resourceful Mrs Conway sets about earning her own living. Phyl and Dolly's rich imaginations and their later literary efforts recall the skill and tenacity of the Turner girls. After Ethel's marriage to H.R. Curlewis, later Judge Curlewis, and until the death of her daughter, Jean Curlewis, she continued to write books for the young. Between 1894 and 1928, Turner published thirty-eight titles, mainly about the genteel urban middle class, including books which were aimed at an older audience, such as *The Story of a Baby* (1895), *In the Mist of the Mountains* (1906), illustrated by J. Macfarlane, *The Apple of Happiness* (1911), illustrated by A.N. Gough, and *The Ungardeners* (1925). For instance, *In the Mist of the Mountains* has four children, Lynn, Max, Muffie and Pauline, left with Miss Bibby while their parents are away. The children soon take second place, as the romance between Miss Bibby and a 'famous novelist' who comes to stay next door takes over. Although the antics of the children move the novel along, the adult romance pre-dominates. *The Ungardeners* (1925) is another adult romance, this time set around the creation of a garden and the battle of wills over its style.

Through her novels Turner explored many of the ideas which absorbed writers of her time, such as the controversy over the importance of heredity versus environ-ment in the development of character; family and the role of parents; the class nature of society; and poverty and its sources. Her heroines are assertive and burdened with a social conscience. Turner believed in the power of a positive upbringing. In *The Secret of the Sea* (1913) she has four babies adopted by the wealthy Lord and Lady Brenchley because they cannot identify their own grandchildren after a shipwreck. The other pair of twins is from a poor family, and it is not until one of the boys discovers an old letter that the truth is out. But Turner's interest is in the twins who are not descendents of the aristocracy, and they are the more spirited and determined pair. There is a suggestion that the Brenchley line could do with the strength and resource exhibited by the 'flannelette babies', a reference to the clothing of the rescued twins. A good environment, however, was of little value without 'intelligence', and 'intelligence' could overcome the obstacles of bad surroundings. Her depiction of Harry, in the 'Cub' series, shows that she rates intelligence above correct speech, as does her picture of Mrs Fitzroy-Browne in *The Family at Misrule* (1895), also illustrated by Johnson, whose motherliness, though she is uneducated, is seen as so much more worthy than the pseudo-refinement of her daughters. In *The Apple of Happiness* (1911) Edna mistakenly believes that money will bring happiness, only to discover that it brings sorrow and the loss of her husband's respect. *Funny* (1926), illustrated by W.E. Wightman, is the story of Owen, sent to live with his uncle and formidable aunt after his father's death. Owen's gift for entertainment is finally recognised, and he goes off to America where he makes his fortune.

Families are the background to Turner's books. Mothers are less influential than fathers, and siblings are more important than parents. In *A White-Roof Tree* (1905), illustrated by A.J. Johnson and others, both parents have died, and the five Dane children have been unhappily living with relatives or working away from each other. At the insistence of the youngest, Una, they set up tents on the river bank and live there together. Turner's beliefs in the necessity of a family living together and the support to be derived from brothers and sisters are clearly shown. *The Wonder-Child* (1901), illustrated by Gordon Browne, is about Challis Cameron, a musical prodigy, whose concerts abroad have deprived the rest of her family of their mother. The incompetent and artistic Mr Cameron and Bartie, Hermie, Roly and Floss struggle on in poverty while Challis earns hundreds of pounds a year. Hermie holds the family together, and refuses an offer of marriage to a wealthy neighbour, who then goes off to the Boer War. When he is wrongly reported killed, Hermie realises she loves

him; Mrs Cameron and Challis return to the bosom of the family, and Mr Cameron's talents are finally recognised.

Turner is not very kind to fathers. Mr Cameron is effete and Captain Woolcot is too ready with the riding whip, but Mr Silver, in *Nicola Silver* (1924), illustrated by Harold Copping, is particularly awful. He makes Nicola carry 500 stones for a wall in one day as punishment for disagreeing with him, locks her up in solitary confinement for a week, and broods, snarls and beats his children until they are in terror of him. Mr Godwin, in *St. Tom and the Dragon*, chains his daughter to the table and, when he is in his cups, whips her until she bleeds. Mr Firth, 'still at heart ... a lonely boy', in *Jennifer J.* (1922), illustrated by Harold Copping, relies on his relatives to mother him and run the household when his wife goes back to England to finish her degree, and it is the 14-year-old Jennifer who bears the brunt of the organisation. Frequently fathers are eliminated, leaving the children to make their own way in the world. In *An Ogre Up-to-Date* (1911), illustrated by H.C. Sandy and D.H. Souter, there is an incident which would delight Freud, when Cathie's real terror of her new stepfather is exacerbated when she sees him 'eating' her mother, i.e. kissing her.

Ethel Turner recognised the class nature of society and saw the need for some intervention, mainly through good works for the poor. *St. Tom and the Dragon* and *King Anne* (1921), both illustrated by Harold Copping, follow the fortunes of Tom St Clair, a very earnest reformer. In the first novel Tom rescues Anne Godwin from a drunken father, and opens the eyes of the brewery-owner to what he is doing to the poor, and in the second he meets Anne King, daughter of an explorer. This second Anne provides warm overcoats and gaily painted carts to the poor denizens of Sydney where Tom has his medical practice. She is impatient with their dirt and ragged clothes, which she could fix in the smallest part of a day's work, and irritated that they cannot discover that life 'can still be no end of a lark'. Tom is tempted to marry her, and even half-heartedly proposes, but Anne is not prepared to share her heart with the 'greyness and ugliness that you [Tom] so deliberately choose', and he is left to get on with his practice. The reader can only breath a sigh of relief that Tom has escaped this heroine. For younger readers, *Betty and Co.* (1903) describes how the disabled Betty and her brother Bern, through the imaginative construction of doll's furniture and clothes, and the intervention of a very business-like neighbour, restore the family's fortunes after their father's death.

Early in World War I, Turner published *The Cub* (1915), which opens on a ship bringing Australians home from Europe, among them the English girl Brigid Lindsay and John Calthrop, the Cub. Brigid has seen some of the horror of the war in Belgium, when she rescued a child, Josette, after the Germans had killed her parents, and Brigid has had her character strengthened in the process. The emphasis of the novel is on this character-building, such as the need to set aside fashion and other trivialities in favour of thinking of others. The Cub is already a reformer. Middle-class women and those who aspire to the moneyed classes are the guilty ones: '...the shops for us, streets of shops, cities of shops, whole continents of shops. The silliness of us, the cheap, sheer silliness and idleness of us', cries Millicent, when her sister Brigid tears the scales from her eyes. See also **War**. In *Captain Cub* (1917) Brigid and the Cub become engaged, after the Cub writes an extraordinarily excited letter to her from the front, to which Brigid replies 'Yes, Yes, Yes', and Brigid is taken to Europe with Mrs Calthrop. *Brigid and the Cub* (1919) furthers Brigid's transformation into a girl with a well-developed sense of duty, and examines her love affair with the Cub during various leaves which he takes in Paris. The three Cub books were illustrated by Harold Copping.

She considered the education of the child a very serious matter indeed. *Miss Bobbie* (1897), illustrated by Harold Copping, describes the education of an 11-year-old who is left with a family of boys for two years. Bobbie's developing confidence and enthusiasm for an active life is frowned on by her elders, and at the conclusion Bobbie is set to 'learn how to be a young lady'. Niall points out that Bobbie predates Judy, as the story first appeared as 'Bobbie, the Story of a Tomboy' in the *Parthenon* in 1890, and Bobbie's determination and irrepressible naughtiness prefigure the more memorable heroine. See also **Girls**. *Fugitives from Fortune* (1909) describes an educational experiment conducted by Mr Jarvie. His attempts to make his children content in the world of nature are not very successful. They all want some of the delights of the city, whether it is pretty clothes or work, and Jarvie finally succumbs. Turner nevertheless saw the powerful effect of education, and whether Mr Jarvie's experiment failed or not, her serious examination of his precepts is a mark of her concern.

Although she recognised disadvantage, Turner's keen sense of class strikes the modern reader as snobbery. Meg's intervention in Pip's romance in *Little Mother Meg* (1902), illustrated by A.J. Johnson, is an instance of Turner's horror of a marriage across classes. In *Laughing Water* (1920), illustrated by Harold Copping, a novel about a large house at Katoomba and the family who live in it, Turner expands on her philosophies of ambition and taste. Clothes and furnishings should be useful and beautiful, and one's ambition should be the very best at whatever one chooses to be, to climb the ladder to 'the top rung of all'. As for love, Mr Lester's advice to a young man is to consider very seriously the 'girl at his side', and eschew 'a gossiping little thing with no mind ... grasping at all money he makes', and prefer a girl 'with a sense of humour and a striding mind to match his own'.

Turner's girls and women may have been assertive and strong-minded, but the author was no feminist. Domesticity was to be preferred to a career for the audience for whom she wrote. In *The Little Larrikin* (1896), illustrated by A.J. Johnson, Linley, a would-be artist, is secretly engaged to Lol's indigent barrister brother Roger, and although her ambition to be a great painter takes over for a time, she sees the error of her ways and returns to Roger and domesticity in straitened circumstances. Niall has suggested that the course of the romance is based on Turner's own experience of engagement to Curlewis. In *In the Mist of the Mountains* Miss Bibby, in her late thirties, has ambitions to be a writer, but when Hugh Kinross, in his late forties, realises that 'if she had a home of her own, that she would never want to touch a pen again' he decides to make her a 'gentle, quiet companion for the autumn of his life'. In *Flower O' the Pine* (1914), illustrated by J.H. Hartley, Flower's sweetness converts her cousin to motherliness rather than a career. *Fair Ines* (1910), on the other hand, is not sweet, and the novel examines the narrow-minded snobbery of a small country town, as a romance develops between a beautiful and unconventional girl and a man who had served a time in prison for a crime he did not commit.

Turner succumbed to a taste for romantic melodrama in some of her novels. *Mother's Little Girl* (1904) relates how Ellie sells her sixth child to her sister Alice when she cannot afford to keep her. The reconciliation between mother and child occurs after Sylvia, the child, finds true happiness within her real family. In *The Camp at Wandinong* (1898), illustrated by Frances Ewan and others, an old admirer of Mary, the mother, arranges for the family to come into wealth by placing a gold nugget in the diggings where the children have been playing.

Some of her creations have remained as touchstones for the Australian character. Judy Woolcot is discussed elsewhere. See

Seven Little Australians. Lol Carruthers in *The Little Larrikin* is one of Turner's happiest inventions. His wild and undisciplined life gives the novel its charm. Lol is the antithesis of the sweet little angels who peopled Victorian children's books. He swears, fights, exploits his prettiness and is rude to the servants, and his vitality dominates the book. *John of Daunt* (1916), illustrated by Harold Copping, is in a similar mould to Lol. He is also disobedient and irrepressible, but more tamed than his predecessor. See also **Germans**.

Gum Leaves (1900), illustrated by D.H. Souter, contained 'An Ogre Up to Date', as well as extracts, poems, fairy stories, instructions on making a sofa, how to make the home more comfortable, ideas for games, and other practical advice. *The Raft in the Bush* (1910) is a fantasy, illustrated by H.C. Sandy and D.H. Souter. King Billy builds a raft which will save all the animals when the drought breaks, and the antics of the animals and Billy and his wife Mary make up the story. *The Sunshine Family* (1923), written with Jean Curlewis, illustrated by D.H. Souter, H. Bancks and others, first appeared in the supplements of the Sydney *Sun*. Mr and Mrs Sunshine decide to take their children to Sydney for an education. The children attempt an escape, but they all eventually set off, to encounter bushrangers, tigers and some astounding adventures. The innocent toughness of Dad and Mother's practicality take Sydney by storm, in a comic story which has many of the characteristics of 'Ginger Meggs'. Turner was the first writer for children to deal sympathetically with city life and to recognise the pleasures of the urban environment. In *Nicola Silver* Nicola is given a week of fun in Sydney, where she is introduced to the delights of shopping, in contrast to the dreariness of the hard work she has to do on the farm.

Turner also wrote short stories, plays and poems, which are often found published with her novels. *Betty and Co.* contains twelve stories and plays, *A White*

Roof-Tree has two plays and stories. *The Camp at Wandinong* also contained *The Child of the Children*, later published singly in 1959. One of her poems, *Walking to School*, illustrated by Peter Gouldthorpe in 1988, appears in *An Ogre-Up-to-Date*.

Turner is frequently sentimental, priggish, and resolves problems too easily. Poverty can be overcome through hard work, freshly laundered curtains and wholesome cooking; her heroines, in their sprigged muslins and pretty ribbons, are generally conventional women of their time. But her respect for those who grasp the moment, her portrayal of lifelike children and families, and her ironic style lift her above her peers. For *Seven Little Australians* (1894), *Judy and Punch* (1928), *Little Mother Meg* (1902) and *The Family at Misrule* (1895) see **Seven Little Australians**. Further reading: Niall, *Seven Little Billabongs;* Poole, *The Diaries of Ethel Turner.*

TURNER, GWENDA (1947–), born Kyogle, NSW, studied graphic design at Wellington Polytechnic, NZ. In *The Tree Witches* (1983) Annie, Shirley and Pam make friends with 'Addi, addi, chickeri, chickeri, ooney, pooney om pom alari, alla balla whisky, Chinese salt', the new boy in the neighbourhood. *Playbook* (1985) follows the activities of primary school children as they cook, build and play outside. In *Daydream Journey* (1982) Molly reminisces about visiting Grandma in the country, and in *Snow Play* (1986) Anna and Willie play winter games. *Once Upon a Time* (1990) looks at a family's day, hour by hour. In *Creepy Cottage* (1985) and *Catnip Mice and Tussie Mussies* (1985) Amy and Clare observe the changing seasons in the garden of a nearby cottage and make items for the school fair (instructions included).

TURNER, HELEN. For *Under Cook's Flag* (1924) see **Cook**, Captain **James**.

TURNER, LILIAN WATTNALL BURWELL (1867–1956), born Lincoln, UK, journalist and writer, came to Australia with her sister Ethel in 1881. Like Ethel, she edited *Iris* and *Parthenon*, and wrote extensively for the young, publishing over twenty books for the teenage reader. In 1904 she won first prize in an open competition organised by the Melbourne branch of Cassell, for *The Lights of Sydney: or, No Past is Dead.*

Her romances for older girls began with *Young Love* (1902), illustrated by J. Macfarlane. *April Girls* (1911) is an account of the various romances between the Hopes, the Redgraves, and other neighbours. Turner was interested in women's rights, but it is not discernible in this novel. Her male characters moon after silly girls who lisp, giggle and throw tantrums. *Stairway to the Stars* (1913) is more positive. A group of young people move from Sydney to London to develop their abilities as authors or artists. Turner explores her characters' ability to recognise and accept their limitations and weaknesses as well as their talents. In *War's Heart Throbs* (1915), Cynthia, flighty and self-centred, is transformed when war is declared into a serious, tireless worker for the Red Cross. The novel examines how the people at home in Australia are affected by the war. All these books were illustrated by J. Macfarlane. In *Peggy the Pilot* (1922), illustrated by F. Dewar Mills, Peggy is one of seven children. Turner looks at gender stereotyping, and Peggy imagines a world where women have the same freedoms as men. *The Happy Heriots* (1926), also illustrated by Mills, are another family of seven. The family moves to the country to 'Tree Tops', next door to eligible young men with a mysterious mother. *There Came a Call* (1930) is the story of David Fordyce, journalist, who falls in love from afar with the rich and beautiful Elfrida Ann Bennett. When Elfrida goes to live in poverty with her father in Sydney, and David and his sister also seek their fortune there, the two meet. It is only after David has won £1000 in a parachute jump, and Elfrida Ann has returned to Melbourne that they swear undying love for each other. *Two Take the Road* (1931) illustrated by 'Sutcliffe', describes a romance between Virginia and Bardolph. *Ann Chooses Glory* (1928), also illustrated by 'Sutcliffe', is an account of a struggle between love and duty. When we meet Ann 'her face was besmirched with oil and grease ... she wore no stockings, but had thrust her feet bare into a pair of dirty sand-shoes ... She was sitting tailor-fashion and disconsolate hard by a most disconsolate-looking motor-car, with one hand grasping a spanner.' Ann has a fine voice, and does take up the offer of singing training in London at the end of the book. *Lady Billie* (1929), illustrated by Mills, set in England, recounts Wilhelmina's transformation from hatred to love towards her Australian stepmother and stepsisters. Billie is another of Turner's heroines to reject the domestic life, preferring to be a secretary or to learn to drive a car than to develop the skill of mending lace or cooking a meal.

An Australian Lassie (1903), illustrated by A.J. Johnson, introduces Elizabeth Bruce, aged 10, and her various attempts to transform her family's fortunes. She fails in an appeal to her hard-hearted grandfather, gets to know the heir to her grandfather's fortune, John Brown, and sets off for boarding school at the conclusion of the novel. *Betty the Scribe* (1906), also illustrated by Johnson, is its sequel. Betty is now 17 and wants to be a writer, but her independence is restricted by her responsibility for younger brothers and sisters after her mother's death.

Paradise and the Perrys (1908) and *The Perry Girls* (1909) are also about the genteel poor. In the first, Addie, Mavis, Theo, Enid and their mother develop a teashop, Paradise, into a thriving business. In the second, Addie marries a shepherd, Enid further displays her selfishness and Theo meets the man of her life. Their resource-

fulness and marriageability save the family fortunes. *Three New Chum Girls* (1910), also illustrated by Macfarlane, describes a family's emigration from England after bankruptcy, and its attempt to make a living off a remote and harsh property. Turner looks at social attitudes to men and women, portraying a boorish brother and sisters who work very hard for very little, raising arguments about women's independence and the role of home-making.

In *The Girl from the Back-Blocks* (1914) Joan Darcy is sent off to school, much against her wishes, but accepts it after developing some friendships. When the schoolgirls share their ambitions, a few want to marry, but others want to be nurses or acrobats. Joan wants to ride her horse around Australia. *Jill of the Fourth Form* (1924) is another school story. Jill is so indulged that she becomes impatient with her soft world, and pleads to go to boarding school. Her early difficulties there are soon overcome, and she displays the plucky spirit that was concealed beneath a spoilt exterior. Other novels include *Written Down* (1912), *Rachel* (1920) and *Nina Comes Home* (1927).

It is inevitable that Lilian Turner's novels are unfavourably compared to her sister Ethel's strong character development and tightly constructed plots. Lilian does not write as consistently well as Ethel, although she has some of the same irony, and she is more ambivalent in her acceptance of the social mores of her time. In *The Noughts and Crosses* (1917), illustrated by Stanley Davis, for instance, she examines the tyranny of a severe Victorian family autocrat, the chilling Judge Lynn, whose rule all the children wish to throw off. To escape from him, 17-year-old Mona marries 43-year-old Stephen. But Turner softens the impact by having Mona fall in love with her husband, and submit to the requirements of housekeeping and marriage. Similarly, she baulks at Mona's sister Daisy taking her life into her own hands, preferring to depict her submission to her father's dominance on the grounds of propriety. Lilian Turner's most interesting heroines, such as Mona Lynn and Theo Perry, are unusual in their less than enthusiastic response to domesticity and their longing for independence, and these coupled with Turner's confidence in the capacity of women to perform practical tasks have more in common with women writers for adults of the period than the children's writers who were her contemporaries.

TURNLEY, COLE (1919–), born Melbourne, is a grandson of E.W. Cole (q.v.). He compiled *Funny Picture Book No. 3* (1951) and has written *Cole of the Book Arcade: a Pictorial Biography of E.W. Cole* (1974).

Turramulli the Giant Quinkin (1982) by Percy Trezise and Dick Roughsey was Commended in the 1983 Picture Book of the Year Awards. Turramulli the Giant, whose name means thunder, was the most dangerous Quinkin. When Moonbi and Leealin are chased by Turramulli, the three of them fall off Quinkin Mountain, but the children are caught in the arms of the Timara Quinkins and Turramulli falls to his death. See also *The Quinkins*.

27th Annual African Hippopotamus Race, The (1969) by Morris Lurie, illustrated by Elizabeth Honey, won 1986 YABBA for Younger Readers. It is the story of Edward Day the hippopotamus, aged 8 and weighing two and a half tonnes, who wins the race down the Zamboola River, beating the Mighty Sebastian. Sebastian resorts to cheating by grabbing Edward's leg, but Edward's friend Barney saves the day by pulling Sebastian's bathing trunks down. This short, funny novel has exuberant characters and a pacy style.

U

Uhu (1969), written and illustrated by Annette Macarthur-Onslow, won the 1970 Book of the Year Awards. Uhu is an owl, 'a defiant white ball of fluff with enormous blackcurrant eyes', who falls from a tree in the Cotswolds, England, and is cared for by the family to whom Minnie (q.v.) the cat also belongs. Uhu grows up, breaks a leg, and is identified as a female before another fall results in tragedy. The watercolours and line drawings of Uhu conjure up the sweep and rush of a large bird.

ULLIN, ALBERT (1930–), born Frankfurt-on-Main, came to Australia as a child. He established the first Australian specialist bookshop for children's books, in Melbourne in 1960. The bookshop, named 'The Little Bookroom' after Eleanor Farjeon's classic, has a logo designed especially for the shop by Edward Ardizzone. Ullin has been active in the Australian Booksellers' Association and the CBC, and has been Victorian president of both organisations, the latter from 1984 to 1985. He has compiled the 'Little Ark Children's Calendars' for Allen & Unwin, in which major Australian illustrators are represented. He was awarded the Dromkeen Medal in 1986.

Unbelievable! More Surprising Stories (1986) by Paul Jennings won YABBA for Older Readers in 1988. See **Unreal! Eight Surprising Stories**.

Uncanny! Even More Surprising Stories (1988) by Paul Jennings won YABBA for Older Readers in 1989. See **Unreal! Eight Surprising Stories**.

Uncle Gustav's Ghosts (1974) by Colin Thiele was considered Worthy of Mention in the 1975 Book of the Year Awards. Uncle Gustav first sees an apparition on the road at night, but he is not the only one to glimpse Maria Rollenberg in her wedding gown, or the awful spectre of her murderous husband. Just when the community believes that their bones, found by Benny, Ossie and Louisa, have been properly buried, allowing the ghostly Maria to rest in peace, another incident seems to show that they are right back where it all began. Thiele has used the German settlements in the Barossa Valley as the background to his novel, in which the robust characters see poltergeists which can *almost* all be explained as figments of their rich imaginations.

University of Queensland Press was established in 1948, but publishing for young readers was first began in 1986, with the appointment of Barbara Ker Wilson as consultant editor. The press publishes around ten new novels each year, and although Canadian, Irish and NZ authors are represented, the list is predominantly by Australian authors, such as Brian Caswell, Judith Clarke, Allan Collins, Michael Noonan and Maureen Pople.

Unreal! Eight Surprising Stories (1985) by Paul Jennings won YABBA for Older Readers in 1987 and was Secondary Winner of KOALA in 1990. It includes 'The ghost that haunts the outside dunny', 'Lucky lips', 'Cowdung custard', 'Wunderpants' and other scatological delights. *Unbelievable! More Surprising Stories* (1986) won YABBA for Older Readers in 1988. Nine stories, each capped with a clever twist, describe why the punk ghost cannot pass his spook exam, how Mr Bin rejects ballet dancing in favour of dentistry, how Grandad escapes from the nursing home with the help of a very small dragon, and so on. Another nine stories appeared in *Uncanny! Even More Surprising Stories* (1988), which again won YABBA for Older Readers in 1989. The stories relate the adventures of a ghost who haunts a tip looking for his false teeth, a spaghetti-eating competition, an evil tightrope-walking scarecrow and other oddities. These collections have humour, original-ity and an unselfconscious style and engage a wide readership.

Useless Donkeys, The (1979) by Lydia Pender, illustrated by Judith Cowell, was Commended in the 1980 Picture Book of the Year Awards. The Quigley family's two donkeys, Garibaldi and Peccadillo, are charming but useless. When they are stranded during a storm and refuse to be rescued, the children row across to them to keep them company. Cowell's detailed watercolours portray the wild storm and its aftermath.

UTEMORRAH, DAISY (1922–), born near Derby, WA, is an elder and storyteller of the Mowanjum people, and a writer and teacher. She has written one of the Aboriginal Dreaming stories edited by Pamela Lofts, *Dunbi the Owl* (1983), and a collection of poems, *Do Not Go Around the Edges* (1990), illustrated by Pat Torres. The latter is her life story from when she was separated from her people to her rein-tegration in her own community as an adult, interspersed with poems which draw on the spirituality of the Wunambul people. 'Do not go around the edges/or else you'll fall./No good that place/or else you'll slip.' See also **Aboriginal Dreaming Stories**.

V

VALLELY, DAN (1945–), born UK, has written *The Rungawilla Ranger* (1986), illustrated by Trish Hart, a verse story about the robbers Butch 'Chidna and Koala Kid, who are routed by Big Red, the Rungawilla Ranger. See also **Bushrangers**. *The Great Possum Creek Bushfire* (1988), illustrated by Yvonne Perrin, is a poem where the animals become the fire-fighters. 'By the time that they were finished/The flames were quite diminished/And relief was plain on every face in town./Twelve hours, they had fought it/And sure as I report it/With exhaustion every creature then fell down.' *The Possum Creek Stories* (1989), *Possum One, the Outback Rocket Ship* (1981), also illustrated by Perrin, are in the same series. Vallely has also written *Professor Cockatoo's Amazing Weather Dust* (1989).

Valley Between, The (1981) by Colin Thiele won the 1982 Book of the Year Awards. Benno Schulz is 13, and has just left school, delighted at the prospect of helping his father run their farm at Gonunda, SA. Benno ambles through the summer days of the 1920s — inadvertently exposing himself in hand-knitted woollen bathers, carrying a scarecrow on his back like an apparition, squirting the Pastor in the eye with Daisy's milk — at the centre of every minor and major catastrophe. Thiele's gallery of eccentric characters, hair-raising incidents and childlike pranks provide a background to Benno's observation of the relationships and rivalries of the adult world.

VAN LOON, JOAN (1946–), born Melbourne, and **JOHN** (1942–), born Brabant, Holland, wrote and illustrated *I Remember Georgie* (1983), which celebrates an old house and garden, and the special relationship which developed between the child, Anna, and Georgie, one of the three elderly sisters who lived there. *Jelly, Chips and Caramel Whips* (1986) is in verse. Willy McMullen threatens to run away to Lucy's house, where wonderful things are allowed to happen, but Mother says that she will come too. They have also written and illustrated *The Mt Martha Monster* (1987) in Macmillan's 'Southern Cross' series. Joan Van Loon has written *Chaos in Acland Street* (1990), illustrated by Mervyn Pywell, in which Gloria's new puppy walks down a busy street, disrupting the shoppers. John has illustrated *Black Sorrow* (1980) by Reginald Ottley.

VAUGHAN, MARCIA KAY (1951–), born Tacoma, Washington, USA, came to Australia in 1981. *Pewzer and Bonsai* (1985), illustrated by Megan Gressor, is a humorous book for young readers about two Sydney mice. In *Wombat Stew* (1984), illustrated by Pamela Lofts, a crafty dingo is outwitted by other animals when he wants to make a stew out of a wombat. *Where Does the Wind Go?* (1986), illustrated by Karen Hopkins, is a verse story in a folding book where the flowing illustrations mimic the wind of the story. *Still Room for More* (1989), illustrated by Craig Smith, is a cumulative story about a pig's washing machine. With Richard Vaughan she has written *Adam's Apple* (1989), illustrated by Coral Tulloch, which follows the ups and downs of a lunch apple, after Adam drops it on his way to school. *Sly, Old Lockjaw Croc* (1990) is illustrated by Rodney McRae. In *The Mystery of the Missing Map* (1991), illustrated by Witold Generowicz, two children search for a stolen map, with the whereabouts hinted at in the pictures. *The Sea-Breeze Hotel* (1991), illustrated by Patricia Mullins, describes how Sam saves the fortunes of the hotel by using the winds to fly his kite. Mullins's tissue-like kites lift above the building, so that the sky is 'alive with kites'.

Verity of Sydney Town (1950) by Ruth C. Williams, illustrated by Rhys Williams, won the 1951 Book of the Year Awards. During Macquarie's governorship of the Colony of NSW, when her father is absent, Verity is sent off to a farm by the unfeeling Mrs Flintley. There she has the standard pioneering adventures, including fighting fires and bushrangers. Verity's hardships are those of a well-to-do girl who for a short time finds herself without the comforts and privileges of her class, but her manners and good breeding ensure that she is always recognised as the lady she is.

VERNE, JULES (1828–1905), born Nantes, France, writer of science fiction and adventure stories, wrote an adventure story about two children in search of their father which has a large section set in Australia. The novel first appeared as *Les Enfants du Capitaine Grant* in 1867, and in later editions was variously titled *The Mysterious Document* (1876), *A Voyage Round the World* (1877), *On the Track* (?1905) and *Among the Cannibals* (1906). Mary and Robert Grant seek the help of Lord Glenarvan and his wife Lady Helena, who have found a garbled message in a bottle discovered inside a shark's stomach, which provides evidence that the ship-wrecked Captain Grant is still alive. With the geographer savant Paganel, they travel to South America, aboard Glenarvan's ship the *Dunbar*. The second part of the novel, 'On the track', takes them to the coast of Australia, where the party journeys from Adelaide to Twofold Bay by land, encountering Aboriginal People, escaped convicts, and every strange animal Australia possesses. Verne's geography is rather

muddled, and his natural history a little elementary, but his enthusiasm and wit are infectious. "'Malefactors, transported into this reviving and salubrious air, are regenerated in a few years. The effect is known to philanthropists. In Australia all characters improve", said Paganel. "But then, Mr Paganel, you, who are already so good," said Helena, "what will you become in this privileged land?" "Simply excellent," answered Paganel, "tout simplement excellent."' After two years of voyaging, including the company being threatened with becoming a Maori supper, Captain Grant is found alive and prospering on Maria Theresa Island.

Very Best of Friends, The (1989) by Margaret Wild, illustrated by Julie Vivas, won the 1990 Picture Book of the Year Awards. When James dies suddenly, the grieving Jessie banishes his cat William from the house, only to readmit him when she sees his deterioration. Jessie's changing feelings and readjustments are shown in Vivas's sensitive watercolours. See also **Death**.

VILLIERS, ALAN (1903–82), born Melbourne, led an adventurous life, which included sailing on a whaler to the Antarctic, an experience described in *Whalers of the Midnight Sun: a Story of Modern Whaling in the Antarctic* (q.v., 1934, republished 1949). *Stormalong, the Story of a Boy's Voyage around the World in a Full-Rigged Ship* (1937), illustrated by James Fuller, tells the story of a two-year voyage with a group of boys from their point of view, as Stormalong and Hardcase travel aboard the *Joseph Conrad*. The adventure captured the local imagination, and when the *Joseph Conrad* arrived in Melbourne in 1936, Stormalong, the bosun, spoke to children on the 3LO children's session. *The Cruise of the 'Conrad'* (1955) is another account of the real-life adventure. In *Joey Goes to Sea* (1939), illustrated by M.T. Caldwell, Joey is a kitten aboard the same ship, and *Pilot Pete* (1953) is about a porpoise who helps mariners around the South Pacific. *And Not to Yield: the Story of the Outward Bound* (1953) describes the origin of the school for young adventurers, and *The New Mayflower* (1959) relates the building and voyage of a replica of the ship which took the Pilgrims to America.

VISKA, PETER (1946–), born Perth, animator and illustrator, has illustrated *The Junk Eaters* (1987) by Nan Hunt; *Far Out, Brussel Sprout!: Australian Children's Chants*

and Rhymes (1983), *All Right, Vegemite: a New Collection of Children's Chants and Rhymes* (1985) and *Unreal, Banana Peel: a Third Collection of Children's Chants and Rhymes* (1986) by June Factor; *Bilge* (1988) by Doug MacLeod; *Let 'er Rip, Potato Chip* (1988) and *That Awful Molly Vickers! Poems and Rhymes Demanded by Children* (1989) by Virginia Ferguson and Peter Durkin; *Carmen Out to Play!: a Collection of Children's Playground Games* (1990) by Heather Russell; *Snug as a Bug! Scenes from Family Life* (1990) and *Duck*

Keiran O'Grady loved the trams that rattled, day and night, past their tiny flat at Bondi. He loved the strange gnashing sound of the wheels on the silver rails.

In the morning he and his little sister Isabelle watched through their big front windows as the trams criss-crossed in front of them, laden with people on their way to work.

The Tram to Bondi Beach (1981) by Libby Hathorn. Illustrator: Julie Vivas

Under the Table (1991) by Gwenda Beed Davey; and *Horrible Humans* (1990) by Max Dann. Viska also contributed to 'Kaboodle' (q.v.), with 'The Hedge and Mr Snip' for *Hedge Island* (1989) by Peter Durkin and Virginia Ferguson.

Visual Arts Board Awards were given from 1974 to 1976. From 1977 the awards were combined with the monies provided for the Picture Book of the Year Awards (q.v.). **1974** Kilmeny and Deborah Niland for *Mulga Bill's Bicycle* (1973) by A.B. Paterson; Ron Brooks for *The Bunyip of Berkeley's Creek* (q.v., 1973) by Jenny Wagner; Dick Roughsey for *The Giant Devil Dingo* (q.v., 1973). **1975** Roger Haldane for *Magpie Island* (q.v., 1974) and Robert Ingpen for *Storm Boy* (q.v., 1974) both by Colin Thiele; Deborah Niland for *Stuff and Nonsense* (1974) compiled by Michael Dugan. **1976** Ted Greenwood for *Terry's Brrrmmm GT* (q.v., 1974); Ron Brooks for *Annie's Rainbow* (q.v., 1975).

VIVAS, JULIE (1947–), born Adelaide, is a watercolourist who studied at the National Art School, Sydney, and also trained in architecture and interior design. She has illustrated *The Tram to Bondi Beach* (q.v., 1981) by Libby Hathorn; *Dim and Dusty* (1983) by Joan Dalgleish; *Possum Magic* (q.v., 1983) and *Possum Magic Birthday Book* (1984) by Mem Fox; and *The Grandma Poss Cookbook* (1985), which introduces the wonders of Australian party fare, including pavlovas, pumpkin scones and lamingtons. *Wilfrid Gordon McDonald Partridge* (1984) is also by Mem Fox. Vivas illustrated Margaret Wild's *The Very Best of Friends* (q.v., 1989) and *Let the Celebrations Begin!* (1990); *I Went Walking* (1989) by Sue Machin; and Richard Tulloch's *Stories from Our House* (1987), and *Stories from Our Street* (1989). *The Nativity* (1986) has a text drawn from the Bible. See also **Religion**. *Nurse Lugton's Curtain* (1991) is a story by Virginia Woolf (1882–1941). Nurse Lugton dozes off, and the animals on the curtain she is sewing leap off the fabric to drink at the beautiful Millamarchmantopolis. Vivas's work has a vulnerable beauty, with illustrations which depict with affection the grace of children and animals. Vivas was awarded the Dromkeen Medal in 1992.

W

WADE, GRAHAM (1931–) illustrated many of the Jungle Doctor books by Paul White; *Kippy Koala's Christmas Present* (1987) by Win Morgan; *Snowy: the Story of a River* (1975) by Howard Guinness; the novels of Denys Burrows; *Everyday Inventions* (q.v., 1972) by Meredith Hooper; and *Kamilaroi* (1978) by John Ferry.

WAGNER, JENNY (1939–), born UK, came to Australia in 1948. She has written scripts for television, including the ABC's 'Bellbird' serial. *The Werewolf Knight* (1972), illustrated by Karl Homes, is based on the ballad of Marie de France. Feolf is cured of his wolfish ways when the Lady Fioran releases him through her love. *Peter and the Zauberleaf* (1973), illustrated by Giulietta Stomann, is the story of a lonely boy who takes a magic leaf as his friend until he is able to establish human friendships. The search for identity is further explored in *Hannibal* (1976), illustrated by Karl Homes, about an eccentric rabbit who develops a taste for meat, and takes over from the farm dog.

John Brown, Rose and the Midnight Cat (1977) by Jenny Wagner. Illustration: Ron Brooks.

Wagner's singular imagination is displayed in three highly original picture-books illustrated by Ron Brooks, *The Bunyip of Berkeley's Creek* (q.v., 1973), *Aranea: a Story about a Spider* (q.v., 1975) and *John Brown, Rose and the Midnight Cat* (q.v., 1977). In *Jo-Jo and Mike* (1982), illustrated by Ann James, Mike is so busy painting signs that Jo-Jo, his dog, is always locked inside. When Jo-Jo breaks out and causes havoc, Mike and Jo-Jo leave town, and Mike decides to paint his own pictures. In *The Machine at the Heart of the World* (1983), illustrated by Jeff Fisher, the machine controls the world, under the guidance of Theobald. When Theobald tires of the machine and goes to bed, the townspeople greedily take it over. Theobald must return to save the world from itself. In *Goanna* (1988), illustrated by Noela Hills, a goanna learns a savage lesson when his home is destroyed by the expansion of a town. See also **Conservation**. *Amy's Monster* (1990), illustrated by Terry Denton, is about a homesick girl who summons up a monster to defeat her two horrible twin cousins.

The Nimbin (1978), illustrated by Inga Moore, was Wagner's first full-length novel for children. Philippa finds a small hairy creature in her beach bag. The Nimbin's passion for chocolate biscuits, condensed milk and sweets leads Philippa into accusations of theft, until, as the end of summer draws near, the Nimbin leaves. See also **Fantasy**. *Return of the Nimbin* (1992) is its sequel, and *Message from Avalon* (1990), set in a haunted house, is another novel for older readers.

WAKEFIELD, S. A. (SYDNEY ALEXANDER WAKEFIELD) (1927–), born Sydney, farmer and writer, lived in England for much of his childhood, returning to his birthplace after World War II. For his fantasies about Bottersnikes and Gumbles, see **Bottersnikes and Gumbles**. In *Captain Deadlight's Treasure* (1990), illustrated by Julie Mac, all Mr Porter wants is to transform the *Peppermint* into a pleasure ship, but when he finds a treasure map he is pursued by Black Jack, and the ghost of Captain Deadlight.

WALKER, KATE (1950–), born Newcastle, NSW, has written picture-books, short stories, scripts and novels. Her realistic books include *Marty Moves to the Country* (q.v., 1980), which describes a friendship, and *The Letters of Rosie O'Brien: a Convict in the Colony of New South Wales 1804* (1988), illustrated by Paul Borg. Rosie is transported to NSW for stealing a lace handkerchief. Her father is already there, and in a series of letters home to her sister, Rosie relates her experiences, meets up with her convict father, and asks her mother and sister to join them to take up a holding near Richmond, NSW. Some of Walker's stories are in the form of folk-tales. *The Frog Who Would be King* (1987), illustrated by David Cox, turns the traditional story on its head, the frog becoming a prince and the princess becoming a frog. In *King Joe of Bogpeat Castle* (1987), illustrated by Margie Chellew, the king is poor until he turns his castle into a cheap eating kitchen. *Tales from the Goodland* (1988), illustrated by Gillian Campbell, contains seven stories, like folk-tales, about a beautiful valley. *The First Easter Rabbit* (1989), illustrated by Marina McAllan, is a picture-book. Henry is born in a chicken coop, and his efforts to paint stones to look like eggs are so beautiful that he becomes the first of a long line of rabbits. *The Dragon of Mith* (q.v., 1989) also draws on legendary tales, but with a very liberated heroine. *The Alien Challenger* (1983), illustrated by Peter Lewis, is an apparently sinister video game, until its surprise owner reveals its origins. *Burying Aunt Renie* (1989), illustrated by Margie Chellew, is in Methuen's 'Dimensions' (q.v.) series and has stories and biographical material. *Peter* (q.v., 1991) is her first book for older readers, and raises issues of gender and sexuality. See also **Sexuality**.

WALKER, KATH, see **NOONUC-CAL** (NUNUKAL), **OODGEROO**

WALKER, MAXINE (1927–), born Swan Hill, Victoria, has written a series of critical essays about children's writers, *Writer's Alive! Current Australian Authors of Books for Children* (1977). Walker has an extensive private collection of children's books.

WALL, DOROTHY (1894–1942), born Wellington, NZ, came to Australia in 1914. Wall had been trained in art at Wellington, and throughout her life sup-ported herself through commercial assignments such as fashion drawings and book jackets, and her books. *Tommy Bear and the Zookies* (1920) has a koala as its central character, although his expression is less innocent than that of the later Blinky Bill. The Zookies are small fat creatures with bear-like limbs. *The Crystal Bowl* (1921) by J.J. Hall is illustrated with similar creatures, combined with human figures displaying elegant drapery and swirling tresses. *Jacko the Broadcasting Kookaburra* (1933) and *The Amazing Adventures of Billy Penguin* (1934) by Brooke Nicholls introduced a further range of bush animals,

Stout Fellows (1936) by Dorothy Wall

including a koala which Nicholls had named 'Blinky Bill'. For the books which developed around this character see **Blinky Bill**. She also illustrated *Australians All: Bush Folk in Rhyme* (1934) by Nelle Grant Cooper. Ginger Pop describes the life of the bees to Bridget in *The Tale of Bridget and the Bees* (1934). *Brownie, the Story of a Naughty Little Rabbit* (1935) follows the adventures of Velvet Paws, Brownie's mother Mrs Bobtail, and Brownie, a naughty rabbit, as mischievous as Blinky Bill was to be. Taking a character out of *Blinky Bill, The Quaint Little Australian* (1933), Angelina Wallaby, she added Chum, a small boy, and Flip, the 'biggest and bulgiest frog in the bush', and Um-Pig to create *Stout Fellows: Chum, Angelina Wallaby, Um-Pig and Flip* (1936). The four friends travel through the bush to Long Ago to find Chum's home.

Wall wrote and illustrated *The Rainy Day* (1937) and illustrated *Mickles and Muckles* (1939) by Dorothy Mellor; these were publicity booklets published by the Commonwealth Bank to promote thrift in schools. *Horrie Kiwi and the Kids* (1984), about a pair of kiwis and their offspring, retold by David Harris, was probably written before Wall arrived in Australia, and was unpublished until it was discovered in Angus & Robertson's files. Wall's strong designs and impudent humour present animals overcoming human difficulties with a cheeky individuality. Further reading: McVitty, *Dorothy Wall*.

WALLACE-CRABBE, KENNETH (1900–83), born Inverell, NSW, wrote *The Story of Otto or How They Fissioned the Atom* (n.d.), illustrated by the cartoonist Wally Driscoll. It is a humorous story about how Otto the Atom felt when it was split and made into an atomic bomb. Wallace-Crabbe also wrote and illustrated picture-strips for magazines, and wrote, illustrated, edited and published *Cross Roads*, a fortnightly magazine, which ran for three years from 1939.

WALLER, CHRISTIAN (YANDELL) (1894–1954), born Castlemaine, Victoria, studied at the National Gallery School, Melbourne, and was married to the muralist Napier Waller (1893–1972). She designed stained-glass windows for Melbourne churches at Brighton, Camberwell, Canterbury, Frankston, Ivanhoe and North Melbourne and for St Barnabas's, West Wyalong, NSW. *The Great Breath* (1932) is a book of seven of her lino-cuts. Waller illustrated Hume Cook's *Australian Fairy Tales* (1925) (see **Fairies**) and the first Australian *Alice's Adventures in Wonderland* (1924). Her illustrations for May Paten's *The Adventurous Elves: an Authoritative Fairy Story* (1926) are characteristic of the period, although they have a strength and boldness which is more clearly seen in *The Gates of Dawn* (1977). The latter was published over twenty years after her death, from plates made when she was using her own press, the 'Golden Arrow'. Her powerful linocuts and pen-and-ink illustrations

The Gates of Dawn (1932) by Christian Waller

make a striking comparison to the delicacy of the fairy pictures of Ida Rentoul Outhwaite or Margaret Clark.

WALLINGTON, VIVIENNE (1937–), born Adelaide, is a librarian and novelist. In *Somewhere* (1982), illustrated by Murray Frederick, Ben shares a secret house with Lucy and Susan, which is consolation for his fear of abandonment. Kate in *Butterfingers* (1986), illustrated by Astra Lacis, is a clumsy girl surrounded by critical adults.

WALSH, AMANDA (1943–), born Melbourne, has written and illustrated a series of picture-books about Egrin, a wizard, who seems unable to avoid trouble. Egrin paints a picture of himself which comes alive as his wicked alter ego in *Egrin and the Painted Wizard* (1972); in *Egrin and the Wicked Witch* (1977) he inadvertently releases a very angry witch who has to be turned into a butterfly before she can be contained; in *Egrin and the Hungry Troll* (1988) he befriends a troll who has designs on small animals and teaches him how to cook. *The Mysterious Hubbub* (1990), where the frozen sounds of a battle go off like fireworks before peace is restored, shows Walsh's fine eye for colour. *The Buried Moon* (1991) is a traditional tale calling on the fear of darkness. Her simple texts suggest the value of kindness without didacticism, and Walsh uses pen and ink and splashes of watercolour to great effect, creating character with gentle satire.

WALSH, GRAHAME L. (1945–), born Roma, Queensland, has written *The Goori Goori Bird: from a Legend of the Bidjara People of the Upper Warrego* (1984), illustrated by John Morrison. It is the story of a devil bird who preys on Aboriginal children, and explains the origins of the Milky Way. *Didane the Koala: from a Legend of the Bidjara People of the Upper Warrego* (1985), also illustrated by Morrison, tells how Didane the warrior

koala threw his powerful boomerang into the sky, causing seeds to grow in the Carnarvon area. See also **Aboriginal Dreaming Stories**.

'WALTERS, HUGH' is the pseudonym of **WALTER HUGHES** (1910–), born Bilston, UK, an English author who writes science fiction. For *Blast Off at Woomera* (1957) and *The Domes of Pico* (1958) see **Science Fiction**.

Waltzing Matilda (1970) by A.B. Paterson, illustrated by Desmond Digby, won the 1971 Picture Book of the Year Awards. The familiar poem is illustrated with distinguished oil paintings, often across a double-page spread. Landscape and period are evoked through changes in colour and light, expressive of the swagman's impending doom.

Wandjina: Children of the Dreamtime; Aboriginal Myths & Legends (1968), selected by Roland Robinson and illustrated by Roderick Shaw, was Commended in the 1969 Book of the Year Awards. It is a collection which combines Dreaming narratives and post-invasion stories, such as 'The gold of Billy Bulloo'. No specific cultural context is defined, and the stories are drawn from Aboriginal People across Australia. Shaw has used the forms of Aboriginal art for the stylised illustrations.

War. The wars in which Australians have participated have been represented in children's books since the Boer War, the first international conflict which involved Australian soldiers. Donald Macdonald's *How We Kept the Flag Flying: the Story of the Seige of Ladysmith* (1900) describes the war for adults. Ethel Turner's *The Wonder-Child* (1901) was also written at the time of the Boer War, and her soldiers are camped in Sydney before leaving for South Africa. Nearly a century later it is possible to see the Boer War in perspective, and Bruce Tanton's *Time's Lost Hero* (1990) evokes the horror of the times. The historical significance of the weaponry used during the Boer War, the development of camouflage, the use of trenches and the War's bloody battles are recalled, particularly through descriptions of the seige of Ladysmith.

World War I generated an upsurge in patriotism, created the Anzac hero, and introduced a source of adventure through the threat of spies. In Joseph Bowes's *The Young Anzacs, a Tale of the Great War* (1918) Aboriginal Jack, Jock and the Irish Tim go off to the war with great excitement. 'The declaration of war by Britain was made upon her enemies and answered in every dominion, commonwealth, colony and dependency throughout the vast Empire by a rousing chorus of passionate loyalty ... Jack's being thrilled with an indefinable ecstasy ... ' In *Three Real Bricks* (1920) by T.E. Grattan-Smith the brave and resourceful young Australians (one of whom speaks German) unmask cruel and sneaky German spies who plan to sabotage an Australian troopship. Ethel Turner's *Captain Cub* (1917) and *Brigid and The Cub* (1919) are also set during World War I, and while there is a great deal about the need to join up and support the Empire, there is little about the bloody nature of fighting. *War's Heart Throbs* (1915) by Lilian Turner emphasises allegiance to England. 'England expects every woman to do her duty, which is to knit socks and make pyjamas and flannel shorts', says Cynthia. As the young men leave school to defend the Motherland, in Lillian Pyke's *Max the Sport* (1916), they carry with them the noble behaviour tested out in the cricket match, vindicated in a VC for Max. *A Prince at School* (1919) by the same author has schoolboys unmasking more German spies. Mary Grant Bruce's World War I trilogy, *From Billabong to London* (1915), *Jim and Wally* (1916) and *Captain Jim* (1919), shows a more realistic view of the outcomes of war. Jim's inner

conflict over whether to enlist or stay at home is considered in the first of the trilogy. Although the novels echo vague notions of decency and Empire, Jim's sentiments reflect the issue of personal honour rather than nationalistic fervour. At one point Norah and Jim are enthusiastic about the adventure of war, but Bruce shows how foolish this is by describing war's horror. *Jim and Wally* has detail of the Flanders trenches and descriptions of fighting.

These books show how committed these writers were to Australia's involvement in the war, inspired by patriotism, and the need to rally to the defence of the Anglo-Celtic way of life. Dale Collins's *Anzac Adventure: the Story of Gallipoli for Young Readers* (q.v., 1959) follows the same tradition, with accounts of the Gallipoli experience. Cliff Green presents a little-known incident in World War I in *The Boy Soldiers* (1990), in which 15-year-olds were being prepared to be conscripted into the army. Will is a pacifist, and his refusal to be a part of army training leads to the contempt of his friends and brutality from the officers.

Novels which deal with World War II present a more critical approach, although the spies are still there, this time Japanese. 'Coutts Brisbane's' *The Secret of the Desert* (1941), illustrated by John Turner, is an anti-Japanese adventure story about an entomologist found murdered in the Cape of Carpentaria. As the murder is unravelled it is found that the Japanese plan to invade Australia's north-west. In Bruce's two novels about World War II, *Peter & Co.* (1940) and *Karalta* (1941), her concern about war and its toll has deepened. In *Karalta*, Jan, an English girl, is evacuated to Australia, and uncovers a German spy in a country town. Bruce's honest appraisal of foolishness and her ability to compose an interesting story is in dramatic contrast to Morwell Hodges's *Bob Berrell in North Australia* (1947). This improbable story is set in Cooktown, where a Japanese film crew is the front for a spying operation. More recent reflections on World War II are seen in Mavis Thorpe Clark's *Nowhere to Hide* (1969). It is set in Gippsland, where two German prisoners of war attempt to sabotage the Yallourn power station. The war forces the children to grow up too quickly. Clark provides details of rationing, shortages and wartime innovations such as the gas producer on the Buick. Max Fatchen's *Closer to the Stars* (1981) is set in 1941 in a rural district where pilots are being trained for active service. Paul's sister is to be married to a young airman, who is killed abroad, and Nancy's baby is born at the end of the story. Paul learns that war is no game, but has tragic outcomes. Margaret Balderson's *When Jays Fly to Barbmo* (q.v., 1968), which is set outside Australia, looks at the German invasion of Norway through the eyes of Ingeborg, a girl who is also searching for her origins throughout the book.

Junko Morimoto's *My Hiroshima* (1987) recreates that terrible event at the end of the war in the form of a picture storybook. Christobel Mattingley has written two anti-war books, *The Angel with a Mouth-Organ* (1984), illustrated by Astra Lacis, and *The Miracle Tree* (1985), illustrated by Marianne Yamaguchi. *The Angel with a Mouth-Organ* is a story of a European family separated by the exigencies of war who experience great sorrow before they find each other again. In *The Miracle Tree* Taro returns from war to find Nagasaki in ruins and his wife Hanako lost. Through a tree which he plants he is reunited after twenty years with Hanako and her mother. The futility of war and its tragic effect on relationships is explored. Another book in the same vein is Michael Noonan's *McKenzie's Boots* (1987), about a 15-year-old who lies about his age to join the army. His experiences fighting the Japanese belie the propaganda about the enemy barbarians. J.M. Couper looks at the anguish of young men caught in the controversial conscription ballot during the Vietnam War in *The Thundering Good Today* (1970).

The enthusiastic patriotism of novels written in the period of World War I shifted to a much grimmer position during World War II. The contemporary novel is more likely to be concerned with the need to maintain peace than to promote the glory of war.

Ward, Lock is a publishing house, founded in 1854 by Ebenezer Ward and George Lock. Ward, Lock & Co. acquired the publishers Charles Beeton, taking on *Mrs Beeton's Book of Household Management*, and W. Tegg, gaining the 'Peter Parley' (q.v.) books. The firm published periodicals, including the *Windsor Magazine*, popular literature by authors such as Guy Boothby and Rider Haggard, and guidebooks. In 1884, William Steele, a senior member of staff, set up a branch in Melbourne, where he handled the firm's publishing until his death in 1918. Ward, Lock published the books of Ethel Turner, Lilian Turner, Jean Curlewis, D. Lindsay Thompson, Mary Grant Bruce and the NZ author Isobel M. Peacocke, and while some of the correspondence between these authors and Steele is extant, Ward, Lock's premises in London were twice destroyed by fire, in 1911 and during an air raid in 1940, so that many of their records were lost. In the 1970s Ward, Lock became a subsidiary of the Pentos group.

WARDLEWORTH, PAULINE (1929–). For *The Land of Ideas: an Anthology of Stories for Children by South Australian Writers* (1986) see **Collections**.

Warnayarra — the Rainbow Snake. See **Aboriginal Dreaming Stories**.

WATEN, JUDAH (1911–85), born Odessa, Russia, wrote *Bottle-O!* (1972), illustrated by Walter Mitchell, for Cassell's 'Patchwork Paperbacks' series, about Jacob Bonosky, who collects and sells bottles in the Melbourne suburb of Carlton between the wars. His novel *Alien Son* (1952), based on his family's experience in

WA before World War I, has made a greater mark on young people's reading. The difficulties of the European immigrant are evoked through the perennial optimism of Father and the despairing fear of Mother that the children will lose their culture as the new country increasingly absorbs them. This picture of a culturally rich Jewish life against a background of prejudice is an important contribution to an understanding of the immigrant experience.

WATKINS, ALLAN (1921–), born Newcastle, NSW, is a writer of adventure stories. In *Pillars of Crystal* (1972), illustrated by Hal English, Mark, Johnny, Susan and Peter accidentally discover a cave system and disturb a burglar's plans. When the children are lost in the subterranean chasms, a crisis of leadership occurs, and Mark's weaknesses are revealed to Johnny. *Danger Island* (1972), also illustrated by English, is set on the Barrier Reef. Jeff and his cousins Nancy and Stephen, with the help of an Islander, Billy Tamiko, uncover an attempt to smuggle the proceeds of a robbery out of Australia. *Blow Up a Storm* (1974) is set in Fiji. With his aunt Susan and a friendly journalist, Richard Miller, Greg Reynolds is able to expose a group of drug-dealers and release his kidnapped father. In *Sky Tramps* (1975) Duffy Clayton's father Col is a crop-duster, moving around in search of work, while Duffy longs to settle down. Duffy's gift of second sight enables him to help catch two bank-robbers, and discriminate between the innocent, a blond Viking, and the guilty, a dark Italian who speaks poor English.

WATSON, INA MAUDE has written *Silvertail: the Story of a Lyrebird* (1946), illustrated by Walter Cunningham, an account of the life cycle of the lyrebird. *Larry: The Story of an Australian Seagull* (1961), illustrated by Margaret Senior, follows the life of a silver gull, born on a Bass Strait island. Larry becomes caught in twine, and is rescued by a boy and his aunt, who nurse him back to health, then free him. Larry finds a mate, and the cycle begins again. Incidental information is given about the migration habits and life cycle of birds.

WATSON, MAUREEN. For *Kaiyu's Waiting* (1984) see **Hodja Educational Resources Cooperative**.

WAYRBA, the West Australian Young Readers' Book Award, launched in 1980, was the first of the Readers' Choice Awards to be established in Australia. It is conducted by the ALIA School Libraries Section (WA Group), and aimed at readers aged 9 to 15, to provide a balance to the awards selected by adults. Two lists of thirty books are compiled by the group from titles submitted by young readers, who rate the books from 'terrific' to 'awful' on a four-point scale. It is not restricted to books by Australian authors, and is awarded in two categories, Primary, Years 4 to 7, and Secondary, Years 8 to 10. **1980** *Tales of a Fourth Grade Nothing* by Judy Blume and *My Darling Villain* by Lynne Reid Banks. **1981** *Sadako and the Thousand Paper Cranes* by Eleanor Coerr and *Don't Hurt Laurie* by Willow Roberts. **1982** *Superfudge* by Judy Blume and *The Forbidden Paths of Thual* (q.v., 1979) by Victor Kelleher. Special Award for most popular Australian title: *The Cockroach that Wrote a Symphony* (1979) by Trevor Todd. **1983** *Samantha on Stage* by S.C. Farrar and *Goodnight Mr Tom* by Michelle Magorian; Special Award: *The Hunting of Shadroth* (1981) by Victor Kelleher. **1984** *George's Marvellous Medicine* by Roald Dahl and *Did You Hear What Happened?* by Gloria Miklowitz. **1985** *The BFG* by Roald Dahl and *The Secret Diary of Adrian Mole* by Sue Townsend. Special Award: *When We Ran* (1981) by Keith Leopold; **1986** *The Witches* by Roald Dahl, *The Growing Pains of Adrian Mole* by Sue Townsend. Special Award: *Hating Alison Ashley* (q.v., 1984) and *People Might Hear You* (q.v., 1983) by

Robin Klein; **1987** *Selby's Secret* (q.v., 1985) by Duncan Ball, *The Eyes of Karen Connors* by Lois Duncan and *Back Home* by Michelle Magorian. **1988** *Grandma Cadbury's Trucking Tales* (q.v., 1987) by Dianne Bates and *Dead Birds Singing* by Marc Talbert; **1989** *Matilda* by Roald Dahl and *When the Phone Rang* by Harry Mazer. Special Awards: *The Ghost and the Gory Story* (1987) by Duncan Ball and *Unreal!* (q.v., 1985) by Paul Jennings. **1990** *Selby Speaks* (1988, see **Selby's Secret**) by Duncan Ball and *Redwall* by Brian Jacques. **1991** *Selby Screams* (1989, see **Selby's Secret**) by Duncan Ball and *Mossflower* by Brian Jacques. In 1991 the Hoffman Award for the highest ranking Australian authors apart from the winners was instituted in honour of Leila and Norm Hoffman, and was won by *The Paw Thing* (q.v., 1989) by Paul Jennings and *Lockie Leonard, Human Torpedo* (q.v., 1990) by Tim Winton.

'WEBB, JACQUELYN', see **PEARCE, MARGARET LORRAINE**

WEBB, MELISSA (1960–) has illustrated *Annabel's Ghost and Don't Tell Lucy* (1983) and *Games* (1986) by Robin Klein, and *The Dingbat Spies* (1984) by Joan Flanagan.

WELD, ANN has compiled *Fractured Fairy Tales and Ruptured Rhymes* (1990), illustrated by Craig Smith. See **Nursery Rhymes**. *Christmas Crackers: Australian Christmas Poetry* (1990), illustrated by Katherine Stafford, includes poems by Max Fatchen, Bill Scott, Michael Dugan, and Colin Thiele.

WELDRICK, VALERIE, born Lithgow, NSW, has written two time-slip fantasies. In *Time Sweep* (1976), illustrated by Ron Brooks, Laurie meets a poor boy, Frank Kilderbee (based on a real settler, Frank Kerribee 1850–1918), whose fortunes he transforms. Weldrick explores how the present acts on the past, through the repercussions created when a boy educated in the twentieth century is thrown into the rough and tumble of low life in London. *The Blakely Ghost* (1980), illustrated by Sylvia Isaac, is a gentle parody of theatrical types. Australian Michael, staying with his aunt who works at the Blakely Blythe Theatre, London, is the only one who can see the ghost of Fred, a mischievous boy. Fred was killed saving his sister in 1908, and Michael arranges a meeting between the ghost and Fred's 84-year-old twin sister, allowing Fred to finally rest in peace.

WELLS, ANN E. (1906–), born London, UK, was a missionary teacher in Arnhem Land. For her two series which draw on that experience, *Tales from Arnhem Land* (1959), *Rain in Arnhem Land: Further Adventures of Three Aboriginal Children on the Far North Coast of Australia, and Some of the Stories of Their People* (1961) and *Skies of Arnhem Land* (1964), all illustrated by Margaret Paice, and *The Dew-Wet Earth*, *Daybreak* and *Stars in the Sky* (all 1973) see **Aboriginal Dreaming Stories.**

WELLS, ERNEST (1902–) wrote two books for children, both excellent fantasies, both with delightful illustrations. In *The Bubble Galleon: a Holiday Pantomime* (1934), with pictures by R.W. Coulter, Tiel Quintillian, Commissioner for High Time, takes the children to the world of Baste in a bubble, where they join the company of the Tight Friends of Baste. This inventive and intriguing fantasy of Australian landscape and character, such as the Gibba-Gunyah of the Paroo, and Harry Dale the drover, is without condescension. *Master Davy's Locker: a Story of Adventure in the Undersea* (1935), also illustrated by Coulter, continues the adventures of Ian and Margery, when they set off to save the world from the destruction of the Tide Pendulum, this time with the help of Masterman Ready, the Flying Dutchman, the Compleat Angler and other fabulous inhabitants of the sea.

WESLEY-SMITH, PETER (1945–), born Adelaide, wrote *The Ombley-Gombley* (q.v., 1969) and has contributed poems to collections such as *Vile Verse* (1988), edited by Jane Covernton. *Hocus-Pocus: Nonsense Rhymes* (1973), illustrated by Ib Spang Olsen, was adapted from a text by the Dane Halfdan Rasmussen.

WEST, R. V. For *The Luciflins and the Duck that Laid Easter Eggs* (1945) see **Bushfire**.

WESTBURY, ATHA. For *Australian Fairy Tales* (1897) see **Fairies**.

Whalers of the Midnight Sun: a Story of Modern Whaling in the Antarctic (1949, but originally published in the UK in 1934) by Alan Villiers, illustrated by Charles Pont, won the 1950 Book of the Year Awards. An unruly gang of boys from Hobart sign on the *Pelagos* and the six smaller steamers which make up a Norwegian whaling fleet bound for the Antarctic. Among them is Ocker Stephens, whose young brother Alfie stows away as the ships leave Hobart. Although the affairs of Ocker and Alfie shape some of the action of the novel, for the most part it is taken up with the experience of whaling — the chase, the terrible death of the whales, and the hardships and mortal dangers which the whaling men faced. The beauty and loneliness of Antarctica is drawn as the men and boys battle the ice, at times forced to travel across it by foot. Although too full of detail to maintain its pace, and out of step with modern attitudes to the hunting and slaughter of these great mammals, *Whalers of the Midnight Sun* remains a tribute to the toughness required for deep-sea sailing, and a testament to the courage and resource of the early whalers.

WHEATLEY, NADIA (1949–), born Sydney, wrote two books about a Greek immigrant family, *Five Times Dizzy* (q.v., 1982) and *Dancing in the Anzac Deli* (1984). *Five Times Dizzy* was made into a television series in 1984 for SBS television. *The House that was Eureka* (q.v., 1985) is a historical fantasy. *1 is for One: a Counting Book* (1985) has ten nonsense rhymes reproduced three times in separate covers. See also **Counting Books**. *The Blooding* (1987) is set in an established logging community. A group of conservationists challenge the town, demanding that the logging cease. A battle ensues — both ideological and physical. Colum's father and grandfather have depended on the timber industry for a living, and Colum is jolted into a conflict between his loyalty to his family and his response to the bush, a struggle mirrored in the battle between the 'Greenies' and the timberworkers. Is Col going to accept the traditional male role of the loggers, or break away from that way of life and acknowledge that part of his nature which his sensitivity to the bush symbolises? This is a passionate book in which a conservation issue is presented in deeply personal terms. *My Place* (q.v., 1987) looks at the history of Australia through a piece of land. Wheatley edited *Landmarks* (1991), a collection of short stories. Her writing is characterised by a variety of narrative techniques, and a strong social conscience.

WHEELER, LORRAINE (1932–), born WA, has written *Pretend It's Christmas* (1984), set in a rural community. It is discovered that a mystery disease is killing adults. A group of children find themselves alone, and develop the physical resources and the determination to survive until the disease appears to have run its course. In *The Silver Cat* (1989) Cathy and John travel across Greece in their pursuit of a ruthless fur trader who wants to use the skins of their beautiful Siamese cats. In *The Battle for Big Bush* (1991) Paul, Jody and Andy save a forest area.

When Jays Fly to Barbmo (1968) by Margaret Balderson won the 1969 Book of the Year Awards. It is set in Norway in the time of World War II. Ingeborg, her father and Aunt Anne-Sigri, and the enigmatic Wood Troll, live on an isolated farm. Balderson shows the oppressiveness of the long winter, the fear of the German invasion, and the difficulties of farming in this stern region. Ingeborg survives a lonely winter, and when the Germans invade, she finds a refuge and discovers her mother's people, the nomadic Lapps. See also **War**. This novel about a girl growing up was an early example of the adolescent novel in Australia, and unique in its setting.

When the Wind Changed (1980) by Ruth Park, illustrated by Deborah Niland, won the 1986 YABBA Picture Book. Josh's speciality is making grotesque faces, so horrible that he is able to frighten the savage dog next door. He is warned of the terrible consequences of making faces, and one day the wind changes, and it happens — he is stuck with the worst face of all. But the face so terrifies a robber at his father's bank that Josh becomes a hero, although there is a clever twist at the end. Park and Niland have taken an everyday saying to make a picture story-book which exploits every humorous possibility.

Where the Forest Meets the Sea (1987) by Jeannie Baker was an Honour Book in the 1988 Picture Book of the Year Awards, won the YABBA Picture Book for 1988 and was Primary Winner of KOALA in 1990. Using a brilliant collage of natural materials, the artist creates the Daintree rainforest from the dinosaurs to the uncertain future, seen through the eyes of a boy. An award-winning film of *Where the Forest Meets the Sea* was made by Film Australia in 1988, directed by the author.

Whistle Up the Chimney (1981) by Nan Hunt was Commended in the 1982 Picture Book of the Year Awards. When

Mrs Millie Mack burns old railway wood in her fire a train materialises in her living room. She becomes a train-watcher instead of a knitter. Millie Mack also appears in *An Eyeful of Soot and an Earful of Steam* (1983), in which Millie's cat, Tom Bola, falls on to the express train. In *The Whistle Stop Party* (1990), also illustrated by Smith, Mrs Millie Mack goes to a retirement party. Millie, the train and Tom Bola are further revealed in Craig Smith's bold illustrations.

Whitcombe & Tombs, a NZ publisher, of Christchurch and Auckland, produced books for the Australasian market. Some of the series published by Whitcombe & Tombs include the 'Southern Cross' series, which began around 1888, the 'Imperial and Pacific Readers' and 'Whitcombe's Story Books'. Titles include *Rossiter's Farm* and *The Cousin from Town* by Mary Grant Bruce, *The Elfin House* and *Mr Spider's Walk* by Evelyn Dare, and retellings of adult works, such as *Geoffry Hamlyn in Australia*, an adaptation of the Australian part of Henry Kingsley's *Geoffry Hamlyn*. McLaren estimates that over twelve million copies of 'Whitcombe's Story Books' were printed between 1908 and 1962. Their series, 'Australian Gift Books for Boys and Girls', contained stories and photographs by Australians. Further reading: McLaren, *Whitcombe's Story Books*.

WHITE, MARY (1928–), born Whitley Bay, UK, settled in Australia in 1967. In *Breakup* (1974) Mike, Tony and Frank attempt to stop an expressway and run up against the law. In *Dominic* (1977) the hero has a special relationship with his artistic mother which is threatened by her friend John. Another friend, Ron Semple, helps Dominic deal with his own selfishness. Anna in *Mindwave* (1980) is blind, and menaced by her brother Ted. Anna establishes mental contact with an English boy, Pete, and is eventually reconciled with her brother and her disability. For *Paint a Dream* (1980), illustrated by

Elizabeth Honey, see **Sport**. In *Three Cheers for Nineteen!* (1981), illustrated by Rosemary Wilson, Felicity is lonely until she meets the creatures who inhabit the numbers in the lift. *Martha Thompson: Wondercook* (1988), illustrated by Shirley Peters, is about a girl who aspires to be a cook. *Sally and Rebecca* (1989), illustrated by Dee Huxley, is written under the name Mary Baylis-White. The story is told to Clarissa by her grandmother, Sally. When Rebecca arrives at Sally's school during World War II, a lifelong friendship begins, and Sally becomes aware of the suffering of the European Jews for the first time.

WHITE, OSMAR (1909–91), born NZ, came to Australia in 1914. He was a journalist, adventurous war correspondent, and radio and television scriptwriter. He wrote many episodes of the television series 'Homicide', and novels and studies of places and people for adults. *Super-Roo of Mungalongaloo* (1973), illustrated by Jeff Hook, began the adventures of the famous explorer Angus McGurk and his camel, Cathie Khan. In *The Further Adventures of Dr. A.A.A. McGurk, M.D.* (1981) Cathie learns to ski and the pair set off for Mount Everest, and in *McGurk and the Lost Atoll* (1983) they are cast away among the head-hunting islanders of Ohoho-Ohaha. See also **Humour**. White's characters are as outrageous as their adventures.

WHITE, 'UNK' (CECIL) (1900–86), born NZ, arrived in Sydney in the 1920s. His comic drawings appeared in the *Bulletin* and newspapers throughout Australia, notably his comic-strip 'Freckles', which he drew for the *Sunday News*. White was an official war artist. *Bear Folk, Bluey and Jacky* and *A Penguin Party* (all 1941) were published by Frank Johnson. They are simple stories for very young children with bold, cartoon-like illustrations and little text. *The Aussies are Here* (1943) is a collection of patriotic verses with clever caricatures, such as Wing Commander Wagtail with Sergeant Pilot Bunny, or the Diggers 'Roo and Cockatoo: 'We're Aussies two, and full of vim,/And soldier fame we're out to win./We'll drive the foe right from our door,/Let's cheer and cheer and win some more.' *Twinkle, Twinkle Southern Cross* (1943) is a parody of Jane Taylor's 1806 rhyme, 'Twinkle, twinkle little star', using swaggies, Mrs Roo, Wombat and the Southern Cross. *Unk White's Boat Book for Little Jack Tars* (1943) is a colouring book. White also illustrated local histories.

WHITE, ZITA (THERESE MARY ZITA WHITE) (1933–), born Brisbane, has written *Ride Across the Ocean* (1959). Jem and her family leave their horses behind in England, but when Jem meets Pam she is able to teach the Australian girl some of the expertise she has learnt. White edited *A Race of Horsemen* (1963) and *How to Ride a Horse* (1973), a guide to horsemanship for young people. White also wrote *The One-Day Ponies* (1958).

White Crane, The (1983) by Junko Morimoto was Commended in the 1984 Picture Book of the Year Awards. In this Japanese folk tale, the beautiful Otsuru repays her debt to an old couple by miraculously weaving silk for them to sell, but when their curiosity overcomes them, and they see Otsuru's true form, she has to leave them. The setting is the winter landscape of Japan.

WHITFELD, JESSIE MARY (Mrs OWEN HARRIS) (1861–1964), born Sydney, also used the name 'Mary Feld'. She spent her childhood at Sydney Grammar School, where her father was the Classics Master. Her sister Ellen was one of the first female students at Sydney University, and her brother Hubert became the Vice-Chancellor of the University of WA. In 1890 she wrote a story for the *Illustrated Sydney News*, 'Gnomes and Nails', which was illustrated by Percy Spence. *The Spirit of the Bushfire* *and other Australian Stories* (1898), illustrated by G.W. Lambert, is a collection of fairy stories. In the title story, the Spirit of the Bushfire is defeated by the raindrop elves, and in other stories the author suggests explanations for natural phenomena, such as the Southern Cross, or the coconut. Whitfeld places her stories squarely in Australia.

Her novels for older readers were written to show 'the cultured, domestic life of the better-class settlers' as opposed to 'rousing tales of prairie and forest'. *Tom Who Was Rachel* (1911), illustrated by N. Tenison, is about Rachel Thompson, the daughter of the Samford children's stepmother. Whitfeld's five children are not always nice to each other, argue about small details such as what colour to make John Bunyan's legs in a painting book, and are located within a loving family. In *The Colters: an Australian Story for Girls* (1912), also illustrated by Tenison, there are another five spirited children, who write poetry, argue and play with Tommy Blitho, the grocer's son. In *Gladys and Jack* (1914) Gladys is transformed from a snobbish and selfish prig into a more concerned person through the influence of the bush and its perils. Although domesticated, Gladys and her girlfriend Tom retain their firm belief in women's suffrage. Tom's admirer Mr Manning says: 'Your world would be a queer place … when we have women intermeddling in all affairs of state.' She replies: 'It is a queer place now … and I should like to see how it works with men and women managing it together. Only when they do have Woman's Suffrage I hope the world will give it a fair trial — say a few thousand years — before they expect much or decide to condemn it.' Whitfeld left Australia for Oxford in the 1930s. She also wrote books for adults. An unpublished manuscript by Whitfeld is held at the Lu Rees Archives, with an introduction by her granddaughter, Alison May Brodrick: 'Valley and the Winged Horses: a Fairy Tale of the Australian Bush.'

WHITING, MARY BRADFORD, an English novelist, wrote *Josee: an Australian Story* (1890). Although the author never visited Australia, *Josee* contains a vivid description of early Melbourne on Saturday night. 'Saturday night is market night all the world over, and in Melbourne, no less than in London, the poorer parts of the town are filled with an eager crowd, buying, selling, shouting, gazing and bargaining.' The novel is the story of an orphan girl taken in by a country man and his rather harsh wife. See also **Families**. *Wallaby Hill* (1895), celebrating the civilising influence of the cultivated English settler, shows how a self-sacrificing schoolmaster brings tenderness and piety to a rough bush township. The countryside is described with fervour: 'The sun blazed down remorselessly, and the dust poured into the coach in clouds. No trees, no water, no hills came to break the monotony of the sand; any plants or bushes that might have managed to exist had been eaten by rabbits, countless multitudes of which were to be seen on either side of the track, the only living objects that met the eye.' Conversely, in *Peggy and Pat: a Tale of the Australian Bush* (1931) the Meredith family and housekeeper arrive in Queensland to find happiness and fortune. '"I am quite ashamed to think how I dreaded it for Pat and Peggy', says Mr Meredith. 'I was wrong in my ideas of Australia. I have learned that the life out here makes young people strong and self-reliant and full of goodwill to others.'" Other books by Whiting include *A Daughter of the Empire* (1919) and novels for adults.

Who Killed Cockatoo? by W.A.C., see **CAWTHORNE, WILLIAM ANDERSON**

Who Sank the Boat? (1982) by Pamela Allen won the 1983 Picture Book of the Year Awards. Reminiscent of John Burningham's *Mr Gumpy's Outing* (1970), many animals board a boat which sinks under their cumulative weight. The puzzle lies in just who was responsible. The story is told through strong pictorial characterisation and witty asides.

WHYTE, J. H. wrote *Fortunatus: a Romance* (1903), illustrated by Phil Ebbutt, an incident-packed saga of a virtuous young man's rise to fortune. Fortune finds wealth on the goldfields and then returns to England.

WIGHTON, ROSEMARY (1925–), born Adelaide, established the first *Australian Book Review* with Max Harris in 1961, which was published until 1974. From 1961 to 1970 there were annual supplements which reviewed children's books. She has written a critical history, *Early Australian Children's Literature* (1963), revised in 1979 (see **Criticism**) and selected *Kangaroo Tales: a Collection of Australian Stories for Children* (1963), illustrated by Donald Friend. See **Collections**.

WIGNELL, EDEL (1936–), born Echuca, Victoria, is a freelance writer and former teacher. She has written around thirty books, and many short stories and informational articles. *A Boggle of Bunyips* (1981), illustrated by Bob Graham, and *A Bluey of Swaggies* (1985) are collections of short stories with specific themes. *A Boggle of Bunyips* contained the outline of her novel for older readers *Escape by Deluge* (1989), in which Shelley frees an ancient bunyip trapped in a Melbourne drain. See **Bunyips**. *Crutches are Nothing* (1982), illustrated by Tony Irving, is a collection of twelve stories about disabled children, from writers such as Alan Marshall, James Aldridge and Eleanor Spence. Wignell has written picture-books, such as *Spider in the Toilet* (1989), illustrated by Margaret Power, and *Raining Cats and Dogs* (1987), with illustrations by Rodney McRae, in which two bored children

draw animals which come alive. She has contributed to reading schemes. For Macmillan's 'Southern Cross' she wrote *Fiorella's Cameo* (1987), illustrated by Helen Glenn, *The Tie Olympics* (1987), illustrated by Robert Roennfeldt, *Missing* (1987) and *What's your Hobby?* (1987). For Harcourt, Brace & Jovanovich's 'Spectrum Yellow' series she has written *Mischief Makers* (1989), illustrated by Heather Campbell, which has recommended tricks for April Fool's Day, and *Big April Fools* (1989), illustrated by C.S. Severn, which shows how the South American Miranda learns about April Fool's Day.

For beginning readers she has written *The Ghostly Jigsaw* (1985), illustrated by Bruce Treloar, in which Richard meets his ancestors when he is on a school camping trip; in *A Gift of Squares* (1986), illustrated by Catherine Bradbury, Emma finds acceptance through making a patchwork quilt; in *The Car Wash Monster* (1986), illustrated by Kim Lynch, two children lose their fear of a car wash, and in *Marmalade, Jet and the Finnies* (1987) Jessica has problems providing for her cat, Marmalade, when she stays with her father. The heroine is on a fruit and vegetable diet in *You'll Turn into a Rabbit* (1988), illustrated by Astra Lacis, and her lettuce diet has spectacular effects. *Amanda's Warts* (1989), illustrated by Heather Campbell, provides various cures for warts. *What's in the Red Bag?* (1988), illustrated by Kate Rogers, was developed from a 1986 television serial. Amy's attempt to take her cat on a holiday is foiled, but Liz is able to smuggle her dog into the caravan park. Wignell takes her own childhood experiences and observations and places them in a modern context.

WILCOX, CATHY, born Sydney, studied at Sydney College of the Arts, and has worked overseas and for the *Sydney Morning Herald* as a cartoonist. Wilcox has illustrated *A Proper Little Lady* (1989) by Nette Hilton, *Bold, Bad Ben* (1989) by

Ann Jungman, *Bus Fuss* (1989) by Sandra McCuaig, *Boris and Borsch* (q.v., 1990) by Robin Klein, and a collection of nursery rhymes, *In the Old Gum Tree* (1989). See **Nursery Rhymes**. *Throw Away Lines* (1991) is a collection of her cartoons. Her animated characters emerge from freely drawn sketches.

Wild Brother (1954) by Mary Elwyn Patchett, illustrated by John Rose, was Highly Commended in the 1955 Book of the Year Awards. It is the story of Warrigal and Shula, two dingoes, and a kangaroo dog, Kylie. Shula learns hate from Frank, a dingo-hunter, who ill-treats her, and affection from Steve the storekeeper, who releases her into the wild. She mates for life with Warrigal, although one season is spent with Kylie, Steve's dog. The novel concludes with Warrigal's dominance assured. Shula and Warrigal are reunited, and Kylie's pup is cared for by Steve. Patchett has drawn on her knowledge of station life and the wild animals of the bush for a dramatic portrait of three proud dogs presented without sentimentality or anthropomorphism.

Wild Dog Frontier (1951) by 'William Hatfield' (Ernest Chapman) was Commended in the 1952 Book of the Year Awards. Set around Cooper Creek, the first part of the novel deals with how Jerry learns to use a .22 rifle with the help of a gun expert from Sydney, Joe Brown. There are lengthy lessons on which gun is best to use in which circumstance, and how to deal with a variety of targets. Boy and man blaze away, mainly at dingoes, killing eleven in one day. Later, the drought and the need to clear Dad's name from the suggestion of stealing cattle is woven into a land use program in which the family is involved. The novel is a reminiscence of life without electricity or advanced farm machinery, when values were clear-cut and a straight left to the jaw solved most problems.

WILD, MARGARET (1948–), born Eshowe, South Africa, came to Australia in 1973. She has been a journalist and editor. Her first picture-books presented a small girl learning things about her world. In *One Shoe On* (1984), illustrated by Hannah Koch, Kathy practices all week to dress herself. *Kathy's Umbrella* (1986), also illustrated by Koch, describes the creative uses 4-year-old Kathy finds for her birthday present. Both are in Hodder & Stoughton's 'Picture Stoats' series. She extended the everyday into the strange with *There's a Sea in My Bedroom* (1984), illustrated by Jane Tanner, a clever mixture of fantasy and reality in which a boy overcomes his fear of the sea. In *Something Absolutely Enormous* (1984), illustrated by Jack Hanna, Sally decides to knit a THING, and cannot stop. When it is finished, it makes a new Big Top for the circus, and Sally takes to cooking with the same enthusiasm. In *Something Rich and Strange* (1990), illustrated by Janet Bridgland, Rebecca is passionate about food until Emma diverts her. Only when his beard is shaved does Nicholas's father get rid of the possum, field mouse and robin which inhabit it in *Creatures in the Beard* (1986), illustrated by Margaret Power. In *Harvey Jackson's Cubby* (1990), illustrated by Keith McEwan, Wild compares two boys' cubby houses, one imaginative, the other more sophisticated but restricted by reality.

In *The Diary of Megan Moon (soon to be rich and famous)* (1988), illustrated by Shirley Peters, Megan is an opinionated and selfish child who believes that everyone should set out to make her life easier. Megan has written a book, *Destruction of the Poltergeist*, which is rejected until Anne Ingram agrees to meet her over lunch. There are sub-plots involving her family and her teacher's love affair with a young man, providing background to a tongue-in-cheek novel. *Mr Nick's Knitting* (1988), illustrated by Dee Huxley, tells how Mr Nick knits a patchwork quilt of scenes observed from a railway carriage for his friend Mrs Jolley.

The Very Best of Friends (q.v., 1989) is a story of death and loss. In *Remember Me* (1990), illustrated by Dee Huxley, Wild looks at ageing. Ellie helps Grandma to remember the details of her day, but Grandma remembers without help the important things like the milestones in Ellie's life. *Let the Celebrations Begin!* (1991), illustrated by Julie Vivas, takes the reader into Belsen, as the women and Katya make stuffed toys out of their rags for David and Sarah. When the liberating army arrives, the party begins. Wild's spare language, full of meaning and deep layers, and Vivas's subtle art, create a life-affirming picture-book. *A Bit of Company* (1991), illustrated by Wayne Harris, explores how the lonely Molly and Christopher find companionship. *Thank You, Santa* (1991), illustrated by Kerry Argent, is a correspondence between Samantha and Santa. In *The Slumber Party* (1992), illustrated by David Cox, a birthday party with seven guests shows the diversity and individuality of Jane's friends. *The Queen's Holiday* (1992) is a fantasy about Queen Victoria. In *Beast* (1992), a book for an older age group than Wild's picture-books, Jamie is terrified of a bully at school and a roaming beast which circles his house at night. How his fears are overcome depends on how Jamie can contend with Brendan and the evil Gamesmaster, and also how Brendan can survive.

Wild presents characters out of the usual mould, and in situations which test their imaginations. In doing so she has extended the scope of the picture-book.

Wild River (1949) by Bernard O'Reilly was Highly Commended in the 1950 Book of the Year Awards. The Dawson children, Buller, Jan and Mike, help their father defeat a gang of ruthless prospectors who want to steal the uranium ore which John Dawson has found on his property.

The good luck and resourcefulness of the children is stretched beyond credibility at times, but the detailed descriptions of the countryside and the authenticity of a life outdoors, as the children ride across mountains and valleys to meet their father, add strength to an exciting story. See also **Adventure Stories**.

WILDER, CHERRY (née GRIMM) (1930–). For *The Luck of Brin's Five* (1977), *The Nearest Fire* (1977) and *The Tapestry Warriors* (1983) see **Science Fiction**.

William Tell (1991), illustrated by Margaret Early, was an Honour Book in the 1992 Picture Book of the Year Awards. The text was based on Johann Christoph Friedrich von Schiller's play *Wilhelm Tell* (1804), and the accurate details of costume and setting are an elegant tribute to the seven hundredth anniversary of the unification of Switzerland. The illustrations, contained in decorative borders, suggest the period of the thirteenth century, and present an old story still relevant today.

WILLIAMS, MAGDALENE ('MACKIE') (1921–) is a member of the Nyul Nyul people from the Beagle Bay area in northern WA. Williams is a speaker of the language, which she records, and the custodian of many traditional stories, such as *The Story of Crow* (1987), illustrated by Pat Torres, which was written in Nyul Nyul by Williams and in English by Torres.

WILLIAMS, PAUL (1946–) has written drama for radio and television. For *The Adventures of Black Ned* (1990) see **Bushrangers**.

WILLIAMS, RHYS (1894–1976), born Sydney, was an engraver, commercial artist and painter. He illustrated the *Boys and Girls Adventure Book* (1946), containing Ali Baba and Robin Hood, and the books of his wife, Ruth Williams.

WILLIAMS, RUTH (1897–1982), born London, UK, was an artist and writer. Her early books included *The Adventures of Georgie Grub* and *More Adventures of Georgie Grub* (both 1946), *Our Friend Rodney* and *Pirates' Gold* (both 1945). In *Timothy Tatters* (1947) a scarecrow travels across Whittigan's Farm. *Verity of Sydney Town* (q.v., 1950) recalls the early days of settlement, and *The Aboriginal Story* (1955) is an informational book. Williams's books were all illustrated by her husband, Rhys Williams.

WILLIAMS, SUE, see **MACHIN, SUE**

WILLIAMS, WILLIAM LLOYD (1902–?69), born Buninyong, Victoria, was a teacher and editor of the Victorian *School Paper*. *Round the World with Billy Bear* (1938), illustrated by Dick Ovenden, is a series of picture-strips, which had originally appeared in the *School Paper*. *Red Gum Bend: Stories of the River Murray* (1945) relates the history of the Murray through stories told to Red Gum by a personified river. *The Silver Bone* (1948), illustrated by Dick Ovenden, is a humorous fantasy. Harold leaves his kennel behind on a quest for the elusive silver bone, only to find that friends are more important than riches. Williams displays his sense of the absurd in Harold's slow and literal thinking, as he bumps into trees, teams up with an owl and a rabbit, and learns the value of showing his teeth to enemies. *History Trails in Melbourne* (1957) is a history of Melbourne's streets and buildings. *First Flights: Drama for Junior Grades* (1952) is Book 1 in Mullens's Plays for children, and contains seven plays, from a singing game to a dramatisation of Ulysses and Circe.

'Willie Winkie Zoo Books' were a series written by Mrs Andrew Rule Osborn, illustrated by Ida Rentoul Outhwaite. There were six books: *Teddy Bear's Birthday Party*, *The Naughty Baby Monkey*, *The Guinea Pig that Wanted a Tail*, *Peter's Peach*, *Fuzzy, Wuzzy and Buzzy*, and *The Quarrel of the Baby Lions* (all 1918). Wee Willie Winkie tires of sending children to sleep, so he goes to the zoo. Each book deals with situations in the life of zoo animals. Jimmie the guinea-pig wants a tail, so Wee Willie Winkie gives him one, only to find that when Jimmie is picked up by the tail his eyes fall out! Sadly, he realises that 'a tail is no good to a blind guinea pig'. Amusing animal characters are presented in novel situations.

WILLMOTT, FRANK (1948–), born Melbourne, has used urban themes to illustrate the difficulties of adolescent life in the later part of the twentieth century. His first book was *Breaking Up* (q.v., 1983). In *Suffer Dogs* (1985) Eric's mother cannot afford to support him, and he is sent off to a country town. He feels unwanted, but finds some comfort at the novel's conclusion in a determination to make his own way. *Here Comes the Night* (1986) is an account of four months in the life of an emotionally disturbed boy, James Raynor. This complex plot and mixture of strange characters and situations has some telling observations on the adolescent subculture. Willmott co-edited *Crazy Hearts* (1985) with Robyn Jackson, a collection of short stories, and contributed *My Dad at Home* (1985) to Hodja's multicultural series. Willmott's novels encourage young people to think for themselves, to develop a sensitivity to the world around them, and to demand a say in the direction of their own lives.

'WILLO AND BILLO', see **'Wongabilla'**

WILMOT, FRANK, see **'MAURICE, FURNLEY'**

WILSON, BARBARA KER, see **KER WILSON, BARBARA**

WILSON, ERLE (b.1898), born Dundee, Scotland, naturalist, has written two collections of legends, *The Green Frog,* *and Other Far-away Stories* (1939) and *Far-away Tales: Nature Myths of Sea and Shore* (1954). *Churinga Tales: Stories of Alchuringa — the Dream Time of the Australian Aborigines* (q.v., 1950) is an early collection of Aboriginal Dreaming stories (q.v.). *Coorinna, a Novel of the Tasmanian Uplands* (1950) was widely used in schools in the 1950s and 1960s. The rare Tasmanian wolf, Coorinna, has a lifelong battle with a shepherd and his dogs, learning how to avoid traps and the dangerous gun. See also **Animal Stories**. Wilson tells strong stories about the Australian environment and its people. He has also written books for adults.

WILSON, KEANE (MOIRA WILSON) (1916–) has written *Pip of Pyalong* (1949) which describes Pip Raynor's holidays at his father's sheep station. In *Pip and Andrew — Schoolmates* (1949) Pip is boarding at Brooklands and chums up with Andrew James. Pip and Andrew and the portly George save an important scientific formula from a gang of desperate men in *Pip and Andrew in Danger* (1950) through a few well-aimed handfuls of pepper and a boiling teapot. *Nicky at Tumbaringa* (1950) relates how English Nicky proves her salt to the Australian Midge, and *Look After Arthur* (1955) describes the conversion of the sheltered city boy, Arthur, into a courageous country boy, through the example of his cousins, Toby and Pat.

WILSON, LORRAINE (1939–), born Echuca, Victoria, has produced successful school readers in many languages, such as *City Kids* (1978–81, 1986), *Country Kids* (1982–83, 1985, 1987), and *Footy Kids* (1982, 1984).

'WILSON, Rev. T. P.' was the pseudonym of Samuel Clark, one of the 'Peter Parleys' identified by F.J. Harvey Darton. Apart from his 'Peter Parley' books, he won first prize in a competition run by the Committee of the United Kingdom Band of Hope Union, for the 'two best

tales illustrative of temperance in its relationship to the young', in 1869. The novel was *Frank Oldfield: or, Lost and Found, a Tale* (1870). The story begins in Lancashire. Frank Oldfield and Hubert Oliphant travel to the Victorian gold-diggings and SA. The story of Frank's descent into an early death due to his 'increasing fondness for intoxicating drinks' is counterpoised to Samuel Johnson's flight from a drunken father, after Frank has signed the pledge. Samuel makes a triumphant return to his home, to find his father reformed: Frank is lost forever. See also **Adelaide**.

WILTON, ELIZABETH M. (1937–), born Adelaide, contributed *The Foolish Fairy, The Lost Bangle, The Little Sea-Dragon, Pretty Foot, The Twins and the Christmas Tree* and *The Twins and the 'Tortle'* (1967), all illustrated by Virginia Brown, to Rigby's 'Reading Development' series. *A Ridiculous Idea* (1967), illustrated by Sandra Hargrave, follows the fortunes of the Haydon children whose father is missing when they arrive in SA. Helped by their Scottish neighbours and the farm labourer, Tom, and their strong religious faith — they are Quakers — they put the farm into order. Wilton describes the physical and emotional difficulties of the young family, and the uncertainty of Sarah, the eldest. *Riverboat Family* (1967), also illustrated by Hargrave, is set on the Murray at the time of Federation. The English Bruce's unhappiness, which appears as snobbery and superiority towards his Angus cousins, is really an expression of his own sense of dislocation. See also **Murray River**. Another river story is *Riverview Kids* (1971), illustrated by Deborah and Kilmeny Niland, in which a community is threatened with eviction to make way for a freeway. The children and elderly residents band together to save the area, and an important bond is established. Wilton contributed *A Riverboat Captain* (1970) to the Oxford 'Early Australians' series. *Red Ribbons and*

Mr Anders (1970), illustrated by Richard Kennedy, is set in Denmark. Kristin has an ingenious idea to get rid of the town's swarm of cats and bring back the storks to nest on the roof-tops. Wilton has written books which relate actual historical adventures, such as *On the Banks of the Yarra: a Story of William Buckley and John Batman*, *A Remarkable Obstacle: a Story of Lawson and Blaxland*, *Adventure Ahoy! A Story of Bass and Flinders* and *The Unknown Land: a Story of Captain Phillip and Bennelong* (all 1969). Wilton's interest in families under stress emphasises the resourcefulness which children acquire in hard times.

WINCH, GORDON (1930–), born Kyogle, NSW, writer and academic, has contributed titles to Rigby's 'Reading Rigby' series. In *Barrington's Board Shorts* (1984), illustrated by Katrina van Gendt, a pair of magical shorts enables Barrington to overcome his rival. In *The Five Bike Family* (1983), also illustrated by van Gendt, Robyn and her family have no car, but they do have a bike each. *Enoch the Emu* (1986), illustrated by Doreen Gristwood, is a humorous account of why the male emu sits on the eggs. *Mulga Bill Rides Again: a Book of Australian Poems Kids Can't Put Down* (1988) has poetry drawn from authors from C.J. Dennis to Robin Klein. With Maurice Saxby, Winch edited a collection of writings about literature for children, *Give Them Wings: the Experience of Children's Literature* (1987).

WINCH, MADELEINE (1950–), born Melbourne, is an author, painter and illustrator. She illustrated *Edward Wilkins and his Friend Gwendoline* (1985) by Barbara Bolton, which features a determined cat. In *Come by Chance* (1988), which she wrote and illustrated, 'Come by Chance' is the name of a derelict house, a haven for animals during a harsh winter.

WINCKLER, RUBY (1886–1974), illustrator, studied at the Julian Ashton School, Sydney. Although her two children's books, *The Arabian Nights' Entertainment* (1915) and *Who's Who in the Land of Nod* (1915) by S.S. Vanderbilt, were published in the USA, Winckler was a neglected artist until interest in her was revived by her inclusion in the 1985 Golden Age of Australian Fantasy Exhibition. Winckler was a friend of the Lindsays, and Robert Holden's *Koalas Kangaroos and Kookaburras* (?1988) suggests that her strong line and intricate patterning rival Norman Lindsay's work.

Wind Comes, The (1974) by Ron Forbes, illustrated by Francia Forbes, was Commended in the 1975 Picture Book of the Year Awards. The wind is everywhere, in the valleys and the mountains, in the country and the city, even in people's mouths. Brilliant colours and flowing tissue-paper collages sweep across the pages.

Windmill at Magpie Creek, The (1971) by Christobel Mattingley, illustrated by Gavin Rowe, was Highly Commended in the 1972 Book of the Year Awards. Tim is frightened of heights and of magpies who attack him. He is forced to confront both terrors after his father's accident, and finds the resources within himself to do so successfully. Despite its simple telling, the novel presents the triumph of firm resolve over fear.

Window (1991) by Jeannie Baker won the 1992 Picture Book of the Year Awards. This wordless picture-book, executed in Baker's magical collages, examines the changes which occur as a boy looks out through a window frame. From an idyllic bushland the vista is transformed into a city, complete with car park and graffiti. The boy, now a man with his own baby, finds another idyll, but the city looms on that horizon, too. The cover illustration shows the whole landscape, and the window as part of a greater dimension.

Winged Skis (1964) by Elyne Mitchell, illustrated by Annette Macarthur-Onslow, was Highly Commended in the 1965 Book of the Year Awards. Barry Milton, his parents, his friend, Michael Hastings, and the Austrian ski instructors from Thredbo, range the mountains, occasionally led on by a mysterious lone skier. The novel describes the techniques of skiing, the pleasure of excellent performance and the beauty of the mountains. See also **Sport.**

'Winners' and **'More Winners'** were television series for upper primary and junior secondary students produced in 1985 and 1990 by the Australian Children's Television Foundation (q.v.). Books and videos were issued together to encourage reading. There were eight titles in the first series. *On Loan* by Anne Brooksbank explores Lindy/Mai's cultural duality. See also **Immigrants**. In *Room to Move* by John Duigan, Carol is being pushed by her father to be an Olympic champion, but discovers friendship and dance with Angie. While he is hanggliding, Mike finds himself in the future in *Quest Beyond Time* by Tony Morphett. He joins forces with Katrin and together they retrieve a healing medicine to save the people. Mike must reassess his own values in the light of the courage and faith of the Murray Clan and the others who live in a harsher world. See also **Science Fiction**. *Top Kid* and *The Paper Boy* are by John Hepworth and Bob Ellis. In *Top Kid* a clever boy must decide whether to win a quiz honestly or with the help of the compère. In *Paper Boy* Joe Riordan has to support his family when his father is out of work. *The Other Facts of Life* by Morris Gleitzman is about the poverty and oppression in the world. Ben's first flush of moral awareness is frustrated, as his concern for others is beyond the comprehension of his materialist family. *Just Friends* by Jan Sardi depicts a girl and her family who are going through difficult times. *Tarflowers* by Terry Larsen explores the emotions of a mentally disabled boy, Kev, and his struggles to keep his independence. The 'More Winners' series contained *Second Childhood* by Morris Gleitzman, in which Mark and his friends become characters from the past; *Boy Soldiers* by Cliff Green, which examines conscription and a boy who is a conscientious objector; *The Big Wish* by John Hepworth and Steve Spears, a fantasy in which C.W. has the chance to wish for anything; *The Journey* by Jane Oehr, in which Ada must seek her inheritance; *His Master's Ghost* by Tom Shapcott and Roger Simpson, set at a musical camp disturbed by a ghost; and *Mr Edmund* by Tom Shapcott and Steve Spears, where a new boarder persuades Cherry and Sam that they can realise their dreams.

WINTON, TIM (1960–) has written novels for adults. *Jesse* (1988) was his first children's book, a picture-book illustrated by Maureen Prichard, describing how Jesse becomes lost, and is brought home by a cow. Winton's funny and astute *Lockie Leonard, Human Torpedo* (q.v., 1990) is for older readers. *The Buggalugs Bum Thief* (1991), illustrated by Carol Pelham-Thorman, recounts the uproar which occurs in Buggalugs when the inhabitants wake up to find their posteriors purloined. Winton uses the vernacular of youth, laced with local colour, for his likeable characters.

Wirrun is the Aboriginal youth who defeats the evil forces in Patricia Wrightson's *The Book of Wirrun*. See *The Ice is Coming*.

Wish and the Magic Nut (1956) by Peggy Barnard, illustrated by Sheila Hawkins, won the 1956 Picture Book of the Year Awards. Wish is a 'koala bear' (*sic*) who wishes to be something better than he is. He finds a nut which grants his wishes, and Wish becomes a kangaroo, a possum, and a platypus. The outcomes are not always what he expects, so Harry the platypus explains to Wish that he has to work for what he wants. Hawkins's bush animals are accurately drawn and funny.

Wish Cat, The (1966) by Jean Chapman, illustrated by Noela Young, with photographs by Dean Hay, was Commended in the 1967 Book of the Year Awards. Lisa, the naughty Siamese cat, arrives after Margaret had wished for her secretly. Margaret is worried when Lisa's demanding ways bring chaos, but the family comes to accept that life with a cat with personality is not always easy.

WITHERS, FANNY (née FLINN) (1858–1933) came to Australia from England in 1882. She was the wife and active supporter of the artist Walter Withers and ran a small private school in Heidelberg, Melbourne. She became interested in the plight of poor children, and wrote *Boarded Out: a Story Founded on Fact* (1907), copies of which she sent to politicians and people of influence, in the hope of reforming the situation of children sent away from their natural parents. Brenda, Meta and Nellie are sent to live with the vicious Mrs O'Malley when their mother dies of tuberculosis. Meta retains her finer feelings, but the lives of Brenda and Nellie, and the other children for whom Mrs O'Malley is paid board, become corrupted by the ill-treatment they receive. Tragedy and starvation are always present in *Boarded Out*, and although the novel was not primarily intended as a children's book, it would have been read by adolescents, and it is about the lives of children. It chronicles the desperation of the 'undeserving poor' in Victorian times. The solution, according to Withers, is ' … a big home … with the best women in it as nurses and teachers, where every child bereft of parents, or discarded by them, shall have its chance of life and love, and shall grow up to be a useful citizen, instead of a probable curse to the community'.

WOLKOWSKY, MAREA (MARIA PRERAUER), born Sydney, was the arts editor of the *Australian* from 1977 to 1991. She is a music and opera critic, a journalist and novelist, and writes a column for the *Bulletin*. Her first children's book was *The Enchanted Pancakes: a Fairy Tale for Children* (1946), illustrated by W.H. Davies. In *Perilous Journey: a Story of Adventure in Elizabethan Times* (1947) Hal Munday, a London apprentice, is engaged on a mission to deliver Good Queen Bess a pendant which has been secretly poisoned by the sinister Captain Moone. In *Australian Adventure* (1965) Peter and Margaret come from England to Australia to live on their uncle's sheep station. When Margaret becomes lost she is found by Aboriginal Palpara, who relates Dreaming stories to her. Palpara is threatened with death, but a Sydney doctor intervenes, and Palpara recovers and replaces the evil medicine man. Wolkowsky captures the conflict between the lifestyles of white and black, and questions the assimilationist views of the 1960s.

WOLLASTON, TULLIE CORNTH-WAITE (1863–1931), born Port Lincoln, SA, was an opal dealer. *The Spirit of the Child* (1914) is a collection of philosophic letters from a father, 'Clukiton-Warden', on nature and life, addressed to his children. He travels from Australia to England, taking inspiration from the sea voyage. Adults would find the formal and discursive style more appealing than children. His *Opal: the Gem of the Never-Never* (1924) is a semi-autobiographical account of his working life.

Women's Movement Children's Literature Co-operative was a discussion group set up in the early 1970s in an effort to counter sex-role stereotyping, particularly of girls, in children's literature. At the time there were few books which did not portray girls as 'passive princesses, cry-babies, nuisance sisters or nonentities', so the group wrote, published and marketed their own books. Their first book was Judith Bathie's *The Witch of Grange Grove* (1974). Muriel the witch expressed how the group felt: 'Boys or girls, what does it matter — all children should have the chance to find out what really interests them and what they enjoy doing.' An association with Wren publishers followed, and later Sugar and Snails Press (q.v.) was formed. The co-operative moved from a counter-sexist to a nonsexist position, concerned to combat racism and stereotyped depictions of class. Titles include fiction and informational books, often emphasising career possibilities. For instance, in Carol Pavey's *The Go-Cart Money* (1977), illustrated by Margaret Haines, Louise wants to be a racing driver, and saves all her money. She foils a bankrobber by scaring him with a huge balloon. Their early titles were cheaply produced, not attractive in appearance, and were self-consciously didactic, but the co-operative's critical style and innovative publications have influenced mainstream publishers' awareness of sex-role stereotyping in books for children, resulting in more powerful princesses and fewer pretentious princes.

Wonderland of Nature, The (1964), written and illustrated by Nuri Mass, was Commended in the 1965 Book of the Year Awards. Through the activities of Tess and Chris, the author's children, the book introduces children to the variety of nature, dealing with rocks, insects, plants, shells and physical phenomena such as electricity and magnetism. The style is conversational and the book is profusely illustrated.

WONG, DAVID (1951–), born Indiana, USA, studied at the Bauhaus School, Chicago, Illinois. He has worked as an illustrator, graphic designer and woodworker. He illustrated three novels by Katherine Scholes: *The Boy and the Whale* (1985), *The Landing: a Night of Birds*

(1987) and *The Blue Chameleon* (1989). His delicate black-and-white and colour drawings depict the stormy sea and skies of Bass Strait, the arid desert, and the bird and animal life which inhabit them.

Wongabilla appears in three fantasies written by William Haynes and William H. Williamson under the pseudonym 'Willo & Billo'. *Wongabilla and His Baby Wallaby* (1943), *Further Adventures of Wongabilla and His Baby Wallaby* (?1945) and *Scout Chief Wongabilla and His Pal Digger* (1945) contain stories built around World War II in Papua New Guinea. Wongabilla, a 'little Fuzzy Wuzzy', is adopted by Australian soldiers when his home in Papua New Guinea is burnt down by the Japanese. He forms a troop of scouts, the Python Troop, with the help of Digger, his pet wallaby.

Wood, Wire and Fabric: a Saga of Australian Flying (1968) by John Goode was Commended in the 1969 Book of the Year Awards. It opens with the flight of the first aeroplane designed, built and flown by an Australian — John Duigan's, in 1910–11, at Spring Plains, between Mia Mia and Heathcote, Victoria. The work of Lawrence Hargraves and historic flights such as those of Harry Houdini, Ross and Keith Smith, and Charles Kingsford Smith are described. There is information on the establishment of commercial air companies, such as Qantas, details on Australian airports, and a chapter on aircraft manufacture in Australia. The role of the Air Force is considered, and some predictions made on Australia in the Space Age. An appendix lists all aircraft made in Australia since Duigan's. The book is illustrated with excellent photographs complementing an informative text.

WOODBERRY, JOAN (1921–), born Narrabri, NSW, wrote four books about Rafferty, an irrepressible scallywag. See ***Rafferty Rides a Winner*** (1961). For *Come Back, Peter* (1968), illustrated by George

Tetlow, see **Death**. *A Garland of Gannets* (1969) was illustrated by Elizabeth Lord. For *Ash Tuesday* (1968), illustrated by Max Angus, see **Bushfire**. *The Cider Duck* (1969), illustrated by Molly Stephens, is a picture-book about a duck who gets drunk on apples, is plucked by the land-lady of the Eider Duck Inn, and becomes the tavern's mascot. In *Little Black Swan* (1970), illustrated by Carol Lawson, Mark observes the life of a pair of swans. When the cob is killed, the pen takes her cygnets up the Derwent River to Bridgewater away from the hunters, in a gentle and affecting story. Woodberry has also writ-ten books for adults.

WOODS, BARBARA wrote *The Adventurous Koalas* (1944) and *The Pig with the Straight Tale* (1944), both illustrated by B.E. Pike, and *The Ringtail Family* (n.d.) and *The Apple Elves* (?1940), both illustra-ted by Betty Pike. For *Tales for Tinies* (1943), illustrated by Donald Gunn, see **Fairies**.

Worm Weather (1971) by Christobel Mattingley, illustrated by Carolyn Dinan, was Favourably Mentioned in the 1972 Book of the Year Awards. There are seven in Wendy's family, and each member has different ideas about what is fun. Wendy and her Grandpa like to grow vegetables and flowers, but most of all Wendy likes to study the worms which appear in wet weather. Her fascination wins her a prize, and a greater respect within the family. Mattingley's picture of a happy family and a determined girl is created in a simple text for young readers.

WORTHY, JUDITH (1937–), born Perth, has worked in advertising and pub-lic relations, and written adult novels as Ann Preston and Catherine Shaw. She has contributed to reading schemes, such as Rigby's 'Reading Rigby' series, with *Barney, Boofer and the Cricket Bat* (1980) and *Old Joe* (1981). Her animal stories include *Search for Tiger* (1977), illustrated

by Jill Gluch, in which Mouse saves his cat from the bulldozers when his street is demolished, and *Simon's Secret* (1983), illustrated by Lorraine Hannay. The secret is a white, blue-eyed kitten, which, like Simon, is deaf. A lonely boy experiences the pleasure of a pet and finds friends. Worthy writes about children searching for acceptance. Helen shares a balcony garden with Mrs Patching in *Garden in the Sky* (1980), illustrated by Murray Frederick, and is helped to stand up to a bully. *Finch's Island* (1985) is the hide-out where Finch goes to avoid school. He is joined by Miranda, lost on a bushwalking expedition. Their Robinson Crusoe lifestyle comes to an end when Finch breaks his arm. The novel conveys the fun of camping out and the development of a friendship. See also **Lost in the Bush**. In *The Magpie Tree* (1987), illustrated by Sandra Laroche, Chris and Tessa must fight to save the tree which has been the nesting place for their pet magpie for many years. *Amy the In-de-fat-ig-able Autograph Hunter* (1990), illustrated by Ann James, becomes famous herself when she catches a bank-robber. These realistic novels are laced with humour. More fan-tastic, in *The Incredible Runaway Pumpkin* (1981) the pumpkin grows to an enor-mous size when Colin feeds it with a chemical mixture, and in *Dragon on the Handlebars* (1984) only Mai and David can see the dragon on David's new yellow bicycle, but it disappears when Mai satis-fies David's need for a friend. *Eyes* (1988), illustrated by Beba Hall, is a picture-book in verse, which explores the eyes of ani-mals and insects.

WRIGHT, DOREEN. For *King Clyde of Brewarrina* (1980) see **Aboriginal Dreaming Stories**.

WRIGHT, JUDITH ARUNDELL (1915–), born 'Wallamumbi' Station, Armidale, NSW, is a poet. Her first chil-dren's book was *Kings of the Dingoes* (1958), illustrated by Barbara Albiston.

The wise Pomeranian William, and Benbow, an enthusiastic and clumsy red setter puppy, set off after their owners, who have gone on a beach holiday. They meet the laconic Jake, a drover's dog, rescue the Australian terrier Emma from Dirty Dick the Dingo and his gang, become local heroes, and find the family they love in an exciting story, with brave and sensible characters. *The Day the Mountains Played* (1960), illustrated by Annette Wright, is a picture story-book about two Aboriginal children, Darri and Cobadong, who climb Buderim mountain. When their people are attacked by the Doolamai, the mountains themselves help the children to send the invaders back to their own country. *Range the Mountains High* (1962), illustrated by I. Waloff, relates how Mrs Cherry and her children, Hugh and Joanna, ride through the mountains to join their father at a mining settlement. As they reach the most precipitous area, they are taken under the wing of two bushrangers, Dick Faulkner and his associate, Harry Reilly. See also **Bushrangers**. *The River and the Road* (1966) is a historical adventure set in a settlement on the Great North Road from Sydney, by the Hunter River. Maxwell learns that an ex-convict, Ned, has come to avenge his brother's death at the hands of a heartless landowner, Mr Carn. Max and Murdo, an associate of the convict, save Ned and Carn — one from further imprisonment, the other from death. Wright's picture of family life, her recognition of the displacement of the Aboriginal People, and the delicacy with which she brings the countryside alive, make a fine novel. See also **Historical Novels**. Her collection of poems *Birds* (1962) was written for her 13-year-old daughter, and was illustrated by Annette Macarthur-Onslow. *Country Towns* (1963), illustrated by Margaret Duce, was one of Oxford's 'Life in Australia' series, and *Henry Lawson* (1967) one of their 'Great Australians' series. Apart from the fast-paced *Kings of the Dingoes*, Wright's novels

move gently. Her characters are often contemplative, despite the dramas in which they are involved, and her work is invigorated by her fresh approach to history and her evocation of the natural world.

WRIGHTSON, PATRICIA (1921–), born Lismore, NSW, was assistant editor, then editor of the NSW *School Magazine* from 1964 to 1975. She has edited two collections, *Beneath the Sun, an Australian Collection for Children* (1972) and *Emu Stew, an Illustrated Collection of Stories and Poems for Children* (1976), republished from the *School Magazine*. Her first novel was *The Crooked Snake* (q.v., 1955), followed by *The Bunyip Hole* (q.v., 1957) and *The Rocks of Honey* (1960), all three illustrated by Margaret Horder. *The Rocks of Honey* involves the discovery of a stone axe which had been put in a secret place before white people came to Australia. It introduced the themes which she later pursued in more depth: the balance of nature, in this case an ancient axe which is disturbed from its resting place, and the mystical role of Aboriginal People, here, the unassuming Eustace Murray, who gains confidence as the novel develops. See also **Aboriginal People in Children's Fiction**. Her interest in shyness, seen in Winnie, the timid girl who appears in *The Rocks of Honey*, is further developed through Lindy Martin in *The Feather Star* (q.v., 1962). *Down to Earth* (1965), illustrated by Margaret Horder, is a science fiction novel, in which Martin the Martian is cared for by George and Cathy. Martin's fresh view of contemporary urban life makes the other children reassess their role in it. *'I Own the Racecourse!'* (q.v., 1968) is a study of a disabled boy, Andy.

Since *The Rocks of Honey* Wrightson's work has increasingly featured Aboriginal Dreaming stories, culture and people. In *An Older Kind of Magic* (q.v., 1972), illustrated by Noela Young, she introduced Aboriginal spirits, the Bitarr, Pot-Koorok, Nyol and Net-Net, who live under the

Sydney Botanic Gardens, using Roland Robinson's *The Man who Sold His Dreaming* (1956) and Aldo Massola's *Bunjil's Cave* (1968) as her sources. Her admiration for the special relationship between the land and Aboriginal People was unusual at the time she wrote this book and her next novel, *The Nargun and the Stars* (q.v., 1973). Allowing her interests free rein, she took an Aboriginal hero as the focus of her three books about Wirrun: *The Ice is Coming* (1977), *The Dark Bright Water* (1978), and *Behind the Wind* (1981). See **The Ice is Coming**. Wrightson has used elements from Aboriginal tradition, such as the Njimbin or the Nargun, and incorporated them into her own epic landscape.

Night Outside (1979), illustrated by Jean Cooper-Brown, relates how Anne and James, searching for their budgerigar, find eccentric elderly people who live on the streets. Wrightson combined her interest in the elderly and her absorption with Aboriginal stories in *A Little Fear* (q.v., 1983). *Moondark* (1987), illustrated by Noela Young, is an ecological parable, told through the dog Blue. Again, Wrightson uses the idea of balance and the reciprocity of all aspects of the earth, linking these themes with Aboriginal culture. When nature is disturbed by human settlement the animals call on the ancient spirit of Keeting, Brother Moon, to restore harmony. In *Balyet* (1989) Wrightson reconstructs a legend, this time contrasting an impulsive girl, Jo, with a wise old woman,

Mrs Willet. The story of Balyet, cast out from her people, is re-enacted when Balyet tries to capture Jo to assuage her terrible loneliness. *The Old, Old Ngarang* (1989) is in Methuen's 'Dimensions' series, and contains two stories and extracts from her other novels, with biographical details. *The Sugar-Gum Tree* (1991), illustrated by David Cox, is a book for younger readers, about the fluctuating friendship between Sarah and Penny, their arguments and gestures of reconciliation.

Apart from the gravity of the themes which Wrightson has explored, always lightened by humour, her strengths as a novelist lie in her command of language, characterisation and setting, and her exceptional imaginative powers. Her assured use of conversation can be identified in the speech of Wirrun, which accurately represents Aboriginal English. Her ability to make children and adults recognisable people, such as Uncle Charlie and Aunt Edie in *The Nargun and the Stars* or Andy in *'I Own the Racecourse!'* is an indication of her mastery of character. Her depiction of landscape is seen at its best in the Wirrun books, although her evocation of the timelessness of the Australian land can be traced back to *The Nargun and the Stars*. While she has maintained a preoccupation with place and time, and an interest in the outsider, Wrightson has examined a range of characters in her varied novels. She was awarded the Hans Christian Andersen Medal for writing in 1986, and the Dromkeen Medal in 1984.

Y

YABBA (Young Australians' Best Book Award) is an award in three categories — picture-book, book for younger readers and book for older readers — for the most popular books selected yearly by Victorian children. The award is made by the YABBA Council, which has representatives from the School Section of ALIA, the School Library Association of Victoria, the Victorian Association for the Teaching of English, the Australian Reading Association, the Australian Booksellers and Publishers Association and the National Book Council, as well as interested individuals. The first awards were made in 1986 on International Children's Day. **1986** *When the Wind Changed* (q.v., 1980) by Ruth Park and Deborah Niland; *The 27th Annual African Hippopotamus Race* (q.v., 1969) by Morris Lurie; *Hating Alison Ashley* (q.v., 1984) by Robin Klein. **1987** *Animalia* (q.v., 1986) by Graeme Base; *Sister Madge's Book of Nuns* (q.v., 1986) by Doug MacLeod; *Unreal! Eight Surprising Stories* (q.v., 1985) by Paul Jennings. **1988** *Where the Forest Meets the Sea* (q.v., 1987) by Jeannie Baker; *My Place* (q.v., 1987) by Nadia Wheatley; *Unbelievable! More Surprising Stories* (1986 see **Unreal!**) by Paul Jennings. **1989** *The Eleventh Hour* (q.v., 1988) by Graeme Base; *The Cabbage Patch Fib* (q.v., 1988) by Paul Jennings; *Uncanny! Even More Surprising Stories* (1988 see **Unreal!**) by Paul Jennings. **1990** *The Monster Who Ate Australia* (q.v., 1986) by Michael Salmon; *The Paw Thing* (q.v., 1989) by Paul Jennings; *Space Demons* (q.v., 1986) by Gillian Rubinstein. **1991** *Counting on Frank* (q.v., 1990) by Rod Clement; *Finders Keepers* (q.v., 1990) by 'Emily Rodda'; *Round the Twist* (q.v., 1990) by Paul Jennings.

Yagan of the Bibbulmun (1976) by Mary Durack, see *The Courteous Savage*

YANDELL, CHRISTIAN, see **WALLER, CHRISTIAN** (YANDELL)

YARWOOD, ALEXANDER TURNBULL (1927–). For *Growing up in the First Fleet* (1983) see **First Fleet**.

Year of the Currawong, The (1965) by Eleanor Spence, illustrated by Gareth Floyd, was Commended in the 1966 Book of the Year Awards. When the Kendall family moves to Currawong Crossing, near Macebridge, Elizabeth finds a talent for pottery, Alex can pursue his fascination with history as the children try to save an old mine from demolition, Terry has new material for her stories, and Chess is intrigued by the local minerals. Spence creates realistic children, and the novel shows much of the promise which was to be fulfilled in later books.

Young Australia, see **Annuals**

Young Australia A.B.C., The, see **Alphabet Books**

'**Young Australia' series** was a reading scheme devised by Angus & Robertson in the 1960s and 1970s, using adaptations of classic stories. Titles included Frank Clune's *Ned Kelly* (1970) and *Burke and Wills* (1971), C.J. Dennis's *Merry-Go-Round* (1975), and books and extracts by K. Langloh Parker, Ruth Park, Ethel Pedley, Norman Lindsay, Leslie Rees, and Dorothy Wall.

YOUNG, NOELA (1930–), born Sydney, has illustrated many books for writers such as Duncan Ball, Hesba

Brinsmead, Irene Gough, Christobel Mattingley, Ruth Park, 'Emily Rodda' and Patricia Wrightson. Her first illustrations appeared in Enid Bell's *David and his Australian Friends* (1952). *Exploring Australia* (1958) by Eve Pownall showed her versatility, and in John Gunn's *The Humpy in the Hills* (1960) and *City in Danger* (1962) her drawings of active children and animals are full of character and emotion. These talents are even more apparent in Irene Gough's *One Sunday Morning Early* (1963). Three children collect ripe paddymelons with intense concentration, a cat moves sinuously across the page, and a landscape of Japanese simplicity reflects the mood of the poems. Lydia Pender's *Morning Magpie: Favourite Verse* (1984) gave Young scope for a range of images.

Using her own text, Young illustrated *Flip the Flying Possum* (q.v., 1963) and *Mrs Pademelon's Joey* (1967), which relates the small adventures of Joey as he leaves his mother's pouch for the first time, enabling Young to explore again the unselfconscious elegance of small animals. *Keep Out* (1975) is set in the inner city, and displayed over double pages are Young's watercolours of a plan view of Sydney terraces. Nine very individual children peeping through a paling fence, and the rough and tumble of a busy building site, are drawn in accurate perspective.

The Special Present and Other Stories (1977) by Christobel Mattingley, *The Enemies* (1985) by Robin Klein, *Birds Fly* (1986) by Letitia Parr, and *The Best-Kept Secret* (1988) by 'Emily Rodda' are among Young's best work. She is an astute observer of the world of animals and children, and her ability to portray character is combined with a high degree of technical skill, fresh and accurate representation, and an apparent affection for her subjects.

Youth Annual, see **Annuals**

Youth Writes, see **KIRSTEN, MARCIA**

Z

ZANGALIS, CAVELL. For *New Year for Children*, *Easter for Children* and *Christmas for Children* (1982) see **Hodja Educational Resources Cooperative**.

ZOFREA, SALVATORE (1947–), born Borgia, Italy, came to Australia when he was 9. He studied at the Julian Ashton School and began exhibiting when he was 18. Zofrea has won the Sulman Prize three times. His paintings are the vehicle for Stephanie Claire's *The Painted Statue* (1987) and *Three Golden Rainbows* (1989), and are deeply religious pictures, rich in metaphor and vision.

BIBLIOGRAPHY

Adelaide, Debra, *Australian Women Writers: a Bibliographic Guide*, London: Pandora, 1988

——, *Bibliography of Australian Women's Literature 1795–1990*, Melbourne: Thorpe, 1991

Alderman, Belle and Lauren Harman, eds, *The Imagineers: Writing and Illustrating Children's Books*, Canberra: Reading Time, 1983, Reading Time publication No. 5

Alderman, Belle and Margaret Hyland, *Lu Rees Archives of Australian Children's Literature: a Guide to the Collections*, Canberra: CBC, 1989

Alderman, Belle and Stephanie Owen Reeder, eds, *The Inside Story: Creating Children's Books*, Canberra: CBC, 1987

Alexander, Alison, *Billabong's Author: the Life of Mary Grant Bruce*, Sydney: Angus & Robertson, 1979

Anderson, Hugh, ed., *The Singing Roads: a Guide to Australian Children's Authors and Illustrators*, 2 vols, 4th edn, Surry Hills, Sydney: Wentworth, 1972

Australian Dictionary of Biography, Melbourne: Melbourne University Press, 1966–

Australian National Bibliography, Canberra: National Library of Australia, 1961–

Australian National Bibliography, 1901–1950, 4 vols, Canberra: National Library of Australia, 1988

Authors and Illustrators Scrapbook: Featuring 24 Creators of Australian Children's Books, Adelaide: Omnibus, 1991

Borchardt, D.H. and W. Kirsop, *The Book in Australia: Essays towards a Cultural and Social History*, Melbourne: Australian Reference Publications in association with the Centre for Bibliographical and Textual Studies, Monash University, 1988

Bradbury, Keith and Glenn R. Cooke, *Thorns and Petals: 100 Years of the Royal Queensland Art Society*, Brisbane: Royal Queensland Art Society, 1988

Bratton, J.S., *The Impact of Victorian Children's Fiction*, London: Croom Helm, 1981

Bridges, Doreen, *Helen Palmer's Outlook*, Sydney: Helen Palmer Memorial Committee, 1982

Briggs, K.M., *The Personnel of Fairyland: a Short Account of the Fairy People of Great Britain for Those who Tell Stories to Children*, Oxford: Alden Press, 1953

Butler, Roger, *Melbourne Woodcuts and Linocuts of the 1920s and 1930s: an Exhibition Based Around the Print Collection of the Ballarat Fine Art Gallery, 2 August–6 September 1981*, Ballarat, Ballarat: Ballarat Fine Art Gallery, 1981

Cadogan, Mary and Patricia Craig, *You're a Brick, Angela!*, London: Gollancz, 1976

Carpenter, Humphrey and Mari Prichard, *The Oxford Companion to Children's Literature*, Oxford: OUP, 1984

Chisholm, A.H., *The Making of a Sentimental Bloke*, Melbourne: Georgian House, 1946

Choate, Ray, comp., *Illustration Index to Australian Art: Reproductions in Art Monographs and Exhibition Catalogues*, Bundoora: La Trobe University Library, 1990

Clarke, Patricia, *Pen Portraits: Women Writers and Journalists in Nineteenth Century Australia*, Sydney: Allen & Unwin, 1988

Crewe, Judith, *Children's Literature for Multicultural Australia*, Ultimo, NSW: Library Association of Australia, School Libraries Section, NSW Group, 1986

Darton, F.J. Harvey, *Children's Books in England: Five Centuries of Social Life*, 3rd edn, rev. Brian Alderson, Cambridge: CUP, 1982

Day, A. Grove, *Louis Becke*, Melbourne: Hill of Content, 1967

Dean, George D., *A Handbook on E.W. Cole: His Book Arcade, Tokens and Medals*, Tarragindi, Qld: G.D. & G.F. Dean, 1988

Dent, J.M., *The House of Dent*, London: Dent, 1938

Dermody, Susan, John Docker and Drusilla Modjeska, *Nellie Melba, Ginger Meggs and Friends*, Malmsbury, Vic: Kibble Books, 1982

Docker, John, *In a Critical Condition: Reading Australian Literature*, Ringwood: Penguin, 1984

——, *The Nervous Nineties: Australian Cultural Life in the 1890s*, Melbourne: OUP, 1991

Doyle, Brian, comp., *The Who's Who of Children's Literature*, London: Hugh Evelyn, 1968

Dreyer, Anne, *Kindergarten of the Air as I Knew It*, Blackburn South, Melb.: Anne Dreyer, 1989

Drury, Susan, *Writers and Writing*, Melbourne: Nelson, 1979

Dugan, Michael, comp., *The Early Dreaming: Australian Children's Authors on Childhood*, Milton, Qld: Jacaranda, 1980

Dunkle, Margaret, ed., *The Story Makers: a Collection of Interviews with Australian and New Zealand Authors and Illustrators for Young People*, Melbourne: OUP, 1987;

and *The Story Makers II: a Second Collection of Interviews with Australian and New Zealand Authors and Illustrators for Young People*, Melbourne: OUP, 1989

Dunstan, Keith, *Ratbags*, Sydney: Golden Press, 1979

Dutton, Geoffrey, *Snow on the Saltbush: the Australian Literary Experience*, Melbourne: Viking, 1984

——, *Sun, Sea, Surf and Sand — the Myth of the Beach*, Melbourne: OUP, 1985

The Early Australian Booksellers: The Australian Booksellers Association Memorial Book of Fellowship, ABA, 1980

Ellis, Vivienne Rae, *Louisa Anne Meredith: a Tigress in Exile*, Sandy Bay, Tas.: Blubberhead Press, 1979

Ewers, John K., *Creative Writing in Australia: a Selective Survey*, 5th edn., Melbourne: Georgian House, 1966

Factor, June, *Captain Cook Chased a Chook: Children's Folklore in Australia*, Ringwood: Penguin, 1988

Farjeon, Eleanor, *A Nursery in the Nineties*, London: OUP, 1960

Ferrier, Carole, ed., *Gender, Politics and Fiction: Twentieth Century Australian Women's Novels*, St Lucia: University of Queensland Press, 1985

Fiske, John, Bob Hodge and Graeme Turner, *Myths of Oz: Reading Australian Popular Culture*, Sydney: Allen & Unwin, 1987

Frost, Cheryl, *The Last Explorer, the Life and Work of Ernest Favenc*, Townsville: Foundation for Australian Literary Studies, James Cook University of North Queensland, 1983

Gash, Lyn, A History of the Australian Broadcasting Commission's Children's Session c.1929–1945, unpublished History thesis: Monash University, 1975

Germaine, Max, *Artists and Galleries of Australia*, 2 vols, Sydney: Craftsman House, 1990

Gibbs, Desmond R., Victorian School Books: a Study of the Changing Social Context and Use of School Books in Victoria, 1848–1948 with Particular Reference to School Readers, unpublished Doctoral thesis: University of Melbourne, 1987

Gibney, H.J. and Ann G. Smith, *A Biographical Register 1788–1939: Notes from the Name Index of the Australian Dictionary of Biography*, 2 vols, Canberra: ADB, 1987

Gibson, Ross, *The Diminishing Paradise: Changing Literary Perceptions of Australia*, Sydney: Angus & Robertson, 1984

Giuffre, Guilia, *A Writing Life: Interviews with Australian Women Writers*, Sydney: Allen & Unwin, 1990

Green, H.M., *A History of Australian Literature, Pure and Applied*, vol. 1: 1789–1923; vol. 2: 1923–1930, Sydney: Angus & Robertson, 1961

Halliwell, William K., *The Filmgoer's Guide to Australian Films*, Sydney: Angus & Robertson, 1985

Hazell, Anne M., *Reflections of Reality: Female Roles in Australian Adolescent Fiction*, Canberra: Auslib, 1989

Healy, J.J., 'The Lemurian Nineties', *Australian Literary Studies* 8, 3, 1978

Hergenham, Laurie, ed., *The Penguin New Literary History of Australia*, Ringwood: Penguin, 1988

Herr, Twila, ed., *The Aboriginal Motif in Children's Literature*, Hobart: University of Tasmania, 1982

Hill, Marji and Alex Barlow, *Black Australia: an Annotated Bibliography and Teacher's Guide to Resources on Aborigines and Torres Strait Islanders*, Canberra: Australian Institute of Aboriginal Studies, vol. 1. 1978, vol 2. 1985

Holden, Robert, *Koalas, Kangaroos and Kookaburras: 200 Australian Children's Books and Illustrations 1857–1988*, Sydney: James Hardie Industries, ?1988

——, *Picture the Koala: a Light-hearted Look at Children's Book Illustrations*, Catalogue of an exhibition curated by the James Hardie Library for the Power House Museum at The Mint, September 1986 to January 1987

——, *Twinkle, Twinkle, Southern Cross: the Forgotten Folklore of Australian Nursery Rhymes*, Canberra: National Library of Australia, 1992

Holden, Robert and Andrew Mackenzie, *Snugglepot and Cuddlepie and Other Fairy Folk of the Australian Bush*, An exhibition of the work of May Gibbs and Peg Maltby, 1986

Horgan, John, ed., *The Golden Years of Ginger Meggs 1921–1952*, Menindie, SA: Souvenir/Brolga, 1978

Hutchings, Patrick, *The Art of Elizabeth Durack*, Perth: Angus & Robertson, 1982

Hutchinson, Garrie, Wiregrass: *A Mythical Australian Town: The Drawings of Percy Leason*, Melbourne: Lothian, 1986

Jacobs, Joseph, *English Fairy Tales: Being the Two Collections English Fairy Tales & More English Fairy Tales*, London: Bodley Head, 1968

Jordens, Ann-Mari, *The Stenhouse Circle: Literary Life in Mid-Nineteenth Century Sydney*, Melbourne: Melbourne University Press, 1979

Jenkins, Ida Elizabeth, *Good Rowing! A Reminiscence about the ABC Children's Session and the Argonauts' Club*, Sydney: ABC, 1982

Kellow, Henry Arthur, *Queensland Poets*, London: Harrap, 1930

Ker Wilson, Barbara, comp., *The Singing Tree: a Selection of Mary Gilmore's Poetry for Young Readers*, Sydney: Angus & Robertson, 1971

Kerr, Joan, *Dictionary of Australian Artists. Working Paper 1: Painters, Photographers and Engravers 1770–1870, A-H*, Sydney: Power Institute of Fine Arts, 1984

Kirk, John Foster, *Allibone's Dictionary of English Literature and British and American Authors*, Philadelphia: Lippincott, 1891

Kramer, Leonie, ed., *The Oxford History of Australian Literature*, Melbourne: OUP, 1981

Lees, Stella, ed., *A Track to Unknown Water: Proceedings of the Second Pacific Rim Conference on Children's Literature*, Metuchen, N.J.: Scarecrow Press, 1987

Lindesay, Vane, *The Inked-in Image: a Social and Historical Survey of Australian Comic Art*, Melbourne: Hutchinson, 1979

Lippmann, Lorna, *Generations of Resistance: the Aboriginal Struggle for Justice*, Melbourne: Longman Cheshire, 1981

Liveing, Edward, *Adventure in Publishing: the House of Ward Lock 1854–1954*, London: Ward, Lock, 1954

Lofts, W.O.G. and D.J. Adley, *The Men Behind Boys' Fiction: a Collective Biography of all British Authors Who Ever Wrote for Boys*, London: Baker, 1970

Lord, Mary, comp., *Directory of Australian Authors*, Carlton, Vic.: National Book Council, 1989

Macartney, Frederick T., *Furnley Maurice*, Sydney: Angus & Robertson, 1955

Mackenzie, Andrew, comp., *Walter Withers: the Forgotten Manuscripts*, Melbourne: Mannagum Press, 1987

McLaren, Ian F. with George J. Griffiths, *Whitcombe's Story Books: a Trans-Tasman Survey*, Parkville, Vic.: University of Melbourne Library, 1984 and Supplement, 1987

McVitty, Walter, *Australian Children's Authors*, Melbourne: Macmillan, 1986

——, *Authors and Illustrators of Australian Children's Books*, Sydney: Hodder & Stoughton, 1989

——, *Dorothy Wall, the Creator of Blinky Bill: Her Life and Work*, Sydney: Angus & Robertson, 1988

——, *Innocence and Experience: Essays on Contemporary Australian Children's Writers*, Melbourne: Nelson, 1981

Malan, Kerry, ed., *On Writing for Children: Nine Papers from the Annual Lectures in Children's Literature*, Brisbane: Queensland University of Technology, 1991

'Memoir of Jeannie Gunn' by Margaret Berry, in Mrs Aeneas Gunn, *We of the Never-Never*, Melbourne: Hutchinson, 1983

Miller, E. Morris, *Australian Literature from its Beginning to 1935*, 2 vols, Melbourne: Melbourne University Press, 1940

Miller, E. Morris and Frederick T. Macartney, *Australian Literature: a Bibliography to 1938 Extended to 1950*, Sydney: Angus & Robertson, 1956

Modjeska, Drusilla, *Exiles at Home: Australian Women Writers 1925–1945*, Sydney: Sirius, 1981

Moran, Albert, comp., *Australian Television Drama Series 1956–1981*, Sydney: Australian Film, Television & Radio School, 1989

Muir, Marcie, *A Bibliography of Australian Children's Books*, 2 vols, London: Deutsch, 1970, 1976

——, *Charlotte Barton, Australia's First Children's Author*, Sydney: Wentworth Books, 1980

——, *A History of Australian Children's Book Illustration*, Melbourne: OUP, 1982

Muir, Marcie and Robert Holden, *The Fairy World of Ida Rentoul Outhwaite*, Sydney: Craftsman House, 1985

Muir, Marcie and Kerry White, *Australian Children's Books: a Bibliography, vol. 1 1742–1972, vol. 2 1973–1988*, Melbourne: Melbourne University Press, 1992

Murphy, Margaret C., *Women Writers and Australia: a Bibliography of Fiction, 19th Century to 1987*, Parkville, Vic.: University of Melbourne Library, 1988

Murray, Scott, ed., *The New Australian Cinema*, Melbourne: Nelson, 1980

Murray, Sue. *Bibliography of Australian Poetry 1935–1955*, ed. John Arnold, Sally Batten and Katie Purvis, Melbourne: Thorpe in association with the National Centre for Australian Studies, 1991

Nesdale, Ira, *The Little Missus: Mrs Aeneas Gunn*, Blackwood, SA: Lynton Publications, 1977

Niall, Brenda, *Seven Little Billabongs: the World of Ethel Turner and Mary Grant Bruce*, Melbourne: Melbourne University Press, 1979

Niall, Brenda, assisted by Frances O'Neill, *Australia Through the Looking-Glass: Children's Fiction 1930–1980*, Melbourne: Melbourne University Press, 1984

Nieuwenhuizen, Agnes, *No Kidding: Top Writers for Young People Talk about Their Work*, Chippendale, NSW: Pan Macmillan, 1991

Norrie, Ian, *Mumby's Publishing and Bookselling in the Twentieth Century*, 6th edn, London: Bell & Hyman, 1982

O'Leary, Zoe, *The Desolate Market: a Biography of Eric Lambert*, Sydney: Edwards & Shaw, 1974

O'Neill, Terence and Frances (comps), *Australian Children's Books to 1980: a Select Bibliography of the Collection Held in the National Library of Australia*, Canberra: National Library of Australia, 1989

Phelan, Nancy, *The Romantic Lives of Louise Mack*, St Lucia: University of Queensland Press, 1991

Pierce, Peter, ed., *The Oxford Literary Guide to Australia*, Melbourne: OUP, 1987

Pike, Andrew and Ross Cooper, *Australian Film 1900–1977: a Guide to Feature Film Production*, Melbourne: OUP, 1980

Poole, Philippa, ed., *The Diaries of Ethel Turner*, Sydney: Ure Smith, 1979

Prentice, Jeffrey and Bettina Bird, *Dromkeen: a Journey into Children's Literature*, New York: Henry Holt, 1987

Prentice, Jeffrey and Bronwen Bennett, *A Guide to Australian Children's Literature*, Melbourne: Thorpe, 1992

Rae, Richard, *Cartoonists of Australia*, Sydney: View Productions, 1983

Reade, Eric, *History and Heartburn: the Saga of Australian Film 1896–1978*, Sydney: Harper & Row, 1979

Robinson, Moira, ed., *Readings in Children's Literature: Proceedings of the National Seminar on Children's Literature at Frankston State College, 1977*, Frankston: Frankston State College, 1977

Ryan, John, *Panel by Panel: A History of Australian Comics*, Sydney: Cassell, 1979

St John, Judith, ed., *The Osborne Collection of Early Children's Books 1566–1910: a Catalogue*, vol. 1, Toronto: Toronto Public Library, 1975

St John, Judith with the assistance of Dana Tenny and Hazel I. MacTaggert, *The Osborne Collection of Early Children's Books 1476–1910: a Catalogue*, vol. 2, Toronto: Toronto Public Library, 1975

Saxby, Maurice, *A History of Australian Children's Literature, 2 vols*, Sydney: Wentworth, 1969, 1971

——, *The Proof of the Puddin': Australian Children's Literature 1970–1990*, Sydney: Ashton, 1993

Saxby, Maurice, ed., *Through Folklore to Literature: Papers Presented at the Australian National Section of IBBY Conference on Children's Literature, Sydney, 1978*, Sydney: IBBY Australia Publications, 1979

Saxby, Maurice and Gordon Winch, eds, *Give Them Wings: the Experience of Children's Literature*, Melbourne: Macmillan, 1987

Simkin, John, ed., *Subject Guide to Australian Children's Books in Print*, Melbourne: Thorpe, 1991

Simpson, E.R., *The Clelands of Beaumont: a History of 26 Generations of a South Australian Family*, Adelaide: Beaumont Press, 1986

Souter, D.H., *A Ticket in Tatts*, ed. with an afterword by Stephen Williams, Ringwood: Penguin, 1988

Southall, Ivan, *A Journey of Discovery: on Writing for Children*, Harmondsworth: Penguin, 1968

Spearritt, Peter and David Walker, *Australian Popular Culture*, Sydney: Allen & Unwin, 1979

Spender, Dale, *Writing a New World: Two Centuries of Australian Women Writers*, London: Pandora, 1988

State Library of Victoria. Mason Family Papers MS 11625. Frederick T. Macartney Papers MS 10519. Cole Papers MS 10111

Stewart, John, *An Encyclopaedia of Australian Film*, Frenchs Forest, NSW: Reed, 1984

Stodart, Eleanor, ed., *Writing and Illustrating for Children: Children's Book Council of the ACT Seminars 1975–1980*, Canberra: CBC, 1985

Stone, Michael, ed., *Children's Literature and Contemporary Theory*, Wollongong: New Literatures Research Centre, University of Wollongong, 1991

Stratton, David, *The Avocado Plantation: Boom and Bust in the Australian Film Industry*, Sydney: Pan Macmillan, 1990

Tennant, Kylie, *The Missing Heir: the Autobiography of Kylie Tennant*, Melbourne: Macmillan, 1986

Thomas, Alan, *Broadcast and be Damned: the ABC's First Two Decades*, Melbourne: Melbourne University Press, 1980

Turner, E.S., *Boys Will be Boys: the Story of Sweeney Todd, Deadwood Dick, Sexton Blake, Billy Bunter, Dick Barton et al.*, London: Penguin, 1976

Turnley, Cole, *Cole of the Book Arcade: a Pictorial Biography of E.W. Cole*, Hawthorn, Victoria: Cole Publications, 1974

Ward, Martha E. and Dorothy A. Marquardt, *Authors of Books for Young People*, New York: Scarecrow Press, 1964

Walsh, Maureen, *May Gibbs, Mother of the Gumnuts: Her Life and Work*, Sydney, Angus & Robertson, 1985

Walker, Maxine, *Writers Alive! Current Australian Writers for Children*, Perth: Westbooks, 1977

Walker, Shirley, ed., *Who is She? Images of Women in Australian Fiction*, St Lucia: University of Queensland Press, 1983

Who's Who of Australian Children's Writers, Melbourne: Thorpe, in association with the National Centre for Australian Studies, 1992

Who's Who of Australian Writers, Melbourne: Thorpe, in association with the National Centre for Australian Studies, Monash University, 1991

Wighton, Rosemary, *Early Australian Children's Literature*, Surrey Hills, Vic.: Casuarina, 1979

Wilde, William H., Joy Hooton and Barry Andrews, *The Oxford Companion to Australian Literature*, Melbourne: OUP, 1985

APPENDIX

1946 *The Story of Karrawingi the Emu* (1946) by Leslie Rees, illustrated by Walter Cunningham.

1947 No award.

1948 *Shackleton's Argonauts* (1948) by Frank Hurley, illustrated with his photographs. Highly Commended: *The Australian Book of Trains* (1947) by J.H. and W.D. Martin, *Beetles Ahoy!* (1948) by Ada Jackson, illustrated by Nina Poynton, *Bush Cobbers* (1948) by 'Musette Morell', illustrated by Edwina Bell, *Ponny the Penguin* (1948) by Veronica Basser, illustrated by Edwina Bell, *The Story of Shadow the Rock Wallaby* (1948) by Leslie Rees, illustrated by Walter Cunningham.

1949 No competition.

1950 *Whalers of the Midnight Sun* (1934, first Australian edition 1949) by Alan Villiers, illustrated by Charles Pont. Highly Commended: *Bush Holiday* (1948) by 'Stephen Fennimore', illustrated by Sheila Hawkins, *Bush Voyage* (1950) by Dale Collins, illustrated by Margaret Horder, *Bonza the Bull* (1949) by Dora Birtles, *The Secret Family* (1948) by Esmée Rice, illustrated by Pixie O'Harris, *Wild River* (1949) by Bernard O'Reilly, *Little Brown Piccaninnies of Tasmania* (1950) by Jane Ada Fletcher, illustrated by Margaret Senior, *The Story of Kurri Kurri the Kookaburra* (1950) by Leslie Rees, illustrated by Walter Cunningham, *Bluecap and Bimbi* (1948) by Leslie Rees, illustrated by Walter Cunningham. Special Mention: *Lyrebird Garden* (1949) written and illustrated by Dagma Dawson.

1951 *Verity of Sydney Town* (1950) by Ruth Williams, illustrated by Rhys Williams. Highly Commended: *Starland of the South* (1950) by W.A. McNair, illustrated by William R. Taplin. Commended: *Carcoola* (1950) by Nourma Handford, *Kiewa Adventure* (1950) by Allan Aldous, *Spear and Stockwhip* (1950) by Richard Graves, *Churinga Tales* (1950) by Erle Wilson, illustrated by Sally Medworth.

1952 *The Australia Book* (1952) by Eve Pownall. Highly Commended: *Cousins-Come-Lately* (1952) by Eve Pownall, *The Blue Wren Series* by various authors. Commended: *Wild Dog Frontier* (1951) by William Hatfield, *Carcoola Adventure* (1952) by Nourma Handford.

1953 *Good Luck to the Rider* (1953) by Joan Phipson and *Aircraft of Today and Tomorrow* (1953) by J.H and W.D. Martin (Joint winners).

1954 *Australian Legendary Tales* (1953) by Katherine Langloh Parker, edited by Henrietta Drake-Brockman. Highly Commended: *Southward Ho! with the Hentys* (1953) by Fitzmaurice Hill, *Fighting Ships of Australia and New Zealand* (1953) by Frank Norton.

1955 *The First Walkabout* (1954) by Norman Tindale and Harold Lindsay. Highly Commended: *Wild Brother* (1954) by Mary Patchett. Commended: *The First Hundred Years* (1954) by Helen Palmer and Jessie McLeod.

1956 *The Crooked Snake* (1955) by Patricia Wrightson. Highly Commended: *John of the `Sirius'* (1955) by Doris Chadwick, *Penguin Road* (1955) by Ken Dalziel, *Birds of Australia in Colour* (1955) by Lyla Stevens.

1957 *The Boomerang Book of Legendary Tales* (1957) edited by Enid Moodie Heddle. Highly Commended: *The Brown Land was Green* (1956) by Mavis Thorpe Clark, *Makers of the First Hundred Years* (1956) by Helen Palmer and Jessie McLeod, *The Boomerang Book of Australian Poetry* (1956) edited by Enid Moodie Heddle.

1958 *Tiger in the Bush* (1957) by Nan Chauncy. Highly Commended: *It Happened One Summer* (1957) by Joan Phipson, *Pacific Peoples* (1957) by Lyndsay Gardiner.

1959 *Devils' Hill* (1958) by Nan Chauncy and *Sea Menace* (1958) by John Gunn (Joint winners). Highly Commended: *The Silver Brumby* (1958) by Elyne Mitchell. Commended: *The Bunyip Hole* (1957) by Patricia Wrightson, *Exploring Australia* (1958) by Eve Pownall, *Australian and New Zealand Ships of Today* (1958) by Frank Norton.

1960 *All the Proud Tribesmen* (1959) by Kylie Tennant. Commended: *Rangatira (The High-Born)* (1959) by Norman Tindale and Harold Lindsay, *Anzac Adventure* (1959) by Dale Collins, *The Summer in Between* (1959) by Eleanor Spence.

1961 *Tangara* (1960) by Nan Chauncy. Commended: *Doctor with Wings* (1960) by Allan Aldous, *Silver Brumby's Daughter* (1960) by Elyne Mitchell, *Lillipilly Hill* (1960) by Eleanor Spence.

1962 *The Racketty Street Gang* (1961) by L.H. Evers and *Rafferty Rides a Winner* (1961) by Joan Woodberry (Joint winners). Commended: *The Hole in the Hill* (1961) by Ruth Park, *The Forbidden Bridge* (1961) by Betty Roland, *The Sun on the Stubble* (1961) by Colin Thiele.

1963 *The Family Conspiracy* (1962) by Joan Phipson. Highly Commended: *Bushland and Seashore* (1962) by Robin Hill. Commended: *Quest for Golden Dan* (1962) by Frank Kellaway, *The Feather Star* (1962) by Patricia Wrightson, *A Picture History of Australia* (1962) by R.M. Crawford, *The Australian Pet Book* (1962) by 'John Wotherspoon'.

1964 *The Green Laurel* (1963) by Eleanor Spence. Highly Commended: *The Roaring 40* (1963) by Nan Chauncy. Commended: *Storm Boy* (1963) by Colin Thiele, *Threat to the Barkers* (1963) by Joan Phipson, *One Sunday Morning Early* (1963) by Irene Gough, *Jamie's Discovery* (1963) by Betty Roland, *Fires and Firemen* (1963) by Carol Odell.

1965 *Pastures of the Blue Crane* (1964) by Hesba Brinsmead. Highly Commended: *Winged Skis* (1964) by Elyne Mitchell, *Jamie's Summer Visitor*

(1964) by Betty Roland. Commended: *High and Haunted Island* (1964) by Nan Chauncy, *The Courteous Savage: Yagan of Swan River* (1964) by Mary Durack, *A Day at the Zoo* (1964) by Carol Odell, *Wonderland of Nature* (1964) by Nuri Mass.

1966 *Ash Road* (1965) by Ivan Southall. Highly Commended: *By the Sandhills of Yamboorah* (1965) by Reginald Ottley. Commended: *Indonesian Journey* (1965) by Ivan Southall, *The Year of the Currawong* (1965) by Eleanor Spence, *February Dragon* (1965) by Colin Thiele.

1967 *The Min-Min* (1966) by Mavis Thorpe Clark. Highly Commended: *Cocky's Castle* (1966) by Celia Syred. Commended: *The Wish Cat* (1966) by Jean Chapman, *The Golden Lamb* (1966) by Irene Gough, *Roan Colt of Yamboorah* (1966) by Reginald Ottley, *The River Kings* (1966) by Max Fatchen. Special Mention: *Beat of the City* (1966) by Hesba Brinsmead.

1968 *To the Wild Sky* (1967) by Ivan Southall. Highly Commended: *Midnite* (1967) by Randolph Stow. Commended: *Mathinna's People* (1967) by Nan Chauncy, *Blue Above the Trees* (1967) by Mavis Thorpe Clark, *The Fox Hole* (1967) by Ivan Southall.

1969 *When Jays Fly to Barbmo* (1968) by Margaret Balderson. Highly Commended: *'I Own the Racecourse!'* (1968) by Patricia Wrightson. Commended: *The 'Loyall Virginian'* (1968) by George Finkel, *Let the Balloon Go* (1968) by Ivan Southall, *Children of the Desert* (1968) by P. and N. Wallace, *Wood, Wire and Fabric* (1968) by John Goode, *Cricket the Australian Way* (1961, revised and enlarged 1968) by Jack Pollard, *Wandjina: Children of the Dreamtime* (1968) by Roland Robinson.

1970 *Uhu* (1969) by Annette Macarthur-Onslow. Highly Commended: *Blue Fin* (1969) by Colin Thiele. Commended: *Finn's Folly* (1969) by Ivan Southall, *The Bates Family* (1969) by Reginald Ottley, *Six Days Between a Second* (1969) by Marjory O'Dea, *Over the Bridge* (1969) by Deirdre Hill, *The Ombley-Gombley* (1969) by Peter Wesley-Smith.

1971 *Bread and Honey* (1970) by Ivan Southall. Highly Commended: *Story of China* (1970) by Lo Hui-Min. Commended: *James Cook, Royal Navy* (1970) by George Finkel, *Climb a Lonely Hill* (1970) by Lilith Norman.

1972 *Longtime Passing* (1971) by Hesba Brinsmead. Highly Commended: *Windmill at Magpie Creek* (1971) by Christobel Mattingley. Commended: *Hughie* by David Martin. Favourable Mention: *Worm Weather* (1971) by Christobel Mattingley, *Minnie* (1971) by Annette Macarthur-Onslow.

1973 *Family at the Lookout* (1972) by Noreen Shelley. Highly Commended: *An Older Kind of Magic* (1972) by Patricia Wrightson. Commended: *Everyday Inventions* (1972) by Meredith Hooper.

1974 *The Nargun and the Stars* (1973) by Patricia Wrightson. Highly Commended: *The Spirit Wind* (1973) by Max Fatchen. Commended: *The Fire in the Stone* (1973) by Colin Thiele, *The Bunyip of Berkeley's Creek* (1973) by Jenny Wagner.

1975 No award. Highly Commended: *Callie's Castle* by Ruth Park. Commended: *Magpie Island* (1974) by Colin Thiele. Worthy of Mention: *Uncle Gustav's Ghosts* (1974) by Colin Thiele, *Faces in a Looking Glass* (1974) by Noreen Shelley.

1976 *Fly West* (1974) by Ivan Southall. Highly Commended: *A Dog Called George* (1975) by Margaret Balderson. Commended: No awards. Worthy of Mention: *Mr P. and His Remarkable Flight* (1975) by David Martin, *Patchwork Grandmother* (1975) by Nance Donkin. Special Mention: *Hey Phantom Singlet* (1975) by Simon French.

1977 *The October Child* (1976) by Eleanor Spence. Highly Commended: *The Cats* (1976) by Joan Phipson. Commended: *Hebe's Daughter* (1976) by Celia Syred.

1978 *The Ice is Coming* (1977) by Patricia Wrightson. Highly Commended: *A Candle for St Antony* (1977) by Eleanor Spence. Commended: *The Curse of the Turtle* (1977) by Thomas Roy, *The Lieutenant* (1977) by Jack Bennett.

1979 *The Plum Rain Scroll* (1978) by Ruth Manley. Highly Commended: *Boori* (1978) by Bill Scott. Commended: *The Pochetto Coat* (1978) by Ted Greenwood, *Come Danger, Come Darkness* (1978) by Ruth Park.

1980 *Displaced Person* (1979) by Lee Harding. Highly Commended: *Once There was a Swagman* (1979) by Hesba Brinsmead. Commended: *The Gould League Book of Australian Birds* (1979) by Don Goodsir, *River Murray Mary* (1979) by Colin Thiele.

1981 *Playing Beatie Bow* (1980) by Ruth Park. Highly Commended: *Darkness Under the Hills* (1980) by Bill Scott. Commended: *Jandy Malone and the Nine O'clock Tiger* (1980) by Barbara Bolton, *The Seventh Pebble* (1980) by Eleanor Spence.

1982 *The Valley Between* (1981) by Colin Thiele. Highly Commended: *Behind the Wind* (1981) by Patricia Wrightson. Commended: *Cannily, Cannily* (1981) by Simon French, *Rummage* (1981) by Christobel Mattingley.

1983 *Master of the Grove* (1982) by Victor Kelleher. Highly Commended: *The Left Overs* (1982) by Eleanor Spence. Commended: *Five Times Dizzy* (1982) by Nadia Wheatley, *Toby's Millions* by Morris Lurie.

1984 *A Little Fear* (1983) by Patricia Wrightson. Highly Commended: *Penny Pollard's Diary* (1983) by Robin Klein. Commended: *The Devil's Stone* (1983) by 'Helen Frances', *Breaking Up* (1983) by Frank Willmott.

1985 *The True Story of Lilli Stubeck* (1984) by James Aldridge. Highly Commended: *Eleanor, Elizabeth* (1984) by Libby Gleeson. Commended: *Me and Jeshua* (1984) by Eleanor Spence, *Dancing in the Anzac Deli* (1984) by Nadia Wheatley.

1986 *The Green Wind* (1985) by Thurley Fowler. Highly Commended: *Little Brother* (1985) by Allan Baillie. Commended: *The House that was Eureka* (1984) by Nadia Wheatley, *The Changelings of Chaan* (1985) by David Lake.

1987 *All We Know* (1986) by Simon French. Honour Books: *Taronga* (1986) by Victor Kelleher, *Space Demons* (1986) by Gillian Rubinstein.

1988 *So Much to Tell You...* (1987) by John Marsden. Honour Books: *I am Susannah* (1987) by Libby Gleeson, *Deezle Boy* (1987) by Eleanor Spence.

1989 *Beyond the Labyrinth* (1988) by Gillian Rubinstein. Honour Books: *The Lake at the End of the World* (1988) by Caroline Macdonald, *Answers to Brut* (1988) by Gillian Rubinstein.

1990 *Came Back to Show You I Could Fly* (1989) by Robin Klein. Honour Books: *Merryll of the Stones* (1989) by Brian Caswell, *Thunderwith* (1989) by Libby Hathorn.

1991 *Strange Objects* (1990) by Gary Crew. Honour Books: *The Farseekers* (1990) by Isobelle Carmody, *The Family Book of Mary-Claire* (1990) by Eleanor Spence.

1992 *The House Guest* (1991) by Eleanor Nilsson. Honour Books: *Change the Locks* (1991) by Simon French, *Peter* (1991) by Kate Walker.

CHILDREN'S BOOK OF THE YEAR AWARD: YOUNGER READERS

1982 *Rummage* (1981) by Christobel Mattingley, illustrated by Patricia Mullins.

1983 *Thing* (1982) by Robin Klein, illustrated by Alison Lester.

1984 *Bernice Knows Best* (1983) by Max Dann, illustrated by Ann James.

1985 *Something Special* (1984) by 'Emily Rodda', illustrated by Noela Young.

1986 *Arkwright* (1985), written and illustrated by Mary Steele.

1987 *Pigs Might Fly* (1986) by 'Emily Rodda', illustrated by Noela Young. Honour Books: *Sister Madge's Book of Nuns* (1986) by Doug MacLeod, illustrated by Craig Smith, *All about Anna and Harriet and Christopher and Me* (1986) by Libby Hathorn, illustrated by Steve Axelsen.

1988 *My Place* (1987) by Nadia Wheatley and Donna Rawlins. Honour Books: *Looking Out for Sampson* (1987) by Libby Hathorn, illustrated by Ann James, *A Paddock of Poems* (1987) by Max Fatchen, illustrated by Kerry Argent.

1989 *The Best-Kept Secret* (1988) by 'Emily Rodda', illustrated by Noela Young. Honour Books: *Melanie and the Night Animal* (1988) by Gillian Rubinstein, *Australopaedia* (1988) edited by Joan Grant, illustrated by Design students at Phillip Institute.

1990 *Pigs and Honey* (1989), written and illustrated by Jeanie Adams. Honour Books: *Papa and the Olden Days* (1989) by Ian Edwards, illustrated by Rachel Tonkin, *The Dragon of Mith* (1989) by Kate Walker, illustrated by Laurie Sharpe.

1991 *Finders Keepers* (1990) by 'Emily Rodda', illustrated by Noela Young. Honour Books: *Boris and Borsch* (1990) by Robin Klein, illustrated by Cathy Wilcox, *Mervyn's Revenge* (1990) by Leone Peguero, illustrated by Shirley Peters.

1992 *The Magnificent Nose and Other Marvels* (1991) by Anna Fienberg, illustrated by Kim Gamble. Honour Book: *Misery Guts* (1991) by Morris Gleitzman.

PICTURE BOOK OF THE YEAR AWARD

1952–54 No award.

1955 No award. Highly Commended: *Things My Family Make* (1955) by Sue Lightfoot, illustrated by Peter Clark. Commended: *Mr Koala Bear* (1954) written and illustrated by Elisabeth MacIntyre, *Mirram* (1955) written and illustrated by Margaret Paice.

1956 *Wish and the Magic Nut* (1956) by Peggy Barnard, illustrated by Sheila Hawkins.

1957 No award.

1958 *Piccaninny Walkabout* (1957) written by Axel Poignant, with photographs by the author.

1959–63 No award.

1964 No award. Commended: *Flip the Flying Possum* (1963) written and illustrated by Noela Young.

1965 *Hugh's Zoo* (1964) written and illustrated by Elisabeth MacIntyre.

1966 No award.

1967 No award. Special Mention: *Naughty Agapanthus* (1966) by Barbara Macfarlane, illustrated by Margaret Lees.

1968 No award. Commended: *Sharpur the Carpet Snake* (1967) by Lydia Pender, illustrated by Virginia Smith, *Moggie and Her Circus Pony* (1967) by Katharine Susannah Prichard, illustrated by Elaine Haxton, *Puffing Billy* (1967) by Esta de Fossard, illustrated by John Mason.

1969 *Sly Old Wardrobe* (1968) by Ivan Southall, illustrated by Ted Greenwood.

1970 No award. Commended: *The Ha Ha Bird* (1968) written and illustrated by Penelope Janjic, *Donovan and the Lost Birthday* (1968) by Marion Ord, illustrated by Penelope Janjic, *John the Mouse Who Learned to Read* (1969) by Beverley Randell, illustrated by Noela Young, *Obstreperous* (1970) written and illustrated by Ted Greenwood.

1971 *Waltzing Matilda* (1970) by A.B. Paterson, illustrated by Desmond Digby.

1972 No award.

1973 No award. Highly Commended: *Joseph and Lulu and the Prindiville House Pigeons* (1972) written and illustrated by Ted Greenwood. Commended: *Barnaby and the Rocket* (1972) by Lydia Pender, illustrated by Judy Cowell. Special Mention: *Art Folios No. 1* (1972) by Paul Milton.

1974 *The Bunyip of Berkeley's Creek* (1973) by Jenny Wagner, illustrated by Ron Brooks. Commended: *The Giant Devil Dingo* (1973) written and illustrated by Dick Roughsey.

1975 *The Man from Ironbark* (1974) by A.B. Paterson, illustrated by Quentin Hole. Commended: *The Wind Comes* (1974) by Ron Forbes, illustrated by Francia Forbes, *Djurguba* (1975) written and illustrated by Aboriginal trainee students of Kormilda College, Darwin.

1976 *The Rainbow Serpent* (1975) written and illustrated by Dick Roughsey. Highly Commended: *Annie's Rainbow* (1975) written and illustrated by Ron Brooks, *Terry's Brrrmmm GT* (1974) written and illustrated by Ted Greenwood, *Aranea* (1975) by Jenny Wagner, illustrated by Ron Brooks.

1977 No award. Highly Commended: *ABC of Monsters* (1976) written and illustrated by Deborah Niland. Commended: *Tell Me Another Tale* (1976) by Jean Chapman, illustrated by Deborah and Kilmeny Niland.

1978 *John Brown, Rose and the Midnight Cat* (1977) by Jenny Wagner, illustrated by Ron Brooks. Highly Commended: *The Lighthouse Keeper's Lunch* (1977) by Ronda Armitage, illustrated by David Armitage. Commended: *The Sugar-Plum Christmas Book* (1977) by Jean Chapman, illustrated by Deborah Niland, *The Aboriginal Children's History of Australia* (1977) written and illustrated by Aboriginal children.

1979 *The Quinkins* (1978) written and illustrated by Percy Tresize and Dick Roughsey. Highly Commended: *The Trouble with Mr. Harris* (1978) by Ronda Armitage, illustrated by David Armitage. Commended: *The Riverboat Crew* (1978) by Janet McLean, illustrated by Andrew McLean, *The Oath of Bad Brown Bill* (1978) written and illustrated by Stephen Axelsen.

1980 *One Dragon's Dream* (1978) written and illustrated by Peter Pavey. Commended: *The Useless Donkeys* (1979) by Lydia Pender, illustrated by Judith Cowell, *Sinabouda Lily: a Folktale from Papua New Guinea* (1979) by Robin Anderson, illustrated by Jennifer Allen.

1981 No award. Highly Commended: *Marty Moves to the Country* (1980) by Kate Walker, illustrated by Bruce Treloar. Commended: *Mr Archimedes' Bath* (1980) written and illustrated by Pamela Allen.

1982 *Sunshine* (1981) by Jan Ormerod. Highly Commended: *The Tram to Bondi Beach* (1981) by Elizabeth Hathorn, illustrated by Julie Vivas. Commended: *Whistle up the Chimney* (1981) by Nan Hunt, illustrated by Craig Smith, *Bumble's Dream* (1981) written and illustrated by Bruce Treloar.

1983 *Who Sank the Boat?* (1982) written and illustrated by Pamela Allen. Highly Commended: *The Train* (1982) by Witold Generowicz. Commended: *Tin Lizzie and Little Nell* (1982) written and illustrated by David Cox, *Turramulli the Giant Quinkin* (1982) written and illustrated by Percy Tresize and Dick Roughsey.

1984 *Bertie and the Bear* (1983) written and illustrated by Pamela Allen. Highly Commended: *Possum Magic* (1983) by Mem Fox, illustrated by Julie Vivas. Commended: *The White Crane* (1983) adapted by Helen Smith, illustrated by Junko Morimoto, *The Friends of Emily Culpepper* (1983) by Ann Coleridge, illustrated by Roland Harvey.

1985 No award. Highly Commended: *The Inch Boy* (1984) adapted by Helen Smith, illustrated by Junko Morimoto. Commended: *Home in the Sky* (1984) by Jeannie Baker, *Ayu and the Perfect Moon* (1984) written and illustrated by David Cox.

1986 *Felix and Alexander* (1985) written and illustrated by Terry Denton. Highly Commended: *A Piece of Straw* (1985) adapted by Helen Smith, illustrated by Junko Morimoto. Commended: *Clive Eats Alligators* (1985) written and illustrated by Alison Lester, *First There was Frances* (1985) written and illustrated by Bob Graham.

1987 *Kojuro and the Bears* (1986) adapted by Helen Smith, illustrated by Junko Morimoto. Honour Books: *Animalia* (1986) written and illustrated by Graeme Base, *Murgatroyd's Garden* (1986) by Judy Zavos, illustrated by Drahos Zak.

1988 *Crusher is Coming!* (1987) written and illustrated by Bob Graham. Honour Books: *Where the Forest Meets the Sea* (1987) by Jeannie Baker, *The Long Red Scarf* (1987) by Nette Hilton, illustrated by Margaret Power.

1989 Joint Winners: *The Eleventh Hour* (1988) written and illustrated by Graeme Base and *Drac and the Gremlin* (1988) by Allan Baillie, illustrated by Jane Tanner. Honour Book: *My Place in Space* (1988) by Robin and Sally Hirst, illustrated by Roland Harvey and Joe Levine.

1990 *The Very Best of Friends* (1989) by Margaret Wild, illustrated by Julie Vivas. Honour Books: *Grandad's Magic* (1989) written and illustrated by Bob Graham, *The Journey Home* (1989) written and illustrated by Alison Lester.

1991 *Greetings from Sandy Beach* (1990) written and illustrated by Bob Graham. Honour Books: *Counting on Frank* (1990) written and illustrated by Rod Clement, *Hector and Maggie* (1990) by Janet McLean, illustrated by Andrew McLean.

1992 *Window* (1991) by Jeannie Baker. Honour Books: *William Tell* (1991) adapted and illustrated by Margaret Early, *Hist!* (1991) by C.J. Dennis, illustrated by Peter Gouldthorpe.

THE SHORT LIST

1982 *The Inside Hedge Story* (1981) by Gillian Barnett, *Closer to the Stars* (1981) by Max Fatchen, *Wait for Me! Wait for Me!* (1981) by Thurley Fowler, *Cannily, Cannily* (1981) by Simon French, *Rummage* (1981) by Christobel Mattingley, *A Tide Flowing* (1981) by Joan Phipson, *The Valley Between* (1981) by Colin Thiele, *Behind the Wind* (1981) by Patricia Wrightson. **Picture Book**: *Ice Creams for Rosie* (1981) by Ronda Armitage, illustrated by David Armitage, *The Tram to Bondi Beach* (1981) by Elizabeth Hathorn, illustrated by Julie Vivas, *Whistle Up the Chimney* (1981) by Nan Hunt, illustrated by Craig Smith, *The Steam Train Crew* (1981) by Janet McLean, illustrated by Andrew McLean, *Aktil's Bicycle Ride* (1981) written and illustrated by Inga Moore, *Sunshine* (1981) by Jan Ormerod, *A Pet for Mrs Arbuckle* (1981) by Gwenda Smyth, illustrated by Ann James, *Bumble's Dream* (1981) written and illustrated by Bruce Treloar.

1983 *Longtime Dreaming* (1982) by Hesba Brinsmead, *Master of the Grove* (1982) by Victor Kelleher, *Toby's Millions* (1982) by Morris Lurie, *The Dragon Stone* (1982) by Ruth Manley, *Three Way Street* (1982) by Bron Nicholls, *The Watcher in the Garden* (1982) by Joan Phipson, *The Left Overs* (1982) by Eleanor Spence, *Five Times Dizzy* (1982) by Nadia Wheatley. **Picture Book**: *Who Sank the Boat?* (1982) written and illustrated by Pamela Allen, *Tin Lizzie and Little Nell* (1982) written and illustrated by David Cox, *Ralph the Rhino* (1982) written and illustrated by Tony Edwards, *The Train* (1982) by Witold Generowicz, *Thing* (1982) by Robin Klein, illustrated by Alison Lester, *Moonlight* (1982) by Jan Ormerod, *Battles in the Bath* (1982) written and illustrated by Peter Pavey, *Turramulli the Giant Quinkin* (1982) written and illustrated by Dick Roughsey and Percy Trezise.

1984 *Bernice Knows Best* (1983) by Max Dann, *The Devil's Stone* (1983) by 'Helen Frances', *Waiting for the End of the World* (1983) by Lee Harding, *Junk Castle* (1983) by Robin Klein, *Penny Pollard's Diary* (1983) by Robin Klein, *People Might Hear You* (1983) by Robin Klein, *The Long Night Watch* (1983) by Ivan Southall, *Breaking Up* (1983) by Frank Willmott, *A Little Fear* (1983) by Patricia Wrightson. **Picture Book**: *Bertie and the Bear* (1983) written and illustrated by Pamela Allen, *The Friends of Emily Culpepper* (1983) by Ann Coleridge, illustrated by Roland Harvey, *The Sparrow's Story at the King's Command* (1983) written and illustrated by Judith Crabtree, *Possum Magic* (1983) by Mem Fox, illustrated by Julie Vivas, *The Magic Saddle* (1983) by Christobel Mattingley, illustrated by Patricia Mullins, *The White Crane* (1983) adapted by Helen Smith, illustrated by Junko Morimoto, *The Boy who Painted the Sun* (1983) by Jill Morris, illustrated by Geoff Hocking, *The Magic Firesticks* (1983) written and illustrated by Percy Trezise and Dick Roughsey.

1985 *The True Story of Lilli Stubeck* (1984) by James Aldridge, *Adrift* (1983) by Allan Baillie, *Eleanor, Elizabeth* (1984) by Libby Gleeson, *Papio* (1984) by Victor Kelleher, *Hating Alison Ashley* (1984) by Robin Klein, *Penny Pollard's Letters* (1984) by Robin Klein, *Something Special* (1984) by 'Emily Rodda', *Me and Jeshua* (1984) by Eleanor Spence, *Dancing in the Anzac Deli* (1984) by Nadia Wheatley. **Picture Book**: *Home in the Sky* (1984) by Jeannie Baker, *Ayu and the*

Perfect Moon (1984) written and illustrated by David Cox, *Arthur* (1984) by Amanda Graham, illustrated by Donna Gynell, *The Angel with a Mouth Organ* (1984) by Christobel Mattingley, illustrated by Astra Lacis, *The Inch Boy* (1984) adapted by Helen Smith, illustrated by Junko Morimoto, *There's a Sea in my Bedroom* (1984) by Margaret Wild, illustrated by Jane Tanner, *Wilfrid Gordon McDonald Partridge* (1984) by Mem Fox, illustrated by Julie Vivas.

1986 *Little Brother* (1985) by Allan Baillie, *Firestorm* by Roger Vaughan Carr, *The Green Wind* (1985) by Thurley Fowler, *Halfway Across the Galaxy and Turn Left* (1985) by Robin Klein, *The Changelings of Chaan* (1985) by David Lake, *Apples from Hurricane Street* (1985) compiled by Clare Scott-Mitchell, illustrated by Louise Hogan, *Miranda Going Home* (1985) by Eleanor Spence, *The House that was Eureka* (1984) by Nadia Wheatley. **Junior Book**: *Edward Wilkins and his Friend Gwendoline* (1985) by Barbara Bolton, illustrated by Madeleine Winch, *One Night at Lottie's House* (1985) by Max Dann, illustrated by David Pearson, *Burke and Wills* (1985) written and illustrated by Roland Harvey, *Paolo's Secret* (1985) by Elizabeth Hathorn, illustrated by Lorraine Hannay, *The Enemies* (1985) by Robin Klein, illustrated by Noela Young, *The Boy and the Whale* (1985) by Katherine Scholes, illustrated by David Wong, *Charlie up a Gum Tree* (1985) by E.A. Schurmann, illustrated by Bruce Treloar, *Arkwright* by Mary Steele. **Picture Book**: *Watch Me!* (1985) written and illustrated by Pamela Allen, *Sebastian Lives in a Hat* (1985) by Thelma Catterwell, illustrated by Kerry Argent, *Bossyboots* (1985) written and illustrated by David Cox, *First There was Frances* (1985) written and illustrated by Bob Graham, *Felix and Alexander* (1985) written and illustrated by Terry Denton, *Clive Eats Alligators* (1985) written and illustrated by Alison Lester, *A Piece of Straw* (1985) adapted by Helen Smith, illustrated by Junko Morimoto, *The Story of Chicken Licken* (1985) written and illustrated by Jan Ormerod.

1987 Older Readers: *Riverman* (1986) by Allan Baillie, *All We Know* (1986) by Simon French, *Taronga* (1986) by Victor Kelleher, *My Sister Sif* (1986) by Ruth Park, *Space Demons* (1986) by Gillian Rubinstein, *Blue Days* (1986) by Donna Sharp. **Younger Readers**: *Melissa's Ghost* (1986) by Michael Dugan, illustrated by Elizabeth Honey, *All about Anna and Harriet and Christopher and Me* (1986) by Elizabeth Hathorn, illustrated by Stephen Axelsen, *Boss of the Pool* (1986) by Robin Klein, illustrated by Helen Panagopoulos, *Sister Madge's Book of Nuns* (1986) by Doug MacLeod, illustrated by Craig Smith, *Pigs Might Fly* (1986) by 'Emily Rodda', illustrated by Noela Young, *Farmer Schultz's Ducks* (1986) by Colin Thiele, illustrated by Mary Milton. **Picture Book**: *Animalia* (1986) written and illustrated by Graeme Base, *The Wild* (1986) written and illustrated by Bob Graham, *Kojuro and the Bears* (1986) adapted by Helen Smith, illustrated by Junko Morimoto, *Creatures in the Beard* (1986) by Margaret Wild, illustrated by Margaret Power, *The Nativity* (1986) adapted and illustrated by Julie Vivas, *Murgatroyd's Garden* (1986) by Judy Zavos, illustrated by Drahos Zak.

1988 Older Readers: *Obernewtyn* (1987) by Isobelle Carmody, *I am Susannah* (1987) by Libby Gleeson, *The Paperchaser* (1987) by Penny Hall, *Rattling in the*

Wind (1987) selected by Jill Heylen and Celia Jellett, illustrated by Maire Smith, *The Makers* (1987) by Victor Kelleher, *So Much to Tell You ...* (1987) by John Marsden, *Deezle Boy* (1987) by Eleanor Spence. **Younger Readers**: *A Paddock of Poems* (1987) by Max Fatchen, illustrated by Kerry Argent, *Looking out for Sampson* (1987) by Libby Hathorn, illustrated by Ann James, *Lucky* (1987) by Elizabeth Hutchins, illustrated by Robert Perkins, *Birk the Berserker* (1987) by Robin Klein, illustrated by Alison Lester, *The Landing: a Night of Birds* (1987) by Katherine Scholes, illustrated by David Wong, *My Place* (1987) by Nadia Wheatley and Donna Rawlins. **Picture Book**: *Where the Forest Meets the Sea* (1987) written and illustrated by Jeannie Baker, *Crusher is Coming!* (1987) written and illustrated by Bob Graham, *Pheasant and Kingfisher* (1987) by Catherine Berndt, illustrated by Raymond Meeks, *The Long Red Scarf* (1987) by Nette Hilton, illustrated by Margaret Power, *Tucking Mummy In* (1987) by Morag Loh, illustrated by Donna Rawlins, *What's That Noise?* (1987) by Mary Roennfeldt, illustrated by Robert Roennfeldt.

1989 Older Readers: *Megan's Star* (1988) by Allan Baillie, *Deepwater* (1987) by Judith O'Neill, *You Take the High Road* (1988) by Mary Pershall, *Answers to Brut* (1988) by Gillian Rubinstein, *The Lake at the End of the World* (1988) by Caroline Macdonald, *Beyond the Labyrinth* (1988) by Gillian Rubinstein. **Younger Readers**: *Australopaedia* (1988) edited by Joan Grant, illustrated by design students at Phillip Institute, *Melanie and the Night Animal* (1988) by Gillian Rubinstein, *Wiggy and Boa* (1988) by Anna Fienberg, illustrated by Ann James, *Split Creek Kids* (1988) by Roger Vaughan Carr, illustrated by June Joubert, *Callie's Family* (1988) by Ruth Park, illustrated by Kilmeny Niland, *The Best-Kept Secret* (1988) by 'Emily Rodda', illustrated by Noela Young. **Picture Book**: *The Eleventh Hour* (1988) written and illustrated by Graeme Base, *Drac and the Gremlin* (1988) by Allan Baillie, illustrated by Jane Tanner, *Edward the Emu* (1988) by Sheena Knowles, illustrated by Rod Clement, *My Place in Space* (1988) by Robin and Sally Hirst, illustrated by Roland Harvey and Joe Levine, *Ali Baba and the Forty Thieves* (1988) illustrated by Margaret Early, *Mr. Nick's Knitting* (1988) by Margaret Wild, illustrated by Dee Huxley.

1990 Older Readers: *Merryll of the Stones* (1989) by Brian Caswell, *Thunderwith* (1989) by Libby Hathorn, *The Red King* (1989) by Victor Kelleher, *Came Back to Show You I Could Fly* (1989) by Robin Klein, *Skymaze* (1989) by Gillian Rubinstein, *Balyet* (1989) by Patricia Wrightson. **Younger Readers**: *Pigs and Honey* (1989) written and illustrated by Jeanie Adams, *Papa and the Olden Days* (1989) by Ian Edwards, illustrated by Rachel Tonkin, *The Extraordinary Magics of Emma McDade* (1989) by Libby Hathorn, illustrated by Maya, *Onion Tears* (1989) by Diana Kidd, illustrated by Dee Huxley, *Following the Gold* (1989) by Bill Scott, *The Dragon of Mith* by Kate Walker, illustrated by Laurie Sharpe. **Picture Book**: *I Wish I Had a Pirate Suit* (1989) written and illustrated by Pamela Allen, *A Nice Walk in the Jungle* (1989) written and illustrated by Nan Bodsworth, *Grandad's Magic* (1989) written and illustrated by Bob Graham, *The Journey Home* (1989) written and illustrated by Alison Lester, *The Very Best of Friends* (1989) by

Margaret Wild, illustrated by Julie Vivas, *A Proper Little Lady* (1989) by Nette Hilton, illustrated by Cathy Wilcox.

1991 Older Readers: *Farseekers* (1990) by Isobelle Carmody, *Strange Objects* (1990) by Gary Crew, *Brother Night* (1990) by Victor Kelleher, *The Devil's Own* (1990) by Deborah Lisson, *Speaking to Miranda* (1990) by Caroline Macdonald, *The Family Book of Mary-Claire* (1990) by Eleanor Spence. **Younger Readers**: *Boris & Borsch* (1990) by Robin Klein, illustrated by Cathy Wilcox, *First at Last* (1990) by Julia McClelland, illustrated by Ann James, *The Black Duck* (1990) by Eleanor Nilsson, illustrated by Rae Dale, *Mervyn's Revenge* (1990) by Leonie Peguero, illustrated by Shirley Peters, *Finders Keepers* (1990) by 'Emily Rodda', illustrated by Noela Young, *Captain Deadlight's Treasure* (1990) by R.A. Wakefield, illustrated by Julie Mac. **Picture Book**: *My Cat Maisie* (1990) written and illustrated by Pamela Allen, *Counting on Frank* (1990) written and illustrated by Rod Clement, *Greetings from Sandy Beach* (1990) written and illustrated by Bob Graham, *Magic Beach* (1990) written and illustrated by Alison Lester, *Hector and Maggie* (1990) by Janet McLean, illustrated by Andrew McLean, *Scallywag* (1990) written and illustrated by Jeanette Rowe.

1992 Older Readers: *Change the Locks* (1991) by Simon French, *Del-Del* (1991) by Victor Kelleher, *Mandragora* (1991) by David McRobbie, *Letters from the Inside* (1991) by John Marsden, *The House Guest* (1991) by Eleanor Nilsson, *Peter* (1991) by Kate Walker. **Younger Readers**: *The Wolf* (1991) by Margaret Barbalet, illustrated by Jane Tanner, *The Magnificent Nose and Other Marvels* (1991) by Anna Fienberg, illustrated by Kim Gamble, *Rain Stones* (1991) by Jackie French, *Misery Guts* (1991) by Morris Gleitzman, *Do Not Go Around the Edges* (1991) by Daisy Utemorrah, illustrated by Pat Torres, *The Sugar-Gum Tree* (1991) by Patricia Wrightson, illustrated by David Cox. **Picture Book**: *Window* (1991) by Jeannie Baker, *William Tell* (1991) adapted and illustrated by Margaret Early, *Hist!* (1991) by C.J. Dennis, illustrated by Peter Gouldthorpe, *Enora and the Black Crane* (1991) written and illustrated by Arone Raymond Meeks, *Dog In, Cat Out* (1991) by Gillian Rubinstein, illustrated by Ann James, *Let the Celebrations Begin!* (1991) by Margaret Wild, illustrated by Julie Vivas.

1993 Older Readers: *A Cage of Butterflies* (1992) by Brian Caswell, *A Long Way to Tipperary* (1992) by Sue Gough, *Pagan's Crusade* (1992) by Catherine Jinks, *Looking for Alibrandi* (1992) by Melina Marchetta, *Take My Word for It* (1992) by John Marsden, *Galax-Arena* (1992) by Gillian Rubinstein. **Younger Readers**: *The Bamboo Flute* (1992) by Garry Disher, *Blabber Mouth* (1992) by Morris Gleitzman, *The Web* (1992) by Nette Hilton, illustrated by Kerry Millard, *The Fat and Juicy Place* (1992) by Diana Kidd, illustrated by Bronwyn Bancroft, *Leaving it to You* (1992) by Wendy Orr, *Titans!* (1992) by Michael Stephens, illustrated by Kim Gamble. **Picture Book**: *Belinda* (1992) by Pamela Allen, *Grandad's Gifts* (1992) by Paul Jennings, illustrated by Peter Gouldthorpe, *Rose meets Mr Wintergarten* (1992) by Bob Graham, *Lucy's Bay* (1992) by Gary Crew, illustrated by Gregory Rogers, *Where's Mum?* (1992) by Libby Gleeson, illustrated by Craig Smith, *Looking for Crabs* (1992) by Bruce Whatley.

ACKNOWLEDGEMENTS

The authors would like to thank the following individuals, institutions and companies for supplying black and white illustrative material.

Individuals

Jeannie Baker for *Millicent* (Andre Deutsch, 1980) p. 38; Charles Blackman for his illustration from *Alice's Adventures in Wonderland*, edited by Nadine Amadio (Reed, 1982) p. 55; Astra Lacis Dick for her illustration from *The Angel with the Mouth-Organ* by Christobel Mattingley (Hodder and Stoughton, 1984) p. 252; Kay Druce for *Popsy and the Bunny Twins* (Offset Printing Co., 1946) p. 139; Elisabeth MacIntyre Eldershaw for *Katherine* (Australian Publishing Co., 1946) p. 275; Ennis Honey for *Youth Annual* (W.H. Honey, 1930) p. 28; Robert Ingpen for his illustration from *River Murray Mary* by Colin Thiele (Rigby, 1979) p. 232; Alan Maltby for Peg Maltby's illustration from *Ben and Bella Down on the Farm* (Murfetts, 1947) p. 285; Patricia Mullins for her illustration from *The Magic Saddle* by Christobel Mattingley (Hodder & Stoughton, 1983) p. 309; Kay Overton for Ethel Jackson Morris's illustration from *The White Butterfly and Other Fairy Tales* (De Garis, 1921) p. 304; Klytie Pate for Christian Yandell Waller's illustration from *The Gates of Dawn* (Gryphon Press, 1977) p. 437; Genevieve Rees for her illustration from *The Man in the Red Turban* by David Martin (Hutchinson, 1978) p. 296; Margaret Senior for her illustration from *The Australia Book* by Eve Pownall (Sands, 1952) p. 33; Jean Elder Towns for her illustration from *Robbie's Trip to Fairyland* by Phyllis Johnson (Murfetts, 1946) p. 146; Noela Young for Walter Cunningham's illustration from *Digit Dick and the Lost Opals* by Leslie Rees (Sands, 1957) p. 131.

Institutions

The McLaren Collection, Baillieu Library, University of Melbourne for *The Gilpins and Their Fortunes* by W.H.G. Kingston (SPCK, 1889) p. 24; *Holidays at Hillydale* by Dame Mary Daly (Yoralla Hospital School for Crippled Children, 1973) p. 121; *Australian Fairy Tales* by Atha Westbury, illustrated by A.J. Johnson (Ward, Lock, 1897) p. 153; *Coppertop* by Harold Gaze (Melbourne Publishing Co., 1919) p. 159; *The Secret of the Australian Desert*, by Ernest Favenc, illustrated by Percy Spence (Blackie, 1896) p. 163; *'Possum* by Mary Grant Bruce, illustrated by J. Macfarlane (Ward, Lock, 1917) p. 184; *Australian Adventures* by W.H.G. Kingston (Routledge, 1884) pp. 227 and 247; *Seven Little Australians* by Ethel Turner, illustrated by A.J. Johnson (Ward, Lock, 1894) p. 227; *Gray's Hollow* by Mary Grant Bruce, illustrated by Stanley Davies? (Ward, Lock, 1914) p. 228; portrait of Donald MacDonald from *Childhood in Bud and Blossom* (Atlas Press, 1900) p. 272; portrait of Ethel Pedley from *Dot and the Kangaroo* by Ethel Pedley (Thomas Burleigh, 1899) p. 339; *Dick* by Mary Grant Bruce, illustrated by J. Macfarlane (Ward, Lock, 1918) p. 378. The Research Collection of Children's Literature, State Reference Library, Perth, WA for *The Hut in the Bush* by Robert Richardson (Oliphant, Anderson and Ferrier, 1883) frontispiece; *Cobbers: Australian Children's Annual* (1938) by 'John Mystery' p. 29; *Champion Library* p. 120. RMIT for *An Alphabet: Being a Book of Designs and Rhymes* by Students of the Applied Art School (Working Men's College, 1932) p. 22. The Spastic Centre of New South Wales and The NSW Society, c/o Curtis Brown, (Aust) Pty, Ltd, Sydney for *A Little Bush Poppy* by Edith Graham, illustrated by May Gibbs (Lothian, 1915) p. 180. State Library of

Victoria for *The Demon McGuire* by F.H. Grundy (Gibbs, Charland and Co., 1870) p. 196; E. Minnie Boyd's illustration from *Waratah Rhymes for Young Australians* by Louisa Anne Meredith (Day and Son, 1891) p. 297.

Companies

Angus and Robertson for *Teens* by Louise Mack, illustrated by Karna Birmingham (Angus & Robertson, 1927) p. 54; *Children of the Dark People* by Frank Dalby Davison, illustrated by Pixie O'Harris (Angus & Robertson, 1936) p. 74; *Counting on Frank* by Rod Clement (Collins, Angus & Robertson, Anne Ingram, 1990) p. 100; *Gumbles in Summer* by S.A. Wakefield, illustrated by Desmond Digby (Collins, 1989) p. 130; *Dot and the Kangaroo* by Ethel Pedley, illustrated by Frank Mahony (Angus & Robertson, 1899) p. 135; *The Enchanted Forest* by Ida Rentoul Outhwaite (A. & C. Black, 1921) p. 155; *Joseph and Lulu and the Prindiville House Pigeons*, by Ted Greenwood (Angus & Robertson, 1972) p. 194; *Blue and Gold Day* by Margaret Balderson, illustrated by Roger Haldane (Angus & Robertson, 1979) p. 199; *I Wish ... I Wonder* by Dee Huxley (Collins/Anne Ingram, 1989) p. 223; *The Magic Pudding* by Norman Lindsay (Angus & Robertson, 1918) p. 282; *Grandad Barnett's Beard* by Kristine Church, illustrated by Kilmeny Niland (Collins/Anne Ingram, 1988) p. 316; *Mulga Bill's Bicycle* by A.B. Paterson, illustrated by Deborah and Kilmeny Niland (Collins, 1973) p. 337; *The Big Book of Pegmen Tales* by Ella McFadyen, illustrated by Edwina Bell (Angus & Robertson, 1959) p. 340; *Pigs Might Fly* by Emily Rodda, illustrated by Noela Young (Angus & Robertson, 1986) p. 366; *Gidja* by Dick Roughsey and Percy Trezise (Collins, 1984) p. 369; *Stout Fellows* by Dorothy Wall (Angus & Robertson, 1936) p. 436; *The Bubble Galleon* by Ernest Wells, illustrated by R.W. Coulter (Angus & Robertson, 1934) Endpiece. Ashton Scholastic for *Wombat Stew* by Marcia Vaughan, illustrated by Pamela Lofts (Ashton, 1984) p. 263; *Enora and the Black Crane* by Arone Raymond Meeks (Ashton, 1991) p. 293; *Digging to China* by Donna Rawlins (Ashton Scholastic, 1988) p. 358. Education Shop for Marjorie Howden's illustration from *Holidays: The Victorian Readers Second Book*, Department of Education, Victoria (Government Printer, 1953) p. 219. Era Publications for Donna Gynell's illustration from *Educating Arthur* by Amanda Graham (Era, 1987) p. 32. Roland Harvey Studios for Roland Harvey's illustration from *My Place in Space* by Robin and Sally Hirst, illustrated by Roland Harvey and Jo Levine (Periscope Press, 1988) p. 203. Kangaroo Press for *The Trouble with Peggetty* by Mary Small, illustrated by Irene Sibley (Kangaroo Press, 1984) p. 389. Lothian Books for *Greetings from Sandy Beach*, written and illustrated by Bob Graham (Lothian, 1990) p. 190. Thomas Nelson for *Tinka and the Bunyip* written and illustrated by Brownie Downing (Nelson, 1966) p. 137. Omnibus Books for *Creatures in the Beard* by Margaret Wild, illustrated by Margaret Power (Omnibus, 1986) p. 351. Oxford University Press for *Dusting in Love* by Max Dann, illustrated by Terry Denton (Oxford University Press, 1989) p. 122; *Felix and Alexander* by Terry Denton (Oxford University Press, 1985) p. 165; *One Day: a Very First Dictionary* by Ann James (Oxford University Press, 1989) p. 236; *The Journey Home* by Alison Lester (Oxford University Press, 1989) p. 258. Penguin Books for illustrations from *My Cat Maisie* by Pamela Allen (Penguin, 1990) p. 20; *Animalia* by Graeme Base (Penguin, 1986) p. 43; *Whispering in the Wind* by Alan Marshall, illustrated by Jack Newnham (Nelson, 1969) p. 75; *Kangaroo Tales*, edited by Rosemary Wighton, illustrated by Donald Friend (Penguin, 1963) p. 103; *One Dragon's Dream* by Peter Pavey (Nelson, 1978) p. 109; *Jack in the Bush* by Barbara Giles, illustrated by Betty Greenhatch (Kestrel, 1983) p. 182; *Drac and the Gremlin* by Allan Baillie, illustrated by Jane Tanner

(Viking Kestrel, 1988) p. 410; *John Brown, Rose and the Midnight Cat* by Jenny Wagner, illustrated by Ron Brooks (Kestrel, 1977) p. 434; *Salt River Times* by William Mayne, illustrated by Elizabeth Honey (Nelson, 1980) p. 95. Reed Books Australia for *Marty Moves to the Country* by Kate Walker, illustrated by Bruce Treloar (Methuen, 1980) p. 419 and *The Tram to Bondi Beach* by Libby Hathorn, illustrated by Julie Vivas p. 433. Walter McVitty Books for *Hist!* by C.J. Dennis, illustrated by Peter Gouldthorpe (Walter McVitty Books, 1991) p. 189; *Farmer Schultz's Ducks* by Colin Thiele, illustrated by Mary Milton (Walter McVitty Books, 1986) p. 300. Weldon Publishing for *Minnie* by Annette Macarthur-Onslow (Ure Smith, 1977) p. 269.

Every effort has been made to contact and acknowledge copyright holders. Where the attempt has been unsuccessful the publisher would be pleased to hear from the illustrator or publisher concerned.

Tiel Quintillian.